To Wayne,

my new friend.

Eric Gordon

Gay Pride Weekend
1997

Mark the Music

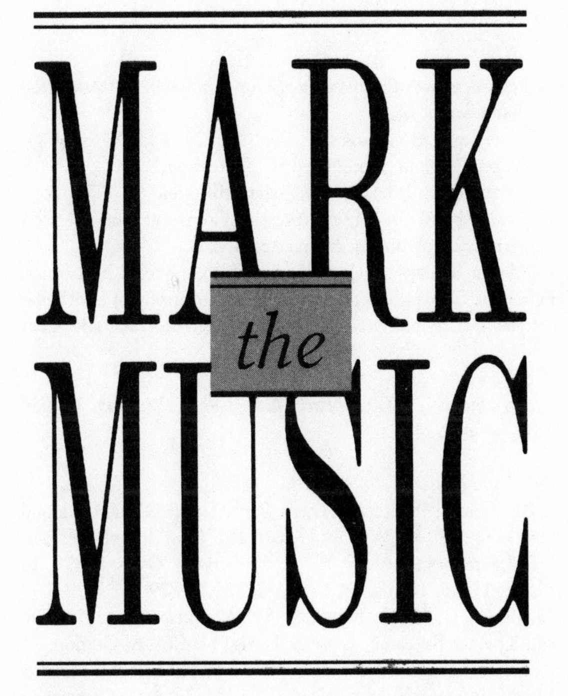

The Life and Work of Marc Blitzstein

ERIC A. GORDON

St. Martin's Press New York

Grateful acknowledgment is made for permission to reprint from the following:

Letters quoted on pages 57, 76, 108, 221, and 287 copyright by Aaron Copland, reproduced by permission.

"Invitation to Bitterness" by Marc Blitzstein (p. 175). Copyright 1939 by Arrow Music Press, Inc. Copyright renewed. Used by permission of Boosey & Hawkes, Inc.

"Skid a lit day . . . . visa" (p. 358). Copyright by Leonard Bernstein. Copyright renewed. Used by permission of Jalni Publications, Inc., publishers, and Boosey & Hawkes, Inc., sole agent.

Photo credits:

Part One: R. T. Dooger; Part Three: Talbot; Part Four: William and Gwen Sloan.

Photo sources:

Part One, 3, 48: Stephen Davis; Part Two, 24: David Diamond; Part Three, 30, 32: William Hewitt; Part Four: Josephine Davis; 1, 2: Laura Goldsmith; 5, 36, 47: Christopher Davis; 6, 8, 9, 10, 11, 12, 13, 15, 16, 17, 18, 19, 20, 26, 27, 28, 29, 31, 33, 34, 37, 38, 39, 40, 41, 42, 43, 44, 46, 49, 50: Wisconsin Center for Film and Theater Research; 7: Joyce Davis; 14: Eric A. Gordon; 21: Library of Congress Federal Theatre Project Collection, George Mason University Library, Fairfax, Va.; 23, 25: Arthur Zipser; 26, 28: Kenneth Cantril; 35: Morris Golde.

Library of Congress Cataloging-in-Publication Data

Gordon, Eric A.
Mark the Music.

Discography: p. 575
1. Blitzstein, Marc. 2. Composers—United States—Biography. I. Title.
ML410.B6515G7 1989 780′.92′4 [B] 88-29891
ISBN 0-312-02607-2

First Edition
10 9 8 7 6 5 4 3 2 1

My field is musico-dramatic, musico-lyrical, and just plain music. If I find myself tending in composition largely towards writing music for voices, for the theater, for films, for radio and television, it is because I am a product of my time—and my time is one of urgency and direct communication in the arts. If it be argued that such a formulation of mine might destroy my chances for "immortality" (and as a serious composer I assure you that I too have that bee in my bonnet), then I can only say that greater artists than I have faced their moment squarely in their work, and have not lost their prestige with posterity on that account. Subject-matter, as such, can never make or break a work of art. Its lasting qualities depend on the artist's personality, on the equation of content-and-form, and on a lot of other intangibles. I am content to have my work undergo the test of repeated hearings, of Time, and of Tarnish.

—Marc Blitzstein,
from a concert program at Severance Hall, Cleveland, Ohio, January 18, 1948

The man that hath no music in himself,
Nor is not moved with concord of sweet sounds,
Is fit for treasons, stratagems, and spoils;
The motions of his spirit are dull as night,
And his affections dark as Erebus.
Let no such man be trusted. Mark the music.

—William Shakespeare,
The Merchant of Venice, Act V, scene 1

Contents

PART THREE

PART FOUR

Sections of photographs follow pages 206 and 446.

Acknowledgments

I would like to thank the following people and institutions for their help in ways both large and small. The biography of Marc Blitzstein would be vastly different without their contributions.

William Abrahams, Maurice Abravanel, Milton Adolphus, Harold Aks, Eddie Albert, Ben Algase, Chaya Amir, Robert Anderson, Cécile Armagnac, Arnold Arnstein, Ed Arrow, Pamela Askew, Lyn Austin, Rudy Avelar, Luiz Heitor Corrêa de Azevedo, Jean Bach, Ben Bagley, Evžen Balaš, Muriel Balash, The Balch Institute, Bill Ballantine, Kaye Ballard, Lucinda Ballard, Rick Barnett, Lisa Barone, Michael Barrett, Liat Barzilai, Rosalyn Baxandall, Howard Bay, Adelaide Bean, Betty Bean, Jack Beeson, Robert Russell Bennett, Eric Bentley, Joanne Bentley, Victor A. Berch, Arthur Berger, Charles Berigan, Burton Bernstein, Shirley Bernstein, Jonathan Best, Karl Bissinger, Steven Blier, Anthony A. Bliss, Adrienne Fried Block, Louise Bloomfield, Abba Bogin, Elaine Bonazzi, Susan L. Boone, Shirley Booth, Jean and Leonard Boudin, Sir Adrian Boult, Paul Bowles, Brandeis University Library, Henry Brant, George Braziller, Arnold Broido, Hal Bromm, David Brooks, Susan Rand Brown, Tally Brown, Karen Browning, Perry Bruskin, Samuel Brylawski, Leonard Burkat, Alan Bush, Tony Buttitta.

Kenneth Cantril, Carmen Capalbo, Carol Brice Carey, Alice Carlin, Elisabeth Carron, Elliott Carter, Yvonne de Casa Fuerte, Joanna Cazden, Erika Chadbourn, Cecile Chan, Carol Channing, Schuyler Chapin, Chappell Music Company, James R. Cherry, Jerome Chodorov, Myron Clement, Ronald L. Cohen, Arthur Cohn, John Collis, Columbia University Libraries, Betty Comden, Jane Connell, Bert Conway, Mary Cooley, Brenda Lewis Cooper, Frank Cooper, Aaron Copland, Norman Corwin, Jerold L. Couture, Elizabeth Goldbeck Coward, Chandler Cowles, Donald Crafton, Nives Mutti Crandall, Cheryl Crawford, The Curtis Institute of Music.

Minna Lederman Daniel, Anita Darian, Robert D'Attilio, Joyce Davis, Sonia Davis, James DeCou, Olive Deering, Norman Del Mar, Agnes de Mille, Edwin Denby, E. de Sabata, Ruth Berghaus Dessau, Irene Lee Diamond, Daniel G. Dietz, Annette Dieudonné, William Dillard, Edna L. Dolber, Melvyn Douglas, Alfred Drake, Paul Draper, David Drew, Martin Bauml Duberman, Ruth Dugan, David Dunaway, Helen Durant.

Jean and William Eckart, Georg Eisler, Bess Eitingon, Nancy Elliott, Anita Ellis, Lehman Engel, Roger Englander, Alvin Epstein, Al Erlick, Harvey Estrin, Alice Esty, Robert Fagles, David Farneth, Ellen Faull, Susan Feder, Michael Feingold, José Ferrer, Richard Fetters, Jonathan Fey, Charles Fidlar, Verna Fine, Hy Fireman, Geraldine Fitzgerald, Richard Flusser, Charles Henri Ford, Ruth Ford, The Ford Foundation, Lukas Foss, Irma and Lewis Fraad, Ellis Freedman, Sanford Friedman.

Adrienne Gaiton, Marc Galanter, Zalmon H. Garfield, George Gaynes, Felicia Geffen, Charles Gellert, Bernard Gersten, Steve Gianakos, Mira Gilbert, David Gockley, Willis B. Goldbeck, Al Goldberg, Robert E. Goldburg, Harry M. Goldman, Milton Goldman, Laura Goldsmith, Sylvia Goldstein, Frederic A. Gordon and Janny van Houwelingen, Ilse Gordon and Neil Shapiro, Jack Gottlieb, Lloyd Gough, Morton Gould, Richard Greeman, Tammy Grimes, John Simon Guggenheim Memorial Foundation, David Hacker, Daron Aric Hagen, Alexei Haieff, David Hall, John Hall, John Hammond, Pauline Hanson, Louis Harap, Ruth Harizy, Charles Harmon, Lou Harrison, Jack Harrold, Diane Hart, Helen Harvey, Peter Harvey, Herbert Haufrecht, Harry Hay, David and Leonora Hays, Hans Heinsheimer, Skitch Henderson, Scott Heumann, John Highkin, Robert Hill, H. Wiley Hitchcock, Barbara Hocher, Rosemary L. Hogg, Charles Holland, Hanya Holm, Wanda Toscanini Horowitz, John Houseman, Jane Pickens Hoving, Francesca Humor, Charles W. Hunt, Joseph Hurley, Leo Hurwitz, Frank Ilchuk, Stuart Isacoff, Christopher Isherwood.

Robert Jacobson, Newell Jenkins, Jess Jessen, Phyllis Joffe, Robert Joffrey, Joan Kahn, Edward Kallman and Dorothy J. Farnan, Garson Kanin, Ralph Kaplan, Sidney Kaplan, Louise Karbownicki, Hershy Kay, Alfred Kazin, Leon Kellman, Michael Kerker, Richard A. Kimball, Gershon Kingsley, Arthur Luce Klein, George Kleinsinger, Marion Knoblauch-Franc, Al Kohn, Bernard Koten, Kim Kowalke, Samuel Krachmalnick, Tommy Krasker, Harry Kraut, John F. Kreidl, Mark Kristalovich, Gail Kubik, David Labovitz, Sharon B. Laist, Henry W. Lauterstein, Geoffrey Suess Law, Jeffrey Lawrence, Pearl Lazar, Paul Lazarus, Evelyn Lear, Will Lee, Robert Leiter, Bennett Lerner, Jim Levas, Jack Levine, Maurice Levine, Robert Lewis, Arthur and Ruth Lief, Robert L. Lind, Leon Lishner, Caroline Lloyd, Jo Sullivan Loesser, Michael Loring, Lucille Lortel, Otto Luening, James Luse.

Michael Mace, Joseph Machlis, Bruce T. MacIlveen, A. B. Magil, Pamela Main, Richard Maltby, Jr., Ken Mandelbaum, Max Margulis, Anna Markard, Charles Martin, Josephine Martin, Freya Maslow, Lawrence Mass, Samuel Matlovsky, John Mauceri, Jan McDevitt, Kean K. McDonald, Nadia McMurry, Gustav Meier, Wilfrid Mellers, Murry Melvin, Burgess Meredith, Metropolitan Opera Association, Edna Ocko Meyers, Elizabeth Michael, William B. Milam, Betty Millard, John Miller, Sheilah M. Miller, Glenn Mitroff, Eugene Moon, Michael Moon, Paul Moor, Larry Moore, Jerome Moross, R. Stephen Mudgett, Herman E. Muller, Caroline C. Murray, National Academy of Arts and Letters, National Archives and Records Service, Lois Nettleship, Robert P. Newman, The New York Public Library, Rose Nichamin, Maralin Niska, Alex North, Russell

Nype, Russell Oberlin, Eileen O'Casey, Shivaun O'Casey, Anne O'Malley, Leo R. O'Neill, Jerry Orbach.

Ruth Page, Matthew Paris, Donald Pechet, Beverly Pepper, David R. Perrigo, Priscilla Gillette Perrone, Joseph Petrocik, Joan Peyser, The Free Library of Philadelphia, City of Philadelphia Records Department, Helen Phillips, Carl Piermarini, Josephe Pierre-Louis, Joseph L. Pollock, Charlotte Rae, David Rayfiel, Arthur Reis, Jr., Emile Renan, Ralph Reuter, Abraham Ribicoff, Tony Richardson, Trude Rittmann, François Dujarric de la Riviere, Lynne W. Robbins, Paul Robeson, Jr., Earl Robinson, Jim Robinson, Rebecca Rohman, Elissa Rolick, Harold Rome, Shoshana Ron, Ned Rorem, Helen Rosen, George Ross, Wolfgang Roth, Vicki Rovere, Michael Rubinovitz, Julius Rudel.

Olle Jane Z. and Carl Sahler, Mary Saliba, Eric Salzman, Victor Samrock, Harold E. Samuel, Ralph Satz, Morris U. Schappes, Augusta Weissberger Schenker, Martha Schlamme, William Schuman, Charles Schwartz, David Scribner, Pete Seeger, Edith Segal, Nina G. Segrè and Frank Furstenberg, Robert Serber, Howard Shanet, Harold Shapero, Charlotte Shapiro, Moshe Shaul, John Sheehan, Paul and Sara Sheftel, John Shepard, Grigory Shneerson, Amy Shottenstein, Florence and Mike Siegel, Steve Siegel, Elie Siegmeister, Kyriena Siloti, Charles Silver, Louis Simon, Robert Simon, Berenice Skidelsky, Leo Smit, Gregg Smith, Muriel Smith, Oliver Smith, Paul Snook, Anna Sokolow, Joseph Solomon, Anna Sosenko, Val W. Spielberg, Roberta Starkweather, Harry Stein, Joseph Stein, Lee Stern, Mimi Stern-Wolfe, Roger L. Stevens, Edith Stewart, Allan Stinson, Beatrice Straight, Lys and Randolph Symonette.

Jerome Talbert, Gregg Tallman, Prentiss Taylor, Telford Taylor, Harry Ransom Humanities Research Center at the University of Texas at Austin, Peggy Thomas, Sada Thompson, Tazewell Thompson, Virgil Thomson, Francis Thorne, Sally Lou Todd, Monte Amundsen Tozzi, Jerry Trauber, C. A. Tripp, Barbara W. Tuchman, George and Ethel Tyne, United States Department of Justice (Federal Bureau of Investigation), United States Department of State, United States Federal Records Center—Philadelphia, Vladimir Ussachevsky, Joseph Valiquette, Willard Van Dyke, Jackie Veglie, Andrea Velis, Frances B. Venard, Joseph Viertel, Ellen Vliet, Andrew and Zina Voynow, Victor Voynow, Marion Wade, Michael Wager, Candace H. Wait, David Walker, Aileen Ward and the members of the Biography Seminar at New York University, Steve Watson, William Weaver, Beveridge Webster, The Kurt Weill Foundation for Music, Estelle Loring Weinrib, Eugene Weintraub, Hugo Weisgall, Glenway Wescott, Monroe Wheeler, William Wilderman, Denise L. Wilkinson, John Willett, Michael Willhoite, Harold W. Williams, Patricia Willis, Tiba G. Willner, Yale University Library, Victor Yellin, Max Youngstein, Henrietta Yurchenco, Benjamin Zemach, Arthur Zipser.

I owe at least a paragraph of very special thanks to certain people, important for their close friendship with Blitzstein or their familiarity with his work, who gave me their unflagging cooperation. Space—not the depth of my gratitude—allows me only to mention their names: Mordecai and Irma Bauman, Leonard

Bernstein, David Diamond, Morris Golde, William and Luellen Hewitt, and Leonard Lehrman. John Mueter gave me many hours of valuable musical guidance.

I give warm thanks to Mary L. Galanter, a cousin of Marc Blitzstein, who housed me for a week in Madison, Wisconsin.

I am indebted to my literary agent, Frances Goldin, who placed this work with the best publisher I could possibly have found, and who sustained a sincere personal interest in the book throughout its writing. My editor at St. Martin's, Michael Denneny, has done a superbly sensitive job with this manuscript. Recognizing, with me, the scant likelihood that another full-scale biography of Marc Blitzstein will appear in this generation, he has allowed me the room to explore comfortably the content and meaning of Blitzstein's life and work. I would be honored to have the chance to work with Michael again. My thanks also go to Michael's assistants, Keith Kahla, Sarah Pettit, and Darlene Dobrin. Carol Edwards, copy editor, and Amelie Littell, managing editor, deserve my deep gratitude for saving me from numerous infelicities. Andy Carpenter, Glen Edelstein, Judith Stagnitto, and Doris Borowsky, designers, have created the book beautiful that Marc Blitzstein deserves.

My parents, Naomi B. and Victor M. Gordon, supported a portion of the research for this book, for which I will always feel obliged. Early on, my father offered to create the index, and he has done so lovingly. I also thank the other members of my family who offered every possible encouragement.

A separate word of gratitude goes to those who read this manuscript, or parts of it, before it went into the final editing process. Their suggestions were invaluable: Rick Barnett, Mordecai and Irma Bauman, Ann Berkhausen, Carmen Capalbo, Stephen and Joyce Davis, Christopher and Sonia Davis, David Diamond, Frances Goldin, Naomi B. and Victor M. Gordon, William and Luellen Hewitt, Kim Kowalke, Leonard Lehrman, Carol Oja, Earl Robinson, Lee Stern, and Paul Weidner. If in any places I have failed to follow their excellent advice, I have in the end only myself to blame for the errors of fact or interpretation that may remain.

When in 1978 I first met Josephine Davis in Philadelphia to discuss the prospect of my writing a book about her brother, she concluded our talk by inscribing my name in her address book. "Biographer," she wrote. The confidence that simple notation showed kept me on a steady course throughout the long research and writing stages that followed. I dearly wanted her to be able to hold my book in her hands; but this was fated not to be. Both she and her husband, Edward Davis, Trustees of the Estate of Marc Blitzstein, died in 1987. I am happy, however, to acknowledge the irreplaceable assistance they gave me. They allowed me to work at my own pace, neither pushing nor withholding, making numerous gestures of encouragement along the way. Their two sons, Stephen and Christopher Davis, who now jointly administer the Estate of Marc Blitzstein, have been equally helpful.

I consider it a privilege to have enjoyed full access to Marc Blitzstein's letters, diaries, and other papers and now to be able to quote from them. He poured intensity, concentration, and depth of observation into his correspondence, and I am pleased to bring as many excerpts to light as I do in this book. As Blitzstein's wife Eva Goldbeck left no other survivors, rights to her letters, diaries, and manuscripts also lie with Stephen and Christopher Davis. I am especially grateful to The State Historical Society of Wisconsin, principal repository of Marc Blitzstein's papers, and to the administrators of his Estate for permission to quote from the papers of both Blitzstein and Goldbeck. I also owe my profound thanks to members of The State Historical Society of Wisconsin staff: Menzi L. Behrnd-Klodt, Josephine Harper, Paul Harper, Harold Miller, Christine Rongone, and George Talbot.

My sincere apologies go to any whose assistance I have inadvertently failed to recognize.

As to sources, wherever I have quoted published and unpublished letters, manuscripts, working notes, diary entries, lyrics and the like, these are all to be found in the Marc Blitzstein Papers, Archives Division, The State Historical Society of Wisconsin and at the Wisconsin Center for Film and Theater Research (WCFTR) in Madison, Wisconsin, whose staff member, Maxine Fleckner Ducey, has been extremely helpful, particularly in supplying photographs for this book. In some cases, for the sake of sparing the reader unnecessary tedium, I have not provided notes dating Blitzstein's detailed working notes on each of his theatrical productions, or dating diary entries. Sometimes Blitzstein did not date such notes; but even when he did, all of these can be located in the appropriate folders in his papers. In every instance, however, I believe I have made the context and approximate datings abundantly clear for any but the most meticulous student of Blitzstein's thinking. For another class of direct quotes deriving from sessions with interviewed subjects, I have also not provided notes: My acknowledgments indicate all their names. All other sources for cited material are identified in the relevant notes.

Preface

I make no claim that Marc Blitzstein is *the* great American composer. But who is? There has certainly never been any agreement on that score. Though it might prove an amusing exercise, it would ultimately be pointless to try to name one.

Still, much can be learned from the life of one who may not be *the* greatest. In an article for the magazine *Modern Music,* Blitzstein once said:

> A cultural epoch is made up not only of the perfect work of geniuses, but also of the combined efforts of lesser talents, a whole geological formation of them. With them wiped out, the genius exists without subsoil, becomes isolated, ingrown, "eccentric."[1]

Whether or not he was a genius, Blitzstein was unlike anyone else. Here was a figure on the American cultural scene unique in his own day and inimitable ever since. This was an American artist who honestly struggled to know himself, know his country and its culture, know humanity, and whose work still stands out as a serious esthetic project. And it may well be argued that Blitzstein was the most controversial composer America produced in his generation.

Blitzstein is often regarded as the social conscience of American music, spurring his audiences to think about our less-than-ideal set of social relations. Many of his works for the theatre were written for their own time. Some, we can see today, were ahead of their time. Though prophetic in certain aspects, they fell short of the total integration of elements needed to convince his critics. If relatively few of Blitzstein's works were successes in their time—at least few of them considered whole—in another respect he achieved brilliantly what he set out to do, and what few since have tried: Almost without precedent he created an American music theatre that spoke convincingly in American idioms. His sense of the American language derived not from Viennese operetta nor from the European operatic stage but from a sharp observation of the speech, vocabulary, and inflection of the entire range of American social classes, from society matrons to shop foremen to unemployed immigrant laborers. Blitzstein did not frequently devise novel musical techniques; for the most part, he was content to use the methods he found at hand. But in his daring subject matter, and perhaps more importantly in the authentic native prosody he developed, Blitzstein's accomplishment stands out as that of an original creative spirit.

Aside from the stage works, there are the instrumental pieces and the songs, which almost no one knows. Some of them may yet go on to represent the composer even more than his theatrical projects. Whatever final judgment Blitzstein's work receives, the fact remains that so many parts of even his most problematic compositions are profoundly affecting. His music still communicates to us, and I don't know how the measure of an artist is taken if it doesn't at least include that.

If Blitzstein played a distinctive part in the consciousness of his era, still he breathed the same oxygen as the others of his generation. While serving a vatic role in his time, he was very much of his time. And that was an important period, for before the 1920s the American composer was a relative oddity, and by the end of Blitzstein's life in the 1960s the American composer had truly become a phenomenon.

This book focuses on Blitzstein's life, but it is definitely a life *and* times. I have felt it critical to paint him in a landscape not all of whose contours will be instantly recognizable. Those knowledgeable about American music in the twentieth century will find substantial information here about its left wing. Those who know American political history will discover much new to them in this treatment of a radical composer. Those widely read in theatre, film, or dance will see some familiar terrain covered here, but from a different point of view: that of the composer.

Twenty-five years after his death, Blitzstein's reputation has largely rested on his operas *The Cradle Will Rock* and *Regina* and on his translation of Kurt Weill's *Threepenny Opera.* While I have not in any way downplayed these works or their importance to Blitzstein's career, others to which he devoted equal or greater creative energy have their own lives and power. It was fully as absorbing for me to research *No for an Answer, Reuben Reuben, Juno,* and *Sacco and Vanzetti* as his better-known pieces.

It may be worthwhile to mention how I became interested in Blitzstein. In 1977, for the fiftieth anniversary of the execution of Sacco and Vanzetti, I was preparing a radio program of musical selections relating to the case. Someone mentioned an opera on the subject, which led me to Blitzstein's uncompleted work. Through his Estate and the courtesy of his sister, Josephine Davis, I obtained piano-vocal scores of two arias from the opera. Friends recorded them and they were played, not on the radio, as it turned out, but at a public commemoration in Connecticut. Then, through with Blitzstein, I completed writing my doctoral dissertation.

When I finished, I promised myself that I would never take on such a huge project again. But not long afterward, I had occasion to program *Regina* on the radio. CBS had just rereleased its 1958 New York City Opera recording, and by chance its title-role performer, Brenda Lewis, was on hand at the Hartt College of Music for a between-the-acts interview. In the course of preparing for that interview, and from my meeting Ms. Lewis, I became convinced that Blitzstein was a fascinating and sadly neglected composer—more than a composer, a commanding presence in twentieth-century American culture.

As I looked further into his career, I came to realize the irony that I, a lover of opera and theatre since my teens and one deeply influenced by the social upheaval of the 1960s, had had to wait until 1977 to hear Blitzstein's name. No friend or mentor in my younger days had ever thought to make me aware of his work. Having studied some German in high school, I treasured my recording of *Die Dreigroschenoper (The Threepenny Opera)* with Lotte Lenya—I hadn't even known about Blitzstein's famous English adaptation, also starring Lenya! I do not blame society for my own ignorance; yet I concluded that if I, a reasonably socially aware operagoer of long standing, had never come across Blitzstein's name other than incidentally, then surely he remained an unknown quantity to the public at large, certainly to the wider public outside New York. I threw away my resolve not to commit myself again to a huge project and in the fall of 1978 started digging in.

Two doctoral students had devoted dissertations to limited aspects of Blitzstein's career: Paul Myers Talley, in "Social Criticism in the Original Theatre Librettos of Marc Blitzstein" (University of Wisconsin, 1965), and Robert James Dietz, in "The Operatic Style of Marc Blitzstein in the American 'Agit-Prop' Era" (University of Iowa, 1970). I acknowledge them as important starting points and references for my own research.

In the absence of other critical studies of Blitzstein's work, I soon began to ask myself, Should this be a musicological treatise, an examination of the sociology of his works, an intimate biography, a life and times? I have leaned toward the latter definitions, knowing that a thorough musicological treatment of even one of Blitzstein's operas might run to two or three hundred pages with musical examples. Yet I have tried to include enough about the works so that a reader can appreciate what motivated Blitzstein to write them. Some readers, no doubt, would prefer more musicology; others will just as assuredly feel that I have included too much already. If this biography encourages further interest among music scholars or performers, I will feel enormously gratified.

In the end, what I offer is necessarily but one writer's view of Blitzstein and his work and time. I have followed the particular line of thinking of no one source, neither his friends nor professional colleagues nor family, though I have drawn from them all. I can only hope that the image of Marc Blitzstein as I present him is a true one to those who knew him.

I have not set out to prove any particular theory of culture with Marc Blitzstein as my guinea pig. His career, more than that of many of his contemporaries, shows an unambiguous relation of music to ordinary life, and that, I believe, is worth documenting. I am led to one main conclusion, however, and I am not ashamed if it is not an original one: that, for one reason or another, our society throws away its past, to our enormous impoverishment. Whether for reasons of politics, fashion, or commerce, our culture generally discourages interest in the past. Our images of the twenties, the thirties, the forties, the fifties are reduced to but a few shards, a few slogans, a few notions gathered from who knows where. Any legitimate act of restoration holds within it the seed of protest against the almost willful forgetfulness, if not destruction, of the American epic. If this book helps to fill in the puzzle of American life in this century, I am content.

PART One

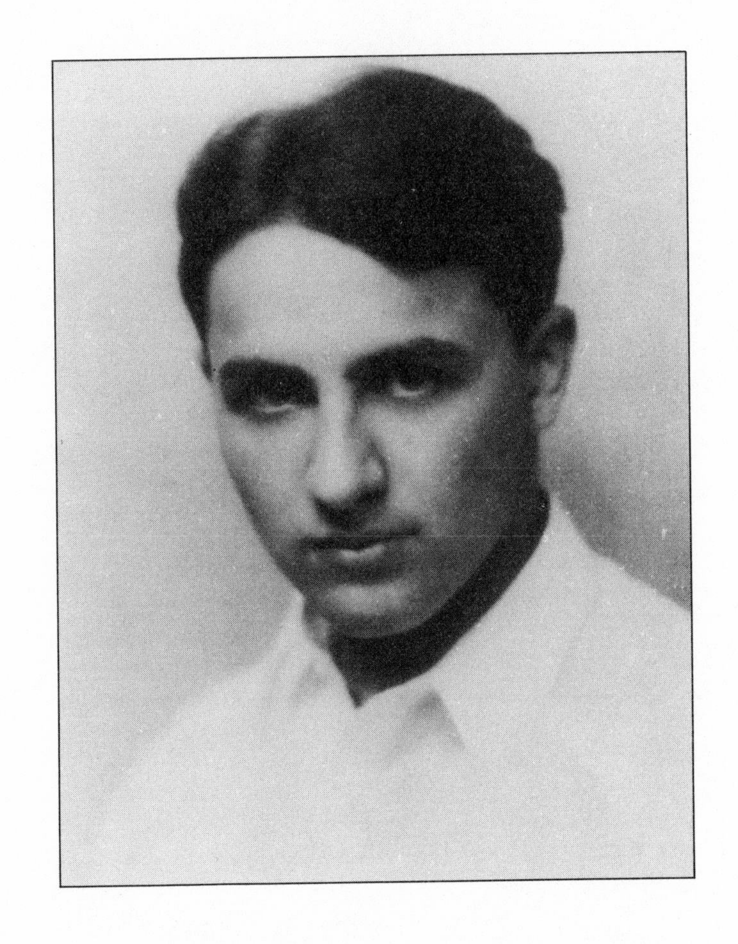

1

THE BRAT

1905–1917

"Mumsie, are you sorry? Are you sorry, mumsie?"

Hannah Galanter lived in a little town outside of Odessa. Her mother (née Ashkenazy) was crippled, and Hannah took over the maternal role. She took her little brothers to *cheder*—religious school—and while she waited in the back of the room, she picked up reading, writing, and arithmetic. The rabbi could observe this, of course, but permitted it. Odessa on the Black Sea and the towns bordering on the Austro-Hungarian Empire (such as Husiatin, where Hannah's brother Zelig settled) knew something of the Enlightenment, the liberal, questioning spirit that showed Jews a way out of the pale.* The border areas produced clever tradespeople skilled in many languages and experienced at commercial transactions involving different currencies, transshipping, smuggling, and frequent bribes to the guards. Many a Jew, and many a revolutionary under pursuit by the czar's police, escaped Russia through these towns whose roads and river crossings the Jews knew so well.

In due time, in the early 1870s, Hannah's father found a proper husband for her. As the story goes, Moses (Moishe) Lionel Blitzstein was so good-looking that

*Hannah's family ancestors may well have gone from Galanta, a Slovakian town near Pressburg (Bratislava today) to eastern Galicia and then across the Russian border into the Ukrainian provinces of Podolia and Kherson.

his prospective father-in-law was afraid to ask too many questions. As a practical joke, a friend of Moishe's told him that his wife-to-be was cross-eyed. So Moishe traveled to her town, sneaked up to the window, confirmed that nothing was wrong with her, and then agreed to the marriage. Naturally, the couple had never met before the wedding day, but it turned out to be a successful union.

The bridegroom came from a large family whose earliest traceable members were a David Blitstein, born around 1787, and his brothers Abraham, Chaim, and Moishie. Many a Jewish name reflected the trade of its carrier, and some suppose that Blitzstein is one such: "lightning-stone" might have meant a maker of flintstones. But *blit* is the Russian pronunciation of the Yiddish word for blood, and bloodstone—a green ore flecked with red hematite—was considered a lucky stone that could stop bleeding and add years to life. Some early ancestor probably chose the name for its charm value: One genealogist of the family asserts that David Blitstein lived to the age of 110. From village to village and country to country, wherever members of the clan crossed borders and settled, the name underwent numerous transformations. Relatives of the Blitzsteins include people named Blitstein, Blistein, Blitshtein, Blaustein, Bluestein, Bloystein, Bluestone, and various shortened forms such as Blitsh, Blits, Blitt and Stein.[1]

For nearly a decade, Hannah and Moishe Blitzstein searched all of Europe for a home. They first moved to Bessarabia, then tried England. They lived for four years in Liverpool. They went back to the Continent, where restless Moishe still insisted on moving from place to place. Of the couple's eleven children, four died in infancy. In 1879 their son Samuel Marcus Blitzstein was born; aside from another son, Jacob, the surviving children were all girls: Alberta, Jenny, Rose, Sophie, and the youngest, Mary.

The last stop on the Blitzsteins' European peregrination was Southampton, where Hannah, tired of the odyssey and caring for her infant daughter, wanted to settle and put down roots. But Alberta died there at the age of five. To escape the sadness, Hannah now declared herself ready for the final journey, and in February 1889 they boarded a ship bound for America. Their original destination was Chicago, but as it so often happens, they remained in their port of entry, Philadelphia. Hannah would not travel any farther.

The Blitzsteins ran a distinctly assimilationist household, more Russian than Jewish. If they knew Yiddish, they did not speak it at home. Inclined toward socialist ideas and decidedly unreligious, Mrs. Blitzstein did not bother to keep a kosher kitchen. As the only literate woman in the neighborhood, she wrote letters for everyone who came to her. Marcus and Anna—they both anglicized their names—took the side of "the masses" but had trouble liking individuals. They guarded the privacy of their own family and kept outsiders at emotional bay.

At first they opened a tobacco business. They did well at it, and friends asked them to help invest their savings for them. Within a few months, they began financing steamship tickets—*Schiffskarten*—for immigrants to America. Often, when the newcomers would arrive, they stayed in the Blitzsteins' three-story dwelling at 431 South Fourth Street, which also housed the banking operation.

There would frequently be as many as twenty people at the dinner table. The confidence they inspired led to more and more transactions until, in the same year of 1889, they were in a position to open M. L. Blitzstein & Company—"Banking in all its branches," read its letterhead. In time, they erected a modest-sized limestone building, in an otherwise all brick neighborhood, on the northwest corner of a 27-by-75-foot lot at Fourth and Lombard streets in Philadelphia. Appropriately enough for this immigrant bank, they chose as their symbol the image of a ship's steering wheel superimposed on an anchor. Specializing in the immigration financing business, the Blitzstein Bank brought to Philadelphia large numbers of Russian Jews who for years would pay a small weekly sum in repayment of their debts. Two other such banks, Lipschutz's and Morris Rosenbaum's, performed similar functions. And this population grew exponentially. In 1890 Philadelphia had fewer than 10,000 Eastern European Jews; by 1910 it was home to over 100,000, and by 1930, more than 200,000. As the "workshop of the world"—so the city called itself—Philadelphia housed a great variety of industries: garments, hats, carpeting, metal works, railroad cars, sugar refining, shipbuilding, publishing, pianos. The bank enabled Jewish immigrants and working people to adapt to their new life in America and to bring over the other members of their families who had remained in Russia.

Marcus Lionel Blitzstein died of heart disease in February 1897 at the age of fifty-one, his death unnoticed by Philadelphia newspapers. Aside from seventeen-year-old Sam, the only other son who had lived long enough to emigrate to America was Jacob, who as a teenager took long trips on his bicycle. On one such excursion, in October of 1898, returning to Philadelphia from Atlantic City, he ruptured his appendix and died at the age of eighteen. By that time, several of the Blitzstein children had married and a next generation was starting up. To them, Anna was known as Babushka. Everyone in the family had their accounts in the Blitzstein Bank and several family members worked there. After her husband's death, Babushka ran the bank herself, turning for support to her son Sam and to her eldest son-in-law, Constantine Borisevich Voynow, married to Sophie.

Jenny married William Tutelman, a wealthy shirt manufacturer whom many of the relations found ignorant and crude, and moved to Oak Lane, Pennsylvania. They were the first in the family to own an automobile. They named the first of their four children Mark, after Jenny's father. Rose went to medical school and became the first woman obstetrician and gynecologist in Philadelphia. She shared a house at Fourth and Buttonwood with a pharmacist, Fanny Slobodkin, and both had their offices there. Fanny always had a supply of rock candy for the children when they passed by.

At twenty-one, Sam married a woman one year younger than he, who bore his mother's name. He had threatened that unless she married him, he would commit suicide. Anna Lewytski, born in Russia into a family of seven or eight children, had come to America as an infant. The family (which later shortened its name to Levitt) settled in Baltimore before they moved to Philadelphia, when Anna was one and a half. Her father had an apparel business and her mother,

Clara, had been friendly with Babushka in various Jewish and civic-improvement organizations. Though not dull, Anna was no intellectual. She was well brought up and reasonably cultured, but she seemed hardly a prize catch for a Blitzstein. In her own family she was held up to her cousins as a model young lady, but the Blitzsteins offered only the most perfunctory acceptance. Sam himself, a man of limitless charm and vivacity, was not an achiever by nature. As he was already established in his position as a steamship ticket agent at the bank, college was out of the question. In time, he found himself more and more attracted to street-corner café talk about socialism and other political notions. His career became secondary. Eventually, he spent a minimal amount of time at the bank.[2]

Sam and Anna's first child was a girl, Josephine, born in 1902, before the couple's first anniversary. On March 2, 1905, Marcus Samuel Blitzstein, named for his grandfather and father, was born at 419 Pine Street, in what is now referred to as Philadelphia's "Society Hill."

In their home, there was a succession of broad-footed Polish maids, just off the ship, who always preferred to work either in bare feet or in worn-out men's shoes. They taught Jo and Marc little peasant games, counting off rhymes on their fingers. One time, a black maid discovered Marc and Jo spying on her having sex with a boyfriend and locked them in a closet as punishment.

As children, Jo and Marc spent their summers at Babushka's house in Atlantic City. Babushka, who had trouble dealing with women and preferred the company of men, always favored the angelic Marc over Jo: For one thing, he was the only grandchild who could be expected to carry on the Blitzstein name.

Early on, Marc developed a taste for candy corn and two jujubes after dinner. From a traumatic childhood event, he also acquired an understanding of dramatic effect. He later recalled the incident:

> What I remember first is horror. I was three; the kitchen of our house at Fourth and Lombard Streets in Philadelphia gave on to a backyard, where there was an outhouse. On a Monday morning in June, I must have asked my mother in the kitchen to undo my panties so that I might use the outhouse. In the backyard there was a flurry of Monday clotheswashing going on, with specially-hired help; dripping garments on the lines, pails of water and boiling starch, sunlight and steaming bricked pavement are all clear in my memory. Then a blank (when I try to recall)—a blank like the report of a gun. I am told I talked to a kitten in the yard, backing up meantime towards the outhouse; and landed squarely into a pail of boiling starch. The burn covered back and buttocks. I remember next a sofa, placed in the dining-room beside the kitchen; a sofa on which the injured child was laid upon his belly, so he could have company all during the day, and be undisputed monarch of things and people in the room. And I remember the child, inexorably eking the last drop of sympathy from parents already shattered by guilt, looking pitifully up: "Mumsie, are you sorry? Are you sorry, mumsie?" Began the relentless career of a charming, talented, self-salving brat. . . . The accident had as one result

> a series of night-attacks, "spasms," accompanied by delirium and screaming; occasionally I would come to during an attack, and continue it with nice theatrical flair and plausibility.[3]

One psychological theory that attempts to explain the origin of artistic talent has it that creativity may be the successful sublimation of rage. If as a child Blitzstein learned to convert his feelings of injured innocence into theatre, the psychologists may be correct.

The family's earliest memory of Marc's first experiments at the piano was Marc picking out a tune he had heard his father whistle in a piercing sibilant timbre, then adding a second tone to the melody line. "Look, Aunt Mary, wif double notes!" he shouted gleefully upon his amazing discovery. At the age of three, he would sit at the piano and play by ear. Babushka once discovered him there with his pants gathered about his feet, as he was still unable to button them up. Lessons began at age five, when it was evident that he had perfect pitch, and he shortly learned to read music. The story is told that when the teacher came to the house, little Marc would go to Babushka and beg for the money to pay for the lesson. Anna considered this display somewhat distasteful—her mother-in-law, a rich woman, forcing the child into such an act of humiliation.

Soon, outfitted in the little white dress that both boys and girls wore for formal occasions in the early years of the century, he would give family recitals, playing selections such as the airs from *The Tales of Hoffman* and Mendelssohn's "Spring Song." Blocks had to be installed on the pedals so that Marc's legs could reach them. He enchanted those about him with his recitations from memory of stories and poems read to him but once. As a preschooler, he demanded to be taken to school with his sister as a "visitor." Once in the classroom, he would participate fully, outshining all the older children.

A favorite game that Marc used to like playing with Jo also involved his humiliation. In a version of Princess and the Pauper, Marc played the beggar, cringing in the gutter, and Jo played the magnanimous rich lady. She would take him in and clothe him with a curtain or some other swatch of material. She would feed him—usually slices of greasy banana—and he would be grateful. He thrived on pity and largesse. It was as though he knew his own flaws, even imagined an inherent unworthiness, and considered his family's adoration of his young talent to be baseless, or certainly exaggerated. Through the game, repeated often in his childhood, he could reestablish his true persona, claim his private reality.[4]

Once, when he was about six, Marc persisted in annoying his Aunt Mary while she was trying to study. To be rid of him, she recited Sir William Watson's little poem:

April, April,
Laugh thy girlish laughter;
Then, the moment after,
Weep thy girlish tears.

"Take that and go set it to music," Mary said, and to her relief he disappeared from the room. Not an hour later, he reappeared, and to her astonishment played through his song for her.

Constantine von Sternberg was Marc's music teacher. As much as Marc later admitted to being "a great show-off; kid prodigy stuff—things that I hate now," when his teacher gave him gold stars on his lessons, he became "still more vain and obstreperous." At age seven he played for the first time in public: the Mozart *Coronation* Concerto with Sternberg at the second piano.[5]

As secularists, Sam and Anna provided Jo and Marc with no formal Jewish education, but Anna felt they ought to have some kind of moral instruction. For a while she sent them to the Ethical Culture Sunday school, which seemed to leave no lasting impact on either child. Sunday afternoons, Sam took them to the Socialist Literary Society, which met at the South Broad Street Theatre.

Marc loved to visit his father at the bank, located in the heart of the Jewish shopping district. All of its employees were Jewish, several of them Blitzstein or Galanter family members. Sam paid them well—in the early 1920s he hired the first woman bank teller in Pennsylvania for a grand forty-five dollars a week. Marc liked waiting for Sam to take him out to lunch because it gave him the chance to play with the office equipment. He would punch in long columns on the adding machine and then go over the tape manually to check its accuracy. He also liked it when Sam whistled and when he gave his frequent impromptu recitals on the "bones"—spoons or knives. Marc loved the sharp rhythmic clickety-clack that Sam created to accompany some overheard tune. At lunch, Marc sat in on Sam's informal conclaves with his left-wing cronies, a pastime Anna did not share.

Constantine Voynow, Jo and Marc's uncle, was perhaps the most Russified of the whole clan, more Russian Orthodox in his customs than Jewish. Trained as an electrical engineer, tall and handsome, he and Aunt Sophie married in 1892, had five sons, Gregory, Lionel, Andrew, Paul, and Constantine, Jr. (called Cutch), and a single daughter Vera. Early on, as of about 1910, he had a Stanley Steamer automobile. He had the first phonograph in the family, with a big horn and the famous white Victor dog. He built Vera a dollhouse big enough for four children to play in and fitted it with electricity at a time when the rest of the family still used gas and Welsbach lamps. A socialist atheist like the rest of the family, he was nevertheless fond of creating an elaborate Russian Christmas just for the spirit of it, complete with a tree (the biggest on the block), a crèche decorated with electric lights, and the exchange of gifts. The whole Blitzstein clan would gather at the Voynows' for the holiday. Babushka would give each of the grandchildren a two-and-a-half-dollar gold piece and then "hold" it from year to year. None of them seems to recall ever having seen the accumulated principal.

Lionel Voynow (called Leo), an employee of the bank, was a natural piano player. Marc, much younger and still in need of blocks on the pedals, would teach him popular tunes. Then they would play four-hand improvisations together in Chinese, Indian, Yiddish, and other modes, to everyone's immense amusement. For all these exciting reasons, the Voynows became Jo and Marc's favorite cousins, with Andy, just a few months younger than Marc, the closest of all.

Anna Levitt had two sisters, Sadie and Reba, and several brothers spread out across the country. But distance, in some cases, and the generally low regard the Blitzsteins held for the Levitts meant that their relations on their mother's side played little lasting role in Jo and Marc's family life.

In June of 1912, after eleven years of marriage, Sam and Anna Blitzstein filed divorce papers. Their social outlooks were too disparate and Sam disliked playing the role of family man. After Sam left, Anna was practically destitute. Abandoned by their father, Jo and Marc often appeared poorly dressed, and the Levitt family sacrificed considerably to help Anna and her children. Babushka gave Anna minimal amounts of money to live on, but Jo had to go to her personally to ask for enough to pay the rent and the coal-delivery man. Through such mechanisms Babushka tried to make the separation so uncomfortable that Anna and Sam would find some means of reconciliation.

In 1914 Anna's mother died. By this time, support from the Blitzstein family had all but dried up in the failure to make the marriage whole again. With her principal source of comfort gone, Anna decided to take the children to California to stay with her sister Sadie.

The three Blitzsteins moved in with Sadie and her kindly, somewhat effeminate husband Herman. Sadie ran a women's dress shop on the boardwalk in Venice, and together the extended Levitt family took care of the children. Through her charm and bearing, more than on the basis of any experience, Anna landed herself a position as head hat buyer for Bullock's in Los Angeles.

An exceptionally bright boy, Marc had already skipped two grades in the Philadelphia schools and now, at the age of nine, entered junior high school in Venice. He continued private piano lessons for two years with Katherine Montreville Cocke, a friend and adviser of the pianist and composer Rudolph Ganz, and for another year with Julian Pascal. Among Marc's treasured memories was seeing Charlie Chaplin and other movie stars from nearby Hollywood visiting the beach. He continued his performance career by playing for any number of charity benefits that Anna and her sister arranged. Lady editors and society writers gave over whole columns of praise to the wunderkind.

"I became a most insufferable brat," he admitted as an adult; "precocious and spoiled, I didn't have to work nearly hard enough for my success, and I was completely cut off from my own contemporaries and really didn't know how to get on with them at all."[6] His brilliance and natural gifts, as well as his unique status in the family as the youngest and the only boy, predisposed a somewhat narcissistic development.

"Much was made of me," he recalled of these California years:

> I had bobbed hair, wore Lord Fauntleroy collars, sat on ladies' laps when I wasn't playing the piano, and was generally insufferable. I remember a series of gifts as follows: a banana, (which I stuffed in my mouth at one try, thereby earning a new prodigiousness), a fancy cup-and-saucer, a tricycle.[7]

Jo led a far less charmed existence. While her younger brother practiced the piano for hours on end, she earned her keep by cleaning and scrubbing at Aunt Sadie's house. Her resentment of this early discrimination was the main reason why as a grown woman she refused to do housework.

In 1917 Anna took her children back to Philadelphia. They needed a father. Marc and Jo, now twelve and fifteen, had lived for three years almost exclusively in the company of women. More important, Marc had outgrown his teachers in California. Only back east could he continue to grow musically.

2

STUDIES

1917–Fall 1926

"You shall not take my nose, it's all I've left!"

When Anna and her two children returned from California in early 1917, Marc entered the eighth-grade class, graduating in June. By the time he entered West Philadelphia High School for Boys in September 1917, the family lived at 4204 Parkside Avenue. Jewish migration from South Philadelphia had begun transforming the school's formerly all-Christian student body, much to the dismay of the WASP parents, who resented the changes in the neighborhood. Part of the mystique Marc cast on his schoolmates—they dubbed him "Blitz"—was his recounting of the pleasures of Venice beach, to such an extent that the other boys wondered why he ever returned east.

While other thirteen-year-old boys were avidly scanning the newspapers to follow the progress of the war in Europe, perhaps to discover the names of their older brothers in print, Marc spent his spare time composing for the piano. His meticulously catalogued "Opus 4, no. 1," bearing the date of March 1918, is "Waterfall," a quiet barcarole in a gently rocking 4/4 with triplets. An "Andante" from November of the following year is a seven-minute piece, again in 4/4 with no meter changes, cast in phrases reminiscent of Stephen Foster, but with soulful chromatic passages à la Rachmaninoff, ending in a Bachian ornament and resolution. The following month, the "Persienne" of Marcus S. Blitzstein featured iridescent splayed chords to be rendered "in mystic mood," salon music at its most imitative.

One of Aunt Mary's chums from Cornell, Berenice Skidelsky, used to return frequently to Philadelphia from her home in New York where, under the pen name of B. C. Noar, she published book notices in the New York *American, Vogue,* and elsewhere and spoke professionally on public affairs. Mary always spoke of her nephew Marc and the intellectual prowess he displayed. "The fairies seem to have been gathered thickly around his cradle when he was born!" Berenice wrote in her journal. On one visit, Berenice attended a party and reencountered the fifteen-year-old, whom she had not seen since before he left for California.

> I danced twice with him, and following the lead of his alert and darting mind, went hither and thither into channels of life interpretation, hardly suited to a dance; nor yet to an average person of his years.
>
> But he is certainly not an average person. This week I received a letter from him which in manner and matter is absolutely amazing for fifteen. . . .
>
> A combined maternal and pedagogic impulse in me rises to the challenge. The chance to take part in the guidance of a splendid young brain is very alluring. I wish this unusual child lived in the same city with me—what a marvelously interesting thing it would be to help him grow!
>
> Of course his infant precocity, and his manifold talents, may peter out and lead him eventually into mediocrity. I asked Dreiser once if he had been a precocious youngster, to which he replied: "Good Lord no! I was as slow as molasses!"
>
> History is too full of budding geniuses who, as someone has said, turn into blooming idiots, for one to place too much faith in early indications. Still, there is no question about the aliveness of this boy's mind; and the indications point also to potential depths. As for any notable exercise of his talents—time alone will tell.[1]

Eighteen years older, the somber, serious Berenice became a confidante. Marc felt freer to express himself to her than to anyone else. "I am a great puzzle to myself in many ways," he confessed to her, asking for her understanding. It was the beginning of a lifelong friendship. Often, when Marc traveled to New York, he would spend the night at Berenice's apartment, as would Jo on occasion.

By now Marc was in his senior year and living with his mother and Jo closer to town at 1418 South Broad Street. His grades in Latin, English, and French were in the mid-90s; in social studies, drawing, mathematics, and in a semester of banking procedures, he scored in the 80s. He sang in the glee club for two years and participated in the dramatic club. He stood first in his class and thereby delivered the valedictory address in June of 1921. He had grown to his full adult height of five feet, seven inches. His eyes of blue-gray never seemed to rest under his crown of brown hair.

Because of a childhood case of rheumatic fever, Jo stayed out of school for a year. And because of his skipping ahead, Marc had advanced. Thus they wound up in the same class of 1921—she, of course, at the West Philadelphia High School for Girls. Jo was an achiever, too. She was president of the Owl Club, the school literary society. In her senior year she participated in an essay contest sponsored by Swarthmore College. When the college called Jo Blitzstein in to claim the first prize, they discovered that she was a girl and gave the prize to someone else: The contest was open only to boys. Still, her grades and accomplishments made her second in her class and the salutatorian of her year.

Ever a ladies' man, Sam had a succession of affairs and tried his best to woo Berenice into marriage. But up to 1920 his divorce from Anna had not become final because she could never prove adultery. One day, taking a ride in Atlantic City with a friend, Dr. Segal, Anna mentioned that she knew of Sam's affairs but was unable to prove anything. To which Dr. Segal replied, "I think I can help you," for he knew of Sam's affair with his own wife, Pauline. The discovery led to a final divorce settlement in May of 1920. The Segals had three girls. The oldest, Vivienne Segal, had already begun what was to become a long and notable career in the musical theatre. The middle girl, Vera, danced with Isadora Duncan's troupe. The third, Louise, while not well known in any way, impressed Marc and Jo as the only true flapper in their circle.

As things worked out, Anna married Dr. Segal in 1921. Shortly after, when he began suffering heart problems, Jo found that Anna was incapable of providing the attention he required and she took his care upon her shoulders. The marriage lasted only two years before his death. Anna recuperated from the blow with her relatives in California.

Marc and Sam, meanwhile, had developed a warm, easy friendship hardly characterized by the standard father-son tensions. Sam loved concertgoing with Marc; and Marc, in turn, showed concern for his father. Once, when Sam had been hospitalized, Marc visited, finding him attended by a prim woman of middle age. "So why couldn't they get a pretty young nurse for you?" son teased father. "Not that you'd be sleeping with her, but at least you'd have something better to look at."

During his high school years, Marc developed an abiding love for swimming. He and his cousin Andy would take a canoe out at Ventnor on the New Jersey shore and test each other for endurance, one rowing, one swimming in the coastal inlets. Once they rowed into a blind alley, hidden by high swamp grass on both sides, and then into another and another. For hours they were lost, screaming for help, swarms of mosquitoes making a tasty meal of them while the midday sun burned. Eventually they came out at Chelsea and took public transportation home, red as much from embarrassment as from the sunburn.

Marc attended as much theatre and as many concerts as he could. He heard the first Philadelphia performance of Stravinsky's *Firebird.* He heard all the great pianists of his day. Once he went home after a recital by Vladimir Horowitz and sighed, "I could never play like that." Daunted by such a strong role model, he turned further in the direction of composing. One ambitious project for a boy of fifteen was his *Marche Vainqueur—A Festival March for Complete Orchestra,* composed in August 1920. Fundamentally not the most engaging material, it is inflated and overly orchestrated, sounding more like Berlioz or Meyerbeer than Sousa or Ives. Yet it shows a disposition toward rhythmic vitality somewhat off the beaten track, and a taste for spicy chromatic harmonies. The fact that he prepared separate orchestra parts suggests that he anticipated a performance or that one took place, perhaps at his high school.

In the fall of 1921, Jo at nineteen and Marc at sixteen both entered the University of Pennsylvania, Marc under a full merit scholarship. While adjusting to the routine of his new environment—"coffee chats at 10:30 A.M.; three-hour conversations on girls, Bach, and psychoanalysis; walks at midnight with a few intimates"—he allowed himself time to compose poems and read hungrily. Among writers, he was fond of Rupert Brooke and George Meredith, and he thanked his mentor Berenice for the introduction to James Stephens's work.

"And I do not dislike the co-eds dogmatically; at least I think not," he wrote to Berenice. "They're either violently familiar, and that always bewilders me (who am timidly trying my first-legs in sex), or they're up-stage and offish. I know that if you were now a co-ed, you'd be as much annoyed at them as I am."[2] Concluding a poem describing some mangled efforts at seduction in a park, he asks:

> *I like to think I moved her;*
> *Or was it she wept at my clumsiness;—*
> *Or wasn't I in it at all?*

The concluding line suggests that he might have begun questioning the nature of his sexuality.

After returning from California, he studied composition with William F. Happich. His piano studies in Philadelphia included work with Maurits Leefson from 1917 to 1918 and with D. Hendrik Ezerman at the Philadelphia Conservatory of Music from 1918 to 1922. His work shortly won recognition. Competing in April 1921 in a Philharmonic Society of Philadelphia contest open to undergraduate music students of the city, Marcus Blitzstein was named a gold medalist. The prize included a performance at the Academy of Music, the orchestra conducted by Josef Pasternack. On February 5, 1922, Marc donned an ill-fitting tuxedo borrowed from someone shorter and fatter—he couldn't imagine owning one and he would not allow his father to buy one. He played the Saint-Saëns Concerto no. 2 in G Minor to a tremendous outpouring of audience affection for the young master not quite seventeen years old.

The pianist "showed wonderful command of his instrument and displayed a masculinity of touch that was really surprising," said one Philadelphia critic. "There is little of the academist about Mr. Blitzstein," wrote another: "He sought emotional expression and found it. The applause that broke forth at the end of the concerto was a spontaneous response to the player's appeal." Called back again and again for bows, Marc pleased his newfound public with a solo of Tchaikovsky's "Troika," revealing, in a third critic's account, "fresh subtleties of technique and interpretation." Even after the awkward boy had thrown his hands upward to indicate he had no more to play, "the audience clapped loudly, determined that this youthful star should twinkle once again."[3]

Marc sent one of the more jubilant clippings to Berenice in New York. "But even more interesting to me was the letter that accompanied it," she recorded in her journal.

> He tells of having continued "on the emotional upstroke" until four days after the concert, and then (the implication is) of having plunged down into the depths.
>
> I read very much between the lines of his letter. He has much suffering ahead of him, no matter what his successes. Already his deepest intuitions are warning him that even in success one does not touch reality, does not rend the mysterious veil between us and that absolute truth with which we long to be dazzled but no faint glimmer of which, even, we are able to catch.
>
> He is bewildered; to have it publicly proclaimed that he "possess[es] something more than talent; it does not shoot wide of the mark to state that he has genius," is apparently far from soul-satisfying. Then if this does not measure up, his soul begins to query, what does?
>
> And so he sets forth upon the journey whose goal is the realization that nothing does—that there must always be (for temperaments such as his) the lure of the just-beyond, which will dim the here and now.[4]

In his academic work at the University of Pennsylvania, Blitzstein did well. In his freshman year he received the grade of "Distinguished" in two English courses (composition and history of the English language), two French courses (advanced reading and advanced grammar), Latin (Ovid), and philosophy (ethics). In psychology (mind and body) he was "Passed."

During his adolescence, Marc continued working at his creative writing, employing a consciously crafted, highly descriptive style, with a vocabulary well developed for one his age. In the first and only pages he wrote of a novel, the maid Mollie always put "one or two things out of place in her housecleaning. It was once suggested by Leo that it might be the last remnant of taste in Mollie; subtle asymmetry is certainly an artistic canon." In his poetic attempts, he displayed that streak of morbidity and self-pity that would never entirely leave him. "Dying," only one among several such efforts, dates from November 1922.

Watch me, I'm about to go.
There will be but one black flare,
You will poise on your tunnel of air
Until I sink and die. Then woe,
Expressed in noisy tears.
This the merry scheme devised.
                    O wait there
Tight and high, agonized

Until I move and die.
Rare
Joy to have you hung upon your breath,
Waiting for my death!

Present as a kind of echo is his indulgent cry of "Are you sorry, mumsie?" from his childhood burn.

In a sonnet written about the same time, he showed his first leanings toward parody. Beginning with the lovesick line, "You took my heart away, and left a shell," and continuing in this vein for twelve lines of perfect scansion and rhyme scheme, he concludes unexpectedly with this couplet:

Now that I'm heartless, senseless, soul-bereft,
You shall not take my nose, it's all I've left!

In his formal studies, as early as 1922 Marc devised a "Musicredo" in which he articulated a series of beliefs concerning composers, performers, styles, and instruments—the violin "a much overestimated instrument, and the viola a much undervalued one." He saw in jazz "a significant and important phase of music; . . . given creatively intelligent apostles and enthusiastic rallyers, it should produce those authentic pieces of art, of which it so far evinces no slightest promise." In the same year, he later claimed, he wrote nine preludes for piano, but apparently only one has survived.

During Marc's college days, he shared a top-floor room with his father at 4122 Girard Avenue, a three-story household that included Babushka, Aunt Rose (who had moved her medical offices to the ground floor), and the entire Voynow family. (The eldest son Lionel, with whom Marc had played four-hand piano as a child, had died in the influenza epidemic of 1918.) As the male head of the household, Uncle Constantine could be both watchful and undercutting. He would shush other members of the family when he heard Marc practicing, so they wouldn't disturb him. But often, when he went into the house and found Marc at the piano, he would remark, "Oh, you're *playing*"—pointedly implying Marc's failure to use his time in any more productive fashion.

Marc frankly worried his relatives. Aunt Rose, in particular, saw him nearly killing himself with exhaustion, practicing the piano and composing several hours a day while still maintaining a full course of studies at the university. Early in life, Blitzstein recognized that both from his class position and his musical talent he had inherited a great privilege. He worked himself extremely hard, and with rare self-discipline, to earn it.

Blitzstein had outgrown the resources of piano teachers in Philadelphia and began commuting to New York to study with Alexander Siloti at his apartment in the Ansonia Hotel. He was Siloti's first American pupil. Then nearly sixty, Siloti, early in his life, had studied music theory with Tchaikovsky at the Moscow Conservatory, and from 1883 to 1886 was a piano student of Liszt in Weimar. Back in Russia, he taught at the Moscow Conservatory, his first cousin Rachmaninoff among his prize pupils. At the time of the 1905 uprising, Siloti and Serge Koussevitzky organized a series of symphony concerts independent of official sponsorship, in which they attempted to present works of a modern harmonic idiom, but the authorities intervened and stopped the new music. After the 1917 Revolution, Siloti left Russia, settling in New York in 1922, where he taught at the Juilliard School of Music from 1925 on.

From the start, Siloti took to Blitzstein well, as did his wife Vera, the eldest daughter of Pavel Tretyakov, the Russian art collector. She served as her husband's secretary, but Blitzstein considered her his "musical mother." They conducted their relations in French for the most part. Mrs. Siloti wrote to him once early in their friendship how *"un maître est heureux d'avoir des disciples pour continuer dans l'univers son idée et son idéal* [a master is happy to have disciples to further his idea and his ideal in the universe]."[5] At one lesson, Siloti gave *"à mon chère* [*sic*] *M. Blitzstein"* a copy of his book *My Memories of Liszt.* At the Silotis', Blitzstein also enjoyed meeting the many Russian émigrés who passed through, including Stravinsky.

For three years, Blitzstein took two lessons a month with Siloti; with trainfare, each visit cost the youngster twenty-seven dollars. He proudly claimed Siloti as his teacher, thereby making himself a musical "grandson" of Liszt, but he never recorded his reactions to Siloti. Though a superb performer, Siloti was not a great teacher. His manner was tyrannical, permitting no discussion. He offered no analysis and no intellectual response to music, relying instead on pure feeling. He would play, and from hearing him, a student might understand Siloti's approach. Yet he was a superb technician, full of physical tricks and exercises to help a student master the keyboard.

Whatever Blitzstein divined from Siloti, each time he returned from New York he would entertain his college friends with tales of adventures with his stepsister Vivienne Segal and her wild theatre crowd. And for the further amusement of his friends, he had somehow picked up a trick of facing away from the piano keyboard, reaching his arms up over his shoulders, and playing backward. At parties all through his life, this sure-fire stunt guaranteed him an attentive reception.

In his second year at the university, Blitzstein distinguished himself in philosophy, English, and French, passed psychology, and in sociology rated "Good." He began and later withdrew from Sanskrit 6, a course on the history of Indian culture and institutions. In the required physical education course he was "Not Passed," however. Though he liked gymnastics, he much preferred swimming as his exercise. He simply skipped most of his physical education classes, believing on principle that this should not be a required subject in an academic institution.

Probably for reasons of illness, Blitzstein took a leave of absence in January 1923. But skipping gym classes happened to be the one point on which the head of the department would not yield, and a passing grade in physical education was a prerequisite for reentry and a renewed scholarship. Marc's Uncle Constantine, a respected civil engineer, aside from being president of the Blitzstein Bank, went personally to plead for an exception in Marc's case, but the department head remained adamant. The Blitzstein family could well have afforded to keep Marc in school, but Marc felt that the decision was unfair and refused to return. Thus his undergraduate career came to an unanticipated end after the first semester of his second year. In any event, Marc had already begun studying with Siloti, and on one visit, when Marc was considering his future, his teacher offered him some peremptory counsel. "It's either music or college, if you want to be a musician," he said. Armed with that advice, Marc now enjoyed the freedom and time to study music all the more seriously.

A regular patron of The Music Shop on Sansom Street and of the Theodore Presser Music Company, where he bought his musical scores, he devoured the available literature on music as well. He read such publications as the *Musical Quarterly* and *La Revue Musicale* faithfully, inserting reproving marginal notes on the authors' statements. In one article on Scriabin, Blitzstein foretold an aspect of his own future, writing, "How horrible a thing it is to have one's musical intentions analysed by a 'critic.' "

During his leave from school, Marc kept busy studying, practicing, composing, concert- and theatregoing. Not only did he see the Moscow Art Theatre's production of Maxim Gorky's *The Lower Depths,* but Gorky himself—on tour with the company and apprised through his socialist connections of some good comrades in Philadelphia—spent his nights at the Blitzsteins' house. Blitzstein continued his work with Siloti in New York until 1926 and often stayed over to see such plays as Eugene O'Neill's *Welded* and *Desire Under the Elms.*

Jo ended her career at the University of Pennsylvania at around the same time that Marc ended his. In 1923 she married Edward Davis, a hardworking, likable lawyer, thirty years old. He came from a fiercely Orthodox Jewish family and had suffered through a strict upbringing and his father's rabbinical aspirations for him. He shared the Blitzsteins' secularism, putting all religious considerations behind him. Politically, he was something of an anomaly: While a pioneer in labor law, representing a number of unions in their formative stages, he stuck close to a conservative Republican line. Somehow he managed to rise above the Blitzstein family's tireless, fevered disputations over the varieties of revolutionary socialist thought, rarely joining in but enjoying the often amusing show from the sidelines. A man of exceptional probity, he appeared several times over the course of his long career at the top of the bar association's list of endorsements for judgeships, but each time he refused to hand over the required ten-thousand-dollar contribution to the Republican Party coffers. Marc soon came to prize Ed's company.

If she had not married, Jo might not have finished college anyway, for the Blitzsteins—Babushka in particular—might have thought it unseemly for her to complete her education after Marc had left school. Whatever the case, Jo always felt a physical revulsion every time she passed the Theodore Presser music shop. To her it represented everything she had had to sacrifice to further her brother's talents. Marriage at twenty-one may have been her best escape route to independence.

Fully conscious of the ways Babushka, then Anna and Sam and her aunt in

California, and Swarthmore and society in general favored boys over girls, and Marc over her, Jo decided early in her maturity to repress her natural feelings of jealousy. What good could come out of nurturing anger? Instead, sensing that in her strength of personality she was hardier than either Marc or her mother, she traded her resentment for an almost desperately protective love of Marc. After all, it was hardly his fault that he had been coddled and fussed over since birth. Whatever pressures they had been subjected to in childhood, the fact remained that no one else in Jo's life could approach him for wit, for a host of shared sensibilities, for intellectual rapport, for emotional closeness.

The following year, 1924, Alexander Smallens, newly appointed staff conductor with the Philadelphia Civic Opera, had a concert engagement in France. He invited Marc to join him on a two-week European trip. Almost twice Marc's age at the time, Smallens not only admired Marc's talent at the piano: He also felt attracted to him physically. In a town on the Brittany coast, Smallens introduced Marc to intercourse, which the nineteen-year-old found painful and rarely tried again. By this time, Blitzstein's sexual orientation had stabilized more certainly as homosexual; but from then on, though he liked his men masculine, he preferred to assume the dominant role in sex. Rumors continued for years to the effect that Marc and Alexander Smallens were lovers. Apparently their physical relations ended on that trip to France, but they did remain good friends and artistic collaborators for a long time afterward. When Marc talked about his homosexuality with his steady confidante Berenice, she imagined a hormonal root to it, citing the work of Krafft-Ebing and Havelock Ellis, and thus forgave it as an unchangeable element in his psychology.

That same summer he returned with his cousin Andy to the West Coast to see his mother. They took passage to California on a slow freighter wending its way through the Panama Canal and up the Mexican coast. "The folks here are almost besides themselves with joy," Mumsie wrote in anticipation, "and are planning for you to have a nice time."[6]

The voyage on the S.S. *Finland* of the Panama Pacific Line turned out to be memorable. Not long out, Andy and Marc were sitting on the boat deck, Andy reading *The Picture of Dorian Gray,* when a crew member spotted them and engaged them in conversation. This literate Scotsman, Donald McKillop, had a book of Wilde's poetry in his room and shared the two cousins' interests. When McKillop's watch was over, he met Marc on deck and on request sang "The Road to the Isles," "The Eriskay Love Lilt," and other Scottish songs. Marc quickly jotted down their melodies in a notebook. Then they repaired to a public room with a piano and Marc played accompaniments to McKillop's hearty singing. The Scotsman proceeded to recite Burns's "Tam O'Shanter" and so the journey passed with a fine new friend.

Marc and Andy debarked in Los Angeles and the ship continued to San Francisco. They stayed in a basement room of Marc's aunt's house in Venice. Another near-relative, Pearl Chern, lived close by; she had remembered Marc from his passage through Chicago on the way to California in 1914, and the three of them went on excursions to Riverside, San Bernardino, and especially, because Andy thought of becoming an architect, to see the old Spanish missions. From her ladies' clothing store on the boardwalk, Aunt Sadie had many friends. Marc always laughed recalling the time he was playing the piano for a clutch of these chattering women and one of them asked in bewilderment, "How can them little hands make so much noise?"

After a month, Marc and Andy took the train back home. But before they went, the *Finland* returned to Los Angeles and Donald McKillop visited them. As he recalled many years later:

> You had me sing for your friends "Ye Banks and Braes o' Bonnie Doon." On finishing the song, I was surprised to see tears in the eyes of one of your lady guests. I wondered if it was the pathos of the words that had moved her, or if she, too, had suffered like the lady of the song: "And my false lover stole my rose, But ah! he left the thorn wi' me."
>
> On parting with you in Los Angeles, you were good enough to give me another invitation to come to Philadelphia when you would return. How flattered I was, when you told me that Maxim Gorky had slept in the same room as I was to sleep in.[7]

Mary Curtis Bok, heiress to *The Ladies' Home Journal* fortune and wife of its editor, had been instrumental in promoting and funding the Settlement Music School in Philadelphia. By 1923 she had become so impressed with the talent of its most advanced students that she decided to create the Curtis School of Music for those aspiring to professional careers, and in October 1924 the first classes were held in three buildings off Rittenhouse Square. Having heard of these plans, Marc was in no hurry to return to the University of Pennsylvania, with or without a scholarship, and he entered the new music school as one of its first students, with composition as his field of specialization. On his application—now definitively as Marc Blitzstein, having dropped both his middle name and the final syllable of his given name—he listed his race as Jewish, nationality as American, and for religion drew a straight line to indicate none.

Rosario Scalero was Blitzstein's principal composition teacher, as he had been for Virgil Thomson and would later be for Samuel Barber, Gian Carlo Menotti, Lukas Foss, and many more. Endlessly, Marc wrote out scales, modulations, chord progressions, and counterpoint for Scalero, using medieval and Early Renaissance *canti firmi* as a melodic base. A mediocre composer himself, the conservative Scalero disallowed any exceptions to the rules. Blitzstein also took courses in early music, dictation and sight singing, keyboard harmony, orchestration, and Roman literature, never receiving a grade lower than an A-minus.

As always, he attended all the concerts he could. Stravinsky's *Rossignol* and *Petrouchka* in January 1925 with the Philadelphia Orchestra were significant in Blitzstein's burgeoning consciousness of the modern. His attraction was ever to the new, to whatever seemed to throw over the established canons and offer fresh models. In his studies of Russian music, he saw Mussorgsky's music as a seminal influence on later composers, with its "atonality, strongly modal in movement." He recognized the splash and finesse Rimsky-Korsakov's orchestrations gave to Mussorgsky, and saw, too, how they denied the essence and genuineness of the music. He preferred the more austere, meditative Debussy to the more extroverted Ravel. He quoted Jean Cocteau: "Music is not always a gondola, a race horse or a tight rope. It is also sometimes a chair." In an essay on the popularity of conductors, he used as one measure of quality their receptivity to younger American composers. Already conscious of the sociology of music, he discussed the treatment of the orchestra as a matter of civic pride: It is "on its way to joining that limbo of public pets in company with the park, the playground and the Bigger and Better cars."

Svarga, a pantomime suite for chamber orchestra, was one of Blitzstein's student works, composed in six movements between October 1924 and February 1925, with revisions that July. Set in the land of the Sanskrit gods, the scenario centers around Indra, a Samson-like figure of strength who takes hearty draughts of soma (wine) and after a prolonged bellyache dies, casting from him his sword, symbol of his energy. Other characters are Agni, the fire god, two Maruts (wind gods), two Apsaras (Svarga girls), and a mortal maiden. At the conclusion, where Indra's sword has fallen, plants and flowers rise from the earth. There is no record of any collaboration on *Svarga,* nor of any performance. Notable is the deadly effect of the wine in this early work. Aware of his father's propensity toward drinking and perhaps afraid of the tendency in himself, Blitzstein would return again and again to this theme.

The first documented performance of Blitzstein's music took place in late 1924. In their early married life together, Jo and Ed threw themselves into Jasper Deeter's new suburban theatre project in Rose Valley, fourteen miles south of Philadelphia. Deeter's Hedgerow Theatre produced O'Neill, Shaw, Shakespeare, Milne, Pirandello, and a host of new plays, in a few of which Jo acted. On December 6, 1924, Deeter introduced the world premiere of *King Hunger,* a Soviet play by Leonid Andreyev. Mordecai (Max) Gorelik designed the production and Deeter directed and acted, along with Edward Biberman and Ann Harding. The program credits the music to Marc Blitzstein. Written in a stylized, propagandistic mode, the play features characters such as Time, King Hunger, Death, The Workers, The Driftwood of the City, Judges, Soldiers, The Hungry Ones, An Artist, An Engineer; and settings such as A Belfry Overlooking the City, The Interior of a Factory, A Cellar, A Courtroom, A Ballroom, and The Public Square. The only surviving music from this score is for the Public Square scene, a "macabre dance" for violin and piano with castanets. This kind of politicized symbolism in the theatre, its lessons worn prominently on the sleeve, would exert a powerful fascination for Blitzstein.

Preparing to enter his second year at Curtis, Blitzstein appealed for a full scholarship. The $145 he had paid for the first year was "money extended by my father with the proviso that my work was to be of such merit as to render any payment this year unnecessary," he wrote to William Walter, executive director of the institute. But Walter arranged only a partial scholarship of one hundred dollars.[8]

At Curtis, Blitzstein also composed a series of piano pieces: "Pavane," "Variations on Au Clair de la Lune," "Sarabande," "Danse Basse," and "Danse Haute." He wrote three songs to texts by A. E. Housman and, in 1925, four settings of Walt Whitman texts: "Joy, Shipmate, Joy!" the chromatic, Hugo Wolf-like "After the Dazzle of Day," the Ivesian "As If a Phantom Caress'd Me," and the impressionistic "What Weeping Face," the last dedicated to the singer Lisa Roma. Cautiously dissonant, these songs feature eminently singable vocal lines. In "As If a Phantom Caress'd Me," Whitman's evocation of sex and of society's oppressive regard for homosexuals clearly resonated deeply for Blitzstein.

> *As if a phantom caress'd me,*
> *I thought I was not alone walking here by the shore;*
> *But the one I thought was with me as now I walk by the*
> *shore, the one I loved that caress'd me,*
> *As I lean and look through the glimmering light, that*
> *one has utterly disappear'd,*
> *And those appear that are hateful to me and mock me.*

Blitzstein indicated a few words to be spoken rather than sung, already showing an influence from the new German treatment of the voice known as *Sprechstimme.*

As a critic, Blitzstein tried his hand with an article called "My Lady Jazz," published in February 1926. The work under discussion was Gershwin's Concerto in F, as performed by the composer and the New York Symphony under Walter Damrosch. "The concerto as a whole seems faintly disappointing," said the twenty-year-old; sections of it sounded "rather facile and cheap. . . . The Charleston rhythm employed throughout is, after all, simply a single and quite ephemeral trick; to have used it so importantly seems rather a pity, since it almost fixes a specific date upon the concerto, and lends to its future evaluation the ambiguous virtue of an antique." He concluded his comments memorably:

> So much has been said as to the importance of jazz, and its inevitable effect upon the music of the future, that one prophecy more or less will not much matter. For my part, I do not see why the fox-trot should not take its place beside the gavotte, the minuet, the polka and the waltz—dance forms which it resembles in every respect at the moment, except that of treatment by a great composer. To be sure, it is less decorative than the minuet—but then, of course, life today is much less ornamental than the day of the measured three-four parade. The influence of jazz will probably be as far-reaching as that of the waltz—which is to say that it will prove an engaging dance idiom, justified by its own charm, and quite outside the development of musical form.[9]

Extending his interest in dance, Blitzstein wrote program notes a few weeks later for a recital by Riva Hoffman, a seven-year veteran of Isadora Duncan's troupe, in which he praised her willingness to present the abstract art of movement without reliance on decor and costume. Isadore Freed accompanied her at the piano, a young composer Blitzstein would later reencounter from time to time.

On July 13, 1926, Blitzstein was the soloist with the Philadelphia Orchestra in the Liszt Concerto in E-flat, conducted by Henry Hadley. Blitzstein's fee was three hundred dollars. The concert took place in the auditorium at the Sesqui-Centennial International Exhibition as part of the celebration of 150 years of American independence. The pianist scored a tremendous success; the audience recalled him repeatedly to the stage for an encore. One critic cited his "technique fully adequate to the demands of the concerto and beautiful tone, sonorous in the louder passages and soft and poetic in those of a lyric nature." "The poetry of power was there," wrote another, "adjacent to the most delicate of fairy notes, sweeping through stirring transitions. It was delightful, and those who heard the young man were amazed at his skill and his age."

In his own analysis of his playing, Blitzstein referred to that French technique of *jeu perlé*—the pearly touch, a relaxed, flexible, genteel manner fleeting across the top of the keys à la Chopin. "I have a feeling that my point of view is close to the method," Blitzstein jotted down in a personal memorandum. But "I'm lighter and heavier than *jeu perlé;* when I mean it, I sink and bang away; when I don't, you almost don't know the music is there." His sinking and banging away might have been facilitated by the very structure of his hands, for while the hands themselves were not large, his stubby fingers were of approximately equal length and his stretch was wide. The muscles of his hirsute arms reached powerfully into each digit.

However, nothing could persuade Blitzstein that performance should be his true calling. Already, the reviews announced, he planned to study abroad the coming season. In the fall of 1926, the huge extended Blitzstein family gave a grand farewell party for Sam and Marc at the Russian Inn on Locust Street, a restaurant close by the Academy of Music where musicians, writers, and the Philadelphia intelligentsia gathered. Sam sailed for Le Havre in September and Marc followed on the *Mauretania* on October 9. After accompanying him on a short continental tour, Sam deposited his son in Paris, where Marc would remain to study with Nadia Boulanger.

3

DONNER UND BLITZSTEIN

Fall 1926–Fall 1929

". . . there are definitely cardinal sins—sins against oneself, against one's law."

Once Sam had left him on his own in Europe, Blitzstein felt himself in flight from "home, friends, family, old tricks and tracks," as he expressed it to Berenice. He tried to rid himself of the idea that he might always be the sightseer. But in time, once his life had settled into regular patterns, he came to feel at home in Paris. Blitzstein rented a sixth-floor room on the rue de Rennes in Montparnasse. "Most of the 'artists' give me a rectal pain," he continued to Berenice; "they have made a Greenwich Village of it here.

"I have started studying composition with Nadia Boulanger, an incredible Spartan woman; her musicianship is limitless, she is entirely charming, and she likes me. Next week I see Ravel; he won't teach anyone, I know, but I'm hoping for some valuable criticism."[1]

Ever since Aaron Copland had first gone to study with Boulanger five years before, a steady stream of young Americans had gone to Paris for her tutelage. At the least, one season with her had become the obligatory *tournée;* some composers stayed in Paris for years to soak up the rich broth of her musical wisdom. In her dark, almost medieval cloister of an apartment, she gathered about her the leading musical talents of France and the world. To be more specific, not of the whole world but of the Franco-Russian tradition, whose undisputed leader was Igor Stravinsky, under whose sway an entire generation or more of American music would emerge. The severe German and Austrian movements, headed by Arnold Schoenberg, lay outside her favor. She sought the expression of joy, emotion, poetry, and spirit in art, not agonized fear and cold mathematical calculation.

Parisian concert life hummed with excitement. Blitzstein's letters home contained sharp analytical précis of the major happenings he attended. He sprang to alertness particularly when any American music was played. He spoke, for instance, of Vladimir Golschmann's performance of two symphonies by George Antheil:

> They are for me tragic things; the tortured, strained product of a talented and vain mind, determined to be original, determined to say that last and perfect *mot* which will forever dispose of the classics; the causal motif is literary, not musical; the result is a terrific flabby structure, betraying familiar angles and plastering, and impotent, ponderous, a colossal waste; the expression of a GREAT IDEA.[2]

At the end of January, Blitzstein continued his series of Walt Whitman settings with "O Hymen! O Hymenee!" an eerie, panting apostrophe to fleeting love, employing dissonant bitonality and incorporating a daring vocal glissando:

> *O why do you now cease?*
> *Is it because if you continued beyond the swift moment*
> *you would soon certainly kill me?*

Another work written directly under Boulanger's aegis, and dedicated to her that same month, was a Whitman setting that he titled "Gods." The text begins, "Thought of the Infinite—the All! Be thou my God. Lover divine and perfect comrade!" and goes on to salute the ideal man, death, great ideas, time, space, shape, and sun all as gods—anything and everything that exalts the spirit. Composed at this time for voice and piano, the slow hymnlike piece, cosmic, unsentimental, and basically tonal, challenges the listener with frequent changes of time, key, and rhythm.

Boulanger considered these early compositions truly gifted and she was clearly impressed with his abilities at the piano. On January 27, shortly before he left Paris, they played together at the Ecole Normale de Musique de Paris. They performed a two-piano version of *Padmâvatî,* Albert Roussel's opera-ballet based on an Indian legend. *Padmâvatî* had had its premiere in Paris less than four years before. Boulanger wrote for Blitzstein a most favorable "To whom it may concern" letter:

> Having had the musical joy to have Mark [*sic*] Blitzstein as pupil for several months, I could not praise too highly his gifts—*Born musician,*

> he is especially bright minded—and gives the greatest reasons to believe he is to become a *true* great artist. What he has already accomplished is of unusual quality. This said in the most serious and sincere feeling.[3]

Marc left Mademoiselle Boulanger at the beginning of February and went directly to Berlin—Boulanger was upset by this—to seek out the twelve-tone advocate, Arnold Schoenberg. Except for those older musicians too committed to Romanticism to appreciate the new trends, most composers fell into one school or another; no one could be a partisan of both Stravinsky and Schoenberg. Blitzstein was not the first American to study with Schoenberg—Adolph Weiss had preceded him—but he was the only American to study with both Boulanger and Schoenberg.

There had obviously been no prior arrangement to study with him, for on February 12, 1927, Schoenberg addressed Blitzstein at the American Express office on Charlottenstrasse, asking why he wished to show him his compositions. Only under the most persuasive circumstances could he possibly take on another student at this busy time. Apparently, Blitzstein was persuasive, for a week later, Schoenberg invited Blitzstein to call on him at the Akademie der Künste.

Once enrolled in Schoenberg's course, Blitzstein made little secret of his antipathy to the twelve-tone system. At most, he indicated his reluctant respect. Only Roberto Gerhard, a Schoenbergian "*malgré moi*," as he put it, shared Blitzstein's irreverence. Besides resisting Schoenberg's technique, Blitzstein felt offended by his intense national chauvinism. One day Schoenberg told him, "It is only since the war that you American composers have been cut off from your source of supply, which is Germany, and have been writing Franco-Russian music. Ten years before the war you were all writing German music; and ten years from now you will all be writing German music again."[4]

Schoenberg turned out to be right but, at first, not the way he meant. For in Berlin, entirely apart from Schoenberg's powerful influence in the conservatory, a new style had begun to emerge out of popular culture. In the cabarets there were Kurt Tucholsky and his like, creators of satirical songs that drove home the inadequacies of the supposedly liberal Weimar democracy. On the increasingly politicized stages of Bertolt Brecht, Erwin Piscator, and the left-wing agitational theatre movement, a simpler and more direct music, like that of Kurt Weill, caught hold. And a sophisticated composer like Hanns Eisler, himself a student of Schoenberg, was actually spending his time writing "mass songs" for political rallies, demonstrations, and marches sponsored by the German left. Only much later, after the Second World War, did the musical establishment turn again to Schoenberg's twelve-tone system.

"I have been working for a month with Arnold Schoenberg," Blitzstein wrote from the Pension Stossinger on Augsburgerstrasse to William Walter of the Curtis Institute:

> I disagree with him more and more. He would make of music an inert, dead pattern, fit only for the laboratory. But he is undoubtedly one of the

> greatest intellectual musicians alive—and as an opposing force to test one's own quality against, he is superb. Even to have found out his theory directly from him, makes the studying with him profitable. I have an uneasy suspicion, however, that my silence will be unable to hold out much longer in the face of his insistent demands to sacrifice beauty on the altar of Scheme—and there will be an explosion."[5]

Blitzstein distrusted almost everything about Schoenberg. He found his formulaic approach inappropriate: "Rationale convinces him his things are beautiful," the American wrote in notes for a later lecture. Concerned with the grammar and vocabulary of music, "and not with the vitality-giving element or life of his compositions," the German let his fantasy loose only in rhythmic matters. Schoenberg's formal concerns Blitzstein found antiquated: Schoenberg would apply dodecaphonic theory to traditional forms used by all the nineteenth-century masters. Blitzstein furthermore felt that Schoenberg wrote badly for the piano and wind instruments, and well only for strings. "Pedagogically, he wants his pupils *not* to compose. Of some fifty or seventy-five, only a few are still writing; . . . he approaches their work with a scissors; something almost pathological about it." He attributed the "hyper-individualism" of Schoenberg's "desperate, hysterical" work to the "frustration and defeat of an age which persisted in divorcing art from life, forcing spirituality into mere pomposity."[6]

Despite the common later assumption, there is no evidence that Blitzstein met Weill, Brecht, or Eisler during his time in Berlin, other than perhaps in passing. The group he found at the Schlichters Café debated incessantly the virtues of an imagined Amerika versus the future in Bolschewismus. These were the artists of the Novembergruppe—the painters, the photographers, and the writers and poets. Max Dungert, the painter and secretary of the Novembergruppe, became an especially close friend. Among the musicians, the Dada influence remained, with Hans Heinz Stuckenschmidt leading them on "for the death of beauty, the death of art, and the resumption of laughter." Stefan Wolpe counted himself in that crowd, too. Blitzstein went to one concert of piano sonatas by Hans Dammert, Stuckenschmidt, and Wolpe and left impressed by Wolpe's "very last note being the closing of the piano, as though putting the final stamp on all piano-music to come."[7]

Among those Blitzstein befriended in Berlin were Stella Simon, a wealthy New York photographer, and her son Louis, who had finished at the Yale Drama School and now studied with Max Reinhardt. Like artists in many media, she wanted to experiment with film, to see in particular if it could succeed as an abstract art form. She created a scenario for a fourteen-minute study using no actors as such, but only their hands, more or less telling a story against a background of deco design. Laconic titles in Gothic German script provide the barest suggestions of a plot concerning a love affair with a coquette at a party or festival.

With Miklos Bandy as Simon's co-director, *Hands* (*Hände* in German) featured photography by Leopold Kutzlub and design by Hans Richter. Simon asked Blitzstein to write the music for the film. Blitzstein scored it for pianola but did not record it at the time. Musically, there are three major episodes, rather lively in spirit, divided from one another by sparse, austere passages that in places approach a chorale structure. The first of these episodes is playful and tuneful, with a music-hall sound, balletic and very French in spirit, updated Offenbach à la Poulenc or Milhaud. The second large section, also light in feeling, borders on jazz, with Gershwin-like chromatics. The third episode is more expressionistic, with driving machine rhythms. At a single screening of *Hands* in Berlin, the composer accompanied at the piano.

Blitzstein took his first trip to London that May—and probably his first airplane ride. At the last minute, Lorenz Hart cabled Stella Simon, asking her to come over for the premiere of his new show with Richard Rodgers, *One Dam Thing After Another.* (A British writer named Ronald Jeans also contributed material for this revue.) Stella invited Marc to go along for the ride, which in those early days of commercial aviation was quite an adventure. First they took a German plane to Hanover, then flew in an open-cockpit affair to a Dutch airport, and from there in a British plane across the Channel to London.

Blitzstein continued to be fascinated by Whitman's poetry. In May, still studying with Schoenberg, he composed the song "As Adam." As if through a veil of mysterious reverie, he set this suggestively alluring text from *Children of Adam:*

> *Behold me where I pass, hear my voice, approach,*
> *Touch me, touch the palm of your hand to my body as I pass,*
> *Be not afraid of my body.*

He would later designate this and three other of his Whitman settings as "Songs for a Coon Shouter," indicating that he had in mind for their delivery something less of the art song's finesse and something more like vaudeville. Coon shouters took off on black subjects, humorously and usually in the denigrating fashion typical of the times, but they were for the most part white women. Since Whitman's poetry addresses far more universal themes, and since the popularity of coon shouters had passed by the end of the First World War, it is obvious that Blitzstein intended only a certain theatrical style, not a comment on race.

Blitzstein's work with Schoenberg amounted, in the American's words, to "a series of wrangles and frustrations." In the end Schoenberg said, "Very well. Go ahead, you write your *Franco-Russische Hübschmusik* [Franco-Russian pretty music], but please stay in my class—you play the piano so well."[8] By the end of the term, however, Blitzstein had seen and heard enough of Schoenberg. They parted on polite but not particularly friendly terms.

In his absence from America, compositions Blitzstein had left behind with a number of performers received their first public performances. In January 1927, Charles Naegele played two brief piano works at New York's Aeolian Hall, "Pavane" and "Variations on Au Clair de la Lune"—the latter "a harmless skit," according to *The New York Times,* the first occasion that newspaper mentioned Blitzstein's name.[9] The following month, Elizabeth Gutman sang the Whitman setting "As If a Phantom Caress'd Me" at a New York League of Composers concert; *Musical America* announced the event and published Blitzstein's photo with the article. And that April, Lisa Roma sang another Whitman song, the elegiac, plaintive "What Weeping Face," at the Academy of Music in Philadelphia, with Nicolai Mednikoff as accompanist.

Over the summer, still in Berlin, Blitzstein sketched out a sonata for piano, and with all his recent work returned to America in August. His months in Paris had brought his academic study up to a near fluency in French; and by the time he left Berlin, he had acquired a fair competency in German. Marc had been writing home with complaints about chronic abdominal illness, and when he got back, Jo persuaded him to have his appendix removed. He settled in for the fall at 1826 Spruce Street in Philadelphia, sharing quarters with Papa.

Aunt Mary's husband, Marcus Zamustin, an importer and an amateur violinist, also collected instruments and amassed a fine collection of sheet music. He reportedly owned both a Guarneri and a Stradivarius and would lend them, and his sheet music, to soloists and members of the Philadelphia Philharmonic Society. Liking the music of George Gershwin, he encouraged Marc for his own good to give up the Schoenberg style and go for a more commercially viable type of music. Still wanting to explore the furthest limits of modern music, Marc was not receptive to this advice.

Hoping to piece out his income, he tried giving private piano instruction. He taught Aunt Mary's daughter Laura for a while—unsuccessfully, because she was terrified and embarrassed to have her older cousin, and such an accomplished virtuoso, wasting his time with her. As for his other students, he reported to Berenice, "My seminary continues. Sweet girls, luscious bodies, the apartment stinks of their glorious perfume after they leave, the money keeps rolling in."[10]

Late that year, the Philadelphia *Record* reported that the ballet-spectacle *Megalopolis* would shortly be on view, probably at some little theatre in town. "This opus, drawing upon the combined talents of Blitzstein, Julian Levi, and Gillespie, three prominent Boulevardiers," the "Around the Town" columnist reported, "threatens to entertain us with the most modern of modern music, decors, and plot." Levi, a widely recognized painter who had lived in Paris, had given one of his works to Jo and Ed as a wedding present. Abraham Lincoln Gillespie—Linc—a mystical poet who had adopted the idiom of James Joyce, collaborated with George Antheil and lived in New York. Extensive sketches of the three-scene work exist, with separate titles for eighteen musical numbers, some of them obviously comical (an atonal "Furioso" opening the third scene includes a "Dance of the Whirling Methodics" and is scored for buzz saws, electric fans, and riveting machines). But apparently Blitzstein did not complete it, and it remained unproduced. Some of his *Megalopolis* material probably went into his ballet for full orchestra called *Jigg-Saw,* a suite in five sections completed the following year. Opening with "Prelude," the work continues with "The Belly-Dancer and the Salvation Army," "Liberty Throws a Party," "Buck and Wing," and the "Cotton-Pickers' Shuffle."

Stella Simon had in the meantime returned from Berlin with a print of *Hands.* Together with the composer, however, she felt her film needed some trimming before she showed it. Blitzstein wrote an accurate description to her son Louis:

> We have worked like the very Trojans cutting the film—but as both Ed & Stella have written you of that, I can only give you my impression of the thing. At first I was horribly disappointed; it seemed such a burdensome, long, unwieldy opus; monotonous, unarticulated, *German.* Some of those faults have been mitigated by the extra slashing we did; but not all, to my mind. The greatest fault seems to be the lack of any definite rhythmic scheme; after that the fact that as a *story* it doesn't quite get across, (since the hands [soli] are not always identifiable) and as a pure abstract study it misses fire by being too long and by having whetted one's appetite *for* a story. In spite of all this, it remains an extraordinarily interesting and stimulating film.[11]

Among the projects Blitzstein wanted to finish before the end of the year was the Piano Sonata he had sketched in Berlin. With Schoenberg's influence behind him now, he began thinking of the Sonata, his first composition written since leaving his last teacher, as "in a sense, my Opus 1." In one movement with eight sections of varying tempo and length, he presents his first and second subjects, with developments, recapitulations, coda, and extended grand finale in cadenza style with repeated glissandi. In the middle of the piece is a third subject that, with its elementary childlike canon, suggests both the primitivism of the 1920s and the composer's own sense of humor toward classical forms. He has eliminated "padding" by substituting measure-long pauses for the usual transitional passages. These brief silences stimulate a psychologically unsettling feeling as powerful as his expressionist dissonances. The overall sense is of a sparse number of musical ideas persistently reworked with barely noticeable variations.

The League of Composers scheduled the six-minute Sonata in a New York concert of all-American music on February 12, 1928. The reviews reported how it went:

> His affair was a bumptious little sonata for piano, thumpingly well played by himself. He is just twenty-three and his music is like that—full of subconscious blaque [*sic,* read blague] and self-conscious piano tricks. Part of it seemed to be Don Marquis's Mehitabel taking a night off and chasing a family of mice up the keyboard in a playful rage of squealing glissandi. But just the same there were deftness and real promise in the little piece.

> This young man is an out and out modern. He rejoices in the insistent repetition of a note and in the short exclamatory, even angry phrase. He can make his piano sing, but apparently is better pleased to make it bark. And his harmonies are very bitter musical speech. If anything of import resulted it would be well, but nothing comes out of it save the now shopworn lot of modernistic mannerisms.[12]

Back home in Philadelphia, echoes of the concert continued to resound as more reviews came in. Blitzstein took offense at the level of glib commentary passing for criticism in the serious music journals: "I am treated as either a lunatic or a baby," he told Berenice; "but I discover in myself a stolidity."[13]

During the fall, he had scored his Whitman setting "Gods" in two alternative ways: for soprano with horn and string ensemble, and for mezzo with solo cello and strings. These versions provide a sensitive coloration and sustain the dramatic tension in a manner the piano cannot. The first performance, in the latter version (arguably the less interesting of the two), took place only three days after the Sonata premiere, on February 15 in the Pennsylvania Athletic Club Ballroom. Fabien Sevitzky—who had shortened his name not to be confused with his uncle Serge Koussevitzky—conducted the Philadelphia Chamber String Sinfonietta, and Ruth Montague sang. For the most part, the reviews were unfavorable: "highly modernistic and queerly off key," wrote one critic. Another thought it "a work of obviously earnest intent, but is melodically maundering modernist music, unalluring in effect." Only one reviewer appreciated it: "The music is modern, but carries out admirably the spirit of the text."[14]

But there was little time to fret about unappreciative reviews, for on March 13 a Society for Contemporary Music concert at the Academy of Music in Philadelphia was to feature Blitzstein with the Sonata again, and Nelson Eddy, then a star of the Civic Opera Company, singing "O Hymen! O Hymenee!" and "As Adam," two of his Whitman settings, as "Two Coon Shouts." In addition, Blitzstein would serve as pianist for Roy Harris's fiendishly tricky Sextet. Billboards announcing the event at the Academy "display my name three times," he told Berenice, "in blue and red print, enormous in size, and very, very gratifying. I must find out the name of the printer, and buy him a lollypop."[15]

On a program that also featured works by Frederick Jacobi and Emerson Whithorne, Blitzstein's contributions were the *succès de scandale.* The Sonata came first, and the Philadelphia critics went wild. They had never heard such a thing in all their concertgoing lives. "It might be called a Sonata in One Round for two heavyweights," wrote Arthur D. Pierce in his Camden *Evening Courier* review entitled "Donner und Blitzstein," "the contestants last night being Blitzstein himself and a Baldwin piano."

> It was Blitzstein's round. With a left jab that all but drove the ivory off the keys and a pummeling right hand technique, the product of Messrs. Baldwin was quickly swatted into submission.
>
> Yet with all the thumping, glissandi, tone clusters and other freaks of piano technique, the musical result was incredibly trite. The chief theme of the Sonata was pounded out baldly and contained neither beauty, originality, nor interest. Had the piece been labeled "Impressions of a trolley car with a flat wheel," I might have appreciated it more.[16]

The machine-age metaphors ran thick. Writing for the Philadelphia *Inquirer,* Linton Martin outdid them all in his "Modern Music Has a Curious Clinic—

Audience in Academy Foyer Hears Strange Patients from the Violent Ward—Contemporary Society's Concert Makes Stone Driller Seem Mild as Mozart." "The concert was mostly a masterly marshaling of musical mediocrity when it wasn't a triumph of tonal trash," he wrote in summation, luxuriating in the alliteration. And in particular:

> Whimsically to suggest that the stone drilling machine at work farther up Broad street sounded relatively like Rossini after Marc Blitzstein's "Sonata for Piano," for instance, would doubtless earn such epithets as "granny" and "mossbach" [*sic*] from those who have an axe to grind—and possibly to wield upon the unconvinced. So it should here be emphasized that no complaint is made this is not music of sweetness and light, but because it was just desperately dull.[17]

As for Eddy's work in the Whitman songs, Pierce wrote:

> The vocal part of these "songs" is tremendously effective. There is elemental power and terror in them and repetition of the second one did not dim the original impression. The piano accompaniment, however, is of the same stripe as Blitzstein's Sonata, thumpy and foreign in mood to the voice. Nelson Eddy sang these difficult numbers with vocal magnificence.[18]

W. R. Murphy, taking cognizance, no doubt, of the newfound interest in black music as sung so well by Paul Robeson, wrote of the songs:

> The results seemed to indicate a talent gone awry. The coon shouts revived a form that used to be, but more melodiously, rife in vaudeville years ago when some leather-lunged variety dame or damsel would voice them, echoed by the pickaninnies which were always a part of her turn. Mr. Blitzenstein [*sic*] has doubtless taken ken of the popularity of the spirituals and thought that there might be a place for the other negroid half chant, half lyric, partly uttered and partly sung.[19]

Mr. Martin returned to the composer's pianistic effects: "Mr. Blitzstein pounded the piano in a way that suggested the desirability of an S.P.C.A. for the protection of defenceless pianos."[20]

Blitzstein sent the clippings to Louis Simon in Berlin, "thinking you might be amused":

> I am treated everywhere with contempt, condescension, or outright vituperation. Thank Heaven I have the sense of humor to keep me from a persecution-delusions-of-grandeur complex. Aaron Copland and some others are for me—the "profession" takes me more or less seriously—so I'm not quite alone.[21]

Perhaps in New York, the most sophisticated music critics would not descend to such lowbrow commentary. But even there, it was precisely their antiquated values and lack of up-to-date information that had led the League of Composers only a few years before to found the magazine *Modern Music.* In it, composers—as critics—might expose the progress of their profession to a wider public. Outside of New York, music criticism remained by and large desert territory, where no one, and especially no American attempting to create modern sounds in music, could expect to receive a fair, informed hearing in the press.

Marc and his father genuinely liked one another and often attended musical and social events together. Their good friend Madelin (Maddie) Leof, an editor and publicity writer the same age as Jo, and her best friend, often accompanied them. Acquaintances of the family suspected a romantic interest between Marc and Maddie. Her father, Dr. Morris Vladimir Leof, a Russian émigré, was a beloved and highly individualistic Socialist Party member, a follower of Eugene V. Debs, and the doyen of a regular Sunday-night salon where radicals of many stripes gathered from near and far for passionate discussion. His common-law wife Jenny—for ideological reasons they had never formally married—was also Russian, a tough, no-nonsense suffragette from an old-line radical family; albeit she possessed an understated sense of humor and was totally devoted to her mate.

One day in late May 1928, Sam and Maddie showed up together at Sam's sister Mary's house. "It looks like you're getting married, the way you're dressed," Mary said offhandedly. "We are," Maddie replied. Their decision truly shocked the family and all of Philadelphia society. After all, Maddie Leof was young enough to be Sam's daughter. Marc felt as surprised as anyone: For one thing, he had to get used to the idea of having acquired a new set of "grandparents." But he believed that when the tumult died down, the arrangement would work. In any case, like Jo, he knew his parents well enough by now to recognize when not to interfere.

Blitzstein saw Paul Hindemith's short opera *Hin und Zurück* on April 22 in a program of the Philadelphia Society for Contemporary Music, and he reviewed it in his first article for the magazine *Modern Music.* Although he found Hindemith's forward-then-backward technique "practically exhausted" by film—he cited a recent Jean Cocteau movie for example—he appreciated the fact that "the score is compact, rich and witty, beautifully proportioned to the trivial nonsense of the libretto and yet so complete in itself that one could long for a concert performance. . . . Satire and commentary are projected by what is the only valid musical method, implicit directness." Importantly for Blitzstein, everything Hindemith wrote was "usually a model for succeeding compositions of like form."[22]

From the model of *Hin und Zurück,* Blitzstein conceived his own first opera together with Ronald Jeans, the British writer for the theatre and an early collaborator with Noël Coward. He had also contributed to Rodgers and Hart's *One Dam Thing After Another.* Jeans had come over to America with a new

British revue and Blitzstein met him in New York. They agreed to write a farce parodizing the type of upper-class drawing-room comedy popularized by the British playwright Frederick Lonsdale. When Jeans had completed the text, Blitzstein prepared to compose the music that summer.

During the spring of 1928, Blitzstein completed his first application for a John Simon Guggenheim Memorial Foundation award. Proposing to work in 1929–30 on a full-length opera, a string quartet, and an orchestral composition, he added that he wished to research the evolution of the sonata form, especially concerning himself with contemporary expressions, and to compose sonatas based on his findings. This work would carry him back to Paris and Berlin, and to Russia as well. In support of his project, he gave as references an imposing cast of figures: Nadia Boulanger, Pierre Monteux, Alexander Smallens, Lazare Saminsky and Alexander Siloti. The latter described his former piano student as "a gifted and highly educated composer as well."

Mrs. Edward MacDowell, widow of the composer, accepted Blitzstein's application for a stay as a MacDowell "colonist" from June 15 to August 1, 1928. His projects for the summer included the one-act opera with the text by Ronald Jeans—already scheduled for performance in Philadelphia the following season—and the completion of a cantata for women's voices and small instrumental group. He had begun it that spring and based it on Whitman's lines, "Out of the cradle, endlessly rocking."

During the day, Blitzstein occupied a remote cabin in the woods, where a staff worker would bring his lunch so as not to interrupt the flow of work. Though he would be at the artists' colony for only six weeks, he hastened, in his pride and fastidiousness, to have personal stationery printed with the Peterborough, New Hampshire letterhead. He also wrote to Henry Allen Moe of the Guggenheim Foundation, adding Mrs. MacDowell to his list of references.

The summer of 1928 at the MacDowell Colony was crowded with composers. Aside from Blitzstein, there were Aaron Copland, Lewis Isaacs, Douglas Moore, Harold Morris, Max Oberndorfer, Raymond Vickers, and a sizable contingent of women: Mrs. H. H. A. Beach, Marion Bauer, Louise Crawford, Mabel Daniels, Mary Howe, and Ethel Glenn Hier. Among the writers, Gerald Sykes, a friend of Aaron Copland, and Dorothy and DuBose Heyward, authors of the play *Porgy*, were there, as well as Edwin Arlington Robinson, who had won the Pulitzer Prize for poetry earlier that year, and a thirty-four-year-old writer, Chard Powers Smith, who would become Robinson's biographer.[23]

Present also was a book reviewer, translator, and novelist named Eva Goldbeck. She was a meager slip of a woman, at five feet, three inches, and had brown hair and green eyes. Eva's European background, level of general culture, and openness to fresh ideas caught Blitzstein's attention.

Once installed at the four-hundred-acre, deeply wooded colony, Blitzstein began what would become a lifelong practice of inviting friends to visit him on his working holidays. From New York, Berenice came up, though her holiday ended when she stepped off a deceptively high ledge and wrenched an ankle, making her immovable for the rest of the weekend. She soon sensed that Marc's new friend Eva resented her presence.

Born in Berlin in 1901, Maria Luisa Eva Goldbeck was a few years older than Marc. She was the only child of Edward Goldbeck, a liberal journalist, and Lina Abarbanell, a Berlin-born soprano from a distinguished Sephardic Jewish family, who sang light opera roles at important theatres all over Central Europe and recorded a score of her most cherished arias. Composers such as Oscar Straus, Franz Lehár, and Edmund Eysler had written songs and even entire operettas for her. In 1905 she came to America to sing the role of Hänsel in *Hänsel und Gretel* at the Metropolitan Opera, and in successive years starred in numerous imported shows in America, chief among them Lehár's *The Merry Widow.*

By 1910 Abarbanell decided to settle in America and her husband and daughter joined her in the Chicago area. She continued to appear on the stage for another twenty-five years, introducing works such as *Madame Sherry* and *Flora Bella*—early American musical comedies—while Edward pursued his career as an editorial writer for the Chicago *Tribune* and political commentator for the German press in Europe.[24]

Eva grew up in Evanston, a not very attractive child much in the shadow of her charming, extroverted mother. Her parents—Mutzi and Putzi to Eva—hosted a weekly soirée on Sundays in their large house on Ridge Avenue, to which performers, writers, and musicians from New York and Europe frequently went. Eva and her childhood neighbor Monroe Wheeler attended, openmouthed at the sophisticated comments they heard, forbidden to say anything but yes or no in answer to a direct question for fear of wasting the guests' time. Together they explored literary interests. The British stream-of-consciousness writer May Sinclair was one of Eva's favorite writers. Eva also attended lectures and purchased all the pamphlets by Emma Goldman, excitedly adopting anarchist principles.

At the time of the First World War, Edward Goldbeck's pro-German sympathies lost him his job. For a time he was even under house arrest. From then on he turned his pen toward more literary pursuits, translating plays from the German as possible vehicles for his wife, and writing chronicles of American life for European publications. But he had become effectively unable to support himself, and they had to make do with Lina Abarbanell's income from her stage appearances. After the war they moved to New York so that Lina could make herself more available for work.

From 1917 to 1920 Eva studied at Northwestern University, graduating summa cum laude with a Phi Beta Kappa key. After graduation she taught Latin in Rockville, Indiana, for a year. In February of 1922 she married a second cousin, Cecil Goldbeck, to the intense distress of both sets of parents. They divorced only two years afterward, though they remained the closest of friends. They frequently traveled together, and when in America she continued to enjoy the peace of Cecil's family home at Sag Harbor, Long Island.*

Working as circulation manager for *The Dial* for a couple of years in the early twenties, Eva had already begun writing short stories, book reviews, and translations and continued on this course, publishing in the New York daily press and such magazines as the *Saturday Review, The Bookman, The Freeman, The Nation, The New Republic, Smart Set,* and the *Menorah Journal.* One of her stories, sold to Johnson Features as a Sunday syndicate under the pen name of Eleanor Gordon, told of her five-day adventure hitchhiking with May Tabak from New York to Chicago in 1925. Another story a year later related the internal factional squabbles at the Provincetown Little Theatre, and included mention of Bobby Edwards's production of *The Provincetown Follies,* "one of the very, very few operatic works ever written on the ukulele."

Eva's many friendships in the literary and art world included such men as Lewis Mumford, Yvor Winters, Clifton J. Furness, and his protégé Elliott Carter. She had another close friend, the writer Glenway Wescott, serve the divorce papers to her husband Cecil. In the mid-twenties she had an extended affair with the painter William Gropper. Among her liberal circle, she counted many homosexual men and women, and modeled positive characters on them in her stories and novels. Indeed, it could be said that in several of these men, such as Furness and Wescott, she inspired deep love, though not of a sexual nature.

By the time she was accepted at the MacDowell Colony for the summer of 1928, she had already spent a season at Yaddo, the artists' colony in Saratoga Springs, New York, and had written at least two substantial works of fiction and a play. For subject matter she gravitated to unhappy childhoods, fear of the world, emotional blockage, and strained personal relationships. Eva kept her journal in a microscopic scrawl that often threatened to dwindle into nothingness, and maintained bulky correspondences with her friends, in which she poured out her soul. In one diary entry from January 1927, she recorded a disturbing event: "I had a dream the night before last foretelling my death—without circumstances given, merely name and date on an index card—in Washington (at least that was the scene of the dream) on September 5, 1935." The dream, and its prophesied date, continued to haunt her.

For her livelihood, she wrote weekly reports—based on gleanings from the press and on her own attendance—for Metro-Goldwyn-Mayer on German and French theatre and film productions, alerting the Hollywood company to possibly lucrative commercial properties.

In 1928 Eva Goldbeck had a twelve-page excerpt from her novel-in-progress published in *The Second American Caravan,* an annual survey of current writing edited by Alfred Kreymborg, Lewis Mumford—both personal friends of hers—and Paul Rosenfeld. The story concerned a severely troubled and withdrawn

*Despite their divorce, Eva retained her legal identity as a married woman: A passport issued on December 17, 1928, names her as "Mrs. Cecil Goldbeck." Subsequent letters from her father also addressed her thus.

seven-year-old boy with a drunken father and an invalid mother. Of the mother, Goldbeck said, she "might be sick, but when an animal was sick it always either got well or died, and his mother did neither," a striking image that Blitzstein absorbed deeply; he often later referred positively to the virtue of "animal health." Publication of her story no doubt conferred a measure of distinction on the twenty-seven-year-old writer.*

Prentiss Taylor, a graphic artist only twenty years old that summer and on the first of four sojourns at the MacDowell Colony, remembered well the day Blitzstein arrived. The guests had all assembled for dinner in Colony Hall when the town taxi drove up and out climbed a precise, carefully dressed young man, self-conscious in his new surroundings. Everyone turned to look at the new member of the colony. Eva Goldbeck stunned them all into embarrassed silence when she blurted out, "Who's this fairy coming?"

Soon enough, Eva's sardonic remark proved the right gloss on Blitzstein, though it may be that she had jumped so spontaneously to her flippant conclusion that it never sank into her consciousness. But if his mannerisms didn't make his orientation obvious, there was his odd behavior: Every afternoon, Blitzstein would take a bath, powder himself generously, then stretch out stark naked on his bed in the dormitory, leaving his door open.

By the time Blitzstein arrived, Eva and the writer Chard Powers Smith had already begun an affair. This connection came about more out of physical need and availability than love. Smith described her in his journal soon after the affair had started: "Eva Goldbeck—feline, rapacious, brilliant, lecherous, disillusionized, hard-boiled, violent, fearless, unscrupulous, exerting a lusty pull without any endearing charm, without tenderness."[25] In later years, the friendship, though not the affair, survived.

Despite her first impression, Eva soon felt an attraction to Marc and showed her manuscripts to him. He replied with several pages of handwritten criticism: "Heavy, unbelievable . . . an overloaded sense of importance . . . should have been handled lightly . . . the novel loses balance . . . three people, fraught with anticipation and foreboding, find—just what they expected . . . bad psychology . . . hifalutin verbiage—especially during conversation." His judgment may have seemed harsh, but no doubt she felt impressed by the close reading this twenty-three-year-old musician had given her work. In any case, she was accustomed to rejection. Numerous publishers and critics gave her similar reactions, though often with positive encouragement. In most cases, it was the daunting length of her manuscripts—six hundred pages or more—that scared editors away. One wrote, "Either your work is of the major significance of a Proust or a Thomas Wolfe, or it is doomed to oblivion. You will easily realize what reluctance we had to answer that fundamental question."[26]

*In the same *Caravan* a two-page poem by Kathleen Millay, "Sacco and Vanzetti," on the two anarchists executed by the Commonwealth of Massachusetts only the previous August must also have come to Blitzstein's attention. In stark, committed language suited to a possible choral reading, its five sections bore these titles: "2 A.M. August 23, 1927," "From the Cross," "Outside the Pale," "Justice," and "Civilization."

From *A Word Out of the Sea,* Blitzstein's Whitman cantata written at the MacDowell Colony, only three movements survive: the third, fourth, and fifth. They are short mood pieces—three or four minutes each in duration—written for a small ensemble of four sopranos and four altos, with soprano and alto solos, oboe, clarinet, bassoon, piano, and string quintet. Blitzstein scored the work delicately, using his instruments in a spare, transparent, soloistic fashion. Comprised of little more than text fragments, this intimate chamber cantata, of an unknown number of projected movements, never received a performance.

Blitzstein also set Ronald Jeans's libretto for *Triple-Sec* that summer in Peterborough, occasionally demonstrating to the other colonists at informal gatherings after dinner what progress he had made on it. He dedicated the score to Alexander Smallens. Its story is concise: A maid and a butler are straightening out the library at Lord Silverside's town house, conversing about the forthcoming marriage of their employer. A stranger appears, insisting that she speak with Lord Silverside. They try to discourage her from staying. At that moment Silverside arrives with Lady Betty, his intended bride. It seems, however, that the stranger is already married to Silverside, at which disclosure Lady Betty faints. Amidst attempts to revive her, the opera ends.

What gives the piece interest is not its story. Nor is Blitzstein's music inherently so attractive—all conversational recitative with no arias or set pieces, composed in a rakish idiom of tonal ambiguity to a chamber orchestra accompaniment. It is the Dadaist staging that makes the opera work. For the assumption of the work, announced by a Hostess in a prologue, is that we are enjoying the drama while eating supper—more to the point, while drinking copious glasses of champagne and getting drunker by the minute. Thus, the maid touches the switch on a lamp, but a different light goes on; the butler stirs the logs in the fireplace, and another lamp lights. Halfway through, the butler leaves the room and returns as one character but played by two singers dressed alike; the same occurs with Lord Silverside and the Stranger. Then, as the opera gets ever sudsier, the characters appear in triplicate, and finally there are eight butlers fetching water for the fainted lady. In the end, the scenery rocks from side to side, as though the audience was quite drunk by now; the lights flash on and off; the characters get all entangled with one another; and before the curtain falls, according to Jeans's stage directions, "A Dragon rears its head above the turmoil, green with red eyes."

The work is slight but effective. At less than fifteen minutes in length, it does not overstay its welcome. Blitzstein's first venture into opera, *Triple-Sec* would shortly become, for its size, a major success.

Blitzstein returned home to Philadelphia in August, envious that Aaron Copland and his friend the writer Gerald Sykes could remain in bucolic Peterborough. He was as envious of the continued working holiday as of the opportunity to be near Eva Goldbeck, whose company he found himself missing. For her part, Eva missed Chard Powers Smith, but also recorded in her journal, "In a minor way I miss Marc too." In a letter to Smith, she admitted to her "German gravity," and beyond that, to a constitutionally depressive frame of mind:

> I have a sense of being condemned to my own life, which might bring either glory or resignation—but at present is only the thing which may be giving rise to my drabness. This summer has made me finally (finally up to the present moment) realize the second-rateness of both my life and work; but even out of such discouraging facts something more positive and redeeming than drabness ought to come.[27]

Back home, Blitzstein once again faced his future. He paid a visit to the sound-film factory at Camden, New Jersey, to witness the new process of recording movie scores. Teams of four composers worked with a staff of copyists to churn out music-to-order. A rush job could be completed in a day if necessary. Victor phonograph equipment would record the music in one or two takes. The orchestra of about sixty musicians was comprised of top-flight professionals who, for ten dollars an hour and double time for over eight hours a day, had deserted the best orchestras in New York and Philadelphia. Blitzstein struggled with Vitaphone's offer of a steady "composing" position at what seemed a fabulous salary, but the job demanded a commitment of five years, and he feared that in the meantime his technique for more artistically satisfying composition might evaporate. In the end, he rejected the offer. He explained his dilemma to Berenice: "It came to a toss-up between a) giving up my real work permanently and b) reconciling myself to a life in which barely adequate money is earned sporadically. I have chosen b). A great load off my chest, I can tell you."[28]

Among his sporadic earnings he could count the receipts from a series of ten lecture-recitals, offered both at his home on Spruce Street in Philadelphia and at a willing sponsor's apartment on East Ninety-third Street in New York. In ten lessons on "The Modern Movement in Music," he gave the ladies the benefit of his prodigious knowledge of contemporary music, beginning with the premoderns, then covering developments in each major Western nation, and concluding with the development of black jazz and its white offshoots.

Blitzstein's intense, driven style of presentation, his boyish looks joined with a sophistication far beyond his years, and his ability to play absolutely anything at the piano combined to make his lectures a popular society event and helped to stimulate interest in the concert music of his own time. Part of his charm involved the strong opinions he rendered so freely. At the age of twenty-three, he came to his material with his formal education completed, his ideas about music essentially formed, and with such an obvious command of his field that he quite mesmerized the registrants in his seminars.

He hastened to reassure his students that, historically speaking, in music "there is really no such thing as revolution, but only revolt. Revolt plays an important part in the evolution of an art, which comprises a) tradition, b) revolt, c) compromise, d) new tradition."[29] He would amuse, too, as when he told them of his preference for inexpressive names for compositions, so as not to introduce extramusical associations: "Thus, the finest title any piece can have, is Symphony in E flat, or Opus 34 no 3—and the most awful title a work can have is 'Fairies frolicking upon the moonlit meadows.' "

Not far into his lectures, in discussing the French composers, he showed his appreciation for Francis Poulenc, especially the fact that Poulenc used influences from Parisian folklore. By contrast, we in America "ignore completely the possibility of a similar music coming out of the city. But the ballads of the streets, the best work of 'tin-pan Alley' can be just as important as any country-tune or Plantation spiritual." Recalling his two-piano experience with Nadia Boulanger, he referred to the work of Albert Roussel: "That *Padmâvatî* has never been given in America is but another indictment on the already overloaded list that can be handed to the Metropolitan Opera Company."[30]

Turning to Russia and Italy in his fourth lecture, Blitzstein cited widespread ignorance about musical happenings on the Soviet scene. But "the building-up of societies to strengthen the bond between Russia and us is at last resulting in something like an authentic comprehension, and a growing, although by no means official, sympathy." No doubt, his father's enthusiasm about developments in revolutionary Russia, and the deep support he had seen in Germany for Communism, had stimulated the young composer's imagination. He continued:

> I for one don't shudder at the so-called degradation of an art being used as propaganda. It seems to me an essentially snobbish and nouveau-riche attitude of bourgeois origin, which feels that the arts must be kept holily intact from obscene life-implications, and maintained after the fashion of candles at an altar.

In Italy, where Mussolini was already in power, though not yet with his later ferocity, composers had been installed in official positions as leaders of the new music movement. Using both the Soviet and Italian examples, Blitzstein concluded:

> There can be no doubt that the ideal situation for the self-respecting artist is such a one; in which he feels himself essential to the community, and recompensed for the importance of his work accordingly, not by a patron, upon whom depends the money, but by a fixed fund, established nationally.[31]

It was a recipe for some kind of state-supported art that he was proposing, assuming that the artist would not be beholden to a specific ideological program.

Excerpts from Kurt Weill's operas figured into his repertory for discussion in the fifth lecture on Germany. Because Blitzstein's own music would later turn so much toward Kurt Weill's approach, it is worth looking at what he thought this early of Weill. He had seen several shorter operas in Berlin, but knew *Die Dreigroschenoper,* which had opened in Berlin only that past August, only by reputation. According to Blitzstein in 1928, Weill was

> an extraordinarily clever musician; as far as I am concerned he hasn't a thing to say in his music; but it is sprightly, gay music usually, written in an extremely dissonant and fashionable idiom. . . . His best work, I think, is a farce comedy, to text of Georg Kaiser, entitled *Der Zar lässt sich photographieren,* an uproarious play, in which the music is lively,

> entirely cerebral, and to me uninspired. . . . As music it appears to me little more than drivel; Weill always takes the easy way out; instead of one single musical idea for a situation, the score is made up of thousands of little fragments, all stuck together, and making a kind of mosaic pastiche out of the thing. . . . His music is essentially ugly because it is characterless; yet he is clever enough to keep the rhythms always going, they all have push and go. Weill is young yet; good things may yet come out of him; but at present he is letting his librettists, whom he chooses wisely, do all of his work for him.[32]

In subsequent lectures, Blitzstein covered Stravinsky and Schoenberg, Hindemith and Bartók. He noted that Krenek's *Jonny spielt auf* had just been produced at the Metropolitan Opera, the title role performed by "a black-face comedian, instead of a real negro, the dear trustees of the Met not being able to stand for a love scene between a black man and a white woman." Otherwise he dismissed the opera as "trash," "rotten nineteenth-century stuff."[33] In his concluding thoughts about American music, he couldn't help observing that the route through which jazz was beginning to filter up to classical music came through Jews—Copland, Gershwin, Irving Berlin, and Richard Rodgers. Even the most famous of the white coon shouters—Nora Bayes and Sophie Tucker—had been Jews.

That fall, Eva came to the city from Sag Harbor to attend Copland's lectures at the New School and to see Marc. Marc came to New York every two weeks or so, staying with Berenice, to give lectures, take books and scores out of the New York Public Library music collection, and see Eva. "He is busy and tired and unhappy giving society music lectures," she wrote in her journal. "I was excited about seeing him again and then (as with Chard) it was not so exciting." Still, she concluded, "it's very comfortable, very friendly and stimulating, very nice."[34]

Toward the end of the year, Blitzstein composed the last of his Walt Whitman settings, one more erotic than the other: "I Am He" and "Ages and Ages." With "O Hymen! O Hymenee!" and "As Adam," they would form a group scheduled for performance at the Little Theatre in New York on Sunday, December 30, at the first Copland-Sessions concert of the season. These two most recent additions, from *Children of Adam,* are saturated with an expansive adoration of flesh. Perhaps Blitzstein was stimulated by the free-for-all atmosphere he had found, and to some extent experienced, in Paris and Berlin. The former is set to bluesy, Gershwin-like harmonies:

> *I am he that aches with amorous love;*
> *Does the earth gravitate? does not all matter, aching, attract all matter?*
> *So the body of me to all I meet and* [Whitman: *or]* *know.*

"Ages and Ages" displayed an open celebration of sexuality fused with Marc's impulsive music:

Ages and ages returning at intervals,
Undestroy'd, wandering immortal,
Lusty, phallic, with the potent original loins, perfectly sweet,
I, chanter of Adamic songs,
Through the new garden the West, the great cities calling,
Deliriate, thus prelude what is generated, offering these, offering myself,
Bathing myself, bathing my songs in Sex,
Offspring of my loins.

In a preview article published in *The World* the day of the concert, Blitzstein explained his esthetic choices:

> Several people have questioned my use of a jazz idiom with the Whitman words; it seems to me perfectly natural to couple two media whose implications are alike universal, and whose methods are alike primitive; both jazz and Whitman contain a primal and all-pervading sex-urge. I hope these songs explain this fact and themselves.[35]

In his choice of a black singer, Benjohn Ragsdale, Blitzstein retained something of the "coon shout" flavor he was after, and reinforced the alliance between "primitive" jazz and sex. At the same time, his choice concretely supported the entry of black performers into the world of serious music, a commitment he honored consistently throughout his career.

Eva went to the concert and wrote in her journal how tense Marc seemed, but also how beautifully he played. The baritone "had a rough voice and very little of the feeling. The songs are grippingly exciting." Berenice Skidelsky gave the party after the concert. Eva wrote:

> Ragsdale and other Negroes were there, but the "mixing" didn't work as it should naturally have; everybody too self-centered. Aaron didn't think it was a good concert. . . . Marc was white, tired, intense and charming—a bad combination, but in him very nice. We said goodbye in a crowd of people—and in a second's look, so close it seemed to be under the cover of my hat, Marc made it a perfectly complete goodbye.[36]

In Arthur Mendel's understated review in *Modern Music,* called—and who knows how maliciously—"First Fruits of the Season," Mendel alluded subtly to Adam's shame: "Marc Blitzstein hid his talent completely behind his collection of *Coon Shouts.* I suppose that is one form of modesty."[37] But other critics went wild, obviously enjoying the field day the occasion had provided for their most excoriating tirades. Marion Bauer's *Musical Leader* review, "A Furious and Outraged Audience, A Debasing Program," recalled Blitzstein's comment about Whitman's "all-pervading sex-urge." "It is exceedingly bad taste to have brought it into the concert hall," fumed Bauer. "Mr. Blitzstein may have made use of interesting rhythms which were presented by Benjohn Ragsdale, baritone of the Hall Johnson Choir, but their union with Walt Whitman's lines was incongruous and debasing."[38] Olin Downes in the *Times* referred to Blitzstein's music, "of such poor, weak and childish character as to afford no justification for public performance. Some of it was of a singularly repellant puerility."[39]

Only a few positive glimmers appeared in the wake of Blitzstein's shocking experiment in the concert hall. Samuel Chotzinoff observed in *The World* that *Children of Adam* had at one time been "considered a stain on the white radiance of *Leaves of Grass,*" suggesting that intelligent people today no longer think so, and that the composer's settings were "inwardly no doubt aptly expressive of the poet's important message."[40] And Pitts Sanborn, hinting discreetly but obviously at the homosexual content of the songs, said: "To me they were, in Scriptural phrase, the abomination of desolation, but another listener whose opinion always carries weight with me assures me that they were as a matter of fact richly charged with talent. I earnestly hope he is right."[41]

Blitzstein may not have written the songs consciously intending to *épater le bourgeois.* However, he certainly enjoyed the extravagant attention he earned. "My concert was, it seems, a great success," he reported to Louis Simon. "I was picked out by all the critics for especial vituperation," and he went on to cite the choicest morsels of disapproval. There was the positive side, too: The critic "Paul Rosenfeld came back-stage & said my stuff was the only music on the program worth listening to, & that I had a 'rich & warm talent.' This at a mediocre performance of one of my minor things (Ragsdale was at moments superb, at moments execrable)."[42]

On the third of January 1929, Eva sailed for Europe on the *American Banker,* Marc planning to go in the spring. He telegraphed from Philadelphia to her ship: PILGRIM TO THE SHORES OF PARIS MAY PARIS BE YOUR MECCA. MARC. Cecil Goldbeck was in Europe now, and Eva, continuing to work for Metro-Goldwyn-Mayer, preferred to live more cheaply abroad. She also preferred to keep some distance from her parents.

The infamous Piano Sonata continued its course. Keith Corelli played it at Boston's Jordan Hall in February on a program of "New American Music, Reflecting the Most Progressive Tendencies," and repeated it in Montreal in May. And, unafraid to welcome the upstart composer into its midst, the MacDowell Club of New York City invited Blitzstein in early March to make some remarks on contemporary music and play the piano. He presented the Sonata, as well as the *Piano-rag-music* of Stravinsky and a Sonatina by Chávez.

The notoriety Blitzstein gained from such bombshells as the Sonata and the Whitman songs only seemed to excite further interest. What might he come up with next? The League of Composers wanted to find out, and programmed a new Blitzstein work for a St. Patrick's Day concert in New York that also included works by Henry Cowell and Harold Morris, whom Blitzstein had met at the MacDowell Colony. For this occasion, the composer prepared a new work in three movements. He had written the first movement, "Toccata," the previous June, and may not have conceived it as part of a larger work. The second movement, "Air," dates from February 1929, and the third, "Rondino," bears the late date of March 12, 1929. The toccata, marked *presto,* and skittish much of the way through, is played *martellato,* with a *subito pianissimo* ending that suggests the sound of a marimba. The air differs greatly, a noble, Purcellian confection with trills and sixteenth-note ornamentation, its meter switching between 4/4 and 5/4.

It was in the third movement that Blitzstein reminded his listeners that his name still spelled trouble. In the words of an unidentified critic:

> Mr. Marc Blitzstein, one of our most recent terrorists of sound, studiously slammed the lid of his piano four times during the course of his contribution to the concert of the league of composers [*sic*] in Steinway Hall last night. A ripple of mirth spread gently over the audience and Mr. Blitzstein looked disgusted. The title of this peroration was cryptically inscribed: *Percussion Music for the Piano.*

Actually, the reviewer somewhat understated the total effect, in that the score calls for several moments where the performer slaps the lid of the piano, shuts the lid, and opens the lid, all these actions marked *sempre forte.* (No doubt, the initial inspiration for these effects had been Stefan Wolpe's more quiet use of the piano lid in the sonata Blitzstein heard in Berlin.) Most reviewers failed to remark on the piece as a whole, though Marion Bauer, so recently scandalized by the Whitman songs, felt that the new composition "had much of interest and for the most part was pleasing." The *Musical Courier*'s critic found the third movement—except for the "useless ornamentation" of the lid-slamming—"easily the best work of the evening," distinguished by its "rhythms, counterpoints, and contrasting ideas." Proud of his new piece and of the reception it got, the composer wrote to Louis Simon, "I achieved one good notice and the usual atrocities from the press."[43]

The forthcoming Philadelphia premiere of *Triple-Sec* took up much of Blitzstein's time that spring. For weeks he rehearsed with the singers and instrumentalists of the Society for Contemporary Music, "under it all a slightly sick feeling—nausea and some terror," he revealed to Berenice. "I may have written a completely unplayable score! and yet, the law of averages would indicate that *some* of it will sound. Such excitement!"[44]

One interruption in Blitzstein's preparations for the premiere of *Triple-Sec* was a lecture on "Music of the Impressionists" that he gave at the end of March for the Civitas Club. A more historic interruption was his first and only performance at the Metropolitan Opera in New York. As a benefit for the National Music League, the League of Composers presented a double bill of Monteverdi's *Il Combattimento di Tancredi e Clorinda* and the widely heralded American stage premiere of Stravinsky's *Les Noces,* conducted by Leopold Stokowski, with décor by Serge Sudeikin. The date was April 25, 1929. Stravinsky's score calls for four pianos, and four composers talented enough to play his music played it: Blitzstein, Copland, Frederick Jacobi, and Louis Gruenberg. Blitzstein traveled to New

York to rehearse regularly in a space rented from the Harlem branch of the YMCA. The evening was an astounding success.

Another brief distraction involved Marc's mother. For a year or so in the late 1920s, after Dr. Segal's death, she had broken out on an adventure of her own. Perhaps at Marc's suggestion, she experimented with life in Paris, where she counted the writer Ford Madox Ford among her friends. In April of 1929, she decided to settle down again and marry William Levy of Pittsburgh—"very nice, indeed," her son remarked to Berenice unexcitedly.[45] Jo and Ed hosted the ceremony in their house. Mama—no longer mumsie to her adult children—moved with Levy to Pittsburgh, but after a few years, during which Marc saw little of her, they divorced. Subsequently she moved to Ventnor, New Jersey.*

Triple-Sec received its premiere on Monday, May 6 at the Bellevue-Stratford Ballroom, along with Alfredo Casella's *Pupazzetti* in its first Philadelphia performance as a ballet, and Schoenberg's *Pierrot Lunaire,* for which Blitzstein served as pianist in the chamber ensemble. Alexander Smallens conducted the entire evening, and James Light, of the Provincetown Playhouse, did the staging. Ruth Montague, who had performed "Gods" the year before, played the Hostess. Once again, as in the recent performance of his Whitman songs, Blitzstein used a black singer, Albert Mahler, for Lord Silverside, thus making the absurdity, and the possible affront to public sensibility, that much stronger for its time. He saw no meaningful way now to express himself politically or socially on the race issue, but at least in this manner he could show his sympathies.

"A resolutely cultural audience submitted heroically" to this rather advanced program, wrote H. T. Craven in the Philadelphia *Record* the next day. "Blitzstein's piece is not so funny. Its satire is crude, its extravagance rather puerile, and its origins may be traced to Stravinsky and the Metropolitan's freak opera *Jonny Spielt Auf.*" Yet, Craven had to admit, "Gales of laughter welcomed this novelty."

> Composer Blitzstein has burlesqued his own stuff in fluent atonal, cacaphonic style, with injections of xylophonic jazz . . . and all the now familiar furniture of musical extremism. Librettist Ronald Jeans has made Lord Silverside a Negro.† He has a love scene, all in fun, mind you, with a white lassie. This is going the Metropolitan one better, since "Jonny," of *Spielt* fame, is, in the American production, only a Caucasian blacked up like a minstrel.[46]

Good memories of the opera lingered behind, and soon more would be heard of it.

Before he left for Europe two weeks later, Blitzstein wrote an article on "Four American Composers" for the July–September issue of *This Quarter.* The men he discussed were Copland, Antheil, Sessions, and Carlos Chávez, the Mexican

*In the late 1940s, when her son had already become famous, she reassumed her first married name of Blitzstein.

†This is not, in fact, specified in the libretto.

composer. Among Copland's works, Blitzstein considered the Piano Concerto and the *Lento Molto* for string quartet his most important. But he cautioned that "the duty of a composer is to compose," and Copland was exhausting himself with lectures, performing, writing articles, and producing concerts. "There are always others to do this second and third rank musical drudgery," Blitzstein cautioned, though he might well have been addressing his own future.

Most significantly, Blitzstein observed that American music had not yet developed a "school," a particular atmosphere out of which the truly creative individuals would emerge: So far the American composer "has dug out his method, his means, without benefit of an indigenous American musical culture." While rejecting artificial attempts to create such a culture, Blitzstein betrayed a restless longing for one. To a large extent, his Whitman settings had achieved what he was looking for: a musical language marked by American inflections joined to a quintessentially American poetry. Off and on for years to come, he continued his search for a modern national idiom, though frequent digressions, such as his surrealistic opera about British lords and ladies, show that he had other formal concerns as well.

Blitzstein sailed for Europe on the *Berengaria,* with Copland on board as well. Blitzstein also had with him the libretto to his next opera, by George Whitsett. A good friend of his, Whitsett worked for a Philadelphia publishing company and dabbled in writing himself. Blitzstein agreed to set his exotic text, called *Parabola and Circula.*

Cecil Goldbeck returned to America for the summer, and Marc appeared in Paris just in time to fill the gap in Eva's life. They saw one another once or twice, and again on May 26, Eva recording the date in her journal:

> Marc came around, as I hoped he would, and we had dinner: with a cocktail before—and he told me that he is homosexual. He thought I knew. I was dumbfounded, and almost chagrined that I hadn't—I should have trusted my instinct (his walk, like Clifton's, observed the first day in Peterborough and again the other night, here) instead of all other indications. But they completely fooled me. I swallowed my chagrin at my idiocy, in a quick recovery which I think was decently done, since he seemed very pleased with me all evening. Of course after that—out of that—we had a good talk.[47]

Thereafter Marc made no further secret of his orientation as they pursued their friendship on an almost daily basis. Copland (infatuated with the twenty-year-old composer Israel Citkowitz, also in Paris), Elie Siegmeister and his wife Hannah, and Roy Harris often joined Marc and Eva at dinner parties, art openings, ballets, and concerts. Minna Lederman, editor of *Modern Music,* was there that summer—everyone was there, it seemed—and was present with Marc one night at a bar that catered to gays and their friends on the famous rue de Lappe where several such establishments existed. For some reason, Marc broke out into uncontrollable weeping, and Alexander Smallens left with him to take him home.

In a note to Eva in the nearby town of Juziers, where she boarded and where Copland, Citkowitz, and Harris also stayed at times, Marc reported on another evening with Alex: "Chance threw . . . Allan [Ross] Macdougall and even two sailors in our way the first night, and there was hell to pay. I am supposed to be on the road to moral perdition. Ruin. Oh, well. We leave Tuesday—for Brittany or Savoie." At the time, Eva thought, "Marc is my best antidote for sentimentality: his magnificent clarity and mental courage!"[48]

One night in Paris, at the invitation of some friends, Minna and Marc attended Prokofiev's new ballet *The Prodigal Son* at the Opéra, a Diaghilev production with Balanchine's staging. Minna later described the occasion:

> Afterwards, Marc, tremendously exhilarated and always gallant no matter how scant his pocket money, took us off to the Bal Colonial. This was held in a large hall where brilliantly dressed French West Indian Negroes gyrated nightly in what I think of now as a kind of muted Twist. Each couple, the man separated from the woman by a few inches, moved in tiny circles, bound together apparently by magnetic control. It was quite sexy, yet decorous. But our hosts found it indecent and so the evening ended with Marc humiliated and in a rage.[49]

It may have been then, or another occasion that Lederman remembered from that summer in Paris, that she went with Marc to the Opéra ticket window. Loudly and as irascibly as possible, he demanded that the box office exchange his tickets for different seats. After some fancy juggling on the box office manager's part, which resulted in seats not appreciably better than the ones Blitzstein had started out with, Marc gleefully confessed to Minna that he only did it to test his French!

In the calm of his life away from home, Blitzstein could reflect on his developing career. Something, he felt, was lacking. He needed the distance from home to sort out his needs and priorities. In Europe, he could do that, away from family and from the temptation to feed his sense of vanity. Of course, the freer sexual climate of Europe permitted him to explore his desires. "I really ran away from America, as I feel you know," he wrote to his sister Jo, from a little rented room near Deauville on the Normandy coast where he and Alexander Smallens had settled:

> One of the reasons was that I was actually beginning to enjoy the nickle-plated adulation coming my way. Had I gone in for it seriously, I should have been doomed—a neat provincial "artist" taking in the shekels, and "believing" in himself.[50]

By August, Blitzstein had settled down in Cannes to complete *Parabola and Circula:*

> I spend mornings and late afternoons working—but from 2 till 6 I lie on the champagne-colored beach and guzzle sunlight. When it gets too hot I step into the sea (3 steps and you tread water), idly duck and dive and swim, return, shake myself like a happy dog, and breathe in the sun again. I have decided that the sun is my god—my inspiration, my life. I can't afford to be without it.[51]

By this time, he was ready to disclose more of his inner life to Jo. From now on, she could have no illusions about her brother, whatever his growing involvement with Eva.

> I am nearing an adjustment which will be productive of many things. I think I have often given the impression (even to people who are close to me, like you) of a mental organism so in control that the emotional aspect had gone sterile, or wasn't born yet. That has been a very small part of the truth. What actually went on was a mechanism, built up of fear, which *tried* to douse the emotional urge; but which was much less powerful than that urge. I knew it was bad for me; I lacked courage to express the emotional—sexual *au fond*—thing. I think you guess—you know—what all this is about. It has become imperative at last that I cut out the "balance," the "control" (I am a pretty good actor, I project well, nearly everybody thought it was the real thing), and let out what has been secret and furtive in me for so long. Shame is the largest single enemy; the sense of being sick, of living a diseased life, is another—the social obstacle, the individual one. I have reasoned it out, this time with my mind; until now what has gone on has been an instinctive process of self-protection, with my mind playing handmaiden to my cowardice—evolving more-or-less successful methods of diverting the issue. Now, I accept what I am; really, knowing all it involves. . . . In this light, it is absurd to assert that there are no sins; there are definitely cardinal sins—sins against oneself, against one's law. My sin is, has been, vanity of this special sort; the willingness to corrupt my nature.
>
> Maddie knows about me; the label, at any rate.[52]

At the same time, Eva began admitting to herself the gradual transformation of her feelings. To her journal she confided, "he has come to mean even more in this month I haven't seen him; has become eternalized, so to speak. . . . That quality of integrity toward self is of course what I admire most—and what I hope most to have." Two weeks later, reporting Cecil's view of the matter, she continued: "If I must have an affair, he hopes it could be with Marc—and I know that if the sex were there I would be in love with Marc—perhaps I am in a way anyway (I must find out)."[53]

With Marc's definitive revelation posted in the mail to his sister, he joined up with Copland for a week to make the rounds of German opera houses. In Frankfurt they saw Gluck's *Orpheus and Euridice,* in Wiesbaden Kurt Weill's *Dreigroschenoper,* and in Darmstadt an all-out production of Hindemith's new opera *Neues vom Tage.*[54] There Blitzstein found the directors of the Hessisches

Landestheater interested in *Triple-Sec;* he hoped that one more audition of the piece would persuade them to produce it, possibly as early as December.

Aaron asked incessantly after Eva. "Why are you so wise in some things," Marc wrote to her, repeating Copland's question, "and such a frightened little girl in others?" It had been an awkward week, though. As he and Copland shared opinions of each other's music and writing, as well as comparisons of "types" to whom they felt attracted, they also grew estranged in a way, Aaron retreating into his familiar mode of impassivity.[55]

September found Blitzstein safely nestled in Salzburg—Louis Simon's recommendation. There he would remain until the first week of January 1930. Still blooming with late summer flowers, the city of Mozart's birth exerted a powerful charm. Rooming houses there had little luxury to offer, but prices were cheaper than in Paris: A good meal could be had for forty-five cents, and a room for anywhere between nine and fifteen dollars a month. In a letter to Eva in Paris, Marc tempted her to join him there, writing of visions of gardens everywhere, the solace-giving grandeur of the surrounding mountains, and the spectrum of social types from a slightly frayed aristocracy down to genuine peasants. Soon he settled—with the Volkert family—in a museumlike room filled with old pitchers and dishware, religious objects, and antique furniture, near the Neuthor at 1 Reichenhallerstrasse.

The revelation to Jo was bound to call forth a response in equal measure. Marc was quick to answer her letter:

> I am not shocked at your incestuous instincts; as you must know, I have known about them as long as you have—perhaps longer; a great portion of our "rapport," and the largest part of the reason we understand each other in a unique way, is engendered by it. I have no such inclinations (I couldn't have); but I have always known that you are and probably always (ultimately) will be the most important person for me. This is hard saying, & will possibly wreck our first meeting after I return; we must be ready for that. Whether or not my homosexuality can be traced to an original & repressed feeling for you, can only be guessed at. It was more likely due to a childhood among women (including Uncle Herman), and a natural distaste for boys' activities. It has only been very recently, as I have written you, that calm and an attendant indifference to "public opinion," "consequences," etc. have arrived,—making it possible to tell you, who should above all people have been told, about it. (Actually, I couldn't bear the thought; superficially, I told myself I was sparing you pain. But the sort of pain you will have, if at all, is an inferior one, totally unjustified, and unworthy.) So, to go back, the only people I told, were those who mattered less to me—try-outs.[56]

He was right. He knew himself well. Jo would remain the most important person in Marc's life. And anyone could see that despite the fact of having her own family—Ed and her sons Stephen and Kit—Marc was always the most important person to Jo. He did say, however, in response to her reaction to this letter, that he had "no intention of wearing my sexual heart on my sleeve. That is, would be, absurd, & would indicate a sense of defense, shame & bravado I don't feel." Especially, he agreed to keep the news from Mama and Papa—though "I feel that he already knows & might actually be helpful."[57]

Eva joined Marc in Salzburg; and for a time Cecil Goldbeck, with whom Eva remained in a close friendship, did as well. Cecil had by then developed the beginnings of a life in the world of letters and had just completed, with Freeman Hedges, a novel called *The Ablative Case.* Bright enough, Cecil did not match Eva's far-ranging intellect. He often gave her some needed down-to-earth advice, but more usually he tolerated Eva's tortured spirit with a noxious bonhomie. At all times, he showed himself on the conventional side; he was a safe and dull person. The three did not live together and only saw one another for an hour or so a day, or for dinner.

Eva felt confused about Marc. He had asked her to come and be with him, but only as a friend. She showed something of her present concerns when she applied for a Guggenheim Foundation grant that October and proposed a new novel, her fourth: "A poor young musician marries a girl whose chief characteristic is her capacity for devotion." The plot thickens from there, involving "his egocentric philosophy" and the idea that "she loves too much and too possessively." As for Eva's impressions of Jo, she recalled to Cecil:

> The ecstatic way he mentions any detail about her, so ecstatic as to be a little ridiculous except in love . . . ; and a general knowledge of Marc, make me know that she is the only one he has yet loved . . . ; he will always love her most deeply, regardless of the passions he will certainly have. She is closest to him, by blood, by habit, feeling, everything: she is "home"—this from him himself—and that is what he most needs. . . . Theoretically it is quite logical: the narcissus business developed throughout, in the artist, the homosexual, the sister-love.[58]

After half a year in Europe, Marc gave Berenice a progress report. As for his love life, he mentioned "wild and small affairs . . . with twenty (since May 15!)" He also relayed the excellent news that Schotts Söhne, the famous Mainz music publishing house, had agreed to publish *Triple-Sec,* with Edwin Denby's translation into German as *"Die Sünde des Lord Silverside."* He felt confident of a production the following February in Darmstadt, with other productions on the Continent sure to follow. And Schotts could hardly wait to see Blitzstein's new opera.[59]

In Philadelphia the previous February, Blitzstein had written a song called "When life is quite through with" to an E. E. Cummings text. Now, in Europe, he decided to expand the one song into a suite of five Cummings settings, *Is 5,* and dedicate them to Jo. The other songs are "After all white horses are in bed," "You are like the snow," "Mister, youse needn't be so spry" and "Jimmie's got a goil." Several years later, the Cos Cob Press, founded by Alma Wertheim, published this last Cummings number in a collection of American songs.

In addition, so Blitzstein reported to the Guggenheim Foundation in his second application for a grant, Cummings was writing a one-act opera libretto for him, entitled "The Termites"—of which there is no evidence. Blitzstein also planned an orchestral work, a wind quintet based on Euler's diagrams, a sonata for trumpet and piano, and a string quartet. He added to his application the names of Douglas Moore and Aaron Copland as references.

The main project on which Blitzstein worked that fall of 1929 was the opera to George Whitsett's libretto, *Parabola and Circula,* obtuse, elliptical, and replete with geometric and grammatical terms. The opera is set in a cubistic "World of Forms" where plants, flowers, and even light all have strange shapes. Man-made objects, too, such as paths and wells and benches, are "trigonometric" and barely recognizable. If the tangible world is unreal, it is also true, according to the synopsis, that "Any resemblance to drama is incidental."

Parabola and Circula, baritone and soprano, live in perfect love with one another and with their adopted children, Rectangula and Intersecta, tenor and soprano, until "Doubt, circulating like a homeless and craven wind in the infinite void inhabited by the Forms, enters the no longer flawless consciousness of Parabola, causing him for the first time to look upon this angelic union with queri[c]al eyes." Parabola's friend Prism, a tenor, quickens Parabola's doubt, which Geodesa and Linea, bass-baritone and contralto, further confirm. In the end, Parabola's doubt grows into danger, which finally destroys Circula. By the time Parabola realizes what has happened, it is too late. "The higher sophistication while making it easier for doubt to enter has offered no ready means for combating it."

Though resemblance to drama is intentionally beside the point, certain reflections of the Garden of Eden story, and of *Othello,* can hardly be denied. Years later, Blitzstein summed up the opera's theme in terms that suggest his own emotional constitution: "The characters played out a cruel jest on the impossibility of perfection or even satisfaction in the matter of human relationships, especially in the matter of love."[60]

He included two ballet scenes. The first one, showing the bower of perfect love, "should verge slightly on the ridiculous, with effusiveness and playfulness; if possible it should be a flying ballet, with the dancers attached to wires so that they can leap and fly over the stage." The second, a pas de deux for Parabola and Circula, shows a "ritual love-scene"—"This should be quite serious and beautiful." The opera, which he dedicated to Eva, turned out "much larger and heavier than I had dreamed," Blitzstein wrote to Berenice. Well over an hour in length by the time he finished it on November 7, it would require cuts from his 555-page orchestral score before any opera house on the Continent would commit itself to a production.[61]

With its abstract, fairy-tale–legend quality, the opera suggests the dream-like symbolism of *Pelléas et Mélisande*—indeed, Blitzstein highly respected Debussy the innovator. But he adopted a simple musical language modeled more on Poulenc, Milhaud, and Satie—tonal, chordal, and conservative in its faint modernism, though not without flavor. His well-crafted vocal lines offer little specific differentiation among the characters. The writing is melodious throughout, with a comfortable flow—hardly the angular, jutting music with wide intervals one might expect. Naïve, inoffensive, the score shies away from musical novelty: All sense of the new went into the scenario instead. Whether or not the exotic staging would carry the music sufficiently was open to question.

The composer felt pleased with the opera only in spots. He appreciated the effort more for the focus it placed on his defects as a composer. "The only way I can state it is that in my compositions, I have as yet no face," he wrote Berenice. "The structure is clear and solid, the métier becoming what it should be, and the urge to get it out as strong as ever. Perhaps in my new work for orchestra (half-done) I am beginning to expose features. What a penalty one pays for having been precocious!"[62]

Through this opera, his longest project so far, he came to see how completely the composer cuts himself off from the world. Often, in conversation with Eva, for instance, his mind would be only half-present: "I am dull, forgetful, commonplace," he wrote to Jo. Yet he accepted his fate: that for short or long periods, whatever the demands, he would need to shut himself off from society. "Please be assured," he said, "I am happier than I have been in a long time; and I see before me a life in which this sort of happiness is due to continue, since it is based upon the most constant thing one can hope for—beloved work. In many ways I have been, am, lucky."[63]

The stock market crash affected Blitzstein only slightly at first, as he felt secure that no one he knew was connected closely to it. What he could not realize immediately was that the crisis would shortly bring the more fragile financial institutions tumbling down in its wake, the forty-year-old M. L. Blitzstein Bank among them. With most of the Blitzstein clan's money invested there, many members of the family became paupers virtually overnight. Marc's uncle Constantine Voynow, president of the bank, retired. His son, Marc's cousin Cutch, the good-natured head cashier at the bank, started a restaurant, then turned to one nonlucrative job after another. Even Marc's rich uncle William Tutelman was reduced to making a living as an appliance repairman. Babushka fortunately did not live to see it—she had died just a few months before.

On Christmas Eve, Marc returned once again to the subject of his sexuality in a letter to Jo. She had been completely understanding; he couldn't have asked for a warmer reception to his news.

> By the way (this is for information) don't get the idea that I have a repressed horror for women. I believe I should be medically classed a bisexual, since I have had sexual experience with women, and liked it. That also Europe has done for me; I decided it was silly for me not to find out everything possible about myself; and so went through a series of self-imposed experiments in Cannes, which convince me that I'm quite there. If ever the social gesture is demanded of me (and I go so far as to

consider marriage for me as a possible social gesture), I can accept it or reject it as I choose, without any fear of incapacity.

As to Papa—it's inconceivable that he suspects nothing. Remember, he's lived with me for years, during which I was certainly no virgin. Certain circumstances must have opened at least one eye.[64]

From September 1929 in Salzburg, the idea of a three-act opera, *The Traveling Salesman,* had occupied his thoughts. Squeezed among other projects, it would continue to do so for the next year. He filled seventy pages of a notebook with scenario, character studies, technical and esthetic ideas, but no music. This fairy tale without virtue concerns the rise of Virgil Sweet from his small-town dreams of success, garnered from get-rich-quick sales magazines, to nothing less than the presidency of the United States. Mediocrity prevails by fluke.

Imagining the mode of presentation, Blitzstein outlined several choices. One might be the "vaudeville and small-time burlesque angle," permitting a wide range of musical genres, including "whatever of the circus-technique is involved." Another might be the "fantastic" approach, in which "Virgil's life should be the holiday-game of Fate." He also considered the "communistic view," by which he meant that both music and plot can be "grasped by the average intelligence—which by no means precludes power or profundity. . . . But it need not be 'communistic' in propaganda—it need not 'hasten the revolution.' " Clearly the influence of Weill and Brecht, and of Hindemith's opera *Neues vom Tage,* is present in this avoidance of a highbrow idiom, in the presentation of a social critique without immediate solutions. Finally, Blitzstein was conscious of the "classic, universal viewpoint," which would tie the opera not just to the here-and-now but to "a permanent *Geist.*"

In this work about salesmanship, Blitzstein grappled with concepts of taste and fashion, indistinguishable terms for most of the world. A significant passage in his notes, written at the age of twenty-four, articulates a philosophy about art that stayed with him in the years to come. It suggests the kind of debate he faced every time he had to choose the style and form of his work:

The real work of art is composed inevitably of elements which contain both good and bad taste, the application of these latter terms changing as eras come and pass. A reaction to an over-absorption in "good taste" like the art-period just passed (when all values seemed to have gone up in smoke—the only judgment that seemed to carry weight or make an impression was "that's in awfully good taste"), a reaction to this is found in the Surrealists, who, insisting they work automatically and without forethought, manage to make their works peculiarly offensive to the older good-taste idealists. But they err, bourgeois-fashion, in an exaltation of bad-taste (that is, bad, judged by what was good) and the whole question remains a seemingly important one, whereas it should be relegated to one of little or no significance.

Already, Blitzstein is profoundly antibourgeois, without necessarily adhering to a particular ideological response; neither is he mesmerized by the fetish of originality.

For the music to *The Traveling Salesman,* Blitzstein planned to use every kind of ballad: the sentimental ("I wouldn't let a dog out on a night like this"), the narrative ("The Face on the Barroom Floor"), the "pick up your tears" cheer ballad, the "nut" ballad in the style of "Bananas," the patter song, the coon ballad in the form of a blues, the ballad with "sick rhymes," a prisoner's song, and even sea chanties, all distributed among the characters in appropriate solos, duets, ensembles, and choruses. Stealing through the opera, appearing at crucial moments, is a trio of Fates named Teddy, Eddy, and Freddy, who embody aspects of the salesman's demonstration techniques: "One spins, one twists, one cuts." Blitzstein imagined his trio performed by the vaudeville comedy team of Lou Clayton, Eddie Jackson, and Jimmy Durante.

Virgil has his opposite, the daughter of a financier, whom Blitzstein describes as "a hard nut to crack." In love with Virgil, she is, indeed, based on Eva, suggesting a certain identity between Virgil and Blitzstein himself. She is "fearless and honest—she hates to ask money of someone willing to give it, but doesn't mind asking, forcing even, somebody who isn't. She alternately hates and loves V., and always hates herself." As for Virgil, "he takes it timidly, not loving her, being flattered and at the same time afraid."

The *Traveling Salesman* notebook is rich in detail: Many ideas for scenes would crop up in subsequent works. By the following summer of 1930, he abandoned the opera, no doubt because in May of that year, George Antheil's opera *Transatlantic* premiered in Frankfurt; it also took a presidential campaign for its theme, rounded out with a wealthy financier and a love story, and used jazz and a parody of popular music as its chief idiom.* Nevertheless, Blitzstein predicted that in isolating the theme of the individual considered in response to social forces, he had found "my theme for a long time to come." For the time being, he postponed his attention both to a specifically American subject and to composing in the "communistic"—that is, harmonically popular—mode.

*Competition with Antheil's opera did not dissuade George Gershwin, whose musical *Of Thee I Sing* opened in December 1931, also reveling in presidential follies.

4

EVA

Winter 1930–May 1932

"I shall have to start learning things about people I thought I knew."

Shortly after the beginning of the new year, 1930, and the new decade, Marc and Eva wended their way to Berlin, visiting Vienna, Prague, Leipzig, and Dresden on the way. In Vienna, Blitzstein played through *Parabola and Circula* for the eminent music-publishing house of Universal Edition, who did not take the work but who did give its composer letters of introduction to the intendants of three major opera houses in Germany. Blitzstein pursued these leads, and Dessau, at least, seemed interested in producing it in collaboration with their local Bauhaus artists. In Leipzig he attended the premiere of Krenek's *Life of Orestes*—"an outrageously cheap and long-winded-work"—and met his fellow American composer George Antheil for the first time. In Berlin Marc and Eva heard Stravinsky play his *Capriccio.* At another concert, of the Novembergruppe, Blitzstein liked only one item, a song cycle by Hanns Eisler. "As for Weill," Blitzstein wrote to Stella Simon, "the greatest thing I resent in him—not having expected more—is his total lack of cleverness. His idea of a 'sonk' is an outlandish mixture of German beer-drinking ditty and American ballad, accompanied a la marcia by jazz-band instruments betrayed into a Sousa formula."[1]

Schotts Söhne informed Blitzstein that they were not interested in publishing the score to *Parabola and Circula;* perhaps they had financial reasons now. And none of the opera companies wanted to produce it, either. Against this background, Blitzstein soon came to see that it no longer represented him, did not reflect his values, said nothing he wanted to say. It dropped into his "composer's trunk," that repository from which he would draw for works written in decades to come.

Berlin's cold climate discouraged a long stay, and by now Marc had decided on Capri for the rest of the year. He let it be known, none too subtly, that Eva might or might not figure in his life there, vacillating between inviting her and saying no. On February 3, Eva attended one of Berlin's famous lesbian balls, and on the eighth she wrote in her journal:

> Marc, Patty, Cecil, I, fairy balls, broke. I urged Marc to go into one (too expensive for all of us) alone; he didn't. Later he said to Cecil, "I wanted to, but Eva insisted I should, and you know what her personality is like—I felt I had to resist it, and not go." *This* is how he feels about my "oppressiveness."[2]

In Eva's absence from the city for a few days, Marc left for Capri, staking his claim on the island. She followed only three days later, but the implication was unmistakable: She would remain there more or less as his guest. He loved the isolation there. From his rooms in the Villa Floridiana—they had separate apartments—he could look down the slope to the farms, and beyond them to the blue Tyrrhenian Sea. In the heat of the day he swam and paddled about in a *sandolino,* a one-seat punt, avoiding the tourists on their set route: "the whole Capri scene amuses and entertains me like a well-made play or meal," he wrote to Berenice. It is "an enchanted isle," he told Louis Simon. "The fairies are gone, one or two disconsolate Lesbians walk the mythological paths; Mussolini has been here with a comb."[3]

The idyll of life in the semitropics—and maybe the absence of prospective bed partners, if Mussolini had indeed routed out all the homosexuals—just about convinced Marc of his love for Eva. They began sleeping together on occasion, culminating in mutual declarations on his twenty-fifth birthday, which they celebrated grandly. But the euphoria was bound not to last.

His project for the month of March was the Romantic Piece for Orchestra, which Alexander Smallens had promised he would try out with the Philadelphia Orchestra, and which Marc dedicated to Eva. He completed both a piano score and a full score that was written for a huge orchestra plus piano and heckelphone. Though competently written and well constructed, the eighteen-minute work lacks both sufficient contrast and development. Like *Parabola and Circula,* it possesses no truly distinctive voice, and moves from section to section with an academic sameness. It is "Romantic" not in the sense of big, sweeping melodies but in the orchestral concept: much doubling of parts, which adds up to a monumental, Bruckner-like tone, but which also deprives the work of individual character. Of course, such a compositional technique had become a cliché by the 1920s. Charitably it might be said that Blitzstein was parodizing the Romantic spirit, but in fact it appears as though he was trying to get his feet wet writing for a big orchestra.

In his absence, a League of Composers concert in New York, including remarks by *New York Times* critic Olin Downes, featured three of his new E. E. Cummings settings. The program misspelled his first name with a *k*—Blitzstein must have been getting used to these maulings of his name by now. Radiana Pazmor, an important new-music performer of the day, sang to Edwin McArthur's accompaniment, closing the program. Of "You are like the snow," the most serious of the three songs, one unidentified critic said, "This impressionistic, modernistic song has moments of rare beauty, which both Miss Pazmor and Mr. McArthur displayed to advantage. 'Mister Youse' and 'Jimmie's Got a Goil' were rowdy and amusing and were received with gales of laughter and enthusiasm."

In other news from home, Copland wrote a chatty letter to both Eva and Marc from his new home in Bedford, New York, mentioning the recent Copland-Sessions evening:

> Our first concert was notable for the discovery of a new 16 year old composer—really talented, Henry Brant. From the way Alex [Smallens] flew into the green room after the concert and yelled, "Aaron, I want to meet this boy," I knew I had discovered something. As Eva says, "Won't it be fun when all the little boys grow up."[4]

That April, Blitzstein composed a string quartet, which he sometimes referred to as *The Italian,* in four movements—*allegro, grazioso* (or *allegretto*), *presto possibile,* and *lento,* an unusual close inspired by Bartók's Quartet no. 2. This, too, he dedicated to Eva.[5]

In the same Clarke's Music Tablet as the quartet, Blitzstein sketched a "Cantatina for Women's Chorus and Percussion," quite a fresh idea for its day. Apparently never finished, it was conceived for two soprano and two alto parts, who sing popular sliding chromatic harmonies, while the percussionist plays a hefty role with a specifically jazz-band scoring. The piece features scat lyrics with multilingual catch-phrases. Already accused of writing musical nonsense, the composer now had his singers enunciate meaningless syllables purely for their aural effect, a technique deriving more from jazz than from operatic fioritura. Another work from this period is the three-minute-long 1930 Scherzo for piano, a hard-edged, antiromantic, polytonal affair marked *presto* that sounds like speeded-up silent movie music. Like the Sonata, it features scale passages of a machinelike ferocity.

Toward the end of April, Alexander Smallens sent Marc notice that the League of Composers was sponsoring a competition, and he suggested that Marc write a ballet. One morning, Marc told Eva that he had thought of three possible subjects, two mythological themes and the story of Cain. "Oh, my God, Cain!" Eva blurted out, and there was a mutual shock of recognition that this was it. He threw himself into the project with an eager fury, and for weeks it consumed both him and Eva. He suffered through a series of small nervous illnesses, he lost weight, and his whole appearance seemed transformed. Eva witnessed this fever of creation, and though she continued to work on her novel, *The Broken Circle*, she found the utmost contentment in Marc's presence and, for the first time in her life, in subordinating herself to her love for him. The discovery of being "an average woman like any other" delighted her, but the happiness was necessarily incomplete: It would have required the equal exchange of love from Marc, and this didn't come.

Blitzstein divided the ballet into two scenes with continuous music and an interlude between them. In the first, set in Eden, we witness Abel offering his sacrifice of a lamb to God, and its grateful reception. Cain makes his offering of fruits of the land, but it is rejected. In his anger, he kills his brother, and Jehovah (a baritone whose voice comes through a speaker placed at the top center of the auditorium) challenges the murder in a slow, authoritative, oratorio-style pronouncement with long note values. Upon Cain's admission, Jehovah curses him: He shall labor the soil in vain, he shall wander alone over the earth, and he shall be marked for life. No one shall kill Cain, under pain of sevenfold revenge.

In the second scene, set in a great city, the generations of Cain are shown as the city is built. In a festival number, the crowd drunkenly celebrates the completion of the building. Noema, daughter of Lamech, dances voluptuously. Cain appears, dressed in rags from his endless wandering, and Lamech kills him. When the people turn the body faceup, they discover from his mark that it is Cain. The voice of Jehovah again issues a curse upon Lamech, and upon all the people, and as they raise their heads, they all show upon their brows—to the intended shock of the audience—the mark of Cain the killer.

Blitzstein's philosophy here is that all people, as the children of Cain, are killers: "murder is our heritage."[6] Overall, in the music to this half-hour ballet, he shows great plasticity of form and a classic nobility of expression befitting a biblical subject. His broad emotional range extends from the tenderness of Abel with his lamb to the frenzied bacchanal of the city-builders. Much of the score is modal and tonally centered, some of it polytonally, none of it overly dissonant. Consistent with the Bible's austere directness of rhetoric, Blitzstein uses no complex musical devices. He orchestrated *Cain* immediately upon completing it in mid-June, and also prepared a piano score.

This was the fourth work he dedicated to Eva, who considered it "his first great work," though out of it a gross contretemps emerged. Cecil had imagined that so many dedications might prove a source of embarrassment—to her parents, for instance—and Marc delayed placing her name on the manuscripts. Eva perhaps never understood Cecil's point; she feared that Marc held back because Jo or Aaron or Alex might think he was in love with her. It took months before the misapprehension could be cleared up.

The moment Blitzstein finished the score, he fell into a "postpartum" depression, really more a crisis. "My only real reaction when I think of *Cain* is one of shame," he said to Eva; though when he thought about it further, he realized that he would be ashamed not of his work but of himself being unable to face possible failure. In any case, from then on it seemed evident that Eva had been useful as a sounding board during the process of creation, but now her presence was futile. She could do nothing to alleviate his pain as an artist. "It's between me and my work," Marc told her, shutting her out. The limits of the friendship had been reached; if she could not get love from Marc, now it looked as though she could not get the "mental intimacy" she craved, either. Marc, too, felt the loss of his illusions about their affair in the tense weeks that followed. Of his depression over the work, he confided to Jo:

> I know I have written the best thing in my career. Yet I have made a failure; no one else will know it, I do. I'm not mature enough to do a *Cain;* someday I shall be. I lack humility; one has no business to tackle a subject so overwhelmingly magnificent at my age; I get all the richness, and the scope, not the implications.
>
> Yet Cain is the work which has given me vision for works to come. I may yet be great![7]

By this time, the Theatre Guild in New York had decided to revive its *Garrick Gaieties,* a revue format suitable for introducing short sketches by new composers. Louis Simon, who did the costumes for the show, talked up *Triple-Sec* for possible inclusion. An incredulous Blitzstein objected: "The skit is both under and over the heads of that sort of public; they will be bored by the theme, and uninterested in the only justification for it—the music." He instead proposed as more likely material some of the pop songs he had tossed off:

> One's called "Start in Lookin'," is pretty hot as to words, and would need a Holman-Waters-Smith voice (one line goes:
>
> *I've lost a lot of time*
> *Believing you were my maybe*
> *I wouldn't toss a dime*
> *For you're not head or tail to me, Baby.)*
>
> This one may be too rough for you. The other one is for a boy-and-girl presentation, all about wanting love:
>
> *He: Me oh my,*
> *The season's high*
> *For wide affection*
> *Once I start*
> *I'll lose my heart*
> *To some collection.*
> *She: I'm so hot*
> *I haven't got*
> *discrimination*
> *Mike and Ike,*
> *They look alike,*
> *It's sex-starvation.*

> Then there's that sad inferiority-song I sent Sterling [Holloway]. If he's with you, maybe you can work that one in. Is this the sort of stuff you mean? It's all crap to me, done in off moments, as relief from the real work, when my funny kind of mind has to be turning out some tune or other. I don't take any of the songs seriously or with cherishment, and I won't be at all offended if they fail to please. However, if there's anything to be made on them in the way of—what-is-it?—kudos, I'm agribble. I suppose you'll do the necessary business of copyrighting.[8]

Louis Simon was sold on *Triple-Sec,* however, and he managed to place it in the revue—though on its advance ticket order form, the Guild advertised music by "March Blitzstein." Alexander Smallens came up to New York to rehearse the pit orchestra in this uncustomary advanced music, and to conduct the first night. Philip Loeb directed. Imogene Coca played Lady Betty III in *Triple-Sec,* and also appeared in other sketches. Called in the program "a modernistic operetta which is not to be taken too seriously," Blitzstein's piece, the fifteenth on the program, opened the second half. For the New York production, unlike the premiere in Philadelphia, the role of Lord Silverside was played by Ray Heatherton, not by a black man.

Wilella Waldorf wrote of *Triple-Sec* that it "kept working toward something without ever getting much beyond the usual opera burlesque."[9] Brooks Atkinson summed it up well for *The New York Times* the same day when he said that though "labored in the beginning, it finally emerges into excellent musical satire."[10]

Toward the middle of June, letters started pouring in to Blitzstein from a host of friends and well-wishers, reporting the success of *Triple-Sec.* Zealous admirers assured him that he was now on the road to Broadway fame. But he downplayed their exaggerated enthusiasm, knowing that musical standards on the Great White Way had hardly shifted so radically. He wrote to Jo acknowledging the news, "As I read between the lines half the applause comes from an audience who don't know what it's all about, but accept it as a spoof on grand-opera; and half is from the snobs (Van Vechten, etc.) who are delighted to go slumming a bit, and discover a diamond in the rough, so-to-speak. However, who cares?"[11] The piece stayed in the revue for 150 performances (it was dropped in October), and Blitzstein recovered sixteen dollars a week for it.

Not everyone liked it—Cecil went to see it and wrote his impressions, perhaps a touch jealously, to Eva:

> Marc's *Triple Sec* still opens the second act and is the poorest thing on the bill and is boring. . . . The orchestra score seems more pointless than the piano score (as it was played by Marc) and I discovered to my horror that the stuff the actors had to sing was, just as I always suspected and you denied, putting the blame on Marc's voice, absolutely without any toune [*sic;* read tune] or tone or beauty of any kind whatever; they all sounded exactly as Marc sounds when he accompanies himself with his voice. I fear you do the piece a compliment when you say it's [*sic*] place

is in a revue rather than in an opera; it's [*sic*] place is no where except on a piano as merely a piano piece, without voice. It is then at least not boring. . . .[12]

In any case, despite private reservations about how he might face up to failure, it was *Cain* that excited Blitzstein at the moment. "If it ever gets produced in New York," he wrote to Berenice, "I expect it will knock them dead. (This is pardonable conceit, a hangover from the creative momentum.) I have made a passionate work, and I suppose I'm a bit surprised." Exhausted from his marathon of inspiration, he thought of taking a brief rest. He explained what would become over time virtually his philosophy of life—the idea that worth comes not from who one is but from meeting the obligation to produce: "The sense of guilt is so often with me (in connection with my work), that I catch echoes of a sense of duty (to life?) behind it; which would mean a morality moulding itself around me. Is it so? I shall march forth and greet it."[13]

Needing to relax, and needing the distance from one another, he and Eva each sought out other company at the end of July. Marc headed for the south of France, leaving his steamer trunks in storage in Capri, and Eva went to Paris. They took the same train together as far as Genoa. Eva had some brief affairs—one with Maxwell Bodenheim—trying to overcome the sense of failure with Marc. By now, she felt convinced that Marc was a confirmed homosexual and admitted to Cecil that between them "the actual physical passion plays a practically negligible part." Neither Marc nor Eva had much desire for it. Nor did Marc show any attraction for other women; to the contrary, he had teased her in Capri with reports of his assignations with men.[14]

From the end of July through most of August, Blitzstein stayed in Cannes, where he renewed his acquaintance with George Antheil. Marc berated him in a letter to Eva for his "ass-licking to achieve good publicity." But also, "He had one good—very penetrating—criticism of my work. He said he thought it too well-made, of a technical perfection close to sterility. It's a good criticism because in the large it includes the perception of my over-intellectuality. But I suppose that's not very difficult to discern."[15]

Back in Paris, Marc and Eva saw one another almost daily, though they stayed in separate hotels. Eva presented him with copies of the turgid poetry she had written in Capri on their parting, but the terms were different now. Downing large quantities of alcohol throughout this unusually rainy season, they talked openly, Marc convinced that whatever cherished memories he retained about the past, he had to free himself of Eva. "I have to find out whether you own me or I own you," he told her. "There was one evening," Eva wrote to her confidant Cecil, "when I was very drunk, got hysterical, and spilled my whole desire to commit suicide; with the result that Marc was shocked, not by my troubles so much as by a sudden coming home to him of all the troubles of humanity, into going on a three-day drunk."[16]

During his stay in Paris, Blitzstein spent a weekend in September with Boulanger at her summer place in Gargenville to hear her reactions to the year's work. She heard all of *Parabola and Circula* and *Cain,* and to Marc's immense relief, pronounced them great: The ballet, she said, "*C'est une trouvaille* [a discovery]." He gave her an original copy of the score to his April String Quartet, and she found it "wholly admirable," "perfect writing for strings." While in Paris, he also played the piano for a Copland work at a concert on September 23. By the beginning of October, he was back in Italy.

Blitzstein sailed for home on the *Conte Grande,* departing November 8. It was a stormy voyage and he was both sick and depressed. In part, it was *Cain* that weighed so terribly on him—the expectation of how it might be received, but also the "misery of relinquishing [it] to the past," as he wrote to Eva from shipboard the day before landing. "I feel stricken. And then, suddenly, everything clears (or blacks out) and I can only remember that tomorrow I shall see Jo again."[17]

Indeed, Eva felt that Marc returned home sooner than originally intended because of Jo. Admitting her jealousy to Cecil, Eva concluded, "The point is that Jo's existence makes me completely unnecessary to Marc, and that it is almost more than I can stand." She knew she was irretrievably in love with Marc, would never simply get over him, and knew, too, that in an ultimate sense, Marc was not available to her.

> My physical cowardice keeps me from suicide, and some moral superstition in me even restrains me from the words "I want to die," which are really all I feel. I suppose I shall live on until I die naturally, and then resent death like hell; but what is the use of living like this, just barely keeping from daily collapse—and sometimes not even that. . . . I have what you would call hysterics almost every day.[18]

Within just a few weeks, Blitzstein settled into an apartment at 149 West Tenth Street in New York, and was back in the swing of musical events. In a lengthy missive to Eva in Juziers, he began and ended with statements either calculated or just unself-consciously designed to discourage her from holding the torch for him:

> Only one thing, of the things I find in America, remains steadfast: Jo. We have come together beautifully; a union conditioned by her hero-worship of me, and my reluctant acceptance of it. (How recently the reluctance would have been absent!) This is real and good.[19]

Then he continued with other news. Alex adored *Cain,* and Aaron said Marc had "improved immensely."[20] Stokowski said he would perform the Romantic Piece at the end of the season—he arranged for the copying of parts—and would do *Cain* in a full staging the next season.

He seems quite willing that Marc Chagall should do the sets and Balanchine (who will be here then) the choreography. [He] sent in a swell letter to the *Prix de Rome.* So did Fritz Reiner, who fell for *Parabola and Circula,* and would like to give a performance. . . .

My father's bank closed last week or so. A terrific run; everything gone to smash. I rushed home for some days, found myself perfectly useless on a battlefield strewn with corpses; and returned to New York. What will happen is still vague; bankruptcy has for the moment been avoided. . . . My father has become an old man through it. Maddie, thank God, remains both cheerful and useful. They have moved out of 1826 [Spruce Street]. I don't think I will be called upon to support Papa—at any rate just yet; but I am disturbed . . . ; the little money I had blew up, that's all. . . .

So far there has been no opportunity to pursue the "junk" idea of making a lot of money. Three new jazz songs are to be tried over by Ethel Merman a famous torch-singer; maybe I'll sell them. . . .

Only last night a boxer, really charming and affable, walked, after a beautiful hour, away with my watch . . . the one that went so often to the Capri jeweler. I shall have to start learning things about people I thought I knew.[21]

The bank had remained solvent for well over a year after the crash. Until December 1930 it still actively competed as a ticket agency, but a sudden run on its accounts forced it to close, throwing all its employees out of work, including a number of family members. Relatives with accounts there lost their savings, but the bank did manage to repay its other customers. The other Jewish immigrant banks of Philadelphia went out of business at the same time.*

If Blitzstein's reputation on the East Coast was growing, his international renown increased, too, with Henry Cowell's appreciative article in the German magazine *Melos.* In February of 1931, he revisited Philadelphia's Society for Contemporary Music to give a lecture-recital based on his European gleanings of recent developments in music. Unlike radio in the United States, German radio was free from domination by private broadcasters and advertising, and Blitzstein considered the medium a "magnificent cultural spur to young composers." He also introduced his Philadelphia audience to the new simplicity of Kurt Weill's music for *Die Dreigroschenoper.* "It is for me, not so good," he reported.

I find it a combination of Russian cabaret music and the sort of American bellowing baritone who sings By the Shores of Mandalay. But you will see for yourself; I am going to give you a sort of imitation of the way Carola Neher in Munich, or Roma Bahn in Berlin sang this particular song; it

*A second cousin of Marc's, Jacob Galanter, worked at the bank, as had his fiancée Mary. They had married in 1927, and Sam asked her to leave, feeling that a husband and wife should not both be on the staff. When their only child was born in February 1931, they named him after Mary's father, Mordecai, but called him Marc, telling Sam it was because Marc Blitzstein was such a nice and talented young man.

> is also the new style of performance in Germany, French grace in combination with American nonchalance, two qualities often sadly lacking in German renditions heretofore.[22]

Then, seated at the piano, he rendered the "Barbara Lied" in his rather good singer's voice, closely mimicking, as he was expert at doing, the German performers.

Amid the family's financial difficulties, Marc completed his application for the Prix de Rome and began work on a piano concerto. Papa depended on Marc's success for his morale, and with Jo encouraged him to accept the award, and a sojourn in Rome, if he won it. Others in the family tried to hold him back, however, saying he owed it to his father to stay home and help support him. He expressed his quandary to Eva:

> This *would* be the correct ironic moment to be giving birth again to music. It is happening again; I am about to make a better piece than *Cain.* The piano concerto; with a slow quiet beginning for the solo-instrument which is monstrous, it is so beautiful.[23]

But work on the concerto stopped when a second opportunity for Blitzstein to write a film score arose.

The last of the Copland-Sessions Concerts held in America, March 15, 1931, featured music and films. Hugh Ross conducted a small orchestra composed of thirty members of the Philharmonic-Symphony Orchestra in a program including three Ralph Steiner films and one by Cavalcanti. The concert was held at the Broadhurst Theatre on West Forty-fourth Street. Copland had relied on Eva as his agent in Europe to pay for copies of the films to be sent.[24] Roger Sessions's *The Black Maskers* and Copland's *Music for the Theatre* rounded out the evening.

Composers had only just begun to perceive opportunities for work in the film medium, hoping to reach far beyond the concert hall and far beyond the hackneyed music used until then. Abstract films, such as those by Steiner, seemed the most appropriate place to begin employing serious scores: *Mechanical Principles* and *H_2O* had scores by Colin McPhee. Blitzstein's score, prepared in the early months of 1931 under the patronage of Alma Wertheim, accompanied Steiner's *Surf and Seaweed.*

Blitzstein's score includes tiny, awkward depictions of rock and seaweed formations, illustrating the various segments of the film: "Seaweed in Sunlight," "Swirling Seaweed," "Lorelei Coming," "Lorelei Passed," "Open Sea Coming," "Open Sea," and others. The scoring is for winds, trumpet, string quartet, and piano. Richard Hammond, in *Modern Music,* hailed the music's "lean simplicity and instrumental economy completely in character with contemporary composition. Savoring of the small orchestra rather than of symphonic complexity it gave an excellent commentary on the film and was, at all times, more than mere background and not in the genre of representational music."[25]

Several days before the concert, Marc met Eva's parents for the first time. He was impressed by Edward Goldbeck's erudition and mental acuity, noting, too, a sense of futility underlying his existence. When Marc played through the score of *Cain,* wanting so much for Eva's parents to like him and his work, Edward became uncharacteristically excited. Marc invited them to the concert of film music, reporting to Eva how disappointed they were, "and well they might be":

> It was a wild and hectic evening, fruitful of not much except chaos. Everything had been rehearsed insufficiently, and went accordingly. I worked—*slaved* really; I played the piano-parts in five of seven numbers. My suite is good—a minor triumph at the moment, which Aaron persists in considering a major one. Compared to the piano concerto I am now doing, it is merely a nice work.[26]

Another report of the evening comes from Ralph Steiner:

> The music was not recorded, but was to be played by a sizable orchestra in synchronization with the films. I knew almost nothing about splicing films, so they kept breaking during the performance. The projectionist would hurry to rethread the projector while the poor orchestra leader went mad slowing the orchestra down to get back into synchronization. When one film happened to end with the end of the music a loud cheer of relief went up from the whole audience.[27]

The sixteen-minute Suite Blitzstein derived from *Surf and Seaweed* for a slightly more modest instrumentation is in five movements, dedicated to Alma Wertheim. It is by turns playful and eddying, ruminative and melodic, lyrical and menacing, highly tonal against passages of polytonality, with a choralelike climax before ending mysteriously on an unresolved chord. No record exists of any performance of the Suite.

As a critic, Blitzstein wrote three major review articles for *Modern Music* that winter and spring of 1931. There were weeks when it seems that all he did was attend concerts. In trenchant and often devastating phrases, he would sum up the principal qualities of a piece of music, saving his rare praise for works of exceptional merit. Pointed in his opinions, he often aimed for a memorable archness of expression. Rarely—but sometimes—he would reverse himself years later, acknowledging the change as a sign of personal growth.

Hearing the new instrument devised by Maurice Martenot and later bearing his name (as *ondes Martenot*), Blitzstein preferred it to Leon Theremin's similar ether-wave invention; but the work in which it was featured, a Symphonic Poem by Levidis, the critic found "pseudo-oriental, pseudo-Scriabinic, pseudo-romantic, pseudo-everything." On the same concert, however, Stokowski programmed a "magnificent" Sarabande by Buxtehude, and Blitzstein asked, "When is Buxtehude's greatness to be made known to us extensively?"

Early in the year, Blitzstein took the occasion of a League of Composers concert to blast Copland's *Piano Variations:* "Pain is the whole keynote, and a stunning rebound from pain." "Monotony" and "harmonic thinness" marked the piece: "The *Variations* lack variety," he wrote, placing intellectual honesty above friendship. Copland's characteristic trait is "doing much with little." Blitzstein's damning vocabulary contrasted sharply with his evaluations of Stravinsky's music. The *Capriccio,* which he had heard conducted by Otto Klemperer the year before in Berlin with Stravinsky at the piano, he called a "tour-de-force" under Koussevitzky with Jesús Sanromá. "The work is like a Swiss watch—neat as a pin and as decorative, and containing an enormously detailed and complicated mechanism."[28]

Established European composers also felt the sting of Blitzstein's critical lash in the pages of *Modern Music.* Bartók's String Quartet no. 4 was "a disappointment": "the reaction to repeated performances is a steady dwindling of interest." On the American premiere of Alban Berg's opera *Wozzeck,* Blitzstein had little good to say. Bristling against the school of his teacher Schoenberg, he declared the work "too typical, too little individual," with an "essential unbalance and essential irresponsibility." In light of what he was clearly still striving for in his own composition, he criticized Berg for the lack of "connection between the form used and the emotion projected."[29]

Turning to the dance, a lifelong love, he considered that of all the women in contemporary choreography, including Doris Humphrey, Agnes de Mille, Tamiris, and Mary Wigman, Martha Graham was "the one to get excited about." He also liked Benjamin Zemach, formerly of the Habima Hebrew Theatre. His Jewish folk ballets are "deeply rooted in a racial spirit, and his imagination derives immense fertility from the contact." In one of his dances, Zemach also chanted.[30] The combination of media impressed Blitzstein, who immediately and excitedly wrote to Eva in early February:

> I have seen the man to play *Cain* . . . , not tall, but powerful and rather ugly in body—muscular, a blunt eloquence . . . barely tamed, and rooted in the race; with a sudden elvishness or tenderness, or that wisdom so old it has gone trivial or a little rotten. I play *Cain* to him tomorrow.[31]

Zemach began improvising several scenes from *Cain* in his studio, with himself playing Cain, Fred Berk as Abel, and Katya Delakova as Cain's Wife. Berk left the company, however, and Zemach discontinued work on the project. After a year or so, Blitzstein asked Zemach to return the score. That is as close to performance as *Cain* ever got.

Eva, still working for MGM in Paris, luxuriated in self-pity. Without Marc she seemed cut off from her moorings. As she asked Cecil in one of a number of letters filled with doubt as to her future, "Don't you see that the whole point is that he is important to me and I am not?" She speculated that she had been the woman figure in Marc's life, helping him to mature, but also necessary for Marc to leave behind; intellectually she could accept this fate, but never emotionally. It was no use returning home, either: There her mother would only question her about her health and her personal life, her affairs, Marc, and her potential for a nervous breakdown. Only Marc could decide if and when they would be together and, maddeningly, she claimed, he wrote so seldom with detailed information about his life, his work, his family, his plans, and his intentions toward her. "I expect to be terribly unhappy with Marc within range; but this way I am not even sane."[32]

Aside from working on his piano concerto and the *Surf and Seaweed* score, Blitzstein met with Cecil a number of times during the same period. "We make a sort of pretense at writing jazz-songs together," he wrote Eva. "Nothing will come of it, since they have all been punk; but I get a feeling of doing something in the Broadway field. Then he leaves and I go back to the *concerto.*" Indeed, he admitted in the same letter that considering his father's poor financial position, he was half-tempted to give up composing for a year to make some real money.[33]

One popular song of Blitzstein's from around this period—to his own text—is an archly poignant, revealingly self-descriptive number called "What's the Matter with Me?" In all likelihood the "sad inferiority song" to which he had referred the year before in a letter to Louis Simon, it is one of a series Blitzstein would write over the course of his life, in which he wonders whether love will ever come his way:

When I was wearing baby dresses
Other kids' distresses
Drowned out all my noise.
Then, when I came to school in knickers,
You should hear the snickers
From the other boys.
And I suppose I am to blame,
If it's always been the same,
For I go to and fro like a rubber bag.
I thought that trousers' longer span
Would show the world my manhood,
Just another gag.

Now love is in the air,
I'd like a little share,
But no one seems to care,
Tell me, what's the matter with me? . . .

O, I suppose some day,
When I am old and worn and thin,
Someone will come my way,
And dust me off and take me in.
I'm trained in all the arts,
My heart's like other hearts,
I've all the essential parts,
Tell me, what's the matter with me?

At the end of March, Claire Reis came through with a five-hundred-dollar commission from the League of Composers for a small work to be performed the next season. At first, Blitzstein proposed a ballet, and Reis replied, "Rabelais (if not *too* expurgated) sounds good."[34] Then he changed his mind and turned to Hemingway's short story "The Killers" for a one-act opera. Perhaps its theme of gangsterism attracted him, as it had Brecht and Weill in Germany. Eliminating the story's one female character, Blitzstein devised a scenario in three scenes for eight male singers and an ensemble of seven instruments. The amoral professionalism of hired assassins may have held wider social implications for the composer. Most striking is the scene in which the killers inquire about the usual arrival time at the lunch counter of the man they are to kill: It bears an unmistakable likeness to the Drugstore scene from *The Cradle Will Rock* of five years later, and can be considered a source for that episode showing a compromised, complicitous morality. However, the League was wary of "The Killers" and Blitzstein abandoned it around the middle of May after writing only eight or nine pages of music. Instead, the composer chose as his source Book III of the *Argonautica* of Apollonius.

Blitzstein did not win the Prix de Rome. Even if it had been inadvisable at that time to leave the family for financial reasons, another reason for staying in America emerged: His nephew Stephen underwent a serious double mastoid operation that spring which required multiple blood transfusions, and Marc would have been reluctant to be so far away.

For two months, beginning on May 25, he enjoyed the quiet of the third-floor Tower Studio at Yaddo, the artists' colony in Saratoga Springs, New York, where he overlooked an edenlike vision of lakes and surrounding woods and reveled in the luxurious service. There he met the young writer Emanuel Eisenberg, with whom he would collaborate on some minor projects a few years later. On this first of several visits to Yaddo, he worked on the Piano Concerto and on his commission piece, an eighteen-minute opera called *The Harpies.* Soon after settling in, he wrote to Eva:

> It seems to me clearer than ever before that I am fighting against time; (I remember ridiculing your assertion you were to die at thirty-odd)—there is no time, and there is so much to be done. I, who want above all to write music which is least like my nature—music which grows out of peace, has no spectacularity—I seem fated by equipment and circumstance to be a nervous brilliant erratic composer.[35]

Actually, his first days at Yaddo were not so quiet: He truly feared there might be little time left for him. On arriving, there was

> a sudden conviction that I had caught syphilis; a pain, strange markings on my penis, a remembrance of an evening which might have caused it. In my nervous state, it was a conviction. I rushed to the Schenectady hospital for a Wassermann test; waited five days in agony; contemplating

suicide among other things; working furiously on the "Harpies" with an insane sense of honor to the League, two hundred and fifty dollars of the prize having already been given me. The Wassermann was negative; I was sure they were wrong, inefficient; went to a good doctor in Saratoga. It appears to be a slight kidney ailment, with referred pain at the penis; really nothing. I can hardly believe it yet; I have lived with the torment so long.

Which, baby, is the ashamed confession of an infant.[36]

A spoof set in ancient Thrace, *The Harpies* has eight characters, neatly balanced between tenor and soprano principals, a group of three female Harpies, and three male Argonauts. At the center is Phineus, a sightless oracle, who attempts to enjoy his dinner but is constantly attacked by the Harpies. Not only do they steal his food, they emit a powerful stench as well. Along come the Argonauts with their chief, Jason, who will fight off the Harpies if Phineus will assure them of their continued favor among the gods. When the battle is all but finished, Iris appears as a messenger of the gods, promising that Phineus will now and forever be safe from the Harpies, whom she sends off to other foul tortures. The prophet can now eat his meal, and the curtain falls.

This third opera by Blitzstein is the first composed to his own text, and though the content is slight, some hints of the composer's concerns glimmer through. All-knowing and all-seeing Phineus admits he is "powerless to help or hinder," to which an Argonaut adds the lament, "To know all, and to be able to do nothing!" Jason concludes that "It can't be good to be an oracle." Covertly, Blitzstein approaches here the dilemma of the intelligentsia: If the contradiction between knowledge and action is to be resolved, ideas must be backed up by militant deed. The Harpies may also represent Depression conditions in that they frustrate the human need for basic sustenance—food, work, shelter.

Thematically, *The Harpies* satirizes the mythological operas of Gluck and other preclassical composers. Musically, with its trios of Harpies and Argonauts drifting in and out of radio-commercial style, barbershop harmony, and implicit references to the Valkyries and the three genii of *The Magic Flute,* it is a send-up of Stravinsky's neoclassical style. The score is written for eight players—winds, double bass, and piano. Suffused with sprightly humor, the text is a clever blend of stuffy "translationese," rank modernisms, and spicy slang. Blitzstein finished the piano score in July, orchestrated it soon after, and dedicated the work to his mother.

Over the summer, Cecil occupied Marc's West Tenth Street apartment. He had taken to acting as something of a spy for Eva, informing her of Marc's movements and especially of his feelings about her. At the same time, in her letters to Cecil, Eva often quoted whole passages of Marc's letters to keep him advised. Shortly after Marc had passed through town on his way to see the family on the New Jersey shore, Cecil affected shock as he reported to Eva on Marc's medical condition. Unaware that Marc had already fully apprised her of it, he wrote, "It astonishes me that he exposes himself to syphilis or any v. d."; and he advised her that if anyone wanted to sleep with her, she should have him use a condom. At the same time he let her know of his forthcoming marriage to Edith Betts—"she is very nice," he said, and what's more, she had been a virgin before meeting Cecil.[37]

Eva had been pressuring Marc to come to Europe and see her; at the same time, Aaron wrote from Tangier that summer, encouraging her to join him and Paul Bowles there. Apart from missing Marc and feeling that their contact had to all intents ended, she had medical problems with which to deal: in April, tumors removed from one breast, and in July, a dilation and curettage. Until well into July, Marc was planning another visit to the MacDowell Colony in September, and would not commit himself to a trip. Finally, he agreed to accept Eva's offer to pay for the trip, but only for three weeks or so and only on condition that wherever they stayed, he would need a piano to work on the orchestration of the concerto. She wavered back and forth between exultation and despair over his visit. Feeling "not worthy," she predicted in her journal that "Even if he leaves with friendship, I shall have been disposed of." Cecil put in his words of advice to Eva; as usual, conventionality won the day, to destructive and selfish purpose, considering that with his forthcoming marriage he would well like to see Eva similarly paired off and out of his way:

> If he should say that you chose him, he didn't choose you, and therefore as a real man he couldn't permit himself to marry you; please point out to him the facts, which are that he chose you in the beginning and kept at you for a long time till he had got you in love with him and then almost at once cooled off or edged off. Therefore the manly thing for him to do is to marry you![38]

On August 9 Blitzstein sailed third class on the S.S. *Lorraine* bound for Le Havre. En route, he kept a diary-letter in which he remarked on the other passengers, and he sent it off to Jo upon arrival. Soon after boarding, he witnessed the meeting of two "fairies"—"One, from first class, with blondined hair and cap to match," the other "an amazing little old lady of 21; ravaged, gray-faced and fattish, with an incurable tendency to comb his hair in the teeth of a constant wind." Amused by their banter, Blitzstein listened to them chat across a porthole for hours. One of them referred to "the grandest man" he had seen on board, who, in the course of the conversation, turned out to be none other than Blitzstein himself! His report was Marc's way of reminding Jo of his own capacity for attraction to men, while distancing himself from any hint of effeminacy.

On board the *Lorraine* and seated at Blitzstein's table, a brutish Mediterranean type kept making offensive comments about Jews. "The thing will probably come to a head if he keeps it up," Marc wrote. A few days later:

> The anti-semite has discovered all. He took it surprisingly, proving himself not even a good bigot. Realizing I was more his "class" in intelli-

gence than the other two French saps at our table (he had been addressing all his witty remarks to me), he sufficed with a "you don't look like one," and proceeded to forget that he hated jews, and to remember how stupid were the provincials of France.

Blitzstein's consciousness was further aroused by the presence on board of a group of deportees, expelled for some unknown reason but not on charges of espionage or Communism, "as I had fondly hoped," he wrote. He mulled over the theme of politics in art, and in a sudden burst conceived a new opera based on the Sacco and Vanzetti story, each character to be played by a chorus, showing the "background of the capitalistic machine against a radical individual." He imagined a severe limitation to such an opera, however: "it does at the moment appear that only Soviet Russia would be willing to perform it."[39]

"Something wonderful has come into his face—his eyes: illumination," Eva reported to her journal once Marc had arrived in Paris. For a while, as he played through the Piano Concerto for her, they seemed to recapture the old feeling that *Cain* had inspired. They agreed, at least, on the permanence of their feeling for one another, even if it amounted only to a "friendship-love" without sex. "I can't be good enough," she wrote in her journal.[40]

While Marc was there, Cecil returned to his campaign to get Eva married off:

> Plenty of homosexuals marry, lots of them very successfully. He knows you wouldn't object to his having outside homosexual experiences so long as he stuck to you; that should be enough. It would too make a man of him; he certainly isn't one now. He greatly needs the experience marriage with you would give him; he can't get it any other way or through anyone else.[41]

But by the end of the visit, Marc told her he did not want her to return with him to America.

On his return, Marc wrote Eva a newsy letter about Cecil, about possibilities for *Cain* with Stokowski the following season, about receiving a promise of patronage for the next year, about a sore finger where part of a nail had to be removed, and about his trip home. On the boat he had met Henry Wadsworth Longfellow Dana, the Harvard professor of drama who had just spent eighteen months in Russia studying the theatre, and who promised to try and get Blitzstein's imagined Sacco and Vanzetti opera performed there. Most of all, and most thrilling to Eva, Marc had unaccountably changed his mind about her:

> When can you come, darling? The thought of you, our life, has done absolutely incredible things to me. . . . You must come. I went over the whole business on the boat; it was a miracle how all the cautions and doubts had vanished in the light of our final understanding.[42]

Not a week later, Marc wrote to Eva again, uncontrollably ecstatic with anticipation:

> Why am I so buoyant on the subject of New York? I seem to own everything, nothing stands in my way. . . . This is clear. Thought over; the "situation" has been scanned; I want you here, or wherever I am, from now on. . . .
>
> So much we went over! I want to go over it again, to be sure of it all—just now the list: you change in principle; no illness, To love—be in love with your inferiority complex; adjustment (can be called "illness.") Literature; music; you and Jo; you in New York; make it soon! My past year; your idea of it, and mine. Being "sorry" for me. Your sense of my value apart from you. The homosexuality; finding a "wisdom" about it. And more.[43]

Jo and Eva also exchanged letters: Jo assured her that she must be right for Marc if he could feel that strongly. Eva wrote back more knowingly, recognizing that "Marc's relation to you is the basic one in his life. I am much clearer about that than about how any other works in."[44]

By the first of October, Marc had moved from West Tenth Street into new quarters at 16 Grove Street at a rent of ten dollars a week. He described the place to Eva as "a comfortable furnished room which has the advantage of a private bell, and thus the benefits of an apartment—re guests, etc." Eva arrived in New York toward the end of the month, and Marc was able to secure another room for her in the same building. Now for the first time in America, they would live together—almost. "Splendid; a private place, and yet together," Marc wrote to his sister. But so far no one in his family had met Eva, and he cautioned Jo not to tell Papa and Maddie about her and this arrangement. "I would not be going into details, a 'Platonic marriage,' etc., I think that when we actually get married will be time enough. He (and Maddie) will be putting two and two together during that time."[45] Eva must have felt even more closely drawn to Marc when, at the end of November, Cecil remarried.

As capitalism sank daily into deeper and deeper paroxysms of despair in the early 1930s, the Soviet system seemed to hold out increasing promise to the West. On November 7, 1931, well-wishers of the Revolution gathered for a fourteenth anniversary concert program that featured excerpts from operas, cowboy and labor songs, a vocal sextet performing Negro songs directed by Hall Johnson, contemporary dance by the Martha Graham group, and Blitzstein at the piano with contemporary American music.

At the end of the month, as if in confirmation of capitalism's decline, Claire Reis wrote to Blitzstein about the future of his commissioned opera, *The Harpies.* The Depression had become "so great that we cannot raise enough money for the stage programs of small works this year," and with that she released the League of Composers' option on the piece.[46]

In the Grove Street quarters, Blitzstein finished orchestrating the Piano Concerto, which he dedicated to a patron, Alene Erlanger. He also heard that Stokowski wanted to perform *Cain* with the Philadelphia Orchestra, and one night in November at a performance of *Wozzeck,* he provided him a complete set of parts. But then he could get no information from the maestro even as to when he would schedule a rehearsal. "Still on the qui vive about the prima donna Stokowski," he wrote to Jo. "The man *is* a bastard!"[47] Finally, in the first week of January, unannounced to Blitzstein, Stokowski distributed the parts at a rehearsal of his orchestra and played through a third of it before deciding he didn't like it. The composer was infuriated not to have been informed, and Stokowski's frigid letter accompanying the return of the parts hardly helped. Howard Hanson and Fritz Reiner expressed some interest in *Cain* but without result.

Blitzstein had sent the score of his concerto to Vienna to be considered for the International Music Festival, but just after the new year it came back, rejected because funds would not permit any orchestral performances. On January 12, though, Blitzstein played through his concerto for Reiner, who called it "one of the best and most expertly done works by an American." According to Eva's journal, Reiner wanted to program it in April—featuring Blitzstein as soloist—with Roger Sessions's *Black Maskers* and the Copland Symphony, but Blitzstein feared that Reiner would lack the courage to offer an all-American concert. It was not programmed.

Koussevitzky expressed no interest in the concerto, and Stokowski only vaguely offered "let's play it through in rehearsal" someday; judging from the experience with *Cain,* this was hardly a likely prospect.[48] Eugene Goossens wrote more affirmatively, though in the end nothing came of his enthusiasm:

> I have just finished reading through your *Concerto* and find it very stimulating. Its clarity of speech is refreshing after so much of recent romantic effusion, (though this doesn't mean that I am opposed to romanticism!). But piano concertos have become so stereotyped that your work, by contrast, seems all the more interesting. On your return from Europe I would like to hear you play it.[49]

In form, Blitzstein wrote, the concerto "follows the Nineteenth century model, except that it begins with an extended prelude for the solo instrument. The last movement is a double passacaglia in which two themes are deployed alternately and simultaneously, affording considerable opportunity for many types of contrapuntal devices and treatment." The movements are titled *Moderato molto; allegro—Largo assai—Allegro non troppo.* Without key signature, the twenty-eight-minute work is marked by frequent meter changes. The writing is taut, ironic, and fresh, a machine-age rhapsody, consistently surprising, never resorting to clichés and complacencies. The composer exploits a wide range of technical resources without resorting to his old percussive tricks—indeed, he includes no percussion at all in his orchestra; and he imposes a rigorous and effective balance between the solo instrument and his orchestra. The concerto was by far Blitzstein's best orchestral writing to date.

As critic, Blitzstein found the midwinter season of 1931–32 tame, smelling of the past, suspenseful with impatience for a new great man to present himself on the music scene. He scorned the *Lyrische* Suite of Alban Berg, dismissing it as a typical product from Schoenberg's musical son: "one is reminded of a child-prodigy, with its brilliant cerebrality, physical sickliness, and strained nerves." He had no use for the "array of gaudy tinsel and facile junk topped by Ravel's *Bolero* and Respighi's *Pini di Roma*" that Toscanini brought before the public. "It is about time also"—the critic's ire mounted—"that someone punctured the myth that Toscanini makes this cheapjack music sound better than it is. He doesn't, he simply makes it sound more expensive."[50] Gershwin's new Second Rhapsody was "pretentious," full of "war-horse pianisms of Liszt," "excessive climaxes," and, most damnably, "easy, and extremely catchy tunes."[51]

By contrast, Blitzstein showed more interest in functional music, music with purpose. He considered Mosolov's *Iron Foundry* among the most successful composed in the "machine" esthetic, "whose day is happily about over." Hindemith's *Wir bauen eine Stadt,* as performed by the children of the Henry Street Settlement, was a piece of *Gebrauchsmusik** in the vein of Weill and Brecht's *Der Jasager.* And he loved Lazare Saminsky's program of Jewish liturgical music at the New School.

In the field of contemporary opera, so woefully unesteemed in America, *Maria Egiziaca* "turned out to be bad music even for Respighi, which is almost being superlative." Meanwhile, "from the Metropolitan, of course, nothing could be expected; and it met expectations to the letter." "I find it difficult," he wrote in review of Jerome Kern's *The Cat and the Fiddle,* to go to "operettas of the 'charming' school." Among the spectacles in New York, Blitzstein appreciated revues and musical comedies such as Gershwin's *Of Thee I Sing* and Irving Berlin's *Face the Music,* observing with pleasure that topical theatre—*Zeitstück*—and satirical cabaret were now becoming popular in America, as they had been in Germany five years before.[52]

Blitzstein could not shake the idea that new forms, and a new man to offer them, were required. In January and February of 1932, he worked on his Serenade for string quartet. He had come to see that many composers combated the spectre of listener boredom by writing music with multiple changes of pace, harmony, and melodic style every few bars. In this piece he attempted another theory: that interest could be maintained by altering harmonic textures without tempo changes. (Again the Debussy influence is present: In his *Nocturnes,* for instance, Debussy opposed the idea that something has to "happen" in music; music might exist only for effect and color, without drama.) To each of his three movements Blitzstein gave the same marking—*largo.*

He gave this work, too, to Eva, on his birthday. That day Copland came to hear the quartet, and Eva recorded his reaction: "Aaron's acceptance was whole-hearted, amazingly unself-conscious (unashamed of having held off so long), delighted, delightful." On March 26 Marc attended the first rehearsal of the piece by the Hans Lange Quartet in Philadelphia, calling Eva excitedly afterward:

*Music for use, written to encourage school and amateur performers.

"It's a wonderful piece!" he said. After living with the work for a few weeks, Lange wanted to "sound forth, tremolo, expressive and make it sound like a mood-piece, groping, tentative," she wrote in her journal. "But Marc has another rehearsal Wednesday, and I think will bring them into line. Lange, very German, respects composers, and also the work."[53]

Eva recorded a political argument with Marc that spring. Both agreed that Communism was the goal toward which they would strive. Marc felt that intermediate palliative measures for the individual, such as patronage from the rich, were not worth going after, and that society would get much more oppressive before the new order arrived. Eva thought that in the meantime it was not wrong to look after one's own interest, a disagreement she feared might one day place them on opposite sides of the barricades. In distancing herself from Marc's asceticism, perhaps she was protecting herself, or what was now left, for she experienced further medical problems in April—more cysts removed from her breasts. Her doctor forewarned that at the first signs of cancer she should have a double mastectomy. Marc wept for hours after Eva's operation.[54]

Eva was well enough to accompany Marc to the First Festival of Contemporary American Music at Yaddo, which Copland organized at the end of April and beginning of May. Jo and Ed drove up to attend as well. Jo was able to take time off from her full-time job at a Philadelphia radio station, where once a week she did interviews with stage personalities. Numerous premieres, including the Serenade, studded the program. Despite—or perhaps because of—a faithful rendition of his score by the Hans Lange Quartet, Blitzstein failed to win the audience to his new theory. "I felt very quiet inside, perfectly satisfied," Marc wrote into Eva's journal, "as though a best-beloved child had been put to rest. I need never hear it again. It filled the room, with all those people, and it filled me, and it was supposed to fill you."[55] No one liked the piece. However, it became the most talked about, and later on in the festival, two of the composer-pianists present sat down and entertained their confreres with a four-hand burlesque of the piece, with Bernard Herrmann conducting. In *Modern Music,* affording more space to the Blitzstein work than to any other, Alfred H. Meyer called it "one of the misfits" of the festival. "The matter of this music often has a darksome Hebraic cast suggestive of Ernest Bloch. . . . The ingenuity of his attempts to conquer the unconquerable leads one to suspect him of an inherent talent above the ordinary."[56]

Oscar Levant recalled the quartet in his memoir, *A Smattering of Ignorance,* as "one of the greatest presumptions toward an audience that I had ever encountered in any composer. . . . It was like a meal consisting entirely of stained glass, with different dressings." After Blitzstein's piece, Levant went onstage to perform his own Sonatina, which he admitted was "unweighty" and had a "banal second movement." Eva considered it "Broadway (lower) & noise." When he had finished, Blitzstein told him, "Now try to write a little *music.*"[57]

Three days of discussion about the future of composers and music in America followed the concerts. Some urged composers to write more music for high school and college orchestras and choruses, but Blitzstein countered with his observation of a certain "regression of material that has contaminated even the composers who aren't writing *Gebrauchsmusik.*" Instead, he proposed that American composers adopt some new formal structure and work within it, to see whether, in the variety of responses to the challenge, a national school might emerge. When others answered that forms would, or would not, naturally emerge over time, Blitzstein said, "Sure. But one way to hurry the future is to start with a form as a hypothesis and work in it without looking for immediate results." Yearning for the signs of a new awakening, he concluded, "We want to push evolution by initiative." Eva noted the response: "Israel [Citkowitz], who is really interested, 'thanked' Marc for the stimulation and let it go at that."[58]

The Yaddo conference was also the occasion for Copland to state his case for the improvement of the composer's lot, particularly in two areas: performance fees and a heightened respect for new efforts in American music on the part of the press. It was a clarion call that, more than Blitzstein's appeal for a new form, summoned composers to a new sense of self-worth and that put newspaper editors on notice that they could no longer afford to dismiss new music with the old customary ignorance.

Directly after the conference, Copland wrote to Marc and Eva, wishing them well on their forthcoming trip to Europe. "I despair of seeing an intelligent review of your quartet," he said. The critics simply could not believe a piece marked *largo, largo, largo.* Then he added his own conclusion as a private criticism: "The moral is: Always cajole a listener, never frighten him away. I mean it seriously."

"I dreamt about Eva last night," Copland continued. "She was in bed and in the tone of Mary just after the Immaculate Conception announced to me that she was going to have a child! And I said: SO SOON?!"[59]

5

IN PURSUIT OF FORM

June 1932–January 1935

". . . beer, light wines, and subsidies for young composers?"

By June 15, 1932, Marc and Eva had settled at Dubrovnik, the Croatian town on the Yugoslavian Adriatic resplendent with Gothic and Renaissance palaces: "a blue and white, fortunately ridiculous apartment in a noisy peasant home; with a nice private beach," Eva recorded in her journal.[1] She continued writing up reports for MGM, and he prepared his lectures on "Form in Music" and "Masterworks of Modern Music" to be delivered early in 1933. They tried to ignore repeated notices from Paris of Eva's unpaid medical bills from the year before.

For his fourth opera, he began working on the sudden inspiration that had struck him the summer before on the S.S. *Lorraine:* a choral treatment of the Sacco and Vanzetti theme. Once again, as in *Cain,* he treated the subject of murder, and once again he strove to create a new musical form. In *The Condemned,* each of the four characters is scored for chorus, with no solo voices, suggesting a kind of Everyman relevance. In fact, among his working notes, Blitzstein jotted down the names of over thirty revolutionaries, from the Maccabees and Socrates through the figures of the French Revolution, the nineteenth-century Marxists and libertarians, John Brown, the Haymarket anarchists, and Eugene V. Debs. Without naming Sacco or Vanzetti, he left the specific reference open to other interpretation.

The thirty-five-minute opera takes place in the Death House, and the choruses take the parts of the Condemned, the Wife, the Friend, and the Priest. As the central character, the Condemned is most highly articulated, with four-part male voices. The Wife is scored for two soprano parts and one alto part; the Friend is two bass parts; and the Priest, two tenor parts. Only the Priest has a distinctive musical voice—liturgical chant style, with highly contrapuntal baroque devices. Blitzstein drew diagrams of the platforms and ramps to be placed on the stage to hold his ninety-six singers, who were to be hidden in groupings behind curtains and revealed at appropriate moments in the opera. For movement, Blitzstein specified that his choruses range about the stage but not act as one. Caught in sleep, for instance, the Condemned should be shown in all aspects of sleep, from complete exhaustion through semiwakefulness.

On the morning of the execution, the Wife visits her husband, who urges her to be strong. The Friend comes to say that though there is no hope for staying the execution, the world knows that "you are to die, killed by a nation for your faith in man. . . . You shall be our martyr. It is a glorious death." When the Priest arrives, the Condemned denies God, suddenly repents, then returns to his atheism: "I need no heaven. The earth shall one day be enough. All men are my brothers." After his final good-byes to the Wife, the full chorus climaxes the opera in a broad, quasi-"religious" celebration of his martyrdom and final glory. The work can be described as a kind of requiem cantata, a ritual coming-to-terms with a nation's sentence of unjust death, ending in an unresolved bitonal chord.

"It's a tense opera—katharsis comes only at the end," Marc wrote to Jo in Philadelphia,

> and the question is if it comes too late to do any good. Each scene moves with a narrow, hemmed-in formula, doggedly regular; the harmonies mostly bleak, hollow, underdone, occasionally passionate. It is this open quality in the vertical line, and closed one in the horizontal which gives the work its special and personal character.[2]

Marc's natural tendency was to call this "far and away my best work," and Eva, too, viewed it as "the greatest music Marc has written . . . a conjunction of genius and the epoch." They had their good days together, even "moonlight"—their code word for sex—"for the first time in a long time."

But writing *The Condemned* was not as stimulating as *Cain* or other works had been, in part because he sensed Eva's lack of involvement. When she resented his lecturing her about Russia, he questioned her dedication to Communism. She chose to see the downside of his enthusiasm: "Russia: always—for over a year now, anyway, in our minds as his future; in my mind as the thing after me." Her morbidity always close to the surface, she confessed on her thirty-first birthday that summer that "if I were to die now I would feel that my life had been in the right place." In early September they moved from the peasant house ("always yelling and noise, horrid rooms, horrible people") to the equally crude Villa Corovič at Mlini, about ten miles down the Adriatic coast from Dubrovnik. Then they moved again to the Pension Lucič, resentful that the Corovič house might one day bear a plaque saying *The Condemned* had been composed there.[3]

Early in September, when Blitzstein had almost completed the opera, he heard from Vera Siloti that the Russian-born conductor and Siloti pupil Albert Coates and his wife were then at their Lago Maggiore home. Coates had been asked to return to the Soviet Union to organize opera and orchestra performances there, beginning the next year. Perhaps, Blitzstein thought, he would be interested in presenting *The Condemned.* In addition, the Soviets had sponsored an opera competition, and *The Condemned* seemed to fit their requirements perfectly. Without delay, Blitzstein arranged to visit them to play through the opera up to the final scene, which had yet to be written. They proved overwhelmingly enthusiastic about the opera. Mrs. Coates, whom Blitzstein described to Eva as "a dried-up hawk of an English creature," claimed for herself the role of its "godmother." Marc telegraphed Eva: TRIUMPH COATES SAYS UTTERLY ORIGINAL RUSSIA WILL INVITE ME TO DEMONSTRATE MEYERHOLD PROBABLE REGISSEUR. Blitzstein wanted to get to Russia the following spring to work for a few months and help to prepare a production of the opera. "My wife will accompany me," he later wrote Coates, anticipating the next stage of the relationship.[4]

Before he returned to Dubrovnik, Blitzstein savored a few moments with an old master. Waiting in Venice for the boat, he "remembered just in time that Monteverdi worked there," he wrote Eva. "So I rushed to the library and spent part of the day copying three of the old madrigals *in ms;* they actually let you take it to your seat to copy!"[5]

Jo tried hard to like Eva; in a way, she did like her, as intellectual company. However, she was also envious of Eva's special position so close to the source of creation. When she heard the good news about Russia, she wrote to Eva from her desk at the radio station:

> I think I'm trying to say that Marc is "right." That you are so essentially right with him. And the Opera, a kind of perfected off-spring. That's so badly put. But there it is. Somehow, I feel a little sad. I don't think it's jealousy; my necessity for Marc and his for me; doesn't include constantly seeing each other. At least we have had to make it that kind of relationship. And I do feel that you are the one person I could bear to have Marc as you do. So my sadness is probably something else. It's all mixed up with a great joy.[6]

Blitzstein had already sent in his 1933 Guggenheim application. After his sojourns in Berlin and Salzburg, he was now claiming total fluency in German; and after his stay in Capri, he could manage Italian well, too. Among his references, he added the names of Roy Harris, Fritz Reiner, Randall Thompson, Robert Russell Bennett, Eugene Goossens, and Dorothy Lawton, head of the Fifty-eighth Street music library, a branch of the New York Public Library. His plans included a three-act opera, an orchestral work, and some smaller works; but in addition, he desired "to evolve a new elastic form," along the lines he had proposed at Yaddo a few months before. Of course, he joked to his sister, everything might be different now, with the election of Franklin Delano Roosevelt that November. "Does that mean beer, light wines, and subsidies for young composers?"[7] Once having seen Coates, however, he proposed to the foundation that instead of his former project, he use his grant to help him go to the USSR, attend rehearsals and performances of *The Condemned,* and study the musical situation there.

Toward the end of November the composer finished orchestrating *The Condemned.* He wanted to dedicate it to Eva, but she objected this time. It should be for his father, she said, or to the memory of Sacco and Vanzetti. Blitzstein returned to America in December, while Eva waited in Paris for definite news about Russia to break. She looked back on the last six months as "the idyllic Jugoslavian period," with not more than three weeks of "stews." On board the *Bremen,* Marc contemplated his relationship with Eva and concluded that despite the "rows, rages, prolonged irritations," "we are for each other, forever." "You are my wife," he told her, "in the greatest sense of the word." Prokofiev was on board and related a disturbing rumor that Coates had broken his contract to go to Russia. Many of the other passengers had just come from Russia, and Blitzstein had the opportunity to hear some useful information. "It is mixed with an amount of ghastly first-hand data about Russian beaurocracy [*sic*], hardships of living, etc. (One particular story about seeing one's manuscripts confiscated or destroyed at the border really got me for a moment!)"[8]

Blitzstein expected a performance of *The Harpies* in January by the New York Opera Repertoire Company, but this production, too, did not take place. Marc played through *The Condemned* for Eva's parents one day, prompting them to send a telegram to Philadelphia for his family's benefit: MARC WAS ADMIRABLE THOUGHT DICTION EASE SUAVE AUTHORITY LOVE FROM BOTH. Clearly they felt more and more impressed by Eva's choice of a mate.

Prokofiev's rumor was correct: Albert Coates did not assume his conducting position in the Soviet Union, nor did Blitzstein win the Guggenheim grant; so Eva joined him a month later. The rest of that winter and spring, they lived in Philadelphia in a brightly decorated apartment at 1408 Spruce Street, with Marc's basic income deriving from his lecture series. They still hoped to get to Russia somehow and get *The Condemned* performed.

The future of the opera seemed particularly grim once Aaron Copland had seen it. "How are we to be moved for half [an] hour about one situation which abstractly gets us but not really?" Copland asked. He criticized the paucity of action, uninteresting melodic lines, the monotony of an all-choral piece, and harmonies with "a kind of unpleasantness." In short, "written very much under the sign of Oedipus," this was "music one has to respect rather than love."[9]

But Blitzstein held on to the idea that his opera "should be as little realistic as possible," knowing that in such a form it would lack a sense of pathos and tragedy. For him, then, form was all: The listener simply would have to dig in deep to understand and appreciate the message. Blitzstein would not spoon-feed his musical or political thoughts. Unfortunately, for this second opera to his own text, the poetry is dreary, inelegant, flat, too static to convey its intended sentiment. This is a case where the opera would sound far better sung in a language the audience did not understand.

Since the runaway success of *Triple-Sec,* Blitzstein had written three operas, none of them with a chance of being performed.

The January-February issue of *Modern Music* carried Blitzstein's thought-piece "Popular Music—An Invasion," in which the author—an "outsider" to popular culture, as he put it—decried the by then common use of dance forms in works for the concert hall. The generation that sought new sources in such material, as well as in folk music, was "in full flight from 'culture,' high-mindedness, and civilized music." Though he did acknowledge early contributions exploiting this vein, such as Stravinsky's *Sacre du Printemps, Les Noces,* and the "neo-primitive" ragtime pieces, as well as Copland's 1926 Piano Concerto, Blitzstein felt that the jazz idiom had just about reached its saturation point for modern composers. No one, after all, could possibly raise the level of popular music, with its conservative harmonies and standard symmetrical phrases. "The material is still predominantly Yiddish, with strains of negro and Celt."[10]

Blitzstein also came down hard against the practitioners of *Gebrauchsmusik,* "music for use" written by well-trained composers for amateurs, for family parlors, for students: "this German child of an American popularism on one side and a Russian Communism on the other, postulates a utilitarian music." But it served neither to lead nor to educate; rather, it "pandered." In a particularly memorable passage, he bristled against Berlin's composer-idol:

> Success has crowned Kurt Weill, with his super-bourgeois ditties (stilted *Otchi Tchornayas* and *Road-to-Mandalays*) harmonized with a love of distortion and dissonance truly academic; the "sonx" go over, the "modernisms" get sunk. This is real decadence: the dissolution of a one-time genuine article, regurgitated upon an innocent public, ready, perhaps even ripe to learn.[11]

Perhaps Blitzstein had taken a lesson from his teacher Schoenberg, who was known for having said, "Franz Lehár, yes; Weill, no. His music is the only music in the world in which I can find no quality at all."[12]

What was going on in Blitzstein's mind? Here was a consummately trained composer, a man struggling to find a new form that could express fresh musical ideas. At the same time, this form should enable the composer to address issues of the day. In Blitzstein's case, he was not entirely sure what he wanted to say about the issues; at least he knew he was not bourgeois. In Germany, Weill, Hindemith, and Krenek had used popular music as a base, while others continued to believe that the twelve-tone and other advanced systems could be applied to practical use. Blitzstein himself had attended one plumbers' union concert in Berlin featuring a completely atonal piece commissioned from Schoenberg's student Hanns Eisler that called for freedom and justice. The workingmen grappled heroically, if not very successfully, with this knotty, unapproachable music. Composers thought they were being useful to society, while not compromising their technique, indeed, while elevating the popular musical taste. Continuing reports from the Soviet Union suggested, too, that composers, like workers in the other arts, still enjoyed unrivaled creative freedom to link the most avant-garde trends with the new society's high sense of purpose.

Of course, with Adolf Hitler's accession to power on January 30, 1933, everything changed in Germany. The conservative reaction in the USSR would follow under Stalin a year later. A new kind of *Gebrauchsmusik* would become the order of the day—Aryan Kultur under the Nazis, and the narrow, often capricious constraints of socialist realism under the Soviets.

Blitzstein gave his lecture-recitals on "Form in Music" beginning that January. He conducted his Tuesday series under Civitas Club sponsorship in Brooklyn, and on Sundays presented the same lectures in the suburb of Rose Valley, under the auspices of the Hedgerow Theatre. He kept two more series going in Philadelphia. He also lectured in Douglas Moore's class at Columbia University. At the Philadelphia Art Alliance, he addressed an audience in April on the subject of "American Music and the American Public," exploring his concern about relinking listeners to a new music they felt they could not understand.

"We must make home, America, a fit place for composers to live in; we must give them a social nucleus which will fructify their activity as composers," he told them. Arguing for some kind of subsidy program, he dismissed government support as "a utopia too remote to be hoped for." Private patronage was no shame as long as no one equated investment with return. "Art in the garret is by now exploded: you can write just as good music with food in your stomach as when you are starving, and you can write more of it." He cited the example of Charles Ives, who around 1900 "was easily the equal of Debussy or Ravel," but who retired from the musical scene disgusted with the critics' and the public's lack of interest. "You are part of that public," he challenged in conclusion. If music is to grow in America, he asked, "What are you going to do about it?"[13]

Eva attended some of his lectures and committed her impressions to her journal: "delivery couldn't be better: natural and dignified, effective and yet 'straight' . . . solid . . . even if, as we agreed, it's a 'pernicious form of entertainment.' "[14]

The marriage Marc and Eva had planned for months took place on his twenty-eighth birthday, March 2, 1933. They appeared before Judge Theodore Rosen that Thursday at Philadelphia's City Hall. Local papers and *The New York Times* mentioned the event. "Dearest Marc," wrote Lina Abarbanell to her new son-in-law the following day, "The second of March will never go by, I hope, so long as I live without my heart being filled with love and gratitude for the happiness that was yours and Eva's." She must have felt relief at the normalization of the relationship, and content with the security and peace that would now come to her only child.

Eva may have believed that in time Marc could come to love her in a physical way. In any case, marriage would serve to bind her all the more tightly to the man she loved, the man without whom she couldn't live. Marc's reasons for marrying were more complex. He entertained no illusions of changing his sexual preference; after five years of knowing Eva, he had no thought of suddenly being attracted to her. Marriage must simply have seemed the next and only logical step, and it couldn't hurt him to be publicly perceived as heterosexual. As he had once expressed it to Jo, "I go so far as to consider marriage for me as a possible social gesture."

The marriage did not alter the essence of the relationship. Rarely, but more likely never sexual with one another anymore, they simply found—Marc in Eva and Eva in Marc—the sharpest mind around with which to spar. She resented what she interpreted (and always pointed out to him) as his immaturity. But she endured his temperamental displays with patient forbearance, perhaps in a way that Marc maneuvered her into—pitying him his weakness, feeling sorry for his depressions and emotional poverty. When he emerged from one of his funks, she observed in her journal only half-humorously, "a Turkish Bath and I usually share honors!" In return, Eva received his boundless solicitousness as to her diet and physical comfort. Not far beneath the surface, each feared that the other would soon find a more suitable partner. On her first birthday as Mrs. Marc Blitzstein, he gave her money so that she could work on her novel for a month, begged her to "stay with me," while in the same letter imagined for her "someone who will be your type, who will offer his all, including his Bobby,* and who will wrench your loyalty to me."[15]

As something of a wedding present to Marc, Eva composed a five-page analysis of his music—not for publication—emphasizing his intellectuality and objectivity fused, as they rarely are in music, with a gift for dramatic expression. She entertained confident hope that his works would be heard a hundred years from then:

> Blitzstein may be called a "neo-classic" composer not only because he partakes of what we call the classical ideal and makes use of some classical procedures, but because his music makes us feel that it will be regarded as we regard the classics by future generations. He is a radical composer, aside from the profound originality of his mind, in that he forecasts the musical development that must take place meanwhile.[16]

In the wake of *The Condemned,* she believed that it remained far from the culmination of his lifework: "It suggests, for instance, that at some time Blitzstein will write a great comic work in music stemming directly out of this great tragic work."[17]

Having premiered the Serenade marked *largo, largo, largo,* the Hans Lange Quartet continued to show faith in it. On April 9, 1933, they performed it in

*Marc and Eva's word for penis.

New York, and a week later, two of its movements on an all-Blitzstein program on WEVD. Filling out the broadcast, Blitzstein played the Piano Sonata and three dances from *Cain.* Eva remained in Philadelphia, having had a nonmalignant cyst removed from her breast only a few days before. He telegraphed her, DEAR DARLING PITY ME A LITTLE. Lina Abarbanell heard the broadcast and wrote about it to her daughter: "Marc was simply *swell* over the radio the other night—but on account of the young moderns who had gathered in the same room with us and who jabbered incessantly I almost became a Hitlerite."[18] String quartets must have been on Blitzstein's mind that month, because he made a two-piano transcription of Copland's *Lento molto.*

The MacDowell Colony asked both Marc and Eva back for the summer. In view of Eva's recent setback in her health, however—the aureole on both breasts having been removed—and because they had come to recognize their addiction to sea and swimming, they declined the invitations. On May 29, joined by a five-month-old pedigreed German shepherd that they named "Very Tentative," or Very for short, they moved for the summer to an almost neighborless house five minutes' walk from the ocean, about a mile and a half from Bethany Beach, Delaware. At $125 for the entire season, they passed their first summer of marriage together, with separate bedrooms and separate workrooms, Marc's with an upright piano installed. Three times a week they took their dinners with a Mrs. West in her hotel a twenty-minute walk away. She relished the rich material for gossip provided by a local composer and his wife—who must be wealthy, she surmised, since "she knew all those languages." Every time she introduced the Blitzsteins to her guests and the locals, she made a point of observing that the couple maintained separate bedrooms. On alternate nights the wife of the farmer a few hundred yards away cooked for them. They enjoyed the exposure to the Atlantic temperament: One day they had "perfect 'flying' weather," then a terrific northeaster. Eva recalled in her diary, "I am a child of the north, Marc said, and he of the south—but better, he of the sun and I of the sea." Very proved a delight to have around.[19]

The composer's principal musical accomplishment of the summer was a Piano Solo that lasted just under ten minutes. In four movements, marked *con brio, cantabile, scherzoso,* and *vivace,* he further explored the atonal patterns set forth in the Sonata, the Piano Percussion Music and the 1930 Scherzo. "Marc's piano piece is new for him," Eva wrote: "*genuinely* humorous, a fling, gay but substantial, robust and much more willing to be easy (in themes) than ever before. He finished the third movement, a delicious tiny thing today."[20] Eva's critique is most generous. Zesty overall, the Piano Solo is a rather ungrateful, tuneless mélange of modernity, closing with a dazzling firecracker of sound. In the second, Bach-like movement he allows a quiet poignancy to emerge, with hints of the slow, meditative melodies that became more characteristic of his later writing. Describing the piece for its premiere some months ahead, he said his aim was "to repeat nothing and to develop nothing," simply indicate by the music the mood he felt at the time. A second piece begun that summer was Discourse—for clarinet, cello, and piano—in which Blitzstein experimented with twelve-tone rows and the usual inversions and retrogrades, his most adventuresome composing to date. But his sketches remained fragmentary; he just didn't have the will to finish a piece so redolent of Schoenberg.

Eva had continued working for MGM all summer, but she left the beach house at the end of July to look after her father in New York; at sixty-seven, and already with a bad heart, Putzi was now suspected of having cancer. His doctors were pessimistic. In Eva's place, Marc's mother came for a visit, to cook for him, wash up after him—he was almost helpless around the house—and remind him ostentatiously of all she did. He grew impatient with her, as he and Jo frequently would, moving back and forth between feelings of filial obligation and resignation over her limitations. He would "simply let her prattle away on any subject she chose," he confided to his wife. "Her capacity for utter triviality has increased to the point where a recital of the bus-schedule from her apartment to the center of Pittsburgh takes fifteen minutes and is done with passion, thoroughness and care."[21]

Back at Bethany Beach for her birthday, Eva appreciated the cocktail party Marc prepared for her, which was complete with eggs stuffed with caviar, shrimps, toast with a topping of red peppers and egg yellows, garnished with holly leaves—everything just for two. It was one of Marc's specialties in life: Not an accomplished cook by any means, he was expert at mixing drinks and setting out a table of hors d'oeuvres. Friends loved to watch him as he carefully measured the correct proportions, delicately sliced lemons and cheese, and tastefully arranged trays with crackers and olives.

All the good food, and perhaps a certain security in being married again, had helped Eva put on weight that summer. But at a hundred pounds she felt, "I am really unpresentable now"—and of course she meant that she felt too fat, not too thin.[22] Doctors had not yet widely identified the psychological condition known as anorexia nervosa, but clearly this is the underlying syndrome from which Eva suffered. Consistent with the later view of anorexia, she no doubt experienced some gender ambiguity in her childhood: She could not begin to emulate her mother, the charming, ebullient, and famous actress. Instead, she took after her dour, cerebral father. She chose men over women as her friends, and many of her male friends were gay; she much preferred their company, wanting so much to be accepted not as a woman but as an intellectual equal. The usual feminine frivolities and diversions were not for Eva. Above a hundred pounds, she might have begun to look womanly, and that she could not have tolerated.

"New Blood in American Music," an article by the prolific music writer David Ewen about Blitzstein and Israel Citkowitz, appeared in the *Musical Courier* that September. Of the *Surf and Seaweed* score and the Percussion Music for the Piano, Ewen did not think much. But, especially in contrast to Citkowitz's "more effeminate and tender" music, he gave unrestrained praise to other works:

> Marc Blitzstein is definitely a vigorous and original voice in modern American music. His songs, *Is Five,* are charged with an electricity that makes this music glow with each bar. This is hard, brilliant, dynamic

> music, endowed with a vitality representing a new experience for the tired musical ear. In *"Gods"* . . . Blitzstein reveals a musical imagination fertile and unhampered. New sounds are explored, new tonal expressions created with telling effectiveness.[23]

Meanwhile, having decided on New York for the winter, the Blitzsteins had no place to live. Money was tight, as he wrote to Stella and Louis Simon: "I imagine the New Deal is for you about what it is for us so far—just another shuffle. (We indeed, are being faintly cynical, since our incomes remain Depressional, yet must cover a cost of living which has turned suddenly National-Recovering.)"[24] For three weeks they imposed on Lina and Edward, Eva ever chafing to be free of what she saw as her mother's hypocrisy and sense of duty. Marc found a small studio room at 17 East Ninth Street. They felt cramped by the forced intimacy there and anxiously sought a way out.

The lecture-recitals, all-important to Blitzstein's income during his periods of residency in the States, continued that fall. In New York, in the home of Adolph Lewisohn at 881 Park Avenue, he gave six Monday evenings on "This Modern Music." Patronesses for the series—vital to recruit a sizable subscription—included Mrs. Leopold Stokowski, Mrs. Alexander Siloti, and Claire Reis of the League of Composers. Blitzstein repeated this series in Philadelphia at the Mellon Galleries. Among the points he liked to stress was that the idea of revolution in music was hardly new: He cited Beethoven as an example many in his audience could appreciate, and included both Mussorgsky and Monteverdi in his list as well. He also liked to contrast the Romantic spirit to the Classical: The personality of the creator stamps the Romantic age, whereas in the Classical period, primacy goes to the created object. In the eternal fluctuation between these polarities, Blitzstein would have seen himself, and many contemporary composers, embracing the Classical philosophy as a counterweight to Mahler, Strauss, and the other post-Wagnerians. The Brooklyn Institute of Arts and Sciences also hired him on three Sunday afternoons in November to present illustrated talks on Debussy's *24 Préludes,* Stravinsky's *Sacre du Printemps,* and Schoenberg's *Pierrot Lunaire.*

Among the first arrivals in America from Hitler's Germany was Arnold Schoenberg. His presence would be salutary, Blitzstein wrote, in that "his almost fanatical academicism" might encourage American composers to shape up their "technically bad" skills. Awed by "his insistence on genius, on perfection, in his ruthlessness with the near-perfect," Schoenberg's pupils suffered "the danger of paralysis and despair." Indeed, most of his students had long since given up composing—laudable enough a result if one wants less bad music around, Blitzstein felt, but lamentable because "a cultural epoch is made up not only of the perfect work of geniuses, but also of the combined efforts of lesser talents, a whole geological formation of them. With them wiped out, the genius exists without subsoil, becomes isolated, ingrown, 'eccentric.' " In such sentences, one can read Blitzstein's own willingness to be judged historically.

As reviewer and as composer, Blitzstein sought out the new "proletarian" music, still standing at a critical distance from the early manifestations of leftist culture. He remarked unfavorably about a satirical piece by Lan Adomian "which he hopes is Communist propaganda": "Music very like the early Prokofieff (say, *Chout*), not very competently scored or formed." As for Elie Siegmeister's *May Day,* it "seemed like illustrative movie music, too long, and wooden at crucial moments where it should have been galvanizing."[25] At a benefit concert for the Communist magazine *New Masses,* the best music was from the agitational repertory of the Soviet composers Popoff, Davidenko, and Scheinin. But, Blitzstein demanded, "Why perform a quartet of the Soviet composer Miaskowsky which gives off the heavy salon smell of the Czarist composer Miaskowsky?" Why confuse the experimental, challenging joyousness of a liberating revolution with the second-rate academic products of the *ancien régime?*

Again, Blitzstein attacked an attempted fusion of popular music with concert music. The subject was Paul Whiteman's "Sixth Experiment in Modern American Music." "This concert is bastardization to please capitalist trade, with a vengeance. *Les domestiques s'amusent.* Dolled-up, lisping Frenchy polysyllables, the music is at any moment likely to let out a 'soitinly,' a 'goil-friend,' and a 'terlet-water.' "[26]

On February 5, 1934, closing his lecture series at the Mellon Galleries in Philadelphia, Blitzstein organized "A Concert of Premieres," either American, Philadelphia, or, in the case of his own work, world premieres. Philadelphia Orchestra players, a few soloists, and a small chorus took part. He announced to the press that he would introduce *Gebrauchsmusik* to America in this program. As his example of the genre, he included Nicholas Nabokov's *Echo Collector,* a piece for family use in which the audience joined. Reflecting his interest in the new Soviet composers, he scheduled a Shebalin Sonatina for Piano and seven songs from Hindemith's *Das Marienleben,* Anton von Webern's Three Pieces for piano and cello, two sonatinas by Chávez, Aaron Copland's *Vitebsk,* and his own Piano Solo, composed the previous summer at Bethany Beach. Soprano Tilly Barmach performed, with Nabokov, Copland, and Blitzstein playing in their own works. The Webern pieces produced hysterical laughter.

Blitzstein was happy to have his Cummings setting "Jimmie's got a goil" published by the Cos Cob Press in 1934, as well as an excerpt from *Cain* published that same year by the Rice Institute in Houston. Other American composers, such as Adomian and Siegmeister, actively emulated the working-class music of their Soviet counterparts. Charles Seeger, the musicologist and composer, wrote for *Modern Music* one of the most emphatic and eloquent appeals for this new style in his article "On Proletarian Music." Musicians, he argued, had to begin identifying themselves as "secondarily" in the proletariat. Once they had made this leap of consciousness, they could see that workers today were rejecting the classics in favor of the new militant composers. "The morbidity, the servile melancholy, the frenetic sexuality, the day-dreaming flight from reality that permeates much of music of the nineteenth century cannot be regarded as fit for a class with a revolutionary task before it." He urged composers to connect the revolutionary technique of bourgeois music to the revolutionary content the workers wanted. In time, music would come directly out of the working class—at first, technically unadvanced, but with the proper marriage of technique and content, "then we have art-products of the highest type." For the composer, meanwhile, there were three paths open: fascism, isolation, and proletarianism. If composers withhold themselves from the working class, he predicted, "they will live lives of equivocation, opportunism and frustration. Let them join it openly and their talent will be strengthened, their technic purified, a content given to it and they will have a wider hearing—not of sophisticated individuals who half disdainfully tolerate them, but of the great masses who welcome them with hungry ears—not an audience of hundreds, but of millions."[27] Ecstatic prophecy!

In accordance with the new ethos, *New Masses* sponsored a contest for a May Day song on an Alfred Hayes text. It was to be published in the magazine and sung by the massed working-class choruses of the city, who would be joined by the thousands of May Day marchers setting off from Union Square that year. Blitzstein submitted a piece, along with Copland and a number of other composers.

Interested enough to hear and report the new proletarian experiments, and with *The Condemned* and his new May Day song "Into the Streets May First" behind him, Blitzstein still traveled what Seeger would have called the path of isolation. At the same time that Seeger's views appeared, Blitzstein showed himself still struggling with the future. He wondered, what will take the place of the primitivist, the neo-classicist, and the popularist phases just now coming to an end? Of the latter movement, infected with "the virus of jazz," he wrote about Ernst Krenek and his opera *Jonny spielt auf*, and about Kurt Weill and *Die Dreigroschenoper:* "They are unfortunately committed to a policy of effusive virility and stormy protest, with the result that their music, so far, is for the most part loud and fast." He valued music with purpose, strength, and commitment, politically motivated or not, but music of a high professional standard. Slumming, simplifying, coddling, writing down to the masses or congratulating the comfortable: These he could not abide.[28]

Blitzstein had not yet decided to commit himself to the new proletarian music as a full-time preoccupation. Neither did he care to stay in America to witness the unfolding of the new movement. That fall, through an introduction provided by Claire Reis, he met Dorothy Elmhirst of the wealthy Whitney family, who with her husband Leonard ran the famed Dartington Hall school in England.* She had asked the acclaimed German experimental choreographer Kurt Jooss to join the faculty of the dance program at the school the following spring, and she needed a composer to collaborate in new works with him. She was so impressed with Blitzstein that she interviewed no one else for the job. Blitzstein was certainly aware of Jooss's 1932 ballet *The Green Table*, a pacifistic work depicting the diplomatic world sidestepping any active measures to prevent war, but he

*By a previous marriage to Willard Straight, she had three children, two of whom, Beatrice and Michael, later led theatrical careers.

must have known, too, that the left had widely criticized it for abstaining from showing any active solutions to the problems of world peace. Nevertheless, he decided to accept the Elmhirsts' offer. After a farewell champagne supper courtesy of Putzi, who was still quite ill, Eva and Marc left on March 5 on the S.S. *Champlain* for England.

Upon arrival at Dartington Hall, they found a strange concoction of old-fashioned aristocratic manners, complete with butlers and maids, and the advanced educational philosophy the school promoted. Founded in 1925, the school tried in many ways to realize William Morris's turn-of-the-century dream of elevating the domestic and minor arts to a high level of self-sustaining crafts—with experimental farming, contemporary furniture-design workshops, a textile mill, and a pottery department. The estate incorporated a castle, part of which dated back to the eighth century, and ancient monkish rooms in drafty towers fit for a Gothic novel, all set in South Devonshire not far from the bleak coast of Cornwall. Eva particularly found it tiresome to sit through three long and large meals plus two teas a day and try to maintain polite conversation. Overall the quality of the teachers there—for the 158 students—did not impress them much, though distinguished composers Edmund Rubbra and Alan Rawsthorne had both spent time working at the school. They also found a baffling arrangement at the dance school. Elmhirst's brother Richard ran part of the school, his wife acting as its manager; and Margaret Barr, a Martha Graham-trained dancer with her own accompanist, ran the other half. When Kurt Jooss entered the picture, he would create a third faction. Exactly how Blitzstein would be used had still not been decided.[29]

The question was settled soon enough. Jooss, in exile from Germany, unexpectedly brought over with him his composer-accompanist Frederick A. Cohen, who had written the score to *The Green Table.* Together they declared no need for Blitzstein's services. In any case, the dance program's budget would not support two resident composers. In the upshot, Margaret Barr left Dartington Hall because she would not compete with Jooss. Also, her own political stance appears to have been further to the left than Jooss's, as she soon established her group in London and began dancing before pro-Soviet audiences. Mrs. Elmhirst apologetically but graciously honored her commitment to the Blitzsteins by paying their full salary for the rest of the year. This left them free to leave Dartington Hall, which they did immediately. They consulted the daily newspapers to check the exchange rates in the Mediterranean countries, and by Easter they had relocated to Mallorca.[30]

After a week of traveling around the island, searching for the right spot by the sea, they found quarters on a little bay called Cala Guya, near the town of Cala Ratjada at the far eastern tip. The toylike fishing village had a single dirt street and claimed no particular tourist interest except the estate of Juan March—possibly the richest man in Spain, a legendary banker with important sidelines as an international smuggler. In Mallorca, Eva found the Spanish cigarettes the equal of her lifelong beloved Luckies. With food for the two of them amounting to no more than six or seven pesetas a day (less than a dollar), and with a month's wages for a maid at sixty pesetas, the locale and the price were just right. In an article called "House-Hunting in Mallorca," Eva showed that her journalism, though perhaps less rewarding to her as a writer than her novels, could communicate an adventuresome spirit and a well-informed yet poetic point of view that she rarely captured in the more introspective prose of her longer efforts.

They had hardly settled into their bungalows and into their routine of morning and afternoon work sessions when the long-expected cable arrived on April 26 from one of Lina's close friends: TERRIBLY SORRY EVA BUT PUTZI HAS GONE. MUTZI SENDS HER LOVE AND ASKS CONFIRMATION OF EDWARDS WISHES REGARDING CREMATION. MARTHA. Marc had somehow managed to lose his wallet, with $175 in it, just after a visit to the bank, so money had become suddenly that much tighter. Eva could not afford to return to New York, but she invited Lina to come to Mallorca to help recover from Edward's death. Lina did not go, however, nor did she accept invitations from both Jo and Maddie to stay with them in Philadelphia; to ease her loss she moved from the memory-laden Somerset to a room at the Barbizon-Plaza on West Fifty-eighth Street, and there she remained until the end of her life almost thirty years later.

The theme of a new orchestral piece came to Blitzstein on May 2, and for the next six weeks he tore away at it. The *Orchestra Variations* begins with a slow, uneventful, even unattractive theme with strong overtones of the "Dies Irae"—Putzi's death may have been the immediate inspiration for the idea. Blitzstein then puts his largish orchestra through an amazing and impressive set of twenty variations, some as fleeting as four bars long, others mostly in the range of ten to twenty bars. The longest variation, and the central event of the work, is number 12, a fugue in ninety-four bars. The writing is skillful throughout, almost a concerto for orchestra that uses the full orchestra sparingly, with many felicitous touches of color; he clearly wished to distinguish his work from the *Orchestervariationen* of Schoenberg, whose "almost mechanical discipline" showed a lamentable "need for a totally organized art."[31] Blitzstein's piece comes to a climax in the eighteenth variation, somewhat reminiscent of the *Sacre du Printemps.* A slower, majestic nineteenth variation leads into a *molto lento* finale with some of the same feeling as the beginning of the piece, which ends *pianissimo,* dying away in a mild dissonance on the strings. The closest affinity is to Stravinsky in the use of older traditional devices expressed in modern, though fairly mainstream language. Approaching the dimensions of a symphony, the work lasts about fifteen minutes. This work, along with the Piano Concerto, shows Blitzstein as a master of contrapuntal composition; if he downplayed technical complexity in his operatic and vocal writing, to which he turned almost exclusively after this, it must be seen as a conscious choice intended to bring out his text better.

He finished orchestrating the *Variations* on June 11. The dedication was again to Eva, though the circumstances had been somewhat distinct from the creation of earlier works, as Eva had not been working in close proximity to Marc's piano and had not heard the piece in the process of its writing. Marc had wondered for a time, but not too wrenchingly, whether the dedication should be to Dorothy Elmhirst.[32]

Blitzstein had not won the *New Masses* May Day song contest. Aaron Copland won it with his setting of the Alfred Hayes poem, and it was duly published and sung by hundreds of men and women rallying at Union Square that day. But the fact that Copland had lent his prestige to the left-wing movement, visibly led by the Communist Party, encouraged other composers to do likewise. The Workers Music League maintained a collection of left-wing music, and Blitzstein's contribution was deposited in it. "And I have put your name on file with the [Pierre Degeyter] club as one whom we knew 'where he stands,' " wrote Charles Seeger to Marc. "This means we expect to see you when you return." Seeger extended some friendly advice to Blitzstein, too, in case he was moved to write more proletarian music. "The mass song, which is to be sung by large crowds not because it is taught to them but because they have heard it and want to sing it, has some definite limitations that you must know about before trying again."[33]

In July, Blitzstein did try his hand once more at writing proletarian music, this time a cantata called *Workers' Kids of the World Unite!,* sometimes referred to as the *Children's Cantata.* In eight sections, to be sung in unison or in dialogue format by a children's chorus, its crude propaganda makes no attempt to reflect the speech or thought of the young.

After an opening chorus of "Workers' Kids of the World," the children sing "My Father's a Tailor." They name other jobs, as well as the work their mothers do—or did: What these families all have in common is unemployment. In the following "Don't Cry Kids," the children address themselves to Mister Mayor: "Listen, tell us where you stand—along with some few hundred ritzy girls and boys or with the kids of those who work by the millions." A solo "Speech" comes next: "Three cheers for the revolution." The fifth episode, "Choosing a Leader," poses the chorus in response to a solo voice. The chorus asks, "If we choose you for a leader, will you be a leader or a boss?" and the chosen one promises to lead the masses through strikes against the bosses. "Hail to our new leader!" cry the children to a kind of Caesar's march, in rhetorical terms more of contemporary Soviet political film than of grammar school.

Next, the children write a letter to friends and fellow workers' children abroad:

Dear Comrade, I take my pen in hand
to write to you in ev'ry foreign land,
wherever you may be. We must unite,
be strong in unity.
We both are poor
we live in misery
You and I and ev'ry worker's child.
Our fathers and our mothers are oppressed,
the rulers of one land are like the rest.

In the seventh chorus, "Listen Teacher": "We ask you, we tell you, we warn you, tell us what is true." In the second stanza, "Listen Preacher": "We'll be no longer mild and meek, nor turn the other cheek, for this cheek and the other cheek have both been slapped too hard." In the final section, "Riddles," Blitzstein echoed the current thinking of the left in this year of misery:

> *Who is it who makes promises*
> *and smiles, and talks on the radio*
> *and makes promises and smiles*
> *and talks on the radio and talks on*
> *the radio and talks and talks and*
> *talks and smiles. Who is it? Roosevelt!*

The cantata is full of catchy tunes and rhythms, never exceeding an octave and a third in range. Written to be easily understandable by a children's chorus, the music nevertheless avoids being trite. Its simplicity is deceiving, for underneath the straightforward vocal lines he has placed a sophisticated, acerbic piano accompaniment that typically straddles and modulates keys ambiguously. Hanns Eisler is a clear model; but whereas Eisler wanted his mass songs actually to be sung by the masses, this cantata is too dissonant in the accompaniment ever to achieve any genuine popularity. Though this kind of agitational composition offers few standards that later generations of composers, or even Blitzstein himself, would choose to adopt, the piece can be judged a modest success within the narrow parameters Blitzstein set for himself.

These months in Mallorca may have been Marc's happiest time with Eva. Living through Putzi's death together linked them closely, and there was, as always, the shared creation of new work. "I am, today," he assured her on her birthday in August,

> back at that first exalted mood we had here in the Cala Guya—of feeling, each, that we have a genius working beside us, to be protected, revered, frightened of and confident for—and that the genius is our lover, we are married to the genius! Everything else can go phutt for the moment—we are solid.

That he wrote for children, however clumsy the cantata turned out, may be related to some thoughts of having children with Eva. In fact, she had stopped menstruating in April, though tests showed it was due to her anemia, not to pregnancy. In any case, the cantata was an act of faith in youth, and a declaration that Blitzstein was ready to assume his place among the musical proletariat. As a couple, Marc and Eva would embrace, if not always each other, the newly adopted ideology of Communism. The *Orchestra Variations,* written immediately before the *Children's Cantata,* was the last piece of pure concert music he would write for many years. That he could write both works in such proximity shows the range of musical languages at his command.

Possibilities of working with Kurt Jooss at Dartington Hall revived. In deference to the Elmhirsts, their benefactors, Marc and Eva left Mallorca during the middle of September to visit the school for discussions.* Though they remained at the school for almost a month, the talk was inconclusive, and they left for Paris. From there, still on the Elmhirsts' payroll, they would decide on a cheaper place to settle. In a week, toward the end of October, they found themselves in Brussels. They rented separate apartments—Marc had a piano moved into his—and fully expected to stay awhile.

On the evening of Saturday, November 17, Marc and Eva attended as spectators a meeting of the Fourth Congress of the Jeunesses Communistes Belges, which they had heard about by chance. Just before leaving, they bought several pamphlets to read later. When they left the front door of the hall, plainclothesmen detained them and hauled them to the police station, ostensibly on suspicion that their passports and residency permits were not in order. There they were searched and then thrown into separate prison cells for the night. In the morning, at the Sûreté, the chief informed them that they would be deported to France on a train leaving in two hours, never answering the Blitzsteins' inquiry as to the charges. He also refused to allow the Blitzsteins to accompany the police back to their rooms so that they could pack properly and safeguard their manuscripts.

Once in Paris, they cabled the American consulate in Brussels, asking for the protection of their papers and for the opportunity to clear their names. The consulate obliged by sending an officer with the Belgian police during the search of Eva's and Marc's rooms; it also took responsibility for giving the bags, with the manuscripts inside, to American Express for shipment to Paris. Though the Blitzsteins protested that as artists they were interested in all things cultural and philosophical, the consulate accepted the police interpretation that they would never have been invited to such an exclusive meeting unless they had been known to the Communists. According to the police, their presence at such a gathering constituted an "unwarrantable interference in Belgian politics," thus providing sufficient grounds for expulsion.

In Paris, American embassy officials told them they had been extremely foolish to attend such a meeting in Brussels but that in France they would be safe from similar harassment. The Blitzsteins had failed to appreciate the jangle of European tensions over the Saar region, recent murders with political overtones in Marseille, and the fall of the Belgian cabinet only two days before. Nor could they have known that Belgium and France in recent months had taken to regularly dumping their "undesirables" on one another—and that the Blitzsteins' Jewish name had hardly been of help.

For eleven days they wore the same clothes in which they had been arrested, until finally their luggage arrived. To their great relief, all of Eva's novel and all of Marc's music were there. Writing home to Jo with details of the deportation,

*A story Blitzstein often repeated later has it that he had been itching to leave Mallorca and get back to the States to join the radical cause; and when he admitted this to Eva, she said, "I know. I've had the bags packed for a week." Presumably there is some germ of truth to this story, but how could she have had the bags packed without his knowledge? It also fails to account for the couple's peregrinations for the next three months; indeed, the story may have served to cover up certain events in the next three months.

Marc asked that nothing be divulged beyond the immediate family for the time being, until their names could be definitively cleared. "Sooner or later, of course, the whole thing will come out; we want it to, we feel every case of this kind must be exposed to the hilt . . . ; since we have an entirely clear conscience there can be no harm in ultimately spreading the story." Most of all, once the thrill of adventure had passed, they resented being stuck with the expense of it all, and the higher cost of living in Paris.[34]

Blitzstein did not hesitate to explain to Dorothy Elmhirst his sudden return to Paris. She responded compassionately to her "homeless, accused, bereft" friend:

> Your experience has set us all agog, and I should like to march straight up to the Belgian prime minister and tell him what I think. . . . Before your second letter came I had gone up to London to put the case before the American Embassy staff. Mr. Johnson, first secretary, was very sympathetic but he said, "You must realize that this sort of thing is happening all over Europe today, and we can do nothing to prevent deportations."

A few days later, she wrote:

> I don't know what you can do over the difficulty of being branded as communists. I imagine it would be difficult to obtain an impartial hearing though I sympathize with your desire to clear your name. Authorities are not in the mood for reasonableness, and I imagine that once you are listed as dangerous in one country information will be passed along to others. The best advice that I can get is that you should take up with the State Department at Washington the matter of "removing the stigma," rather than attempt to do it from any European centre.[35]

She offered to help them return to America, but they did not feel quite ready to leave Europe.

In her room in the attic of the Hotel de l'Univers on the Left Bank near the Sorbonne, Eva translated speeches by Brecht, reviewed books, and conducted interviews for articles. Her chief subject was Alfred Kerr, the German theatre critic and writer, bitter in his denunciation of playwright Gerhart Hauptmann for going over to the Nazis. In addition, she began organizing her notes toward a lengthy article about Dartington Hall, and another about Brussels as a tourist attraction. She also made sure to send her maternal grandmother a birthday note in December—by now Grossmama had moved into the Jewish Home for the Aged in Berlin.

As a reviewer, Blitzstein still continued to tramp around the Parisian concert, theatre, and film circuit. Most of the music he heard was escapist, "graceful and meaningless tripe" pandering to "the pleasure-seekers." Josephine Baker played in Offenbach's *La Créole,* set in "Louis-Philippe and Martinique, a windfall combination for the bourgeois scene designer."

Kurt Weill's *Marie Galante* lasted only a week: As a German Jew, Weill was unpopular in Paris. Blitzstein heard him play through the score to Franz Werfel's text "The Road to Promise," renamed *The Eternal Road* when Max Reinhardt's long-delayed production of it finally opened in New York two years later. Blitzstein described this Jewish pageant in *Modern Music* as Weill's best though most uneven work, employing his proven formulas. "The questionable intelligence involved in using the same general style for the Middle-Western *Mahagonny* and the Old Testament *Road to Promise* evidently does not bother him."[36]

In another room at the same little hotel with Eva, Blitzstein attempted a daring analysis of Stravinsky for the *Musical Quarterly,* which appeared the following summer. He tried to relate the numerous transformations in Stravinsky's style to social evolution, citing the rudimentary work in materialist musicology by Soviet writers Tchemodanoff and Lebedinsky, but, unsatisfied with the lack of guidance there, he returned again to the question of form. Revered as he may be, Blitzstein concluded, Stravinsky could not answer current musical problems. If music is a "delayed articulation" of the culture of a period, according to Marx, then Stravinsky seemed to be escaping from reality with his "luxury products." The later works "imply the existence of a settled, serene, unshakable world, to which they are ornamental contributions." Blitzstein looked instead to "younger and fresher talents to combine the new discipline with an ideology that more truly reflects the reality of the day. We may expect from them a rebirth of the spirit that makes music an integral part of the cultural community, and molds it into new epochal forms—forms that are with life, not separated from it, nor against it."[37]

With these thoughts posted to America, he felt prepared to give a definite answer to Kurt Jooss on the possibilities of collaboration during the next year:

> I have come to feel more and more that the only kind of stage-work I want to do now is one of social and political import. I should be unhappy with any other sort of theme; and I should be unsatisfied even with a ballet which depicted conditions without exposing the social revolution as goal. This will not come as news to you, I think; it is simply that in the last weeks I have strengthened and intensified my conviction. Not because of the episode in Belgium, of course; that was a purely personal example of something I had always known existed.

Although Blitzstein had held out the hypothesis that some mutually agreeable theme might later bring him and the choreographer together, Jooss replied that such a work was not in his plans for the foreseeable future.[38]

Toward the end of 1934, Eva and Marc had begun to get on each other's nerves again. They were agreed on the principle of Communism, and that drew them together. But emotionally neither felt whole, and some of their bitterness turned on each other. Putzi's death had left Eva feeling alone and helpless—though she rarely required any huge justifications for such feelings—and weighing only ninety pounds. "If I die thirty years from now it will be no better for me than if I died now," she confided to her journal on New Year's Eve. Marc had composed nothing since the summer; he felt restless with inactivity, wanting to return to New York for stimulation, but had no specific urge or plan. Finally, impatient to get started on something new, and feeling politically unwelcome in Europe, they decided to change course. On January 17 they set sail on the *Corinthia* for home.

6

IN THE VANGUARD

Winter 1935–May 1936

"Slow death, quick death, take it as it comes . . ."

On their sudden return to America in early 1935—a surprise to the family—Marc and Eva moved into the Leof-Blitzstein house at 322 South Sixteenth Street in Philadelphia. At first, the family thought of making a grand cause célèbre out of the Belgian incident. But in the end, Marc thought it would jeopardize his chances for work. Also, for the case to be effective, it would have to be argued that Marc and Eva were *not* Communists, a pointless campaign given their manifest sympathies.

Neither Papa nor his wife Maddie could quite understand how Marc could be so in love with Eva. She seemed to give him so much trouble. How often they would see Marc on his knees before a seated Eva, asking whether there was anything he could get for her, do for her. But they continued on with their daily routines at the house, incorporating her into it. Maddie had become a proficient publicist for theatrical shows and for left-wing causes, working from the single room she and Sam occupied in the house. Her other function was to keep Sam as healthy as possible. Diagnosed with pernicious anemia, he would often overdo things, stressfully arguing politics, shaking his finger at any and all who disagreed with him, questioning their basic intelligence. Maddie struggled to limit his consumption of alcohol, insisting that he stay away from it at least until cocktail time, and then trying to keep him down to one "drinkee" or maybe two. He was the central figure of the household, and almost every night a clutch of literary and politically minded visitors would convulse to his Jewish jokes and hear him dispense with the fund of information gleaned from the several daily newspapers he read. When they went out to dinner, Sam's favorite gag was to load the pockets of his jacket with the silverware. Then, at the cashier's counter, he would drop a dollar bill, stoop to pick it up, and out would come fistfuls of forks and spoons clattering to the floor.

In Marc's absence from America, Sam's political consciousness had shifted noticeably. Always radical-minded, he had been a supporter of Eugene Debs, the Socialist. Now he took his place on Chestnut Street, selling copies of the Communist newspaper, the *Daily Worker,* and allowed his membership in the Party to be widely known. The concept of the United Front had emerged as the order of the day—a united front of all democratic forces against the threat of fascism. The Party, and the cultural organs in its orbit, had already adopted this political line so as not to repel potential allies. Unrelentingly, Sam would press into people's hands—willing or reluctant—the latest tracts and pamphlets that shed the correct revolutionary light on any subject at hand. "Lenin is the simplest writer in all literature," he would say as he sold a copy of *State and Revolution.* "You can't possibly have any trouble with this one." Once, a young friend of the family was explaining to him her need for a larger room in which to live. "He looked at me and smiled," she related, "and then put his head back and laughed. Then he said, 'Why in the Soviet Union, which is the most wonderful society in the world, you would have to share your little room with three other people.' "[1]

For at least a month, so Eva wrote to Essie and Paul Robeson in London, "we've been busy trying to find out just how and where we can fit in. It's difficult, for various reasons, but to neither of us has New York ever seemed so stirring as it does now."[2] For a time, Eva stayed in New York to be near her mother. There she began poking into the Communist scene in New York: Copland, she found out, was writing music for a "red revue" to be offered that spring by the Theatre Union. As of the first of March, Marc and Eva moved into noisy, dirty quarters at 35 Morton Street in Greenwich Village: two rooms, plus a kitchen and bath for forty dollars a month. Still claiming a responsibility for Blitzstein's year, the Elmhirsts continued to pay him a monthly stipend, lasting at least until June. In between the usual quota of rejections, Eva managed to publish occasional pieces in *The New Republic, Travel,* and other magazines.

At least twenty years before, Jacob Schaefer had begun writing revolutionary music for Jewish choral groups, but he had led a lonely campaign for the cause. More recently, composers, like members of other professions, had come to see the need for more concerted activity, and in 1933 Schaefer, with Charles Seeger and Henry Cowell, organized a seminar on the writing of mass songs. This grew into the Composers' Collective of New York, whose regular members included Elie Siegmeister, Charles Seeger, Ruth Crawford, Lan Adomian, George Maynard, Herbert Haufrecht, Robert Gross, Henry Leland Clarke, Norman Cazden,

Earl Robinson, Alex North, Irwin Heilner, and Amnon Balber. From time to time, Aaron Copland dropped in for a meeting. In addition, Collective members knew all the composers in New York and could approach them to sign petitions and attend organizational meetings and political functions.

Not long after his arrival in New York, Blitzstein ran into Siegmeister at the Fifty-eighth Street music library and asked him, "What's this proletarian music that you're doing?" Right away the émigré-returned-home joined up and became the secretary of the Collective and a member of its executive committee.

One function of the Composers' Collective was to provide "round-table criticism of each other's current productions in proletarian music." Minutes of meetings throughout the year record the approval of Blitzstein's 1930 Scherzo (titled *Bourgeois at Play* for performance on Collective programs), his sketch "Send for the Militia," and the works of the other composers as well. Blitzstein considered the jazz idiom for the most part inappropriate for political music and criticized Alex North for using it too much. Yet he could hardly find fault with North's texts, taken from Langston Hughes. "Negro Mother" was one song, and another seemed to say it all for these men in these times: "Put One More S (in the U.S.A.)." It was a musical gloss on Communist Party Secretary William Z. Foster's book *Toward Soviet America.* [3]

As part of the Collective's activity, it organized a "shock troupe": At short notice, a small number of performers could be called upon to appear before meetings and rallies with selections of appropriately chosen music. Of course, theirs was hardly the full complement of radical music forces in the city; the *Daily Worker* had its own chorus—conducted for a time by Elie Siegmeister—as did the Friends of the Workers' School. Numerous unions and cooperative societies with Communist or other left-wing leadership also sponsored choral groups, mandolin orchestras, and amateur musical theatre units.

The Composers' Collective had actually grown out of the Pierre Degeyter Club, named for the composer of "The Internationale," but by the time Blitzstein entered the proletarian music scene in 1935, the Collective had split off. The Degeyter Club comprised less musically adept songwriters whose sights rarely rose above agitational numbers written to order. Oftentimes these songs were only new texts set to popular tunes or folk-derived melodies of a markedly derivative stamp. Members objected that their work never found its way into the Collective's programs, and that the Collective showed a bourgeois attitude in rejecting this simpler, grass-roots production.

In later years, partly in sympathy with Stalin's insistence on a culture closely tied to popular traditions, and partly in honest recognition of the fact that the Composers' Collective, comprising a membership of strong beaux-arts esthetic orientation, had never produced any truly well-liked revolutionary music, the Communist Party adopted a strong partiality toward folk song. The *Daily Worker* columnist Mike Gold once quoted a worker's commentary on the Collective's work: Their melodies, he said, are "full of geometric bitterness and the angles and glass splinters of pure technic . . . written for an assortment of mechanical canaries."[4] In its intended leadership of the proletariat, the Party assumed the natural successorship to the unorganized agrarian workers and artisans of the preindustrial age. Thus it tried to emphasize the nationalistic roots of its political program. Ever since the inauguration of the United Front in 1935, folk music has been regarded as the special home for the left, enriching its culture beyond what the Composers' Collective was able to contribute, but also limiting the boundaries composers could explore while still expecting a favorable reception.

Personally, Blitzstein had never placed much faith in folk idioms as useful source material for future music. He never succumbed to the Party's preference on this point, nor did he join the majority of former Composers' Collective members who turned toward folk music in the late years of the New Deal era. Whatever might be said about the beauty inherent in almost any folk tradition, by its nature, form in folk music is static, whereas in serious music form grows and develops as part of a composition. And the development of form had been one of Blitzstein's major concerns over the preceding several years. "Folk music for serious purposes is limited," he pronounced in one of his lectures, "and turns out to be a cul-de-sac, if not an actual misalliance."[5] His aim in the Composers' Collective would be to discover a form, or evolve a new arrangement of forms, at once "serious" and popular.

By contrast to folk-music styles, Blitzstein was attracted to what the Germans call *Kleinkunst*, the minor art of musical commentary on events, often within hours after their occurrence, and always written in popular idioms. Cabaret songs, soldier songs, barmaid songs, street songs, material coming out of the Jewish *badkhen* or wedding entertainer's tradition, these numbers were often satirical or risqué. In Berlin the Kurfürstendamm was the center of such activity; Brecht in his early days used to appear, guitar in hand, and croak through his poems at Berlin bars where such performers were welcome. Often producers tried to cash in on the *Kleinkunst* spirit with more lavish productions in larger theatres—in some ways, *Die Dreigroschenoper* partook of the genre. In America, the topical revue had a limited popularity, as much on the college campus as on the legitimate stage; the absence of the tradition and of an audience for it began to be felt only in the thirties, when conditions cried out, as they had not before, for response.

Once again, in 1935, *New Masses* sponsored a contest for a May Day song, to be judged for singability and catchiness among large groups of untrained voices. The Composers' Collective sent out two texts—one by Robert Gessner and one by Eva Goldbeck—to fifty American composers, with a cover letter by the magazine's music editor, Ashley Pettis. Using the militant pseudonym of "Hammer," Blitzstein submitted his entry—in C major, with march-tempo measures of 4/4 occasionally set off by 3/2—composed to Eva's strong-willed poem:

We march. We sing. We work. We fight.
We know that we are in the right.
For you, for me, for everyone,
Fight for freedom!

The workers' parade is the workers' vow
To build a world for workers—now!

"Hammer" did not win the contest; Siegmeister, using the pseudonym L. E. Swift, saw his "May Day Song" to Robert Gessner's text published in the *New Masses.* *

Blitzstein reviewed for the *Daily Worker* the second *Workers Song Book* published that spring. He mixed in healthy praise with some gentle chiding, especially about the English translations of songs from other countries. He found Copland's prize-winning piece from 1934 ambitious but not entirely successful, and Earl Robinson's contributions too long and not sufficiently varied. Hanns Eisler's songs, "Forward, We've Not Forgotten" and "Comintern," were "unconventional in a manner to attract workers, not repel them." And what a difference between Eisler's "stubborn, hard" music of "oppression and courageous resistance" and the workers' songs from the USSR, with their "joyful, unfettered" ardor.[6]

Eisler and his wife had come to the United States on a concert tour to raise funds for the children of persecuted German families. The young baritone Mordecai Bauman accompanied him around the country, offering first American performances in numerous cities of his mass songs already so famous in Europe. Eisler remained from mid-February to early May in New York, and while there served as the judge of the May Day song contest. A huge concert with a thousand choral singers accompanied by the Pierre Degeyter Symphony Orchestra took place there on March 2—Blitzstein's thirtieth birthday—though it turned out to be a musical fiasco because the program had been insufficiently prepared. Eisler also visited meetings of the Composers' Collective as an honored guest, and he offered advice to his American counterparts. (Among other suggestions, he encouraged composers to write mass songs without need of accompaniment, so as to make them more accessible.) *Modern Music* published his "Reflections on the Future of the Composer" in its May–June issue. Here he pointed to the obsolescence of the symphony, the sonata form, and generally all absolute "music for music." These meetings and concerts were enormously persuasive. In Hanns Eisler, Blitzstein had at last found the man for whom he had been searching. Eisler had also been a former student of Arnold Schoenberg, and he had utterly and without apology thrown the strong weight of a thoroughly trained composer behind the workers' movement. His music remained solid, without pandering; furthermore, it put the composer squarely in the public eye with music that obviously served the noble intention of uplifting the artistic standards of the people. What more could be desired?

In addition to her writings and translations, Eva interviewed Eisler to help promote his farewell concert at the Brooklyn Academy of Music on April 19 and

*Blitzstein used a pseudonym because the competition was theoretically blind, but normally he did not use one. Siegmeister and other composers used pseudonyms regularly to obscure their left-wing affiliations.

a banquet in his honor to be given by American composers two days later. Calling him a "scientific composer," she recounted his major achievements, including the fact that in 1932 Leon Lebedinsky, the President of the International Music Congress in Moscow, had named him and Stefan Wolpe the two best adepts of Soviet-style "social realism" in Western Europe. She detailed his escape from Germany on the day following the Reichstag fire, just as the police had gone looking for him, and she reported that the Nazis had smashed 300,000 recordings of his music and burned his sheet music. Even now, the Nazis had a price on him of ten thousand francs. Asked whether he was happy or unhappy being away from Germany, Eisler repeated the words blankly. "Neither," Eva quoted him, as he prepared to return to Paris. "I simply work, you see, as I have always done. I am going on with my work, and it doesn't matter much where I do it."[7]

Eisler's presence at this critical time of ferment coincided with similar developments in theatre and all the other arts. In every field, artists saw their pens and brushes and instruments as weapons in the fight against fascism. The magazine *New Theatre,* organ of the New Theatre League, was a good mirror of the revolutionary movement on the stage. The dancer Anna Sokolow had spent three months in the USSR and reported on developments there for the publication. A young Cheryl Crawford taught on the faculty of the Theatre Collective Studio, a revolutionary training school. Edna Ocko, Emanuel Eisenberg, Ralph Steiner, and Lincoln Kirstein all contributed reviews of left-wing dance and film. In one issue, Mrs. August Belmont of the Metropolitan Opera Guild was severely satirized with a cartoon depicting her crowd of bejeweled ladies seated in an opera box. The caption quoted her saying, "The people must feel that the opera is theirs." In March 1935 Eva collaborated with Ray Ludlow on a commentary for *New Theatre* called "Time Marches Where?" about the film version of the radio show "The March of Time." The newsreel capitalized on the audience's acceptance of what they see as "facts," they wrote, all the while manipulating events to favor governments and business interests, omitting labor stories, and failing to document Nazi advances.

Aside from his May Day contest song that spring, Blitzstein wrote sketches. With his predilection toward *Kleinkunst* and the theatre, they seemed a logical outlet for his talent. One, called "People," was about "the kind of thing a Broadway show once couldn't have afforded": unglamorous poor people, standing on breadlines, sleeping in flophouses, starving, dying, and when lucky enough to get work, dropping of weariness, only to find themselves locked out, sold out.

> *Slow death, quick death, take it as it comes,*
> *From feeding out of garbage cans and rotting in the slums.*

Eva is unmistakably in those lines, as Marc worried more and more about her health. How she had taken the sorrow of the world upon herself! Hunger and destitution about her, she would not eat, thinking it obscene and gluttonous, though at least by this time she had begun to consult a psychiatrist to try and resolve her problems. "Perhaps you are capable only of a low standard of happiness," he told her.[8]

It was the same generation as Yip Harburg and Jay Gorney's song, "Brother, Can You Spare a Dime?" The words are hard, bitter, angry, the themes built up, piled atop one another until overflowing with rebuke of the system.

> *How many times machine-guns tell the same old story,*
> *Brother, does it take to make you wise?*

Aside from the militant texts he wrote, Blitzstein's music itself showed a new form, a new spirit. In music, one refers to a "home" key, or the tonic key, on which the composition is based. In the system of polytonality, Blitzstein's accustomed mode in his avant-garde phase up to this time, the composer wandered between and among keys; the works of that period generally bore no key signature. With his return to America, and with his dedication to Communism and the working class, his music too returned "home" to given keys, to tonality. He soon realized that the European mass song, of which Eisler was the acknowledged master, would sound inappropriate in America. Composers of the left recognized that bourgeois music of radio, film, and recordings served as dream-escape from reality, as a kind of aural drug to depress the population's social awareness. Thus, Blitzstein felt it better to use the devices of Broadway—the thirty-two-bar AABA form, for instance—but elevate their employment to make a more sophisticated music. In part, this explains why his tunes always retain a snaky, uneasy, slightly unsettled sense of tonality wavering between major and minor, with surprising accidentals that often begin to sound "right" only after repeated listening. For that is how he saw his country musically—like a stew of popular tunes made tasty by the dissident spice of protest. The relationship of his music to American popular modes expresses the living, active relationship between the composer and his listeners in which he had come to believe.

The authors of *Stevedore,* Paul Peters and George Sklar, collaborated once again with other writers and musicians, mostly Jerome Moross, on *Parade,* a revue they described as "1935 set to music." Copland did not write any music for the show, as Eva had believed in January that he would, but Blitzstein did. The Theatre Union and the Group Theatre turned down the show; the more classically oriented Theatre Guild accepted it for production as its final offering of the season. *Parade* was the Guild's first musical, though already it planned to open the following fall with George Gershwin's musical version of the play *Porgy.* Its Junior Group had put on the *Garrick Gaieties,* the last avatar of which had offered *Triple-Sec* in 1930. Maddie Blitzstein served as the Guild's press representative.

For the Boston premiere on May 6, handbills announced *Parade* as "a revue with a definite idea and not just a potpourri of songs and sketches about sex and love and the moon above." Initially, it comprised twenty-eight numbers satirizing the New Deal and Roosevelt's failure to live up to his 1932 campaign promises. In one number, "The Tabloid Reds," similar to others in its use of black-and-white captioned cartoon figures, the cast of characters included bomb throwers, policemen, Communists, Mr. Capitalist, Mrs. Capitalist, and Junior Capitalist. The vicious anti-Semite radio priest Father Coughlin, Louisiana demagogue Governor Huey Long, and the lynching of Negroes in the South were other targets. In another scene, an ignorant college professor called for more football and military training as part of the curriculum. V. J. Jerome's poem "Newsboy," made into a stage piece by the Theatre of Action, found its way into *Parade* as well, though it was cut in deference to Boston sensibilities: Governor Fuller and a swarm of his friends paraded themselves right out of the theatre when a character in Jerome's sketch asked, "Have you heard of Sacco and Vanzetti?" Fuller had been one of the judges in the case. Before it was cut in New York, the show ended with a number, "No Time to Sing a Gay Song." In the cast were the well-known New York comic Jimmy Savo, and a young, unknown Eve Arden.

Eve Arden appeared in several scenes, but it was her subtle work in Blitzstein's "Send for the Militia" that stopped the show. Attired in a society matron's flowered dress, wearing a lorgnette and a closely cropped coiffure, she enacted the hostess of a women's tea and discussion club, which has the topic of socialism on the agenda of its afternoon meeting. The song has four stanzas and a chorus, in which the hostess bemoans the dreadfulness of war, discusses the longshoremen's strike in San Francisco, and gives a beggar a dime for dinner. With each insult or threat to her own security, however, or to her banker husband's profits, she calls for the militia, the army, and the navy to put down the rebellion.

The number was nearly cut in Boston for reasons of time. But the stagehands needed to set up Lee Simonson's scenery for the next sketch and, as a solo act, Arden could stand before the curtain to deliver her monologue, to the accompaniment of Blitzstein's chamber orchestra scoring. On opening night the audience applauded Arden so wildly that she was recalled to the stage with half her costume off, already in preparation for her next scene, and the next night the producers allowed her an encore.[9]

Papa and Maddie and Jo went to the New York premiere; afterward they joined Marc and Eva and members of the company, with *World-Telegram* journalist George Ross and his wife Dorothy, to wait at the Waldorf bar for the morning reviews. On the next night, Jo and Marc saw the show again, only to witness Eve Arden forget her lines in "Militia." She turned to the conductor and quite audibly said, "You'll have to start all over again." Jimmy Savo later did the same thing. Eva told these incidents to her mother, then in St. Louis: "But that always happens the first few nights, if I remember rightly—doesn't it? Especially, of course, in a failure."[10]

Though theatregoers in the upper balconies shouted their violent approval and *New Theatre* published several of the show's sketches, few of the established critics found *Parade* amusing. Most thought it dull, propagandistic, strident, and tasteless, though in virtual unanimity they singled out Miss Arden's "Send for the Militia" as exceptionally good. For the seven weeks that the show ran,

Blitzstein earned 4 percent of the gross receipts, clearing under $160 for the use of his material. The Theatre Guild lost $100,000 on the show. Possibly it would have survived longer if the Theatre Union, with more experience in radical theatre and a more receptive audience, had produced it. Though the times were ripe for full-length revues of this type, it would be two more years before another producer dared to put one on. In the meantime, Blitzstein personally received good publicity; he was asked to appear with Eve Arden doing "Send for the Militia" at a benefit for the Theatre Union, and he received an invitation to meet Elmer Rice. What he absorbed from the radical revue format, he would soon put to good use.

During the heady months of spring and summer of 1935, two publications appeared to help spread the word of musical radicalism, *Music Vanguard* and *Music Front.* The former, edited by Amnon Balber, Max Margulis, Charles Seeger, Lan Adomian, Henry Cowell, and Elie Siegmeister, with Blitzstein mentioned as a future contributor, contained book reviews, concert notices, articles about black music, Brecht's "Notes on Translating Songs of Struggle," and a lengthy report on the First International European Olympiad of Workers' Music and Song, which was held that June in Strasbourg, only twelve miles from the German border. Siegmeister and Balber wrote a criticism, with musical excerpts, of Shostakovich's opera *Lady Macbeth of Mtzensk.* Two articles appeared on German music: "A Nest of Singing Birds" on the new crop of fascist songs, and another on the concentration camp interns' theme song, "*Die Moorsoldaten*" ("The Peatbog Soldiers"). Aaron Copland struck the right note for this readership when he stated in its pages, "No more Schoenberg. The music I write must have more pertinence than Schoenberg's had even to his own Vienna."

Designed as a worthy companion to *Art Front* and *Film and Photo Front, Music Front* was the intended monthly organ of the Pierre Degeyter Music Club of New York City. Its crude standard of criticism reflected the militancy and arrogance of this, perhaps the American left's most uncompromising period. Plaudits for the exalted position of Soviet composers balanced appeals to support Communist candidates in the fall elections. The magazine warned of the signs of fascism at home: Clifford Odets's *Waiting for Lefty* had been banned, and its actors arrested, in many cities; in San Francisco, the Pierre Degeyter Club headquarters had been raided and its piano smashed. *Music Front* attacked the musicians' relief work being offered by federal agencies at "Mr. Roosevelt's coolie wage-scale," and observed with dismay the protests Leopold Stokowski had received when on one of his concerts he programmed "The Internationale." Finally, they published an appeal that Blitzstein must have found inviting: for the creation of librettos to operettas, operas, and oratorios dealing with the life of the working class.

In the search for a summer place with a rental of not more than $125, Eva wrote to Elliott Carter, then in Saugatuck, Connecticut, for suggestions. She had thought of the Westport area, or perhaps somewhere along the Hudson River. "I wonder why you don't mention Cape Cod," he replied, "for I am sure that you could find a deserted ocean spot up there." Eventually, that is where they turned, leaving the city on July 4. Three weeks later, after staying at an inn in Provincetown, they were able to move into separate one-room shacks at the Coast Guard station at Peaked Hill Bars, directly overlooking the dunes and the sea—"the most beautiful place in America that I know," Eva said. Once Marc had a piano moved in, he was ready to proceed with his music. The coast guard staff brought in their supplies and mail, and in gratitude for their services, Marc and Eva threw a party for them. They served hors d'oeuvres and drinks, Eva reported to her mother, and Marc played jazz for five hours. While Eva was supposed to be "convalescent," Marc proved "very popular with the boys." "Peaked Hill," the composer thought, "makes one quite Whitmanian."[11]

One of the projects that preoccupied the Blitzsteins during the summer was the Downtown Music School. It had just been founded in December of the previous year; as soon as Marc and Eva settled in New York, they had thrown themselves into its activities, and now Marc served as its administrator. Known as the Workers Music School while still a part of the Workers School at 35 East Twelfth Street (where Communist Party headquarters was located), it became a separate entity and moved to two floors at 799 Broadway. It affiliated with the American Music League, and had a faculty of twenty and a student enrollment of 240 in the first year. The school itself organized a number of performing groups and in time adopted the New Singers, under Lan Adomian, who became the head of its choral department.

Many of the leading figures on the New York musical left participated in the work of the Downtown Music School. Blitzstein, Henry Cowell, Wallingford Riegger, Charles Seeger, and Elie Siegmeister taught composition and music history. Copland offered to teach privately the student submitting the best instrumental work and mass song in a competition Blitzstein and Israel Citkowitz judged; Earl Robinson won the scholarship. Max Polikoff taught violin. Aube Tzerko, recently arrived from Toronto with a strong personal recommendation from Artur Schnabel, taught piano, as did Joseph Machlis. The school offered classes in several other instruments, as well as chorus, counterpoint, harmony, ear-training and sight-singing, orchestration, music criticism, and music appreciation. There was even a children's bugle, fife, and drum corps.

Aside from the low rates the school charged for its classes, the policy of this institution placed it squarely within the arsenal of the class struggle. It announced itself as "primarily for workers," growing "directly out of their demand for good musical education for themselves and their children." The program clearly distanced the school from expensive conservatories, "racket" schools, and charitable and settlement institutions that "estrange the worker from his problems and those of his class." The school aimed to develop its students politically as well as musically "to help build the united front."

Publicizing the school took its toll: Lilly Popper, a piano teacher, head of the children's department, and administrator, was actually arrested and had to appear in court for passing out promotional leaflets. Blitzstein wrote numerous letters to raise funds for the school during that summer at Peaked Hill. The school required support of fifteen hundred dollars a year to continue, and at the beginning of the fall term the school's assets amounted to less than twenty dollars. He wrote to Dorothy Elmhirst, who turned him down. He also tried Elizabeth Ames at Yaddo, Bess Eitingon, Claire Reis, Colin McPhee, and many more. Eva suggested that someone should write an article promoting the school in the *Young Worker,* and she put forward the name of Chester Kallman, the son of her left-wing dentist. Young Chester had already written several class-conscious poems much ahead of his fourteen years both in literary power and in knowledge of the radical movement. The Blitzsteins wrote press releases for the opening of the fall season and planned a November benefit concert at Town Hall.

A minor crisis blossomed into a flurry of letters to and from V. J. Jerome, writing for the National Agit-Prop Commission of the Central Control Commission of the Communist Party. It involved Lan Adomian, for some reason on Party discipline for a year, meaning that he could assume no administrative positions in the organizations of the music front. But the Downtown Music School needed him to direct the choral department, and members of the Party fraction at the school defended him to Jerome, who at last relented. By November, Norman Cazden wrote to Adomian officially "erasing" him from the membership roster of the Composers' Collective for nonpayment of an accumulated $2.50 in dues. Ashley Pettis, who had taught piano at the school, resigned that fall because he had found another full-time job.

The sketches Blitzstein worked on that summer, together with those he had written during the preceding months in America, represented something different for him. Eva told her mother that one of them had "a tune that should be as popular as Puccini." In her journal she remarked on the new phase in her husband's work:

> Both of us knew he was ready—but now it has come, almost without effort, a perfect "birth"! . . . I think he has found the way to his medium—musically—to form his musical idiom. What we used to speak of as a "new form"—but it comes now out of the psychology, a way of speaking; it is simple, straight, straight from the heart, too, "real." That word has come back! The simplicity he always wanted before—no "words" about it and absolutely communicable, to anyone, and instantaneously.[12]

Impoverished as the school was, so were the Blitzsteins. Eva told Lilly Popper that "we expect to return to New York with at best $50, and no job in sight for either of us."[13] One possibility for the fall was the idea Blitzstein proposed to the Philadelphia Orchestra, whereby he would offer a series of concert-lectures for children, and conduct musical games, tests, and contests. A master of ceremonies would help draw the audience into the performance, and soloists would wear appropriate historical costumes. No one in Philadelphia was interested.

Then, amid the uncertainties of the coming season, a ray of light suddenly shone in the form of a letter from the Chicago choreographer Ruth Page, enclosing her scenario for a ballet called *American Woman.* Page had begun her career with Anna Pavlova, continued with the Diaghilev Ballet in Monte Carlo, then with the Metropolitan Opera, and now headed her own company at the Chicago Opera. She had already begun employing jazz music, abstract dance, and black dancers. She also commissioned scores from contemporary composers. Copland had just written *Hear Ye! Hear Ye!* for her, and had suggested Blitzstein's *Cain.* Privately, Copland wrote him warning that Page and her lawyer husband Tom Fisher "must be watched when it comes to contract-making," though the réclame and the overall experience of a stage production might well be worth Marc's efforts.[14] Despite commitments to the Downtown Music School for the fall, Eva and Marc seriously considered moving to Chicago for part of the fall season to work on the ballet, Eva writing urgently to a real estate friend there to ask about a cheap, quiet apartment.

The scenario of *American Woman* concerned a middle-class woman bored with her husband and the smothering society about her. Shopping around for something meaningful to which she can escape, she encounters a gigolo, a rich tycoon, a spiritual mystic, and a young Communist agitator. All the while she is tailed by a trio of conservatively dressed matronly figures, whom she joins in the end, succumbing to dull routine and the limitations of American business success. Both Eva and Marc made faces at the "individual-suffocated-by-mechanization stuff" that Elmer Rice had already done in *Adding Machine,* but the theme contained moderate enough appeal to Marc. He had toyed with similar ideas in *The Traveling Salesman* a few years back, and his sketch for *Parade* had also dealt with a woman of just that class background. Blitzstein sent Page a copy of his *Cain* scenario, hoping to interest her in that instead, but she never considered it.

On Sunday, September 2, Marc and Eva spent eight hours talking with Page in Cohasset, where her company was performing, and they agreed to proceed with the ballet. After some weeks of failed contractual negotiations, it became apparent that the ballet would have to be postponed to the spring season if Blitzstein was to write the score; eventually the entire project fell through. Presumably, the questionable scenario, the travel, the low payment offered, and the potential difficulties of working with Page, not to mention Eva's health and his own political work in New York, all combined to discourage him. Though the ballet would have provided an opportunity for an attractive variety of musical expression, the ultimate hopelessness and immutability of social conditions would by this time in Blitzstein's thinking have been politically unacceptable. Page pursued her plan for the ballet, however, finding Jerome Moross to compose the score, his first for a ballet, which premiered in Chicago two years later as *An American Pattern.*

Marc and Eva did not return immediately to New York. For the past year or more, Eva had felt negative about accomplishing so little, even declining to celebrate her birthday on August 26. Now, too, as if to confirm the downward direction of her spirits, *New Masses* had changed its policy and would only review books of some political significance; its editors returned several of Eva's previously accepted notices. Dr. Leof had diagnosed her case as "overwork, over-stimulation, undernourishment." She had lost more weight still, her body totaling a mere seventy-eight pounds by the end of their stay in Provincetown. In a letter to her friend Clifton Furness asking if Marc and the dog Very could use his Cambridge apartment while she entered a hospital in Boston to be force-fed, she recalled to him the disturbing dream she had had years before:

> in which I was in Washington, D. C. driving in a carriage, and suddenly a library (or filing) card was given me saying "September 5, 1935" and I knew it was the date of my death. . . . You took it seriously, and said "I think it may be quite possible. But what I really believe it is, is a warning. I think you are being given, or will be given, your choice whether you want to live or die." Well, I doubt that; but anyway, the whole winter and until June was a losing struggle against what finally seemed to me a "weakened will to live."[15]

Marc stayed by her at Clifton's. Eva had stayed in the hospital only three days, just enough to begin a new regimen, and then discharged herself to the apartment, her condition of secondary anemia confirmed by further testing. Against all advice, she continued to smoke her Luckies without restraint, coughing in jagged fits, and to drink coffee and liquor copiously, meanwhile virtually boycotting all food. She wrote letters to her friends and editors asking for leads on suitable work; she retyped a four-page report to Mutzi with only minor changes, as if she would be judged for literary style—and at a time like this—by her own mother. By September 10, Marc wrote Lilly Popper, Eva was "already better," but surely this was wishful thinking. Her refusal to take absolute control of herself and of her life placed the burden on Marc of devoting himself to her needs. He found her pitiful but also possessive, and he resented it. Eva frankly wondered whether she had finally burnt the bridge between them.

After a strained parting, Marc drove to Philadelphia—a harrowing ride with no brakes in his car—and deposited Very with Jo. While there, he met a friend of Jo's who had spent the summer with William Morris, the literary and theatrical agent. Supposedly, Marc wrote to Eva, Morris was "crazy to handle me or my stuff. So one of my first duties in New York will be to look him up."[16] The William Morris Agency liked "Send for the Militia," but they wanted to see more before taking Blitzstein on as a client. In any case, Morris himself showed little interest in music as such and preferred to think of Blitzstein as a writer.

Marc also hoped to persuade Bess and Motty Eitingon, famous patrons of music and theatre, to allow him and Eva to live rent-free on their property in Old Greenwich, Connecticut, at least until they were surer of a source of income. The Eitingons agreed to let them have the gardener's cottage. This would be ideal for Eva, Marc thought, as it would place her both far enough and near enough to her mother Lina for comfort. At the same time, another beneficiary of the Eitingons' generosity, Franz Hoellering, had come to the Connecticut estate—"he smells encroachment on his 'territory' with Motty."[17]

Eva in the meantime had decided to consult a friend of Lewis and Sophia

Mumford, the psychiatrist Dr. Henry A. Murray at Harvard. Murray analyzed her case as masochism, complicated by mother problems. Apparently in her first few days of life, she had refused feeding, and in later analogous situations also had rejected both mother and food. Putzi's death had begun the latest cycle of despondency. How to get herself out of the slough was the question, and where to do it—in New York, in Philadelphia, or there in Boston?[18]

The ballet with Ruth Page was off by now, but out of the blue another exciting development arose: On September 19 the Philadelphia papers carried Stokowski's announcement that he had programmed Blitzstein's Mallorca piece, the *Orchestra Variations,* for that season. The composer had hardly counted on it: "I simply left the score at his studio, with the usual lack of hope," he wrote Eva in Boston. "Incidentally, my stock as a composer has gone up considerably since the Stokowski announcement. Motty had me play things to him (*Cain,* etc.) last night, and striving valiantly, actually got to like them."[19]

In the fall, the Blitzsteins moved to 7½ Jane Street in Greenwich Village, occupying two long, starkly white floor-throughs, Eva's quarters below and Marc's above. It was there that Marc wrote a touching, slow song—both words and music—called "Stay in My Arms." Not merely unlike the angry, socially conscious sketches to which he was now committed, it is really a complete antithesis, more like a Gershwin popular song but with a striving reach in its melodic line and some harmonic risks that suggest something closer to an art song. He must have offered it to Eva to help her recovery.

Let's just be
Old-fashioned,
Let's just be lazy;
The world's gone crazy,
So stay in my arms.
I love you,
You love me—
That much is plain, dear;
The rest's insane, dear,
And full of alarms.
Why dance a dance that kills,
Grasping and shrieking?
Such jumping Jacks and Jills,
What are they seeking?
Forget them,
Or let them
Grow dim and hazy;
The world's gone crazy,
So stay in my arms.

For possible use in a revue, Blitzstein detailed an idea for its production: "eccentric, modernistic, futuristic sets, costumes, dances, music, give way slowly (piece by piece) to familiar, lovely, comfortable, luxurious sights and sounds." Indeed, at the same time that fall, Eva gave extensive thought to organizing "America's first topical cabaret" to present artists committed to United Front politics. But she could not find a backer to pay her a living wage while she organized such a project, and she had to abandon the idea.

Another song in the popular mode that Blitzstein wrote in 1935 is "The Way You Are," a slow bolero sung by a woman recounting her lover's imperfections but ending each time with the refrain, "I like you best the way you are."

Once again, it was Guggenheim Foundation application time, and Henry Moe encouraged Blitzstein to try once more. Blitzstein could now add a fair Spanish to his language proficiency and, as references, the names of Carl Engel, editor of *The Musical Quarterly,* Hans Lange, conductor of the Philharmonic Symphony Orchestra of New York, Martha Graham, and Hanns Eisler. His résumé had substantially strengthened by now: He was able to include a reprint of his entry in the United States Section of the International Society for Contemporary Music's "Catalogue of American Composers" and update his application with a bibliography of writings about him, a list of his own publications, and a much expanded list of fresh performances. Aside from further composing, he proposed to write a volume of critical analysis, basically expounding his views on the origins of modern music, current trends, and the crisis in music in America, encompassing all fields of musical activity.

That fall, in the enthusiasm over his newly adopted world view, Blitzstein reached the height of his commitment to a specifically Marxist, materialist music history. To further his own ideological education, he took classes in Marxism at the Workers School, for which he was recommended as a scholarship student by the Composers Collective. Aside from counterpoint and composition, he taught a course at the Downtown Music School called "Social Aspects of Music," reflecting a Marxist position.* In his lectures he stressed the dangers of "forgetting the Marxism because of the music; and forgetting the music because of the Marxism," presaging the emergence of both a large number of composers who in the thirties went through a leftist period but who later returned to their apolitical estheticism, and others who, in their drive to offer the world continually relevant political material, neglected the ever-imposing demands of changing musical values. Never did Blitzstein give up his intense curiosity to hear and be involved in new music of all kinds, and he incorporated this compulsion into his sense of Marxian obligation. He kept up a feverish pace of attending meetings, composing, concertgoing, reviewing, and lecturing. This season's theme was "Masterworks of Modern Music," upon which he expostulated at the Women's University Club in Philadelphia on Monday evenings, in various well-to-do homes in Scarsdale and Hartsdale on Tuesday afternoons, and at the New School on Wednesday nights.

Somehow, amid the crush of activities, Blitzstein found the time to work with

*For a time that fall the school was at loggerheads with the Pierre Degeyter Club, which had set up its own Workers Music School, enlisting the support of *Daily Worker* columnist Mike Gold.

the composer and ethnomusicologist Colin McPhee on a program of Balinese ceremonial music. Along with films of processions, religious events, dance performances, and indigenous gamelan orchestras, the evening of November 6 at the Cosmopolitan Club also featured, aside from a Balinese feast, recorded music and two-piano arrangements of Balinese music, apparently devised by both composers together. Shortly afterward, McPhee asked whether Eva was available to edit his book on the music of Bali, for he knew she was editing George Antheil's book *Music in America* for Harcourt Brace, supposedly for publication in the spring.* Dr. Leof had also written the rough draft of a book combining some of his autobiographical reflections with his views on modern medicine, and Eva worked on it as well. But this, too, remained unpublished.

In connection with the Theater Union's ill-starred production of *The Mother,* which Bertolt Brecht came to America to supervise, and which also brought Eisler back to the United States, *The New York Times* published Brecht's lengthy article explaining his role in the development of German drama. In part, Eva drew on this article, but drew more on her own interviews with both Brecht and Eisler, to write a piece of her own for *New Masses,* "Principles of 'Educational' Theater." Its appearance on December 31, 1935, marked the first time a left-wing readership in the United States had been exposed to Brecht's theories. In the same way that the dramatist opposed "hypnotic" theater, the composer also refused to place his listeners in a romantic, eyes-closed trance. At that time, few in the theatre world, not to mention those among the theatregoing public, yet appreciated the revolutionary "epic" ideas in staging promulgated by the Germans—Brecht, Piscator, and others—and the Russians, above all, Meyerhold. Americans were still attached to representational, Stanislavskian technique, what Brecht would subsume under the term *Aristotelian.*

Eva also translated Brecht's poem, the "Letter to the Theatre Union Concerning the Play 'Mother,'" for the *Daily Worker,* but the features editor Morris Colman refused to print such a long piece, as once already he had devoted his page to the production. Within a few weeks, however, Eva's translation of Brecht's important poem "How the Carpet Weavers of Kujan-Bulak Honored Lenin" appeared in the *Daily Worker,* a job for which V. J. Jerome thanked her, though not before altering her phrasing and holding up publication in his typical magisterial manner.[20] Eva was anxious to see these translations in print so that she could support her prospect of becoming Brecht's translator of choice and agent in America. She met with Brecht in late January to discuss it, not long before his return to Denmark, but without conclusive result: Brecht would hint at, but never give, exclusive rights to any American translator. Among others of his works, Eva expressed particular interest in the *Threepenny Novel,* Brecht's prose adaptation of the stage piece.

While Brecht remained in New York, Eva translated an article on "The Usage of Music in the Epic Theatre" for *Modern Music.* Minna Lederman had especially commissioned this piece and paid both author and translator for their

*Antheil never finished this book for some reason, and despite Eva's efforts it never saw print.

efforts, but she found problems with its didacticism and in the end refused to publish it without alteration. Lederman appreciated all of Eva's hard work on translations and book reviews, but the pay remained miserably low—one cent a word. An article would rarely bring in more than ten dollars.

On the same evening in Eva's flat that the arrangements were made for the Brecht translation, the party moved downstairs to Marc's, where the composer sat Brecht down and played him his sketch that included the song "Nickel Under the Foot." The song reflects the hard-boiled, hard-bitten world view of a young lady economically forced into selling herself. Brecht rose to his feet when Marc had finished, saying, "Why don't you write a piece about all kinds of prostitution—the press, the church, the courts, the arts, the whole system?" Evidently, Brecht's idea took hold, though it would be some months before Blitzstein could settle down to work on it.[21]

Another project of Eva's, advanced in a well-organized proposal, was a book called *Music for Us,* which she called "a first Marxist survey of 20th-century European and American music." Its outline closely paralleled Marc's concerns and theories. Simon and Schuster turned the book down, but its inherent value and timeliness suggest that another publisher might well have taken it. A firm contract would have given Eva a much-needed emotional lift.

Still, Eva persevered. Her ability to work continued, seemingly unimpaired by her now dangerously minimal consumption of food. Late one snowy night, Marc's friend Berenice Skidelsky drove him around and around in her car to see whether there was a place open where he could buy some ice cream for Eva, for by now, with her difficulty in swallowing food, it was one of the few things she could eat comfortably.

On one occasion, a November 8 concert of Virgil Thomson's music at the New School, Marc could not attend and Eva pinch-hit for him. In less than a page, she summed up Thomson's whole esthetic in some choice phrases that sent the composer and his friends reeling from the assault. Written for the salon, she said, his music is "pretentious and frivolous, although it is intrinsically honest and serious." She called it "discreet"—and she punned on Thomson's French model—"Satiesfied" music, which "neither puts itself forward nor belittles itself." "It is a great pity," she wrote in final judgment, "that the tradition invoked by Thomson's music in general is for most of his listeners dead; the evocation therefore gets a mournful response."[22] Surely, Marc would have agreed with this opinion, and may even have prompted some of it. Lederman not only had to face Thomson's wrath—he was convinced the Party had sent Eva to do a polemicist's hatchet job—but had to defend the article in the face of Alexander Smallens's protest resignation from the League of Composers. The magazine was not nicknamed the "Backbiters' Quarterly" for nothing!

With the New York *Journal-American* critic Leonard Liebling as commentator, the International Music Guild held a Town Hall recital on December 1, programming music by Elie Siegmeister, Paul Creston, Hanns Eisler, Evelyn Berkman, Otto Luening, Henry Cowell, and Blitzstein. The New Singers performed two Eisler numbers, including "On Killing," translated by Marc and Eva.

Mordecai Bauman sang, and later recorded, Siegmeister's "Strange Funeral at Braddock," the harrowing story of a fatal industrial accident in Pennsylvania, which was written in an advanced musical idiom not at all like Eisler's mass songs. Blitzstein played two excerpts from *Cain,* which Robert A. Simon in *The New Yorker* found "so good that I'd like to know more of this ballet."[23] Simon then arranged to meet with Blitzstein for a private performance of the entire score.

A few days later, Eva accompanied Marc to a one-man concert of Walter Piston's music at the New School. With a sense of vain inner superiority, Eva scratched on her pad, "He doesn't even seem to know the bourgeois class is falling; . . . conventional inside and out." Blitzstein, reviewing the concert for the Boston *Evening Transcript,* referred to Piston as "the Post-Impressionist of America" and, in a masterful imitation of music in words, cited the "impeccability of the workmanship; although he is addicted to over-precious finales, adding two or three or four extra dreamy notes, refusing to let well enough (a quite ended piece) alone."[24]

On Friday, December 20, 1935, the Friends of the Workers School sponsored a concert and dance to celebrate the first American recordings of revolutionary music, on three Timely disks. Recorded late that year, the six sides included four Eisler-Brecht songs: "In Praise of Learning," with Blitzstein at the piano; "Rise Up" (the "Comintern" song revised to conform to the new, less sectarian Communist line), with Eisler at the piano; "Forward, We've Not Forgotten" (the "Solidarity" song); and the "United Front" song, with Blitzstein's accompaniment; also, the "Internationale" with new pro-Soviet lyrics, with Blitzstein at the piano; and the "Soup Song," lyrics by Maurice Sugar. Lan Adomian led the New Singers both on the recordings and at the concert, with Mordecai Bauman and Felix Groveman performing the solos. The records made more than musical history, for several significant, socially aware artists of the day contributed the cartoon labels: William Gropper, Phil Wolfe, Hyman Warsager, and Russell T. Limbach.

These recordings illustrate a true musical internationalism, with Eisler and Blitzstein's Central European driving march tempos; Bauman's perfect, cultured enunciation, complete with rolled *r*'s; and the fresh, uncouth sound of Adomian's American chorus. As expected, the left press cried "Bravo!" all around; the Establishment press either ignored the releases or condemned them in the standard anti-Communist terms.

Reviewing the late-fall season of 1935, Blitzstein found much good to say of Shostakovich: "the happy product of a society which believes in him and backs him to the limit; and he is practically the first composer in our day to write good music which is also contagious." Thirty-three small pieces by Goddard Lieberson made up a November Composers' Forum-Laboratory concert that Blitzstein found uninteresting; and Lieberson soon afterward gave up serious composing. The reviewer found Stokowski's recent Bach transcriptions "execrable," and Klemperer's presentation of Mahler's Symphony no. 2 "very hard to stomach." Overlong, empty, this was "the hymn of the petty-bourgeois."[25]

Blitzstein also had a crack at Virgil Thomson—of the "*de luxe* set"—occasioned by a Composers' Forum-Laboratory concert. "Thomson's music is at once very ordinary and very finely wrought; so that ordinary ears get troubled because it isn't ordinary enough, and the professionals are bothered because it's all too ordinary." Perhaps it was to embarrass Thomson that Blitzstein reported remarks from the question-and-answer period afterward. Someone asked, "Why should people lend their ears to your music?" and the composer answered, "I have always felt the lending of any part of the anatomy should be an act of simple faith." Another posed what Blitzstein called a "pertinent question about his music's relation to the social scene"; Thomson froze, then countered, "My politics, as well as the source of my income, I consider a personal matter, which I shall gladly discuss privately."[26]

On December 17, the Blitzsteins attended a League of Composers and Cosmopolitan Club concert honoring Kurt Weill and featuring his wife Lotte Lenya (then spelled with a *j*). A "hand-picked public," wrote Blitzstein for *Modern Music,* "applauded all the numbers with equal fervor. Both the music and Lotte Lenja were worth a more discerning response." Finding the song *"J'attends un navire"* "about rock-bottom in melodic cheapness," he thought, "Lenja is too special a talent, I am afraid, for a wide American appeal; but she has magnetism and a raw lovely voice like a boy-soprano. Her stylized gestures seem strange because of her natural warmth; but in the strangeness lies the slight enigma which is her charm."[27] Still resistant to the couple's gifts, Blitzstein could hardly have dreamed how closely his own future would be tied to Weill's esthetic and works. But even then, Eva wrote on her program next to the number "Seeräuber Jenny" from *Die Dreigroschenoper,* "Marc likes."

He also commented on Eisler's music for *Mother;* though the Theatre Union's performance was "wretched," Eisler was a better worker than Weill: He wanted to educate, whereas Weill wanted to entertain. Eisler's music "answers its purpose." He rounded out his review of the season by mentioning the December 7 Town Hall "Music in the Crisis" symposium, vociferously attended in the cheapest sections of the house, the orchestra only half-filled. Copland, Eisler, and Henry Cowell spoke, along with the critic Oscar Thompson; and the New Singers and Mordecai Bauman, with Blitzstein accompanying, provided music. The Downtown Music School shortly reprinted Eisler's remarks as a pamphlet called *The Crisis in Music.* "It is clear to me," Blitzstein reported, "that the conception of music in society, with us these many years, is dying of acute anachronism; and that a fresh idea, overwhelming in its implications and promise, is taking hold."*[28]

In his review of the published pamphlet for a *New Masses* readership, Blitzstein cited Eisler as "probably the first instance of the real fusion of Marxist and musician," and the essay "very possibly the manifesto for the revolutionary music of our time." We composers, he added, remembering Brecht's reaction to

*One fresh idea Blitzstein perhaps had in mind was the New Singers' projected performance of *The Condemned* for the following fall; it was announced in the notes on contributors, though such a performance never came about.

"Nickel Under the Foot," "are the tool of a vicious economic setup. The unconscious (sometimes not so unconscious) prostitution of composers in today's world is one of the sorry sights to see."[29]

In February of 1936, at a Composers' Collective concert presented by the New Theatre League, three singing actors—Gladys Frankel, Thomas Frank, and Nat Fichtenbaum—joined Blitzstein at the piano in his "Sketch No. 1," the streetwalker's scene including the song "Nickel Under the Foot." This was the first publicly performed music from what would become his Brecht-inspired opera *The Cradle Will Rock.* An unascribed review of the concert said of this piece only: "A sensational issue now agitating the New York newspapers is treated from an unusual angle."

As New York correspondent for the Paris *Revue Musicale,* Blitzstein wrote in the early part of 1936 two roundup articles on the New York musical season. In both he devoted space to "Communist" composers. Again he remarked on the futility of searching for indigenous music in jazz, American Indian tunes, and spirituals. "Real roots should appear spontaneously in the music itself," he wrote. Of four new American operas recently performed, he briefly mentioned Antheil's *Helen Retires,* Hanson's *Merry Mount* and Gruenberg's *Emperor Jones,* concentrating on Virgil Thomson's *Four Saints in Three Acts,* "by far the most successful. . . . The agile, precious and decadent music tends towards a mixture of church parody with Satie's style. A scintillating production with Negro actors and singers made a consistently gay and amusing spectacle of it, and the able music incontestably added something. It was a remarkable experience in the lyric theatre."[30]

As for the new opera by Shostakovich, *Lady Macbeth of Mtzensk* marked "the end of the period of combat in modern music." Though too long and uneven, it made for superb theatre. "The subject is naturally conceived and elaborated according to Communist ideology," meaning that the milieu is the real subject of the opera, not an individual abnormality. Blitzstein did not care for the rapidly changing variety of styles employed—they dissipated the overall effect of the work—but he did feel that Shostakovich had taken the modern idiom to a resting plateau, had summed up the potential of contemporary musical resources. The power of this opera would remain long with Blitzstein.[31]

Back in 1927 when Blitzstein had written the score for Stella Simon's film *Hands,* he had not recorded the music. In March of 1936, the Museum of Modern Art's Film Library, which was in possession of a print, arranged with RCA for Blitzstein to perform his piano score and add it to the picture. This version with sound is the one presently available for viewing. At this time, too, Blitzstein added a series of twelve lectures on Stravinsky, Schoenberg, and their progeny to his schedule; these he taught at the New School on Wednesday nights from February through April. During his time there, he and Aaron Copland joined to address "The Composer, the Audience, the Music," a forum which WHN broadcast live. In that speech, Blitzstein complained that the resistance of contemporary audiences to new music bore much of the responsibility for the composer's retreat into the ivory tower, or into "art for art's sake"—Schoenberg was his prime example—and he urged a more active relationship between creator and listener.

Ashley Pettis, who had served as music editor for the *New Masses* and had proven his left-wing credentials, now served as the director of the Composers' Forum-Laboratory in New York, a Federal Music Project undertaking within the Works Progress Administration. The program began in the fall of 1935 and consisted of weekly concerts featuring the music of a single composer, with a question-and-answer period following the performance. The concerts were held at the Federal Music Building on West Forty-eighth Street. In its four-year history, the Federal Music Project sponsored the performances of some 6,327 pieces of American music in concert halls and high school auditoriums around the country.

Blitzstein attended many of the New York series and had reviewed Virgil Thomson's evening. Then he threw himself into a minor tempest regarding Elie Siegmeister's upcoming program. Siegmeister planned to have a choral work performed called "Biography," set to a text by Communist writer A. B. Magil, in which the names Ford, Mellon, and Rockefeller cropped up as the complicit murderers of American working-class leaders. Pettis asked that Siegmeister delete the number from the program because he feared offending the government and these great families of art patrons, but Siegmeister refused on First Amendment grounds. Blitzstein then assumed the role of head cheerleader, circulating letters and a petition to Pettis with the signatures of Copland, Riegger, and as many fellow composers as he could garner. Presumably, he argued, a federal project should be committed to upholding our country's principle of free speech! To his surprise, he found a degree of nervousness among some of the other composers: Colin McPhee wouldn't sign because he was a Canadian citizen, and Virgil Thomson refused because he felt there was an underlying personal issue between Siegmeister and Pettis coming out of disagreement over *New Masses* policy. The protest fizzled out.*[32]

Blitzstein's turn came for an unremunerated Composers' Forum-Laboratory concert on April 15. The major pieces were the String Quartet of 1930, performed by the Modern Art Quartet, and the Piano Concerto, performed, in a two-piano version, by the composer Norman Cazden as the soloist (the only person Blitzstein knew, he claimed, who could handle the tricky part) and by Blitzstein playing the orchestra part. Earlier in the program, the audience heard the composer with his Piano Sonata of 1927; the first movement of the Serenade for string quartet (just one *largo* this time!); and three songs with Mordecai Bauman—"Jimmie's got a goil," phrases from the Dialogue in *Cain,* and "A Child Writes a Letter" from the *Children's Cantata,* the only agit-prop music that represented the new Blitzstein.

In the daily press, only the *World-Telegram* covered the evening. "A large group of eager, forward-looking musicians sat in on the experiment," wrote Louis

*The outcome of this contretemps is not known for sure; most likely, "Biography" was not performed.

Biancolli. The Sonata "showed decided mechanistic leanings," and the cantata excerpt was "vividly worded and scored."[33]

Colin McPhee reviewed the concert for *Modern Music* and wrote of the Concerto that it is

> an excellent and well constructed piece of music. One feels in it primarily a preoccupation with form; the material is perhaps too thoroughly worked out, especially in the double passacaglia which constitutes the last movement. It was difficult to estimate its real value when played for two pianos. As far as I could judge from the score, the orchestra is handled with brilliance and a decidedly personal feeling for instrumentation. Blitzstein has a freshness at times which is most attractive. . . .[34]

A week after the concert, Eva left for Boston to begin a translation of work by Elias Canetti, to see Dr. Murray at Harvard, and to get away from Marc. Lately, their life together had been month after month of nervous strain, self-doubt, fatigue, and "jitters." For his part, Blitzstein concluded that "it is characteristic of me as a person to be without resources (psychological or physical) for any other human being than myself; and this admission, confronted by the person I love, shows me up completely as a person."[35]

Dr. Murray concluded that Eva required either a prolonged psychoanalytical treatment or a complete love relationship; once or twice that spring he also saw Marc, telling him that he was a bisexual "with extraordinary empathy and intuition" and that he should live and act less rationally, more impulsively and experientially. In her frequent letters, Eva appealed to her husband for calm in contemplating their future; for the moment, a separation seemed inadvisable mostly for financial reasons, but it was certainly on both their minds. Marc told her of a strong offer from Charles Seeger to work for the Resettlement Administration in Washington, with possibilities for travel into rural areas to collect and record music. When Seeger asked for an immediate answer, Eva telegraphed her husband, CONSIDER YOUR PREFERENCES AS IF ALONE.[36]

Badly needed income amounting to $350 came along in the form of a contract signed May 2, 1936, with a New Jersey firm called Pedigreed Pictures, Inc., to compose the score for a film, *Chesapeake Bay Retriever.* Written and produced by Mrs. Milton Erlanger and Thomas T. K. Frelinghuysen, it previewed on May 26 at the Chanin Auditorium along with two other films, *The Poodle* and *The Collie,* though Marc would not be in New York to attend. Made with the cooperation of the American Chesapeake Bay Retriever Club, the film starred Skipper Bob, the versatile, all-retrieving pet of Harry Conklin, in the role of Captain Jack, whose rival, Sea King, was played by Anthony Bliss's champion dog, Sodaks Gypsy Prince. The supporting cast was recruited from Mr. Bliss's Chesacroft Kennels.

Blitzstein scored the film for violin, clarinet, bassoon, and piano, and incorporated two songs in the public domain, "Life on the Ocean Wave" and "A-Roving."

As musical counterpoint to the plot on the screen, Blitzstein titled other sections "The Salt and the Spray," "Family Portrait," "Gray Surf," "Pooch Procession" (marked *maestoso*), "Water Trial," "The Prize" (a reprise of the "Procession"), and a "Finale." This music, little more than that of a composer on holiday, is not recognizably Blitzstein. Functional, unsophisticated, chordal and very diatonic, such light entertainment might have been produced by any competent musician. It is not even chamber music in a true sense, as the piano mostly doubles the instruments or provides a regular oom-pah accompaniment. Knowing how overworked Marc had been of late, Eva wrote that when it was finished he should "scrap everything . . . don't do anything; simply sleep, enjoy yourself—fuck—meditate or not, do whatever is best for your nerves and to get rested."[37]

Mordecai Bauman had become the favorite singer on the left. Blitzstein asked him to premiere "People"—his song from the year before, now called "Poor People"—in a radical anti-Nazi dance and drama workshop at the YMHA. The date was May 16, 1936, and it was the second song to be heard publicly that would later find its way into his Brecht-inspired theatre piece. As Bauman sang, Elsa Findlay and her dance troupe mimed the scenario. "Slow death, quick death, take it as it comes," he sang—as Eva desperately tried to hang on to life up in Cambridge.

One musical publication in which Blitzstein participated from the beginning was the organ of the American Music League, *Unison.* Its first issue appeared in May 1936 at two cents a copy. In this number, the AML spelled out its objective: to develop a people's music in the face of the literal bankruptcy as well as the social poverty of the leading musical institutions. Aside from encouraging affordable concerts, amateur musical activity, a close relation between composer and audience, and folk-music traditions, the organization set out "to defend musical culture against fascism, censorship and war." Part of its calling was to run the Downtown Music School. Already some seventeen member groups comprised the AML, including Lan Adomian's sixty-member New Singers. Mordecai Bauman served on *Unison*'s editorial board.

Blitzstein responded to a four-part questionnaire in this first issue, as did Elie Siegmeister and Wallingford Riegger.

> *Unison:* Do you write with a definite audience in mind?
>
> Blitzstein: Since my orientation is toward a proletarian society and a revolutionary art, the answer to this question is yes. It is part of the conscious plan, like deciding to write a string-quartet or a mass-song. This does not at all imply that while composing I concentrate upon anything but the thing at hand.
>
> *Unison:* Is it important to you that you know the reaction of your audience to your music?
>
> Blitzstein: Emphatically, yes. Music is intended for somebody, not nobody. The reaction of the audience can be a guide, a warning, a standard or a blank. (But I assume you mean the audience at large, not one particular concert's audience.)

Unison: How do you visualize the ideal relation between a composer and his audience?

[Blitzstein referred readers to his forthcoming article "Coming—the Mass Audience!" in *Modern Music,* stressing the primacy of the composer's articulation of the life and times about him.]

Unison: What can you as a composer suggest as a means for achieving this ideal relation?

Blitzstein: I feel it part of my function to hasten through musical means, the arrival of a social order which permits such a relation. Music is one of the greatest educational forces we know; it can train, not only our minds, but our blood. Composers must come out into the open; they must fight the battle with other workers.[38]

As he gave these answers to *Unison,* Marc sent a draft copy of his *Modern Music* article to Eva. Blitzstein dreamed of an ideal musical atmosphere in which the general public would show an aroused interest in new works. He recalled that between Beethoven and Wagner, as the middle class grew in numbers and power, audiences expanded from three hundred to three thousand. By modern analogy, the radical music leagues had recently been besieged by requests for music and music education. Blitzstein knew this because he served as the Composers' Collective secretary in charge of booking the Performing Unit, which could supply anywhere from a half hour to an hour and a half's worth of music for a small fee. "The art is renewing itself. A new fact, a new idea is becoming apparent. A public is storming the gates. . . . A thrilling thing is taking place under our noses—an economic thing, which has definite and visible effects on music and musical life; a cataclysmic change such as has happened only once or twice before."

Declaring himself against the "bestially anarchic" sort of "rugged individualism" whereby every composer felt obliged to create his own style, he lauded the Soviet composers, Eisler, Stefan Wolpe, and the American left-wingers. He projected his fantasies: "There is no telling what may happen to Tradition when the huge eager innocent mass, completely earnest, completely without piety, takes charge. . . . It may mean the end of the platinum Orchestra Age," he shouted with warning and doom. "The individual composer achieves his pure ultimate undisturbed individuality only on the basis of a smooth and balanced social machinery; it is his function as a musician to aid in the building of such a machinery," he claimed.[39]

With these words, written for Eva, for his readers in the music field, for the left, and for posterity, he threw himself clearheaded and proud into this people's movement. The one thing lacking in the American operas he saw, in the modest sketches of the left, and in the musical theatre was the one thing he just might be able to supply. Perhaps it was up to him to perform his own Wagnerian integration of the arts, in a single, powerful, American statement of the crisis in music and society, a work paradoxically so much a part of the machinery of the times that through it he might uncover for himself the right form and the right identity as a composer.

From Cambridge, Eva responded with her usual detached editorial comments: Change past tenses to present, clear up vague expressions, develop ideas more about the present state of music than the past. She had clearly read through the article several times and assumed her task seriously. She also wrote to *Publishers Weekly,* protesting that they had broken a promise over a year old in rejecting her article on Sylvia Beach. The sharpness of her mind belied her famished body's steadily declining ability to sustain life: She had by now dropped to seventy-five pounds.

On May 18, Eva telegraphed, saying she would let Marc know shortly when he should come to Boston to see Dr. Murray. By the twenty-first, she was in the hospital and wrote Marc that she needed reading matter, phone calls, and mail. The next day, she wrote to Marc and admitted how deeply she needed trust, belief, and conviction. This brought him to her side.

On Saturday, May 23, Eva again saw Dr. Murray, who felt impressed by her apparently renewed will to live. "It seems that Power is ultimately important to you and without it life is not worth living," he wrote to her on Monday after their session. But he cautioned that she might not always be able to find situations where she could exercise her omnipotence, and he advised a more resilient approach to life. "The main thing now," he concluded, "is to put on weight."[40]

By then it was far too late. Looking in on her early on the morning of Tuesday, May 26, Marc found Eva motionless, dead at thirty-four years and nine months. She had outlived by 261 days her nightmare premonition from nine years before of a September 5, 1935, death.

LINA DEAR, Marc telegraphed, EVA HAS SUDDENLY DIED ONLY A FEW HOURS WARNING NO PAIN I AM HAVING CREMATION PERFORMED TODAY WILL RETURN TO NEW YORK THURSDAY LOVE BE BRAVE MARC. Lina responded: I AM WITH YOU AND OUR EVA MY DEAREST EVERY EVERY MOMENT, and later, I HAVE MONEY READY PLEASE WIRE WHERE TO SEND IT.

The cremation took place on Thursday at Mount Auburn Cemetery in Cambridge. Wanting two or three days of solitude, Marc booked passage on a cargo steamer down to New York. A day out, he released Eva's ashes into the sea off Cape Cod, which she had found so beautiful the summer before. After stopping in New York to see Lina, he headed for Philadelphia and Jo.

Eva must have known that passage from the ending of Jack London's *Martin Eden* where the author puts his head out of the porthole, preparing to drop out into the ocean depth: "He wondered if he ought to write a swan-song, but laughed the thought away. There was no time. He was too impatient to be gone."[41] As her last literary effort, Eva prepared final corrections on an excerpt from her autobiographical novel *The Broken Circle,* scheduled for publication that year in *The New Caravan,* edited by her friends Lewis Mumford, Alfred Kreymborg, and Paul Rosenfeld. She titled the passage "There Was No Time."

The death certificate listed the cause as "starvation associated with a psychosis." Eva had left her own epitaph in the *New Caravan* story. But Marc and she had sometimes talked about whether, at the point of death, they would feel they had done their duty toward life, and Eva wrote out her final report:

We laughed, because it was insoluble, and agreed, "We'll leave a slip at the last moment, just—I've done it or not! A record." I have not done it. My life is wasted. I have not given what I brought. I have not taken what life had to give. Life was wasted. Rebellious—yet relieved, I should be glad to die.

What I have lived most keenly: my lack of living.[42]

7

WHEN THE WIND BLOWS

Summer 1936–Summer 1937

"Find out who he drinks with and talks with and sleeps with . . ."

In the weeks following Eva's death, Blitzstein fell into utter despondency. Were her doctors irresponsible in allowing her to deteriorate so completely? What was the root cause of her unhappiness? Was it just a personal tragedy, or was it the failure of the whole capitalist system to provide work and self-respect for a woman of her special talents? What might he have done to save her? What might anyone have done? Lina, he knew, asked some of these same questions.

Marc's friend Louis Simon, now director of the Federal Theatre Project in New Jersey, saw him shortly after Eva's death. Marc said he wanted to give up composing, at least for a time, and devote himself entirely to finishing Eva's novel. Simon proposed that Marc accept a steady music-related job in one of the Works Progress Administration units, which would combine composing, organizing, and research. And he reminded him of Brecht's suggestion—an opera molded around "Nickel Under the Foot."

But Blitzstein was unable to take up any of his friend's suggestions yet, nor could he bring himself to work on Eva's manuscripts. He wandered about, unable to concentrate, unable to work, plagued by feelings of inadequacy. In May, the Italian fascists had conquered Addis Ababa, consolidating their takeover of

Ethiopia. Now, in July, an upstart army officer named Francisco Franco launched a rebellion against the Spanish government that presaged one more country—where Marc and Eva had lived for some months in 1934—going fascist. What hope was there in this world?

Eva's story, "There Was No Time," appeared in due course in *The New Caravan.* It was the last piece ever published under her name. Marc never discarded any of her writings, letters, journals, or other literary effects, however; perhaps one day someone might come along and express interest in them. For years he kept a photo of her prominently on view in his flat. When he traveled anywhere, he took it with him, as well as her Phi Beta Kappa key and a tiny bear and other miniatures that had belonged to her; and he set these up as a kind of shrine in any room he made his own.

One thing he knew. Not only would there never be another Eva, there would never be another woman. He sustained intense friendships and loyalties to a number of women—Jo, Mama, and Lina above all. But in his erotic life there would only be men; on that point, Eva's death resolved any lingering confusion. He also succeeded in convincing himself that he lacked the emotional resources for the focused love of another person—the kind of judgment that, left unexamined, becomes truer and truer with each passing year. With the exception of one man later on, his romantic life would be characterized by the briefest of affairs, mostly one-night stands with men met at bars or in the local cruising grounds, or with anonymous contacts at the baths. His taste ran toward "real men"—servicemen, sailors, working-class toughs, no pretty boys or Broadway hoofers. Sometimes he would feel crushingly lonely.

By the summer of 1936, the Davises had moved out of Philadelphia to Ventnor, near Atlantic City on the New Jersey shore, where Kit's doctors felt his ear problems would be improved by the fresh air. Marc took some days of solace with Jo and her family in July. An invalid had lived in the Davises' house before they bought it, and for his use a solarium had been installed; its only access was a rickety elevator. Marc occupied that room and began thinking about how to expand "Nickel Under the Foot" into an opera.

Back in the city, still broken and dazed, he met Bess Eitingon one day at the corner of Fifth Avenue and Fifty-seventh Street. Shocked by his appearance, she invited him to Hillcrest, her Connecticut home, where he and Eva had spent a few weeks the year before. There he could have the peace he needed to compose his Brecht-inspired opera.

Before he was free to go, Blitzstein completed a task he had promised to do. As he had made the case in *Modern Music* for composers turning toward the working class, now, in three successive installments in the Communist *New Masses,* he defended the other side of the equation.[1] He began "The Case for Modern Music" by outlining the radical impulse in the post-Wagnerian world. This musical revolution was associated with a similar upheaval in architecture, sculpture, painting, and literature, yet it was still in the "art for art's sake" period. He criticized the "overblown war-lord-boss-hero music of Richard Strauss" and such "safe" modernism as *Bolero* and *The Pines of Rome:* "Modernism has here the function of a cosmetic," he fumed. Of the genuinely radical impulse, little survived.

Blitzstein continued on to a general critique of *Gebrauchsmusik.* It stemmed from the working class's demand for an "art that will bring to it a deeper knowledge of itself and of reality, that will show it a possible new reality." But if *Gebrauchsmusik* had direction, it lacked content. Composers wanted to reach the masses but had little idea what to say.

Enter Brecht. And Eisler:

> The composer is now willing, eager, to trade in his sanctified post as Vestal Virgin before the altar of Immutable and Undefilable Art, for the post of an honest workman among workmen, who has a job to do, a job which wonderfully gives other people joy. His music is aimed at the masses; he knows what he wants to say to them. Communication; enjoyment; knowledge; spur.

Now Blitzstein elegantly brought the argument back to modern music. Atonality "has punctured the chromatic myth." He wrote of the inevitable collapse of the tonal structure almost in the same terms one might discuss the last days of the bourgeoisie. Because modern musical technique has been abused by some does not mean that we must abandon it: It belongs to our time and we need only apply it in a revolutionary manner. It banishes "effusiveness, overstatement, windiness. Certain things have arrived: directness, economy, clarity. Music heaves and sweats much less." We must not ignore the moderns and their lessons, as some of our instinctual proletarian composers would today, he added in an unstated jibe at the leftist philistines of the Degeyter Club.

Motty Eitingon, Russian by birth, had made his fortune in Siberian furs. Bess had worked in the theatre, knew Paul Robeson well, and enjoyed hosting members of the Group Theatre at their estate. They were important backers of Kurt Weill's pageant *The Eternal Road.* In fact, during the summer of 1936, Weill was also in Connecticut writing his first American musical, *Johnny Johnson,* about the sad stupidity of the First World War. In a campground in nearby Trumbull, he gave talks to the Group Theatre on music in the theatre, and Blitzstein attended. Despite their wealth, the Eitingons considered themselves socialists. Of an evening, Motty would read *Das Kapital* in its original German and translate for Bess as he went along. Only the year before, they had traveled to the Soviet Union—his first trip back—to be wined and dined in thanks for concluding his latest deal: five million dollars in dearly coveted Western currency in exchange for rare pelts. The Eitingons employed a staff of household help and supplied plentiful, rich meals to their guests. Beginning sometime in July, Blitzstein occupied a huge room with a balcony in a renovated stable on the property.

The composer had little time to socialize with his hosts or with any of the other guests that summer. Once he started working on *The Cradle Will Rock,* he tore into it manically, completing both text and music in five weeks, "at white heat," as he often recalled it. The action of this "play in music," in ten scenes with flashbacks, takes place in Steeltown, U.S.A., on the night of a union drive. The Moll opens the play. Her assignation with a Gent is interrupted by a Dick, who remarks that the whole town is down in front of union headquarters awaiting the results of the election. Because she won't give him free sex in exchange for "protection," he arrests her. At the same time, the members of the superpatriotic, anti-union Liberty Committee are also arrested by an overzealous Cop, over their loud protests, and all of them are hauled to Night Court, the central locale of the play.

In the second scene, the Liberty Committee members try to cover themselves with the mantle of Mr. Mister, the town boss. They include Dr. Specialist, President Prexy, Professor Mamie, Professor Trixie, Reverend Salvation, Editor Daily, Yasha the violinist, and Dauber the painter. Objecting to their arrest, they say they were trying to prevent the union organizer's speech and were not a part of the crowd. The Moll befriends Harry Druggist, who acts as cicerone for the play. He points to himself, arrested for drunken vagrancy, and to all the town notables, each one of whom has sold out to Mr. Mister in one fashion or another.

Harry's first example is Reverend Salvation, which leads into the first flashback, Scene Three, a Mission. The year is 1915 and the good pastor gratefully receives Mrs. Mister's payoff before beginning his sermon. He preaches peace, according to instruction. In 1916 she reappears with another envelope, and another instruction: He needn't be quite so pacifistic. Rather, "You might mention that you do deplore the *German* side of the war!" By the next year, she is practically mad with visions of steel profits going sky-high and, accompanied by her usual contribution, urges total support for war. Rev. Salvation complies enthusiastically and everyone joins in praying:

Make the world safe for Democracy!
Make the world safe for Liberty!
Make the world safe for Steel and the Mister family!

Scene Four is another flashback, Editor Daily's turn. The scene is the lawn of Mr. Mister's home, and we encounter his children, the vacant Junior and the peevish Sister. They sing "Croon Spoon," a takeoff on vapid popular songs that dull the people's consciousness. Mr. Mister and Editor Daily profess their loyalty to the principle of a free press. Then Mr. Mister says he wants an article framing Larry Foreman, the union organizer:

Find out who he drinks with and talks with and sleeps with,
And look up his past till at last you've got it on him.

When Editor Daily says he'll have to consult with the owner of the paper, Mr. Mister informs him that as of that morning he is the new owner himself, and the editor caves in. Daily also agrees to let Junior be the paper's correspondent in Honolulu, to get him out of the way in case Junior should decide that mixing himself in the union drive might be an answer to his boredom.

The next scene tells Harry Druggist's story. He is tending his shop with his son Steve when Bugs enters. The thug threatens him with a clampdown on the mortgage (owned by Mr. Mister, of course) and warns them that the Polish fellow who always comes in this time every week with his wife for an ice cream soda will be caught up in an explosion to occur shortly at union headquarters across the street. Middle-class Harry, afraid for his security, passively agrees to name the dead man as the criminal causing the explosion, but Steve doesn't like the smell of it. Gus and Sadie appear on schedule and sing tenderly of their baby on the way. When they pay and leave, Steve runs after to warn them, and all three are killed in the explosion. That is why Harry has become a drunkard: In his own way, he sold out to Mr. Mister, lost his son, and brought about the deaths of two innocents and their unborn baby.

A quick change of scene brings us to the Hotel Lobby where Yasha the violinist and Dauber the artist meet by chance. To their horror, they discover that they are both competing for Mrs. Mister's patronage this summer, but they find solace in their mutual disgust at the mores of the rich. They perform a vaudeville patter that is patently insulting to Mrs. Mister, who has arrived on the scene, but it is all above her head. She is thrilled with her role as patroness, and especially with Yasha's favor to her: He had the horns of her Pierce Arrow tuned to play the theme from Beethoven's *Egmont* Overture: ta, ta, ta-ta-ta, ta-ta-ta, yoo hoo! In exchange for her largesse, they agree to serve on her husband's Liberty Committee, even without knowing what it stands for.

"Politics?" says Yasha.

"Cora, we're artists!" Dauber answers. They go into their credo:

And we love Art for Art's sake!
It's smart, for Art's sake,
To part, for Art's sake,
With your heart, for Art's sake,
And your mind, for Art's sake—
Be blind, for Art's sake,
And deaf, for Art's sake,
And dumb, for Art's sake,
Until, for Art's sake,
They kill, for Art's sake
All the Art for Art's sake!

At which, the Pierce Arrow horns play the *Egmont* theme and all exit, croaking a unison "Yoo hoo."

Scene Seven brings us back to Night Court, where the Moll sings "Nickel Under the Foot." Her philosophy recalls Brecht's *Dreigroschenoper:* "First feed the face, and then talk right and wrong":

Go stand on someone's neck while you're takin;
Cut into somebody's throat as you put—
For every dream and scheme's
Depending on whether, all through the storm,

You've kept it warm,
The nickel under your foot.

Enter the hero, Larry Foreman, who explains to the Moll that he's been arrested for giving a speech and passing out leaflets. He also has a committee: "farmers and city people, doctors, lawyers, newspapermen, even a couple of poets—and one preacher. We're middle class, we all got property—we also got our eyes open." In the exultant tempo of a May Day marching song, he shares his vision of apotheosis with the Moll, how the cradle of the Liberty Committee will fall from its high perch in the coming unity of all the workers in Steeltown:

That's thunder, that's lightning,
And it's going to surround you!
No wonder those stormbirds
Seem to circle around you!
Well, you can't climb down, and you can't say "No"!
You can't stop the weather, not with all your dough!
For when the wind blows, oh, when the wind blows,
The cradle will rock!

With a mighty fist he explains to the Moll the difference between an open shop and a closed shop, but before he can continue his speechifying, the Clerk calls for order in the courtroom, and the next case is presented: President Prexy of College University and his Professors.

As a trustee of the university, Mr. Mister insists on extending compulsory military training. The students will be useful in strikebreaking, and Prexy is all too willing to help by calling in three professors, candidates for the job of firing up the students. Two are inadequate—one too intellectual, the other a Tolstoyan pacifist. The third, Trixie, football coach and teacher of elementary French, renders a sample of his pep talk. He is ideal:

Listen, fellas!
Military course—two years?
Tree cheers! Listen fellas!
Army training—Port in a storm!
There's nuttin like a uniform!
Soivice stripes—epaulettes—
Silver Shoit maybe—attababy!
Builds you up!—Alma Mater!
Sex Appeal!
Two years! Tree cheers!
Stick your chest out!
Be a man!

The scene segues neatly into Dr. Specialist's office, where Mr. Mister is undergoing examination. He has a case of bad nerves brought on by his union troubles. The doctor thanks Mr. Mister for making him chairman of the Liberty Committee; it has enabled him to land a prestigious research appointment. But of course there is a price to pay. Ella Hammer, the sister of a pro-union worker who got hurt when he was pushed on the job, has appeared in the doctor's anteroom. Mr. Mister wants the doctor to tell the press that Joe Hammer was drunk at the time, and Dr. Specialist does just that. Ella breaks into "Joe Worker," a revised version of Blitzstein's song "Poor People":

Joe Worker gets gypped;
For no good reason, just gypped,
From the start until the finish comes,
They feed him out of garbage cans,
They breed him in the slums!
Joe Worker will go,
To shops where stuff is on show;
He'll look at the meat,
He'll look at the bread,
And too little to eat sort of goes to the head.
One big question inside me cries:
How many fakers, peace undertakers,
Paid strikebreakers,
How many toiling, ailing, dying, piled-up bodies,
Brother, does it take to make you wise?

The tenth scene, back in Night Court, brings everything together. Larry Foreman sums up how the middle class has prostituted itself to Mr. Mister: "This ain't Russia, no—it's Steeltown, U.S.A.!" The middle class is caught between the bosses at the top and the workers coming up. When Mr. Mister finally arrives to set the Liberty Committee free and settle this whole misunderstanding, he tries to bribe Larry Foreman into switching sides. Blitzstein employs a masterful counterpoint here: Mr. Mister and Larry Foreman are discussing this last-minute offer; the Liberty Committee members urge Larry to accept it; Harry Druggist encourages him not to; and the Moll quietly starts up her "Nickel Under the Foot." Larry refuses Mr. Mister's deal. Suddenly, from outside, the sound of the drums, fifes, and voices can be heard: The workers have voted the union in! And the opera ends with a rousing reprise of Larry's marching song, "The Cradle Will Rock." For the moment, Mr. Mister has been stopped.

The play works on a number of different levels. Most prominently, but also most superficially, it is a plea for industrial unionism of the sort the Committee for Industrial Organization had been urging under its leader, John L. Lewis. Founded in November 1935 amid one of the most extensive strike waves in American labor history, the CIO opposed the American Federation of Labor's old division of workers into individual crafts, a form of organization more appropriate to the age of artisans and small factories. But in the modern steel and automobile industries, structured on a mass scale, it made more sense to unite all the workers into a single union for greater bargaining power.

During the first term of Franklin Delano Roosevelt's New Deal, government guaranteed the right of workers to organize, backed up by the National Labor Relations Act. Larry Foreman's campaign reflects this new policy. Private industry, however, would not give up without a struggle: It financed a huge war chest to support private armies of labor spies and strikebreakers to prevent unions from forming. Communists led a number of union efforts in these mass industries. The CIO began organizing the steel industry in May 1936. Not a single worker among the United States Steel Corporation's 220,000 employees belonged to a union at that time. But by February 1, 1937, the Steel Workers Organizing Committee had forced the corporation to sign a collective bargaining contract. "We are not only fighting for the economic emancipation of the millions of Americans who work for a living," said John L. Lewis, chairman of the CIO, "but we are fighting also for their political emancipation, for the right to live in communities free from corporations' domination to a point that limits and circumscribes their political rights and political actions."[2]

On another level, *The Cradle Will Rock* can hardly be considered a direct appeal to the working class. True, it bears many earmarks of agitational propaganda theatre—agitprop—but it is more an appeal and a warning to the middle class to sort out its priorities lest it be stranded on the wrong side of history and humanity. By his very act of writing it, Blitzstein provided an example of a composer, middle class in origin, who was not afraid to say no to Mr. Mister and to the hundreds of civic-minded anti-labor groups around the country that were variously styled as Liberty Leagues, Citizens Alliances, and the like.

Though Blitzstein admired the "scientific" music of an Eisler, for instance, *Cradle* is far from a carbon copy of that approach. It is exuberant, zesty, urbane, optimistic, and funny. Out of the dying vaudeville tradition, he honed a sharp rapier to thrust at his enemy, economic royalism. If Larry Foreman's arrival in Scene Seven and the ultimate union victory smack of melodrama, with strong Romantic and even naïve overtones, it is crucial to recall that on the labor front a riveting drama of good and evil very similar to it was in fact rocking the nation at just that juncture.

In his earliest drafts for *Cradle,* Blitzstein gave certain characters real names—Mr. Morgan and John L. Lewis for the principal antagonists—and he had a pro-union farmer named Sickle to balance out the worker named Hammer. Then, perhaps remembering the problems surrounding Elie Siegmeister's "Biography," he abandoned the excessive specificity of those names, choosing more cartoonlike monikers; no doubt he was influenced by the sketches in *Parade* that gave the players labels rather than names. Like figures in a morality play, they were not intended to be realistic. But he also knew that under the surface, no one exactly fits the stereotype; he did not completely buy the Soviet esthetic of socialist realism, wherein heroes are supermen. On the villain of the piece: "He is so much the archetype of all the Mr. Misters in the world that he resembles the type not at all; is, in fact, rather eccentric, a distinct individual." On the hero: "He's not very good-looking—a humorous face, and an engaging manner. Confidence is there, too; not self-confidence; a kind of knowledge about the way things probably have to work out. It gives him a surprising modesty, and a young poise." Structurally, the play resembles Clifford Odets's *Waiting for Lefty,* the New Theatre League's prize-winning play from the year before, where the central scene of a union meeting also melts into a series of flashbacks that present the characters.

A detailed exegesis could be offered explaining the sources of Blitzstein's thoughts, but a few points will have to suffice. He had studied two pamphlets closely: "Industrial Unionism" and "Organizing Methods in the Steel Industry," published in 1936 by William Z. Foster, national chairman of the Communist Party and the Party's candidate for President in 1924, 1928, and 1932. Blitzstein was probably familiar with statistics from Anna Rochester's classic study of finance capitalism, *Rulers of America,* published in 1936. It showed that steel prices had risen to 240 percent above their prewar average by the end of 1916; and that only four months later, in April 1917, when the United States entered the war, prices had shot to 370 percent above the prewar level. Similar conclusions arose from Senator Gerald Nye's 1934 study of the armaments industry, which confirmed that J. P. Morgan and the Du Pont interests had propelled the country into the war. Blitzstein was aware of recent student protests against forced military training at land-grant colleges, which resulted in the Reserve Officers' Training Corps's being dropped at certain institutions, or made optional. In fact, earlier he had composed a setting of words from an official War Department Manual (volume 7, part 3), which recommended a variety of solutions for crowd control: air power, tear gas, riot guns, hand grenades. He had included it in the Faculty Room Scene in an early draft, then deleted it.

Blitzstein had certainly seen the leaflet episode in Brecht's play *Mother.* The 1934 Soviet film *Maxim's Youth,* with a score by Shostakovich, had included not only its own leaflet scene but another of a worker mashed in a machine, the factory owner claiming intoxication as the cause of the accident. He knew how popular fundamentalists such as Billy Sunday had joined the patriotic cause by preaching Christian hatred of Germany. Blitzstein felt, as did most of the left, that the war had not been about democracy at all, but about competition among the colonial powers to dominate worldwide markets.

The composer would have known of the effort beginning in 1932 to organize druggists into a union; Harry Druggist remarks at one point that he had been invited to join it. This left-wing CIO union later evolved into the powerful National Union of Hospital and Health Care Employees, known as Local 1199. Once again, and not for the last time, the theme of alcohol abuse enters Blitzstein's dramaturgy through the druggist character. He also knew of California labor organizer Tom Mooney—imprisoned since 1916 on a frame-up over an explosion—around whom a powerful movement arose to set him free. The Drugstore scene suggests a parallel to this then still-pending case; Mooney was freed only in 1939.

As far as the bought press is concerned, almost anywhere Blitzstein might have looked, he would have found confirmation of his thesis. Particularly in the one-industry company towns of the midwest, strong-arm tactics to prevent unfavorable news about the principal employer were more often the rule than the exception. The fearless journalist George Seldes made a career out of exposing the sycophancy of the press, as evidenced in his magazine *In Fact* (to which Blitzstein later subscribed) and in books such as *You Can't Print That.*

The composer had already articulated his views on artists who sold their talents to the highest bidder. As he described his own lecture-recital series to one interviewer, "You know the sort of thing—West 86th Street to #1 University Place—dowagers, debutantes and do-littlers. I was a blender of musical pills. But I made money to live that way; and I also learned how to placate vanity—how useful it could be."[3] But in his Hotel Lobby scene, the vaudeville pair of Yasha and Dauber represent something more. In their effete, petulant yearning to be smothered with food and attention by some rich lady patron, Blitzstein can be seen recalling his old childhood game with Jo, the Princess and the Pauper.

If there is additionally a slightly homosexual characterization to these self-styled *artistes,* which in some productions Blitzstein specifically called for, it serves as a cautionary note to his fellow composers, so many of whom were gay—Aaron Copland, David Diamond, Paul Bowles, Colin McPhee, Lehman Engel, and Virgil Thomson. He seemed to be saying, Don't let a sense of inferiority about your homosexuality cloud your class consciousness. Communists, of course, opposed homosexuality as bourgeois decadence, but in those circles Blitzstein kept his personal life private.

He did manage to make his own hostess Bess Eitingon squirm with self-recognition, though in the end her affection for Marc enabled her to distance herself from the Mrs. Mister image. More likely, the kind of patroness Blitzstein had in mind was the Mrs. Harrison Williams type, who acquired a villa in Capri during one of her marriages to a petty aristocrat, and to whom Cole Porter had referred explicitly in a line from his 1936 show *Red, Hot and Blue.* Mrs. Mister is a close cousin to the society lady of "Send for the Militia," a type—the rich woman with largesse to dispense—that would emerge frequently in Blitzstein's work. Inevitably, the image recalls Blitzstein's early experience of begging his grandmother for the money with which to pay for piano lessons.

Musically, *The Cradle Will Rock* bubbles with delight. It is the full apotheosis of everything that as a critic he had been calling for in music, and which no one else but he could create. It is the work Blitzstein must have imagined when he saw the New Theatre League's repeated appeals for fresh material for the stage. In form, it is a type of modern *Singspiel.* Though based on popular rhythms and song structure, it does not pander to these forms: The composer elevates them to a higher sophistication, hoping with his insights into popular culture to raise the musical as well as the political consciousness of his public. In his use of dance tempos, croon numbers, and what might be called an urban folk style, his models are Mozart, Bizet, and Mussorgsky. In his use of satire and parody, he merely updated the social function of an Offenbach or of Gilbert and Sullivan. Of course, the more recent influences of Brecht and Weill and Eisler are much in evidence. In its own way, *Cradle* is a *Lehrstück,* a "teaching-piece" for its audience, and Blitzstein dedicated it appropriately to Brecht.

Most important, this is a thoroughly American work, not just in its theme or in its tunes, but in the way Blitzstein wrote and set to music the speech patterns of a wide gamut of social classes. Never before in an American musical work had a composer rendered such attentive portraits of workingmen and women, cops, drunks, immigrants, and the middle-class petty bourgeoisie. There are no exotic locales, no flamboyant costumes. Gone are the standard heiresses and counts, the love-struck ingenues and the romantic student princes, as well as their melodies derived from Viennese operetta. Blitzstein's prosody, the fitting of words to music, preserving their proper accents both in tunes and in rhythmic declamation, broke all the rules by its idiomatic authenticity. The composer also wanted to avoid a pompous, operatic "placed" tone in his singers, which would probably obliterate his text in the delivery. Instead, he adopted what Brecht called "*Misuk,*" the kind of untrained singing that could be expected from washerwomen and laborers.

The musical also fulfills Eva's prediction following his completion of *The Condemned:* "At some time Blitzstein will write a great comic work in music stemming directly out of this great tragic work." The work is a lightning bolt of genius, born of the complete and timely fusion of a man's talent, his beliefs, and his soul.

A comprehensive musical analysis would take a volume. There are broad jokes, such as the quotation of "Boola Boola" in the Faculty Room scene, and the "Honolulu" song, a send-up of hundreds of musical "South Sea Island Magic" escape fantasies. (Blitzstein was certainly not oblivious to the music industry's part in romanticizing America's takeover of the Hawaiian Islands as part of its turn-of-the-century imperialist grab for territory.) There is the Gus and Sadie love song in the Drugstore scene, redolent of Eastern European Yiddish melody. If his vocal lines sound cheap, Blitzstein dresses them up in pungent harmonies, irregular rhythms, and nonstandard forms. More subtly, as an in-joke only for musicians, he quoted the melody and harmony from Bach's chorale "*Brunnquell aller Güter*" in the Reverend Salvation scene.

And why the *Egmont* quote for Mrs. Mister's Pierce Arrow? Certainly it was to show the debasement of high art under the command of philistines; but also because the character of Egmont, in the Goethe play to which Beethoven wrote incidental music, is a leader of the Protestant Dutch against Spanish Catholic rule during the Reformation. Beethoven's overture evokes the voice of an aroused nation. Thus, Blitzstein places the contemporary fight against America's reactionary elements within the historical continuum of justice-seeking, and reminds us that there have always been musicians who have aligned themselves with conscience. Indeed, Beethoven's only opera *Fidelio* is itself a rescue drama with similar concerns. In the same way that no one today calls *Fidelio* a "dated" work, a listener should be able to extrapolate from the particular union struggle in mid-1930s America to any situation where greed and corruption are lined up against the people's rights.

Blitzstein completed the score on September 2 at Hillcrest. In the fall, he taught his "Music in the Theatre" course on twelve Monday nights at the New School.

But his main project was to get *Cradle* produced. The William Morris Agency had been interested in Blitzstein's earlier material, particularly in "Send for the Militia." Now he played through the new full-length piece, and the agency decided to take him on as a client. He signed his first contract with them on October 1, 1936, appointing the agency sole and exclusive manager for his career in exchange for 10 percent of his profits and royalties. The relationship began happily and would continue so as long as Blitzstein lived.

Undeterred by past failure to win a Guggenheim award, the composer tried still another time for the 1937 round. He added the names of Lee Simonson, stage designer and director, and Herman Shumlin, producer, to his list of references. He was able to cite the first prize awarded that October to *The Cradle Will Rock* in the New Theatre League competition. He proposed creating a new theatre piece about a brother and sister who, after a series of life experiences, arrive at contrasting positions vis-à-vis society and the world: "one will have lost himself in the process, the other will have slowly come to self-realization and organic growth." In appearance, the new piece would resemble musical comedy or revue, but he would expand the relation of words and music beyond the set number format. Already he was thinking past *Cradle.* Slowly, and with many interruptions over the next four years, this new piece, *No for an Answer,* would eventually come to fruition.

Without too much delay, Blitzstein got a commitment from the Actors' Repertory Company to produce *Cradle;* they had produced Irwin Shaw's antiwar play *Bury the Dead* the previous season. For at least two months, he worked on the proposed production, which was to be directed by the twenty-one-year-old firebrand Orson Welles, but by December the company unaccountably got frightened of the material it had originally found so exciting and they handed it back. In any case, they shortly went broke. Other possibilities included the Labor Stage, the New Theatre, the Group Theatre, and the Theatre Guild, as well as several individual producers. But the material was too politically hot for anyone to handle.

Socially conscious theatre could be found all over New York; indeed, in most major cities of the country there existed outposts of the New Theatre League or other independent producing companies. *The Cradle Will Rock* was not alone in offering a radical point of view. In these years, Communist Party membership was at its height, with many times that number of sympathizers. Certainly in New York they formed a sizable core of theatregoing audiences. Arthur Arent's *One Third of a Nation*—about poor housing—played at one of the Federal Theatres. *Professor Mamlock* treated anti-Semitism; *Hymn to the Rising Sun* raised the issue of race discrimination; *Triple-A Plowed Under* discussed the farm question; and *Chalk Dust* addressed the status of public high schools. Clifford Odets had already made his mark with the blindingly effective strike play *Waiting for Lefty.* Lillian Hellman approached the class struggle in *Days to Come.* Other works treating labor issues during this period of real industrial warfare included *Stevedore, Plant in the Sun, Tide Rising, Marching Song,* and *Steel.* Another play, *Altars of Steel* by Thomas Hall-Rogers, treated the exploitative moves of the steel industry into the Deep South. Edna Ferber and George S. Kaufman's play *Stage Door,* which opened in October 1936 and played 169 performances, made an important character out of a radical playwright whose play about a strike has become a smash hit.*

One evening Blitzstein arranged for the authors of several socially conscious plays—people such as George Sklar, Paul Peters, and Albert Maltz—to hear *Cradle* at his apartment. Joseph Viertel, only twenty-one and author of the antimilitarist play *So Proudly We Hail* that had run on Broadway earlier that season, was there. After Blitzstein's performance, Viertel asked, "So how much would it cost?" The composer replied, "It wouldn't cost so much except for the damned Musicians' Union—they want at least twenty-four men in the pit, top Broadway scale, so many weeks' rehearsal, etcetera, etcetera." Blitzstein was well aware of the irony—a union making trouble for a theatre piece about unions!

Viertel returned home to his father, who had grown up in a socialist milieu but who by this time had become a wealthy theatre builder with many high-level contacts. A private performance by Blitzstein followed within days; perhaps a backer had been found at last. When Blitzstein finished, Viertel's father thanked him very much for coming and showed him the door.

Then Viertel asked his father what he thought.

"Are you crazy?" replied the ex-socialist. "This man is trying to kill me!"

Kurt Weill and Paul Green's *Johnny Johnson* opened in November under the auspices of the Group Theatre. Blitzstein telegraphed Weill: WE NEED YOUR SUCCESS IN AMERICA MY HOPES TONIGHT.[4] After all the acerbic attacks Blitzstein had made over the years against Weill, he had the opportunity at the end of 1936 to make amends. Honorable in his recantation, he wrote of Weill, "He hasn't changed, I have." He might have added, so had the world. For now, with the world burning hot with the Spanish crisis, musicians could no longer write in isolation from mass audiences, at least Blitzstein could not. But this philosophy, by now completely ingested, had been Weill's for years.

The "new musical form" Weill offered in *Johnny Johnson* "is needed in the New York theatre as few things are needed in it." Blitzstein meant the transcendance of the traditional Broadway "number" pattern: the music under dialogue, the rhythmic speech, binding sections, and entr'actes. He perceived some triteness, even some "embarrassing" and "sentimental" writing in the score, but in part the responsibility could be Green's, for it is a "soft-spoken" pacifistic play. "The result," sighed the critic, "is a message so gentle, so barely-whispered that it is missed." Lacking is a sense of cause, of direction. "The play misses because of deep confusion in the poet's mind as to just where real sanity such as Johnny displays would lead him." Blitzstein was not wrong about *Johnny Johnson,* though he was comparing it in his own mind to *Cradle,* whose central character knew exactly in what direction he wanted to go.[5]

*The Hollywood movie version bears little resemblance to the Broadway play; Kaufman commented, "They should have called it *Screen* Door."

If the catharsis of writing *Cradle* helped to restore Marc emotionally from the blow of Eva's death, only time and immersion in the theatre world could help Lina Abarbanell. Since her husband's death, she had decided to act no more. By this time, she had begun working as casting director and co-producer for the theatre producer Dwight Deere Wiman. Some of these shows included *On Your Toes, Babes in Arms, I Married an Angel, By Jupiter, Mornings at Seven, The Country Girl,* and *Green Pastures.* Though Marc and Lina chose not to discuss Eva much—what more was there to say?—her death served as a permanent bond: Marc gave her a loyalty at least equivalent to that he owed his own mother. A second heavy blow came to Lina later the same year: On December 8, 1936, her mother died at the age of eighty-one at the Jewish Old Age Home in Berlin. Marie Abarbanell had survived her husband Paul by seventeen years, and she was buried with him in the Jewish Cemetery in Berlin. Fortunately, she did not live any longer to see what would become of her city and country; within a short time, the Gestapo would begin using the Home as a collection point for transporting Jews to Auschwitz and Theresienstadt. Now, with no one left from her own family, Marc was all Lina had. She was out of town at the time, and Marc wrote to her: "There is only one thing to do—and you and I have told ourselves and each other that over and over again. Work."[6]

The American Music League's magazine *Unison* came out that November 1936 with a blistering attack on the leadership of Local 802 of the American Federation of Musicians. The leadership of this AFL-affiliated union had only recently—at the beginning of 1935—taken over from the previous reactionary union bosses in a rank-and-file revolt, and now, according to the AML, the rebels had themselves become corrupted.

Far more eventful developments were occurring in the auto industry. A campaign to organize the largest of the auto manufacturers, General Motors, had been going on for several years, largely under Communist leadership of the United Auto Workers. Finally, on December 30, 1936, workers occupied the Fisher Body Plant No. 1 in Flint, Michigan, and would not leave despite threats from police, courts, and strikebreakers. Wives of the strikers handed blankets and food through an open window at the plant, and the men continued to sit, waiting for GM to sign a contract. Company thugs patrolled the streets. The press screamed for law and order. President Roosevelt urged Governor Frank Murphy to withhold troops and thus avoid a certain bloodbath. For forty-four days the workers held out, until on February 11, 1937, GM finally inked the precious contract recognizing the UAW. Immediately, workers elsewhere in the auto and steel industries adopted the sit-down tactic.

In March, the companies known collectively as Big Steel agreed to unions. But Little Steel—National, Republic, Inland, Bethlehem, and Youngstown Sheet and Tube—led by Republic's Tom Girdler held out against the unions. By now, Roosevelt had perhaps seen enough union victories and he tolerated Girdler's vicious campaign, which had mobilized support from the clergy, police, and all the professional classes. "A plague on both their houses," Roosevelt said. While

The New York Times published a regular column called "Day's Strike Developments," Little Steel was bringing the story of *The Cradle Will Rock* to life. But who would produce it?

Orson Welles, the startlingly talented director of Project 891, one of the WPA's Federal Theatre Project outlets, had been slated to direct *The Cradle Will Rock* for the Actors' Repertory Company. With John Houseman as his producer, Welles had done an all-black voodoo *Macbeth* in Harlem, followed by Eugène Labiche's *Horse Eats Hat* and Christopher Marlowe's *Doctor Faustus.* Project 891's previous commitment had been to classical theatre, hardly to proletarian operas. Now, without any other definite plans for Project 891, Welles revived his thoughts about *Cradle* and had Blitzstein play it through for Houseman. Without a moment's hesitation, Houseman agreed that this was their kind of material, not that either was any kind of radical. They simply perceived the irrepressible theatricality of the work and the timeliness that made it as fresh as that morning's papers. Perhaps Blitzstein recognized a special kind of irony in the fact that the Federal Theatre Project's headquarters was located on Eighth Avenue near Forty-fourth Street in the old Bank of the United States building, one of the many institutions that had folded in late 1930 just when the Blitzstein Bank went under.

For his cast, Welles chose a mix of Federal Theatre actors, some with practically no experience on the stage and others who were more seasoned. Will Geer, who played Mr. Mister, had played an evangelist preacher in the Federal Theatre's production of *Unto Such Glory.* He had also appeared in *Let Freedom Ring* and in *Bury the Dead.* His political views coincided nicely with those of the show: Once, on the West Coast, he had been severely beaten by thugs from a group called Friends of Germany and was hospitalized as a result. Howard da Silva, who portrayed Larry Foreman, had appeared in both classic and modern plays in New York and in his native Cleveland, where he had directed the Federal Theatre's unit until it closed. In Pittsburgh, he had actually worked his way through Carnegie Tech in a local steel mill. He had acted in the original production of *Waiting for Lefty,* and until now had been employed in a Federal Theatre radio series called "Labor on the March." Hiram Sherman, who specialized in comic parts, was an old boyhood friend of Welles. He played Junior Mister and Professor Scoot. For the role of Harry Druggist, Welles chose John Adair, whom Will Geer remembered as a "rather reactionary young man." Adair supposedly mused about the show, "Oh, if they'd just change this book, what a wonderful Shubert musical it'd make. It's the words that's the trouble. The music is great."[7]

Peggy Coudray had played soubrette roles in musicals and operettas on Broadway. Critics had appreciated her adroit sense of comedy, and she now applied it to her zany but savage characterization of Mrs. Mister. Welles had found Olive Stanton for the Moll. Looking for all the world like a plain working girl, she had never appeared on Broadway before, but her tender, weary voice that still retained the mettle of a survivor fit the role perfectly.

Rehearsals began in March and involved a large cast of solo performers and forty-four members of a mixed black and white chorus, one of whom, a black dancer and choreographer named Clarence Yates, taught the dance steps to the company. Blitzstein himself went on the WPA payroll, receiving the same wage as everyone else—$23.86 a week. They planned a daring May Day opening.

News began to spread. Mrs. Murray Crane, a prominent socialite, invited Blitzstein to play the work at a private soirée in her Fifth Avenue apartment. He gave her an advance sample, making sure to include the Yasha and Dauber scene where they join singing, "Oh, there's something so damned low about the rich!"

Mrs. Crane suggested, "Couldn't you have a violinist play it, instead of a pianist?"

"But why?" Blitzstein asked.

"So that you wouldn't have to use any lyrics!"

So instead of *The Cradle Will Rock,* Mrs. Crane's guests heard Blitzstein play through his score for *Cain,* and he received seventy-five dollars for his efforts.

"Hallie Flanagan has at last heard the *Cradle,*" Blitzstein wrote to his father and Maddie on March 3. He was referring to the head of the Federal Theatre Project, who was increasingly under attack by know-nothing congressmen for the range and sharpness of some of the project's productions around the country. Martin Dies and his House Committee on Un-American Activities were especially critical of what they perceived as outrageous left-wing stances taken within a welfare system for artists that they had ideological problems accepting in the first place. One congressman asked with somber deliberation whether Christopher Marlowe, author of *Doctor Faustus,* was a Communist. Drastic cuts in the program appeared inevitable. "She's crazy for it," Marc wrote home about Hallie Flanagan,

> says its [*sic*] the biggest best etcetc—and is also terrified about it for the Project. So she'll take no responsibility, but is having us—I, John Houseman and Orson Welles—fly down to Washington to show the work to Harry Hopkins. Sometime soon, in a couple of days. I am very skeptical all over again. I've apparently turned out a firebrand that nobody wants to touch.[8]

The more they rehearsed the show, the less sure it looked. Houseman privately began to seek outside backing for an independent production should the WPA fall through. "At last," Blitzstein wrote to his sister Jo,

> the play is on. Definite this time, Houseman and Welles say—but where have I heard that one before? Anyway, I'm orchestrating and rehearsals start Monday. Probable opening May 15, Maxine Elliott Theatre.[9]

From the middle of April, orchestra rehearsals began under conductor Lehman Engel, five hours a day, five days a week. It was certainly a lot of preparation for two dozen players, but in a way, that was the point: The Federal Theatre and the entire WPA existed to give people work.

Though he gave the credit to Edward Schruers so as not to look too self-centered, Orson Welles himself designed a heavy, elaborate production with roll-on illuminated glass-bottomed wagons transporting the sets for each scene. In Scene 4, Junior Mister and Sister Mister would do their number in swinging hammocks. For the explosion at union headquarters ending the Drugstore scene, Abe Feder, the lighting man, would have a powerful searchlight turned directly onto the audience, as if to implicate the public in the action. At the moment when Larry Foreman leads the cast in the final strophe of the title song, the whole stage was to rock back and forth. But Welles kept changing his concept from day to day, which resulted in delays. Still, continued postponements of the opening posed no serious problem. Scheduled to alternate in repertory with *Doctor Faustus, Cradle* could easily open later and the other play would fill in the time gap.

At the same time that spring, Weill's Jewish pageant, *The Eternal Road,* played at the Manhattan Opera House, closing in May after 153 performances and leaving its producer, Meyer Weisgal, with a half-million-dollar debt. Aaron Copland's opera written for high school students, *The Second Hurricane,* also went into rehearsal for a Henry Street Settlement production. Lehman Engel served as the music director, and Orson Welles was to direct. This, too, may have resulted in delays on *Cradle,* but in the end, Welles more or less deserted Copland to ready the Blitzstein, and Hiram Sherman effectively staged *Hurricane. Hurricane* played a limited number of performances in April, and many critics found it dull, a "valuable contribution" to the high school musical literature. It received a radio broadcast, and went on to an unspectacular future of few and far-between performances.

That May Day of 1937, the left marched for Spain, for China, for unionism and more jobs. Among the main slogans was "No WPA cuts!" Later that month, actors playing at the Nora Bayes Theatre on West Forty-fourth Street protested the forthcoming cutbacks by staging their own sit-down strike following a performance. Pickets and demonstrators supported them outside the theatre, while inside the audience joined the actors by staying all night. On May 27, seven thousand out of the nine thousand employees in the New York arts projects of the WPA participated in a work stoppage; some joined a New York–Washington march to forestall the cuts. Members of *Cradle*'s Project 891 joined the actions. Howard da Silva, Will Geer, and Blitzstein, along with other cast members, passed out protest fliers; the composer encouraged da Silva to go into his leaflets routine from the show:

Ain't you ever seen my act?
Well, I'm creepin along in the dark;
My eyes is crafty, my pockets is bulging!
I'm loaded, armed to the teeth—with leaflets.
And am I quick on the draw!
I come up to you—very slow—very snaky;
And with one fell gesture—
I tuck a leaflet in your hand.
And then, one, two, three—

There's a riot. You're the riot.
I incited you—I'm terrific, I am!

Virgil Thomson visited the Maxine Elliott several times to investigate Blitzstein's opera. He couldn't wait until fall to write up his impressions, and so he went into print in the May–June issue of *Modern Music* with his enthusiastic forecast. The libretto, he wrote, is "dramatically effective and verbally bright," while the "musical declamation is the season's best so far, and the orchestral accompaniment is of a rare finesse. . . . I predict a genuine success. The opera has passion and elegance."[10] To spur interest, Minna Lederman also published three scenic sketches for *Cradle* by Edward Schruers.

Blitzstein's photo appeared on the front page of the summer issue of *Unison,* which printed a lead article on the forthcoming premiere of *Cradle.* Blitzstein was "not so keen on the audience which attends the top-hat operas," Unison reported. He compared the new audience for his music to the seventeenth- and eighteenth-century audiences of bourgeois listeners, freshly exposed to music extricated from church or court patronage. Then, in the nineteenth century, Beethoven's *Choral* Symphony and Wagner's *Meistersinger* once again created new audiences for music. "And contrary to the usual notion, one doesn't have to write down to its level," said the composer. "The demands of this new audience, let me emphasize, are at least as stringent as the most artistic audience." *Unison* urged its readers to purchase tickets for the opening night of *Cradle,* sponsored by the Downtown Music School.[11]

Blitzstein's opera, the hoped-for magnum opus of American proletarian music, was only one sign of the flowering of the movement. By the summer of 1937, the American Music League had expanded to twenty-seven affiliated organizations. Concerts had been given for the Spanish Loyalists and for the antiwar cause. New music had been published and had sold thousands of copies—including "Spain Marches" and Maurice Sugar's topical "Sit Down." Courses had been added to the Downtown Music School catalogue, and the school now offered a scholarship to each of the AML member organizations. The Manhattan Chorus had just released seven American labor songs on Timely Records. And Tamiris and her dance company were now appearing at the WPA theatres in the AML's *Negro Songs of Protest.*

In Spain, Franco's German supporters had bombed the medieval Basque capital of Guernica in April. The attack on a militarily useless target probably did as much as anything else to waken world consciousness to the destructive energies of fascism; and yet the United States held firm in its purported neutrality, which prevented aid from reaching the Loyalists.

Domestically, in South Chicago, a confrontation between the police and striking pickets at Republic Steel that Memorial Day concluded with a bloody massacre. Eighty-four were hurt and ten killed. Of the ten strikers mowed down by the police, seven had been shot in the back.

In the wake of this newest episode of labor strife, Blitzstein feared the worst for his opera. "Lots of troubles," he wrote to Jo on June 2. "Mrs. F[lanagan] is getting scared all over again—I suspect the *Cradle* will be suppressed before it opens—nothing definite yet." Only a few days later, things looked better: "First round won—Flanagan brought people from Washington to a run-thru—they are crazy for it, approved it unreservedly—we open June 16—unless something else pops—and the situation is such that anything may pop."[12]

The houseboard announcing the new show went up on West Thirty-ninth Street at Project 891's Maxine Elliott Theatre. Was it an honest mistake or was it some sign painter's wisecrack that told the world about "Lightning by Feder"? In the meantime, some eighteen thousand advance tickets had been sold, mostly to benefit the Downtown Music School and some thirty other leftist causes.

On June 10 the long-anticipated word came forth from Washington: a 30 percent cut in Federal Theatre personnel in New York. Seventeen hundred workers were to be fired. Pickets immediately went up around the theatres. Furthermore, the WPA ordered, no new openings could take place before July 1. *The Cradle Will Rock* was not the only show scheduled to open before that date—a *Carmen* was slated to open, and did, at Newark's Mosque Theatre on June 18, and *Tales of Hoffman* premiered at the Theatre of Music on June 22. But inevitably everyone saw the blow primarily directed at *Cradle*. Immediately the cry of "Censorship!" went up.

Welles flew to Washington to meet with Harry L. Hopkins, head of the WPA, whose secretary told Welles, "It is my job to see that you do not see Mr. Hopkins." He met instead with David Niles, head of the WPA's Information Department; however, Niles remained powerless in the matter.

The final rehearsal performance was scheduled for June 15. Afraid that an official opening would never take place, Blitzstein and the producers made sure that everyone who was anyone in the New York music and theatre worlds would be at the Maxine Elliott that night; for it might be their last chance to see *The Cradle Will Rock* in its originally conceived form. The evening did not go especially well. The performers had been thoroughly rehearsed, but Welles's glass wagons rolled on clumsily and the cast got nervous. The play only picked up on Larry Foreman's entrance in Scene Seven, and then rose to its stirring climax.

The next morning, Federal Theatre press agents got on the phone to announce to the press and to groups with advance tickets that the show was canceled. Simultaneously, however, from her office in the theatre, Houseman's secretary called the same newspapers and organizations to say that the show would definitely go on, somewhere, and to wait for further notice. Armed guards stood at the doors to the Maxine Elliott to ensure that no one removed Federal Theatre property—sets, props, costumes, scores. Howard da Silva, already balding, used a blond toupee in the show. When he tried to leave the theatre wearing it, an alert guard lifted it off his scalp and reclaimed it.[13]

During the day, Actors' Equity apprised Welles and Houseman of its position (later proved mistaken): that the performers could not, while in the employ of the Federal Theatre, appear on any other stage that Houseman and Welles might find. But if the actors could not appear *on* the stage, nothing could prevent them from entering the theatre, taking seats, and performing their parts from the interior of the house. This is what Houseman and Welles proposed to them, not knowing how many, if any at all, would be prepared to argue this neat technicality before Actors' Equity, and possibly lose their Federal Theatre jobs. In addition, Local 802 of the musicians' union, an AFL organization hostile to the tactics of the CIO so loudly promoted in the *The Cradle Will Rock,* declared that as an "operatic" work, *Cradle* would require additional musicians if it played a Broadway house, and the producers would have to pay Broadway scale. Clearly, the orchestra would have to go home; the work could go on with just Blitzstein at the piano.

If the show could proceed without sets, without costumes, without lights, without an orchestra, and likely as not without a cast, the one thing the show couldn't do without was a piano. The project's technical assistant, Jean Rosenthal, borrowed a battered upright instrument from somewhere and got it into a passing truck. On Houseman's orders, she handed the driver five dollars and told him to keep driving around the block. Every few minutes, she called Houseman for further instructions.

News reporters started gathering outside the Maxine Elliott late in the afternoon. Joining them now were hundreds of ticketholders. To quiet their impatience, Hiram Sherman and Will Geer went before them and sang some of the songs from the show to whet the public appetite. All through the day, Houseman assured the press and the public that the show would go on. But where?

As one theatre after another was found unavailable or unsuitable, deep despair descended over the scene in the basement powder room where Project 891's management held out. Finally, close to eight o'clock, the theatre broker whose earlier tries at finding a house had failed got up to leave. For hours since his last failure, he had been timidly begging to be heard, but he was ignored in the crisis. It seems that all along he had been offering the Venice Theatre on Seventh Avenue between Fifty-eighth and Fifty-ninth streets. Why wouldn't it do?

In an instant, the one-hundred-dollar rental fee lay in his hands. As the legend goes, it was raised from the press corps hungrily awaiting the next act of this unbelievable but all too real drama. Yes, the Venice would do just fine!

With 1,742 seats, the Venice could hold more than twice the audience the Elliott could, and word spread quickly among the friends of the Downtown Music School to invite more friends up to the new theatre. By subway, private car, and taxi, people traveled the twenty blocks north to the Venice. But mostly they went on foot, a whole audience marching uptown on a warm late-spring night, gathering more people along the way to be a part of the excitement.

When Jean Rosenthal called about the piano, Houseman directed her to West Fifty-eighth Street. The truck arrived at the Venice, and firemen from the neighboring fire station hoisted the piano up to the stage. Just then a better piano came along, another upright, either from a friend of Houseman or from Blitzstein's landlady—both stories have been reported. The composer promptly had its front ripped off so that it would produce more tone in such a large house.

The Venice had seen better times. Lighting man Abe Feder discovered a single working spotlight in the house. The theatre's principal activity was a weekly

Italian variety show. Stage rear, a huge backdrop depicted the Bay of Naples in gaudy colors, with Mount Vesuvius smoking off to one side. Over the edge of a box hung an Italian fascist flag. Someone ripped it down and the audience cheered.

By ten of nine, every seat was filled. Newspaper reporters and cameramen lined the aisles. There was nothing left to do but begin. No one knew what might happen. Maybe Marc, in his shirtsleeves and suspenders, sweating in the light of the single spotlight, would simply play through *The Cradle Will Rock* and sing all the parts himself, just as he had done hundreds of times at backers' auditions and rehearsals.

Houseman opened with a welcoming speech tracing the history of the production. Orson Welles identified the characters and described the missing elements of his staging. Then he introduced Marc Blitzstein and the curtain rose.

Blitzstein began with the Moll's streetcorner song. He got through the first two or three lines. And then, in John Houseman's recollection:

> hearing the words taken out of his mouth, Marc paused, and at that moment the spotlight moved off the stage, past the proscenium arch into the house, and came to rest on the lower left box where a thin girl in a green dress with dyed red hair was standing, glassy-eyed, stiff with fear, only half audible at first in the huge theatre but gathering strength with every note:
>
> *For two days out of seven*
> *Two dollar bills I'm given . . .*
>
> It was almost impossible, at this distance in time, to convey the throat-catching, sickeningly exciting quality of that moment or to describe the emotions of gratitude and love with which we saw and heard that slim green figure. Years later, Hiram Sherman wrote to me: "If Olive Stanton had not risen on cue in the box, I doubt if the rest of us would have had the courage to stand up and carry on. But once that thin, incredibly clear voice came out, we all fell in line." On technical grounds alone, it must have taken almost superhuman courage for an inexperienced performer . . . to stand up before two thousand people, in an ill-placed and terribly exposed location, and start a show with a difficult song to the accompaniment of a piano that was more than fifty feet away. Add to this that she was a relief worker, wholly dependent on her weekly WPA check, and that she held no political views whatsoever.
>
> *So I'm just searchin' along the street,*
> *For on those five days it's nice to eat.*
> *Jesus, Jesus, who said let's eat?*
>
> That was the end of her song. A flash-bulb went off. The audience began to clap—not sure what they were applauding—the girl, the song, Marc or the occasion.[14]

From then on, those performers who had come to the Venice that night—and it turned out most of them had, including the chorus—rose on cue, wherever they found themselves seated in the house. Duets took place across thirty rows of seats, ensemble scenes involved actors in every area of the theatre. Neither the conservative John Adair, the Druggist, nor Edward Hemmer, the Reverend Salvation, showed up. Hiram Sherman filled in for Reverend Salvation, and Blitzstein himself sang eight other roles that night. And from time to time, his piano was joined by the one instrumentalist who showed up, the accordion player, who played along when he thought it would help. He had not allowed the musicians' union to intimidate him from showing up. As if the performance didn't already resemble a circus, Blitzstein ate peanuts all night!

When it was over, pandemonium broke out. New York had never seen such a night of sheer theatrical defiance. Eventually, Welles quieted the audience down. Dressed nattily in a Palm Beach suit, Archibald MacLeish informed the people that they had just shared in the creation of a historic event, which once and for all had broken down the creaky barrier between audience and stage. He may well have been right, but anyone who was at the Venice Theatre on the night of June 16, 1937, did not need a white-suited expert to tell them what they had just experienced.

The next morning, news of the sensational, daring break from the Federal Theatre appeared on front pages of newspapers around the country. Unquestionably, *Cradle* was a work of searing audacity. But there is also no question that by refusing it a home, the Federal Theatre did the work the greatest favor possible. Whereas the play might have occupied the Maxine Elliott stage for a few weeks or even a few months and then died a natural death, now, overnight, it became an established masterpiece. If anything, the simplified staging, with only piano accompaniment, lent it the spark of spontaneity some viewers felt it lacked in its more cumbersome orchestration. More than fifty years later, *Cradle* still rocks—in part because of its native indestructibility, and in part because of its fabled history.

On the following night, the house remained dark, although the American Labor Party had purchased 360 seats and the International Workers Order had another 150: Welles and MacLeish had flown to Washington to plead with the WPA to allow *Cradle* to proceed. They were refused. But as Project 891 had merely leased the rights to *Cradle* from the New Theatre League, there was no legal obstacle to their launching a commercial production. Herman Shumlin, Lincoln Kirstein and his sister Mina Curtiss, Gifford Cochran, Bess Eitingon, and Arthur Garfield Hays came in as principal backers. Helen Deutsch, press agent for the Theatre Guild, posted $1,525 with Actors' Equity to pay initiation fees for several new members and to guarantee the performers' salaries for two weeks—nineteen of the cast obtained a two-week leave of absence from the Federal Theatre. Equity actors would now receive forty dollars a week, almost twice their WPA wage. As a performer himself, Blitzstein had to join Equity and Local 802 of the musicians' union and, as author, the Dramatists' Guild, which he did, all on the same day. With all his sudden notoriety, Blitzstein began keeping a scrapbook of articles sent in by a professional clipping service. Typically, many newspapers managed to misspell his name again; One AP story reprinted in dozens of papers around the country had it as "Marc Elitzstein."

Houseman immediately ordered a fresh publicity campaign for the show at the Venice; handbills and postcards advertised *Cradle* as "a musical satire." He raised ticket prices from the WPA's top of 55 cents to $1.10, with WPA workers permitted in for 25 cents. A special midnight performance took place on Thursday the twenty-fourth to enable Broadway actors to see the show.

On the historic night of June 16, the Venice was not the only place for protests against WPA cutbacks. At the Lafayette Theatre in Harlem, hundreds of people staged a sit-down strike following a performance of *The Case of Philip Lawrence;* and at the Federal Music Theatre on West Fifty-fourth Street, 250 musicians and their sympathizers refused to budge from the auditorium after a Brahms chamber music concert. Within the next couple of days there was also an all-night sit-down strike for the WPA Music Project, in which a hundred students and thirty instructors took part. The City Projects Council, the WPA workers' organization, planned a mass demonstration in front of WPA headquarters at 70 Columbus Avenue, and it was contemplating a general strike by all 180,000 WPA workers in the city. At the same time, a CIO-led strike of marine workers had closed five of the largest shipyards; and in Ohio, Governor Davey had requested federal intervention in a steel strike. John L. Lewis planned to lead thousands of CIO members on a march to the site of Chicago's Memorial Day massacre for a service of remembrance and protest.

Only two hundred or so attended *Cradle* on June 18—Section 18 of the Communist Party, which had purchased its block of seats in advance. If large audiences did not fill the house, especially readers of the *Daily Worker,* it may be because they had read Charles E. Dexter's unenthusiastic comments. Having been present at Tuesday's dress rehearsal, he wrote, "I want to go on record with the statement that the words are superior to the music and the production, rough as it was in the dress rehearsal, superior to both."[15]

At the Maxine Elliott, box-office staff told callers that there was no production anywhere of *The Cradle Will Rock,* and they would not refund any ticket monies. The WPA, meantime, had lost no time in removing the sets from the premises. They were unceremoniously scrapped, to ensure that they would not be used in any of its theatres.

The actors continued to sit in the audience throughout the two-week run at the Venice, though Welles had taken care to position them in the most theatrically effective spots. Audiences gradually built, and sometimes, encouraged by Orson Welles to join in the fun, participated in the show in unexpected ways. *Time* magazine's June 28 issue may have helped, with its claim that Blitzstein's music was so good it was no wonder that Arnold Schoenberg had regarded him as "his most talented U.S. pupil." By the end of the run, standees crammed in to see it, and the producers scheduled an extra matinee. On Sunday evening the twenty-seventh, WEVD—named for the Socialist Eugene Victor Debs—broadcast *Cradle* at 8:30. Rudy Vallee attended one performance and took three songs from the show, promising to sing them on his radio hour.

The last performance took place on July 1. The Federal Theatre performers who had been granted a two-week leave of absence would have to give up *Cradle* if they wished to return to their regular jobs. In the meantime, though the runaway opera had been in the newspapers almost daily and more than thirteen thousand people had seen its fourteen performances, not a single theatre or music critic formally reviewed the show. Blitzstein somehow hoped that the Federal Theatre would resume its commitment to the work, but the WPA turned it down within the week.[16]

In the weeks following the closing, Houseman announced that *The Cradle Will Rock* would follow the course laid out by other labor shows. It toured the steel districts of Pennsylvania and Ohio. As some of the performers would have to be replaced, casting preference went to those recently dismissed by the WPA, thus enabling them to return to the commercial theatre, as the WPA had always predicated. Interviewed in the *Daily Worker,* Blitzstein said, "I can't regard this work purely from the viewpoint of an artist—I believe firmly in what the play stands for and an audience of steelworkers represents a new public, wide-awake and extremely critical." On one occasion, in an amusement park near Bethlehem, Pennsylvania, no one showed up in the outdoor auditorium where *Cradle* was booked. It turned out the workers were all in the factories working. Will Geer managed to locate a sizable group of Baptists out for a picnic and to cajole them into the theatre, but as soon as the Moll made her first entrance and the audience got the drift of the scene, they stood up as one and instantly departed.

The sudden, traumatic death of George Gershwin on July 11, 1937, ended the career of one of America's greatest amalgamators of classical and popular music. No one would ever replace him. Yet the emergence in 1937 of new operas by Copland and Blitzstein signified that composers working in the classical/popular vein had a future. The Communist writer Max Margulis, in an article called "A New Prospect for Modern American Music," compared the two: "In the long run, *The Second Hurricane* may be judged to possess the profounder artistry, but definitely *The Cradle Will Rock* will rank as the artistic document of our day by day history."[17] The first half of his assessment is debatable; the second half cannot be denied.

PART Two

8

TUNES FOR THE PEOPLE

Summer 1937–Winter 1938

"A song is made for somebody, somewhere, some place.
You don't just write a tune into an empty space!"

Shortly after the Spanish Civil War broke out—just as Blitzstein was writing *The Cradle Will Rock*—a group of literary figures came together to form Contemporary Historians, Inc., in order to produce a documentary film about Spain. The company included Lillian Hellman, Archibald MacLeish, Herman Shumlin, Dorothy Parker, and others. They produced a script and raised an initial three thousand dollars for the radical documentary filmmaker Joris Ivens to begin shooting. When Ivens arrived in Spain, he found wartime conditions unsuitable for setting up a neat scenario, and he utterly changed the plans, enlisting the support and participation of both John Dos Passos and Ernest Hemingway. The latter eventually wrote a terse, poetic script for the sound track.

Ivens settled in the village of Fuentidueña de Tajo, twenty-five miles from the Jarama River. On the main road from Madrid to Valencia, where the Loyalist government had relocated, Fuentidueña was vital to the defense of Madrid. Ivens began filming in January 1937 and returned to New York that May. The film, *The Spanish Earth,* draws clear lines between the German and Italian support to Franco's fascist rebellion on one side, and on the other, the Loyalist government and especially the people who have undergone centuries of exploitation.

Scenes of war, bombing raids and their senseless destructiveness, dead and wounded in the streets and at the front, faces caught in moments of panic, anger, and despair comprise the majority of the footage.

Other scenes develop the story of an attempt to install an irrigation system using waters from the Tagus. The importance of this project was severalfold: It would help feed the populace from these fields recently expropriated from the gentry, and it would help provision the men at the front and the people of Madrid in their defense of the city.

A young soldier from the village, Julián, is brought in to show the tie between the people and the war. Handsome and virile, he is one of those figures always so touching in war, just reaching the age of manhood, made mature by the trial of war itself. Shots of Loyalist government leaders in Valencia addressing the assembled parliamentarians are respectful enough, but they contrast to the more heroic activities of the peasants on the soil and the men of the Fifth Regiment. People are also seen in everyday situations—reading the news, getting shaved, waiting in line for food—and caring for art objects destroyed or endangered by fascist bombs.

Ivens intended to make a film to be used above all to raise money for ambulances and medical supplies. He was less concerned about the artfulness of the finished product. Time and the intense conditions of war prevented a more studied approach. He felt the film might also alert the viewing public to the fact that Spain represented a real test of fascism and its weapons. Even Hemingway had held a romantic image of Spain before going there and witnessing under fire just how the political forces lined up. Perhaps the film would turn the democratic governments' policies away from the nonintervention they stubbornly maintained in the face of mounting gains by Hitler, Mussolini, and Franco. In the end, the film presented little hard information—which displeased some critics, including Hellman herself and viewers of later generations—but it served to galvanize issues and attitudes at the time. Everywhere it was shown, it inspired contributions to aid the fight against Franco—from loose pocket change to thousand-dollar checks from Hollywood actors and producers.

Irving Reis, master sound engineer for CBS radio, worked on the sound track, electronically duplicating the sounds of war. He took earthquake noises from the film *San Francisco* and ran them backward to create the desired effects. In the first version of the film, Orson Welles read Hemingway's narrative. When early viewers found his correct, rotund voice somehow disengaged from the terrible events on the screen, the filmmakers replaced him with Hemingway reading his own script.

By June of 1937 the film was ready to be scored. But as there was neither time nor money for original music, the producers engaged Blitzstein and Virgil Thomson for a different kind of job. At night Blitzstein played piano in *Cradle* at the Venice Theatre, and during the day he worked with Thomson to create a musical montage as the background for the film. They culled through dozens of records Ivens had brought back with him from Spain, and through the folklore collections of Gerald Murphy and Paul Bowles. Some forty selections found their way into the film. Many types of Spanish music are represented, from flamenco to choral pieces performed by miners. In the absence of dialogue, the music arrangers, helped by Helen van Dongen's careful editing, produced moments of telling commentary on the mood and action on the screen.

In *The Spanish Earth,* even without employing his own music—perhaps even because it was not his own—Blitzstein learned much from Ivens that would later be put to good use: about the building of a scene, particularly the rise of tension, the drawing back from it, and then the climax and its aftermath. In one particularly effective scene, three warning voices call out *"Aviación!"* during a bombing raid.

The suffering faces peering into the camera reflect the same agony Picasso captured in his painting *Guernica.* But there is an understated eroticism to the film as well. The final shot is of an unshaven and strikingly beautiful man aiming a rifle as the narrator speaks: "The men who never fought before, who were not trained in arms, who only wanted work and food, fight on."

Ivens, Hemingway, and Martha Gellhorn received an invitation to dinner at the White House upon completion of the film. President and Mrs. Roosevelt, joined by their son Jimmy, two military advisors, and one or two others, were the company. Conversation revolved around the experiences of the film crew during the shooting. Afterward at the screening, to which about thirty others were invited, including Harry Hopkins, Roosevelt inquired about the comparative stamina of French and Russian tanks, but he was not moved enough to reevaluate his neutrality stand. Eleanor Roosevelt wrote about the film in her newspaper column, stating that viewers in America might be insufficiently familiar with landholding patterns in the Old World to be educated by what they had seen on the screen.

The Spanish Earth had its official premiere at the 55th Street Playhouse in New York on the twentieth of August, 1937. Reviews ran the gamut from praise to condemnation, mostly on the basis of its value as propaganda. Some critics would have preferred more "objectivity," a presentation of both sides of the war more evenly. The stark foreboding shocked reviewers unfamiliar with documentary technique and used to glamour and tinsel. Howard Barnes wrote in the *Herald Tribune* the following day that it was "the most powerful and moving documentary film ever screened," citing its "brilliant musical accompaniment" and "compelling artistry." The *New York Times* reviewer, clearly sympathetic with the struggle, wrote that "the Spanish people are fighting, not for broad principles of Muscovite Marxism, but for the right to the productivity of a land denied them through years of absentee landlordship." He claimed that the film was visually more effective than Hemingway's "bitter and unreasoning" narrative. The *Daily Worker,* failing to mention Thomson, further enlarged Blitzstein's contribution by saying he had "written the musical score."[1] (Peter Ellis in *New Masses* corrected this misstatement in his review, which also covered Lillian Hellman's class-conscious film *Dead End*.)

Modern Music delayed its review for almost a year. In his survey of "the Hollywood Front," a somewhat misplaced locale for this film, George Antheil saw the "anti-Hollywood" film as "remarkable" in its rejection of literal underscoring. Nonetheless, contrary to many favorable opinions he had heard and read about the music, he found that the "score does not build. It is not really dramatic . . . it does not play either for or against any specific ideas; it merely strings along" without plan.[2]

In Pennsylvania, *The Spanish Earth* could not be shown until December because of a ruling by the state's Board of Motion Picture Censors banning the film as "Loyalist propaganda," thus outstepping by far its mandate to prevent affronts to public morality. But once it was cleared, Marc's family took prints of the film to countless fundraising meetings; his "grandfather" Dr. Leof was chairman of the Philadelphia chapter of the Medical Bureau and North American Committee to Aid Spanish Democracy and Maddie served as its secretary-treasurer. Jo worked for the group from her home in Ventnor. Marc himself was listed on the Musicians' Committee.*

In the wake of his newfound fame after *Cradle*, Blitzstein signed a contract in mid-August 1937 to write a half-hour work for a CBS radio broadcast in October. The song-play Blitzstein was to write—the first in its genre for radio—could feature a chorus of not more than twelve voices, a cast of not more than nine principals, and an orchestra of not more than twenty-four pieces. For this commission he received $500, with an additional $150 for repeat performances. Before finishing the score, he scheduled another move, to 496 Hudson Street.

I've Got the Tune represents one contribution to a series of commissions by the Columbia Broadcasting Corporation for original scores by contemporary composers. Others in this group included Walter Piston's Concertino for Piano and Orchestra, Roy Harris's *Time* Suite, and Copland's *Music for Radio;* additional works came from William Grant Still, Howard Hanson, and Louis Gruenberg, whose opera *Green Mansions* premiered on radio just a week before Blitzstein's. Few of those composers showed as specific an appreciation for the medium as Blitzstein, perhaps the one quality of the work on which all commentators agreed. Most composers conceived the broadcast opportunity in traditional concert-hall terms.

The idea of a song-play on radio suggested further application: Something along these lines could be "marketed to the movies," Blitzstein wrote in a note to himself. In a publicity article printed a few days before the October 24 air date, Blitzstein referred to the integration of music and drama, citing the examples of *Johnny Johnson* and the work of Hanns Eisler. Wishfully, the composer remarked that unlike the usual practice of throwing in music at the last minute to support weak spots in the film, music could be in on a film from the start—a far cry from his recent experience with *The Spanish Earth.* In any case, what he and Columbia's studio director Irving Reis had in mind was music, combined with sound

*Another documentary production group, Frontier Films, made a film in 1937 called *Heart of Spain*, which was about the career of the Canadian physician Norman Bethune. Paul Strand and Leo Hurwitz worked on it. Frontier's project *China Strikes Back* (1939) involved Jay Leyda, Irving Lerner, Sidney Meyers, and Ben Maddow. Within a short time, Blitzstein would be working with these men on an even larger film.

effects, that tells a story and that exists not just to show off the tenor's high notes. Blitzstein may have been aware of Bertolt Brecht's pleas a decade before for the use of radio as a means of reaching the masses, indeed, as a replacement for the bourgeois theatre. In any case, capitalizing on his notoriety from *Cradle,* Blitzstein quipped that until three years before, he enjoyed the distinction of being the most famous "unperformed" American composer, a claim he had now enlarged by becoming the "forbidden" composer.[3]

I've Got the Tune is intensely autobiographical, as the title implies. Blitzstein relates in five scenes the odyssey of a composer, Mr. Musiker, who has a melody without words. He is looking for the right application of his talents. Musiker has a sidekick in the form of a secretary, Beetzie, whose function is to jot down the words offered to his song. The relationship resembles Don Quixote and Sancho Panza, Beetzie representing both the inanity and brutalization of the working class and at the same time its honest pragmatism and common sense. In no way an intellectual companion for Musiker, she is without a hint of physical attraction. She serves mostly to allow the story to proceed in dialogue form rather than in the composer's first-person narration.

In Scene One we are given the basic problem of the play and introduced to the two main characters, Beetzie describing herself as "the short-hand speed queen." She is proud of her competency: "Dictation is my line, Dictation's where I shine," she sings in a comment Blitzstein may have used to indicate her class position and weak political ideas. Unexpectedly, her vocal line is highly irregular, not at all "proletarian," recalling the modernism of *Triple-Sec* and illustrating the composer's thesis that the working class is ready to hear the combination of advanced musical technique and an advanced political point of view. Musiker vocalizes his tune, calling it the "finest" he ever wrote. This is the melody, not really that interesting to begin with, that will be successively transformed in a dozen ways throughout the song-play, recalling the way Blitzstein would sit at the piano as a youngster and subject a popular tune to a set of ethnic variations. Blitzstein's materialist musical thesis comes out in Musiker's statement, "A song is made for somebody, somewhere, some place. You don't just write a tune into an empty space!"

Scene Two takes place at the Park Avenue penthouse of Madame Arbutus, former Stuttgart society lady whose salon attracted artists, poets, and millionaires. She is addicted to "The New Art," calling herself "Priestess of the New Music," and she declares herself "the true non-conformist." She is, of course, another Mrs. Mister, though this time with a rather more evolved set of esthetic pretensions. Again, Blitzstein identifies the patroness of the arts with the meals she serves, as in the Yasha and Dauber scene of *Cradle:* Madame Arbutus serves chicken salad.*

"You know I once tried to starve, Mr. Musiker," Arbutus says in an uncomfort-

*There is a precedent for Blitzstein's use of this particular menu as a symbol. Four years before, talking about the concept of patronage in one of his lecture-recitals—which he no longer needed to offer—he described the positioning of modern music: "When we do consent to smile upon the little changeling child, it is usually with benefit of much social trimmings and spectacular soirées. Modern music in America may be said to be nourished even today, largely on chicken salad and cocktails."

able allusion to Eva, "but I got to thinking the vilest thoughts!" At this point, she breaks into a one-step with Weillian harmonies, in which she confesses that she stays up late "on Scotch and Art," and in her drunken episodes creates her musical and dramatic works. Later in the scene, after she has transmogrified the simple tune into a Schoenbergian *Sprechstimme* poem, "The moon is a happy cheese tonight" (marked *unruhig,* "uneasy"), she bleats how "it is so grand to be so bored! You can afford the kind of music you can not stand." In this hothouse atmosphere, Mr. Musiker's tune would certainly not do at all.

The next scene brings us to another vision of the sickness affecting the world: fascism. In an induction ceremony conducted by Captain Bristlepunkt for his group of Purple Shirts, Blitzstein includes chanted rote responses:

What's a good American?
A white American!
Who do we hate?
The mongrel race!
What do we do to mongrels?
Kill the mongrels! Kill the mongrels! Yay!

Private Schnook is the inductee at this meeting in the woods, which Mr. Musiker watches from a hiding place. Schnook is forced to bow down to the Captain in a scene that recalls the ancient story of Mordechai in the Book of Esther, who refused to bend to the Persian emperor. In this manipulation of the tune, with the chorus singing open fourths and fifths in a parody of medieval organum, Schnook protests several racist points in the fascist ideology, until the group works him into a final frenzy (at the threat of loss of his clients), and he beats upon a sample "mongrel" they have brought along to teach a lesson. To something like a chorale, marked *grave,* the Purple Shirts extol their leader, while the radio sound-effects men go wild with whistles and bomb sounds, machine guns and pistol shots, the same sort of material on the sound track for *The Spanish Earth.*

The scene presented a vivid rebuttal to the pro-Aryan thinking fairly widespread in America. The same theme of the threatened, bought-out professionals is present, as in *Cradle.* Blitzstein used some of the "crazy-march" from the Building of the City scene in *Cain* in this variation. He was also conscious in this and in the final scene of the people's use of music under fascist conditions: "Remember Peatbog," he wrote to himself. "Perhaps the Fascist concentration camp men sing other words under their breath than the ones they publicly sing with the guards."

Scene Four brings the listener to a rooftop where Mr. Musiker and Beetzie are sunning themselves. There they come upon a young lady whom they rescue from a suicide attempt. In a weepy torch song, again a variation of the same tune, marked *andantino rubato,* the Suicide mocks her saviors:

Now it seems I'm safe and sound.
You must be very proud; indeed,

You've saved a lady in distress.
And you will think me quite hateful,
Because I'm not at all grateful.

The lyrics that follow closely reflect Marc's thinking about Eva and her final despairing years. In fact, his notes on this nameless character say that she never got over her mother's death, which may suggest Eva's sense of guilt over her wish that it might have been Lina, not Edward, who died.

Well, her story's just a bore.
Let's say she lost her way,
And can't search any more.
So must she go on searching?
She will say, what for?
Now you cite the reasons why
Such a death is not worth courting;
That way it's a sin to die
And besides, it's not sporting.
I have no defense.
Nothing else makes sense.
They tell me there's a war;
I don't know what it's for.
The system's not so hot;
I don't care if it's not.
I think I won't be gallant any more—what for?

At which, on a second try, the woman escapes her saviors and jumps to her death—just as Eva had ignored Marc's attempts to help.

In the fifth and final scene, following on the heels of death, comes the apotheosis of the tune. Blitzstein is saying that the effective way out of depression and mourning is to throw oneself into intense, committed activity. We are on the street, and again the sound-effects men show their craft with clanging subway sounds.

"How can you stand the noise, Mr. Musiker?" asks Beetzie.

"I don't mind the noise," he answers. "I like the noise."

"And you a musician, Mr. Musiker!" she responds incredulously, unwise to the machine-music tendencies of this composer.

Beetzie and her employer discuss the myriad styles to which his tune has been subjected: Chinese treatment, Italian organ-grinder, the movies, radio, Tin Pan Alley, all of which with appropriate snatches of variations on the basic tune.

"Maybe nobody wants my tune. I think I'll go back to my Ivory Tower," Musiker moans, upon which a parade comes into view.

Beetzie begins to remark, "I hear in Soviet Russia . . ."

Musiker interrupts her: "What do you know about Soviet Russia?"

"O, a girl gets around," she coyly admits. Perhaps she is not so addled after all, this short-hand speed queen!

In the distance, a May Day crowd is heard singing. The Choral Director urges the paraders on as they sing radical songs to tired old melodies, such as Joe Hill's "The Preacher and the Slave," "Hold the Fort," and "Solidarity Forever." In between measures of these songs, the boys and girls demand "a tune which is original, a true one. Who will compose a song for twenty million strong? All we ask is a song, our demands won't be so modest very long." Musiker offers his song: He vocalizes the melody and the paraders make up words. They invent what turns out to be a banal mass song for May Day, ending the half-hour song-play *allegro maestoso:*

Tomorrow is for us,
So fight, but still be gay!
We'll rule in that tomorrow,
So we sing today!

Until a week or so before air date, Orson Welles had been announced to the press as Mr. Musiker. In fact, *I've Got the Tune* is dedicated to him. But Welles was deep into rehearsal for *Julius Caesar,* his first Mercury Theatre production after *Cradle,* and so he withdrew. Blitzstein himself played the part. As Beetzie, Shirley Booth reproduced the strong New York accent she had used in *Three Men on a Horse.* Mercury Theatre actors performed other roles: Adelaide Klein as Madame Arbutus (Blitzstein had considered Lina for the role), Kenneth Delmar as Captain Bristlepunkt, Norman Lloyd, also from the Living Newspaper company, as Private Schnook, and Hiram Sherman as the Choral Director. Making her American radio debut, Lotte Lenya sang the part of the Suicide. Bernard Herrmann conducted. "These are radiogenic voices," wrote Richard Gilbert in *Scribner's.* "Without the microphone they have no power, but with it and Blitzstein's incisive lines the impact of character is as physical as the jamming in the subway."[4]

The immediate critical reception to *I've Got the Tune* was overwhelmingly positive. Despite the facts that thematically much of the song-play repeated the contents of *Cradle,* and that it was so self-referential, it was a real novelty for radio, and reviewers appreciated that. *Time* called it "wiry-muscled music," and the *Radio Daily* hailed it as "a show that can stand repeating," though CBS chose not to do so. In the *Sun,* Irving Kolodin wrote that "Mr. Blitzstein's score is uncommonly well-wrought, with expert use of the medium, and constant, successful concentration on the problems of making his meaning articulate through speech and music." The *Daily News* writer Ben Gross called it "tuneful, sprightly, colloquial and as up-to-the-minute as today's paper."[5]

Not surprisingly, R. D. Darrell of *New Masses* rhapsodized over the latest triumph of the Party's favorite composer. "The fascist scene and the later snatch of 'Solidarity Forever' must have caused many a genteel dialer to wake up with a start from his Sunday-evening snooze." Addressing *Tune* in another commentary some weeks later, after hearing private transcription records of the program, Darrell called it "so simple, powerful, entertaining, and honest that it's almost too good to be true," and he urged some enterprising record company to publish it on disks. "This is the stuff that many of us have been waiting for hopefully and we have only ourselves to blame if we don't make sure that it is firmly rooted in the permanent repertory."[6]

The left-wing Musicraft Records took up Darrell's suggestion and released the entire song-play on seven disks. Chappell did its part by publishing the fifty-five-page piano-vocal score the following year. During her engagement at the Blue Angel in the spring of 1938, Lotte Lenya included a Blitzstein song, probably her number from *I've Got the Tune.*

Once again, it was Guggenheim application time. Blitzstein increased his roster of references to include Archibald MacLeish, Philip Barry, the playwright, and John Dos Passos. He mentioned that he had also applied for the John Golden scholarship for young playwrights. His description of his new project, *No for an Answer,* was remarkably intimate in tone, indicating that perhaps he no longer took these applications with the same seriousness as before: "The form will range between satire and realism, and will comprise both burlesque and tragedy. Difficult as all ——— to do, but worth it if successful." By this time, the "Rialto Gossip" of the *Times* had already reported Blitzstein at work on the new opera. Toward the end of the year, the *Herald Tribune* projected that it would be finished in January.

For their new venture, the Mercury Theatre, which Blitzstein named, Welles and Houseman took over the old Comedy Theatre, a 687-seat house at Forty-first Street and Broadway, only two blocks away from the Maxine Elliott. The way Welles reshaped *Julius Caesar,* it ran for an hour and three-quarters without intermission. He dressed the show in contemporary attire. Playing Brutus, he got himself up like a Hitler Gauleiter in a slick, double-breasted military outfit. Shakespeare's contempt for the shallow convictions of the masses rose in this production to a scathing call to conscience in these dark years. The image of Caesar, of course, summoned up a wealth of modern referents: Kurt Weill and Georg Kaiser had already written their theatre piece *Der Silbersee* in the waning light of the Weimar Republic, with its searing "Ballad of Caesar's Death."

In Blitzstein, Welles and Houseman knew they had a versatile and compelling composer for the theatre, and they asked him to provide the music for the new production. For his work, he received two hundred dollars and beyond that, 2 to 3 percent of the box office depending on gross receipts, as well as fifty dollars a week later on when the show went on a road tour. This was Blitzstein's first score for a Shakespearean play, and his great success at it sealed his love for the Elizabethan dramatist. He would later write incidental music to five other Shakespeare productions and compose a symphonic piece on *King Lear.*

The only vocal music Blitzstein wrote for *Julius Caesar* was a setting of the Orpheus song from *Henry VIII,* Act III, scene 3, which is often inserted at the moment in Act IV when the unsettled Brutus calls upon his servant boy Lucius for some calming music. The song has just the right soothing quality for such a mood, as its gentle meters rock almost imperceptibly between 3/4 and 4/4. It possesses an authentic Elizabethan flavor, an unexpected accidental near the end retaining musical interest. Reviewers found this scene between Welles and Arthur Anderson (as Lucius) among the most effective in the play. Chappell published the song, with its simple accompanying chords to be played on the piano or ad lib on the guitar or ukulele. The cover prominently advertised it as from the Mercury production.

The frightening pace of the show riveted the viewers' attention, as though they were watching a newsreel of contemporary history pass before their eyes. The play opened, on Caesar's entrance, with a sardonic "fascist" march that inevitably suggested the current European scene. The theme recurred several times throughout the evening, and was played on a booming Hammond organ (an electronic instrument invented as recently as 1935). The score called additionally for trumpet, horn, and percussion. On alternate nights, Blitzstein himself played the organ. Elliott Carter cited the "great effect" of Blitzstein's music in his *Modern Music* review and he predicted that it would be "not easily forgotten."[7]

The production achieved another success in its handling of the crowd scenes. Running over bare wooden platforms, the Roman citizens provided a threatening, ominous sound fully integrated with the other aural devices. Blitzstein took charge of some of the direction, using a metronome to pace the rehearsals of spoken dialogue. Welles's expressionist use of lighting struck New York audiences as exceptionally powerful, the sort of effect known only in Germany and Russia earlier in the decade.

Once *Julius Caesar* opened on November 11, it could have played for months with the rave notices it received. But Welles could not have withstood repeating the same performance night after night. He had to give the public new work to confirm the power of his genius. Thomas Dekker's *The Shoemaker's Holiday* opened in repertory with the Shakespeare play shortly after Christmas. Before it closed, however, *Julius Caesar* hit a record 157 performances of a Shakespeare play on Broadway, shared until that time only by a 1923 *Romeo and Juliet,* starring Jane Cowl.

Welles put *Julius Caesar* onto eleven Columbia Masterworks disks, advertised as the "complete Mercury Theatre version," reportedly the first time an entire, though severely edited Shakespeare play had been committed to records. But this version, featuring the same cast, was less than complete. None of Blitzstein's music was used, the Brutus-Lucius scene being reduced to a strum or two on the lute, as though the boy's song had just concluded. The recording featured an omniscient narrator who confided the entrances and exits to the listener and announced the act and scene changes. It was a pale and unexciting reflection of a mighty event in the theatre.

Mercury Theatre radio casts also recorded two other Shakespeare plays for Columbia, though these were not disk versions of stage productions. Elliott Carter wrote music for *The Merchant of Venice.* For *Twelfth Night,* only the "Handbook for Teachers" accompanying the set identified Blitzstein as the composer. Welles played Malvolio, Eustace Wyatt played Sir Toby Belch, and Will Geer was Sir Andrew Aguecheek. Though the production is more lighthearted and intimate than the *Julius Caesar,* it, too, is a failure on records.

Blitzstein composed two songs for Feste the Clown—performed by LeRoi Operti—one at the beginning and one at the end of the play. The first, "Come away, come away, death," is tender and sad, subtly undulating in a minor key, sung to a lute accompaniment. The unoriginal final song follows a standard ballad form, serving merely to bid the audience farewell. Lost in manuscript form, the music could be transcribed from the records.

With a substantial amount of work for the stage now among his credits, the composer distilled his thoughts "On Writing Music for the Theatre" for *Modern Music.* Rules could be invented, he said, but many of them would necessarily be discarded in the composing process:

> There is only one rule I know; follow your theatre instinct. You discover you've got it very much in the way you first discovered you were a composer. You may be wrong on both counts; but your inner conviction is all you've got.[8]

Over the next few months, Blitzstein entertained for a variety of left-wing causes. Spain drew his attention many times. But perhaps the grandest spectacle in the history of the American left, for which he served as musical director, took place in Madison Square Garden on Saturday, November 13, 1937. Sponsored by the New York State Committee of the Communist Party, "One Sixth of the Earth" took its name from the popular 1926 film by Vertov, *One-Sixth of the World,* and also, by contrast, alluded to Roosevelt's expression describing poverty in America, "one third of a nation." Held at the height of Stalin's terror, to which the Party blinded itself, the extravaganza celebrated the twentieth anniversary of the Russian Revolution. Top Communist Party speakers, including Chairman of the CPUSA, William Z. Foster, addressed the crowds. Two hundred actors and dancers, recruited from the Young Communist League, enacted a four-part program: The October Revolution to the End of Intervention; The NEP (New Economic Policy) to 1924; The First Five-Year Plan and the Triumph of Socialism; and The Struggle for World Peace.

For the first time in America, arena staging was employed—the technique of Soviet director Vsevolod Meyerhold, who was shortly to be executed under Stalin's orders. The unobstructed view from all parts of the Garden represented "the desire of the Communist Party to constantly take the lead in evolving and making use of the newest technique in revolutionary theatre, for the benefit of the widest masses of people," claimed the handbill. Bret Warren participated as stage director, Howard da Silva as director of the Radio Company, and Lillian Shapero, formerly of the Martha Graham dance company, as choreographer. It was announced that Blitzstein was preparing a "hit tune" about the new Moscow metro system, though if he premiered it on this occasion, it has since been lost.

Marc's nephews Stephen and Kit, now twelve and nine years old, came to New York from time to time, sometimes with Jo, later on more often by themselves, to attend their famous uncle's shows. Courtesy of Lina, they saw all of Dwight Deere Wiman's shows, too. Budding radicals nurtured by their family atmosphere, they began writing and drawing for family newsletters and school papers. Marc lovingly introduced them, almost like surrogate children, to his theatrical friends.

For a year, shop workers who were members of the International Ladies Garment Workers Union (ILGWU) had been rehearsing a revue with sketches by various writers and music mostly by Harold Rome. Their idea was a little in-house entertainment, scored for two pianos. A Party man, Charles Friedman, directed, and Benjamin Zemach supplied choreography. Known as *Pins and Needles,* the show featured ordinary people playing themselves, dealing with their own felt realities in song and satire. Memorable numbers were "Sing Me a Song of Social Significance," "Doing the Reactionary," "One Big Union for Two," "(Sitting on Your) Status Quo," and "Not Cricket to Picket." One scene made fun of Brecht's epic theatre style in his poorly understood *Mother.* Politically, the show was pro-union and somewhat left of center without leveling any truly radical social criticism, but it was the first full-length revue since *Parade* had flopped two years before.

After the debacle of the WPA *Cradle,* which had thrust Blitzstein's name into wide public recognition, he prepared a sketch for inclusion in *Pins and Needles.* "FTP (Federal Theatre Project) Plowed Under" parodized a Living Newspaper production of the preceding year called *Triple-A Plowed Under.* Characters included Mrs. Clubhouse (the Hallie Flanagan of the piece), Mr. Bureaucrash, Mr. Zealous, Mr. Stallalong, and four guardsmen. As the author-composer character, Blitzstein created Mr. Hippity Bloomberg (played by Joe Roth). The skit directly attacked the Federal Theatre's squeamishness: Officials prune out of their promised colossal production of Bloomberg's play all references to a boy and a girl, a picnic in the woods, sex, a strike, and a radical; and they eliminate the ballet because dancers are notoriously prone to conducting sit-down demonstrations. Of course they reject the title, "Workers Also Love." As Bureaucrash puts it, "Mr. Bloomberg, don't you think the term 'worker' a bit inflammatory, just now? Controversial and all that?" In the end, all that's left is "The Curtain Rises." But Bureaucrash has an answer to that, too. "Now why can't our play open SMACK like that? Do we have to have a curtain?" Bloomberg faints. Blackout.*

Self-indulgent the skit may have been, but it illustrated the intimate relation Blitzstein felt with his public. It also served as promotion for the forthcoming Mercury Theatre revival of *Cradle.* In fact, on November 27, 1937, the same cold, rainy night that *Pins and Needles* opened at the Labor Stage (formerly the Princess), *Cradle* received the first of a series of weekend performances at the Mercury playhouse. Together with *Julius Caesar,* this meant that Blitzstein had three shows playing simultaneously in New York.

The ILGWU believed that *Pins and Needles* might run for a few weekends

*The script of the sketch has survived, but the music has been lost. As for the rest of *Pins and Needles,* Harold Rome's songs have survived, as they were published, but the sketches have been lost.

at best. But to universal surprise, it became an overnight hit and shortly established itself on Broadway, eventually racking up 1,108 performances in its three-year run. It established a record for longevity for any musical until *Oklahoma!* came along several years later. On February 3, 1938, the cast gave a command performance before President Roosevelt at the White House. There was also a road company that traveled across the country and into Canada for ten months, and another company did union lunchtime matinees. All told, well over a million theatregoers saw the show. But though it touched on some issues of interest to the left, it kept its temper cool. For Heywood Broun, all but Blitzstein's contribution was too tame. "The only really savage satire is directed against the Federal Theater, a movement which worker groups ought to support in spite of its present limitations."[9] As time went on, the revue went through three substantial overhauls and it became politically more and more tame, though the Blitzstein sketch lasted in it for a year and a half.

Hallie Flanagan saw *Pins and Needles.* Years later, after having published *Arena,* her memoir of the FTP, she wrote to Blitzstein, who was then contemplating writing a book, from her position in the Department of Theatre at Smith College. Her view is worth quoting in full.

> March 5, 1947
>
> Dear Marc Blitzstein:
>
> It is courteous of you, though somewhat surprising ten years after the event, to ask for my side of the story of *The Cradle Will Rock.* The inference from the sketch that later appeared about this occurrence in *Pins and Needles* was that I had been instrumental in stopping *The Cradle Will Rock.* The reverse was true.
>
> You remember that you, Jack Houseman, and Orson Welles invited me to a hearing of *The Cradle Will Rock* in Jack's apartment. You played and sang the whole opera. I was tremendously excited by it and said at once we would do it on the project, perhaps very simply, much as it had been done that evening. Orson, however, wanted an enormous show with glass wagons. Remember our discussion on this point?
>
> As rehearsals went on, there was a rumor in Washington that the play was to be stopped. I went to Harry Hopkins and told him that I was concerned for fear some action as that which stopped *Ethiopia* might be taken. He said, "Will you give me your word that this production is something you believe in?" I sketched the action of the play, told him that it was strong, authentic American material with a remarkable score. He said, "I am not going to be in a position to back you actively but I will not fight it. Suppose you get Larry Morris to go and see it."
>
> I took Larry (at that time an assistant administrative of WPA and hence our superior) to see a rehearsal and we had a meeting with Jack, Orson, and a number of other people, after the production. Larry said he thought it was tremendous, that it was likely to get us into some trouble, but would be worth it.
>
> Several days after that, the national directors of all four of the arts projects received an order that no plays, concerts or art exhibits were to

open before July first. (All national directors, while in artistic control of the projects, took orders from WPA on all other matters.) We felt that this was aimed at *The Cradle Will Rock,* which was the only big show soon to open. (Of course we couldn't prove this.) I immediately proposed to the Washington office that they make an exception of *The Cradle Will Rock,* explaining that it was a big show, had been in rehearsal a long time, and must open if we were to hold our actors. Although the officials never admitted that this order was aimed at *The Cradle Will Rock* they stated that no exceptions of any kind would be made. I therefore got in touch with the New York office and suggested that you and Orson come to see WPA officials. I asked that the group come to see me first so that we could all go to see Hopkins together. The next thing I heard was that Orson Welles—I don't know who else was in the party—had taken a plane to Washington, had conferred with WPA officials, and had made them so furious that the government "had relinquished the rights to *The Cradle Will Rock.*"

You are quite right, Marc, that some of this was left out of *Arena.* I would not have said anything in the book to reflect in any way on the Mercury because I was for it from beginning to end, and *Arena* was not a book about my personal feelings. I thought the Mercury was magnificent in spite of the fact that it took away with it some of our best ideas and our best people. However, I never felt that it was either ethical or generous for any of you connected with the Mercury to infer that I had been on the other side. After all, it was at my request that your show was put together on government time and money, and rehearsed for months on government time and money. It was stopped over my protest. I will be very glad indeed if the book that you write makes these points clear.

In connection with the closing of *The Cradle Will Rock,* as at an earlier point when *Ethiopia* was closed, I was tempted to resign in protest. However, I do not believe in resigning; and especially in this case, because it was well known at that time in Washington that the resignation of the national director would be the only excuse needed for closing a controversial project. Important as the issue raised by *The Cradle Will Rock* was, it was not the only issue facing us. The thing that people on the New York project never cared about, never understood, and never took the trouble to find out, is that this is a big country. Federal Theatre was bigger than any single project in it. It included not only *The Cradle Will Rock* but the theatre for the children of coal miners in Gary, Indiana, the enterprise for vaudevillians in Portland, Oregon, the negro theatre in Chicago, the research being done in Oklahoma—and other projects employing several thousand people in other states. Some of the sense of this vast panorama I tried to give in *Arena* and I am glad to have you say that reading the book makes you realize how big Federal Theatre was.[10]

With its one sure hit *Julius Caesar* on their hands, the Mercury Theatre would have been foolish not to revive *Cradle,* its first attention-grabbing play. As a form of tryout, it launched a series of Sunday-night performances as a Worklight

Theatre feature, enabling Will Geer (then in *Of Mice and Men*), Howard da Silva (*Golden Boy*), and Hiram Sherman and John Hoysradt (*Julius Caesar*) to participate. Now Welles decided on a new, more practical staging. Instead of the actors sitting in the audience, he set them up on three rows of chairs on the stage, with the stairs from *Julius Caesar* still in place. As their turns to perform came up, the actors moved forward, dressed in street clothes, using the top of the upright piano as a prop—clerk's desk, drugstore counter. But still there were no scenery, no orchestra, and no special lighting effects.

"Remarkable," commented *Stage* magazine, "how, in an entertainment world drugged with manufactured glamour, they conjure Steel Town out of thin air, set it raw and terrible before your eyes."[11] But in reality, the no-scenery staging of the mid-1930s was not so new: The Greeks had never used scenery. Shakespeare's stage, too, was bare, and the actors presented themselves on it *as actors*, not as characters in "real life" whose drama an unacknowledged audience mysteriously happened to chance in upon. With *Cradle*, the actors and the audience so shared the spirit of the show that with all the traditional elements of theatre stripped away, what remained was the pure joy of just being there together.

On December 5, finally, the critics came. Walter Winchell, who back in June had quipped, without having seen the show, that it contained "no entertainment," now praised it to the hilt, both in his syndicated column and on the NBC Blue Network. "By all means," he advised, "*The Cradle Will Rock* and *Pins and Needles*, two of the better diversions." Brooks Atkinson called it "the best thing militant labor has put into a theatre yet. . . . What *Waiting for Lefty* was to the dramatic stage, *The Cradle Will Rock* is to the stage of the labor battle song."[12]

In the Communist press, Eric Englander reviewed *Cradle* for the *Sunday Worker*. It is "the highest point that popular revolutionary theatre has touched in this country . . . makes almost everything else in town have the air of stale and desperate confectionery." With minor reservations about the role of Larry Foreman and the limited use of the chorus, R. D. Darrell in the *New Masses* claimed that "Mr. Blitzstein is in the groove and just beginning to go to town." Most importantly, "even when you've stopped laughing, you haven't stopped thinking."[13]

The Nation magazine placed Blitzstein's name on its Honor Roll for 1937 in recognition of *Cradle*. Ironically, the honor roll also included Harry L. Hopkins! And *The American Hebrew* listed him on the cover of its "Who's Who Among American Jews—1937" issue.

The continued popularity of *Cradle* encouraged Random House to issue the play in book form. It appeared in a handsome 150-page edition, featuring the music to six of the songs and a preface by Orson Welles. Archibald MacLeish wrote the Foreword, an adaptation of the speech he gave back at the Venice Theatre, in which he called Blitzstein more successful than either Brecht or T. S. Eliot in "assassinating" the tired, passive audience of the past that only came to the theatre to be titillated. Instead, in *Cradle*, there was "a room full of men and women as eager in the play as any actor. . . . The whole feel of the room was of well-wishing and common cause."

Feeling that *Cradle* deserved a long run but unwilling to tie up the Mercury's resources with it, Welles and Houseman contracted with Sam H. Grisman, who only recently had gotten his start with *Tobacco Road,* to co-produce the show. He booked the Windsor Theatre on West Forty-eighth Street. In advance of the January 3 opening, Blitzstein wrote some "Lines on *The Cradle*" for publication in both the *Times* and the *Herald Tribune,* accompanied by Hirschfeld cartoons of him and the production. Tickets were set at 55 cents to a $2.20 top. Handbills screamed, "Suppressed by the Government! Acclaimed by the Critics! Demanded by the Public! Now on Broadway!" They, too, managed to misspell the composer's name. "Blitztein" still led the show from the piano; a good part of the entertainment was watching him putting his cast through their paces, beating out rhythms with his hands, making announcements about the action, and playing the three roles of Clerk, Reporter, and Professor Mamie. Inviting her to "come and wander around and behind the *Cradle,*" Marc wrote to Jo, "We're settled down to good business and prosperity at last! What an ordeal! And I feel fine!"[14]

With the show being billed as a musical play, the musicians' union obligated Grisman to hire ten men as a pit orchestra (later reduced to eight men), each receiving one hundred dollars a week for showing up and doing nothing. Blitzstein chose his men from among the neediest musicians he knew. When the union found out who they were, an official approached him, saying, "You've picked four cornetists, three flute players and three trombonists. That's no orchestra." The composer replied, "That is the orchestra I want to have not play my opera."[15]

More attention followed the new opening: press interviews, William Gropper's full-page cartoon in *New Masses,* a Flatbush rabbi's sermon, based on the play, called "Judaism Pleads with Capital and Labor." Even the *Catholic World* gave the piece a supportive review, calling for a similar effort from a pro-Catholic point of view. Veteran theatre critic Stark Young felt that the ending might have been too simplistic, but overall, "It makes one proud, makes one swell, believing in the reality of talent and impetuosity, chances taken, and the assertion of vividness."[16]

Perhaps the most glowing notice of all was Alistair Cooke's report on the NBC Red Network:

> It will numb you, it will give you the willies, but there is a reason to say it will not depress you. That reason is the astonishing talent of Marc Blitzstein. Without any highbrow preface or any academic fol-de-rols he has found a form of presenting plays which is to my mind the nearest most effective equivalent to the form of a Greek tragedy. There is not a spare line, a spare speech, an extra song, thrown in for the sake of characterization, comic relief, or any other text-book bromides. . . . You watch this play and you see nobody but yourself or what you might become. . . . If you know of a better play written from the other side, go to it.[17]

Not all reviews were so positive; some, for example, could not appreciate the quality of singing that dispensed with a trained operatic tone that Blitzstein wanted in his actors. Others, like George Jean Nathan, simply hated the politics of the piece: It struck him as "little more than the kind of thing Cole Porter might have written if, God forbid, he had gone to Columbia instead of Yale."[18]

During the run of *Cradle* at the Windsor, one of the hottest issues troubling the CIO's organizing drive in the northeast came in the form of Mayor Frank ("I Am the Law") Hague of Jersey City. Singled out in left circles as a prime representative of American fascism, he was known for saying, "We hear about constitutional rights and the free press. Every time I hear those words, I say to myself, 'That man is a Red, that man is a Communist.' You never hear a real American talk in that manner." Hague was in the habit of denying the use of public spaces—auditoriums, streets, parks—to the CIO and others he thought too radical. (In a case brought against him by the CIO and the American Civil Liberties Union, the Supreme Court eventually disabused Hague of this habit.)

Early in January, columnist Heywood Broun attended a meeting sponsored by supporters of Mayor Hague; he remarked that some of the mayor's speakers sounded just like the sold-out professionals in *The Cradle Will Rock.* The famous "Grandmother of American Labor" and Communist Party member, Ella Reeve Bloor, had also attended Hague's meeting, and *Cradle* the following night. Backstage after the performance, she gave the cast an account of her visit to Jersey City. "That Liberty Committee uses almost the same words that they used last night at the Hague meeting about the C.I.O. When Larry Foreman named the list of enemies of labor, I almost hollered out 'And Mayor Hague!' . . . It's remarkable, but if I hadn't known that *The Cradle* was written more than a year ago I would have thought that Marc was writing about Hague."[19] Within days, Blitzstein inserted several lines about Mayor Hague into the show. And in mid-February, scenes from *Cradle* formed part of a Newark fundraising evening for the CIO called "Bring Democracy to Jersey City."

One night, Gary Cooper, with a countess as his companion, sat in the front row of the audience. Howard da Silva remembered, "We threw our lines right at them, the revolutionary lines."[20] Someone else who went to see *Cradle* was a Warner Brothers story editor named Irene Lee Diamond. She met Marc after the show; it was the beginning of a lifelong friendship.

When Virgil Thomson returned to *Cradle* in the pages of *Modern Music,* he called it "the most appealing operatic socialism since *Louise.*" Still "burning with the red flame of social hatred and glowing with the pure white light of Marxian fanaticism, the work turns out to be, curiously enough, the big charm-number of the year." He also reviewed the audience:

> It is roughly the leftist front: that is to say, the right-wing socialists, the communists, some Park Avenue, a good deal of Bronx, and all those intellectual or worker groups that the Federal Theater in general and the Living Newspaper in particular have welded into about the most formidable army of ticket buyers in the world. Union benefits, leftist group-drives, the German refugees, the Southern share-croppers, aids to China and to democratic Spain, the New York working populace, well-paid, well-dressed, and well-fed, supports them all.[21]

It was not only Blitzstein, but Thomson himself, and Copland, Bowles, Rome, Engel, and others who had found a new audience in the left-wing and popular theatre movements. For this new public, they wrote succinctly, creatively, and without that crippling self-consciousness of being judged for the ages.

In his personal demeanor, Blitzstein was changed by the success of *Cradle.* It matured him, made him less of the esthete, and less of the angry young man. It gave him renown as the commanding figure in left-wing music. How many other composers found their names on the front pages of newspapers around the country? He was not the envy of everyone, however. Kurt Weill, not remembered for a generous regard for other composers, saw *Cradle* and noted certain similarities to his own style. He began parading about town asking everyone he met, "Have you seen my new opera?"[22]

9

ODE TO REASON

Winter 1938–Spring 1940

"Make the mind be fire. Make the heart be stone."

Blitzstein had accepted Communist Party leadership on the left, had worked closely with it, publicly supported its line, and wrote for its press. But exactly when he formally joined the Party is unknown. Years later, he claimed it was during the spring of 1938, though his activities of the preceding three years suggest earlier membership. Certainly he had little reserve about professing his views. Walter Winchell reported him with the actor Burgess Meredith at "Tony's the other middle-of-the-night debating, between drinks, whether the country needs more Roosevelt or more Communism."[1]

As a Communist, Blitzstein attended weekly meetings of his Party club, comprising members of the music, theatre, and film professions. It was important to him to belong, to take a stand, to show where he stood. It also was a family matter; the Blitzsteins were active in all the radical causes in Philadelphia. Even so, he did not become learned in the art of Marxist-Leninist polemics. He read the widely circulated Party literature, the endless pamphlets on every burning issue of the day, *New Masses* and the *Daily Worker,* but he never made a serious study of Marx, Lenin, and other Marxist philosophers; he much preferred wrapping himself around a swift-paced detective novel. He endorsed the Party's diatribes against Trotsky without question and happily distanced himself from John

Dewey's anti-Stalinist Commission of Inquiry by signing an open statement of support for the Moscow Trials against the supposed Trotskyists and renegades of the fascist fifth column. Against the background of Nazi successes all over Europe, the Soviet Union "gains strength internally and externally by the prevention of treason and the eradication of spies and wreckers," read the *New Masses* statement. If the Communist thesis suffered serious flaws, at least Blitzstein shared some distinguished company in his error: Harold Clurman, Malcolm Cowley, Dashiell Hammett, Lillian Hellman, Langston Hughes, Leo Hurwitz, Dorothy Parker, Wallingford Riegger, Harold J. Rome, Irwin Shaw, Paul Strand, and Max Weber, to name only a few of his co-signers.[2]

The Party tried to get what it could out of Blitzstein—volunteer work on committees or at least the lending of his name as a sponsor to any number of campaigns, occasional articles for its newspapers, his presence at fundraising events, even entertaining at private Party leadership gatherings. Sometimes the requests came in too thick to handle, but Blitzstein felt flattered, too, and useful. The prestige he lent to the Party was too great to spoil with the kind of prying to which a local club would subject an ordinary candidate for membership. If he was ever asked to stand on street corners selling the *Daily Worker,* he never complied, though a staff member of the *New Masses* once asked him to set himself a quota of new subscriptions to sell among Broadway people.[3]

Blitzstein felt sure of himself, even cocky in his allegiance to the Party. If he entertained any doubts about the Soviet Union—lack of freedom for artists, for instance, or its retrogressive attitude about homosexuality—he kept them out of view, publicly confident that in Stalin the Soviet Union had the father it needed. He would always defer to those Party leaders who spoke with authority and knowledge. But in front of others, not Party members, he often mounted his Union Square soapbox when he perceived anything less than total fealty to the cause. Instantly he leapt into passionate speeches in defense of the poor and oppressed. And if he did not elicit the right response, he could be witheringly sarcastic, insinuating naïveté at best, or willful ignorance and even treason to humanity. Minna Lederman remembered an occasion when "no one was too surprised to see him march into the Russian Tea Room and right out again, refusing to join a composers' gathering because a 'Trotskyite' was present."[4] When he walked along the street and a bum asked for a nickel, he might stop to give the poor soul a lecture about how he should organize, form a union of the unemployed, demonstrate. When he was drinking, the alcohol released all his inhibitions. He could become so unbearably intolerant and abusive at social gatherings that occasionally people asked him to leave. The next morning he would be all apologies.

In the winter of 1938, a year and a half after its first appearance, *Unison* came out with its fifth and last issue. Among its pages was a roundup article featuring the frenetic activity of its founding participant, Blitzstein. During that brief but fateful time, he had risen from recognition only within local radical and avant-garde musical circles to national status. Now, in addition to playing *Cradle* nightly at the Windsor, that spring semester Blitzstein taught a Friday-night course at the Downtown Music School on "Music in Relation to Theatre," the subject on which he was by then the acknowledged dean on the musical left. Tuition was six dollars. Eisler also taught there then; most of the other teachers were Party types as well. Lan Adomian, the choral instructor and conductor of the New Singers, had gone to fight in Spain that year. From his cell at San Quentin, where he had been imprisoned on charges of homosexuality, Henry Cowell kept up his loyalty to the school by writing piano music for its students.[5] In June 1938 the school changed its name to the Metropolitan Music School, and that fall Blitzstein again taught his theatre music course.*

Among the activities of the American Music League in this period were the successful organization of public opinion against the choice of Nazi collaborator Wilhelm Furtwängler as director of the New York Philharmonic, and the circulation of an open letter to Béla Bartók supporting his decision not to allow performances of his works in fascist Germany or Italy. Composers had also formed a committee for the Fine Arts Bill, sponsored by Representative Coffee, to expand and improve the WPA arts projects, but by now it was late in the day for the WPA—it would shortly be dismantled. By June of 1939, Federal Theatre had become a thing of the past.

The first staging of *I've Got the Tune* took place in early February 1938, on a lengthy benefit concert for *New Masses* at the Forty-Sixth Street Theatre, at which Orson Welles spoke. Earl Robinson, Alex North, Hanns Eisler, Aaron Copland, Paul Bowles, Harold Rome, and Virgil Thomson all contributed music to the program. In the fascist scene of *I've Got the Tune,* Count Basie improvised a swing on the "Ya Gotta, Ya Gotta" chorus of the Purple Shirts. For this performance, Blitzstein again played Mr. Musiker; newcomers to the cast included Peggy Coudray as Beetzie, Olive Stanton as the Suicide, Maynard Holmes as the Choral Director, and the Lehman Engel Singers as the chorus. John Amrhein produced the sound effects.

On this occasion, Howard Taubman of the *Times* wrote of *I've Got the Tune* that it is "compact, unpretentious and stirring in total effect. . . . superior in these respects to *The Cradle Will Rock.*" Elliott Carter, in *Modern Music,* observed caustically that "composers want to have their music played more than they want to show their political affiliations," for he doubted the depth of commitment to the *New Masses* cause in some of these musical quarters.[6]

As for Welles, he certainly knew who comprised his public for *Cradle* at the Windsor and had no shame in showing his appreciation. After the warm reception for *Tune* on this benefit, Welles scheduled it to run twice at the Mercury on Sunday nights later that month, on a double bill with Ben Bengal's *Plant in the Sun. Tune* was cast now with Lilly Winton as Madame Arbutus, Lou Polan

*The school retained that name for the next forty-one years until it was forced by creditors to close.

as Captain Bristlepunkt, and Ben Ross as the Choral Director. *Variety* found the piece severely deficient: only "satisfactory enough for the hysterical left audiences, who are not over critical of what is dished up to them."[7]

That March, Blitzstein signed a contract with Chappell, the music publisher, who shortly released sheet music to eleven of the songs from *The Cradle Will Rock* against an advance of three hundred dollars. Attesting to the continued place of player pianos in American musical culture, Chappell also released piano rolls of several of *Cradle*'s hit songs. The complete piano-vocal score to *Cradle* has never been published, however; only, on rental, photocopies of the manuscript score interpolated with the printed numbers. No doubt, Chappell believed in this way it would be easier to control runaway performances staged without payment of royalties. Chappell would remain Blitzstein's exclusive publisher for life, with a couple of very minor exceptions. When the composer sent the *Cradle* songs to the British music critic Wilfrid Mellers, Mellers replied enthusiastically: "Your music is the first convincing answer I've seen to the problem of reinstating the composer as an active member of society. . . . I'll do what I can to make your work known over here."[8]

The Cradle Will Rock lasted through March for a total of 108 performances, a respectable run for Broadway, though far from glorious. If Blitzstein tried to reach, and even help to create a wholly new type of audience for the theatre, he soon saw that even in its heyday, the American left was a finite population. The work can, however, be considered the first American opera to achieve financial success. By contrast to Blitzstein's conception of the new kind of opera America needed, that March at the Metropolitan Opera, twenty-six-year-old Gian Carlo Menotti's first opera, *Amelia Goes to the Ball,* had its New York premiere. Delightful enough, it is politically safe, musically conservative, entirely within the mold of escapist European taste, and just the sort of novelty the Metropolitan would be pleased to offer.

In April, Musicraft released the cast recording of *The Cradle Will Rock,* only slightly cut, the first full-length Broadway show ever to be put on disk. Blitzstein filled in the missing action with his own narration, but whole scenes, including dialogue, remain intact. Priced at $10.50, the set of seven records shortly found its way far beyond New York and into the homes of hundreds of families on the left, where Blitzstein's tunes became true cradle songs to the next generation.

The records received mixed notices. One reviewer claimed he threw them away: "If *The Cradle Will Rock* is an American opera, then Union Square is the cradle of American liberty—yes, we know some folks think it is, but we hardly call them Americans." "The music is scarcely of one piece," wrote Moses Smith in Boston. "Quite properly. For the play is not of one piece, just as American life is not." Almost a year later, Musicraft sent Blitzstein its royalty report for the previous six months. His advance had just been met. "Therefore we now owe you –.15. Will you have it in postage stamps, coffee and, or just let it draw interest until the next royalty check is due?"[9]

After *Cradle* closed, the composer needed both a rest and a period of isolation so he could work on *No for an Answer.* He stayed for a brief time in the Virgin Islands, writing off five hundred dollars from his income taxes that year as a professional expense "for scenic background to write scripts." But he didn't like it there and returned to the Jersey shore. Later that summer, he continued his work-vacation at Camp Intermission at Lake Saranac in the Adirondacks, where he fully played the part of the irritable genius: "everything and everybody stays out of my way until I yell," he wrote to a newly acquired friend, Mina Curtiss, the sister of ballet patron Lincoln Kirstein and an associate professor of English at Smith College. "I am being temperamental, difficult, ill, tired, exalted—in a word grotesque, for me."[10]

Newspaper reports now had it that the fully orchestrated, fully staged *No for an Answer* would be ready for production the following winter. Orson Welles had been promised first look at it; and both the Group Theatre and Billy Rose expressed interest in producing it.

As one of their productions for the 1938–39 season, Houseman and Welles decided on William Gillette's *Too Much Johnson,* the story of a turn-of-the-century rake on the run to Cuba, his mistress's jealous husband hot on the trail. For this show, Welles decided to experiment with several filmed sequences to introduce the characters and situations. In July, filming began in Central Park and around New York, with a cast that included Joseph Cotten as Johnson, Virginia (Nicholson) Welles, Arlene Francis, Ruth Ford, Mary Wickes, and several others, including Marc Blitzstein.

The play opened at a summer stock theatre in Stony Brook, Connecticut, where it received lukewarm reviews. The film sequences could not be edited in time, nor did the theatre have projection facilities. Clearly *Too Much Johnson* was too little ready for the New York stage as the Mercury's first offering of the season, and it was postponed.* The only known stills from these sequences appeared in *Stage* magazine in September 1938. Blitzstein appeared in three of them, once as a French barber carrying a large trunk over his head, again with Mary Wickes and Ruth Ford in a horse-drawn carriage, and finally along the railing of an ocean liner bound for Cuba. The caption remarked of the composer that he is "an excellent comedian as well. The most energetic of the extras, he appears practically all of the time."

With *Too Much Johnson* unavailable to open the Mercury Theatre that fall, Welles shuffled the schedule, and *Danton's Death,* with Blitzstein's music, became the first production of the season. It turned out to be the last by the Mercury Theatre. Far more expensive than anticipated, and always fraught with Welles's intense personality problems, this loosely structured drama by the early nineteenth-century German writer Georg Buechner went into rehearsal in late September. Welles insisted on constant scene shifts and rewriting, aside from

*The unedited footage remained in excellent condition for many years, but a fire at Welles's villa in Madrid in August 1970 destroyed it.

which he was not on the best of terms with Martin Gabel, who played Danton to Vladimir Sokoloff's Robespierre. As producer of the Mercury Theatre radio program also, Welles could not always attend to rehearsals. He left much of the handling of the crowd scenes to the stage manager and to Blitzstein, who had performed a similar function in the *Julius Caesar* production.

Aside from such technical problems as a difficult elevator device onstage that would raise a unit set to different levels from which the actors would play, the gripping drama of revolutionary terror had its political problems as well. By this time, Blitzstein had become one of the Communists' leading advocates in the cultural field. Though most of the way through rehearsals he had conducted himself with cool confidence, suddenly, following the *Daily Worker*'s open discussions of the play's weaknesses in articles published even before it opened, he went to Houseman demanding either substantial changes in the text of the play or cancellation of the production altogether.

His position was that in these days of Moscow trials, the Trotskyists in their protests against the Stalinist machine would inevitably compare Danton to their fallen Russian hero in exile, and Robespierre to the amoral and dictatorial usurper in the Kremlin. And if it was not for the consistent patronage of the Communists in the form of positive reviews and the encouragement of theatre parties, a healthy percentage of the Mercury's audiences would drop away. Beyond that, if the alterations were not incorporated, the Party might actually institute an open boycott of the production, which could be disastrous. Already a number of preview performances had been booked by progressive organizations with Communist backing, such as an October 20 benefit scheduled for the League of American Writers. Since on the advance publicity for *Danton's Death,* Blitzstein's name as composer of the incidental music stood out prominently just below director Orson Welles's, it is clear that the composer's weight and that of the Party expressed through him amounted to something substantial.

Hasty meetings with the Party's cultural czar V. J. Jerome resulted in some textual modifications, and the show was thus "allowed" to go on. The Party did not boycott the play, but neither did they promote it. Previews finally began on October 29. On Sunday the thirtieth, Welles went on the air with his panic-producing radio program "The War of the Worlds," the story of the landing of the Martians in New Jersey that sent thousands of listeners running from their homes in apocalyptic shock. By the time of *Danton*'s official opening on November 2, the waves had calmed somewhat.

Blitzstein wrote several bars of accompaniment on the spinet to a polite salon scene and to other sparse moments throughout the drama. But his main contribution was the introduction of two French Revolutionary songs, "Ça ira" and "La Carmagnole," to which he set English words for the crowds to sing, and two original songs, an "Ode to Reason" and "Ho Christina." "Ça ira" had been reprinted five years before in Moscow in a collection of revolutionary songs, and Blitzstein owned a copy of the book. Beginning as a court dance, the song had achieved its popularity among the Parisian mobs watching the aristocrats being led to the guillotine. Kurt Weill had also used "La Carmagnole" in a 1927 Berlin production of Strindberg's *Gustav III;* and a version of the song called "The American Carmagnole," with words by Harrison George, had appeared in a workers' songbook published in Chicago only two or three years before the Mercury Theatre's *Danton.* [11]

Blitzstein's own numbers have a period flavor to them, but remain hauntingly modern. "Christina," performed by Joseph Cotten and Mary Wickes, was the clear favorite among reviewers; it is a dialogue song between a soldier and the agreeable girl he is trying, without much resistance, to seduce. In only one among a number of Blitzstein lyrics about sex bordering on the abusive, she sings:

Mister Soldier, handsome Soldier,
Mister handsome, handsome Soldier,
Play me mild, or play me rough,
I just can't get enough.

The "Ode to Reason," more of a classical art song, was performed by Adelyn Colla-Negri. In three stanzas, Blitzstein appealed to reason against "temper's hot fire," "jealousy," and "pretense." He called for "honesty unadorned" against "sweet fickle passion," against "doubts" and "vile superstition" and "noble lies"—a stirring anthem for freethinkers of every generation, however ironic in light of his blindness to the depravity of Stalinism. In the final verses he announced the Revolution's and his own atheist creed:

No bell from the constant steeple
Shall sound on the limpid wind.
The destiny of a people
Is cast in the people's mind.
Oh Reason, our constant aid,
For thee is justice made!
With thee goes France unafraid!

Danton's Death had been anticipated with great interest. *Modern Music* published Jan Tichacek's drawing for the set design, a cyclorama covered with eerie, leering Halloween masks. And of course the Party's eye watched the show closely. John Gutman's review in *Modern Music* called for "a more ample score" to help the production. The Communists' *New Masses* carried a review by Ruth McKenney, author of *My Sister Eileen* and its sequel, *The McKenneys Carry On.* She struck just the expected tone, praising the lighting and the "startling and provocative" production. She liked Blitzstein's contributions exceptionally well, predicting that the "Christina" song "ought to be heard frequently around town." As an evening of theatre, however, she found the play a dull and muddled disappointment, for with the issues and events of the period unclear, it was "impossible to figure out what all the guillotining is about."[12] Without crucial Party support for the play, and amid the general exhaustion of the cast and producers, the play folded after twenty-one performances.

Blitzstein signed a contract with the Mercury Theatre the following February to produce *No for an Answer,* the new opera he kept struggling through countless interruptions to compose. But Welles soon departed for the West Coast, where he made *Citizen Kane,* and the Mercury Theatre came to an end. Blitzstein himself began receiving offers to write for Hollywood, where he could have earned upward of seven hundred dollars a week. But the year 1938 produced a higher income than he had ever seen before—over seven thousand dollars—and he must have felt he could survive as a composer for the cause. Years before he had refused big money to write schlock music for the movies. Now he told his friends about the new temptations. When they asked whether he would give in, he said, "I'm fighting it."

Radical theatre groups around the country had by now taken up *The Cradle Will Rock.* The New Theatre League, which had given *Cradle* its prize, controlled amateur production rights to it, as well as to *I've Got the Tune* and "Send for the Militia." At the close of the Broadway production, it began leasing the work out to its affiliate groups around the country.* As early as June of 1938, only two months after it closed on Broadway, Lou Cooper's Flatbush Players, a musical outgrowth of the Flatbush Branch of the Young Communist League, began performing it in Brooklyn. Over the next two or three years, in various locales and with numerous cast changes, they would offer the work dozens of times. One long-running production in Philadelphia went on the boards every Friday and Saturday night for months; Blitzstein was of course the guest of honor whenever he dropped by. The Chicago Repertory Group's *Cradle,* with Louis (Studs) Terkel in the cast as Editor Daily, enjoyed United Mine Workers support; Blitzstein attended, and was photographed with its Illinois District President. In Detroit, the United Automobile Workers featured news of *Cradle* on the front page of its newspaper aimed at Chrysler employees. It became *the* show every left-wing stage wanted to present. Random House reprinted it in early 1939 in *The Best Short Plays of the Social Theatre.*

Leonard Lyons, the Broadway gossip columnist, reported that Arthur Schwartz and J. P. McEvoy had written a musical called "Swing to the Left" about a radically minded playwright. Supposedly, Schwartz said, "If you're still interested in being an actor, Marc, I'd like to use you in our new show."

"What's it about?" Blitzstein asked.

"Frankly, it's about you."

"Well, I won't act in it, but I'll take the job of research director."[13]

The economic situation of American composers remained dreadful. In the serious music field, fees and royalties alone could not support them. Few outlets existed for composers to publish or record their scores. Only a long-running show such as *Cradle* or a much-produced ballet score could bring in enough money to enable a composer to continue writing. Chasing after patrons was a degrading occupa-

*The League acted in this capacity only until the spring of 1941, when it turned over inquiries to the William Morris Agency.

tion. And in mid-1939 the Federal Theatre Project met its death at the hands of a know-nothing Congress: One more outlet for composers was shut down. In 1937 Blitzstein had attended the inaugural meeting of the American Composers Alliance, headed by Aaron Copland and set up to advance the rights of composers. Blitzstein later served on its board of governors. He also joined ASCAP and, at the invitation of Claire Reis, the Composers' Committee of the League of Composers.*

In part to redress the sorry lot of composers, Blitzstein joined Copland, Virgil Thomson, and Lehman Engel to form the Arrow Music Press, a cooperative composers' publishing group. Engel served as president and Blitzstein as vice-president, though Thomson and Copland were the more active members. In its few years' existence, Arrow published a small but distinguished catalogue. At times, when Thomson found himself in disagreement with the others, he would refer to the endeavor as "the American Jewish Composers' Press"; for just as there were those in the musical world who felt that it was controlled by the "Homintern," the homosexual network, Thomson occasionally bristled at what he saw as Jewish control. Another publishing endeavor, the Cos Cob Press, which had included Blitzstein's "Jimmie's got a goil" in an American songbook a few years earlier, merged in 1938 with Arrow.

In 1939, Arrow printed Blitzstein's curious choral piece "Invitation to Bitterness," scored for four-part male chorus with altos supplementing the first tenor line. Set to music of an unattractive hardness, it recalls the spirit of *The Condemned.* Blitzstein had written it for *No for an Answer,* but dropped it from that score because it fell harmonically outside the more popular vein he wished to continue exploring. His text is an anguished cry of revolt and something of a throwback to the agitprop of his *Children's Cantata.* It refers to nothing in particular and refuses all compromise:

Call out. Invite to bitterness.
Armed! so with bitterness,
Armed with ruin and our great need.
Armed then: act: together.
Clear the way.
Make the mind be fire.
Make the heart be stone. Stone.

Between the sourness of the harmonies and the near inhumanity of the words—except that such deep anger *is* so human—Blitzstein had written a difficult piece to program on a concert. What chorus would want to sing such music? In fact, no definite record of any performance of this short work has survived.

Blitzstein's friendship with Billy Rose yielded many fascinating tidbits of gossip over the years—that the composer would write music for the Ziegfeld Follies, for

*When the American Composers Alliance affiliated itself with BMI, Blitzstein withdrew from it.

example, or that Rose would pass along Blitzstein's droll song "Smoking Glasses" (about movie stars who call attention to themselves by hiding behind dark sunglasses) to his estranged wife Fanny Brice. One rumor that aired in the press in the late 1930s had it that Rose and Blitzstein planned to open a "proletarian" nightclub in New York, the "United Front Cabaret." Broadway artists might perform there in topical sketches too radical for the Great White Way, though mostly there would be a house group of artists.

Such a locale for new songs of social significance did shortly emerge in New York, but not under Billy Rose's auspices. The left-wing Theatre Arts Committee established the Cabaret TAC, which held forth at the Princess Theatre on West Thirty-eighth Street on Sunday afternoons and Mondays at midnight. Blitzstein served with Howard da Silva, Robert Gordon, Michael Loring, James Proctor, Hiram Sherman, Jay Williams, Kermit Bloomgarden, and a dozen others on its production committee. Harold Rome and Earl Robinson composed songs; John Latouche wrote lyrics; Leo Hurwitz did staging; Tony Kraber sang ballads. Administrative details were the responsibility of Adelaide Bean, later a cultural editor for the Communist press. It was a good place to ventilate ideas on the left and to give a chance to fresh composers and writers, but most of all to experience the collective thrill of sharing an affirming evening in perilous times.

One early production, in February 1939, featured skits such as "Curse of the Silk Chemise," "Noël Coward Custom," "Picket Line Priscilla," and "It Can't Happen Here," in which Blitzstein sang an anti-Hitler song by John Murray—one of the only times he ever publicly sang anyone else's music and words. For the most part, however, Blitzstein contributed his own material. One of his best songs from the 1930s is "Who Knows?"; it is also referred to as "Let's Be Blue." A slow torch song with a cocktail-piano accompaniment, a takeoff of the "white man's blues," it was performed at Cabaret TAC by Ruth Ford wearing a knee-length Schiaparelli dress with a novel mirror-studded jacket.

Let's be blue—to conventional music.
Let's be gay—where it's publicly gay.
Let's just do—what will take the least doing.
Let's be bored—in the best approved way.
If there's danger, we'll run to cover,
Fleet, discreet, safe and sane;
Sip our tea, take another lover,
Smile and smoke—no strain, no pain;
All our lives—not a hint of ourselves reveal—
For who knows
Where we'd end if we once should think and feel?

Another sketch called "What's Left?" had a clutch of weary lyricists in a Tin Pan Alley song factory bemoaning the exhaustion of subjects in the commercial music market. The boss walks in with a bright idea: Exploit the success of *Pins and Needles, The Cradle Will Rock,* and Cabaret TAC by inventing new, left-wing words to old tunes in the public domain. One by one the writers come up with lackluster, made-to-order lyrics to the "Song of India," "Melody in F," and "Moment Musical" as the spotlight shines on each of them in turn. The best of Blitzstein's lyrics is "Danny Boy":

> *O Danny boy, what union made your union suit?*
> *Your BVD looks most suspect to me;*
> *No label there; such perfidy must bear bad fruit;*
> *An open shop just means an open union suit!*
> *O Danny boy, the buttons on your union suit!*
> *Tears blind mine eyes; for shame, you open shop!*
> *I only hope those buttons on your union suit*
> *Like to the cork upon the bottled soda—pop.* [14]

Early in 1939, *I've Got the Tune* saw another revival, by Lou Cooper's group, the Flatbush Arts Theatre, as a benefit for the New Theatre League at the New School. Blitzstein directed it himself. Company regulars filled the roles adequately, with Buddy Yarus playing both the Chorus Leader and one of the Purple Shirts; under the name of George Tyne he would much later reappear in another Blitzstein show. The composer admired the company's pluck in tackling such a musically challenging piece: "You've got more nerve than brains," he told Cooper. A few months later, they presented it again at the Ninety-second Street Y, also premiering a "metropolitan cantata" called *A Life in the Day of a Secretary,* with words by Alfred Hayes and music by George Kleinsinger. Following these two pieces came a one-man rendition of the Pyramus and Thisbe scene from *A Midsummer Night's Dream,* played by Arthur Zipser, later a Communist Party historian and biographer of William Z. Foster.

On Saturday, May 27, 1939, a fateful production of *The Cradle Will Rock* took place in Cambridge, Massachusetts, sponsored by the Harvard Student Union. Reportedly put together in ten days' time on a thirty-five-dollar budget, this Boston-area premiere starred college students and a few semiprofessionals involved in community theatre. Graduating senior Leonard Bernstein, who had seen the show in New York, served as pianist, assuming the roles of the Clerk and the Reporter. He played the score from memory. With Arthur Szathmary, he co-directed the show as well, and cast his younger sister Shirley in the role of the Moll. (She appeared under the name Shirley Mann, a joke on the Mann Act, for here was a fifteen-year-old high school student playing a hooker on the stage!) Faculty sponsors for the show included Arthur Schlesinger, Sr., the philosopher David W. Prall, and Archibald MacLeish, then at Harvard as the curator of the Nieman Collection of Journalism. Bernstein omitted the Faculty Room scene, considering it a weak link in the show and without important musical ideas.

The Boston *Evening Transcript* critic Moses Smith commented on Bernstein's tempos, which were faster than Blitzstein's, and cited some rough edges and missed lines. Still, he said, in this performance "the separation between the audience and the players was spectacularly annihilated." The *Crimson* reviewed the evening in similarly superlative terms. Elliot Norton, writing in the *Post,* had less favorable things to say. He seemed positively traumatized that "the Harvard proletariat liked it immensely." He considered the play subversive, the author "an unpleasant propagandist but an artist of unquestionable gifts, astride his good white charger, 'Proletariat.' " *Cradle* "makes Mr. Blitzstein seem as mean and vengeful as Mr. Mister," he fumed. The play had been "given with fire, ardor, intelligence and altogether too much conviction for comfort." Another performance took place a week later on June 2 to meet the demand for tickets.[15]

The production had political repercussions. The ultraconservative Cambridge City Council member Michael A. (Mickey) Sullivan protested the indecency of *Cradle* and called for Chief of Police Timothy Leahy to investigate the "Reds" at the university. But a *Crimson* editorial countered that Sullivan had himself recently produced a profascist movie about Spain, and it challenged the politician to state openly whether he regarded the play to be "un-American."

Blitzstein flew up to see the production, later remarking to the press that he was astonished at the brief rehearsal time for such an expert production. Bernstein, said the composer, had played the score better than he had himself. During the afternoon of the premiere, Blitzstein and Bernstein spent hours together walking along the banks of the Charles River and having an extended talk that would make the strikingly handsome young undergraduate a Blitzsteinian for the rest of his life. The composer also liked Shirley as the Moll, telling her she was the equal of, or maybe better than, Olive Stanton. He even requested that she make a recording of "Nickel Under the Foot" for him (she didn't). Clearly he recognized a symbiotic relationship between Lenny and Shirley parallel to his own with Jo. At the cast party following the show, held at a Harvard Square restaurant, Blitzstein delighted the students with highlights from his next work, *No for an Answer:* The ever-present cigarette hanging from his lip as he sang impressed them almost as much as the inimitable way he delivered his songs.

Back home again, Blitzstein told his old friend Berenice Skidelsky about the production and about its extremely talented pianist. "He reminded me of myself at his age," he said, "brash and self-assured." He could hardly have failed to be impressed by Lenny; indeed, the performance turned him into a committed Bernstein fan. In a letter written to acknowledge receipt of the Boston reviews, he complimented Lenny, Shirley, and the entire cast:

> I made it fairly clear, I believe, that it all packed a thrilling wallop for me—second only to the original NY opening. I want to repeat it all; and to wave a bewildered cap in the air (I forget which Ovidian figure *that* is) at the speed, efficiency and talent with which you got it on.
>
> And it was fine to get to know you, and I keep kicking myself that I never managed to hear a note of your music. Which is a reason for us meeting soon again.[16]

Blitzstein shortly left for a summer at Yaddo to forge ahead with *No for an Answer.* He occupied the Tower studio, reachable across a moat. Around the walls of the room, he would tack up all the music for the scene or act on which he was working, necessary for his unusual technique of timing the opera, which he loved demonstrating to visitors.

German refugee scholars were plentiful that summer at Yaddo. But mostly he enjoyed the company of his friend David Diamond, who had dedicated to Blitzstein "The Mad Maid's Song" (to a text by Robert Herrick), and who had just returned from a year in Paris on a Guggenheim grant. At Yaddo the relationship flourished. Two serious composers, both Jewish, had much to share, including their taste for manly men. They would exchange stories of their pickups, local farmers mostly, or the odd garage mechanic found at Jimmy's Bar in Saratoga. They could even dance together in one of the black bars on Congress Street where no one minded what went on—David led, Marc followed. Almost anywhere, in a nearby bar or over lunch, Marc freely carried on clinically descriptive conversations about the most intimate sexual affairs. Out of his affection for David, Marc would openly hug and kiss him, not caring who noticed, so much so that when Copland went up with his boyfriend Victor Kraft and Colin McPhee, he remonstrated with Marc and David. "Boys, stop that!" Copland said, ever concerned to keep unsullied his own status as the dean of American music.

"Even my sex-life has gone completely by the board in behalf of *No for an Answer,*" Marc wrote to Mina Curtiss.

> and if there is any more varied, strange and elaborate sex-life in these United States than at Saratoga just before and during season, I'd like to know about it! Little Diamond comes home nights and brings me stories of his exploits—but stories! But I go right on like one in a dream.[17]

At one point during the summer, Diamond went away for a few weeks. The sex scene must have picked up for Blitzstein. He filled David in on the news:

> Very little happened of interest after you left. I found lots more bed-partners, no amours. . . . The crowd here is stupid and dreadful. . . .
> I threw a party for Gypsy Rose Lee here at the studio. Very gay. . . . You would have died for Paul Engle, who visited. Accompanied by his wife, who is really lovely. That's why you'd have died.[18]

Because his room had been previously booked for the last two weeks in August, Blitzstein had to vacate. He drove over to Mina Curtiss's Chapelbrook Farm in Williamstown, Massachusetts, where he settled happily into a four-room converted blacksmith shop on the property. He worked on *No for an Answer,* slashing out several scenes and eliminating one major character. Evenings, Mina's cook prepared superb dinners. As one of the heirs to the Filene's of Boston family, who had married into even more money, Mina enjoyed the finer things of life; she welcomed Marc into her home to share them. Blitzstein wrote to the director Herman Shumlin, a prospective producer of *No for an Answer,* that he would be finished with it "before the summer is over." "I'm excited about it, and I think you will be."[19]

On September 1 he returned to Yaddo, and Diamond was back there by then, too. But now everything had changed. On August 23, the Nazis and the Soviets had signed a treaty of nonaggression, the so-called Hitler-Stalin Pact, pledging neutrality in case of war. Secretly, the treaty also assigned to each nation its own sphere of influence in Eastern Europe.

Italy had invaded Ethiopia back in 1936. The British and French had timidly facilitated the German takeover of the Sudetenland in 1938, and the dismemberment of the rest of Czechoslovakia the following March. Spain had finally fallen to Franco in 1939 as well. The Soviets were horrified by the obvious fact that the "democracies" cared nothing about the integrity of Europe's borders. Indeed, after more than a decade of Hitler's ranting against Bolshevism, the Soviets concluded that Germany might well be preparing to invade their territory. They decided that if the Western powers could not unite with them to stop the forward march of Nazism, they would at least protect themselves by buying the time to build up their own defenses.

On the first of September 1939, the Germans invaded western Poland. The Soviets overran the eastern half of the country. Each counted on the other's concurrence. This move went too far for France and England, however, and they declared war on Germany. Within the year, also by German leave, the Soviets took over the Baltic countries and invaded Finland. In the ensuing period of nonintervention, Soviet and German cultural policies reversed themselves: Now German orchestras played Russian and Soviet music widely and broadcast it on the radio, while the Soviets recruited Sergei Eisenstein to stage a massive production of *Die Walküre* at the Bolshoi. The full extent of German-Soviet cooperation in other fields, military and intelligence notably, has yet to be exactly determined.

The American Communist Party, like the Communist parties everywhere in the world, was thrown into a tailspin by the sudden, strange apparition of a Soviet Union now friendly with the Nazi regime. For years, Communists had implored the Western democracies to make common cause with the Soviets against Hitler, but Hitler proceeded unchecked, even encouraged by Western appeasement. Was it still correct now to be anti-Nazi?

Blitzstein accomplished little the first week he was back at Yaddo. He no longer knew what political position to take. Several times a day he ran to the main house to answer telephone calls from New York. The poet Delmore Schwartz, a Trotskyist, was also at Yaddo, and Blitzstein nearly came to blows with him over politics. Marc argued with David incessantly and violently. Like many Jews both in and outside of the Party, Diamond could not stomach the German-Soviet treaty, and he disagreed with Marc's unqualified defense of Stalin. Marc tried to engage David's sympathy for the Soviet position, but David would not yield. Then Blitzstein baldly told him how ignorant of the world he was.

At the end of a week, Marc went to New York for a couple of days, almost certainly to confer with his Party comrades. Perhaps the future of his new opera would be endangered by the new developments. It surely appeared as though the Party was falling apart rapidly, with the protest resignations of large numbers of its Jewish members. His own form of "protest," if that's what it was, was to shave off his mustache—perhaps it reminded him too much of both Hitler *and* Stalin—though it shortly came back as his trademark. In New York, he also took the opportunity to visit his old hangout, the Everard Baths, where, in between a number of sexual adventures that he recounted to David on his return, he spotted the painter Pavel Tchelitchev.

Back at Yaddo, Marc fluctuated between moments of hard-bitten political intransigence and other times of extraordinary tenderness toward his friends there. After cooling off from a fiery argument, he would compliment David on his sparkling music and loan him some of the little money he had. He felt pleased that David was reading Malraux's novel *Man's Fate.* "Good for you," he said.

"I don't remember whether this is my eighth or ninth application," Blitzstein wrote from there on September 25th to Henry Moe of the Guggenheim Foundation, exaggerating the number of his tries by two or three, "but I think I must hold a record of some sort for persistence!" This time adding Lincoln Kirstein, Brooks Atkinson, Elmer Rice, and Lillian Hellman to his references, he proposed nothing less than "an extended study of all forms of musical theatre from earliest to most recent times" and, still thinking of *No for an Answer,* the creation of a musical stage work reflecting the results of his study.

Both from the unlikelihood of ever receiving the grant and from the frightening turn of world events, Blitzstein felt heavyhearted; he returned to the city on October 1. There he found that in the still-running, but newly updated edition of *Pins and Needles,* Harold Rome had introduced a skit called "The Red Mikado," satirizing the Soviet-Nazi pact in Gilbert and Sullivan style. Obviously, the left—especially the Jewish left—was not unified behind Stalin's questionable move. But still, the American public did not lean toward joining England and France: As late as 1940 the revue contained the number "Stay Out Sammy," an explicitly anti-intervention song. Was the show prowar or antiwar? Blitzstein wondered.

With Michael Loring, Blitzstein previewed the theme song from his new opera at the Mecca Temple at a December benefit for Spanish refugees. Unlike the short lead time between the composition of *Cradle* and its production, *No for an Answer* became familiar, by its name and by some of its songs, two or more years before its eventual emergence on the stage. Blitzstein also donated an original manuscript score for *I've Got the Tune* to an auction sponsored by the League of American Writers and the Booksellers Guild of America as a benefit for exiled writers. Its purchaser, and the subsequent whereabouts of the score, are unknown.

The Flatbush Arts Theatre once again tackled *Cradle* for a three-night run in December, again led by Lou Cooper. Betty Garrett, who sometimes played Sister Mister for the Flatbush group, sang "Joe Worker" as Ella Hammer, with Buddy Yarus as Prof. Trixie and Junior Mister, and Arthur Zipser as Reverend Salvation and Dauber. The artist Sydney Weiss played Gus.

That December, while Jo and Ed vacationed in Florida, Marc stayed at their house on Church Road in Philadelphia and entertained Stephen and Kit with all the songs from *No for an Answer.* The opera "at last is done," he wrote to David Diamond. "I am very happy. (You see, I am lacking in pride about living off family or friends while I feel I'm doing a real work. . . .)"[20]

Knowing Jo's inordinate devotion to him, Marc consciously tried not to exert an overbearing influence on his nephews, though in celebration of finishing the opera he did buy them a beautiful new sled. As a kind of second father to the boys, he may have wanted to forestall any concern about his "homosexualizing" them; he knew that with Ed as their sober, conservative father often working late hours at his office, it could be tempting but ultimately destructive to steal the boys' affection.

The first of what would become a series of one-man performances of *No for an Answer* took place at the Malin Studios on February 7, 1940, as a benefit for the New Theatre League. The press began discussing the work more and more frequently now whenever details of its forthcoming unveiling were announced. A few weeks later, on February 27, Constance and Kirk Askew hosted Blitzstein for another run-through, as a benefit for the Arrow Press. "We filled the house in two days [*sic*] telephoning," Constance Askew wrote to Virgil Thomson:

> We've heard it—it's superb but the book needs a lot of whacking around. . . . Marc seems quite [a] bit of a brat, somehow—looks thin and worn, seems edgy. Perhaps the Party Line goes down hard, but he's a strict conformer to it.[21]

On March 27, 1940, the blessed and long-awaited appointment to a two-thousand-dollar Guggenheim Fellowship arrived. "May I thank you personally," Blitzstein addressed "My dear Mr. Moe," "for advising me not to be discouraged by eight rejections? The ninth did it!"[22] The Philadelphia *Inquirer,* proud of its native son, featured the story on page one. Also that year, among the seventy-three grants awarded, three other composers won: Alvin Etler, William Schuman, then director of chorus at Sarah Lawrence College, and Earl Robinson, whose plan was to spend his time writing the Carl Sandburg musical *The People, Yes.*

Not long after, Marc and Earl ran into one another. Earl asked, "How's your *No?*"

"Okay," Marc answered. "How's your *Yes?*"[23]

10

IN THE CLEAR

Spring 1940–April 1941

"Go on and ask me how I can be certain,
How I can pick him out like a shot,
And he will never upset my plot,
By actin' dirty and sly
Like the usual guy in a spot . . ."

In the late 1930s, Alfred P. Sloan, chairman of the board of directors of General Motors, believed that most Americans had a poor conception of the problems of capitalism. He decided to fund a series of films that would lay out the workings of the system in easily understood terms, and he donated a sizable grant to New York University to set up an Educational Film Institute to produce these films. To head the undertaking, he chose Spencer Pollard, who happened to be an avid film buff particularly enthusiastic over the documentary work of Joris Ivens.

Shooting on *Valley Town,* the first of the films in the series, had begun in late 1938 in Newcastle and nearby Lancaster, Pennsylvania. Suggested to director Willard Van Dyke by the Steelworkers Organizing Committee, Newcastle had been badly affected by the introduction of automatic, high-speed strip mills in the steel industry, which displaced workers at a rate of thirty to one. Now two-thirds of the town was on relief. Van Dyke's job was to produce a twenty-five-minute film exploring the effects of joblessness resulting from new technology, and proposing new national programs that would assist workers in relocating and would reindustrialize to create new jobs.

Van Dyke lived for four months in Newcastle, winning over the unemployed workers to the necessity of such a film, earning their trust much as an anthropologist might with his informants in the field. Purposely avoiding the use of professional actors, Van Dyke used these same workers on the screen, at certain points in the film having them mouth their lines, which later would be dubbed in by actors' voices. Film sequences show actual steel mills at work, though United States Steel would not permit its new machines to be filmed.

In a naturalist vein, the town itself is the protagonist, as the camera pans across the lonely rooftops, the alleys between the rows of sad, desolate dwellings, and the chimneys no longer belching progress. The narrator is the folksy mayor of the town, an honest representative of his people who is unable to act in isolation. The well-known radio actor Ray Collins, who had often been heard with Orson Welles's Mercury Theatre of the Air and who by 1940 was known to radio audiences as Dr. Benjamin Ordway on CBS's "Crime Doctor," played this sympathetic role. (Afterward, Collins went to California to play the political boss in *Citizen Kane.*) Ben Maddow, who considered himself a "proletarian poet," wrote the script, based on Spencer Pollard's scenario.

The political ideas of *Valley Town* describe exactly the meeting ground between the capitalism of Alfred P. Sloan and the Communism of some of those who worked on the film. In the interest of both would be the reindustrialization of the country: from General Motors' point of view for the sake of greater profits, and from the left perspective for the sake of full employment and for economic and military strength against fascism. For though conceived more than a year before the Hitler-Stalin Pact in August 1939, by the time the film was completed in mid-1940, the left realized that it was only a question of time before the Soviet Union and the United States would be dragged into the year-old war. If the Soviets thought to gain precious time to prepare their industry for war production by staving off the Nazis for some unforeseeable period, the American left now also perceived a stake in economic and military preparedness. As a foretaste of the left's wartime policy of strict obedience to capitalist economics in the struggle against the Axis powers, *Valley Town* shows no unions, no problems of race discrimination, nor any struggle against domestic enemies of democracy, as might be indicated in a production more completely conceived and controlled by left-wing filmmakers. How the populist mayor came to be elected, who his allies are, and what forces stand behind the mill owners, all these questions are left behind.

The mayor also takes care not to blame unemployment on the machines themselves. He only points up the lack of a national program to train and reemploy the jobless workers. Capitalism as such is not the focus. Indeed, contrasting sequences appear of the flourishing town during flush times a decade earlier, with heavy Christmas buying as the summum bonum of a healthy system. These scenes were shot in the relatively more prosperous Lancaster. Of course, to a large extent, the film was already obsolete by the time it appeared because the nadir of the Depression had long since passed, industry was picking up, and a national policy of war preparation had begun.

There was little question of Marc Blitzstein's appropriateness as the composer for *Valley Town.* He played through some of his songs to Van Dyke and others in the company and was engaged immediately, for one thousand dollars. They signed a contract in mid-April 1940, and the score was due by May 5. Naturally, his opera on the steel industry made him exactly suitable, and it helped as well that he already had the experience of three films behind him. Van Dyke had studied violin as a child, had once played saxophone in a jazz ensemble, and enjoyed the company of musicians and composers. He would make whatever musical concessions Blitzstein needed. When the composer at the Moviola found that he needed additional footage to complete his musical ideas, Van Dyke willingly returned to Newcastle to shoot it, even though a year later certain details on the principal actors, such as hairlines and apparel, had changed. When the script called for a monologue by an unemployed worker, the composer suggested a musicated recitative, and Van Dyke readily agreed. He knew he was taking some chances on Blitzstein's ideas but trusted the composer's judgment. When Blitzstein tried to inject his politics, however, Van Dyke had to spurn the advice: He would not warn, for instance, that in the 1920s it only *appeared* as though there were no economic problems. To develop the subtleties and nuances of this point of view would require the resources of a full-length movie.

In the first half of the film, the only voice is the narrator's: In keeping with the theme that the workers have been made obsolete, their voices are suppressed. In the second half, Blitzstein accomplished something toward his ideal of a "film opera," whose sources are easily located in Eisler's score to Brecht's *Kuhle Wampe,* a German proletarian film made a decade before. There, for example, the "Solidarity" song is heard as the mental counterpart to the faces of workers on the screen but is not sung by them. This technique, common enough later on, was up to this time unknown in America. Blitzstein's scoring is for flute, clarinet, saxophone, trumpet, trombone, percussion, piano, and strings, amplified by the sound effects of passing trains, trucks, and factory whistles. Alexander Smallens conducted and Alex North played the piano. Henry Brant, more adept at the "commercial" sound required for film and sought after by many "art" composers for this reason, orchestrated the score to Blitzstein's specifications.

To the opening credits, the composer put a strongly accented, muscled statement. When the mayor introduces himself and the theme of the film, the camera depicts the desolation of the town. Over the tombstones of the workers who have come here and died, Blitzstein plays an appropriate theme marked *grave, tempo morendo.* For scenes in which the energetic steel-rolling mills are busy, he employs playful, jazzy, syncopated rhythms rapidly alternating between 4/4 and 3/4. This section comes about the closest Blitzstein ever wrote to pure machine music, a concept he considered limited. Once, discussing the topic, he concluded that "unfortunately for the idea, the machines themselves began to be perfected just about the time this cult was getting underway, and proved to us that the best machines make the least noise, thus leaving the motto and the theory high and dry."[1] But undeniably, steel manufacturing made plenty of noise, and this passage of the *Valley Town* score provided the composer the one opportunity in the film to liven up what is, on the whole, a very sad tale. At the final bar to this section, Brant playfully penned in the words *"endo dello machino inferno,"* adding a skull and crossbones for extra amusement.

Once the film turns from the sociological and focuses in on a few representative individuals to drive home the points, Blitzstein has the opportunity to write some vocal music. An unemployed worker is seen plodding through the streets of the town, and over him a distraught voice renders a soulful streetwise soliloquy, "What am I goin' home for?" The desperation of family life is a clear function of bad economic times. But he does not sing this passage; it is rhythmic speech integrated with a stop-and-start accompaniment, mostly on the strings.

Without interruption, the film continues to show the inside of the worker's home, where his wife is tending the baby in its crib, preparing a skimpy dinner, counting up the pennies for the week's meager budget, and watching the infernal drip from the sink. Here Blitzstein moves from speech into song, careful to remember his own warning against "sentimentalizing a sophisticated mood" in theatre music. The song "How Long?" is one of the most Weillian songs of Blitzstein's entire output—or as Van Dyke said of it, "It's so Brechtian that it's almost plagiarism"—a blues with sweet-and-sour intervals and a depressed wistfulness:

Oh, far away, there's a place
with work and joy and cheer,
Oh, far away,
Oh, far away from here.

Again, the actress on the screen does not sing the song; she moves about her kitchen while the music tells her story. For a few moments, the husband reenters, his voice-over speaking about the wonders of the modern age; he removes the toaster, presumably to sell it, and walks out the door, leaving open the question whether he will even return. Then the wife's song resumes in almost a dirge. It is a noble piece of music and would have been worth publishing in sheet-music form. The film concludes with a continuous musical passage that leads from the melancholy emasculation symbol of smokestacks being torn down to the upbeat brass fanfare that announces a new national policy of putting people back to work—which would come, of course, in war. *"Endo di movio grande,"* quipped Brant.

When *Valley Town* was completed, it was subjected to a "swear-in" test to determine audience reaction, a method generally used to evaluate commercial advertising. The negative and positive response levels wavered without significant reaction up to the wife's song, at which point both the "like" and "dislike" ratings soared. Van Dyke kept the song. When he showed the film to Alfred Sloan, the tycoon was infuriated with the number. Thinking that "far away" represented not some mythical dreamworld but a real place, Sloan shouted at the director, "They're talking about Russia!" He truly believed the filmmakers had tried to sneak in a message of Communist propaganda. To no avail, Van Dyke tried to reassure him that the workers just wanted to find a way out; Van Dyke had been to Russia in 1935 and had seen for himself that conditions were far from ideal there. No one else on the project had been there to observe children sleeping under bridges at night and begging in the streets by day. Sloan insisted on changes before allowing the film to be distributed. At this point Van Dyke, Blitzstein, and others associated with the film left in despair and would have nothing more to do with it.

A compliant film editor altered the film so that instead of concluding with an as yet unrealized hope for the future, now America was well on its way to a rebuilt economy, and thankfully all have learned the lesson of the 1930s. The singer for the wife's song was changed also, so that instead of a bluesy singing actress, the film now featured a trained operatic vocalist who rendered the words virtually unintelligible.*

Henry Brant, who orchestrated the score, conducted the remake, which was released in the spring of 1941. Curiously, it fell to Joris Ivens, regarded as the international commissar of documentary filmmaking, to console Van Dyke and Blitzstein. He reminded them that after all, the film would soon be irrelevant and forgotten, and that one should be prepared to make far more wrenching compromises in life than this one. With the cautionary reminder to save at least one print of the original for the future, he urged them to put aside their concerns.

B. H. Haggin used the film to take a broad swipe at Blitzstein in *The Nation.* He claimed that though Blitzstein often came up with original tricks, such as that decade-old string quartet marked *largo, largo, largo,* he lacked a true talent for composing. The score to *Valley Town* was a good example: "while it did not offer any music with the significance and power that were required, it did offer a feature that was novel, daring, provocative of controversy." Paul Bowles and Henry Cowell both reviewed *Valley Town* more favorably for *Modern Music,* praising it for its innovations, singling out the husband's soliloquy and the overall skillful scoring. One commentator, Elsie Finn in the Philadelphia *Record,* hailed the photography as a series of images superior to the work of the Soviet master filmmaker Sergei Eisenstein.[2]

When Spencer Pollard proposed other films using the talents of such men as Ivens and Ralph Steiner, Sloan called a halt to the entire project, withdrew his support from the films already in progress, and gave his money instead to the Foreign Policy Association. Van Dyke was hired to make a film for that organization and subsequently embarked on a motoring trip from Caracas to Buenos Aires with Ben Maddow as scriptwriter. They came up with *The Bridge,* dealing with the triangular trade of precious commodities between Latin America, Europe, and the United States.

New York University would later rent out the new version of *Valley Town,*

*The identity of neither singer is known.

its brochure referring to Blitzstein's "stirring musical score." The American Association for Adult Education showed it and produced a classroom discussion booklet on the themes of unemployment and defense, but it never achieved a commercial release. By the time the United States entered the war, *Valley Town* and its message were forgotten. Its subsequent revival—in Van Dyke's original version—emerges from film students' interest in the documentary masterpieces of the 1930s, of which *Valley Town* surely is one. Indeed, after a long career in the medium that involved the creation of dozens of films, Van Dyke claimed to feel prouder of *Valley Town* than of any other work.

During the spring of 1940, Blitzstein participated in several more concerts for Spanish prisoner and refugee relief, at the Mecca Temple and elsewhere, frequently performing songs from the always imminent new opera, *No for an Answer.* Significantly, the Party's attention focused more on the victims of a war already over than on those suffering now during the so-called "phony war" period. According to worldwide Communist thinking, dominated naturally by the Soviets, it made little difference that England and France should be at war against Germany; all of them were imperialist powers and deserved to wear each other down. The Communists pointed out that indeed the belligerents did not seem to be fighting very much; thus, according to Communist lights, this was a "phony war." Perhaps the imperialists were still holding out for some way to join forces against the Soviets. Communists even expected that should England lose the war, it might be for the best, since it would write the final chapter to oppressive British colonialism.

In keeping with this spirit, the Flatbush Arts Theatre put on a production of *Cradle* that April, on the twenty-third anniversary of the U.S. entrance into the First World War. Emile Renan played the Gent and Gus, Arthur Zipser was Dauber, Manny Green (later a manager for Joan Baez) was Mr. Mister, Frank Maxwell was Harry Druggist, and Jane Hoffman was Mrs. Mister; both Maxwell and Hoffman went into professional acting careers. Preceding the Blitzstein work, a musical setting by Lou Cooper set the tone of the evening: "The Yanks Are Not Coming"—this time, American boys would not come to save the world for European imperialism. As Betty Garrett used to sing in another sketch from the same period:

Stop knittin' for Britain,
And pearlin' for Berlin.
There's plenty to do over here.

Although an overwhelming majority of the American public wished to stay neutral in the war, the Party's pro-Soviet, propeace line was tricky. Its defenders were forced to draw nice distinctions between its policy and the anti-intervention stance of such right-wing groups as the America First Committee. With the support of known pro-German conservatives such as Henry Ford and Charles Lindbergh, and other anti-Communist but liberal leaders such as Chester Bowles and the Socialist Norman Thomas, the Committee in effect acted as a cover for continued trade and industrial investment in German capitalism, by now wholly devoted to the war economy.

The fact of a war in Europe naturally made an impact on the cultural scene, and Blitzstein figured the politics of music into his observations for *Modern Music.* Cole Porter's *Dubarry Was a Lady* struck the reviewer as exemplary of a certain mood: "A war is on, and we all have the premonitory jitters. So we are being doggedly Broadway; I mean doggedly tried-and-true." Elmer Rice's *Two on an Island* had musical arrangements by Weill, which Blitzstein thought shabby and trite. The same composer's radio cantata to a text by Maxwell Anderson, *Magna Carta,* seemed "nervously exalted, as though obedient to some tenet of the year that demands composers be musically patriotic." Rodgers and Hart's *Too Many Girls* was "infantile" and *Two for the Show* by Hamilton and Lewis "inept." Of a Viennese-American show called *Reunion in New York,* he held mixed impressions, confessing that he "got emotional at the number 'Where Is My Homeland?,' but maybe I'm a pushover for that kind of thing." Clifford Odets's *Night Music* had opened, with a score by Hanns Eisler that Blitzstein found "in every way a thoroughly good job."[3]

In the same issue, Blitzstein reviewed Oscar Levant's best-selling memoir, *A Smattering of Ignorance.* He regarded the book as a carelessly written piece of wisecracking self-castigation. "Above all," he asked archly, "has he not taken a couple of wicked potshots at me (at once happy and embarrassed to be included in a book devoted to People who Currently Count)? Has he not delivered me over to the lions of snobism and the vultures of venality? I burn with a desire for vengeance." Levant had commented on the ill-received Serenade for string quartet and, for the most part positively, on *Cradle.* In what may have been a sly reference to Blitzstein's homosexuality, Levant had found the "pseudo-virility" of *Cradle* "forced and artificial." On one point Blitzstein found confirmation of his own views: "In the movie-music chapter, there is a wealth of enjoyable new information about why not to go West."[4]

A friend of Marc's, Emanuel Eisenberg, was a moderately talented writer but had an abrasive personality and a deep sensitivity about his unattractive, acne-scarred face. He had material in the 1935 *Parade,* in *Pins and Needles,* and in the Cabaret TAC shows in the spring of 1940. He wrote theatre criticism for the *New Masses* and also worked in the press department of the Group Theatre. Eisenberg had written a "Jobless Blues," and he got Blitzstein to write "Negro" music for it. One night they met at Cafe Society to show the song to Billie Holiday and to ask her opinion. She did not like it at all, and on each of her criticisms, Blitzstein agreed wholeheartedly, thus, in Eisenberg's presence, invalidating their collaboration. Deeply hurt by this betrayal and embarrassment, the lyricist wrote a seven-page letter to Blitzstein chafing at the slight. Why had the composer not discussed his reservations about the song in advance? Eisenberg did not wish to close off the possibility of further work with Blitzstein; rather, he wanted to clear the air for it, if the composer could work with anyone at all.

Eisenberg's missive took on the character of one spurned in love, and this may have been closer to the true nature of his pain; many of his friends assumed him to be homosexual, while others believed he would be happier if he *was* homosexual. Not long after, he went up in a two-seater plane over New York harbor with a leftist pilot friend whom he had asked for flying lessons. Eisenberg panicked suddenly—or he may have chosen this as his means of suicide—and jumped out to his death.

Whatever Eisenberg's personal unhappiness, the incident over the "Jobless Blues" reveals Blitzstein's difficulty with collaboration. Rather than try to correct it, he preferred to encase himself all the more securely within it, just as he had persuaded himself that he lacked a true capacity for love. He raised and discussed some of these problems in a *Herald Tribune* article, "On Collaborating with Oneself," published in conjunction with the premiere of *No for an Answer.*

Blitzstein described his modus operandi, his freedom to range over the entirety of what he had conceived, both lyrically and musically, and to make minor or major adjustments at will. For "I don't write words first, or music first, but both in a discontinuous and muddy stream":

> This possibility of a close-woven texture of words and music, of ideas and treatment, is the one real advantage of collaborating with one's self. There aren't many others. There certainly aren't enough to make plausible the rumor that I insist upon doing the whole job myself. I simply have not found the collaborator who has either the patience or the inner strength to put up with me. In the few instances I have tried working with a poet we managed to get constantly in each other's way—emotionally, ideationally, even geographically.
>
> And yet I know that the introduction of another mind, another psyche, upon the work at hand can be an inestimable boon; it can also be a great time- and energy-saver. For I am a musician, addicted to the theater, not a playwright. If I write plays, it is in order to put music to them. Which means that I must learn the craft of making plays while I am writing them.[5]

The Cradle Will Rock had taken five weeks to write and compose, and was given to the public before a year had elapsed. *No for an Answer* took three and a half years, admittedly with substantial interruptions along the way. *Cradle* is a play in music, or a musical or *Singspiel.* Or as its author once put it, "that Blitzstein—uh—thing."[6] But *No for an Answer* is by almost any definition an opera, "a musical-dramatic work in which there is a pervading and primary relation between the music and the stage-action," in the creator's words. Throughout the course of its composition, Blitzstein wrote and discarded more music, even whole scenes, than he had ever done before. Some scenes he wrote just as practice—background scenes to deepen his understanding of his characters. In all, he estimated that he had written six hours' worth of material for this work. He pulled and tugged at it endlessly, making substantial changes and cuts right to the end. This turned out to be the standard practice in Blitzstein's career.

He apparently didn't mind the deliberation and all the wasted time: For him, the price of collaboration was even higher.

Here is how he introduced the opera in program notes for the subsequent recording:

> The plot of *No for an Answer* deals with a club of Greek-American workers in the U.S.A. It is a workers' social club; not a social workers' club. Its quarters are the back room of a roadside lunchcounter two miles outside Crest Lake, a summer resort. Nick Kyriakos owns and runs the lunchcounter, and he has made the big barn-like room attached to it into the clubroom. The members are the people employed during the season in town: waiters, hotel-workers, restaurant-workers, chefs, laundresses, chambermaids, taxi-drivers. They are now, most of them, without work. The time of the play is around September 15, just after the summer season has closed; the hotels are boarded up, shops and bars closed; a skeleton town, a town like a morgue, waits for next summer. Some of the workers have followed the trade to Atlantic City, Miami, the mountains; but some are forced to stay on. These are the ones we find coming to the Diogenes Club—for comfort, hope, company, enough morale to last out the winter. They hold conversations, meetings, study-classes, socials, card-games, and especially chorus rehearsals. Being Greek-Americans, they equip the action with a Greek Chorus of singing waiters, who keep us informed of plot developments.
>
> It is the life and fate of the Diogenes Club and its little people which forms the opera; tragic episodes, comic interludes, individual love stories, plans, anguish, determinations, setbacks, triumphs. The Club is having a hard time to survive. There is almost total unemployment; besides, the hotel owners' Resort Association, fearing the threat of a union (aliens and a group spirit are an "alarming" combination), worry and harry the Club, and launch an offensive which culminates in the murder of Joe, the Club's leader, and the burning of the Club. This is the main thread.
>
> Then there is also the story of Paul and Clara Chase. Paul is a youngish rich intellectual, who fancies he sympathizes with the workers in their struggle, and wishes to lead them. Really he is a trapped liberal, given to heavy drinking, who finally succumbs to the pressure and pull of his conditioning. His wife, Clara, is drawn into the Club's problems because of Paul's espousal of them; she is a rich girl, sister of a Congressman, who has always believed, without investigation, in the actuality of freedom and democracy in America. She finally emerges into a dawning consciousness of how real is the persecution of little people going on about her.
>
> The opera centers about Joe, who has returned from a Georgia prison term; Nick Kyriakos, his father, who "insists" America be the truly democratic country he dreamed of; Francie, Joe's girl; the other members of the club; and Paul and Clara. When Joe is killed, and the Club is set on fire, the little handful of new "refugees" are left with nothing but their spirit, their song: "No for an Answer." At the end, Nick, with incalculable courage, begins over the dead body of his son to "plan for tomorrow." The chorus behind him catch the fire in his voice; they start slowly to sing

> the final song as he doggedly, methodically, itemizes small gains; a meeting to be held at such a place, a collection to be taken up, a mimeograph machine to be rescued from the fire. The little people will go on.

This, then, is intended more as a musical novel with fully developed characters than as a revue with loosely connected episodes. Indeed, a source for Blitzstein's theme was that whole tradition of Russian novels by Turgenev and others that featured bourgeois youth going out to the countryside or to the working class and throwing themselves into the revolutionary movement, usually with disastrous results. If superficially the labor-organizing theme of *No for an Answer* appears the same as *Cradle*'s, it should be stressed that while *Cradle* deals with the highly concentrated steel industry, the later opera deals with a much harder to organize service sector, decentralized, centripetal, and often involving a transient population only recently arrived in America. The implications go much broader and deeper, suggesting that no class of workers in America should remain unorganized and unrepresented.

As with *Cradle*'s Joe Hammer, Blitzstein uses the name Joe for his hero. By this time, Earl Robinson's song in tribute to IWW labor organizer Joe Hill had become popular on the left. The inevitable inference can also be drawn to Joe Stalin. Just as much a reference can be made to Marc's sister Jo, in her own way one of the "little people" of America, active in so many committees and causes in Philadelphia. In fact, according to her:

> *No for an Answer* was written after Marc had spent part of a winter with me in Ventnor, N.J., where I lived from '36 to '39. A long cold winter in a resort town out of season gave us a chance to see the inside workings of the people who served. We actually spent a great deal of time with 2 Greek cooks and a whole coterie of bright workers who were trying to better their conditions. When Marc got back to New York and began to work on this idea, one of the things that must have struck him forcibly was the rather pathetic role people like us (middle-class intellectuals) played in the lives of these people. In the end they were of more use to us than we to them.[7]

More important than the name, perhaps, are the strength and warmth of the father-son relationship. Nick and Joe enjoy the same easy comradeship that Marc had with his own father.

It is a pity that before the final production of the opera, Joe's clever song "Outside Agitator" was cut. In it, he objects to the way labor organizers are always blamed for coming in and stirring up trouble in nonunionized areas, while at the same time the owners see no problem importing Wall Street lawyers and union-busters to do their work.

The name Clara has its resonance, too: It was Marc's grandmother Levitt's name. Gradually Clara becomes "clear" as to what is happening to traditional American freedoms. Indeed, her moving song about growing up to this wisdom, sung to Paul while he sleeps off a binge, is called "In the Clear." In it, Clara represents Blitzstein's own emergence from his self-conscious, iconoclastic brat-genius period into a mature, disciplined mastery of his craft and social point of view:

Yes, we love your lovely talents,
And your charm it charms us too;
But your charm and talents
Simply happened to you.
Well, they won't see you through.
You're out among bigger boys.
Stop playing with toys.
So I'm in the clear—Hooray for me.
Does it have to be so lonely?

Blitzstein lavished attention on his minor characters, perhaps to such a degree that they distract from the main story. Among them is a lumpen-type named Mike, who out of his poverty and lack of class consciousness becomes a spy for the Resort Association. The composer gives him a brilliant soliloquy of musicated speech, similar in technique to the husband's soliloquy in *Valley Town,* in which he explains his philosophy of life—basically, "get mine." Another is Cutch the choral director (Blitzstein took the name of one of his first cousins), who in his rehearsals symbolizes musically the small gains the union drive tries to consolidate politically. Still another is Bulge, a former Wobbly hobo who befriended Joe riding the rails. He has two big numbers: a deft satire called "Penny Candy," one of Blitzstein's best comedy songs, in which he mocks the upper class's pity for the downtrodden; and "The Purest Kind of a Guy," a birthday tribute to Joe, in which Blitzstein's own interest in men is idealized:

I got a extra sense:
I know what guys is like.
I know what makes em tick
I know what makes em click.
And when a man's okay,
I know it a mile away!
There's a kind of man—
When he passes by:
I can tell that man's
The purest kind of a guy.
Black or white or tan
Ain't the reason why
I will know that man's
The purest kind of a guy.
Go on and ask me how I can be certain,
How I can pick him out like a shot,
And he will never upset my plot,
By actin' dirty and sly
Like the usual guy in a spot;

Well I don't know how I know that I know,
But I know he will not!

Another pair of characters Blitzstein brings in purely for comic relief are the nightclub entertainers Jimmy and Bobbie, who perform privately for the escapist Paul. Their two numbers, fused into one routine, are "Dimples," a silly Broadway Hot-Cha patter, and "Fraught," Bobbie's spoof on torch songs that if for nothing else would place Blitzstein among the highest ranks of musical parodists. Taking off from such tunes as "Body and Soul," "I Get a Kick Out of You," "Mad About the Boy," and "I've Got You Under My Skin," he once called "Fraught" his "Coel Poward number." Cut from the final version of the show was another extended send-up, this time of "The Litt'ry and Artistic Scene, 1930," in which Bobbie and Jimmy depict the vapid, cynical world of writers abroad. It was a world of which Blitzstein had seen plenty when he left to come back home:

I want to be an émigré—the Heming-way,
And walk—and talk—and look the way a hero looks,
In all the very ultramodern books.
Life's only bearable to me in Italy.
When I'm at home in Rome, I'm like the Romans are—
I always do my roamin' near the bar.
I love that cryptic, elliptic mode of speech,
Somewhere's a ruin, somewhere a beach,
Grapes and rapes within my reach—
Oh, ain't it great?
I'm an expatriate!

In the program for *The Cradle Will Rock* at the Windsor Theatre, Blitzstein had characterized his new opera as "concerned with the chances of youth in the modern world." Again, as in *Cradle,* he is not so much preaching to the working class—this would have been presumptuous—as to the middle class of which he was a part. If professionals and intellectuals are to be useful to the workers in their struggles, if they are to help stem the tide of reaction, they must avoid ultraleft romanticism of the anarchist or Trotskyist kind. He had in fact studied the Communist leader Earl Browder's book *The People's Front,* published in 1938, and underlined passages referring to the childish impatience, the so-called "Blanquism" and individualism of pseudorevolutionaries, who "lead the revolution" so far ahead of the working class that none but a few splinter groups dare to join in. Blitzstein's character of Paul Chase represents this tendency to be drawn in one way or another to cults and escapism. Paul accuses Joe of limited sights in promoting "only" a union. By contrast, Blitzstein says, let us instead adopt a sober, disciplined plan in which the working class truly leads. Joe Kyriakos is the working-class hero of the opera. Clara Chase, with whom the audience identifies, represents the middle-class intelligentsia whose support is so crucial. Her consciousness evolves slowly, until by the end she has become a firm pillar of the struggle.

Who leads Joe is unstated, not even hinted at in the opera, but clearly he gets his ideas and his methods from somewhere. In prison he has met Max Kraus, a Jewish lawyer from the International Labor Defense, whom he brings home with him to Crest Lake. Aside from the local farmers and tradespeople enjoined to unite with the hotel workers against the Resort Association and its thug allies, this suggests some kind of left-democratic alliance in the union campaign. Somewhere behind the alliance no doubt stands a shadowy Communist Party.

Blitzstein's "cover" for the Party is consistent with the Party's strategy at the time, and for the most part since: While the Party functioned openly, maintaining an active press and even running candidates for public office, much of the work that it perceived had to be done in this country to combat fascist activity was not specifically Party work. Forming unions, protecting civil rights of immigrants and minorities, preserving the right of free speech, fighting for unemployment benefits, Social Security, and other social legislation, demanding more jobs, organizing against war—all these tasks could and should be the work of much broader sectors, organizationally independent of the Party.

At that time, though, the people most deeply committed to those goals were often Communists. Their vision and their passion moved them to promote these causes at risk of their lives and fortune. Naturally, their point of view helped inform the politics of these struggles. The House Committee on Un-American Activities would call this kind of activity "front" work for the Communist Party. But apart from the dyed-in-the-wool anti-New Dealers, the Communists' influence in these areas coincided in large part with the aspirations of an American people exhausted by the Depression and seeking a way out of the cycle of war. Blitzstein himself serves as a good example in his own field: A talented composer who might have become wealthy and famous by going the commercial route, either in Hollywood or on Broadway, instead commits himself to a career of relative penury in order to write works that will influence his country in a progressive direction.

Among the criticisms made of *Cradle* was that Blitzstein had failed to exploit the resources of his chorus. Not until the end did they really have much to do. In *No for an Answer,* the chorus plays a more central role, though they are not always the "Greek chorus" Blitzstein cites; they are within the action, part of it, not standing on the outside. Thereby Blitzstein shows his understanding of music's function for large groups, as a binding and uplifting force capable of creating a sense of solidarity as few other activities can. His choruses are written in Brecht's *Misuk* style for untrained voices. Much of his choral music is in unison, but sometimes he drifts into the sour harmonies found in "Invitation to Bitterness." The choruses also teach important lessons, such as "Take the Book" ("Workers, do your homework!"), or "The Song of the Bat," applying to the rootless character Mike, in the Hanns Eisler *Gebrauchsmusik* mode:

> *Once there was a war of the Beasts and the Birds.*
> *The two armies asked the Bat to come and join them,*
> *But the Bat could not decide which to join.*

He told the Birds, I'm a Beast,
And told the Beasts, I'm a Bird now.
But when the war was over,
The Bat came to join in the rejoicing.
The Birds flew against him,
So he went where the Beasts were.
The Beasts nearly tore him to pieces.
This is what a worker can learn from the Bat:
He'd better know which side he's on,
And not be torn to pieces
By both sides.

In contrast to the immigrants actively seeking to learn the lessons of American democracy, Blitzstein counterposes the mob of Monktowners that the Resort Association mobilizes against the Diogenes Club and the growing union movement. He never quite defines who comprises the mob, but they are clearly people who feel threatened by the Greeks; perhaps they are underemployed themselves, a lumpen element to whom Hitler so easily appealed in Germany. In their xenophobia they are subject to superpatriotic, fascistic invocations, and are likely subsidized by the resort owners. Blitzstein's portrayal of the mob recalls the easily excitable small-town citizens in Fritz Lang's 1936 film *Fury.* Lang, an anti-fascist immigrant to America, like Nick Kyriakos, insists on America's fulfilling its promise of liberty.

In an attempt to define a place for himself in his America, Blitzstein drafted a statement that easily applies to *No for an Answer* and to the musical contribution he sought to make:

> I love this country. For the matter of that, I love all countries. What I love is people. I am ashamed of the meanness and stupidity which disorganizes people, and I am proud of the insight and generosity which organizes them. If you were to limit me to my nation in the matter of love and loyalty and belief, then I might ask you to limit me also to the region, the state, the city, the street, the house, the room, the corner I call my own, for my exclusive love and loyalty and belief. Really, you are asking me to recline, like the Greek Narcissus, gazing at myself in a pool, with eyes of worship. I am against that; it seems to me that the complex that I am, and the complex that I am not, which is to say the Others, must have a traffic system, must join, must above all *equate,* before my conception of the way things ought to be will be satisfied. This is not nearly so unrealistic as it might sound to ears attuned only to "Number One". What I think I mean is Culture; and I might reduce Culture in definition to the smallest particle of join-up in this sense; wherever different people, plus time, plus experiences, simply living experiences, stack up a shapeless thing that gets shaped by more people, more time, more living experiences, a style is created; and when several of these styles are discovered to have joined, and shapelessly, slowly to have taken on a shape, we have, lo, a Culture.[8]

Blitzstein confessed that he had not started out as a playwright and had had to feel his way. In the end, *No for an Answer* has an overly episodic structure, with some ten scenes in each of its two acts. There is only a fraction of a love song between Joe and Francie; she speaks, wanting to bring him up to date on local developments since he left town, and he sings her name over and over, yearning for her touch. Innovative in form, this is one of Blitzstein's few love songs; what is important about it is how exactly and movingly he communicates the experience of two people in love but in different moods. His comedy songs are interpolated in arbitrary places and do nothing to advance the plot. Even when they minimally help to develop character, they do so for unimportant people in the play. Though he possessed an undeniable gift for words, his belabored libretto often betrays the sense that for him, in these years, the message far outdistanced the poetry.

Yet many of the individual songs are memorable and easily extractable as solo numbers—"Penny Candy," "The Purest Kind of a Guy," "Fraught," "In the Clear." These were the tunes Blitzstein used to promote the show in guest appearances at benefits for over two years. And he continued to employ his own unique combination of speech patterns, rhythmic speech, song, dialogue with and without underscoring, abandoning the standard Broadway habit of actors suddenly stopping the show to break into song.

Beyond that, as a playwright Blitzstein continued to experiment with innovative techniques. For a time he considered illustrating one of Paul's escape mechanisms as a marijuana ballet, incorporating some "high" dialogue, though in the end he opted for the more conventional alcohol. He used the flashback again, but now he divided the stage into halves: On one side characters in the present are discussing events in the past, while on the other side the past is acted out. Some characters even move back and forth between the two sides of the stage. He also considered using a flash-forward: In one early note he wrote, "Maybe—here is a long chance—it all starts in 1937, and goes to 1940, beyond the audience's date—(unless it waits around that long for a performance—ha ha)." Having done so much more work on this opera than on *Cradle,* he believed—he had to believe—that it was by far the superior piece.

Among the characters and scenes originally planned for *No for an Answer,* Blitzstein included a homosexual named Evie (who later evolved into the I've-seen-it-all, possibly gay journalist named Cookie, and ultimately into the sensitive lawyer Max Kraus, of indeterminate orientation). He described Evie in his working notes:

> An old bland tante of a man, personally no longer interested in sex, but he knows all the variations, has probably been through them all. Without convictions, but with a curious honesty; utterly aware, rather wise. No morality, no blindness, no evasions. Funny, a definite comic; clear about everything except values—and he begins to get them as the play goes on (perhaps discusses the need for them immediately.) He becomes [Paul's] duenna, sort of, follows him about, takes care of the messes. Not exactly

in love with him, you gather their relation is not clear, [Paul] tolerates him, soon finds him indispensable. Model: Douggie [Allan Ross Macdougall], Virgil Thomson.

In some ways, of course, the model is Blitzstein himself, a gay man attracted to a bright, straight-acting, hard-drinking, would-be labor hero. One discarded scene set in a dive has a young couple—man and woman—out for some thrills, trying to pick up Mike, the penniless roustabout. In another early draft of a barroom delirium scene, he has Paul drunkenly singing to Evie:

The workers are wonderful. the jews are terrible.
what do you think of women? oh, you're a homosexual.
ought I say -ist? homosexualist? I missed the -ist,
I want to be fair!
oh where is the solace and peace and security?
where is the purity? y'see?
impure! impure! are you sure
you don't mean
unclean, unclean? see what I mean?
take it away; it hots me!

The stream of consciousness, with the references to homosexuality deleted long before the final version of the script, suggests Blitzstein's discomfort with his own orientation. He had no inclination toward effeminacy; his ever-present mustache asserted that, not to mention his cultivated habit of inhaling while his cigarette lay dangling from his lips, the smoke curling into his eyes and causing him to wince from the irritation. No, he was a man, he could be sure of that, but a man who liked men. It was hard to feel good about yourself if you were that way in 1940. Once, in his notes on the opera, he cautioned himself that his Diogenes Club members "don't fuck around enough—show them warm, healthy about sex." But if he wanted to introduce a homosexual character, what types in the literary vocabulary of the day could he refer to if he also wanted to show the homosexual in an equally natural, healthy way? Such types did not exist. Homosexuals were only portrayed negatively, as degenerates, outcasts, perverts, and criminals. In all probability, Blitzstein deleted the scene in order not to fall into an unfortunate repeat of the stereotype. The moment for the positive gay character in popular culture had not yet arrived.

Eventually, like an overdue baby, *No for an Answer* had to come out. The work had been "written and rewritten, brooded over, bathed in sweat, alternately smoothed and slapped," Blitzstein wrote in the *Times.*[9] He had worked on it in St. Thomas, Saranac Lake, Ventnor, Yaddo, Ashfield, Philadelphia, and New York. The composer could tinker with it until doomsday, giving benefit previews for dozens more good causes, but sooner or later he had to declare it ready to be seen. In the meantime, since the Nazi-Soviet Pact of 1939, Communist Party fortunes had declined as its sympathizers became disillusioned. One prominent literary critic, Granville Hicks, had publicly resigned in protest, and many more Party members quietly followed. The Party's press circulation plummeted. If the opera waited too much longer, its base of support in the theatre might vanish completely.

In the spring of 1940, the opera began moving toward production. Random House signed an agreement with Blitzstein to publish the script. A producing company came together, consisting of the Random House editor and publisher Bennett Cerf, writer John Henry Hammond, Jr., Lillian Hellman, producer Lincoln Kirstein, playwright Arthur Kober, and director Herman Shumlin, with James D. Proctor, a playwright and theatrical press agent who later represented Arthur Miller, as chairman. Kirstein and Shumlin had served on the production committee for *Cradle* back in 1937, and Proctor was on the Cabaret TAC committee. (*Time* magazine sniped that the committee "includes several Communist fellow travelers.") They needed about fifteen hundred dollars to give the opera three Sunday-night "experimental" performances with solo piano accompaniment at the Mecca Temple on West Fifty-fifth Street; that amount would pay for the house rental, promotion, music reproduction, and a musical coach. For a full production, they budgeted the show at upward of thirty thousand dollars.

It was a touchy time—1940 and 1941—for an opera whose premise was fighting off the native fascist infection at home and staying out of the war abroad. As Blitzstein pointed out in one newspaper interview not long after the Italians invaded Greece and were repulsed, the opera was written "before people who thought of Greeks primarily as short-order men, had started eulogizing their bravery."[10]

A number of main-line producers liked Blitzstein's music but not the book, and they refused it. Whether or not they agreed with Blitzstein's premise, commercial producers simply could not see the work as a money-maker. Muriel Draper, the full-time agitator for left-wing causes who had become almost a one-woman institution in New York, attended a backers' audition at the home of William Morris, Jr., Blitzstein's agent. Though she called the opera "a work of genius," she bowed out of joining the producing committee, volunteering only to send more possible backers to the next audition.

"Dear Marc," she wrote on March 21:

> If, in this complex world, it became necessary to organize the Moslem population of North Dakota into an Anti-Japanese-Expansion-of-the-Wool-Growing-Industry-to-Australia Committee, with the object of diminishing the strain on Anglo-Japanese relations, for the reason that if the strain increases the relations may break, which in turn would sharpen the attitude of the U.S. against Japan—unadvisable because it would add to the existing world antagonism to the U.S.S.R. in view of the fact [that] the U.S.S.R. wishes to conciliate Japan for the moment, then I would spend another such evening as I spent with your Production Committee last Tuesday at Mr. Morris's.[11]

Director William E. Watts and Blitzstein selected a star-studded cast for the three performances. Perhaps as many as half the cast were Party members. Though they performed for extremely low pay—$18.12 for the performances and

$20 a week for the rehearsals—no doubt they looked forward to a longer run in a full production where their roles would be already thoroughly rehearsed. Martin Wolfson played Nick Kyriakos, and Robert Simon his son Joe. Norma Green played the girlfriend Francie. Lloyd Gough and Olive Deering were Paul and Clara Chase, and Deering's brother Alfred Ryder played the Jewish lawyer Max Kraus. Though only twenty-two and the veteran of a dozen plays already, Deering had never sung on the stage before; she turned out to have a sweet and serviceable voice. Another pair of siblings, Curt and Bert Conway, sang the roles of Bulge and Mike. Members of the Diogenes Club included Martin Ritt, later a prominent Hollywood director, and Hester Sondergaard (sister of Gale). The club's chorus director Cutch was Charles Polacheck, later a television director. Elaine Perry (daughter of the actress Antoinette Perry, after whom the Tony awards are named) sang in the chorus.

As the nightclub entertainers Jimmy and Bobbie, Coby Ruskin (another later television director) performed the "Dimples" number with Carol Channing. Fresh out of her sophomore year at Bennington College and not yet twenty years old, Channing headed for New York and walked into the offices of the only talent agency of which she had ever heard—the William Morris Agency. She fitted the bill exactly for Bobbie and shortly made her Broadway debut singing "Fraught."

German émigré pianist Trude Rittmann, who had known Marc and Eva at Dartington Hall, rehearsed the chorus. This was her first theatrical job in America, the first in what would be a distinguished and largely unacknowledged career as arranger and composer for Broadway. Norman Cazden, Marc's choice as the soloist for his Piano Concerto back in 1936, served as rehearsal accompanist. Marc Daniels, later a television producer, served as production manager. Howard Bay, a veteran of the Federal Theatre and the designer of Hellman's *The Children's Hour* and *The Little Foxes,* supplied minimal sets. *Modern Music* published one of his sketches for the Blitzstein opera, and another was auctioned off to benefit *New Masses.* Lina Abarbanell attended rehearsals to offer notes. Equity had permitted a two-week rehearsal period instead of the customary four, and the musicians' union cooperated by allowing the production to waive the orchestra.

Several of the cast members of *No for an Answer* seemed to be in the show more for their political dedication than for their experience. Robert Simon was a total newcomer. His only work in the theatre until the fall of 1940 had been painting the walls of the radically leftist New Theatre School on West Forty-seventh Street. However, he had the temerity to audition for Blitzstein, and once the composer heard that he could carry a tune, he got the critical role of Joe. Blitzstein had long believed and often stated a simple tenet: "Anybody can sing." For months before the show went into its final two-week rehearsal period, Simon appeared two or three times a week at Blitzstein's apartment for coaching—once again, Blitzstein had moved, now for the first time out of Greenwich Village, to 327 West Fifty-seventh Street.

In late October the American Youth Theatre, a new avatar of Lou Cooper's Flatbush group, offered *Cradle* at City College's Pauline Edwards Theatre. Betty Garrett was in the cast, as well as Emile Renan, who would later reappear in several Blitzstein shows. Blitzstein took Robert Simon to it; Simon remained unimpressed by the music, though he saw how Cooper's cast idolized Blitzstein backstage after the performance. Only a month later, the City College Dramatic Society performed *Cradle* again at the Pauline Edwards, billing their show as the "first New York production with scenery."

The week *No for an Answer* had its premiere also saw the opening of Kurt Weill's newest creation, *Lady in the Dark.* Already the two composers had diverged greatly. While Blitzstein in many ways was still trapped by the principles of agitprop theatre, Weill had gone on to a more operatic and not at all political style of musical theatre.

Just before the opening, Blitzstein experienced a fright: Like Beethoven, he was going deaf. Someone recommended Dr. Lewis Fraad, known to be friendly to both the left-wing and the theatre crowds. Blitzstein explained his symptoms over the telephone and Fraad asked him to come in for an appointment. The doctor examined him thoroughly, then removed the clumps of wax clogging Blitzstein's ears. The patient seemed a little disappointed—being neither deaf nor Beethoven.

The first performance of *No for an Answer* was slated as a benefit for the American Rescue Ship Mission, headed by Helen Keller as honorary chair. Its purpose was to help Spanish refugees find passage to new homes in South America and then supervise their rehabilitation. The organization made the news the day following the premiere, when the press revealed that Eleanor Roosevelt had resigned from its list of sponsors: The State Department, it seems, had revoked the Mission's license to collect funds for relief work abroad.

No for an Answer had a packed and wildly enthusiastic house on its first night at the Mecca Temple. Critically, it got a receptive welcome in many quarters. Brooks Atkinson hailed it, though added political reservations: "In recent years the dramatic stage has had no better example of the power of music to create men and women through song. . . . No labor union ever had a better concertmaster." Nevertheless, Blitzstein hewed "close to the party line": "No one has ever damned Mr. Blitzstein as a member of the bourgeoisie. *No for an Answer* is labor drama, leaning so far to the left that it is practically horizontal." Virgil Thomson considered this opera less interesting musically than *Cradle.* But "no matter what happens to the present work in the way of commercial success or failure, it is a serious work on a noble subject by a major musical author. Nothing can wash that out." Blitzstein shows a keen dramatic sense, he continued, accurate timing, abundant musical invention, and expressive characterization. "He can draw laughter and tears as few living composers can." Trying to head off the expected criticism that Blitzstein's subject matter was inappropriate to opera, Thomson reminded his readers that the standard offerings were not all so tame, either:

> Embedded and fossilized in the repertories of the most conformist opera foundations are subjects that, if treated less stylistically, would be even today social dynamite. Incest, revolution, suicide, miscegenation, black magic, religious heresy, pessimism, free love, and the abolition of private property are glorified and advocated nightly at the Metropolitan Opera House.[12]

Indeed, the Metropolitan's often rather snobbish magazine *Opera News* came out with an unsigned but wholly laudatory review titled "Yes for an Answer."[13]

Samuel Barlow reviewed the opera for *Modern Music,* praising its "spontaneous" music "in just the right American vein which is so conspicuously out of Mr. Kurt Weill's range, for example. It uses, sparingly but authentically, any jazz rhythms it needs, tosses a Gilbert and Sullivan patter over its shoulder, and rises to the real power of its choruses in a natural and vigorous way." Barlow nominated "Fraught" as "the best Broadway song of the year—a Torch Song to end all Torch Songs." "Mr. Blitzstein's esoteric virtuosity at the piano is not news. What is news is that this is an important work, a big work. It is engrossing, exciting and moving." As for the performer of "Fraught," Robert Simon in *The New Yorker* predicted that "you may hear more about a satirical *chanteuse,* Miss Carol Channing."[14]

Ralph Warner, reviewing for the *Daily Worker,* came in with the anticipated accolades. He caviled at the excessive length of the piece and suggested that for greater effectiveness it would work better in a smaller house. But the opera—no, the event—showed the truth about day-to-day America: "Here was a slice of what is called life—the real struggle which goes on behind the scenes of America in these days when the people face their enemies, when their friends waver, when their foes attack, when the people close ranks and defiantly face the future—certain of ultimate victory." The *New Masses* followed up with a paean to Blitzstein's powers: "If some of our music critics are worried about whether this country will ever produce a composer of major proportions, let them stop worrying, for right in their midst is the brilliant and immensely endowed Marc Blitzstein."[15]

In *Our New Music,* published later that year, Aaron Copland summarized the critical opinion of *No for an Answer* when he wrote that "most commentators are agreed that Blitzstein has an unusual flair for dialogue and lyrics but does less well in the construction of a tightly knit dramatic plot." More important to the development of American music, "For the first time in a serious stage work he gave the typical American tough guy musical characterization. . . . No one has ever before even attempted the problem of finding a voice for all those American regular fellows that seem so much at home everywhere except on the operatic stage. If the opera had nothing more than this to recommend it, its historical importance would be considerable."[16]

Among that first Sunday-night audience sat New York City License Commissioner Paul Moss. He may or may not have liked the show, but when he got to his office the next morning, he issued a ban on further performances. His grounds were that the Mecca Temple lacked a theatre license and that the auditorium was full of building violations, principally that the chairs were not screwed down to the floor. He declared that he had personally tried to obtain such a license, for performances at the municipally-owned building would only mean more revenue for the city, but that the Department of Housing and Buildings, the Fire Department, and the Gas and Electricity Department all sustained objections to using the premises. He warned that if anyone tried to present *No for an Answer* the following week, they would be stopped by police and firemen.

To Blitzstein and his producing committee, it looked like a clear case of censorship—an incident all too reminiscent of *Cradle*'s abortive WPA opening. For during the previous year, they pointed out, numerous theatrical companies had used the Mecca stage, including Alfredo Salmaggi with his popular series of operas that drew up to three thousand people. Sniffing another *scandale* in the air, and maybe even riots or violence (which might be good for the box office), the composer proclaimed to the press, "We expect the cops Sunday night but we're going to give a show, license or no license."[17]

Workmen at the Mecca Temple set to screwing down the seats that week in order to guarantee the second performance. A delegation from the producers demanded to see Mayor La Guardia to insist that the ban be lifted. Others influential in the city's cultural life prevailed upon him as well. Under this kind of public pressure, Paul Moss issued a temporary permit, and the show went on the next Sunday without interference from police or firemen. Of course, the attempt at censorship gave Blitzstein the ultimate satisfaction, for it proved his thesis perfectly—that the underdogs in this society do not enjoy basic democratic rights.

New York sponsors of the Highlander Folk School, a labor organizing community in Monteagle, Tennessee, which Eleanor Roosevelt also supported, booked the January 12 performance as a benefit evening. Part of the evening's proceeds were to be directed toward the defense of twelve defendants in an Oklahoma trial for criminal syndicalism. One of them, twenty-two-year-old Alan Shaw, free on bail pending appeal, addressed the Mecca Temple audience.

On that same night, the Museum of Modern Art sponsored a program of music in films. Blitzstein's contribution was *Valley Town,* but since he was playing at the Mecca Temple, Aaron Copland read Blitzstein's comments about his film to the audience. The January 19 performance of *No for an Answer* came off without trouble from the city.

Almost ten thousand people saw the show. Out of the box office receipts, the sponsors were all paid back in full. The remaining $730 would go toward a new, full production, projected to open at the Jolson Theatre in April if the funds could be raised. The producers sought to gather seventeen thousand dollars for a two-week run, with tickets ranging from fifty cents to two dollars. For his orchestration of *No for an Answer,* still not begun as of the Mecca Temple performances, Blitzstein intended to provide a flute, saxophone, two trumpets, two trombones, violin, cello, bass, piano, and traps. Brooks Atkinson dealt with the economics of Broadway in a piece for the *Times:*

> Marc Blitzstein and his associates in the production of *No for an Answer* kept their costs so low that in three performances, sold at a $2.20 top, they paid all their expenses, including salaries for actors and stagehands. There ought to be some food for bitter thought in the fact that a left-wing play is the only new production this year that has been able

> to crack the box-office barriers and let the people in without robbing them first.[18]

No for an Answer, Inc. quickly produced a promotional brochure containing a production budget, statements from Blitzstein and the cast, and quotes from the critics and other individuals devoted to the future of the work—among them, Copland, Paul Robeson, and Metropolitan Opera baritone Lawrence Tibbett. Capitalizing on the perceived censorship attempt at the Mecca Temple, they went further, describing how another kind of censorship works, the censorship of the marketplace. "It would be difficult to find a commercial producer for a people's opera in any season," read the brochure. "This season, the implications of a people's opera are even clearer. Broadway won't touch it."

Therefore, the solution lay in having the opera's audience produce the opera, "the first time in the history of the commercial theatre that the American people themselves would become financially responsible for a theatre production." No for an Answer, Inc. established a plan by which 170 people would invest one hundred dollars each and get the opera onto the Al Jolson stage for its first two weeks. They also set up a drive to sell ten thousand tickets out of booklets of twenty-five coupons, to be purchased in blocks by organizations, at a dollar each (or one hundred tickets for eighty-five dollars).

By the first week of March, six thousand dollars had been pledged in one-hundred-dollar loans. One contributor, S. J. Perelman, gave more than money: He gave the show a legend, for he had written out his check payable to "No Financier." Later that month, Keynote put out the original cast recording of *No for an Answer*—only the second musical in history to be recorded (*Cradle* was first, and *Oklahoma!* would follow two years later). Originally, Decca was to have recorded and pressed the album, but its officials were concerned by the final "Hymn of Hate" chorus, in which the workers sing "They have killed our Joe." Decca concluded that the workers were singing about Joe Stalin.

"But Stalin is still alive!" Blitzstein objected.

"Nevertheless, we want no part of that Red stuff," answered Decca. "This isn't the Kremlin, you know."[19]

In the end, RCA in Camden, New Jersey, made the pressings, and Keynote released the set. For their fees, the contract specified that major artists would each receive ten dollars plus an album; minor artists would just get the album.* Priced at $4.75, the recordings came out in a strange package of three 10-inch disks and two 12-inch disks, with accompanying liner notes by the composer and texts to the choruses.

On March 17, Paul Robeson sang "The Purest Kind of a Guy" at a Madison Square Garden sixtieth-birthday tribute to Communist Party General Secretary

*On the recording, left-wing singer Michael Loring, the first to record Earl Robinson's song "Joe Hill," took the place of Robert Simon as Joe in the "Francie" number. Marc's young friend from Harvard, Leonard Bernstein, who in the intervening time had studied at Blitzstein's old school, the Curtis Institute, also played and sang "Weep for Me"—a drunken solo by the Paul Chase character—on a private recording never released.

William Z. Foster. It was attended by eighteen thousand Party supporters. Later, Robeson recorded the number as one of a widely heralded set of eight "Songs of Free Men." Columbia pressed Blitzstein's ode to Joe Kyriakos appropriately on the same disk as Robeson's famous recording of Earl Robinson's "Joe Hill," both with the singer's longtime accompanist Lawrence Brown at the piano.*

An additional association with Robeson came about on March 7 when Joseph Levine led a chamber orchestra in a shortened, five-scene version of the *The Cradle Will Rock* at the Academy of Music in Philadelphia. The singers came from the New Theatre Acting Company. This was the first time since June 15, 1937, that Blitzstein had heard his orchestration. The evening was a benefit for the Committee for People's Rights, commemorating the 150th anniversary of the Bill of Rights. The artist Rockwell Kent gave the address and Robeson sang a solo version of Earl Robinson's *Ballad for Americans* and a group of songs.

Early in 1941, Blitzstein had applied for a year's renewal of the Guggenheim fellowship, citing all of his recent theatrical and film activity. As the fundraising for *No for an Answer* continued and as the recording began to circulate, newspapers around the country reported March 24 on the new crop of award winners. Blitzstein had won it a second time, and out of eighty-five recipients, it was Blitzstein's photo that most of the press picked up.

By the beginning of April No for an Answer, Inc. had raised half of the sum needed for the production. If the opera was going to be seen this season, the rest would have to be raised very soon. A two-day rally sponsored by the American Peace Mobilization on April 5 and 6 featured performances by the cast of *No for an Answer;* perhaps the producing company believed that more subscribers would come forth from the crowds that packed Randall's Island Stadium and the Mecca Temple on those days. But they didn't, and by April 14, the press announced a postponement until fall.

All of Blitzstein's activities on behalf of left-wing causes had begun attracting attention in Washington. J. Edgar Hoover, director of the FBI, wrote to his New York office on November 8, 1940, regarding the internal security matter of Marc Blitzstein:

> The above captioned individual has been reported to the Bureau as being a Communist Party member who is also a playwright and entertainer. He has sponsored and participated in dramatic productions and balls for the benefit of such Communist Front Groups as the North American Committee to Aid Spanish Democracy and the non-Sectarian Committee for Political Refugees. He attended the Tenth National Convention of the Communist Party and has recently been associated with the various peace moves, having been elected to the National Council of the American Peace Mobilization at the Chicago rally in September, 1940.
>
> Please furnish the Bureau with the present address of Blitzstein

*Toward the end of Robeson's career, "The Purest Kind of a Guy" remained in his repertoire; he included the song on all his Australian programs in late 1960.

> together with any other readily available information reflecting on the advisability of considering him for custodial detention in event of a national emergency.[20]

In the months ahead, FBI agents clipped newspapers and consulted newspaper morgues, looked in phone books and reference books, placed pretext phone calls, visited Blitzstein's draft board, local post office, and finally the utilities company, all in an attempt to locate the composer's present address. They expanded their search to Philadelphia. It took them until December 1941 to find him on West Fifty-seventh Street.

Besides making its own investigation into the lives of its subjects, the FBI also received information from other sources. Some unnamed person reported to the New York office on April 2, 1941, that "one Marc Blitzenstein [*sic*] received a Guggenheim award for musical stage compositions. He is described as a notorious Stalinist and his no for an answer [*sic*] is blatant propagandizing of the Soviet line." Another concerned citizen brought a copy of the Keynote recording of the opera to the FBI office in Memphis, Tennessee. Special agent in charge, E. E. Kuhnel, forwarded the records to Mr. Hoover in Washington "in the event it is desired that a transcript be prepared of the material."[21] The FBI retained the accompanying booklet of song texts in its files but destroyed the disks themselves. They were broken.

1. Hannah (Anna) Galanter Blitzstein

2. Moses (Marcus) Lionel Blitzstein

Sam and Anna Blitzstein, Marc and Jo

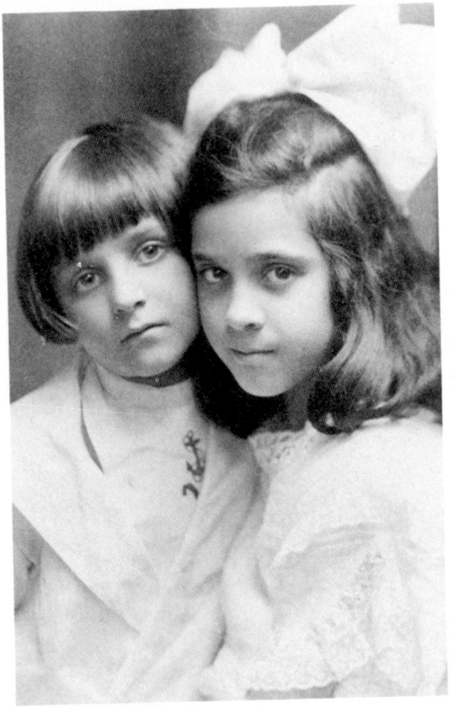

4. Marc and Jo

5. Marc and Jo

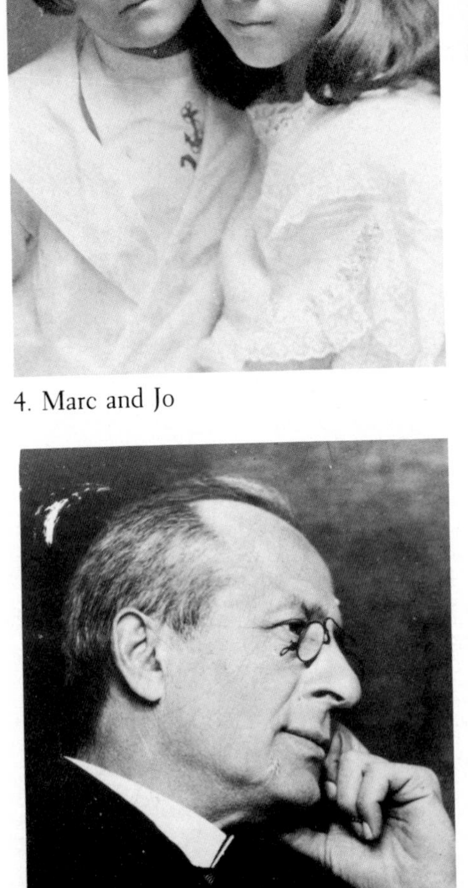

6. Alexander Siloti

7. Berenice Skidelsky

. Alexander Smallens and Marc, 1929

9. Maddie and Sam Blitzstein

10. Marc in Salzburg, 1929

11 & 12. Marc and Eva, early 1930s

13. In Dubrovnik, 1932

14. Lina Abarbanell

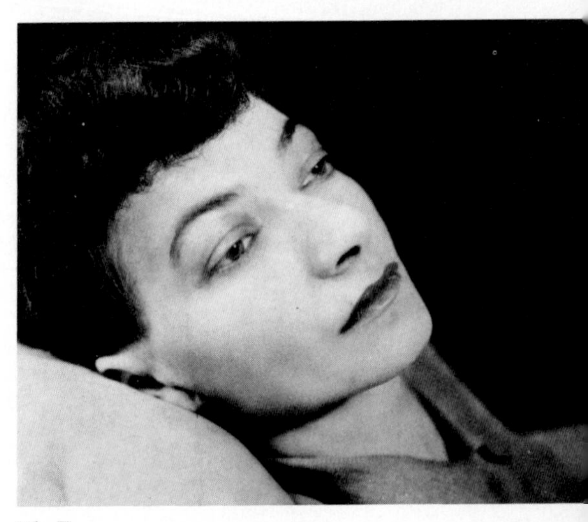

15. Eva

6, 17, & 18. Marc, Eva, and Very at Peaked Hill Bars, Provincetown, 1935

19. Kit, Jo, Stephen, Marc, Mama, ca. 1938

20. Marc and Kit, ca. 1938

21. Rehearsing *The Cradle Will Rock,* 1937

NEW YORK POST, THURSDAY, JUNE 17, 1937

WPA OPERA CAST FEARS SPANKING

Sings Parts From Audience After Production Is Ordered Delayed Until July 1

The cast of "The Cradle Will Rock," a WPA pro-union opera about a steel strike, hoped today that it won't be disciplined.

In a manner completely new to Broadway, the cast presented its show last night after WPA officials had ordered production halted until after July 1 and Frank Gillmore, president of Actors' Equity Association, had warned members against taking part in a nunauthorized play.

The members of the cast got around the two orders by singing and speaking their parts from seats in the audience.

New to Broadway

About 1,000 persons, including 100 standees, listened in mild astonishment but with frequent applause at this method of play production.

The play was given in the Venice Theatre, at Fifty-ninth Street and Seventh Avenue, after members of the audience had followed the cast twenty blocks from the Maxine Elliot Theatre, where the play was first scheduled.

Virtually the only action on the stage was by Marc Blitzenstein, author of the play, who sat at a piano playing the musical numbers while a spotlight focused on him.

Orson Welles, the director, sat a few feet away and made occasional speeches about the action which could not be presented.

The opera, winner of the annual award of the New Theatre League, concerns "Steeltown, U. S. A.," and portrays organized steel workers forcing the villain, "Mister Mister," a steel mill owner, to give them higher wages.

Order Issued Yesterday

The WPA order halting production was issued yesterday and covered all scheduled openings of Federal Theatre Project plays, operas and concerts. Hallie Flanagan, national director, said this was to facilitate reorganization of WPA art projects which must prepare for a twenty-five per cent cut in personnel.

Some of the first-nighters gathered at the Maxine Elliot Theatre at Thirty-ninth Street and Sixth Avenue said grumblingly, however, that they believed the order was a censorship of the play because the play was radical.

They said the present steel strikes might have figured in the order, also, and they demanded that the show go on.

The clamor and the crowd increased. The entire house had been turned over to the Downtown Musi School, 68 East Twelfth Stree where Mr. Blitzstein teaches, and few speeches aimed at placating th ticket holders were not enough.

Will Geer, star of the show, san two of the numbers from the side walk, but this wasn't enough, eithe

Finally John Houseman, manag ing producer of the WPA unit i charge of the production, obtaine telephone permission to use th Venice Theatre. He posted $100. I buses and autos the audienc moved en masse to the new loca tion.

It was 9:45 P. M., an hour afte the scheduled opening, that th strange production began.

An Italian flag draped over a bo was removed just as the curtain wa lifted and this brought cheers.

The audience also applauded vig orously when a song uncompli mentary to college military train ing was sung by a member of th cast seated in the middle of th house.

"This performance was not a po litical protest but an artistic one, asserted Mr. Welles at the close c the opera, two hours later. Archi bald MacLeish the poet praise the "vitality" of the Federal The tre Project in another speech.

The cast believed it had tech nically violated none of the ruling

(Sydney Weiss, 1938)

24. Marc with *(l to r)* David Diamond, unidentified, Colin McPhee, late 1930s

25. *(Sydney Weiss)*

26. At the Moviola, composing the score to *Valley Town,* 1940

11

PHONY WAR, REAL WAR

May 1941–August 1942

"The real fight at last . . ."

One of the acknowledged experts in the field, Blitzstein contributed his ideas on "Music in the Theatre" to John Gassner's volume, *Producing the Play,* published by the Dryden Press in 1941. He cautioned against the use of music at all in the talky, "cerebral" plays of Shaw, Wilde, Ibsen, and Behrman. While proposing that producers "allow the composer really to collaborate," he also advised against a symphonic treatment for the theatre score. Stressing the importance of correct prosody, he recommended a careful look at Virgil Thomson's setting of English words, particularly in *Four Saints in Three Acts.* And for pacing, how could one do better than study Verdi's last operas, *Otello* and *Falstaff?* In his own work, Blitzstein said, his greatest success had been with singing actors, as opposed to acting singers. Where the words were more important than the music, he had his actors perform "a kind of running *parlando,* a speak-singing which sounds horribly difficult theoretically but is the easiest kind of delivery." Rendering plain advice that still holds true for theatre songs, he added: "It requires vocal and mental relaxation; concentrate on the meaning of the song."

That May, members of the New Theatre of Philadelphia, which had enjoyed such prolonged success with *Cradle,* printed up a petition asking Blitzstein to release *No for an Answer* for a Philadelphia production. Marc's father Sam signed to give the appeal extra clout. Blitzstein declined, however, holding off for an October Broadway opening. A request also came in from progressives in Washington, D.C., for a local production there, and Blitzstein gave the same response.

Until the spring of 1941, the left still actively promoted a radical peace. The Almanac Singers—Pete Seeger's group—published a songbook and asked readers to take up their songs and sing "so loudly that all the war-makers and native fascists and enemies of peace will hear you and tremble in the counting houses." Their material consisted of a timely mix of patriotism with unionism and pro-farmer policies, anti-draft and anti-big business philosophy with ample references to 1776. Their song "Plow Under" recalled the days when agricultural authorities "killed a million hogs a day. . . . Instead of hogs, it's men today. Plow the fourth one under."

In just this period, May of 1941, Volume I, number 1 of a new monthly appeared, *The Jewish Survey.* Stylishly printed with twenty-four pages of photographs, cartoons, drawings, and montages setting off its topical articles, it bore the names of several well-known figures on the left on its editorial slate, Blitzstein among them: Dashiell Hammett, Rockwell Kent, Albert Maltz, Viola Brothers Shore, and Max Weber. Louis Harap served as managing editor. Its main themes, echoing the Communist line, stressed support for the Soviet Union, solidarity with blacks, and opposition to anti-Semitic, fascistic elements at home. But the line held its contradictions for Jews, as for everyone: Even as Arthur Miller's article "Hitler's Quarry" cited the beginnings of the Nazi policy of mass slaughter of the Jews, the magazine objected to the growing prowar tendency observable in the mainstream Jewish community.

As it developed, Blitzstein never wrote for *The Jewish Survey.* However, he did sign the call to the Fourth American Writers Congress, to be held at the Hotel Commodore June 6–8, and served as chairman of the drama panel. The Congress represented "the conscious action of writers in defense of culture and peace, against Fascism," and featured such speakers as Edgar Snow, Richard Wright (on "What We Think of Their War"), Dashiell Hammett, Samuel Putnam, Vito Marcantonio, Rockwell Kent, Genevieve Taggard, and Art Young. At the closing concert, the Almanac Singers and the American Ballad Singers both performed, with music by Siegmeister, Robinson, and Blitzstein on the program. Solo acts included Leadbelly, Burl Ives, Tony Kraber, Woody Guthrie, and Josh White.

In that same week, Claire Reis proposed a League of Composers commission to Blitzstein, a member of the Composers' Committee, for the following season. Perhaps she was trying to make up in this way for the League's inability ten years before to produce *The Harpies.* The composer accepted the offer, deciding on the title, *The New York Opera.* Possibly a reworking of *Nine Day Wonder,* announced the year before, it would be a two-hour work requiring two main sets. He envisioned it with a cast of twenty speakers and singers and a chorus of sixteen. Leonard Lyons reported that it would star a Metropolitan Opera baritone "and a hotcha comedienne." The orchestra would be a sixteen-piece jazz band and four violins. Newspapers reported that at this time Blitzstein was also writing an opera called *The Happy Family.*

What survives from *The New York Opera* involves a regular workingman—once again Blitzstein names him Joe—who likes to "figger" things out for himself. A spokesman for the little people, he is antiracist, for full union rights even once the war is on, against appeasement, and, summing it all up in a single phrase, against what FDR had called "the Cliveden Set," a loose cabal of ruling-class mandarins known for their sympathies for fascism. Other material from the projected opera includes a torch song called "Tell Me," in which a character reminiscent of the Suicide in *I've Got the Tune* moans, "Tell me why should I go on?" Little more about *The New York Opera* is known, and nothing of substance about *The Happy Family,* as Blitzstein's notes were lost in transit a year later. By now the struggle against suicide—the ultimate form of escape—had become a leitmotiv with Blitzstein, a theme seemingly always on his mind. Once, at a party, he ran into Alfred Ryder, who had acted in *No for an Answer.* In the midst of a personal discussion, Marc unexpectedly said to him, "You're going to commit suicide before I do."

On June 19, Blitzstein flew out to the West Coast to continue raising money among the film crowd to enable *No for an Answer* to open in New York in the fall. The FBI tracked his movements in Los Angeles. By this time, two-thirds of the required sum had been collected. His Party and other left-wing friends had set up an exhausting round of appearances in the Los Angeles area; and just in case he got bored or lustful, he noted down in advance the address of the Angelus Baths. He stayed with the screenwriter Jerome Chodorov. "Very relaxing trip," he wrote to David Diamond on the twenty-first. "Very enthusiastic welcome. It looks good. Hollywood seems to be a bit more of everything than I had imagined. More reality, and more fake."[1]

If California never exerted the pull for Blitzstein that it did for other artists, it may be that he brought to it unhappy associations from childhood. It was there that he and Jo had been cast upon the charity of relatives after his parents separated. And what if he went to Hollywood and sold out to the studios? Or what if he went to the Promised Land and fell flat? Suppose no one wanted music filled with his singing voice?

The very next day, June 22, before he could begin his series of one-man backers' auditions, the world turned upside down. Without warning, German forces staged a massive invasion of the Soviet Union. In days, they had penetrated over land and by ferocious air power deep into the heart of Russia and the Ukraine. From this moment, the left's characterization of the war as a struggle between imperialist powers no longer applied. Now a neutral, noncapitalist country committed to peace had been swept into the war.

For the moment, Blitzstein's plans proceeded as scheduled. On June 25, he introduced the opera at the home of screenwriter Dalton Trumbo in Beverly Hills, with Orson Welles, Dorothy Comingore, and the John Garfields present. The following day, Blitzstein spoke, along with John Howard Lawson, Albert Maltz, and Georgia Backus, at a Hollywood chapter meeting of the League of American Writers. The program, called "Some Called It Treason," dramatized the report of the fourth American Writers Congress just held in New York. On Sunday the twenty-ninth, Blitzstein performed *No for an Answer* at a cocktail party in Bel Air at the home of the actress Elaine Barrie, which was sponsored by the Hollywood Committee of the American Peace Mobilization. And on July 1, at the Embassy Auditorium, the same organization presented "The Cultural Event of 1941"—Blitzstein performing his new opera.[2]

On his return, relaxing at Jo and Ed's farm and writing material for both *The Happy Family* and *The New York Opera,* he wrote to David Diamond:

> Hollywood was a critical smash, and financially over the top, I think—the returns are still coming in. It became fashionable to discuss "No", and no one dared say he disliked it. I gave six (6!) performances of the work, for everybody from Tories and Second-Avenue-peddlers-turned-Producers—to honest hardworking actors, writers and directors. Welles went overboard. He swears we will make a picture together. . . .
>
> The tide of the war and the world is so gigantically absorbing that nothing can happen to me personally right now that matters a damn. What a moment! The real fight at last—and just as I was beginning to despair of ever being alive to see it!"[3]

"That famous locomotive of history," the *New Masses* editorialized in its July 8 issue, had "taken another sudden turn. And as in 1939, there may be a few who find themselves flung off and sprawling by the roadside because they lost their grip in rounding the bend." With America still not in the war, Communist efforts turned toward opposing those elements in finance and business, and their representatives in Congress, who positively licked their lips in anticipation of picking up the pieces of a mutual German-Soviet destruction. It had only been a few months before, after all, that Ohio's Senator Robert A. Taft had declared that "Victory for communism would be far more dangerous to the United States than a victory for fascism." Now, like other wide sectors of the American public who could no longer ignore the Nazi advance, the Communist Party acknowledged a major policy shift and pledged "its loyalty, its devoted labor and the last drop of its blood in support of our country in the greatest of all crises that ever threatened its existence."

In Moscow, an August 24 mass meeting of Soviet Jews called upon fellow Jews around the world to rise up against the Nazis. In October, as reported by *Jewish Survey,* two hundred prominent American Jews—Blitzstein included, along with Kurt Weill, Lehman Engel, Ira Gershwin, Lincoln Kirstein, Harold Rome, Elie Siegmeister, and many others—broadcast a message of solidarity. Their pledge committed them to "the greatest possible cooperation and fraternity between the two great sections of our people, the Jews of the United States and the Jews of the Soviet Union."

But also in October as it rounded the bend, the famous locomotive of history flung off *No for an Answer.* A *Times* report made it seem as though, with only seven thousand raised out of the twenty thousand dollars needed, the producing committee had decided to abandon the opera. Blitzstein's correction, published on October 19, cited a figure of twelve thousand dollars raised, with an advance ticket guarantee of eight thousand dollars. True, it had taken many more months than originally projected to raise that much, but Blitzstein mentioned the many small donations from average working people: "Our files are full of their letters, and they make pretty exciting reading. They prove that a real culture in this country, from the ground up, is no myth."

> If we have decided not to do the opera in New York at present, it is clearly due to no lack of response or support. It is because we feel that the red-hot urgency of today's war news has relegated all other social themes to a comparatively secondary role. During this emergency we believe the stress should be on plays reflecting the growing unity of all anti-Fascist forces; and particularly we feel that the energies of the people should be concentrated on such plays. But *No for an Answer* is presumably a work of art, not a pamphlet; and the validity of its content holds, if not its immediacy.[4]

That was the end of the opera's career for then.

As drama, *No for an Answer* has its problems, which might have been corrected in a full production. Unquestionably, however, it broke new ground in the furtherance of an American operatic tradition, mostly in Blitzstein's setting of common American speech. Unfortunately for its success, it came at a time when the audience for Blitzstein's politics had dwindled. With increasing tempo, the nation once again prepared both economically and psychologically for war. Unemployment by the late 1930s and early 1940s had slackened as a result and was no longer the most compelling theme for a *Zeitoper.* Perhaps if Blitzstein had been able to concentrate fully on *No for an Answer* in the year or two following *Cradle,* and if he could have premiered it in 1938 or early 1939, it might have gained a wider acceptance.

With no production in sight, therefore, and with a warehouse full of *No for an Answer* recordings, Keynote offered its stock to *New Masses* for promotional use. If a subscriber signed up for more than thirteen weeks, an additional $2.75 would bring him the five-record set. Later *New Masses* repeated the offer in another form: a one-year subscription and the complete set for eight dollars.

Blitzstein now filled his time more with benefit concerts than with work on his new operatic projects. On November 8 there was a long program of Stars for China Today in which he performed. With Paul Robeson, he sponsored a November 29 testimonial concert at Town Hall, saluting Earl Robinson upon the completion of the Sandburg musical *The People, Yes.* For that program, Blitzstein not only sang and played but acted as narrator of the evening as well. Robinson, also a Communist, shortly withdrew his work, however, for the same reason Blitzstein had halted *No for an Answer.*

On December 3, just after the League of Composers had released its formal announcement of Blitzstein's *New York Opera* commission, he wrote to Claire Reis saying that the opera had undergone many changes, with much discarded and still much to do. "I feel guilty and depressed about it—but there it is."[5] Five days later, a day after the Japanese bombed Pearl Harbor, Congress made the formal but long-awaited declaration of war. The new situation detracted even more from Blitzstein's will to linger over an extended work. Though he continued to poke desultorily at *The New York Opera,* he now preferred to devote his energies to pragmatic musical assignments with an immediate purpose at hand.

As in the fields of music, dance, theatre, and graphic arts, film had taken a left turn during the thirties as well. *The Spanish Earth* and *Valley Town* represented high points in American documentary film during those years, but at least a few dozen others had been made as well. Leo Hurwitz's *Sweet Land of Liberty* treated the harassment of dissenters. *Black Legion* revealed the workings of pro-Aryan Klan-type groups in America, such as the Purple Shirts Blitzstein had satirized in *I've Got the Tune.* A government-sponsored film such as *The Plow That Broke the Plains,* filmed by Paul Strand and Leo Hurwitz, with Virgil Thomson's score, called attention to the problems of the Dust Bowl, but it failed to present either the "little people's" point of view or any concrete solutions.

Out of the labor-oriented Film and Photo League and its successor Nykino, Frontier Films came together in 1937 with the aim of producing documentaries on American life on a higher artistic level than newsreels. Most of these included musical scores by sympathetic composers. In 1938 Frontier Films made *People of the Cumberland,* in cooperation with the Highlander Folk School, using a score by Alex North and Earl Robinson; and *Return to Life,* about Spain, with Charles Koechlin's music. *White Flood,* an apolitical film from 1940 about glaciers, featured Hanns Eisler's experimental scoring. Earl Robinson and the American People's Chorus contributed music to another Frontier Films production made in cooperation with the United Automobile Workers.

Some of these same filmmakers wanted to produce a full-length film that in its amplitude of scope could say more and say it with a more highly evolved esthetic. In 1937, Ralph Steiner, Paul Strand, Leo Hurwitz, and Willard Van Dyke began work on *Native Land,* based on the findings of Senator Robert La Follette, Jr.'s Civil Liberties Committee in their investigation of the corporate labor spy network. Leo Huberman's book *The Labor Spy Racket* (1937) also influenced the filmmakers' thinking. After the first shooting session, however, when it became clear that the filming would proceed in widely spaced fits and starts only as funds would allow, Steiner and Van Dyke left to work on *The City,* with Copland's score. From time to time the *Native Land* producers would show rushes from the film-in-progress to raise the money to continue shooting, most of which took place from 1937 to 1939. Eventually, some fifteen thousand people saw portions of it before its completion nearly five years later, and five thousand of them made contributions. Jo Davidson and Reginald Marsh donated artwork to be sold for the film.

Early on in the project, Blitzstein came in as the composer of the score, for a fee of five hundred dollars. He did most of his work in the cutting room in the late summer and fall of 1941, after his return from California. Since he knew Paul Robeson well, he invited him to act as the offscreen narrator; Robeson accepted, donating his fee back to Frontier Films. With such a rich voice at his disposal, Blitzstein could not resist the opportunity to compose for it. Robeson sings two of Blitzstein's songs on the sound track. As he had done in *Valley Town,* Henry Brant assisted with the orchestration. Recording of the music under Lehman Engel's baton took place at the end of September and October.

Several of the key movers in Frontier Films were Communist Party men, including the principal scriptwriter, Ben Maddow (who used the pseudonym David Wolff, as he was employed on a WPA project). In accordance with the Communists' Popular Front policy, the struggle in *Native Land* is not for socialism against capitalism; rather, the film promotes democracy versus fascism. A commonly promoted Party slogan at the time was "Communism Is 20th-Century Americanism"; at its Tenth National Convention in 1938, the Party had declared the object of the democratic mass movement to "restore the lost economic foundations of Jeffersonian democracy," setting aside its agrarian premise, of course. The left was out to reclaim patriotism for its own. Suitably, the narration, the visual imagery, and Blitzstein's music are full of American values: liberty and justice for all. America must live up to its promise. The little people of this land are entitled to their rightful place in society. They cannot and must not be bullied, intimidated, stepped on—those are the methods of fascism.

Musically, Blitzstein's score to *Native Land* is written in his most populist, expansive mode, many cuts above the warmed-over Tchaikovsky that was standard movie music for the day. An occasional folk song or soupçon of a patriotic tune can be heard worked into the orchestra. A mother hums Brahms's "Lullaby" to put her baby to sleep. Blitzstein exploited the opportunity to integrate many extramusical sounds: train noises, church bells, office and industrial machines, sirens, a toy piano, the knocking on a door, and gunshots. The score is full of melodies and extended treatments of them, unlike most film music of the era, which swells and then fades away purely for the sake of the dialogue. For Robeson, Blitzstein wrote a poignant "spiritual" called "Dusty Sun," used in a scene involving a white and a black sharecropper, who are hunted down and killed for wanting ten cents more for their cotton. Shortly after, in fine voice, Robeson sings an upbeat "American Day," celebrating the average man's joy of getting up in the morning for an average day's work. As in the similar scene in *Valley Town* of happy shoppers in the twenties, the music accompanies film passages depicting an idealized nation untroubled by strikebreakers and labor spies. Blitzstein also included substantial cuts from recordings by the Almanac Singers—"Get Thee Behind Me, Satan," played to a striking counterpoint against the sound of a ping-pong game in progress, and the well-known classic "Which Side Are You On?" A lone clarinet later plays another famous union song, "Hold the Fort (For We Are Coming)." The film is eighty-three minutes long, and music plays for perhaps two-thirds of the running time.

The political line shares common ground with Blitzstein's views in *No for an Answer.* Of course, as in Earl Robinson's cantata *Ballad for Americans,* the fact of a black man—Paul Robeson—as singer and as narrator of the elevated text drove home with a certain irony the absence of full democratic rights for a substantial underclass of the American population.

Also consistent with the Party's long-range strategy, it was to be expected that massive social changes would not occur overnight. As in Blitzstein's opera where the consolidation of pro-union, democratic consciousness in the Diogenes Club and on Clara Carver's part, and the salvaging of the important mimeograph at the end, represent the movement's small gains, here also, social struggle is seen as a constant progression from battle to battle, some won, some lost, but always—dialectically—with some advance in accumulated wisdom.

The film enacts a number of seemingly isolated incidents where men—never women—who spoke up against fascism or the Klan are run out of town, blacklisted, or simply killed by a variety of means. At the center of the film, in a twenty-six-minute segment, the entire labor spy system is dramatized. The filmmakers draw the connections between the ordinary secretary who merely answers phones and types out orders and the widespread network involving 41,000 spies and a corporate budget of $80,000,000 that resulted in those individual deaths. The film claims that it was the little people's protests to Washington that gradually forced Congress to investigate and expose this fascist conspiracy against our democracy. The capitalist state is obligated to live up to the Bill of Rights and the rest of its body of laws. For now, at least, the state is the people's tool: FDR's portrait reverently hung in the union hall says it all.

Native Land combines a number of film devices to make its point: narration, music, newsreel, dramatizations, montage, animation. The result is an original feature form something like the Living Newspaper theatre productions of the thirties. Scenes were shot wherever it was cheap and possible, for example, a Ku Klux Klan sequence at Camp Unity in Wingdale, New York, where left-wing summer vacationers donned white robes to act out the script. Though some professional actors appear in the film—Howard da Silva, Bert Conway, Art Smith, and a few others—most are actual workers. A Florida minister who spoke out against the Klan and suffered mightily for it is played by a Rev. Charles Webber. Paul Strand is credited with the photography and Leo Hurwitz with the editing, and both with the direction. William Watts, associate director along with Alfred Saxe, had directed *No for an Answer.* No one made any real money from the project.

Aside from the constant financial problems, there was political resistance. Paramount Pictures, for instance, owned newsreel footage of the infamous Republic Steel Massacre on Memorial Day 1937, but they would not release it for this film. Instead, the filmmakers made do with stills of the day's events.

The first print of the completed film came back December 8, the day war was declared. Now, with the newly transformed international situation, what would become of the film?

Jewish Survey—until the March 1942 issue still with Blitzstein's name on the masthead—immediately went into full gear to promote the war effort. "Every ounce of energy, every resource, every American life at the service of our country and humanity!" it insisted, as other Communist publications did. It named the newspapers that published "defeatist" views, and congressmen such as Dies, Fish, and "appeasement" Senator La Follette, whose filibustering on the war could only serve fascist interests. It also opposed John L. Lewis, former head of the United Mine Workers and leader of the CIO, who now openly identified with Father Coughlin, opposed the alliance with the USSR, and whose daughter Kathryn served on the national executive board of the America First Committee. As the war unfolded, this voice of the Jewish left featured stories on Jewish servicemen, countering such anti-Semitic slander as the widespread "joke" that the Jewish national anthem had become "Onward, *Christian* Soldiers." The magazine reported on the work of Russian War Relief, a government-designated agency, and featured articles on the evolution of the people's underground movement in the occupied countries. It demanded an antilynching law and called for stronger Jewish-Negro unity. Most of all, it called for tanks and bombers for the Red Army, for the opening of the Second Front in the West against Hitler, and for an ever-increased commitment to war production: "Planes, more PLANES, and still more PLANES!!"

In February and March, after years of dreaming about film as an art form truly integrated with music—film opera—Blitzstein's opportunity came. Garson Kanin was directing a ten-minute film called *Night Shift* for the Office of Emergency Management. He asked Blitzstein to serve as scriptwriter and composer. Contrary to the standard practice, Blitzstein was to write his work before the film was shot, much preferable from a composer's point of view. His preparation involved little more than reading the daily press, both Establishment and left-wing. He clipped stories about army slang. He noted developments in the auto industry: how it had delayed conversion to war production as long as it could, how some companies had begun war profiteering, and how top executives had raised their already impressive salaries. He read of disagreement over the issue of double pay for Sunday work, when it was the government itself that would ultimately purchase most of what the factories produced.

The theme of *Night Shift* is the battle for production. "The army doesn't stop," he wrote in his draft of the script, "the navy doesn't stop—what about the soldiers on *this* battlefront, here, where the big push begins?" He quoted current slogans: "Every citizen must work every hour of every day of every week," and "No more business as usual." At the same time, he did not want to see labor suffer loss of benefits or dangerous fatigue from double shifts. Labor should not carry the whole burden of the war. He sought to relate the direct effects of home production on the soldier in battle—helmets that hadn't arrived, food gone bad for lack of refrigeration cars, and always the need for more planes.

Using a two-character dialogue form, he posed the problem: to persuade industry to operate war-production factories on a round-the-clock basis. Writing on the back sides of an early draft of *No for an Answer* to save paper, he asked, "Why are these machines idle at 3:30 in the morning?" The thought recalls the closed-down steel mills of *Valley Town.* "Weren't you informed we're in a war?" the Gal asks the Guy. "Maybe Congress should declare war over again, and louder!" Repeating the theme used in all war, the script tells the viewer that "the men who work this factory are the soldiers behind the lines."

Music for *Night Shift* begins immediately, as a chorus sings out the credits—a device picked up, perhaps, from Kurt Weill's *Der Zar lässt sich photographieren.* When they chant "Written by Marc Blitzstein," the Guy comments, "Never heard of him." Perhaps this was false humility, but without expectation of special distinction Blitzstein thereby humorously accepted his role as worker in the common front for the war effort. The centerpiece of the film is the song "Turn the Night into Day," which Chappell published. It is a forceful hymn to night work in march tempo marked *forte* and *fortissimo* all the way through. "Make work one great relay," he screamed above an orchestra churning out the sound of production:

We know now that we're in a war
against grim and evil powers.
You can't fight that war
only during business hours.

For this project, Office of Emergency Management Film Unit Production No. 50, Blitzstein had considered Ginger Rogers and Bing Crosby as his two singers, but the final choice fell to Kate Smith and Danny Kaye. Smith sang the theme song. Alexander Smallens recorded the score in a New York studio.

Kanin did not complete shooting of the film, however. Washington sent orders to cancel the production, for reasons never made clear—perhaps a policy change, some bureaucratic or budgetary contretemps, or possibly some fear of Blitzstein's political taintedness. Most likely, factories were going on night shifts by spring 1942, and the film no longer had propaganda value. The recording has never surfaced.

Caught in the throes of work on the film, Blitzstein felt the lack of intimate affection that winter and unburdened himself to David Diamond:

> As usual, when I work as hard as now, I have a passionate and completely unrealistic desire to fall in love. Unrealistic since I wouldn't find it if I looked for it, and there's no time to look; but it would be practical in the deepest sense to have it there warm and waiting for me to drop into as I drop out of work. The day-dreaming of a drip.[6]

In his last piece for *Modern Music* for the next year, Blitzstein reviewed *Our Singing Country,* a folksong compilation by John A. Lomax and Alan Lomax, with Ruth Crawford Seeger serving as the supremely conscientious musical editor. He wrote a rave review—"wonderful," "a beauty," "rates with Bartok and Kodaly." Seeger's editing distinguished this volume from the other folk-song collections he had seen, such as Elie Siegmeister's, which Blitzstein considered "all folked up." Impressed with the quantity of Negro songs, work songs, and "social songs" in the book, he cited with strong appreciation one holler called "Make Me a Garment," with "the most astounding recitative quality," its "interval leaping" so uncharacteristic of folk music. It "yields a wild fresh juice. This is what we have all been talking about, when we said that the 'folk art' must stimulate and fertilize the 'fine art.' " Upon which, showing more enthusiasm for folk music than ever before, he put in a plug for urban folk music. Of course, with images of war all about, he may have been personally moved by the final verses:

My true love died the other day
I believe I'll die tomorrow.[7]

"This is a day for action," Blitzstein wrote. "In time of war, everybody, everything must do a job. Music no less than machine-guns has a part to play, and can be a weapon in the battle for a free world." Accordingly, he organized a massive extravaganza to benefit Russian War Relief that was held at the Alvin Theatre on Sunday, May 10, 1942, and he acted throughout as emcee. Titled "Music at Work," the program directed by Robert H. Gordon included a host of talents in a variety of genres—theatre, film, dance, concert and swing music. Leading figures in American culture, not just the left-wingers, signed on as sponsors of the evening.

Highlights of the vast program included a two-piano overture based on Red Army songs, performed by composer Stanley Bate and Blitzstein; Earl Robinson's cantata *Report on the State of the Union,* a John Latouche text based on a Roosevelt speech; a "Pas de Trois for Piano and Two Dancers" to music by Theodore Chanler, produced by Lincoln Kirstein and choreographed by Balanchine; a scene from Harold Rome's *Caleb Catlum's America* with Martin Ritt and José Ferrer, set and costumes by Irene Sharaff, with Rome at the piano; the second part of Copland's Piano Concerto, with Copland and Leonard Bernstein at two pianos; Brecht's play *Strength Through Joy in Dresden,* with Ferrer and Uta Hagen; and a final segment of swing music by Teddy Wilson and his band. Also on this "Cook's Tour of Music," as one reviewer called it, was the clip of a Paul Robeson song from *Native Land,* scheduled for its formal opening the following day.

Virgil Thomson found Chanler's ballet the most interesting item on the program, and Robeson's song "not very good," though he considered Blitzstein's instrumental music in the film "anything but banal." "The whole evening, in fact, seemed to me a bit lacking as, indeed, most of our war shows have been so far, in gusto and humor." Olin Downes saw some "good theatre in this show, and a little promising music."[8]

Native Land played at the World Theatre on West Forty-ninth Street. Critics offered ringing praise for the filmic invention, the impassioned sense of faith in America, and for Robeson. *PM*'s John T. McManus opened his fervent review saying, "Every American owes it to himself to see this urgent, unforgettable film document." The *Times* film critic, Bosley Crowther, chimed in with a superlative notice: "Manifestly, this is one of the most powerful and disturbing documentary films ever made . . . a brilliant achievement . . . with such bite and dramatic intensity as would make the best directors of films take solemn note." *Time* magazine called the film "an eloquent indictment of acts of injustice and intolerance which did happen here and might again . . . a shocking, stinging picture whose realism could never have been achieved in soft-stepping Hollywood . . . , highlighted . . . with perhaps the finest spoken commentary (Paul Robeson) ever recorded on celluloid and an effective musical score (Marc Blitzstein)."[9] That year the National Board of Review of Motion Pictures gave *Native Land* an honorable mention in the documentary category (*Moscow Strikes Back* won the palm).

Pete Seeger of the Almanac Singers appreciated the composer's contributions: "I saw *Native Land* for the 2nd time last week, and just wanted to write you to tell you how swell I thought the music was. I haven't seen any musical background, even in Russian movies, to equal it." In his high school newspaper, Marc's nephew Stephen wrote, "The music is tremendously moving. It does not just follow the photography and the voice; it speaks for itself. It makes itself known and felt."[10]

Pleased as Blitzstein certainly was by these friendly remarks, he must have reveled in *Modern Music*'s assessment:

> Blitzstein's dramatic instinct and abundant talent never fail an instant throughout this film. He has composed a magnificent work which merits painstaking analysis and deep study—more than one viewing makes possible. I was struck by the originality of his musical thought, which, without resorting to modern rhetoric, achieves poignant and grandiose effects. His inspiration, rich and sparkling, seems almost to spring from his feeling for metier, in this instance the metier of special film music. Some of his treatments in this field are unforgettable: the sound of trumpets in the distance, as though they were lost in fog; vocalized choirs; the use of cymbals to make the rhythm of a train an obsession; the voice of a girl singing a tango; a song harmonized for four voices, accompanied by a guitar and the punctuating smacks of ping-pong balls. . . .
>
> The entire sequence called "An American Day" is brilliantly handled. Nothing could give a clearer pictorial idea of what happens when a great nation wakes to a day of work.[11]

But after all the positive notices, there remained the question of the timeliness of the film now that the war was on and the native fascists had beaten a deep retreat. Unity, not discord, should be the theme of the hour. Supporters of the film defended continuing to show it because it proved that the organized march of labor against the fascist-minded corporations had, through its victory, strengthened the collective will of the people to unite in the war effort. Class conflict had been successfully squelched. The film also showed how a democratic society, unlike a fascist one, confronts its own problems publicly and without shame. But the tacked-on ending clearly did not sum up the theme of the film. At its core, anyone could see that *Native Land* saw the corporations as the enemy.

Leo Hurwitz personally visited Communist Party Secretary William Z. Foster in his office to win the Party's backing for widespread distribution. Foster had seen the film, but the Party maintained a strict no-strike pledge during the war and had eased up in other areas of social agitation. He answered by pulling out a drawer, saying, "I've written a book which I'm keeping in my desk until the end of the war for the same reason."

Hurwitz disagreed, thinking that on basic principles—capital versus labor—the left ought to guard its independence even within the United Front.

"Don't worry," Foster reassured the filmmaker, "the class struggle will be back."

At that time, there existed a national system of block-booking into neighborhood movie houses, which was wholly controlled by the major studios. It meant that an independent film such as *Native Land* would be completely marginalized unless it possessed some extraordinary backing. The Party would not push it. Thus, facing the prospect that no one would ever see their film, Frontier Films developed a strategy not unlike the intended audience-sponsored production of *No for an Answer.* The idea was to circulate petitions among unions and other "people's" organizations to show theatre owners that a demand existed for this film and that it would be profitable for them to show it. However, Frontier Films did not have the organizational resources to coordinate such a campaign. In fact, by this time Frontier had disbanded as a film-production unit. In the end, the film ran for two months at the World, achieved only a few further showings in 1942, even fewer the next year, and then sank into oblivion.

Native Land shared the same fate as *No for an Answer*—long in its gestation and deprived of a speedy production, it finally emerged when events had already superseded its theme. The film returned into circulation only in 1974. Since then, film historians have lavished attention on it as a unique and almost entirely forgotten achievement of its era. For this work and for his other independent documentaries, Leo Hurwitz became a belated film hero, sought after by interviewers. *Native Land* certainly stands as Blitzstein's most fully evolved film score, and one of the longest, most important documentary film scores of any era.

Once the Soviet Union had been attacked in June 1941, the Communist Party placed itself in the forefront of the all-out effort to support its armed resistance. But after the U.S. declaration of war in December, sympathy for the cause rose in a symphonic swell. Concert programs and radio broadcasts featured Soviet music as never before, including live broadcasts from Moscow of new music by Shostakovich and others. Fred Waring and the Pennsylvanians sang the "Song of the Soviet Tankmen" from the film *Red Tanks* on a June 1942 NBC Chesterfield program. On the first anniversary of the Nazi invasion, America celebrated "Aid to Russia" Day; in New York the honors to the Soviet Union lasted a week. Orson Welles narrated *Peter and the Wolf* on a CBS Russian-American Festival series during the summer of 1942. Hollywood, too, went into action. Perhaps its most notable tribute to the Soviets was Lillian Hellman's script for *North Star,* with music by Aaron Copland. From this, he extracted two choral pieces, "Song of the Guerrillas" and "The Younger Generation," to Ira Gershwin's texts.

Russian War Relief sponsored a series of Monday-night radio broadcasts called

"Russia Is Singing" in late May and June. They were aired on WINS as part of a campaign to raise six million dollars that spring for the Soviets. Blitzstein chose the music and narrated the programs. In part, Blitzstein's selections can be explained by what was available in the United States, though in many cases there appears to have been only a slight gap between Soviet issuance and American markets. He chose material representing a wide variety of music, from Uzbek, Tatar, Ukrainian, and other regional and ethnic minorities to traditional Russian folk songs, choral selections from operas, pieces from the Yiddish theatre, film music, and war songs. Remarking that art songs were flourishing in wartime Russia, he played "Perikola, the Ladylike Drunkard," based on Offenbach's *La Périchole,* and "The Little Birch Tree," based on a theme from Tchaikovsky's Fourth Symphony.

Accompanying the excerpt from Prokofiev's *Alexander Nevsky* score, "Arise, Ye Russian People," Blitzstein explained that it was "one of the first movies in which *music score* is actually integrated into film. Big subject—but Russians were the first to realize that there was something more to music-in-the-movies than a thin trickle of sentimental sound barely audible behind a love conversation, or a great torrent of lush expansive 1000 bucks-an-hour sound for the spectacular silent moments."

Blitzstein also liked those songs in which the performers were themselves active in the war effort. The number "Arrival of Red Army Nurses at the Front" from the movie *The Girl from Leningrad* was sung by an actual nurse at the front. A tune called "Suliko" starred mechanic and tank driver Eugene "Zhenya" Dormidontov. Blitzstein played a Cossack song and commented that though the Cossacks had often in the past been used to oppress "such minorities as the Jews," their allegiances had changed now: "One of the most famous of the Cossack leaders of today was a Jew. I say was, because this man, Lev Dovator, was killed in battle last December."

It is fitting, the announcer reminded his listeners, to be playing Soviet music, since the Russians themselves are playing British and American music to help strengthen the alliance. He carefully pointed out to any listener yet mystified by the Communists' sudden ideological shifts, that the film *Red Tanks* had been "produced before June 22, 1941; you will see that the Soviet hatred of Fascism and the Fascists and the Soviet's knowledge of its enemy were no sudden trumped up thing."[12]

As part of its work with Blitzstein, Russian War Relief placed in his hands copies of the "Inter-Continent News," daily releases from which, as announcer, he would excerpt and adapt portions to give an up-to-the-minute cast to his programs. One item dated Sevastopol, June 8 impressed Blitzstein with the heroic story of the unsuccessful naval defense of the Crimean city. As he followed successive bulletins on the progress of the campaign, he came to see the story as a symbol of the whole Soviet defense. In the following weeks, he wrote out the words and melody to the "Ballad of Sevastopol." In plodding, almost mechanically persevering measures with a rising motif, he told the story of the warship *Tashkent*'s removing loads of silent civilians in the dark of night, and of the battle spreading from the shores into the streets of the city.

> *Sevastopol fell one July day.*
> *Lift your head, oh noble city.*
> *Lift your head and tell with pride*
> *How you fell, and mounted to glory.*
> *How they fought, how they held, how they died . . .*
> *Oh, whenever men ask courage,*
> *Ask the knowledge to endure,*
> *Ask the fire to fire their veins,*
> *Ask to see the task accomplished,*
> *Ask the will to be unyielding,*
> *Let them call, let them call on your name.*
> *Sevastopol, Sevastopol, Sevastopol.*

To this song, the composer never added the accompaniment it would have needed to be effective. In its existing state it never reached performance, but its sentiment and its melody would not be forgotten.

During that summer of 1942, Marc's nephew Stephen worked at Crown Publishers in New York. Living at the West Side YMCA for a dollar a night, he was only a short walk from Marc's apartment on West Fifty-seventh Street, and Marc was pleased to have him nearby. Together they saw the show *This Is the Army,* for Marc a foretaste of what was to come; by the end of June he had decided to join up. As he wrote to David Diamond, he would soon be wearing "a bright and shining uniform. And I'm looking forward to it."[13]

Not knowing quite what he might expect, he sought letters of recommendation from a number of his contacts so that he might serve in the capacity for which he was best suited—entertainment and the arts. Davidson Taylor, Assistant Director of Broadcasts at CBS, said of him that "He understands the uses of music in propaganda and he has the cause of our country at war very much at heart." Taylor also wrote a separate letter of introduction to Arthur Bliss, Director of Music at the BBC. Robert W. Horton, Chief of the News Bureau for the Office of Emergency Management, provided a letter of recommendation based on his experience with Blitzstein on the abortive *Night Shift.* Blitzstein had "demonstrated great ability in his profession, reliability in performance and an intense interest in the welfare of his country." John Houseman, now serving as Chief of the Radio Production Division of the Office of War Information, described Blitzstein as "a skillful and talented craftsman, able to adapt his talents to the particular needs of his medium." Garson Kanin and Virgil Thomson wrote on his behalf. Copland introduced Blitzstein, who would "spend some time in London," to Ralph Hawkes, the music publisher, and Sir Adrian Boult. Brooks Atkinson spoke of his high regard for Blitzstein's operas: "I do not share Mr. Blitzstein's political point of view. But in my opinion he ranks very high as a composer of serious musical drama."[14]

One more letter arrived, not as part of this series. He had sent portions of his *No for an Answer* score to Nadia Boulanger, now in America in flight from the German takeover of her beloved France. From her studio in Cambridge, Massachusetts, she thanked him for the music, "in which I recognize you, at your best":

> You know how, always, I have attached importance to your gifts, your intelligence, your sensibility. It means a great deal to feel that the man has built what the boy dreamed—and I am more happy than ever to know you.[15]

The last work Blitzstein did on the home front was to write several scripts for the CIO's biweekly "Labor for Victory" radio program aired on WEAF alternately with AFL programs. The latter were tamer by far, emphasizing labor-management cooperation but ignoring all issues of contention. In the first of his programs, he addressed the secrecy of the Congressional Ways and Means Committee sessions when it decided on sales taxes as the method of raising the eight-billion-dollar war chest rather than on taxing the higher income brackets and business profits. President Roosevelt had spoken in a recent address of limiting personal income to twenty-five thousand dollars a year, and Blitzstein had a congressman in his script refer to this idea as "the President's questionable pleasantry." In a didactic interchange between a Montana ore miner, Johnny, and his wife Mary, it is she who encourages him to view the sales tax as a "plot" and to move a resolution in his union supporting the President's idea. Songs drove home Blitzstein's points—and again Henry Brant assisted with the orchestrations. In one number, Blitzstein had his actor, José Ferrer, relate a dream in which money grew on trees and the government did away with taxes ("to beat the axis"):

It seems the big shots
paid every penny,
whatever the demands,
We little guys watched
them win the war,
while we sat on our hands.
They did it with one toy sabre—
no use at all for labor—
Boy, oh boy, that was some dream.

Then, to a slow waltz, Johnny tells his wife not to worry: "on twenty-five thousand dollars a year, we'll get along." The narrator adds that this is the "patriotic American" thing to do.

For another program that aired on August 1, Blitzstein used the expression "The Bullet That's Going to Kill Hitler" as his title. His theme song is "Quiet Girl," shortly picked up for use in Lunchtime Follies programs offered by the American Theatre Wing. "I used to be a quiet girl," a secretary in a factory sings;

the "quiet guy" who held her in his arms now "drills with other arms, and he knows what he's drilling for."[16] A soldier visiting the factory on furlough reassures her that she, too, is helping to win the war, and he brings in a reminder of the night shift. To make a bullet requires "phones-files-letters-orders-bills-Organized!" The girl says, "We want to know that we're doing something important! How can you be happy these days if you're not working in the war effort?" Every secretary, even for a private doctor helping a man get back to work after an accident, helps the war.

Another episode treated the career of Mike Jones, army private. "I've got two buttons now—the old one that says C.I.O., and a new one that says U.S.A.—That's me, Private Mike Jones, C.I.O. and U.S.A." He takes the radio listener on a tour to three fronts where CIO relief supplies are at work: to visit a Newcastle steelworker in England who now is able to work a little longer "on the night shift" because of CIO donations; to see a roadworker in the mountains of South China who uses a first-aid kit sent by American workers; and to congratulate Dmitri Krasavin, oil refinery worker in the Soviet Caucasus, whose wife has just given birth to a baby boy, "another fighter against fascism." The program concludes with a barrage of sound effects—Japanese and German guns and bombs. Mike Jones says, "Maybe we've got some sounds that are just a little louder, and a little more deadly. Maybe we've got a symphony of our own, loud enough to drown out the sound of the Nazis and the Japs." Everyone contributes to the CIO War Relief "a symphony of nickels, quarters, half dollars." That program aired on August 15. It may have been the first time Blitzstein actually thought in terms of a symphonic work in the Allied cause.

Music cues in Blitzstein's handwriting survive from other CIO programs apparently not of his authorship. "Freedom Grows" was one of these, in which the great black orator and liberator of the nineteenth century, Frederick Douglass, comes back to life to advise today's young blacks not to be fooled by pro-Nazi appeals to stay at home and let others fight "the white man's war." It was a tricky issue for the CIO and for the left. True that such vices as segregation, the poll tax, denial of fair employment, and Jim Crow laws still persisted, even in the armed forces, along with the Klan, lynchings, and all manner of everyday discrimination. But the danger of fascism was far worse: Blacks in America at least enjoyed the promise of future improvements. James W. Ford, a leading Communist official, provided a foreword to a reprinted American Civil War address by Douglass, by way of showing the parallel example. But if the left was to gain black support for the war effort, it had to double and redouble its commitment to fight against racial discrimination. The estimated fifteen thousand American Communists who served in the armed forces during the war were the most dedicated activists for integration and racial justice for this reason.

The Selective Service System had by now reclassified Blitzstein 1-A, as he wished, and he requested enlistment. He cleared out his New York apartment, moving his piano and all his possessions to Jo's in Philadelphia. On August 24, he prepared a power of attorney, assigning all rights to Jo, and on the following day he drew up a handwritten will, with Jo as his beneficiary. By August 27 he had reported to Bolling Field Air Force Base in Washington, D.C. On the twenty-ninth, he enlisted, becoming Private Marc Blitzstein, serial number 13082206, attached to the Eighth Air Force in London. "I only hope it works out!" he wrote, perhaps a bit patronizingly, to his friend David Diamond:

> This is exactly what I want, need for realization: the chance to do my own work, fused into the stream of the most terrific events of our time, and right at the field of operations! Not ominous, my boy: thrilling.[17]

How short the years since he had ridiculed army training in the Faculty Room scene of *Cradle;* since Trixie, the naked-chested football coach (also elementary French teacher), blurted out his fulsome praises of the military:

Builds you up!—Alma Mater!
Sex Appeal!
Two years! Tree cheers!
Stick your chest out!
Be a man!

And now Blitzstein would stick his chest out. The FBI, aware of Blitzstein's enlistment, discontinued its investigation for the duration, though a year later they added his name to their list of "persons considered Communist Party Key Figures by the New York Field Division."[18]

The producer Sol Hurok had organized a Town Hall series on Mozart's concertos on six Tuesday evenings beginning in November. In midsummer, he printed his subscription brochure to the series, listing Blitzstein for one evening as the speaker on "Mozart and Our Times," with Clarence Adler as soloist and Leon Barzin conducting members or alumni of the National Orchestral Association.

Blitzstein couldn't make the date. He was now a composer in uniform.

12

EVERY INCH A SOLDIER

August 1942–November 1943

"Of course symphonies must be written now. But if the issues of today aren't clear to you, what kind of symphony?"

At Bolling Field, Blitzstein amused himself by watching aerial maneuvers. The aviation theme grabbed his fantasy from the start. On August 29, the day he became an enlisted man, he sent a picture postcard of the Washington Monument to Leonard Bernstein. "Here, and every inch a soldier," he wrote suggestively.[1] By the first of September he was assigned as an "entertainment specialist," his precise duties as yet undefined, to the United States Army Eighth Air Force attached to Headquarters Squadron. Major William Wyler, the Oscar-winning film director now in uniform, who had directed *The Little Foxes* just the year before, would be his boss in London.

Blitzstein felt surprised by the smoothness of his transition to military life: Happily, he was informed, he need not remove his mustache. Basic training did not detain him long. "I have learned how to really pack a barracks bag," Marc wrote to his sister Jo, readying himself for action:

> so that the two I possess are firmly and securely full, but not too heavy or bulky. . . . I've been very well handled at Bolling Field; now I'm glad to be leaving, because with a background of war, Bolling Field is too much

> like continental Europe's peace-time military service: fun for 19- + 20 year-olds; but after a couple of weeks too soft and colleg-y for grown men.[2]

To his mother Marc wrote on the same day from Bolling Field: "I've already got several fine ideas for small movies, which I plan to present to Wyler as soon as I report to him. I think he'll be impressed. . . . Get busy . . . don't worry—about me, at any rate."[3]

While Blitzstein was at Bolling Field, the husband-and-wife team of José Ferrer and Uta Hagen premiered a farce in Washington, and they invited the composer to attend. That day, Blitzstein had received the latest in a round of vaccine shots, and one of them caused him to collapse right in the aisle of the theatre, drawing all the attention away from the stage. But he recovered soon enough and within days shipped out.[4]

On September 27, a Dutch ship that had once seen service as a tourist boat in the East Indies, now gutted to form a single large room in which all activity took place, departed for Scotland with its cargo of six thousand troops. Blitzstein made the mistake of eating the greenish meat served on board; along with the Red Cross nurses who took the same chance, he entered the ship's hospital ward with a virulent case of ptomaine. The convoy traveled slowly; by the time it reached Glasgow, he had recovered. From there he took a train to Chorley in Lancastershire. Despite the hellish adventure, he was enormously titillated and encouraged by his new surroundings. He wrote to Sam and Maddie on arrival:

> You can be assured I have had a lifetime of experience crammed into these few weeks; I am really beginning to know guys inside out. I find confirmation of all my hopes and beliefs. In short, I find I am for people; I have added to my faith in men a realistic knowledge of them. Give these soldiers I have been with a purpose and they will match any one, any where, for tenacity, courage, good humor—and incidentally, barrack-room wit. I'm having a fine time.[5]

"The one thing I could wish for, and I admit it is basic," he added in a comment to Jo, "is a deeper and more unanimous conviction about the whole effort."

"After a month of unrelieved publicity in the matters of dressing, eating, sleeping, and you-can-guess-what, it is amazing how I relish comparative privacy," he wrote again two days later. "I note Stalingrad still holds! Those Russians!"[6]

On that same day, Blitzstein wrote the first of dozens of V-letters he would send home—those three and a half by five-inch photographic reductions in an inky black, which from time to time defied legibility. Jo faithfully kept them all, stuck into a copy of *Mr. Weston's Good Wine* by T. F. Powys, which Marc had bought back in 1928. How could she know which of Marc's precious letters might be his last? In this one, still cautious of what the censor might blank out, he gave hearty assurances of a safe arrival in England, filled out with paeans to the placid landscape.

Blitzstein gave as much news in his letters as possible. Some projects, however, and often his exact location and movements had to be concealed to pass the censors. Below the surface, his letters took on a gnawing, guilt-ridden quality, acknowledging but somehow also relishing the suffering at not seeing his family "for the duration." He wrote home at least weekly, more often to Jo than to anyone else, almost always asking that his letters be circulated among the whole family. His absence lined up his relations in a solid phalanx behind him: They wrote to him frequently, at his request shamelessly detailing the kind of small talk that would have exasperated him at home, just to reassure him that all functioned normally. They sent packages of foodstuffs and garments; they knitted for him; they sent regular batches of the latest theatrical and musical clippings. The boys sent their writings—poetry and short stories—and they asked their uncle for career and scholastic advice.

As part of the home-front war effort, Marc's mother served as a member of the Army Air Forces Technical Training Command's Sewing Units in Ventnor. She read many of Marc's letters to Jo, though he also took care to write to her separately. There never was a question of Sam and Maddie falling out together—the marriage held up splendidly—but the possibility of Marc's being in danger did bring Sam closer to Anna. This highly politicized family relegated personal problems to a position of very low priority. In most of Marc's letters home, he assured his family of his well-being; and generally he tried to strike an optimistic note about Soviet advances in the east and British and American efforts in Africa and southern Europe. At the same time, he did not let down his guard about the backsliders among the Western allies: He bristled whenever he heard politicians or newspapers issuing statements that seemed to impugn the struggle against fascism.

Laid over at first in a depot camp in western England, Blitzstein was gratified to find a hearty welcome to the Yanks on the part of ordinary Britishers. But it was more than a week before he got to London, and he had become impatient to start working. In London at last, he stopped first at Claridge's, the hotel occupied by American officers, where the Hollywood screenwriter Jerome Chodorov had left word that Blitzstein be admitted to his room on arrival. Chodorov came home one night to the sight of Blitzstein wilting in a hot bath, weeping in relief after three weeks without proper facilities.

By the third week of October, he was assigned to his post. Because of the Blitz, the more elegant sections of London had been evacuated. Apartments in Mayfair had been requisitioned as barracks, and Blitzstein was assigned to one, albeit a coldwater one with four other American servicemen, at 5 Green Street. The British caste system still prevailed, of course, despite the rationing and the purported ceiling on prices, but the American private admired the British fighting spirit none the worse for such social distinctions. He soon found himself drawn to a huge Trafalgar Square rally urging the Allies to open a Western European second front against Hitler—a campaign close to his own heart; for while yet in the States, he had written a "Second Front" song, around the same time that Charlie Chaplin appeared at a Carnegie Hall rally for the same cause. The second front was of course necessary to diffuse Hitler's forces and relieve the pressure on the Soviet Union. Before long the composer found himself trapped in the tube for the night during an air raid—the classic British wartime experience. He also looked into the uninhibited London nightlife during the blackouts. Every imaginable kind of sex could be found on the streets at night. As he recalled it after the war for *New Masses,* "Brother, it's like nothing that's printable."

The Eighth Army Air Force was designed as a strategic unit primarily for long-distance missions. When the time came, however, it would also play a part in the eventual invasion of the Continent. Jerome Chodorov had already settled into his work in its public relations department. Posted in the film unit, he quickly took on Blitzstein as a co-worker. He introduced him to the local eateries and personalities and accompanied him to first showings of films, musicals, and theatre. Blitzstein saw Emlyn Williams in what he called an "execrable" staging of *The Little Foxes.* Among other projects, he worked with Chodorov on scenarios for short films: One had to do with a Flying Fortress named Phyllis, which Eleanor Roosevelt had talked about in a recent column. Using the piano of Louis Dreyfus at the English branch of Chappell's, his publisher, Blitzstein also wrote air force songs.* Another of Blitzstein's steadiest companions during these first weeks in London included the writer Bill White, whose wife Ruth was the daughter of Blitzstein's agent William Morris.

The USO put together material written in part back home and in part by writers employed overseas for a variety of stateside entertainers to perform at soldier camps throughout the war zone. That fall in England, Blitzstein entered the fray as writer and composer of such material. One of his first subjects for a five-minute short was buying war bonds. Martha Raye, Kay Francis, Carole Landis, and Mitzi Mayfair did the number on their camp tour. "Everyone feels I should be most useful doing what I do best," he wrote to David Diamond. "That's more than one up for the U.S. Army—that's practically the millenium!"[7]

Introductions to the famous were easy to come by, especially once the army had moved Blitzstein to Claridge's. In one letter home, he impressed his sister by saying that he couldn't name his new quarters, but General Doolittle and Colonel Oveda Culp Hobby could be found there. At Claridge's also he visited

> the apt. of Laurence Olivier and Vivien Leigh: she lovely in negligee, and an exquisite hunk of lady. . . . All very gay, very lah-de-dah, the war just a thing to talk and read about (for the moment). They all commented on how smart I looked, compared to British privates' uniforms—and then this morning, at inspection, a Major comes by and gives me K-P for a day on account of my brass insignia button ain't shined up enough. Irony? I'll appreciate it later.[8]

Not long afterward, Olivier and Leigh invited him out to their country estate. When he arrived, the actress noticed that he was missing two buttons on his tunic.

*Little of Blitzstein's incidental wartime work has survived; in some cases, the only reference to it appears in his letters home.

"Oh, Marc, let me sew those on for you," she volunteered, an honor—and an anecdote for future retelling—he was not about to pass up.

His swirl of activity amounted to "a dazing mass of *unconnected* experiences." "I can tell you it's one of the experiences of my life—and will, as soon as things begin to move, undoubtedly prove *the* experience." "This is all for now; but if it doesn't tell you that I am living to the hilt; and that being closer to the scene of operations is exactly what I wanted and am getting, then you're no good at reading between the lines."[9]

As a composer, Blitzstein also made the effort to meet his British counterparts. He became especially good friends with Alan Bush and his family. Bush had been in New York at the time of *Cradle* and had met Blitzstein then. He considered "Nickel Under the Foot" "the finest blues ever written." Now he, too, was in his country's army, and he was rehearsing a revue that fall. In the afternoons, Bush invited Blitzstein to use his studio on Baker Street, which was equipped with nothing less than a Bechstein concert grand, "rented from a Miss Mabel Lander, spinster extraordinary, who teaches the Princesses Margaret and Elizabeth, but is also affable to American-Jewish privates by the name of Blitzstein."[10]

As president of the left-wing Workers' Music Association, Bush worked feverishly to promote Soviet music. He toured the Soviet Union himself in 1943, conducting British music and introducing Elgar's *Enigma Variations* among other novelties. Upon his return, he published enthusiastic accounts of the wartime musical scene there, citing a figure of over 200,000 concerts given on the front lines since June 1941. Perhaps because the British public was so much more ideologically attuned to a Labour policy, the British composers, more enduringly than in the United States, displayed a sense of mission in allying with a working-class audience. Vice-presidents of the association included such eminent figures as Lennox Berkeley, Benjamin Britten, Edward J. Dent, Alois Hába, and John Ireland, as well as their correspondent Hanns Eisler in the United States.[11]

Questioned about how Eisler was faring in America, Blitzstein told Bush that to his mind Eisler had "sold out" in California, separated himself from the progressive movement—a fairly widespread opinion of Eisler among Communist music circles. The denunciation caused Eisler's family perhaps more distress than it did the composer himself, who regarded Blitzstein's behavior as a matter of jealousy between composers. For despite the huge reputation he had earned for his mass songs, Eisler's ties to the Communists were never all that zealous.

In his letters home, Blitzstein could not directly state everything he wanted to say. Innuendo dripping with self-satisfaction covered for explicit information. He would refer to "our friends" from time to time, meaning politically compatible types who were of course happy to have Marc Blitzstein in their midst. As he expressed it to Sam and Maddie once, "Our friends are throwing that little party for me this Sunday week"—already he had begun adopting a few British locutions—"at the studio of the daughter of one of England's big bankers, if you please. Thus do the sands of time, etc."[12]

To David Diamond, with whom he shared more of his intimate life than with anyone, he wrote a Christmas card that year: "While at work on your big throw, give a thought, shed a tear for a soldier somewhere in the wilds of Soho, beating down trees that turn out to be Canadian grenadiers in the blackout." And he named for David all the places he would find "amusing": Piccadilly and Hyde Park, of course, the Players' Club, and a pub called the Queen's Brasserie, renamed the Brassiere by those who went there seeking a certain kind of companionship.[13]

Modern Music carried Blitzstein's article on "London: Fourth Winter of the Blackout" in its January–February issue, a résumé of his frenetic theatre- and concertgoing activity. Adrian Boult, with Peter Pears, Astra Desmond, and the London Philharmonic, gave "the finest *Lied von der Erde* I have ever heard. This work is for me by far the best Mahler—almost the only one I can take wholeheartedly." He found Noël Coward's film *In Which We Serve* cold, "class-angled with a vengeance, its author being a very conscious, if not entirely kosher member of British aristocracy." Blitzstein mentioned a number of revues, radio and theatre productions with incidental music, and the dance performance of choreographer Robert Helpmann, who "might be Martha Graham in switched-drag, so startling is the resemblance."[14] For publication he did not include what he remarked in a letter home: "I went to the ballet a couple of times; I saw a very good male dancer, Robert Helpmann, who is most famous for the crack he made when describing his performances for ENSA (USO sort of; playing in factories for the men): 'There we were' (you must imagine him, very airy-fairy and effeminate) 'There we were, buttering up the workers, just as though we liked them!' "[15]

On December 2, 1942, a year since he had last informed Claire Reis of his progress with *The New York Opera,* he wrote again to write *finis* to the League of Composers project. "Most of my stuff including a lot of manuscripts has been lost in transit," he told her, and with them sketches and other material for the opera. "The Army is something of a taskmaster," he continued to Reis, and it was not likely that he would soon return to the piece. "I'm more than sorry; I should have finished the New York Opera before we got into the war." "I'm enjoying London and England hugely," he added. "Musically, the town is not terribly active, from a contemporary point of view, or, indeed, any other. At least, there seems to be no *a priori* objection to music written by a live composer, which is damned white of them, say we all."[16]

In conjunction with William Wyler, who planned a major epic film on the air war, Blitzstein traveled out in early December with a cameraman and two technicians to visit bomber stations. They shot film at several locales for the historical archives and researched the tight relationship between men and their planes, garnering useful information and germs of ideas for stories. At night they occupied bunks in Nissen huts, corrugated-metal, cement-floored half-cylinder structures that housed hundreds of thousands of servicemen during the war. In rank an ordinary private—as were most of the men he met, only in most cases he was nearly twice their age—Blitzstein met the real, unguarded soldier, heard his complaints, witnessed the hardships he endured, and shared some of his commonplace joys. He saw boys barely out of high school suddenly turned men.

Every Flying Fortress had a name, the composer observed. "One has the names of girls under the windows of their respective boy-friends' positions: 'Mary Jane' for the bombardier, 'Sissy' for the co-pilot, 'Virginia' for the tail-gunner. And on one is painted a descending bomb with a bird flying above it, eyeing it dubiously: 'Did I do that?' "[17]

The outfit he wore, and the deliberate activities of the bomb crews he met, shortly provided hardy nuggets for Blitzstein's major wartime composition:

> My field-jacket is wool-lined; my fatigue suit, my galoshes—they have all been waiting for action; + this is it. Well, not the action I see about me—for real "missions" do start and finish at this particular station—but a recording of them, anyway. Mess with the ground-crew, operational intelligence boys, gunnery-instructors—all enlisted men and non-coms. No shit here about removing your cap when you eat, or having your shoes shined and brass buttons polished; the place is designed for business, and all the faces reflect it. Somehow most of the men seem better-looking than the city-variety or headquarters-variety: I think it's the concentration on the job that does something to their expression.[18]

At the same time, he also chanced upon a nugget he would squirrel away for use in a theatre piece after the war was over. In a story in *Stars and Stripes,* the armed forces newspaper, James Aldrige had written "about four American sergeants, inspecting American-made trucks for the Russians in the eastern wilds: how they got along, how they learn Russian, admire our Allies, who apparently adore them, and are ready to stake them against all comers. A humdinger." At present, however, Blitzstein was concerned for his nephew Stephen, imminently eligible for the draft: "I'm convinced he'll handle it," he wrote to Jo, "but I'm not sure I want him to, just yet. If there is any way he could get a year off—either in college or working,—I'd feel lots calmer."[19]

Not long after Blitzstein returned to London, Wyler was dispatched to another assignment; Jerome Chodorov left London; Lina Abarbanell's employer Dwight Wiman went into direct Red Cross entertainment; and the composer acquired a new commanding officer, the arrestingly attractive Col. Beirne Lay, Jr. Blitzstein liked him from the start. One day, Lay asked Pvt. Blitzstein to come into his office and, as Marc reported it to Jo, "he said I am apparently better known to the British than I am to my own army; that having me was like 'having Toscanini as a private' (!) and that he planned as soon as possible to see that the 'crime' of my situation was rectified. Of course I'd like a promotion."[20]

While he waited for the change to happen, Blitzstein wrote more radio material for Martha Raye and Kay Francis, prepared commentary and some translations for a newsreel by Anatole Litvak, and selected music for another short movie. By now Blitzstein had gotten his feet wet. He knew the terrain and knew that in a string of minor ways he was being useful. But none of these little jobs amounted to much. He was capable of doing far more for the cause. It staggered him, then, when Col. Lay volunteered, "I know your abilities, and I think you may be wasted here. What would you like to do?"

Barely skipping a beat, Blitzstein answered: "I'd like to do a big symphony, on flight," and he sketched out the fantasy.

"It's a hot idea," Lay replied, "but there may be complications. I'll try to sell it to General Eaker."

Blitzstein provided a thumbnail synopsis for a four-movement work, with prelude, scored for orchestra and six-part mixed chorus, designed to persuade his superior officers of its worthiness:

> *Theme:* The sacred struggle of the airborne free men of the world, but particularly of the USA and in the US Army Air Force—to crush the monstrous fascist obstructionist in their path; to crush completely the power of an enemy who abuses the very achievements of the air for purposes of persecution, murder, enslavement. The threat is airborne; the fight is airborne; and victory will be airborne. Once the battle is won, free men can resume their historic task in this Age of the Air: the conquest of the skies, men over nature. This is the good conquest, the good enslavement.

He also prepared the defense of his project by citing Shostakovich's Seventh Symphony, dedicated to the besieged city of Leningrad. Not long before, bomber planes had carried the microfilmed score to London and New York for performances shortly after the Russian premiere in March 1942. "The results more than justified the effort," Blitzstein wrote for his officers' edification. "The symphony, symbolizing, even representing courage in the face of withering fire and destruction, was responsible for an immense worldwide wave of enthusiasm and admiration for the people of the USSR and their fighting forces. Music was on the map as a positive weapon in winning the war." This could be done for the United States Eighth Army Air Force. As he had answered his composer friend David Diamond, whom he often addressed in a somewhat tutelary fashion, "Of course symphonies must be written now. But if the issues of today aren't clear to you, what kind of symphony?"[21] There could simply be no defense of "sitting this one out."

Quickly, Blitzstein began lining up support for his project. Imagine! To be paid on army time to create a major musical work completely of his own choosing and design! In a memorandum dated January 9, 1943, Anatole Litvak, Maj. AUS, Signal Corps, commended Blitzstein as "especially qualified to carry out a project such as he has outlined to me—one involving the use of the art of dramatic music in public relations."[22]

The composer even roughed out his conception of the symphony accompanied by film. Begin with camera in a plane shooting the takeoff, then expand to sky and clouds throughout the prelude. Aim for a high tone, like Auden, but not highfalutin, also colloquial where necessary. Use up some of that music in his composer's trunk—from *The Condemned* and *Cain,* from what he could remember of *The New York Opera.*

With the new year came good news: The symphony proposal tentatively approved! Freed from daily inspection and ordinary serviceman's duties, he received a stipend for rations and quarters, and a deadline of eight months to write his symphony. For the time being, though, he kept his family waiting for the specifics. Certainly he might have given more detail, for which he knew they hungered, but a combination of superstition about new projects and some notion of military secrecy gave him the right excuse to create an air of suspense.

He did tell them about his old friend Jimmy Dugan, a former theatre critic for the Communist press in New York, and the mutual favors they performed for one another in London: Marc found Jimmy a job in OWI public relations work, and Jimmy introduced Marc to a Dr. Peter Gorer, pathologist at Guy's Hospital and cancer researcher, who provided Blitzstein billeting in his Highgate house. With his fiancée Gertrude, a German refugee, Gorer lived twenty minutes outside of London, practically next to the cemetery where Karl Marx lay buried. The home was surrounded by gardens and equipped with a fawn-colored Steinway parlor grand and a lovable old chow dog that reminded Marc of his own Very. Now, all his contacts together provided six pianos at his disposal. As Dugan recalled the scene years later:

> The rest of us had worked out accommodations for ourselves in London, but Marc was the envy of all. We made legends of the corporal who never turned out a reveille, never ate army chow, performed no drill, saluted no one, marched nowhere, shot at nothing, and spent his days in a manor house parlor placarded do not disturb, gazing idly over a mile of heath displayed through the open french doors, and just played himself tunes on the pie-anna.[23]

Before the month of January was out, Col. Lay's promise to advance his own private Toscanini came to fruition. On the thirtieth, Marc wrote to Papa and Maddie that he was now Corporal Blitzstein: "Although a certain distinction departs with the 'Private,' which I honestly regret, I will relish the extra pay, not to mention the prestige which goes with my new stripes. Happy little corporal! Maybe I should start looking about for a little Elba room."[24]

Marc *was* happy. He wouldn't have wanted to be anywhere else. Living at the Gorer home, he proceeded with his project. And when the day was over, if he went out drinking in some Soho pub, his beliefs and his work entitled him to vent all the self-righteousness he could muster. If not everyone he met seemed to know what the war was all about, or if someone let loose an anti-Semitic smear, he could justifiably raise his voice in anger and proudly pat himself on the back if he controlled himself from exchanging blows. But he found friends, too:

> in that strange arm's-length relation I always seem doomed to achieve: Dr. Peter Gorer, Dave Scherman, Lee Miller [*Life* and *Vogue* photographers, respectively], Robert and Iris Nesbitt [British producer and his wife]. No deep thing has happened—and it better had, soon. The war status makes these things instantaneous, or impossible, or both at once.

> There is no time for indirection, fancy plays. You look at someone, and it's: "You for me? I'm for you." Then you get drunk, or you don't; then you go to bed, or you don't. If you do, or if you don't, it's immensely unimportant.[25]

On February 16, Marc lifted the suspense with an excited letter home:

> The project has been accepted—an hour ago! . . . so I can spill it. I submitted a plan to do a big lyric-and-dramatic symphony, to be called "The Airborne"—for orchestra, chorus, speaker, singing-and-acting-solos. A concert-work, but one adaptable for radio—or even film production. Four movements and a prelude. To take about an hour in performance; to be exploited in a big way (translations in Russian for Moscow performance, Spanish for Mexico and S. America, French for the underground movt.), with initial London performance radiating repeats everywhere else. A big throw, and to be treated as such. Lt. Tex McCrary, Major Wyler and Col. Lay got steamed up, and began to investigate possibilities of my being released full-time to do the work. Now it has happened, right up to the Air Force Generals. . . . Really on the beam, and I am excited as rarely before. . . .
>
> Dreyfus here of Chappell will publish the work. Lord Rothermere *(Daily Mail)* is prepared to help on exploitation; Richardson of NBC, Majors Redding and Nussbaum of 8th A. F. Pubic [*sic*] Relations are all out for it. Now all I have to do is write the damned thing. Had you gathered I'm very happy?
>
> N.B. Not a word yet to anyone! It *must* be first publicized from this end![26]

With its late-nineteenth-century architecture and gardens, the Gorer home in Highgate reminded Blitzstein of Yaddo. The painter Tchelitchev had lived in the house some ten years before and his paintings covered the walls. Blitzstein traveled into town only once or twice a week. For music paper, he asked his family to deliver the right type to John Houseman, now working for the OWI in New York, who would forward it to London. Despite the vagaries of the English heating system, the composer quickly fell into his typical work routine of long morning and afternoon sessions of struggle over words and notes. As usual, he would write both the lyrics and the music. There were times, writing the *Airborne,* when he wondered how useful he was, remaining out of combat—"chairborne," as he put it. But he satisfied himself that doing the job he did best would in the end be his most valuable contribution. "The thing that gives me most trouble is the style," he wrote to his father and Maddie:

> It has to be fairly colloquial—but it must also contain the germ of real poetry, must have extended line, must give off the sense of non-specific forces. I don't have anything like the same difficulty with the composing. You may recognize little hunks here and there. My past is coming into good service; those weighty laborious desk-drawer masterpieces are sim-

> mered down, condensed, distilled in my memory; and the residuum is what I meant all along. Old Siloti wasn't wrong when he announced I was the kind who would mature late, if at all. I've always remembered his dictum with rancor—because I saw the truth of it subconsciously. Ben Lyon (now a Major in my outfit) shook a warning finger at me yesterday, and said: "Don't look to me for sympathy if you come in with 'Deep in the Heart of Texas.' "[27]

As winter ebbed, Blitzstein found a second home at the Little French Club on Duke Street, one of the many small but flourishing private restaurants that served alcoholic beverages after hours. At this "Hollywood-in-exile," nestled in the house where Chopin had lived, he could entertain fellow Americans who drifted through London on one wartime assignment or another. And he could keep his French in shape, as the Welsh proprietress always had a French refugee clientele on hand. Week after week, as one of the OWI's most knowledgeable cultural workers, he met the leading actors, producers, writers, and other personalities in the art worlds of several nations gathered in London: Carol Reed, Peter Ustinov, and Eric Ambler in the film crowd, for example. And when he dropped by John Lehmann's Hogarth Press to check the proofs of Lincoln Kirstein's new novel, he met the poets Stephen Spender and Louis MacNeice there. "I'm well, flourishing really; and looking forward to that Big Push that keeps getting promised every time one of the Big Boys opens his mouth."[28]

The disparate human and historical forces operating in the world had perhaps never seemed so unified as now, so aimed toward a specific objective. Out of the whirlwind of impressions invading the mind, the artist tried to connect all these heterogeneous realities:

> Spring is here—and we get more news of pillage and plunder and ravaged homes in Russia, in Europe. Somehow, the two facts go together. I look at beautiful gardens, there is the sound of birds, the air is lazy, nothing seems so far away as the war, on the surface; and yet the *truth* of these gardens and sounds is the sending of little children out on the fields of Kharkov to be killed by hidden mines; or the lining up of prisoners against a concentration camp wall to be shot.[29]

> I don't work all day and night, you know—or did you? Now that spring is here, and the holly is doing whatever holly does—I'm doing a little too. The blackout is in my way a bit—we now have daylight until 11 P.M., and again at 4 A.M., which means whoopee must be made in short order—and whoopee isn't whoopee when you come out of a pub to find the sun shining. What kind of a war is this anyhow, one asks—and then gulps, and asks it again.[30]

Other distractions intervened to slow down the composer's pace on the *Airborne.* Blitzstein wrote the translation of a fighting song for the French Resistance; performed a concert of his own music at Cambridge, arranged by Wilfrid

Mellers, the British critic who had championed *Cradle* and *No for an Answer* as such authentically American expressions; gave a BBC radio talk on American music that attracted an estimated two million listeners; and on July 4 returned to the BBC with Frank Travers, the Maxwell House Coffee baritone, singing the Robeson songs from *Native Land.* More introductions were made: to Erika Mann, the daughter of Thomas Mann, to John Steinbeck and Cedric Belfrage. The actor Burgess Meredith had arrived in town; so had CBS's Irving Reis. And Blitzstein had two upper back teeth pulled.

But he continued working on his choral symphony. By mid-June he could report the end in sight. Perhaps he would meet his eight-month deadline. He hoped that his father, in his weakened condition, would hold out long enough to hear the *Airborne,* long enough to see the Allies victorious, long enough to welcome his son home:

> I feel guilty as hell that you have written me several special letters, and this is the first in a long time I've addressed to you personally. Of course you'll understand, you do understand; but the sense of guilt persists. About a couple of months ago, I got maudlin drunk, I remember; and decided to send you a secret special unique and for-all-time intimate letter (the Army provides some kind of particular blue paper for such letters, which are seen by the general, but not our local censor); telling you all about how I felt I had neglected you through the years, all about how much more often we should have seen each other—and so on, and so forth; sentimental to tears I got, over very weak brown ale, which has more or less become my staple drink, largely because it goes through the system so quickly. It's just as well all around that letter never got written.[31]

There was good war news, and good news from home. The Allies had all but wiped up the Germans in North Africa by the summer of 1943; Mussolini resigned; and Stalin had dissolved the Comintern to reassure his Western allies. Stephen had won a scholarship to the University of Pennsylvania—cause for another of Marc's drunken binges. It reminded him, too, of the inexorable advance of years: Jo and Ed were celebrating their twentieth anniversary! From photographs of the life at home, it also looked as though gentle Very was showing his age as well.

An unusual moment of excitement came suddenly in late July when Blitzstein was asked to participate in a live thirty-minute BBC broadcast featuring Alistair Cooke hosting Sam Grafton, Dorothy Dunbar Bromley, and Ed Sullivan in New York, asking questions live to Henry David, Margaret Mead, and Blitzstein in London. The show would be delayed for broadcast a week later in America. "Answering You Americans to Americans" dealt mostly with politics, wartime social developments, and economic planning for the postwar period, but for a few minutes Sullivan and Blitzstein talked about theatre and music in London. Hints of a newly acquired British accent subtly showed in Blitzstein's speaking voice. He happily reported growing British interest in American composers such as

Gershwin, Copland, Harris, and Schuman. And he spoke enthusiastically about the new audiences for music—factory workers at lunchtime concerts hearing Bach's *The Art of the Fugue* for the first time.

> "Marc, I don't know how much time a corporal has in the Air Force, but I got a great idea for you as a composer."
> "Go ahead, Ed."
> "Why don't you compose a new opera to be presented at Rome?"
> "One, for a very good reason. The Rome Opera, as I remember it from 1932, is a lousy opera company."
> "Well, we're going to change that all around!"

"The material wasn't too interesting (it was all impromptu, no script), but the thrill of talking to NY, and having it talk back was *something,*" he wrote to his mother. And to Jo: "we managed to hit the high spots in utter drivel and insignificance for nearly half an hour."[32]

After nearly eight months, the time had come for his superiors to check on the progress of his choral symphony:

> One actually said he got the sensation of something "new" as surely and unmistakably as the time he first saw a Flying Fortress take off into the blue. If that isn't praise from an airman, I'll eat my garrison-cap. I still have a lot to do on the work—and have been more or less granted an extension on it. I like it; and feel that when it jells, it will be what I set out to do.[33]

Still ensconced in the comfortable Gorer home in Highgate, he continued composing, at least until the next interruption. "I've been being very good and proper since the Colonel 'examined' and enthusiastically passed on my job; industrious, with lots of work and sleep, little drinking, and a bit of rock-gardening in my spare time to shave off the curves in my figure."[34]

Blitzstein's method of organizing his composition baffled those who saw him at work. He amassed a sheaf of hundreds of pages of music paper, all that he would require for the entire piece, and inserted his bar lines. Then he would write in a measure of music here, two measures there, another measure several pages later, with many blank pages in between, almost as though the exact length, the arc of the score was completely premeditated, the specific notes to be written in only as composed.

To the displeasure of the American left, hopeful that the war on fascism represented more than a struggle between competing nationalisms, the United States armed forces during World War II remained strictly segregated. Racial discrimination, even a kind of quarantining of American black soldiers into separate units, stood apart from and against all the democratic ideals the left espoused. Indeed, in England, racism on the part of white American troops and their officers had begun to infect the British, whose own racial attitudes at home had never taken the virulent forms known in the United States. Some of the black servicemen themselves were getting discouraged by the cool British welcome. Whites, too, were included when resentful Britishers would say things such as, "There are four things we hate about the Yanks: they're overpaid, overfed, oversexed, and over here."

As a way of forestalling further British antiblack prejudice and of helping to solidify the Anglo-American alliance, army leaders decided to call upon a spontaneously organized black chorus to present a pair of concerts in London's famous Royal Albert Hall. The two-hundred-voice chorus was comprised of members of army aviation engineer units. Though most of them had no formal training, some had sung in church choirs and school glee clubs. A few had begun careers on the stage and radio.

The concerts to be offered on September 28 and 29 were sponsored by the army and by Lord Beaverbrook's *Daily Express,* the newspaper that carried the banner headline reading "Second Front Now"; both Beaverbrook and Sir Stafford Cripps had called for an invasion of Europe before Hitler could defeat Russia. Proceeds from the first concert went to British and American relief organizations. The second concert was free to all members of the Allied armed forces.

Blitzstein was taken off his assignment to help prepare the concert, just the sort of interruption he welcomed because of its solid political ramifications. In addition to rehearsing the choral portion of the program, Blitzstein would write a specially commissioned orchestral work, "dedicated to the United States Army Negro Troops," to be performed by the London Symphony Orchestra. It would be the first musical composition by an American GI written and performed in a combat zone. NBC would broadcast a half hour of the concert to the United States, though not the new Blitzstein piece.

Blitzstein's hosts got married on August 18, leaving Blitzstein in the house while they honeymooned. But he did not remain there for the two weeks the Gorers were away. Instead, he moved into a Nissen hut on the edge of the 8th Battalion post near Ipswich in East Anglia, where the black engineers were busy building airdromes with concrete mixers and pavers. At these stations, crews would fine-tune and repair the planes used in bombing missions on the Continent.* Blitzstein's hut, from which he could look out on the placid English countryside, had the only piano on the base. It was the PX, used for recreational purposes, and he had to squeeze his working hours in between movie showings and Sunday worship services. At other times, men off duty would sleep, snore, relax, play dice, talk, and sing all around him. The move to these quarters ensured that as composer, but also as coach in the spirituals and in Earl Robinson's *Ballad for Americans,* this lone white man would share the surroundings of five hundred black troops and gain their confidence.

*The first all-black fighter unit, the 99th Fighter Squadron, trained at Alabama's Tuskegee Army Airfield in 1941–1943, but black flying crews were not based in England.

Blitzstein felt excited by such intimacy with his singers, many of them only half his own age. "Born singers all," he reported to Mama on September 4, "delightful kids, who call me 'Corporal Marc.' " But shortly he sensed that the white officers actually opposed the concert and would try anything to sabotage it, including an insistence on scheduling rehearsals at the two bases in the towns of Diss and Eye on the same night. He wrote to Jo:

> I feel more like what is fondly called a "People's Artist" than ever in my life. I'm living with negro-engineers. During the day I have a large movie-Nissen-hut to compose the piece in which will be played at the negro-concert. At night I rehearse the chorus in the *Ballad for Americans* and supervise spirituals. Half of them are miles away at another station—so in a jeep I am driven wildly through English villages in blackout night, and take over at the second rehearsal. (The two will be put together in time for the concert.) We stopped last night at a Red Cross Club apparently in the wilderness, where the gayest and maddest jive and lindy-hopping this side of the Savoy was going on. The English like them, they get on fine with them. And as for me I'm treated like "The Maestro."[35]

Blitzstein based his twelve-minute composition on a number of black musical themes, among them two spirituals, "My Lord's Goin' to Rain Down Fire" and "When the Stars Begin to Fall," both of them appropriate in light of the ferocious air war against the Nazis. When he had completed a section or a few measures, he would play it through for the men.

"How does it sound?" he asked. "This is supposed to be you."

Someone answered, "That ain't me. That's Russian or Chinese." Blitzstein tore up the music. At one point, in a passage employing boogie rhythms, a soldier in fatigues produced a set of drumsticks and marked out a beat that the composer gratefully incorporated into the score.

Freedom stood out as the theme of the day. Samuel Barber, also in uniform, dedicated his second symphony to the U.S. Air Forces; in addition, he wrote a *Commando March* for military band and a *Funeral March* based on the Army Air Corps Song. Robert Russell Bennett wrote his *Four Freedoms* Symphony, and John Alden Carpenter his *Song of Freedom,* while Earl Robinson came up with a Jeffersonian tribute called *That Freedom Plow.* Elie Siegmeister's *Freedom Train* and Randall Thompson's *Testament of Freedom* both date from 1943.

Blitzstein's *Freedom Morning* opens with a slow, modal section suggesting the coming of dawn. The mood shares much in common with Copland's *Appalachian Spring,* written the following year. After a long buildup, the piece bursts into a frenetic jazz episode that, like Leonard Bernstein's compositions during the war years, could not have been written without the prior example of Copland's Piano Concerto. Echoes can also be heard of the Virginian composer John Powell's *Rhapsodie Nègre.* When Blitzstein finished the piece, he took the score for copying at the army photostat plant. The sergeant in charge looked at it and in a word revealed his dearth of musical knowledge. "Code?"

In connection with the premiere of *Freedom Morning,* Blitzstein wrote a report for *The New York Times.* "All my belief in the American Negro as an integral and vital part of growing American culture—musical, artistic, civic, human and social—has been strengthened," he said. The black men of the U.S. Army in England sang all the time, creating spontaneous improvisation, harmony, and polyphony. "Singing, to these men, is the very threshold of all feeling, whether happiness, misery or anger." Even their speech was musical, delivered with real melody and real figuration. Of course, he added, they were also good soldiers who had given up pass privileges for the six-week rehearsal period: "I do not want to give the impression that these are irresponsible, singing children. They are grown men, perfectly aware. They know what they're doing in this war—and, what is more, why!"[36]

Ten days before their appearance at Royal Albert Hall, the two hundred choristers left for London for final rehearsals. In typical Jim Crow style, the army isolated them in their own hotel. For the two days before the concert, they were given leave, during which time their white officers expected, and hoped, that the singers would ruin their voices by whoring and drinking.

Roland Hayes, the famous black American tenor who had been active on the concert stage since the early 1920s, flew over from America on his first airplane trip especially to sing at these concerts. Joining the chorus and orchestra in a set of spirituals, he also performed a Bach recitative and aria, and the aria "O Peace, Thou Fairest Child of Heaven" from Thomas Arne's masque of 1740, *Alfred.* True, his voice was now less impressive than it once had been, but his presence would be an inspiration to the troops. Actually, Paul Robeson had been considered first, both because he was so well known in England and because he had made *Ballad for Americans* so famous. But word had it that Queen Mary herself vetoed Robeson on account of rumors of too many affairs with too many highly placed British women.

These concerts marked the first time *Ballad* was performed by a black chorus with a white soloist, twenty-one-year-old Private First Class Kenneth Cantril, from Springfield, Missouri. With his rich bass-baritone that some listeners mistook for Robeson's, Cantril had privately recorded some songs shortly after arriving in England a few months before. Blitzstein had heard his "Ol' Man River" on the radio and had had Cantril brought to his quarters for an audition.

Technical Sergeant Hugo Weisgall, thirty years old, plumpish and already balding, conducted. He was the nephew of Meyer Weisgal, the fundraiser who had backed Kurt Weill's *Eternal Road* and whom Blitzstein ran into in London when Weisgal went to visit Chaim Weizmann. Hugo Weisgall had studied under Roger Sessions and Fritz Reiner and had directed the Baltimore String Orchestra and numerous choral societies. September 28 marked his debut conducting the London Symphony Orchestra, though only recently he had led the BBC Symphony Orchestra in his own composition, *American Comedy—1943.* As it turned out, that night was Rosh Hashonah, the Jewish New Year. Ordinarily, he would have observed it by not working or traveling. He sought out the Chief Rabbi, Dr.

J. H. Hertz, who made a dispensation for the occasion: Yes, Weisgall had to conduct the concert. So he did—and walked home afterward.

A week before the first concert, the five-thousand-seat hall had been sold out. The box office estimated that the demand for tickets might have filled the auditorium five times. As the concert approached, Allied troops landed in Naples; within days they liberated the city.

The evening began with a dramatic drumroll accompaniment as the two hundred uniformed singers marched single file down the side aisles onto the stage to swelling applause. This was the first black chorus to sing at Royal Albert Hall in its seventy-two-year history. *Freedom Morning* opened the program. Though Blitzstein had written a number of works for full orchestra, this was the first time a major symphony orchestra had played one of them. The chorus followed, singing "Over My Head I See Trouble in the Air," only the first of the spirituals to relate specifically to the war theme. Their snappy appearance and the perfect tuning of their voices belied their officers' lack of confidence in them; they had spent their two-day leave in London resting and taking good care of themselves. Roland Hayes and the chorus sang "Go Down, Moses" and "By and By," the chorus continuing with "When the Saints Go Marching In" and "Ain't-a Dat Good News." A bright orchestral work by John Powell came next, *Natchez on the Hill,* then *Ballad for Americans.*

After the intermission, Hayes did the Bach and Arne arias; the chorus sang "Steal Away," "Certainly, Lord," "I Can Tell the World About This," "I Want to Die Easy," "Lead Me," and "Fare Thee Well." *Bamboula,* another orchestral piece, by the black British composer Samuel Coleridge-Taylor, took off from a New Orleans theme. Winding up the program, the chorus returned with "Wade in the Water," "Death's Gonna Lay His Cold Icy Hands on You," and "Deep River"; Hayes joined chorus and orchestra for "Joshua Fit de Battle of Jericho"; and the orchestra concluded with the two national anthems. For its encore number, the chorus performed "Go Down, Moses." Its final words—"Let my people go"—produced a demonstrative effect on the audience: sobs and cheers and frenetic applause.

Notables in the audience included a number of generals and other high military officials and distinguished Allied representatives: Sir Stafford Cripps, British Minister of Aircraft Production; Lord Beaverbrook; Dr. Wellington Koo, Chinese Foreign Minister; Jan Masaryk, Czech Foreign Minister; Lord and Lady Mountbatten; and U.S. Ambassador John Winant. And quite to Blitzstein's surprise, a relative of his turned up as well—Victor Voynow, his cousin Cutch's son, who was stationed in Southampton as a medic. He had read about the concert in *Stars and Stripes* and went to London to attend.

Local critics wrote of the "sheer ecstasy" of the *Freedom Morning* score, of its "thrilling urgency." Private Cantril had been a resounding success in *Ballad for Americans,* leading to his recording three spirituals on the London label soon afterward. The concert turned out to be "the real right thing."

In *The New York Times,* F. Bonavia referred to *Freedom Morning* as a medley, then waxed ecstatic over the chorus:

> The choir had some very special qualities. Its tone was different from that of any other European choir, recalling, in the ease and range of the basses, the choristers of Russia, but avoiding virtuosity and sensationalism with as deep a distrust as that of English singers. In mellowness and blend it equaled anything we have heard, combining perfect discipline with a certain naturalness that fitted admirably some of the music it sang, music that was infinitely touching, utterly devoid of artifice but profoundly sincere.[37]

The American composer Gail Kubik, himself in the air force for thirty-eight months, also reviewed *Freedom Morning* for *Modern Music* as "an effective, vigorous piece. It is Blitzstein's first purely orchestral work in a number of years. It is remarkably successful in sounding just like the Blitzstein of the stage works, and yet, though immensely dramatic, it is convincing as a piece of absolute music."[38]

The day following the second of the two concerts, Marc wrote to Jo. The shows "were sensational, the only word for it. . . . My own part has been recognized, and I think there will be some repercussion. In short, I'm very happy. Earl's *Ballad* came off beautifully. So did my new work, which I think Rodzinski now wants." Immediately the cry rose up for the chorus to offer the same concert elsewhere in England and Scotland, and Blitzstein was asked to go along to supervise the arrangements. "Maybe that's my métier after all, glorified stage-manager."[39]

Before concert dates could be set in other cities, Blitzstein and Roland Hayes accompanied a twenty-four-member chamber chorus of the larger ensemble on a week-long tour of camps and troop halls around the country. Marc was out on tour when he wrote home to Jo on October 8, the first anniversary of his landing in Britain: "The moment for a sententious philosophical statement—luckily I can think of none." The large chorus, with the RAF Symphony led by Hugo Weisgall, subsequently sang at five sold-out concerts in Manchester, Edinburgh, and Glasgow, but Blitzstein stayed in London to resume work on the *Airborne.*

Changes: Peter Gorer's mother returned to England from America, and the house would not accommodate so much company. So Blitzstein moved into a small flat in town, to which Louis Dreyfus of the London branch of Chappell's right away sent a piano. Blitzstein also acquired a new immediate boss, Jock Whitney—John Hay Whitney, future brother-in-law of CBS's William S. Paley.

The utter determination of Blitzstein's black chorus and especially of the air force fliers lent a somber coloration to events. For a period he became moody and serious. He found it impossible to put out of mind a gunner he had met out at a bomber station: The man had reached for his tunic on the rack and mistakenly picked up that of a buddy missing in action. When he tried to return it to the rack, he couldn't, and instead put it on himself. Now he couldn't stop wearing it, and he had become almost mute. Drafts of the *Airborne* Symphony show the composer hard at work trying to musicalize this incident. Could the composer somehow tie together these little human details with the larger issues that framed them? To connect—that was the challenge.

In addition to working on the cantata, Blitzstein wrote an article for the BBC magazine and music to a new OWI film, and gave a lecture to the BBC staff on the use of music in radio. He attended the premiere of Benjamin Britten's Serenade for Tenor, Horn and Strings, sung by Britten's lover Peter Pears on a Saturday afternoon punctuated by falling buzz bombs. He found it overly theatrical, a display of attitude and gesture, and weak in commitment. But then, he didn't understand Britten or his political position, either. As he had written to David Diamond explaining why he never saw Britten:

> I hear he was frightened off by my warning (to him at a party) that the next time we met I was going to ask him how he squared his conscientious objection to the war with doing propaganda work for the BBC, etc. That may be malicious; but then, I am, and with pleasure in certain cases.[40]

He seldom went to the theatre anymore: The escapist entertainment wasn't worth the time or the money, though he did appreciate it when Jerome Chodorov, back in the States now, sent him piles of all the latest Broadway scores. And he loved the attention—the gloves, the socks, the foodstuffs—bundled into packages from home; "I'm certainly not among the forgotten boys here," he wrote in thanks. On Halloween he attended a ritzy cocktail party where frivolity seemed to reign supreme:

> The introduction of a serious topic was always met with by a strained pause, or hilarious laughter, as though something farcical had been said. I was mystified; and wonder how much of that is the same in our own fair land. It was a pleasure to get back into the inky blackout. The airraids have provided little interest and certainly no excitement. Veddy dull.
>
> Actually, I've become more or less a hermit; not new for me, but here people seem to think it strange. I think you know how lonely I can get, and how restless and nearly-rude I am when the substitution of polite conversation and milling-about-among-people is offered me. None of that has changed; during the war, it would be practically staggering if it had.[41]

Wanting the *Airborne* finished up, Jock Whitney scheduled a presentation for November 25 in the novelist Hugh Walpole's former quarters. A strong contingent of Hollywood and Broadway types attended—Ben Lyon, Burgess Meredith, Tex McCrary—as well as an assortment of majors and colonels, to witness Blitzstein at an ancient Welte Mignon Grand pianola tearing through the almost completed work in his old one-man routine of playing, singing, explaining, and tossing pages of music onto the floor. The performance was electrifying, like nothing they had ever experienced.

"Well, gentlemen," said Blitzstein, catching his breath. "That's the opus."

There was a deafening silence, as the officers assimilated what they had just heard. Then a voice spoke.

"Carry on, Corporal."

In military parlance, such a laconic reaction turned out to mean extraordinary support. Blitzstein felt assured of a major send-off for the work.

> Details as yet are not at hand; but I liked the feeling well enough to go out and get drunk on Jamaica rum with Burgess Meredith (who didn't get drunk; but who was at the audition, and who will probably be the speaker in the performance). Now I must work full steam ahead; it *is* about time this one was off my chest.[42]

Jock Whitney obviously thought well of Blitzstein and of the *Airborne*, for another promotion came through. He was now Sergeant Marc Blitzstein.

> I don't know why it should happen right now; things in the Army don't go according to plan, or at least not according to any plan I can dig up; undoubtedly there's a higher order of things, and one should be grateful for small favors. Also I now sport on my left shoulder the flash "US Army Correspondent," which is already proving a vast help in many ways.[43]

13

BILL

December 1943–May 1945

". . . a bang of nightmare glory and chaos."

In December of 1943, Jo's son Stephen turned eighteen. Having begun as a freshman at the University of Pennsylvania in June, he already had a year's worth of college behind him. Now he wanted to join the armed forces, to continue studying languages, and to serve the cause. True, he was a strapping lad, but Marc feared for his youth and inexperience. In the end, Stephen's childhood double mastoid operation kept him out. Other news from home included the fact that Ed had bought a large farmhouse with adjacent acreage in Chadds Ford, a few miles south of Philadelphia in tradition-filled Delaware County. The neighboring countryside had already become well known through the paintings and illustrations of N. C. Wyeth who, as a student at the Brandywine School of Art, had settled in the township. His son and student, Andrew, was also beginning to be recognized.

It was still easy to meet people in London. Blitzstein saw the playwright William Saroyan almost daily in his French dinner club. He saw Irwin Shaw, and for a time he befriended Humphrey Jennings, the English documentary filmmaker. He met an official of the Victor recording company in London, who played for him the master of Robeson's just-released recording of "The Purest Kind of a Guy" from the set of "Songs of Free Men." How strange it was to hear this music: *No for an Answer* seemed worlds away in space and time. He was also delighted to meet Britain's venerated composer Ralph Vaughan Williams, "a charming, delicious old man, remarkably patrician and human at the same time."[1] In a way, it was too easy to meet people:

> I make too many acquaintances, and not enough friends, as is my wont; and everybody else's, to judge from the talk. The place is wide open, but wildly; the camp-following-town-psychology is virulent here as I couldn't have imagined. As one little witty RAF put it at a pub-counter one night, " 'Ere I stand in lonely isolation, blown about by the four sexes."

"The one thing missing is Love, Perfect Love," Marc wrote to his old friend Mina Curtiss. "Still, I should be used to that by now. I am, and take my chances on occasional lechery."[2]

Blitzstein tried to work out the details of the *Airborne* production—who would sing, who could conduct what orchestra. The task of orchestration—perhaps a month's concentrated effort—still lay ahead, too. He would begin this part after Christmas. He hoped for a mid-February premiere in London, broadcast to America by a mixed white and black chorus from the Eighth Air Force, with a New York performance soon to follow.

Early in the year 1944, his commanding officer, Jock Whitney, left for Italy with General Eaker to build the Mediterranean Air Force, which meant another change of assignment. In Blitzstein's next appointment, as director of music at the OWI in London, he was to help promote better cultural ties between the United States and Great Britain. The job meant a parade of working lunches and social obligations, which Blitzstein found a tiresome routine by this time. In theory, he would have time to finish the symphony, but the work piled up; among his other tasks, he was told to assemble a record library of a thousand disks for some as yet unknown purpose.

As one of Blitzstein's collaborative efforts with the British, he wrote a song called "Modest Maid" for Beatrice Lillie. Leonard Lyons, who every week air-mailed copies of all his columns to Blitzstein in exchange for gossip and cute tidbits, referred to the bawdy cabaret number as "I Love Lechery." Lillie did not perform it, however, and it lay untouched among the composer's papers for another decade before he thought of it again.

A proposal for a more virtuosic collaboration with the British came about in February: He agreed to play the solo piano in George Gershwin's *Rhapsody in Blue* on a March 26 all-American concert with the London Philharmonic. "It seems like fun; and I can't resist sending an appropriate cable to Oscar Levant, with some kind of elaborate apology for poaching on his territory. I haven't been a concert-pianist for years; but I think I can make the grade on the piece, which turns out to be not too difficult."[3]

His birthday—and the anniversary of his marriage to Eva—always put Marc in a contemplative frame of mind:

> I'm even told I'm getting fat. And as to being 39, and being concerned—have you forgotten my old wish to be 45? It still holds; I still feel I'll be really in my stride by then. That's six years from now. Speculation: what will the world be like then?
>
> My health? Good. Spirits? Up, down, fine when I work or hear about our Forts over Berlin, or the Russian break-through. Fears? None. Hopes? All kinds: That I will achieve a new blouse (tunic) before the war ends; that "The Airborne" will finally get on; that I won't disgrace myself utterly playing Gershwin's "R in Bl" on March 26; etc., etc.[4]

Thoughts of mortality occurred to Blitzstein when the Gorers had to do away with their blind, senile dog, replacing him with an Alsatian shepherd:

> I went around . . . imagining he was Very in his early days. . . . Is Very still about? You don't have to be tactful about anything; I know time is passing. I feel old these days; the hair's out, and the jowls are growing; and my bones tell it to me. Plenty of energy; but also a new physical pleasure in sitting down and going to bed. Middle-age, here I come.[5]

Jo had written of the possibility that the Philadelphia Orchestra might perform *Freedom Morning.* "Of course I'd be tickled if they did," Marc wrote to his mother, no doubt remembering that Stokowski had once promised to play his *Orchestra Variations* and then backed off. "It would bring you all a step nearer to me, among other things; and it's about time the Phila Orch did something of mine."[6]

Sunday, March 26 came, the event heralded by huge posters in the underground. Hugo Weisgall conducted the London Philharmonic Orchestra that afternoon at the Royal Adelphi Theatre in a program that included Copland's *An Outdoor* Overture, the first English performances of the Symphony no. 1 by Roger Sessions and the suite from Walter Piston's ballet *The Incredible Flutist,* Ernest Bloch's Violin Concerto, with soloist Eda Kersey, and Gershwin's *Rhapsody in Blue.* Through her connections, Lina Abarbanell somehow arranged for Blitzstein to perform on a rare Steinway concert grand. It was a risky, unconventional program for London, a city known for its unadventuresome orchestra concerts. Unexpectedly, the audience received it warmly and the critics hailed it. One reviewer commented on Blitzstein, "who happily did not, like some virtuosos, make our ears the target for pianistic block-busters of deadly execution."[7]

"Concert a great success, everybody happy," Marc wrote to his sister. "I did a theatrical performance of the *Rhapsody;* as once I put it, 'like a real hep-jazz-pianist.' It's the way I feel it should be done."[8]

The concert out of the way now, Blitzstein returned to intensive work at his OWI post. By this time, he knew why he had been asked to assemble such a large record library: The OWI had in fact brought him into its top-secret plan to open a new radio station, the American Broadcasting Station in Europe (ABSIE). CBS producers Brewster Morgan and William S. Paley had gone to London to set it up. The BBC had begun broadcasts of American programs, primarily from Voice of America, as early as January of 1942. The American Forces Network in Britain, a chain of low-powered radio stations, already existed to serve the U. S. army camps and airfields. But ABSIE would be directed toward the Continent, with an initial eight-and-a-half-hours-a-day schedule from 5:30 P.M. to 2 A.M. It would broadcast in English, German, and in eighteen languages of the occupied countries, countering Nazi propaganda with accounts of the war from the Allied side and readying the population for the final Allied assault on northern Europe. One and a half hours of the day would be devoted to music, with English continuity. Blitzstein was named the station's music director. Once again, events—his new responsibilities and, finally, the opening of the second front—overtook Blitzstein's music. For the time being, the *Airborne* was grounded.

For a month before ABSIE went on the air, station personnel practiced their jobs. Soon Blitzstein was able to reveal more details of his new job:

> I find myself running the music part of a beaming transmitter to "them parts"—and that means doing menial jobs like timing records, interviewing difficult Hungarian zigeuner composers, auditioning potential propagandists in the form of French, German, Belgian, Dutch, German, Danish, Norwegian, Jugoslavian and Czech singers who hope to do "political cabaret," getting like programs into shape—and having dummy programs, dry runs . . . and what have you. It's all part of the job. About fourteen hours a day, and no time for yearning, depressed personal troubles, or anything but a little sleep; and not much of that. The "Rhapsody" period is over, the "Airborne" moment not yet at hand—and for the first time, I'm doing something immediately connected with the war, and I mean immediate. . . . Right now I'm too rushed to be happy or unhappy, depressed or exalted. This is non-creative *work*—possibly for the first time in my life. No, I'm not enjoying it, I'm not detesting it—I'm just doing it—and nothing else. And about time, too.[9]

As if he weren't occupied enough, Blitzstein also participated on a weekly quiz show for GIs and British Tommies on the Forces Network, improvising answers on stray subjects. He joined the show in order to learn to speak extemporaneously, but he also enjoyed the opportunity to show off at the piano when a musical question arose.

Blitzstein's passions could dominate him, sometimes to an embarrassing degree, but rarely did he descend to the level of personal abuse. Often glib, charming, and persuasive, his tone could change in an instant. On April 14, Hugo Weisgall repeated *Freedom Morning* with the London Symphony Orchestra in Oxford. The program ended with Smetana's tone poem, *The Moldau.* Blitzstein shocked Weisgall with his comment about the Smetana. Earlier, he had heard Weisgall's *American Comedy—1943* and after this concert, he said to him, "Now that's the kind of music you should write instead of the shit you do." Perhaps he thought Weisgall would laugh it off as a friendly, though misfired collegial joke. Instead, it wounded: Weisgall had trouble composing for several years afterward.

Coincidentally, on that same day and the next, the Philadelphia Orchestra also programmed *Freedom Morning,* led by Saul Caston, associate conductor of the orchestra. In association with the United States premiere, Caston commissioned the black painter Claude Clark, who at that time held a fellowship at the Barnes Foundation, to paint a canvas called *Freedom Morning.* The painting was exhibited in the foyer of the Academy of Music for the concert. By arrangement with London, CBS agreed to relay the performance to a private listening monitor at the BBC, where Blitzstein invited a group of friends to listen.

The performance had its drawbacks; for one thing, much of the fast boogie section had been eliminated. "[I] practically died of homesickness when I heard that Phila Orch sound," Blitzstein wrote home. "The cuts were frightful; easily a third of the work went down the sewer; but the wonderful sound of those strings, and those solo brass!" "When the London symphony did it here, and messed that part up, I kept thinking, *What* an American orchestra could do with it!" Responding to other news from America, he continued, "OK about Very; I had suspected something of the sort, and wasn't too depressed. The boys are right, of course; Very's death does put a demarcation line around a whole lot of things, and punctuates a whole section of my life."[10]

Freedom Morning was respectfully received in Philadelphia. Edwin H. Schloss, writing in the Philadelphia *Record,* mentioned the jazz themes, woven in "with a dignity that refuses to exploit its more blatant possibilities."[11] Vincent Persichetti in *Modern Music,* however, called it "an inconsequential work," "stiffly rendered" and "superficial."[12]

At long last, ABSIE began broadcasting on April 30, 1944, at 5:30 P.M. For the first sound beamed to occupied Europe, Blitzstein chose the typical American banjo—from a Stephen Foster album recorded by André Kostelanetz—followed by station identification and the Toscanini recording of Beethoven's Seventh Symphony. Blitzstein considered the Fifth, with its famous dot-dot-dot-dash opening, the rhythm of "V for Victory," too trite a gesture for the occasion. From his desk in the offices of the station on Wardour Street, Marc wrote to Sam and Maddie on that historic date:

> How much money did you spend, Papa, on my musical training? Never mind; it's worth the doing if the French are to have the "Man I Love" in French, as part of the march towards victory, they shall have it, and as beautiful a performance as I can make it. Luckily I'm also involved with Mendelssohn, Shostakovich, Beethoven, Copland and Blitzstein (who *is* that man?) so that I'm not utterly sunk in the Rat Race of pop stuff. As to "The Airborne," the performance has now got to wait until I can clear a couple of hours a day to finish the orchestration (the completion of which I've been holding off on for reasons best outlined personally, so hold your fire a year or so!).[13]

The station instituted a number of novelties unique to an American enterprise: a fifteen-minute program during the French hour called "Le Swing Club," a program of American march music, and musical segments of the German program made by German prisoners of war under ABSIE supervision. Stars such as Herr Bing Crosby and Fräulein Dinah Shore would sing their most popular tunes in a carefully transliterated version of German and other European languages; from these broadcasts Crosby later acquired the name "Der Bingle." Blitzstein was responsible for providing musical intros and interludes for feature programs; the American program, for example, used "Yankee Doodle" as its theme song. The station also did other war-related work, furnishing music for camp shows, films, and OWI programs and lectures.

Occasionally, a European adviser to the station would complain that ABSIE sought to combat Nazism and Bolshevism by extolling the American way of life and bestowing American civilization on the rest of the world, but such observations fell on deaf ears. On the British left, the Communist organ, the London *Daily Worker,* rebuked ABSIE supposedly for promoting a cautious wait-and-see attitude on the French-language programs instead of stressing the importance of armed struggle.

Blitzstein soon grew accustomed to spending fourteen-hour days at the station supervising a staff of five, as ABSIE originated about half of its programming. Once when he entered the studio, he found the chief engineer Don Drenner playing Richard Strauss's *Rosenkavalier* waltzes not for broadcast but on the audio monitor. "That Nazi!" Blitzstein shouted, appalled and livid, adding obscenities to insults. "How can you stand to listen to his music?" Of course, for Blitzstein, who had never cared for the overblown late-Romantic style anyway, it was easy to dismiss Strauss; the fact that Strauss had cooperated with the Nazi régime gave Blitzstein all the more justification for venting his spleen at an unsuspecting music lover. At the end of the day, often well past midnight, he trudged up the stairs to his flat and flung his body into instantaneous sleep.

ABSIE aired SHAEF-approved news, and many code messages to the European underground. Finally, not long before D-Day, the station broadcast a message from General Eisenhower, Supreme Commander of the Allied Expeditionary Forces, about the forthcoming liberation, which gave advice and encouragement to the citizens of the occupied countries and Germany itself, especially to the underground movements. Marc sent home clippings about the event, writing:

> I was in on the enclosed, and it was really thrilling. Nobody knew it was coming; and we had a hell of a time changing stuff to make way for it. When it came (I was in the actual control room at the time), the effect was startling, almost like a trigger pulled. You would have said the invasion had started. A tiny speck in the moment of history-making; it turns out that, for the time being, I'm quite content to be just that.[14]

On June 3, to the envy of the BBC and all the other stations in Europe, Blitzstein scooped the musical airwaves with the first playing of the sound track Toscanini had contrived for an OWI film, *Hymn of the Nations.* A mélange opening with the *Forza del Destino* Overture, and interpolating "God Save the King," "The Internationale," and "The Star-Spangled Banner"—with Jan Peerce and the Westminster Choir—it scored a tremendous success. "I say without fear of contradiction," he wrote two years later when the film played in New York, "that the Toscanini sound track provided the most potent single musical weapon of World War II."[15]

"I won't begin to describe my excitement or the excitement in these parts," Marc wrote to Jo on D-Day, June 6, 1944. "It probably resembles what you've got":

> The staid English are staid no more—Oxford Circus was a seething mass at lunchtime; around a tobacconists [*sic*] shop bobbies had to keep them away from 1) the radio and 2) a news vendor. There has been no official communique as yet—but the talk is that everything is going "according to plan"—and more. I'm filled with mixed emotions—you know what they are, and why.[16]

The second front! The long-delayed, long-awaited invasion of the European continent! The initial assault was made by 130,000 men landing first at the Baie de la Seine in 20,000 vehicles, 467 warships plus minesweepers, and thousands of aircraft. Soon Cherbourg in the west and Vitebsk in the east would be recaptured from the Germans. It was possible to envision the Allies closing in on Berlin.

> One Canadian sapper I picked up in a pub, told me he had been trained down to the last muscle, and treated for six weeks before the invasion like a thoroughbred horse; he was whimsical about it, with a fine sense of values, too; had been there, sized it up, would be going back. At the moment I don't have any idea what plans are in store for me; but I feel very good and ready for whatever is decided.[17]

Maddie's parents, the Leofs, went up to New York to hear Alexander Smallens conduct the New York Philharmonic at Lewisohn Stadium, where *Freedom Morning* was performed on August 4. WNYC broadcast the concert with a commentary from Blitzstein sent via BBC channels. The New York office of the OWI sent a transcription of the performance to Blitzstein at the London office. "I know what Lina meant by her disappointment," he wrote home; "the slow parts are too slow; the thing doesn't quite hang together, and seems over-cautious and worried in approach. But the sound of the orchestra, and the really fine acoustical recording made up, partly."[18]

If the rendition Smallens gave the piece did not meet Blitzstein's standard, critic Paul Bowles also picked up on its sluggishness. "A pretty uninventive piece," he called it. Considering the conditions under which it came into being, "One can only chalk it up as one of the cultural casualties of the war." "One hopes Mr. Blitzstein will soon have the opportunity to work quietly again in his own room." It took but a few days for the composer to receive clippings of the reviews. "An extremely cool reception, apparently," he wrote to his father. "I can't get upset about it at this long distance; but I did, and seriously, object to Paul Bowles' disdain for working under trying conditions. The poor boy, getting up at the crack of noon."[19]

In early September, the blackout in London was lifted; after five years, Allied bombers had effectively wiped out the German air bases from which bombing flights emanated. On the eleventh, Blitzstein traveled north to the town of Leamington Spa, where the music critic Wilfrid Mellers organized a concert at the Royal Pump Room, a polite tea salon. After the performance of string quartets by Michael Tippett and Benjamin Britten, Blitzstein played excerpts from *The Cradle Will Rock* and *No for an Answer.* Though the material might have sounded abrasive to the audience of local ladies, the composer was able to charm his way through it directly to their hearts. Mellers, born in Leamington Spa, reported that the evening was recalled pleasurably for years afterward.

Once again, Blitzstein was called away from the *Airborne* when SHAEF asked him to compose and supervise the music for a documentary film about the invasion and liberation. Both British and American contributors worked on *The True Glory:* Carol Reed and Garson Kanin (an OSS captain) as directors; Harry Brown, poet, writing bridges connecting the episodic stories; and screenwriter Guy Trosper. Peter Ustinov and the French actor Claude Dauphin were in the project as well.

Blitzstein was among the first Americans to view film footage of Allied advances. With these fresh images in his mind—the liberation of Paris on August 25, 1944, being the very latest—he willingly joined the *True Glory* team. When the film was finished, presumably in a few weeks' time, he would return to ABSIE. As for the *Airborne,* more and more it looked as though it would have to wait until war's end: No GIs could be spared now to sing cantatas.

He moved into new offices in the SHAEF building at 27 Grosvenor Square. How he enjoyed the Allied officers' mystified looks as he had a piano and a Moviola hoisted in! Blitzstein occupied two large top-floor rooms joined by French doors, "with the whole blasted city at my feet; room to walk in, to write and compose, and a beautiful project waiting for me. Is it any wonder that I feel a new lease on energy, terrific vitality and zeal to start?"[20] Both in his rooftop quarters and at Pinewood, the best-equipped English film studio, Blitzstein enjoyed every available resource that he could possibly desire, courtesy of Garson Kanin.

One day, Blitzstein raised some personal money problems to Kanin. "Write a song," Kanin said. "A commercial song. I know Richard Rodgers and Frank Loesser, and if you just prepare the charts for me, I'll make sure they do something with it."

Almost overnight, Blitzstein came up with his answer, the plaint of a soldier overseas. As Kanin remembered it:

Won't it be lovely to get back to love?
Lovely, all the things we can do,
When I get back to you again.
Lovely, and I'm counting the dreams till then.
Darling, this must all end soon.
Darling, we'll be humming our tune,
Looking up at our moon above.
Think how lovely to get back to love.

It was a pretty ballad with just the kind of text Blitzstein abhorred: vacuous, sentimental, pandering. He had written it purely for the exercise, just to prove how, in parody, he could come up with the real, rock-bottom commercial product.

Kanin called everyone in the film unit to gather round and hear Marc play and sing. Palmer Williams, a jeep driver for the unit and later a prominent television producer, leaned on the piano. When Marc finished, there was a pause. Williams stood there with tears brimming from his eyes, then broke the silence: "That's the corniest thing I ever heard!" But they all loved it and urged the composer to let Kanin send it home.

"I don't want my name on a song like that," Blitzstein refused flatly.

"Put another name on it," Kanin answered.

"No. Someone will find out." And that was the last anyone ever heard of Blitzstein's soldier's plaint. He didn't solve his money problems with just any music for the masses.

Earl Browder had formally disbanded the Communist Party in the United States midway through the war as a sign that American Communists placed victory over the Axis ahead of any sectarian politics. In its place, a Communist Political Association came into being that, eschewing the stricter requirements for Party membership, gathered in large numbers of untested sympathizers with the Communists' broad-based but vague "progressive," "democratic" ideals. For a Party adherent abroad in the war effort, as Blitzstein was, membership never involved regular club meetings; in fact, members in the service were asked to withdraw from the Party. All that could be expected of such people was that they do their best in everyday situations to combat racism and national chauvinism and to help win the war. For the 1944 presidential election, Blitzstein and the left-wingers he knew in London worked to get the CIO's message to the troops—Vote for Roosevelt! New Allied entries into Norway, Holland, and Germany proved that America would do well to stick with FDR for a fourth term.

And after that? He wrote to Papa: "How are you? And if it's 'well,' keep that way until I see you. It may not be long now." To his sister, he had written in a less sanguine vein, foreseeing the class struggles that the Communist Party's

William Z. Foster had predicted would reappear in the postvictory world. The war still "looks long and arduous, from the Western end anyway":

> It won't do to get discouraged at this point; still I think it turns out the war we have been fighting for many years longer than this one is still the war to be fought. So keep your eyes bright, and your direction clear and firm.

He had earlier written:

> It's not only that we'd like to get home eventually, if not sooner; we'd also like to get this war won, and the problems of what to do with the victorious as well as the defeated at least started; in short, what the Amgots will do with the Ain't Gots.
>
> When the time comes for trying war criminals, I'm wondering if we don't have a few of our own? But who asked me?[21]

One evening that October of 1944, Blitzstein had a startling, fateful encounter in the Yorkminster, a tiny pub in Soho dating back to Shakespeare's time. Perhaps a dozen customers could fit into it at one time. He turned around and faced a striking blond, bright-blue-eyed boy-man of twenty-four who was about his own height.

"You're Marc Blitzstein, aren't you?"

"Yes, how did you know that?"

"I saw *The Cradle Will Rock,* and I've seen your picture in the paper."

An excellent beginning. Technical Sergeant William Hewitt was a Ninth Air Force radio gunner on a Marauder, just the kind of bombardier the *Airborne* Symphony was all about. His story soon got even better. He melted the composer completely by telling him that when he was transferred from Boreham Air Force Base in England over to a field in France after D-Day, he had actually packed his beloved recording of *Cradle* into his baggage. In fact, in accordance with the practice of naming planes, this gunner had dubbed his the *Blitzbuggy.* That one had been shot down—Marc, whom people sometimes called "Blitz," remembered reading about it—and Bill's new plane was the *Firebird,* after Stravinsky.[22]

Bill and Marc talked till closing time. Bill was a Southerner, a direct descendant of Peter Cooper Hewitt and the Jamestown settlers, and he spoke with an endearing Tidewater accent. His grandfather had fought for the South in the Civil War. He had grown up in North Carolina and had gone to high school in Norfolk, Virginia, though as a rule he couldn't stand Southerners—too racist, mostly. He preferred his Jewish friends; they shared more of his social views. In his bomber unit, where not many Jews flew combat missions, Bill was known as "the Jew-lover." To Marc, he sounded more and more attractive.

Bill had read all the Marxist classics, too; an older brother had got him interested. His mother sang and played the piano; she had attended the Peabody

Institute in Baltimore. Though not a musician himself, Bill possessed a formidable recall and could instantly recognize the themes of hundreds of classical compositions. Trained in radio and code, he had arrived in the European theater in January 1943. On D-Day he flew two sorties over the Continent from his British base. The following day, he strafed a German army train, saw the young farmer-boys-turned-soldiers escaping out into the surrounding fields, and with his 50-calibre machine gun killed hundreds of them, so he claimed, as though he was back home hunting rabbits. By the time he ran into Marc, he was well on his way toward an accumulated sixty-five bombing missions over Nazi targets.

Every two weeks, combat airmen based in France got a three-day pass and a quart of 100-proof rye. Most of them liked to go whoring in London—to reconnoiter the "Piccadilly commandos"—but Bill preferred Bloomsbury and more historic places. His girlfriend lived in Soho, which is why it happened that he stopped in at the Yorkminster that night. Nadia Poliakoff was a well-known Polish Jewish bareback rider in the circus, the daughter of Coco, a famous clown, who had been stranded in England when the war broke out. Bill had in fact fathered a child by her, though she made no marital demands on him. She was only one of Bill's girlfriends; another was a Welsh woman, Dilys Jones, a nurse at a London hospital, by whom he also had a child. A third, Luellen Bowles—Lu—directed the American Red Cross unit at Bill's base.

The next time Bill went to England, he visited Marc in the roof-top studio at SHAEF. He took along his bottle of rye, which they downed together at a single sitting. Familiar with the cliché that nice Jewish boys didn't drink, he was surprised to hear Marc complain about the difficulty of getting scotch, gin, and vodka. Interested as Marc was in Bill, he also liked his rye. "So keep on coming, baby!" he entreated Bill.

To his unsurpassed delight, Marc found out something even more interesting about his stunning new friend: Bill was bisexual. In San Francisco, where he had lived five years earlier for a year or so, he had met men who introduced him to gay sex. Bill truly liked Marc; he felt drawn to the image of the romantic composer and he looked up to Marc, fifteen years older, as if to a father.

It may have been on Bill's second or third visit to Marc's SHAEF studio that he found no one there. He began descending the stairs when he heard a sudden screaming and scuffling coming from the rooms. Bursting into the far room, he found two men stark naked—Marc and a six-foot four-inch Irish guardsman. The Irishman had lifted Marc shoulder-high and was poised to throw him out the open window. Perhaps he had expected some quick sexual release and Marc wanted more.

"Put that man down!" Bill shouted in his sternest voice. The guard complied. Without a word, he put his uniform back on and skulked out. All of the color had left Marc's face.

"My God, you saved my life!" Marc said.

By now Bill had recognized his friend as the soul of reckless indiscretion. "One of these days you're going to get yourself killed," he answered.

On October 29 Blitzstein left for France with the actor Claude Dauphin on assignment for *The True Glory.* Dauphin was a captain in the French LeClerc Division and had participated in the invasion. While Dauphin collected secretly taken film footage and anecdotes about the Resistance and the invasion, Blitzstein interviewed Resistance fighters about the music they sang.

They arrived in Paris only a month after liberation. Once there, Blitzstein discovered that "no one" had collaborated with the Nazi occupiers. But almost everyone had, from the seamstress making delicate fineries to the society dames whose every demand could be met on the black market that flourished under the Germans. Though he found the undamaged city more beautiful than ever—and how much lovelier to see it again with Bill!—he expressed alarm at the terrifying discrepancy between wealth and poverty. Before he left the city, he took Bill on a visit to Nadia Boulanger's home on rue Ballu. Boulanger herself had fled to the United States during the war years, but when he appeared laden with scarce canned goods from the PX, her secretary recognized him, threw her arms around the composer, and cried out, "*Monsieur Blitzstein! Est-ce que c'est bien vous?* [Is it really you?]"

When Blitzstein went to France, the only Resistance music he knew was Anna Marly's tune, "*Chant des Partisans*" (text by Joseph Kessel and Maurice Druon), which the BBC recorded and broadcast to the French underground for morale. When he met for tea with Jean Cocteau, who had spent the entire war unharmed in Paris, even continuing to make films such as *L'Eternel Retour* for Nazi approval, the Frenchman shook his head. With an index finger to his pursed lips, he confidently assured Blitzstein: "You will find no music; it was a *mouvement silencieux.*"

But the American refused to take Cocteau's word. Such a movement must have its music. Luckily, he also met a few individuals who gave him referrals to those in the provinces who could give him the music he was after.

Cocteau arranged for a private showing of his version of *Carmen,* filmed in Italy with his lover Jean Marais and Viviane Romance. He believed that Blitzstein might be able to influence American film distributors. The score faithfully followed Bizet up until the climactic moment when suddenly for a few bars the music broke out into the "*Liebestod*" from *Tristan und Isolde,* a transparent appeal to the German audience Cocteau expected for his work.

"What was Wagner doing there?" Blitzstein asked when the screening was over.

Cocteau fumbled with his reply, claiming an "accident." "Do you think this might hinder a sale in America?"

"If I have anything to do with it, it certainly will," Blitzstein replied. However seminal Cocteau's impact on twentieth-century arts had been, he now had plenty of apologizing to do in Marc Blitzstein's book.

On Monday, November 6, Dauphin and Blitzstein drove out from Paris in a trailer-equipped jeep. Like the bomber pilots who had named their Flying Fortresses for girlfriends waiting at home, Marc christened his vehicle *Jo.* The composer kept detailed notebooks on his trip, filled with a sense of wonder at himself. To be in France! To be heading toward the front! And in the intimate company of a personality known to the French as widely as Clark Gable in America! They passed through Fontainebleau, then headed to the Jura Alps and the Haute Savoie near the Swiss border, a dazzling landscape of cliffs and rushing rivers where the Maquis—the Resistance fighters—had established their most sophisticated campaign.

There Dauphin picked up his first reels of clandestine Resistance film; and there, too, Blitzstein collected several songs from a wealthy printer named Grandchamps who had subsidized a whole unit of Maquis. They heard radio news of FDR's reelection and celebrated with a bottle of Savoie white. They also stumbled on what had to be the most luxurious bomber base of the entire war. At the Beaurivage, a lake resort hotel in Annecy, a B-17 Fortress crew had parked their plane on the grounds nearby. From that private paradise, they went out on sorties, bombed German sites, and returned to their comfortable armchairs. Marc wrote home about the place as soon as he returned to London:

> The "patron" of the hotel, who is also the chef, is as queer as a bedbug, and is madly in love with one of the sergeants, topturret engineer, who knows from nothing about such things. But this is the reason for the fabulous concoctions which turn up at every meal, made with ordinary American rations: tuna fish salad, smoked turkey pie with gobs of heaped asparagus and julienned potatoes, chocolate soufflé ice cream was what we had. The sergeant, too full, got up before the ice cream, saying "Jesus Christ I can't eat any more of this rich food," and the chef went into a small tantrum which was very funny.[23]

In Grenoble on the ninth, Blitzstein met the leaders of an unusual unit of Maquis made up of more than three hundred escaped Russian prisoners. As they sang their songs, Blitzstein transcribed them to music paper. In Lyon he ran into the actor Pierre Brasseur and the troupe he led in *Galilea,* a sort of Living Newspaper show about General de Gaulle. The actors sang their songs for Blitzstein, too.

The fifth column was still very much around; that same night, a Vichy militiaman stole into Brasseur's room and beat him severely with a club. Brasseur appeared for lunch the next day with bloody bandages wrapped around his head, his nose broken and his eyes black. But when collaborators were caught, at least in Grenoble, retribution came swiftly: Within two days after liberation, they were either shot or hanged.

In Grenoble, Blitzstein saw Cocteau's movie *L'Eternel Retour,* also starring Jean Marais. In his diary he recorded his opinion: "Perverted, artificial, Hollywooden, Auric music, not even good sleazy [Max] Steiner; but Marais has great physical beauty."

Back in Paris to resupply, Blitzstein stopped in at the French National Liberation offices, where they proudly produced a copy of their hottest song—Anna Marly's *"Chant des Partisans."* It had been published clandestinely in France as early as September 1943, only a few months after the BBC first aired it. At liberation, people started whistling the song openly in the metro and everywhere. So the radio work had done its job after all!

At dinner with Roger Desormière, conductor and in 1941 the founder of the secret National Resistance Committee of Musicians, Blitzstein got the lowdown on their confreres: "Cortot, Honegger, bad; Auric, Poulenc, Rosenthal, Muench, okay; Sauguet, Messaien, apolitical, talented, unoffending."[24] Desormière supplied examples: Francis Poulenc, George Auric, and Manuel Rosenthal all wrote songs to Resistance poems by Aragon, Eluard, and others, which were performed clandestinely. But Arthur Honegger had gone to Vienna to help with the expected but ultimately aborted German celebration of the taking of Stalingrad. And the dancer Serge Lifar had behaved very badly; one time, he personally invited Goering to the opera. When asked what he planned to do the following winter, Lifar said, "Oh, we're going to Moscow, the Germans will have taken it already, and we'll give a gala ballet festival there to celebrate it." When reminded that his old friend Serge Prokofiev was in Moscow, Lifar answered, "Yes, isn't it a shame, the poor fellow will probably have to be hanged."

The second leg of the French tour began on November 14. Blitzstein and Dauphin headed out to the Alsace front, passing through Verdun, Etain, and Nancy. Evidence of recent fighting was all around: dead animals on the road, bombed-out tanks and German command cars, whole villages reduced to smoking timbers and muddy ruts that only recently had been roads. Crude signs appeared along the way: MINES CLEARED, 20 FEET; MINES CLEARED, 3 FEET; CLEARED TO HEDGES; ROAD AND SHOULDERS CLEARED; MINES! And who was there rationing gas to French jeeps but Jean Marais, a private in the French First Army.

This was really war. For the first time, Blitzstein felt no longer "chairborne." He shared rations in a wrecked barn in Brouville with both French and American boys, exchanging cigarettes and sugar. Within days, many of them would be killed or disabled in the drive on Strasbourg. General Brosset of the French First Army had his men sing for Blitzstein; the next day, he ran his jeep into a river and drowned. His aide, the actor Jean-Pierre Aumont, survived the accident with only a broken wrist.[25] Blitzstein collected three more songs from the sister of Jean Sablon, Germaine Sablon, a nightclub singer now serving as a hospital nurse.

On the third trip out from Paris, Dauphin and Blitzstein traveled to Normandy, now using Claude's French army car—a 1937 Ford. There they saw the most impressive destruction: Caen in ruins, Lisieux and St. Lô heavily bombed. They not only met Marraine, code name for the thirty-year-old Henriette Henry who ran the Resistance movement in Normandy, but they stayed in her home. Posing as an ignorant peasant, Marraine had decoded BBC messages and penetrated German lines twenty times during the war. She turned out to be an excellent cook as well, serving her visitors a gourmet dinner complete with snails. The local partisans sang songs for Blitzstein—again the Anna Marly songs broadcast from London! Before leaving the area, he took a look at the coastline, where only a few months before at Omaha and Utah beaches, the Allied forces had landed. How they had managed to climb over the steep cliffs remained a mystery to him.

For the final jaunt of their trip, Dauphin wanted to visit his fourteenth-century château near Tours, which he owned with his wife Rosine Deréan, a film star who at that moment was making rope in a German prisoner-of-war camp. It had been four years since the actor had seen the castle. The gardener presented Dauphin with the small stock of brandy made on the estate; at twenty bottles a year, the cellar now contained eighty bottles. In part to celebrate the owner's homecoming and in part to share in the wedding festivities taking place that day in the town's eleventh-century church, the travelers enjoyed a royal drunk. And then, with Dauphin's seventeen-year-old son, "a young Adonis" as Blitzstein described him, they returned to Paris. There, the day after Thanksgiving, he would rendezvous at the Astra Hotel with his buddy Bill.

Bill had introduced Marc to his friend Stuart Ottenheimer, the only Jewish combat flier in his unit, for whom Bill had served as best man back home at Kellogg Field. Jews were rare in the air force, and Marc felt a kinship with Ottenheimer. Ottenheimer had lived with a steady barrage of anti-Semitism from the other men; indeed, Bill was virtually his only friend. Stuart was to accompany Bill to meet Marc in Paris. However, on Thanksgiving Day in a sortie over Koblenz, the Germans shot down his plane and he dropped to his death. The following day, Bill told Marc what had happened, and Marc wept bitterly. "I have seen war, peace (very relative), joy, heartbreak, resistance, collaboration, birth, life and death of men and ideas," Blitzstein wrote home.[26]

After five weeks in France and a host of adventures, he wound up with eighteen songs from the Resistance. Of one, *"Le monde libre,"* he made a transcription for solo piano, which the London branch of Chappell published in 1944. Paris had depressed him, especially to see how the known collaborators simply went about their business undisturbed. But the spirit in the rest of the country, where the real fighting took place, moved him. There, the people knew what the fight was all about. No one thought it fashionable to sit this one out.

More fighting still lay ahead, for sure. At the end of December and into the year 1945, the Battle of the Bulge raged mercilessly in Belgium. For two weeks, Bill and his crew got dressed in their full flying regalia, waited for the clouds to clear, then received orders that the mission had been scrubbed. Just before Christmas, the sun shone through a hole in the sky, and they bombed. On one of Bill's last missions, nine of his squadron's planes were shot down and he barely managed to make it back in a crash landing that gave him a slight back concussion—which gave rise to Marc's pun, "Oh, my Aachen back!"

But however severe the casualties now, the end could be seen. Before Blitzstein left France to go back to work on *The True Glory,* there was talk of an American Music Festival to be held in Paris in the spring, with Blitzstein coordinating the programs. Having had the chance to speculate on the postwar political alignment in liberated France, Blitzstein felt encouraged by the role the left would play in the new Europe. He wrote to Jo shortly after returning to London. His words turned out to be prophetic:

> How many times have I written you that it looks as if we in the USA will turn out to be the Old World after the war; and that the big things will undoubtedly happen on the Continent, where there is no longer anything

> to lose or hold on to? The more I think of my impressions of France, the more crystallized this impression has become. . . . There will be a great yearning to come over to France, to Greece, to Yugoslavia, etc., to see the big new things happen; and it will be even more important to stay put, in our own cities, fighting what is bound to be a great reactionary wave.[27]

Work progressed on the film scoring. The composer watched the latest takes at Pinewood with Garson Kanin and Carol Reed. Curt Conway, from *No for an Answer,* worked on casting narrators, and Blitzstein did one stretch of narration himself. "They have got me tied to the mast of my good old Piano-and-movieola [*sic*]," Blitzstein wrote to Sam and Maddie on Christmas Day while doing fire-guard duty at the office, "so that it almost seems like the days when I was turning out *Native Land*—only this one is about 'All the Other Lands,' and how they got liberated."[28]

London seemed so ordinary after the frisson of war. And where was Bill? He had been due in London in mid-December on his way home. Until well after New Year's Day, Marc had received no word. Had he been downed? Captured? Killed?

At long last, news. He confided to Jo in terms she could not mistake as to the nature of his feelings for this man fifteen years younger than he:

> You may have heard from me that I have been sweating out a young guy, Bill Hewitt. . . . Well, now, three weeks later, a long letter comes from him, telling me he has completed his tour, and is on his way to the States (probably to rest, and then begin over again in the Pacific. These kids!) He's going to try to stop over here in England to see me before he goes—but that may not be possible. And so I've written him, telling him to get in touch with you if he makes Philadelphia at all. I want you to know him; in the first place, he is as close to me as anyone I've met here; also his ideas are like ours, from a world point of view; although you may have to worm this out of him, if he goes shy on you. I'm hoping he'll open up, since on the surface he's just another guy. But full of charm and tricks, as you'll discover.
>
> For some reason, which I haven't as yet doped out, he's the warmest personal contact I've made in years. I think it has something to do with the ways in which he's mixed up, plus the instincts he has for being a really fine human being. Now he's apparently off to a commission and the Pacific—night-flying, I think. A baby; 23 years old.[29]

After a two-day struggle, a hundred-man orchestra assembled at Pinewood produced an acceptable recording of Blitzstein's music for portions of the footage. The composer had used a robust, stirring idiom, somewhat tricky in places; the studio musicians could hardly play it. For other parts of the film, for which there was no time to write original music, he selected stock music. In early February, the military overseers of the Anglo-American Film Project viewed a rough cut of *The True Glory.* Though the committee liked what they saw, Kanin and Reed recut the film again and again, trying to stay abreast of the latest war developments. This called for wholesale reworking and rerecording of the music. Such revisions continued until well into the spring.

With perhaps another hour's worth of music to write before the film was completed, Blitzstein had to give up his role in the Paris Music Festival, and he suggested Aaron Copland for the job. "Aaron will come over to do it, I believe," Marc wrote to his sister. "I had suggested he come anyway; and now it looks as if he will bring young Lenny Bernstein to conduct some of it. His, Bernstein's success, is the talk of the music world; and I'm happy about it, because I think he deserves it all. A fine kid."[30] Eventually, however, the festival was called off as too expensive a proposition to mount.

It was hard to know what to think about Bill. Now back home in an air force base hospital, he wrote frenetic reports of his plans for the future. First he wanted to get sent on another tour, to the Pacific. Then he mentioned his doctors' opinion that he needed a discharge from the army and a long rest for his combat fatigue. True, he had hurt his back in one emergency landing, but if the doctors discharged him for that, he would have had to spend weeks or maybe months in a VA hospital. On a psychological discharge, he could simply be released and sent on his way. At bottom was his condition physical or mental?

"I'm glad you've invited Bill Hewitt up to the farm," Marc wrote to Jo in anticipation of Bill's discharge:

> I don't think he'll be nearly as great a problem as he seems in his letters. I've written him (he asked my advice) saying he should try it out for a couple of weeks; then, if it works, he should stay longer, but on a paying basis. That won't please you, I know, especially as he hasn't much money; but I think it will be better for his psychology. There's only one thing to remember; he's a cute little trick in appearance, with a lot of conflicts and real stuff underneath.[31]

To Bill he wrote about the future. Perhaps journalism? "Get cracking, then," Marc advised, "and keep writing; and I'll be back soon, and we'll see each other and have it out, together with a couple of other deep things."[32]

Suddenly the future crashed in on everyone: Without warning, President Roosevelt died on vacation at Warm Springs, Georgia. Londoners stopped American soldiers on the street to offer their condolences. "Gord bless 'im, 'e was a great man," they said to Blitzstein. After a number of these approaches from complete strangers, he learned to say a simple "Thank you," almost as though he had lost a member of his own family. "Now what will Truman be like?" he wrote to Sam and Maddie. "What of his Tory inclinations?"[33] "Great as he was, no single man is indispensable," Blitzstein wrote about FDR to his mother on April 22. "The Russians in Berlin today! And the sickening news of the Buchenwald, Belsen, Ordruf concentration-camps—which we all knew, and wouldn't face or believe. What the holy hell are we to do with such people?"[34]

As always, Blitzstein showed a supersensitivity to criticism of the Soviets. By war's end, conservative elements in both the American and British press began calling for a minimal postwar role for the Soviet Union. One headline in the *Daily Mail,* reflecting fear over the Russians, referred to the forthcoming United Nations meeting in San Francisco as the "San Fiasco Meeting." The American writer Alfred Kazin joined Blitzstein and a group of Americans that night at dinner and witnessed Blitzstein making a scene—throwing the newspaper down, loudly decrying the scandal and disgrace.

Lillian Hellman passed through London on her way back from the Soviet Union and met Blitzstein there. She had been warmly welcomed by the Soviets and was still brimming with positive impressions of the Soviets' war efforts. Out of deference to her friend Marc, however, and out of personal embarrassment, she may not have told this story to Blitzstein: When she met with the Soviet film director Sergei Eisenstein and his wife, the actress Pera Atashova, she had occasion to mention Zina Voynow, a young Russian lady the Hollywood studio had assigned to her film *North Star* to correct the many inaccuracies in Hellman's script. Hellman did not hide her antipathy, calling her "that little Russian bitch."

"Zina?" Atashova replied. "That's my sister!" Zina Voynow, furthermore, had married Marc's favorite cousin, Andrew Voynow, who had worked in the Soviet Union all through the thirties as editor of the *Moscow Daily News* and returned in 1940 to the States.

By spring, it became dismally apparent that after months of labor, Blitzstein's compositional work might never find its way into the eighty-five-minute invasion film. Garson Kanin and Carol Reed disagreed sharply over it. The Englishman considered Blitzstein's music "too Russian, too revolutionary," too much in the Shostakovich mold.

"But you are not a musician," Kanin answered. "I am. You'll have to defer to me on this, Carol."

Sunday, April 22, the same day that Marc wrote to his mother about the President, Maddie cabled Marc. Sam was dying; a question of days, perhaps. He had worked hard, even when overtired in these last few months, on behalf of continued American-Soviet friendship following the war.

Marc had wanted to go home, anyway. The war in Europe was about over, and Bill, now a civilian, was waiting for him in America. On April 24, Kanin requested an emergency furlough for Blitzstein for a short absence home, transport by air. He had served without interruption for thirty-one months and deserved the favor. It was granted, though it would take several days before space on a flight could be arranged from a base in France.

Marc cabled Maddie: CABLE JUST ARRIVED TRYING HARD TO ARRANGE IT CABLE ME REGULARLY UNTIL I LET YOU KNOW DEFINITELY.

In the meantime, Bill had arrived in Philadelphia from his military hospital in Alabama, on Jo's invitation. The timing could not have been more inconvenient. Papa had suffered a severe recurrence of his pernicious anemia and lay quietly in his bed. Maddie and Jo took Bill into Sam's room and introduced him as Marc's friend. Sam took Bill's face in his hands and kissed him.

On the twenty-seventh, Marc received Jo's second cable: SAM ABOUT SAME. FAMILY WELL. BILL CAME FOR DAY. DARLING GUY. AM NOT WRITING LETTERS. MADDIE WONDERFUL.

No flight home from France came through and Blitzstein returned to England on the twenty-eighth. The next day, he found himself at a troop replacement depot, waiting for a slow boat back to the States. That day, the third and final cable came to his London address. Garson Kanin telephoned the news.

Sam had feared losing his only son at war; instead, the son lost his father.

Now, Marc thought, what was the point of even going back to London? Against the background of dissension over his music for the film, Papa's death was reason enough to leave it all behind and call it quits. As his superior, Kanin agreed to Blitzstein's request to return home.

In the end, *The True Glory* uses none of Blitzstein's music. The score is credited to William Alwyn alone, a prolific British film composer. One scene depicts the French Maquis, but the accompanying music appears to be stock musical footage unrelated to any of the eighteen songs Blitzstein had uncovered. Indeed, the film as a whole is scored in the most unoriginal fashion. Neither Blitzstein's research material, nor any original music, nor the Pinewood studio recording has ever turned up. Perhaps in some obscure repository in England or in some U.S. government archive, they will be found one day.*

Kanin recommended a Good Conduct Medal for the wartime composer, and Blitzstein received it that same month. Kanin promised to pack up Marc's papers and belongings and send them on to Philadelphia.

From the British depot, Marc wrote to Jo and Maddie:

> Aside from the grief, now he is gone there is a most intolerable sense of guilt: I neglected him. I saw him too little, I wrote too seldom. I repeat an age-long routine; we all do. . . . I need very badly to be talking to someone; it's the way I feel. People (our people) were so impressed when I told them I was Sam Blitzstein's son, and when he used to tell them he was my father. It's a private thing too; but I discover the other is there. It's bad now to be among strangers, no one who knew him.
>
> This will reach you before I do. The war is closing in a bang of nightmare glory and chaos. I only hope he knew about the join-up with the Russians before he died.[35]

*An *ASCAP Symphonic Catalog,* third edition, published in 1977, lists *Movie Music (Suite)* among Blitzstein's works, a thirty-minute piece available from Chappell. Exact scoring is provided. In his last weeks in Europe, Blitzstein had given the name *Movie Music* to his *True Glory* score when excerpts were to have been played in newly liberated Belgium, though apparently this performance did not take place. Chappell has a huge collection of unorganized musical material stored in a New York City warehouse that for practical purposes is inaccessible. I believe it highly likely that Blitzstein's *True Glory* suite will one day turn up there.

PART *Three*

14

HOME

May 1945–Fall 1946

"Make me find the joy of work again."

Blitzstein was not able to leave England until May 15, 1945. Disembarking after a seven-day voyage home, he telegraphed Jo: ARRIVED SAFELY EXPECT TO SEE YOU SOON DON'T ATTEMPT TO CONTACT OR WRITE ME HERE LOVE. On the twenty-fourth, he returned his steel helmet, gas mask, and arctic overshoes to the army.

Effectively, Blitzstein's army career ended on his return home. How swell it felt now that his old friends could at last see him in uniform. He couldn't wait to see Jo, and Maddie, and Mama and Stephen and Kit and Ed and Lina and everyone. He also couldn't wait to see the hit of Broadway, Bernstein's *On the Town.* And Bill. He met him in New York and they saw it together, their first show after coming home. Blitzstein had good reason to celebrate Bernstein's success: It was the kind of classical and popular amalgam Blitzstein had been espousing for the past ten years. In places, it was not hard to uncover his own influence on Bernstein's music, just as this show would, in turn, suggest new possibilities to Blitzstein. Backstage afterward, Marc ran into Olive Deering, his Clara from *No for an Answer,* who had played a leading part in Moss Hart's air force spectacle *Winged Victory* during the war.

"How marvelous to see you," Marc cried when he saw her. "Now I know I'm really home." With such inflated remarks, he renewed his old practice of working a room for all it was worth. In New York, Marc and Bill also celebrated their homecoming with something for which neither of them had ever especially yearned in the past, but it seemed symbolic after Europe—a good kosher meal!

Sgt. Blitzstein reported to Fort Dix, New Jersey, on June 20 for mustering out. Formal separation from the army took place on the twenty-sixth. He was a free man again, after two years, nine months, and twenty-eight days. His discharge pay of three hundred dollars would help him return to civilian life.

Sam's death had also left Marc with some money, so the immediate future would not be financially rough on him. Of course, with his long-abiding attachment to the nobility of work, he viewed inherited money suspiciously and did not manage it carefully; it was Marc who in those months and first couple of optimistic postwar years generally reached for the tab at dinner.

The whole Davis family, including Maddie, spent the summer of 1945 at the Chadds Ford farm. The pre-Revolutionary house sat on top of a hill. On its veranda the family gathered every evening for martinis before dinner. Down below ran a little stream and alongside it stood a stone spring-house. Bill proposed that he and Marc move into it for privacy, an idea Jo approved, so that they would remain out of Stephen and Kit's view. Before Bill began the renovations—Marc was notoriously inept at household repairs—all they had for furnishings was a bedspread, pink on one side and black on the other. When Bill asked Marc what colors he wanted, Marc said, "Pink and black." So Bill painted the floor a high-gloss black and the walls pink to match the bedspread. They bought a big double bed secondhand and a chest of drawers for fifteen dollars. Stripped down, the chest turned out to be cherry wood. Over the piano, Marc hung a steel engraving of Mozart, with a fragment of music attached.

Bill succeeded, to an extent, in piercing through the fierce mutual protectiveness that characterized the Blitzstein tribe. He and eighteen-year-old Kit became close that summer. He gave Kit advice on riding a horse and shooting a .22 rifle. With the .22, Kit once shot a dove, and Bill showed him how to wring the wounded bird's neck—and with that taught him a valuable lesson in honor. Together they painted the whole interior of the main house. At lunchtime, Marc and Bill usually escaped to the Chadds Ford Inn, a historic dining room and bar where they could drink out of Jo's sight. Most important for Bill, he could relax in the bosom of a loving, tolerant family and ease his mind away from the terrors he had seen—and those he had inflicted—in his more than four years of service. A solid season of wholesome distraction should do a world of good for a man the military medicos had discharged with a psychological disorder.

The war had produced an avalanche of films, recordings, radio programs, stage shows, and writings extolling the USSR as a great ally. The old anti-Communism was out. The new line had it that the Soviet people lived and loved, celebrated and suffered just as Americans did. But most commercial writers and artists regarded the Soviet alliance with the West as a temporary expedient for wartime application only. Once the war ended, the line would change and they would sell their talents to the next cause. Blitzstein, however, took the message to heart.

The war had not rooted out native fascists; they continued to raise their voices against labor, against racial minorities, against Communism. William Z. Foster had been right: The class struggle was back. The tougher battle was yet to be fought on the home front. Perhaps, though, America could at least cooperate with the Soviet Union to preserve the peace and to crush any recrudescence of fascism wherever it might arise. At least that much the left believed it had earned for its unstinting contribution to the war effort.

The political winds began shifting fast, however, even before the war in Asia had come to an end. That July, H. Ralph Burton, chief counsel to the House Military Affairs Sub-Committee, released a list of sixteen U.S. Army officers with Communist backgrounds, clearly intending to impugn their loyalty. *The New York Times* picked up the Associated Press story, and named all sixteen, including Sgt. Marc Blitzstein, whom Burton identified as "one of the foremost activists in communist ranks in the United States." The War Department gave immediate assurances of the named men's loyalty, and in several cases bravery under fire; the story died shortly, without detriment to Blitzstein's career other than the fact that the FBI duly noted his name in print once again. Almost a year later, a more hysterical version of the story resurfaced in the New York *Journal-American,* this time linking the names to atomic secrets and Soviet spy rings, but the charges sounded so reckless that few outside the FBI could possibly take them seriously.[1]

Blitzstein remembered the *Stars and Stripes* article by James Aldrige that he had read back in 1942 about the American sergeants in Russia helping their allies with U.S.-supplied trucks. This became the germ of his next project for the stage, which he worked on all summer at Chadds Ford. He called it *Goloopchik,* an endearing Russian word meaning "little dove" that his father Sam had used (one of Sam's few Russian words). It had to do with three midwestern American servicemen in Russia and the three girls with whom they fall in love—Ludmila, Tanya, and Nina. Marc's nephew Stephen helped him with some Russian words, as he had been studying the language at the University of Pennsylvania.

In his attempt to draw a connection between the wheat fields of Kansas and those of the Ukraine, Blitzstein proposed to solidify the links between the two peoples with *Goloopchik.* He sought to put on the stage his hopes for a more rational, caring world devoted to ideals of universal brotherhood. After all, for what had they fought this war?

In New York, Marc had met Jerome Robbins, the choreographer of Bernstein's ballet *Fancy Free* and the show *On the Town.* Like Bernstein, Robbins was politically on the left; he had even joined the Communist Party for a time. Blitzstein asked him to work on *Goloopchik* and Robbins agreed to direct and stage the dance numbers. Together, Blitzstein and Robbins studied films of Russian folk dance, and Robbins went to the farm for several days that summer to work with the composer.

Blitzstein wrote all the lyrics for the show, but only the American side of the music. For the countervailing portion, he would borrow healthy chunks either from such contemporary sources as Khachaturian, the Red Army songbook, and other collections of Russian and Ukrainian folk songs, or from composers in the public domain, such as Tchaikovsky, Mussorgsky, and Borodin. He had been impressed by the effectiveness of the all-black *Carmen Jones,* which used Bizet's music with an updated book, and he thought a similar use could be made of the Russian classics in his serious-cum-popular fusion.

What survives from the show are an outline of the musical numbers and their sources, several original songs, and lyrics for others. The scenario calls for many dance sequences. His songs have titles such as: "Home for a Hero," "Tree Back Home in Kansas," "Chick Song" (explaining the Russian habit of attaching the suffix "chik" to words), "Mamasha Goose" (an amusing conflation of Russian and English nursery rhymes), a "Drinking Scene" and, at the end, the "Meeting on the Elbe" about the final linkup of the Red Army with the United States Army.

In one song, "Three Sisters Who Did," Blitzstein as lyricist surveyed some of the changes in Russia since Chekhov. Now, he said, "They're looking forward, they're looking skyward":

The singin of the Volga boatman
Ain't so volga as before.
The paradin of the wooden soldiers
Ain't quite so wooden, not any more.

He hailed the significance of the "Meeting on the Elbe," having his chorus sing

And with that clasp of hands
There was sealed the destiny of the future, the world.
And with that slow embrace,
The two flags unfurled.

Some of Blitzstein's translations from his Soviet sources are little better than doggerel, such as this Ukrainian song called "Flying":

We're climbing and climbing up into the space.
We are flying, yes, we're flying all over the place.
We look down and see the detestable foe.
Our super-heavy bombs know the right place to go. Ho!

In his original songs, he was somewhat more inventive, but the results cannot be considered Blitzstein's best. The last lines of "So-o-o-o Beautiful" in which he revived his penchant for lusty lyrics go like this:

It's so-o-o-o beautiful, the romance of a boy and a girl.
It's so-o-o-o beautiful, when they're both giving nature a whirl.
See them lying about in the posies,
What a picture of delicate grace.
See him playfully tickle her toesies,
See her playfully kick in his face.
It's so-o-o-o beautiful, just to grow and to know I'm alive.

Have you noticed a cow and a bull?
Beautiful, beautiful, beautiful,
Beautiful, beautiful, beautiful.

Everyone in the Blitzstein-Leof clan was well aware of the research going on at Los Alamos, New Mexico: Maddie's sister Charlotte was married to the physicist Robert Serber, who worked in direct association with J. Robert Oppenheimer on the team that produced the atom bomb. The couple had spent the war years in Los Alamos, where Charlotte acted as the chief librarian of the document room. She had required special permission to leave the community in April of 1945 to visit with Maddie when Sam lay dying. On August 6 the *Enola Gay,* flying out from the tiny island of Tinian in the Marianas, dropped the first atom bomb on the city of Hiroshima.

Two days later and a day before the second bomb dropped on Nagasaki, Blitzstein began writing the song "D.P." (Displaced Person) or simply "Displaced." In this slow, desolate song of war, he describes a person—whose sex is not suggested by the text—returning to the lone, smoking doorway of what had been home, an image borrowed from his *Airborne* Symphony text. In the context of the musical, it is apparently a woman who had been taken into Nazi custody and now returns to her Russian village. The singer recalls running, almost blindly, and hiding, and also how "they" forced their prisoners to labor painfully.

I remember they took me on a long journey,
Put me by a road near a darkened wood.
Oh, my children! Work is a word
We once found good, my children
This was work, work on work—
Break your back, and still work.
Bitter work, never meant for men.
And now I am home, children—
Make me find the joy of work again.

Now, the people have been freed, but freed for what? "*Make* me," Blitzstein said, not "help me," as if challenging those in power to make life meaningful once again now that they had secured victory. By what magic do they intend to restore the desire for living, with so much destruction, so much death all around? From Blitzstein's point of view, the left had joined the war wholeheartedly, not just to save democracy but to help transform democracy. Bill Hewitt received the dedication of this song.

An effective and affecting piece, "Displaced" helped Blitzstein to begin releasing all the terrible images of war from his mind. He felt all the ambivalence war engenders: Yes, it had been necessary to bomb German trains transporting men and material to the front, but at what human cost? Those peasant boys drafted into Hitler's army, was their blood less precious than ours? And their mothers, were their tears any less grievous?

There is little record of performances of the song. A recording did appear later but barely circulated. Much later, he set aside the text and reused the plangent melody for another work.

Though deep into work on *Goloopchik,* Blitzstein took the time that July to write "The New Suit," also known as "Zipper Fly." The inspiration for the number is unknown. The composer enters the mind of a boy perhaps ten or twelve years old whose most passionate wish is for a new suit all his own, never passed down from an older brother but a real one bought and paid for in a genuine store and, most essential of all, with a zipper fly. Molding a kind of jazz scat mumbo-jumbo prayer around a vocal line that in places sounds suspiciously Chasidic, Blitzstein gave this boy of indeterminate ethnicity a tender characterization equal to any in his entire output. It is perhaps his best cabaret song.

Blitzstein may not have written "The New Suit" expressly for the comic Jimmy Savo, who had played in the 1935 revue *Parade* and had since made a hit for himself in *The Boys from Syracuse,* but Savo soon bought the rights to the song for use in his one-man act. Savo seems not to have used the song, however, and it found no outlet to the public outside of Blitzstein's frequent performance of it at private parties, where it became one of his most requested numbers. Leonard Bernstein grew to love the song and performed it himself. Not until long after its composer's death did the song achieve a place in the familiar Blitzstein canon.*

Papa's death hurt Marc deeply. Even more trenchantly would he dedicate his work to Sam's memory and to Sam's causes. Though in the end it died an abortive death, *Goloopchik* was clearly for Sam. It hurt, too, that the famous Blitzstein-Leof household at 322 S. Sixteenth Street broke up almost immediately; no one had quite realized what a cementing role Sam had played. Now the life drained from it. Maddie had long been friendly with George Ross. A restaurant and theatre columnist, he and his wife Dorothy now ran a theatrical press agency in New York. After the summer of 1945, Maddie joined them in their agency. The Leofs and the Blitzsteins viewed Ross as certainly not of their political stripe; for one thing, he had written a poor review of *No for an Answer,* which Marc begrudged him for years. But he was always good company; waiters would shower him and his party with attention wherever he went. In short time, to Dorothy's shock and to the dismay of the Blitzstein-Leof crowd, Maddie and George began an affair that led in 1952 to their marriage. Maddie's parents moved to New York to be near her, though they felt unhappy there, cut off from their longtime Philadelphia friends. Within a few years, Dr. Leof had to be moved to a nursing home and Jenny grew increasingly paranoid.

There may have been no more exciting place in the world than New York City in 1945. Every week brought new swarms of returning veterans full of hair-raising stories of war and adventure. The city blazed with hope, idealism, optimism.

*The manuscript for "The New Suit" is dated July 1945, though he may only have recopied it then. The song was possibly intended for *The New York Opera,* which never materialized.

America sat triumphant, on top of the world. Devastating and morally questionable as the atomic bomb may have been, in those days hardly anyone raised such doubts. Rather, it seemed to have cauterized the awful wounds of the past. Now, all the creative forces of the world—the artists and the political leaders and the democratic masses—could work together through the United Nations to reshape the globe in a fresh image, create a New Deal for the future, build a humane system and shine its rays into every remote corner of every continent.

Among the returnees at the end of 1945 were the physicist Robert Serber and his wife Charlotte, who visited the East Coast briefly to see their families. Dropping in on Marc and Bill, Serber related the story of how he had so narrowly missed being on a most historic flight. Three planes flew to Hiroshima from Tinian in the Marianas that fateful day: one carrying the Bomb and two with instruments. Serber was on a plane with the camera and he was to film the bombing and its aftereffects. But as the plane reached the end of the runway, the pilot realized that he had forgotten to load an extra parachute for Serber. Without even taxiing back to the hangar, the pilot dropped Serber off right there on the tarmac. The skeletal crew on board the plane would simply have to figure out how to use the camera themselves. As Bill could readily attest, Serber's story joined the hundreds of others that confirmed the sad, old truth: "There's the right way, the wrong way, and the army way."

As the three men traded war stories, controversy inevitably developed over the bomb: Serber defended it as the surest way to end the war. Blitzstein may have gone along that far, but he expressed reservations both from a humanitarian and a political perspective. For now the United States possessed the power to dominate the world with its atomic threat, and he had little doubt where the threat was aimed: at socialism and the USSR.

It didn't take long to see in what direction the country was headed. And it was not hard to internalize the message. As Marc said to Bill and often repeated: "I have three strikes against me, three things the world detests. Number one, I'm a Jew. Number two, I'm a Communist. Number three, I'm a homo composer."

That fall, Marc and Bill tried to find a suitable apartment together—a week here, a few days there, then a place of their own at 134 West Fourth Street. Immersed once again in the glittering theatre scene that fall, Blitzstein always got free tickets to opening nights, and he took Bill to all of them. Some weeks it was night after night of concerts, plays, and musicals. Bill appreciated the attention he received as Marc's buddy, loved the dinners and drinks at Sardi's, and relished the anecdotal encounters with all the famous people Marc knew.

There was the week of the three white ermines, for instance. One night outside the theatre, a deep, rumbling female voice greeted Marc with a big smooch. It was Sophie Tucker, dressed to the nines in an ermine cape. The next evening, who came up to Marc with a splendid welcome home but Gypsy Rose Lee, also dressed in ermine. On the following night at another opening, someone approached him saying, "Oh, Marc darling, how nice to see you!" It was Lucille Ball—and she wore ermine as well. White ermine was clearly the thing to be seen in that season.

Walking on Broadway, they ran into Vivien Leigh and Laurence Olivier, who greeted Blitzstein warmly. Their faces were known to moviegoers around the world, but Bill found just the endearing thing to say to her.

"Aren't you the lady who sewed the buttons on Marc's army uniform?" he asked.

Blitzstein and his immediate circle of family and friends were hardly the only people in America committed to good relations with the Soviets. The National Council of American-Soviet Friendship sought to broaden and strengthen such ties. Far more than a Communist Party front organization, it aimed principally to keep the two most powerful nations on earth on friendly terms in order to stabilize global peace. In 1943, at the height of the war, it had established a Music Committee under Serge Koussevitzky, with the support of such musicians as Aaron Copland, Roy Harris, Fritz Reiner, Dimitri Mitropoulos, Lily Pons, André Kostelanetz, Elie Siegmeister, and Benny Goodman. In April of 1944, not long before the end of the war, Leonard Bernstein had conducted the New York Philharmonic with the Russian Choral Society under Lan Adomian in an all-Russian program benefiting the war orphans of Stalingrad.

The council sponsored a day-long conference on November 18, 1945, devoted to mutual cultural interests. Koussevitzky praised music and art as a challenge to barbarism. Copland, Siegmeister, and Bernstein all spoke as well. Other speakers addressed topics in theatre and literature. Charles L. Child, from the Division of Cultural Cooperation at the Department of State, and Pavel P. Mikhailov, Acting Consul-General of the USSR, also made presentations.

Blitzstein talked about the interchange of popular music, recalling his work with Bing Crosby and Dinah Shore on ABSIE and proposing visits of bands and major singers to each other's cities. He welcomed the integration of styles seen in the work of Bernstein, Jerome Moross, and others. But he also suggested, using the occasion to promote his forthcoming production of *Goloopchik,* that something could be done by way of integrating Russian and American popular styles:

> We are the two greatest nations on earth, and we must develop a sure and friendly and smooth reciprocal traffic system between us, from all points of view. The rest of this century, and I daresay, many more to come, depends on it. Musical culture is, by its very nature, one of the keys to such a traffic system, and so the interchange of popular music takes its place as a significant and urgent task.
>
> What do we do? Shall we take Tchaikovsky's *Piano Concerto* and move it into four-four time and send it to the juke-boxes called "You Are My Heart's Delight" or something like that? No, I don't suggest that. On the other hand, I can see no objection to addition of American (notice I say American, not English) lyrics, especially when the originals themselves are songs. I am not suggesting that we change the mood or tempo or that we pep it up a bit.[2]

Marc's sister Jo probably never became a Communist Party member—in light of Ed's work as a labor lawyer, she may not have wanted to jeopardize his career—but she certainly read Party literature and worked closely in the peace movement with Party adherents. She had no trouble persuading her brother to reappear publicly in his native city on December 7, 1945, the fourth anniversary of the bombing of Pearl Harbor, when the Philadelphia Council of American-Soviet Friendship sponsored a celebration of the Soviet Revolution and U.S.–Soviet relations. The occasion also marked the inauguration of the Samuel Blitzstein Memorial Fund, which would devote itself to public education projects under the direction of the council. "If Sam Blitzstein had lived longer," the program stated, "this is what he would have done. It is left to us, his friends, to continue his work for lasting peace by encouraging friendship between the United States and our greatest ally."

Aside from the presentation of a plaque and an award in Sam's name, the evening at the Academy of Music featured the two national anthems; songs by Russian soprano Tatiana Pobers, including a pair of Langston Hughes settings by Soviet composer Marian V. Koval; speeches by Soviet officials, Eslanda Goode Robeson (Mrs. Paul Robeson), and Seattle Congressman Hugh De Lacy; and Marc playing excerpts from *Goloopchik* at the piano. The following day, one of Blitzstein's early connections to Russian culture died at the age of eighty-two: his old teacher Alexander Siloti.

Blitzstein had signed contracts with James Proctor and Milton Baron as producers for *Goloopchik.* But after a while Jerome Robbins dropped out, feeling that it lacked cohesion. Without a strong book, furthermore, the show held little promise for a commercial run on Broadway. As American policy and public opinion gradually turned against accommodation with the Soviets in the postwar disposition of the world, Blitzstein put off the production. It didn't take long to see the unfeasibility of the project. From that point on, only occasionally would a song or two from *Goloopchik* surface—"Mamasha Goose," mostly—at appearances Blitzstein made for a variety of left-wing causes.

In 1946 Marc and Bill moved to a third-floor studio at 4 East Twelfth Street right off Fifth Avenue, coincidentally just down the street from Communist Party headquarters at number 35. This small apartment barely eight paces square, a corner of it taken up by Marc's baby grand Baldwin, had a tiny alcove for a bed; it would remain Marc's apartment for eighteen years. The neighborhood also housed many of their friends: The actor John Garfield lived nearby, and Leonard Bernstein lived just the other side of Fifth Avenue on West Tenth. Donald Ogden Stewart, the Oscar-winning screenwriter, and his wife Ella Winter, the pro-Soviet journalist, World War Two correspondent, and art collector, had an apartment three blocks away on East Ninth.

The close proximity of these talented, leftish people, all on their way up in the New York cultural world, led to many engaging evenings of fun. Mostly, they liked to play "The Game," an elaborate form of team charades in which anything went. One time at Betty Comden's, the composer Israel Citkowitz offered the phrase *"Kunst der Fuge"* for enactment by Judy Holliday. Her husband David Oppenheim had to guess it. She indicated her crotch for the first word. "Fuck . . . twat . . . piss?" he asked, then "cunt," the correct word. With a gesture to her ear, she then indicated "sounds like" and gave the German fascist salute, and thus he got the first word.

It can hardly be said that Marc and Bill were a quiet, contentedly "married" couple. Neither put any stock in fidelity as an institution, and most of their friends knew it; and Marc could not abandon his habit of going to the Everard Baths. Once he took Bill along to show him the goings-on there. Bill took one look and fled.

"Really, you're not all that naïve," Marc taunted him.

"I just don't go to places like this," Bill answered.

Another time, a pair of toughs followed Marc home from the baths. Marc had already gone up to his apartment when by chance Bill arrived at the front door to the building. "This must be one of his little pansy friends," one of the bruisers said, and they fell on Bill, giving him a thorough beating before a neighbor appeared on the scene and the hooligans fled.

With David Diamond, Bill formed a strong personal friendship, and when they went out drinking together at the White Horse Tavern, Bill would complain that Marc was trying to make him gay. Essentially, Bill's ties with Marc were not sexual. Excited though he might be by the luster of a relationship with so famous and talented a person, Bill remained primarily heterosexual. He kept up his affair with Lu Bowles, the Red Cross director he had met in Europe during the war who was now in New York studying dance with, at various times, Doris Humphrey, Agnes de Mille, Martha Graham, Ted Shawn, and Charles Weidman. Marc could be jealous hearing of Bill's adventures with other men, but the relationship with Lu did not bother him. Marc knew and cared for her. She was an understanding woman who never judged, and he knew what a balm she was for Bill's troubled personality. The three of them enjoyed social occasions together and Marc visited her attentively on a few occasions when she was ill.

When Blitzstein left England in May 1945, his superior officer Garson Kanin sent his musical papers after him in a trunk. But as week followed week and then month followed month, the trunk never appeared. It could only be assumed by the end of the year that the score to the *Airborne* Symphony had been lost—just as on their way over to England, the scores to *The Happy Family* and *The New York Opera* had been. At this point, he had no reason to recompose the work unless for a performance. That fall, he played excerpts for Leonard Bernstein from a few penciled notes, and Bernstein enthusiastically promised to conduct it with his New York City Symphony at City Center, the old Mecca Temple building on West Fifty-fifth Street that the City of New York managed. The premiere performances were scheduled for April 1 and 2.

To complete the symphony, Blitzstein needed an undisturbed retreat. Once again, he asked the Eitingons for their studio at Hillcrest Park in Stamford, Connecticut, where he and Bill stayed almost uninterruptedly from the end of 1945 through March 1946. One additional product of his retreat there was a song called "Chez Eitingon," a rumba detailing the hubbub at the estate with various family members, servants, and guests all engaging in their separate activities. On the surface a grateful occasional piece, it actually bears a mild undercurrent of resentment at the Eitingons' wealth, just as the Yasha and Dauber scene from *The Cradle Will Rock* does—also written at the Eitingons' ten years before.

When Blitzstein had completed three-fourths of the recomposition, toward the end of February, the trunk unexpectedly surfaced in a quartermaster's depot in Boston. The second version turned out tighter—some ten minutes shorter—and as Blitzstein put it to *The New York Times,* "a heck of a lot better piece."[3]

The *Airborne* Symphony is almost the result of a cultural anthropologist's visits to bomber stations, barracks, and briefing rooms. The text shows an intimate familiarity with the realities of air force life, as well as the psychology and the dreams of the average men in the ranks. Appropriately, Blitzstein dedicated the work to the men of the United States Eighth Army Air Force.

It might be thought that the *Airborne* is an example of machine music, but it is not a true representative of that school, such as Frederick S. Converse's *Flivver Ten Million,* Arthur Honegger's *Pacific 231,* or Alexander Mosolov's *Iron Foundry.* Except for a wind machine in one passage, Blitzstein made little attempt to imitate or describe the machinery itself. He concerned himself with the mythological and historical interests in flying and the contemporary social and political use of flight technology. The work treats the machinery of mass ideologies and systems more than the flying machines themselves.

The *Airborne* has its precedents, of course. Two of George Antheil's works for piano, the *Airplane* Sonata of 1921 and his Sonata III of the following year (its third movement called "Airplanes") had dealt with the subject. Emerson Whithorne also wrote a piano piece called "Aeroplane," which he later orchestrated. Italian futurist composer Francesco Balilla Pratella had written an opera just prior to World War I called *L'Aviatore Dro.* James Dunn's *We,* a symphonic poem celebrating Lindbergh's flight, premiered at the New York Stadium in 1927, and August Bungert had written an orchestral work called *The Zeppelin's First Great Journey.* Perhaps best known to Blitzstein was Kurt Weill's cantata of 1929, *Lindbergh's Flight.*

Chances are high that Blitzstein was also familiar with a work by the British composer Inglis Gundry, a favorite of the Workers' Music Association. In the latter part of the war, Gundry wrote an opera called *The Partisans,* dealing with the Resistance movement in a Balkan setting; it premiered in 1946. But in 1942, before Blitzstein began the *Airborne,* Gundry had composed *Five Bells,* a large work for chorus and orchestra—a "naval suite" written during the composer's year in the Royal Navy, replete with bugle calls and a text peppered with slangy naval expressions.

The fact that early on Blitzstein switched from a mixed-chorus to a male-chorus setting for the *Airborne* makes patent sense, but it was also Blitzstein's way of paying tribute to his Albert Hall chorus of 1943 and to such entities as Leonard de Paur's all-black Infantry Chorus, which entertained all over the world and recorded numerous albums. At the same time, Blitzstein was evidently indebted to those dozens of radio cantatas that filled the airwaves in the late 1930s and 1940s, settings of Presidential speeches and tributes to great historical personalities. Norman Corwin on CBS was the most famous practitioner of the genre, with his up-to-the-minute ersatz Auden poetry and inflated music by studio composers. Perhaps Corwin's most famous essays in the form were *They Fly Through the Air with the Greatest of Ease,* an angry denunciation of the fascist bombing of Guernica that aired in February 1939, and *On a Note of Triumph* that aired on May 8, 1945—V-E Day. Similar to Corwin's works, the *Airborne* uses a principal voice as a narrator, or what Blitzstein called the Monitor. Another work that Blitzstein knew was the Czech composer Bohuslav Martinů's war-inspired *Field Mass,* written in 1939 for male chorus and baritone solo. David Diamond was subletting Martinů's apartment on West Fifty-eighth Street for a time, and when Marc visited him there, he examined the vocal score.

Blitzstein divided the *Airborne* Symphony into three movements, each of them subdivided into discrete component parts. The first movement salutes man's inventiveness unleashed by his imagination. In the "Theory of Flight," the Monitor poses the problem: We move on the ground and over the water. But "you know what a man is," he says. Is it conceivable we can also move on the air, be airborne? The chorus muses on this proposition with music like mist rising out of a swamp. The Monitor dreams of a globe shrunken by air power, in terms reminiscent of 1920s Aviation Age travelogues:

> *Laugh it off.*
> *This little thought knocks out a mountain range,*
> *Tears up the jungle. This notion eats oceans,*
> *Puts the desert in its vest pocket,*
> *Has geography for tea.*
> *The barriers to the other side of the world—*
> *They can pack it up now, and call it a day.*

The tenor, backed by the chorus, tells the stories of early attempts at flying in his "Ballad of History and Mythology"—Etana, Phaethon, Icarus, Archytas of Tarentum. The light, playful, minstrel music is tinged with jazz. This is a happy song, showing the pioneer inventor's joy of tinkering. It recalls the upbeat "American Day" number Robeson sang in *Native Land.* To disguise the essentially didactic nature of this episode, Blitzstein doused it in slang, jokes, poor puns, strained rhymes, and Gertrude Stein-like wordage:

> *There was a flying bicycle,*
> *Did everything but fly.*
> *A giant black umbrella kite*
> *Did not go very high.*
> *(It wooden pigeon.)*
> *There was a rocket to the moon.*
> *(No sweller model.)*
> *And as for the balloon.*
> *Oh, every manner of balloon,*
> *And some stayed up all right, and some did,*
> *And some did, and some did not,*

And some went so high,
And some did, and some, did
And some went up and out of sight. . . .
Though they had wings on the brain—
They all went flat on their nose.

Finally, to an accompaniment of tense strings, the Monitor announces that at Kittyhawk, North Carolina, on December 17, 1903, the Wright Brothers' seven-hundred-and-fifty-pound, twelve-horsepowered contraption took flight for fifty-nine seconds at an average speed of thirty-one miles an hour. Blitzstein glides into a soaring, floating Coplandesque theme for an orchestral passage named "Kittyhawk," in which he uses the wind machine. The chorus follows with "The Airborne," a celebration of flight, a salute to man's technical mastery over the elements, ending the first movement.

In "The Enemy," which begins Part Two, the Monitor reminds us of Blitzstein's old theme from *Cain,* that the potential for evil resides in all of us:

Name now an enemy.
You know what a man is:
He yearns, he destroys.
He kills, he builds.

Man has become airborne. Using quotes adapted from Alfred Rosenberg, one of the prime theorists of Nazi philosophy, Blitzstein shows how in the wrong hands technology becomes a means of oppression. To illustrate Nazi myths of blood, race, and hate, the composer uses pompous, imperial martial music with prominent brass, recalling his marches for *Julius Caesar.* Led by a rabid Monitor, the chorus chants out the repulsive Aryan catechism in methodical, mechanical rhythms similar to those he had used in the Purple Shirts' scene in *I've Got the Tune.* The identification of Hitler with the Nazi youth culture contrasts with the spontaneous generosity of American youth that will appear later in the work. Blitzstein represents Italian and Japanese fascism with a snakelike theme. Alongside the unpitched fascist cheerleading, Blitzstein counterposes a series of deranged tunes, similar to something out of *Triple-Sec* or *The Harpies,* or the "Crazy March" from *Cain,* as if to say that the music of the twenties, written without social consciousness, could only eventuate in fascism if it had remained on course.

Touches of Shostakovich characterize the "Threat and Approach" orchestral passage denoting the Nazis' air war on civilization; appropriately so, because it recalls the Soviet composer's *Leningrad* Symphony (the Seventh), devoted to the city under German siege for nine hundred days. In the entire *Airborne* Symphony, this is the music that most resembles a typical 1940s movie score.

"Ballad of the Cities" is first a recitation of seven cities hit hard by Axis bomb attacks—Guernica, Warsaw, Manila, Rotterdam, London, Malta, and Leningrad. It was important for Blitzstein to mention Guernica as the "starting point" of the Second World War—even though the bombing of that Basque town was an episode in the Spanish Civil War—in order to underscore the complicity of the Western democracies in the origins of the war. (Until shortly before the premiere, Blitzstein had named Coventry instead of Manila, but he made the change no doubt so as not to include two cities in the same country and to include at least one Asian city.) Then Monitor, chorus, and the baritone and tenor soloists tell what those wounded cities looked like, felt like, and sounded like after the raids: rubble, dust, a child crying, voices straining to be heard through the chalky air.

Blitzstein based his vision of these cities on news reports, miles of film footage—beginning with *The Spanish Earth* and all the way through film of the liberation—and on what he had seen and experienced in London and France. In fact, he used as his melodic motif the "Ballad of Sevastopol," written before he enlisted. It was the same atmosphere he had summoned up in his song "Displaced." From out of the rubble, his chorus cried, "Are you coming? We can hold out. Are you coming?" And, responding to these appeals for the opening up of the second front, the chorus of liberators answers, "Hold out, oh cities. Hold out until we come. We will be coming. Soon. Hold out"—a new version of the union song "Hold the Fort," but on a more tragic, worldwide scale.

The second movement concludes with a "Morning Poem," spoken by the Monitor without any musical accompaniment. Here, he pays quiet tribute to the British pilots who had begun bombing the Continent well before the Americans got themselves settled in England. But Blitzstein does not wax heroic. The pilot goes out for an early-morning promenade in the sky just to feel the exhilaration as he dips and glides, mounts and floats, turns upside down, improvises in the cool air. This is a moment of respite in the symphony, a time to leave ideology behind and look at a single man taking a few minutes of airborne sport.

The composer did not wish to rule out humor in war. The opening section of the third movement, the "Ballad of Hurry-Up," is genuinely amusing:

You know him—the young American?
Fresh from high-school, straight out of college, green from the office and the farm and the shop and factory?
The brash, the young, the funny, the noble—the brash young funny noble American
Turned flier, turned ground crew, suddenly turned Air Force overnight.
Iris in, train down, focus on him, for one example.

The Monitor's language here shows the origins of this music in Blitzstein's idea for a film-accompanied score.

This ballad uses a democratic, colloquial language, contrasting to the Auden- or Stephen Spender-like tone of the higher-flown "Morning Poem." Here the composer uses barbershop harmonies—the kind of spontaneous music the black engineers in the East Anglia repair battalions invented as their choral pastime—to celebrate the common man. Recalling the tinkering, experimental themes of the first movement, Blitzstein shows these grease monkeys and airfield builders and bomb crews willing, untroubled, striding free, the way he saw them when he lived with them writing *Freedom Morning.* They have no complexes, just the ordinary human responses, when the air force orders them to "Hurry up, hurry up, hurry up—and wait." A mission is called and the men prepare for it. The chorus gives us an intimate look at a whole crew of these young men dressing for the sortie:

Put on your old gray undershirt.
Put on your long-handled drawers.
Your heavy socks, and your sky-blue
Electrically-heated bunny-rabbit suit.
Your wired shoes, your fleece-lined boots.
Your cover-alls and flying helmet
With goggles and ear-phones attached.
Heavy jacket, heavy pants,
And don't forget to bring out the
Oxygen mask and the throat-mike and the
Parachute-belts and your O. D. gloves
And your thick electric gloves
And the cord to connect up the electrically-heated suit with.

Then, with all at the ready, the mission is scrubbed; the men take off in reverse order—and perhaps Marc displayed here some homoerotic interest—all their aforementioned gear. Voices from the chorus interpolate their comments: "Snafu, brother," "Tarfu, slug," "Fubar."* Without question, Blitzstein applied here something of what he had learned about building excitement from the filmmaker Joris Ivens in *The Spanish Earth*—"*Aviación!*"—then pulling back in order to launch an even more gripping attack.

"Night Music," gentle, suave, melodious, dreamy thought, sets the mood for the "Ballad of the Bombardier," another close-up, this time of a nineteen-year-old writing a letter home to his girl, Emily, before his flight. He is at that special, poignant age of youth grown into sudden manhood that Blitzstein always found so attractive. The baritone solo croons this semiarticulate letter with its reduced vocabulary and touching sentiment and its slight cowboy jaunt that shows a similarity of mood to the opening of Copland's Clarinet Concerto:

The words are like a wall, Emily,
I cannot write at all
What you are to me.
You are my heart's one cry.

*Acronyms for "Situation Normal, All Fucked Up"; "Things Are Really Fucked Up"; "Fucked Up Beyond All Repair (or Recognition)"—or "fouled up" for more delicate ears.

If you were nearby,
You could tell me why,
So easily.
Write me you will be true, Emily.
Write me I am to you
What you are to me.

Though the song doesn't say it, the implication is that the letter may reach Emily but that the boy never will. The song borders on kitsch, something like the one Blitzstein wrote for Garson Kanin and the boys on the film project to which he was too embarrassed to sign his name. But in its context and in the suppleness of its line, "Emily" becomes an affecting, almost commercial-radio art song. Marc told Bill he wrote it thinking of him.

"Iris out: bombardier to crew. Crew to squadron. Squadron to group," continues the Monitor again in film talk. It's the big picture again. On the imaginary screen, the skies fill up with planes. From all the united nations, the sound of the rendezvous is heard. As in Toscanini's *Hymn of the Nations,* men and planes have at last rallied to the people's cry, "Open up that Second Front!" To words recalling Churchill and Roosevelt's wartime speeches, Blitzstein injects French boulevard music suggesting D-Day. This is the fight, the thrust, the victory.

And without pause, the composer opens into a full-throated chorus of glory with bells ringing out the news. His huge mass song with full orchestra, chorus, speaker, and soloists turns into a secular victory mass: "The Open Sky" at long last, the airways free to roam in, the sky cleared for freedom.

In peace, though not without grief, men wend their way back to their farms and homes as Blitzstein strikes an American pastoral mode. But the Monitor warns us:

Watch this victory:
Whose victory? Whose glory?
Shall men, once again ready to resume the conquest of the
skies,
Once again be stopped? Once again create—
The enemy?

What class, and what new myth of invincibility, will turn victory into arrogance, turn the mastery of technology into rule by might? By April 1, 1946, when the *Airborne* Symphony received its first performance, the left could already sniff the odors of a new imperialism.[4]

As the composer had told *PM* in an advance promotional article:

> The music here is what I call "idiot music," very martial, very bare, rather Teutonic in orchestration, lots of brass. . . . I have taken a risk in the ending of the *Airborne.* Most symphonies, you know, end on a single note, maybe triumph, maybe tragedy. But a symphony about our times cannot have that luxury—you cannot do that and be honest with yourself.

> No victory is unqualified victory, no glory is unqualified glory. So the *Airborne* ends in conflict. There is a great paean of triumph over the enemy, sung by the chorus, but a single voice—the narrator—begins to jab in the note of warning! Warning![5]

For almost an hour, the composer keeps a whole symphonic and choral palette occupied. Though he uses large forms, he never forgets the little people, the personal element, the human scale of war. In his shifts of scale and focus, he manages to hold audience interest and at the same time convey both musical and textual messages.

In the course of writing the symphony, Blitzstein prepared a series of character sketches, additional material he knew he would discard but that he wrote just for practice to get the feel of his men and material. For example, he wrote lyrics for one of the ground crewmen he had met in England, the man who wore the tunic of his comrade missing in action and who had gone into a deep depressive state. Another sketch was the "Ballad of the Grease-Monkey and the Gunner" in which Jake the tail gunner and Eddie the ground crewman, both from Kentucky, are bosom pals. Jake is shot down, and Eddie advances to take his place. He is shot down, too. The Monitor concludes the episode, saying, "Get that gallant enemy, that noble enemy, get him for Eddie and for his friend Jake."

In certain instances, Blitzstein's final version fails to convey all the meaning he intended, as evidenced by his discarded lyrics. For example, his series of "Connect two facts" in "The Enemy" aims to establish the links between very disparate events, but it fails to convince:

> *Connect two facts:*
> *This gardener whistling under the somewhere sunlight;*
> *And one other fact:*
> *Twelve men, being stood against a wall.*

His idea was to connect phenomena, connect people, tie concern and accountability for one another into a worldwide community so that discrete crimes could not be ignored and grow into criminal systems later on. The makers of *Native Land* had used the same technique: By their sheer weight and proximity to one another, the piling up of images and facts would teach the viewer to look deeper for the meaning of separate events. In a very late version of the "Open Sky" section, he wrote, then deleted verses that would have made the connections clearer:

> *Now do we know that the slum in Glasgow*
> *Is a threat to the little electrician in Memphis?*
> *That the corpses piled high in Belsen*
> *Are the responsibility of the gardener in Kent,*
> *the butcher in Marseilles.*
> *One enemy down.*
> *What of the new enemy—outside, inside?*

Musically, too, in the language he selected—an integration of popular with more elevated forms—Blitzstein stressed an interdependence of the two cultures on one another, as other composers had done especially during the war—Bernstein, Copland, Weill, and Richard Rodgers in *Oklahoma!* Though written for the concert hall, the *Airborne* Symphony exudes its conceptual origins as a film score to be heard in conjunction with visual imagery. It is, far more than a recording could suggest, a highly theatrical event for the audience.

If this symphony is about more than just flying and World War II, if it begins to explore more broadly the relation of human culture to technology, then it achieves its end by citing one example of this relation. Like the high-speed steel mills Blitzstein had depicted in the film *Valley Town,* air power itself is not the enemy. However, we must watch technology when it is the pawn of the dishonest, the self-serving, or the malicious—as Blitzstein had warned in *The Cradle Will Rock* to watch medical science in the hands of a Dr. Specialist.

Similarly, Blitzstein attacks the ideology of hate, not the perpetrators as racial or cultural types; for next time around, or in some ways even now, the haters could be—us. In one draft of his text, which recalls his old theme of universal responsibility from *Cain,* he wrote:

We are guilty, as long as there is guilt.
What did we know?
What wouldn't we know?
Glance at the face—the face is bland.
Go on, make your cartoon
A bucktooth for the unsavory jap—
A pock marked swarthy bulging strut of chin for the massive duce
The blue-eyed blonde with fat rolls for a neck which is the ineffable Aryan
Heiling his weak intense masturbatory Führer.
Make your cartoon, remember the face is bland, the face is average.
The killer really looks like you or me.
Know him by his nature;
Know him by his act.

For performers, Bernstein recruited the eighty-five male voices of Robert Shaw's Collegiate Chorale. Walter Scheff, a Juilliard graduate, sang the baritone solo, and Charles Holland, a black singer from Norfolk, Virginia, performed the challenging tenor part. "Charles, you should be at the Metropolitan," Bernstein told him, knowing that blacks were not welcome in that sacred temple of art in 1946. Orson Welles spoke the role of the Monitor. Leo Smit, a composer, played the piano for the New York City Symphony.

A full house greeted the performers at City Center on the night of the premiere, Monday, April 1. The program began with two Mozart works, the Overture to *Abduction from the Seraglio* and the Violin Concerto in D Major, with Werner Lywen as soloist. The symphony followed intermission.

At the end of the performance, Blitzstein jumped to the podium to embrace Orson Welles, then shared a particularly warm embrace with Bernstein. The audience responded with such prolonged applause that Bernstein had to calm them down with an impromptu speech in which he congratulated everyone, including himself—and the audience for its taste and awareness.

Reviews came out in the next morning's papers. Overall, the critics tended to separate the composer's less than original music from the impact of the work as a whole. Virgil Thomson, in the *Herald Tribune,* noting the Norman Corwin style, called the *Airborne* Symphony "an ingenious piece of musical work and far from uninspired," "masterful but not entirely satisfactory," the performance "a triumph of efficiency." "His tunes are both distinguished and singable. And his whole invention, melodic, contrapuntal and orchestral, has a higher degree of specific expressivity, a clearer way of saying what it means, than we are accustomed to encounter in the work of American composers." Olin Downes in *The New York Times* wrote: "Not often has a new symphony had such an approving reception in this city. The work gripped the audience by its subject and its music-dramatic treatment." He declared it "a significant score, in its quality, expressive purpose and relation to urgencies of today," though he found the music itself "superficial and derivative."[6]

Grena Bennet, music critic of the New York *Journal-American,* took the Symphony for the epochal statement Blitzstein intended it to be: "It is a saga of men. Men that we must never forget, just as we must never forget Pearl Harbor. . . . It is a moving and sincere work that should be performed on every national holiday just as our national anthem."[7]

Douglas Watt brought no sympathy to his review: "It is somewhat useless to criticize the work. To me, it said nothing new or fresh or moving and, in its studied use of familiar tragedies, it occasionally seemed a little callous. It is scarcely profound, more of a musical poster, but I appreciate that there is an audience which responds happily to these clichés."[8]

On the left, both Louis Harap and Sam Morgenstern reviewed the *Airborne* Symphony for the *Daily Worker.* Harap cited the triumph of the piece as "a major event in American music history. . . . To say that this is the finest musical to come out of the war from an American composer is not enough. It is among the best to emerge from the war from any country." Morgenstern was more critical, especially of what he saw as the musical disunity of the piece. Wallingford Riegger in *New Masses* talked about the movement to incorporate the serious and the popular in contemporary music. Blitzstein had used the popular idiom but not sunk to the bottom with it. His text was "the product of an enlightened political thinker, endowed with an unusual musical talent and possessed of a boundless faith and an intense purposiveness in communicating his message, not to the select few but to the multitude." The *Airborne* is "written in a style easily understood by the average GI Joe."[9]

Musical America called the music "as dated as Beethoven's *The Victory of Wellington,* and probably will be no better known within two seasons. It is too time-bound, both in topic and style, to survive. There is a Hurry Up and Wait chorus which should have a transient popularity with T-B-B choirs; and the song of bombardier writing to his girl (baritone solo) has Hit Parade possibilities. Beyond these, the outlook is not rosy."[10] Chappell did, in fact, publish these two numbers separately.

In a more considered article, Harold Clurman pronounced perhaps the wisest opinion in his acclaim for what he considered "the best show in town":

> The talent is theatrical, showmanlike, even Broadway, and has a new sophistication—that of the youthful urban intelligentsia nurtured in the thirties. It is urgent, unsure of its true aim, real even if its motives are mixed, expressive of a confused agitation that is energetic, unripe, warmly sentimental to the point of the saccharine, worried, even hysterical at times. . . .
>
> The success of this piece is salutary. It is good for American music. It is good for our public to hear the actual find direct expression in the concert hall as it found expression once in the theater (*Waiting for Lefty, The Cradle Will Rock,* etc.). Should this work prove ephemeral, it is still important as a pioneer piece for those ultimate syntheses which will one day come, perhaps through another generation of artists. . . . Even what is "corny" and pretentious in the *Airborne* is part of an American consciousness trying to find itself amidst the ubiquitous commercialism in which the ambitious artist must perforce live.[11]

In the composer's first conception, he thought big for the *Airborne,* hoping for approximately simultaneous performances in the major world capitals, in appropriate translations and, as long as the score was not changed, perhaps with some ingenious staging. If the work had been filmed, it first would have had music, then visual accompaniment. Blitzstein was committed to writing for his times, but without a production at the ready, the times often flew by him. If his symphony had somehow been able to be performed during the war with anything like the major excitement of which Blitzstein had dreamed, there is little question that it would have made a profound impact.

In the Soviet Union, the systematic excision of names from all public mention, coupled with the doctoring of photographs, could create nonpersons virtually overnight. But American culture produces its own form of social amnesia. A year after V-E Day was rather late in this culture for a big war symphony. Consumerist society had moved on to other stages, and to many ears, the *Airborne* seemed already dated. How many people wanted to hear about the second front any more? Indeed, in these two or three postwar years, America welcomed to its shores hundreds of former Nazis, as scientists or simply as informants and good prospective U.S. citizens if they talked in a sufficiently anti-Communist way. What major musical work is seen and felt today as the great American commemoration of the Second World War epic through which this country lived? What major works can even be named? Blitzstein aimed for his work to be for America what the Shostakovich *Leningrad* Symphony still remains for the Soviets. If it never achieved anywhere near that status, the explanation is only partially to be found in the work itself. By contrast, Soviet composers thirty and forty years after the end of World War II, or what they call their Great Patriotic War, are still writing works honoring the defenders of Soviet soil, memorializing their twenty million dead.

At its time, however, the *Airborne* Symphony captured tremendous attention. Blitzstein received both the 1946 Music Critics Circle Award and the Page One Award of the Newspaper Guild of New York for the work—but no Pulitzer Prize. Also, possibly as a result of the acclaim given to the symphony, that spring he became a member of the board of directors of the League of Composers. The symphony's text was later published in *Radio's Best Plays,* with six pages of musical manuscript reprinted.[12]

Also that spring, Blitzstein received a one-thousand-dollar American Academy of Arts and Letters award, "for the vigor, timeliness, and dramatic power of his composition." The prize did not result from the premiere of the *Airborne,* however. Aaron Copland had prompted it, citing the operas *The Cradle Will Rock* and *No for an Answer* as "two of the most original works in that form composed in this country." At the awards ceremony on May 17, members of the New York Philharmonic under Howard Hanson played three excerpts of a Suite from *Native Land,* Blitzstein's first attempt to recirculate some of the music to his prewar film score.

Shortly on the heels of the American Academy award, the Koussevitzky Music Foundation offered Blitzstein a one-thousand-dollar commission "for a musical drama or opera suitable for performance at Tanglewood." Koussevitzky hoped the work might be ready for the 1947 season. On the heels of the *Airborne,* composed to his own text, the composer gravitated toward adapting an existing play rather than creating one out of his own imagination. But what play?

O'Neill's *Anna Christie,* perhaps? No, " 'Atmosphere' just choked up the essence," Blitzstein wrote in a rundown of possible choices—"I got bored before I started." *Awake and Sing* by Clifford Odets? No, "too cosy, too 'family-drama' with no chance for spread anywhere." Shaw's *Saint Joan*? "Imagine walking deliberately into the contractual complications that old boy would automatically set up!" *Sons and Lovers* by D. H. Lawrence—"very good, earthy, full of meat—but so full of plot-detail,—an opera?"

He returned again and again to the subject in conversation with Bill. Bill suggested Nelson Algren's *The Man with the Golden Arm.* "I wouldn't touch that with a barge pole," Marc answered, picking up one of Bill's expressive Southernisms.

They talked of a possible musical based on *The Gilded Age,* the collaborative novel by Mark Twain and Charles Dudley Warner about post-Civil War Washington: corrupt congressmen on the pork-barrel circuit, all the while professing the highest of ideals. Maybe the composer could recruit someone such as Lillian Hellman to write the libretto.

Bill mentioned some of the other plays he had seen. He suggested Hellman's new play due on Broadway that fall, *Another Part of the Forest.* But Marc was scheduled to provide music for that anyway.

"Well, what about *The Little Foxes?*"

Yes, why not? The grasping Hubbard family in the sluggish Alabama of 1900; decadent aristocracy, burgeoning progress, black sharecroppers, the beginning of jazz. The finest play written in America, Blitzstein thought, turned into "something as real musically to Americans as Italian opera is to the Italians." With a salute to Shostakovich, a kind of *Lady Macbeth of Bowden, Alabama.* Certainly, Meredith Willson's syrupy Swanee River score to William Wyler's prewar movie had in no way exhausted the musical potential steaming up from this rich native humus.

> I no sooner decided than I was in love with the idea—a real infatuation, even to the desperate uncertainty as to whether my urge was reciprocated. I wanted to make an opera of the *Little Foxes*—but did the *Little Foxes* want to be made into an opera by me? I mapped out quickly in my mind how I would make the hard-hitting play about the first blossoming of industrial capitalism in the South conform to what I wanted an opera about it to be; I found spots for spectacle, action, "laughs," almost none of which were in the play proper.

Blitzstein approached the playwright with his idea. Hellman looked at him astonished, then answered him: "Of course you may do it if you really wish to, but I don't know how you can add anything to the Hubbards that will make them any more unpleasant than they are already."

The contract they signed entitled Hellman to approval of the opera and one third of all royalties. By the middle of May, he set to work putting *The Little Foxes* to music.

Pro-Soviet musical activity continued. As an outgrowth of the National Council of American-Soviet Friendship's music committee, and of the impulse to lend further life to the wartime alliance, a separate American-Soviet Music Society came into being in February 1946. Composers Blitzstein and Bernstein, Henry Cowell, Morton Gould, Elie Siegmeister, and others were active in it, as well as Olin Downes, music critic for *The New York Times,* Margaret Grant, dean of the Eastman School of Music, and Gladys Chamberlain, director of the New York Public Library's music collection. Koussevitzky served as chairman and Aaron Copland presided over its meetings. Betty Bean was executive secretary. As Koussevitzky defined its motivation at an early meeting: "The post-war world cannot exist without the friendship of these two great countries, vast in land, rich in soil, young in spirit. And it needs the help of Art."[13]

The society's national advisory board had thirty-five members who were committed to the exchange of scores, promotion of recordings and educational information, and sponsoring concerts of both popular and concert music. Major figures in the musical world, such as Walter Damrosch, Claudio Arrau, Paul Robeson, Bruno Walter, Fritz Reiner, Dimitri Mitropoulos, Joseph Szigeti, Arthur Judson, and Yehudi Menuhin made monetary contributions of anywhere from ten to two hundred and fifty dollars for the furtherance of the society's goals.

On May 2, the Greater New York Committee for Russian Relief sponsored a Carnegie Hall concert of modern American music to benefit the First Central Medical Institute of Moscow. The black conductor Dean Dixon led his American Youth Orchestra in a program of Bernstein, Copland, and Siegmeister. In addition, the audience heard *The Last Speech,* a cantata on FDR by Lou Cooper, the producer of amateur stagings of Blitzstein's work before the war. Blitzstein performed excerpts from his musical-in-progress that was announced for production in the fall, though in fact *Goloopchik* had made very little progress since his initial burst of energy the previous summer. Muriel Smith, the black soprano, sang Gershwin songs, "I Hate Music" by Bernstein, and "The House I Live In" by Earl Robinson; Isaac Stern performed pieces by Kabalevsky, Prokofiev, and others.

> Mr. Blitzstein captivated the large audience with his singing and playing of a round of songs from his as yet unnamed music comedy on which he is now working. It deals with two [*sic*] Americans in Russia, and judging from the cleverness of the composer's own text for the songs presented and the snappy character of their music, the work should prove a big success when it reaches the stage.[14]

On May 9, a piano recital by Alexander Brailowsky, sponsored by the American-Soviet Music Society for its own benefit, commemorated the first anniversary of the end of the war in Europe.

In the weeks since the premiere of the *Airborne* Symphony, Bernstein had traveled to Prague to conduct American music at the International Music Festival, the first year of what would become the well-known Prague Spring Festival. At 5 P.M. on May 26, the General Motors Symphony of the Air broadcast the *Airborne* on the NBC network, and Bernstein made his debut with the NBC Symphony Orchestra. The same soloists performed, except this time with Blitzstein himself as the Monitor (Orson Welles had previous commitments). A surviving transcription of the broadcast shows Blitzstein sounding fresh, enthusiastic, high-pitched, and perhaps a touch overexcited. In an intermission talk by C. F. Kettering, a vice-president of General Motors, the sponsor ironically promoted both atomic energy and continued bomb testing—the very antithesis of Blitzstein's warning!

Charles Mills reviewed the broadcast for *Modern Music.* He considered it a "brilliant score" with "some good emotional kicks" that works "in a fairly stirring way in spite of its indifferently integrated materials." "Like a fairly good 'grade B' movie, one might like it and recommend it to someone else, but one shouldn't go a second time."[15]

On the day following the broadcast, the American-Soviet Music Society sponsored a concert at Times Hall featuring contemporary Soviet and American chamber music. Muriel Smith sang a group by American composers, including Ned Rorem, Siegmeister, and Blitzstein ("Displaced" and "Mamasha Goose"). Arthur Gold and Robert Fizdale, the duo-pianists, performed three works by other American composers, Paul Bowles, Virgil Thomson, and Norman Dello Joio, whose *Rhumba* received its first performance at this concert. A trio by Shostakovich and a first New York performance of Shebalin's Sonata for Violin and Viola, played by Joseph and Lillian Fuchs, represented the Soviets.

A week later, a group of Soviet writers arrived in the United States at the invitation of the American Society of Newspaper Editors and the State Department. The American-Soviet Music Society gave a reception for them on June 6. On behalf of the society's concert music committee, Blitzstein gave Ilya Ehrenburg a copy of Eugene Ormandy's recording of Prokofiev's *Alexander Nevsky*, and Morton Gould presented an album of Soviet popular songs recorded by Harry Horlick, to show what Americans were doing for Soviet music. Expressing the society's interest in stimulating cultural exchange, Elie Siegmeister handed Ehrenburg the music to five American ballads and asked that the Russian poet give these to Soviet composers to work into chamber pieces for performance in the United States the following season. In turn, the Soviet composers sent a group of old Russian folk songs for American composers to set.[16] A few days later, the radio playwright Norman Corwin left for Moscow, taking with him for the Union of Soviet Composers recordings of Copland and Siegmeister with the composers' inscriptions to Shostakovich, Miaskovsky, Prokofiev, and Glière. Moscow concerts of American symphonic music on July 3 and 5 and a concert performance of *Porgy and Bess* showed the Soviets' interest in reciprocation.

For a while, New York seemingly couldn't get its fill of the *Airborne* Symphony. The composer appeared on Hildegarde's program "The Penguin Room" on WEAF July 3, where she sang the bombardier's song, "Emily." Norman Barasch wrote for the program, as well as Joseph Stein—on his first writing job—with whom Blitzstein would collaborate on a major theatre piece more than a decade later. After Hildegarde mentioned how thrilled she had been by *The Cradle Will Rock*, Barasch and Stein came up with this winning dialogue with Blitzstein:

> "I have an idea you made even greater history when you wrote the *Airborne* Symphony."
>
> "Well, when I wrote that I was really in the money."
>
> "How come?"
>
> "I was a sergeant in the Army."
>
> "Oh, yes, the program said you were commissioned to write that by the Army's Eighth Air Force."
>
> "That's right, Hildegarde. And believe me, that was the only commission the Army ever gave me."
>
> "Well, it worked out fine. Oh, and I heard somehwere that you lost your original score of the symphony somewhere in Europe."
>
> "Not exactly—it was on a ship that was torpedoed."
>
> "Really?"
>
> "Yes, and I always thought that was rather a violent way to criticize music."[17]

At which point, Harry Sosnick and his orchestra were cued in to begin "Emily" for Hildegarde.

Exactly a week later, Laszlo Halasz conducted the full Suite from *Native Land* at Lewisohn Stadium, a twenty-five-minute work in seven segments and a finale. Film music often lacks cohesiveness, and certain of the reviewers found the Suite too disparate in focus to stand up on its own as a concert piece. They missed the visual element. But other critics found it forceful and effective, at times gratifyingly melodic. Louis Biancolli mentioned the "crisp, fiery idiom" of the work and called it "one of the sturdiest film scores heard in recent seasons. The Blitzstein touch is in the slashing rhythms and probing colors . . . the challenging bursts of passion, the social satire, implicit and explicit."[18]

Ed Davis sold the Chadds Ford farm in 1946, so it was unavailable for the summer. But Blitzstein preferred in any case to stay with Bill at Mina Curtiss's property in Ashfield, Massachusetts. They lived in the guest house, the little fairy-tale cottage straight out of the Brothers Grimm where Marc had stayed before the war and where Mina had once again installed a piano for him. Mina loved both Marc and Bill in her weepy, enveloping immensity and gave them the run of the woods, the pond, and the swimming pool. It was an idyllic retreat where Marc could begin working on his next project.

They visited Tanglewood often, where Bernstein worked with the students and conducted. That summer he led the American premiere there of Britten's *Peter Grimes,* an opera whose subtext can easily be read as a defense of the homosexual in a society that fails to understand his condition. Felicia Montealegre, the determined woman Bernstein eventually married, spent the summer there to be near him. But he had already begun living an active gay life and simply ignored her much of the time. Perhaps Felicia wanted to make him jealous: On several occasions, she slipped off with Bill for the kind of romancing both of them missed.

In the fall the American-Soviet Music Society sprang back into action, sponsoring the first American appearances of two distinguished Soviet singers: soprano Zoya Haidai, People's Artist of the USSR and a Stalin Prize winner, and Ivan Patorzhinsky, leading bass of the Ukrainian State Theatre of Opera and Ballet, a deputy of the Supreme Soviet of the Ukraine, and a holder of the Order of Lenin. The two singers would be the first musical representatives to come from the Soviet Union in the postwar era. Haidai and Patorzhinsky had preceded their October 5 Town Hall concert by a five-week tour of Canada, and intended to continue on to several other American cities with their program of Russian and Ukrainian songs. But as soon as they entered the United States, the Department of Justice demanded that they register as foreign agents, under penalty of a thousand dollars or two years in jail. This, despite the fact that at the same time other foreign artists, such as the pianist Dame Myra Hess and the actors of the Old Vic Company, had no such problem.

As they were not foreign agents but artists invited to perform in the United States, the singers refused to register. They gave their one concert in New York and left for home, a host of positive reviews following them. In subsequent days, newspapers around the country reprinted a protest letter to the Justice Department signed by Koussevitzky, Copland, Howard Hanson, director of the Eastman School of Music, and Douglas Moore, composer and head of the music department at Columbia University. Olin Downes dealt with the issue in a lengthy Sunday *Times* piece:

> If this ruling, applied with special interpretation, as it would seem, to the Ukrainian artists, is made a precedent it will unquestionably lower an iron curtain of non-cooperation and ill-will and have a generally stultifying effect upon every artistic activity of international significance in the world. Should other nations, thereupon, make reciprocal restrictions in the field of art, as they did years ago retaliating upon us in matters of tariffs and passports, then we are well back on the way to the narrow nationalisms, misunderstandings and resentments which begat the second World War.[19]

America had started building a cultural wall. The cold war in music had begun.

For Blitzstein the concert season began that fall in Philadelphia. The Art Alliance sponsored his lecture-recital on October 22, 1946, at the Ethical Culture Auditorium. His theme was modern American music, and he performed Ives's "Serenity" along with his own early Whitman setting, "As Adam." He pointed to the amalgam between popular and serious music and illustrated his theme with a song from Weill's *Dreigroschenoper* and a ballet sequence from Bernstein's *On the Town.* He played the "Toreador" song from *Carmen Jones* and excerpts from *No for an Answer* and the *Airborne* Symphony. The *Record*'s reviewer observed Blitzstein's "tendency to pontificate. . . . The listener felt that any disagreement on his part with Blitzstein's statements would be regarded by the speaker as a violation of fact and of the laws of reason," a sharp, but clear judgment on Blitzstein's commanding manner.[20]

But the main event for Blitzstein that season was the revival of the *Airborne* Symphony on October 28 and 29, this time with Robert Shaw as the Monitor; it was paired with Mendelssohn's *Italian* Symphony. On the thirtieth, Bernstein recorded the *Airborne* Symphony for RCA Victor.

Hugo Weisgall, who had conducted *Freedom Morning* in its London premiere, served after the war as an assistant military attaché, then as cultural attaché with the United States Embassy in Prague. While there in 1946, he persuaded the Czech recording company Supraphon to issue a set of ten pieces of American music, using Prague's FOK Orchestra under his baton. Though the plan did not materialize in full, Weisgall did record his own *American Comedy* and *Freedom Morning,* the only professional recording the piece ever received; it was also the only recording of any purely orchestral work by Blitzstein during his lifetime. Though Weisgall produced a polished performance both in concert on September 28 and on the recording, the obscurity of the label guaranteed a minimal American distribution.

In "An Analysis of Prokofiev" that Blitzstein wrote for *Soviet Russia Today* in November 1946, he spoke of his Soviet counterpart as "a mature equilibrated composer doing a positive and historic job." His description closely mirrored his own view of himself: Prokofiev had surpassed the "wandering émigré" period of his youth, when the "still-expatriated" Russians were writing "piddling academic or destructive pieces." With the *Airborne* Symphony behind him, Blitzstein saw in Prokofiev "a master at the height of his resources, dynamically rooted in, and joined to, the most forward-looking, social basis of his day and age." As though announcing a five-year plan, Blitzstein affirmed that "the period now, in the USSR, is musically one of clear consolidation. . . . The soil and the conditions are right."[21] If only the conditions could be right for a people's composer in America.

That month, November 1946, Blitzstein's political commitments on the left aroused renewed FBI attention. "It is desired that this case be reopened and the subject's activities brought up to date with a report," J. Edgar Hoover directed the New York office. "You should endeavor to obtain legally admissible evidence which will prove the subject's membership in or affiliation with the Communist Party and knowledge of the aims and purposes of that organization."[22] The New York office complied, filing numerous and frequently repetitive reports over the next several years.

15

LITTLE FOXES

Fall 1946–March 1948

"I Played the Piano (for the CP)."

If by the fall of 1946 Blitzstein had come to see *Goloopchik* as in all likelihood unproducible, he had not given up the prospect of working with Jerome Robbins. They came up with the idea of an approximately fifteen-minute ballet with lyrics, called *Show.* Numerous drafts of a scenario exist; if one were to realize a final scheme out of them, it would go something like this: The manager of a major department store on 14th Street—or possibly 42nd or 125th Street, but in any case it has a racial mix among its employees—welcomes the audience to the gala summer show. Each department has chosen a male and a female to model the latest designs in the show window. The winners of this contest, heavily advertised in the tabloids, will be declared king and queen of the show and will receive a week's vacation in Miami plus a one-hundred-dollar bonus. The manager is sure to announce that of course the contest is fair and free of any discrimination, the judges being the owner's wife, an assistant to the publicity director, and a famous nightclub comedian. The real judge, he adds, is you, the audience.

The first couple, Variation I, does a frisky nightclub number, and the second, Variation II, performs to a torchy Hollywood song inspired by cheap magazines. In Variation III, it is clear that we have the superior team: Uncluttered by any commercial imagery, this couple is a real find. They simply grow toward each other in the most classic but natural pas de deux conceivable.

The problem is that the third couple is a black boy and a white girl. Stymied by this unforeseen and wholly impossible choice, the judges select the second pair as the winners. In the final scene, dancing begins around a punch bowl at the celebration party. Black males pair off with black females, and whites with whites. The rejected black boy and the white girl are left not dancing. In one of Blitzstein's thoughts about the scenario, he has the black boy throwing his punch glass out into the audience.

By the end of January 1947, Blitzstein had become unhappy with the Robbins collaboration. Apparently, Robbins had proceeded to make substantial revisions in the scenario, but he allowed Blitzstein to go on writing music for the old script. Perhaps other factors intervened or the distractions of other projects, but the work broke down. Blitzstein was left with a substantial ballet score but no producer or choreographer. For the time being, he put it aside, though he extracted some of its individual numbers as piano solos.

Before getting much further on *The Little Foxes,* two stage productions brought Blitzstein back into the theatre during the fall of 1946. Probably some of the easiest money Blitzstein made in the postwar years was his work on Hellman's new play *Another Part of the Forest,* the story of the Hubbard family in the period of Regina and her brothers' childhood—a "prequel" to *The Little Foxes;* it starred Patricia Neal and Leo Genn. In Act Two the script calls for some background music, which continues through about ten pages of dialogue. For this job Blitzstein used Leopold Mozart's Divertimento for String Trio in D Major and an arrangement of the thirteenth-century Gregorian chorale "Urbs Beata Jerusalem," "as found in my old Richter 'Counterpoint' book," Blitzstein noted privately, "and which has haunted me since I was twelve." Blitzstein was paid $750 for providing incidental music. Kermit Bloomgarden produced this latest Hellman play and the playwright herself directed it. After playing Wilmington and Detroit, it opened in New York at the Fulton Theatre on November 20, 1946, running for 182 performances. Almost none of the reviews mentioned Blitzstein's name; this was possibly the farthest-back background music he had ever supplied. The show gave Hellman the chance to meet Bill Hewitt. She liked talking with him—a fellow "emancipated Southerner," as the left liked to refer to antiracist whites from south of the Mason-Dixon line.

Again, and for the first time since the war, Blitzstein's path crossed with Cheryl Crawford's. She served as managing director of the American Repertory Theatre. One of her productions, opening at the International Theatre at Columbus Circle on December 19, 1946, was a double bill of Sean O'Casey's *Pound on Demand* and Shaw's *Androcles and the Lion.* Margaret Webster directed the Shaw play, Wolfgang Roth designed light, airy scenery and costumes, and Blitzstein composed a score for English horn (and oboe), clarinet, trumpet, trombone, drums and percussion, and piano (and Hammond organ). Music played at various points throughout both acts of the play, but there were no songs. For this work, Blitzstein received payment of $500, plus $12.50 for each of the 160 performances. Reviewers found the score "admirably economical," "evocative and appropriate."

Bill tried his hand at writing short stories, dreamt of being a playwright, and sketched out a novel on race relations. But he rarely managed to complete anything. Some internal psychological mechanism left over from a childhood under a tyrannical father prodded him to a sense of failure. Marc encouraged him. "Send things out," he'd say, and he personally recommended Bill's stories to Lincoln Kirstein and other literary friends. Financially, Bill had scant reason to be ambitious, for on top of his separation pay and the two thousand dollars he had saved, his 50 percent disability pension from the service would always be there for as long as he lived, to tide him over from one procrastination to the next.

By the fall of 1946, Marc had delved deeply into work on *The Little Foxes*. As an early riser, he found it hard to have Bill in the apartment all the time. Through Motty Eitingon, Bill got a position as a fur cutter in one of Eitingon's shops—an anomalous situation because Bill was one of the few non-Jews in the Communist-led Furriers' Union. Lunch hours he spent away from the shop: The union officers took the workers' time to offer them political harangues that he could not abide. "Bill works at his job and doesn't complain openly," Marc wrote to his nephew Kit, then in Colorado Springs studying art.[1] Bill quit after a year, tried going to school for a while at the University of North Carolina and in Miami, but gave up and returned to New York.

Late in the fall of 1946, the first and, as it turned out, the only issue of the *American-Soviet Music Review* appeared. Its fifty-two pages chock-full of reviews, career updates, news of recordings, publications and premieres, future plans, feature stories, and letters endorsing the Society's aims were mimeographed but well laid out and professionally written. Columns and articles spread far beyond the limits of reporting Soviet music to an American readership: It equally covered developments in American music for a Soviet audience. For just as in the thirties when American composers sought a new public among the working class, now, if relations didn't sour too badly, a huge, receptive public for their music seemed to be waiting in concert halls all across the Soviet Union. Indeed, in a world of few foreign outlets for American music, the American-Soviet Music Society was, according to the *Musical Courier*, "the only American organization which is actively engaged in an appreciable exchange of music with another country."[2]

In January 1947 the American-Soviet Music Society announced which composers had been asked to write the pieces of chamber music in the exchange program: Lev Knipper and Alexander Mosolov on the Soviet side, Quincy Porter and Burrill Phillips on the American. By the middle of April, Porter had finished his Sextet on Soviet Folk Tunes (later rechristened String Sextet on Slavic Folk Songs), and by June, Phillips had composed his quartet, a Partita for Piano and Strings. The society also sponsored a public forum on "Music and Musicians in the Soviet Union," which featured Norman Corwin, recently returned from the USSR on his world tour as the first recipient of the Wendell Willkie "One World" Memorial Award. Once again, Corwin conveyed the Soviets' hunger to hear more American music. He reminded his listeners that Henry Cowell, Elie Siegmeister, and Alex North had all received handsome fees from the Soviet publication of their works.

Mordecai Bauman, by then living in Cleveland teaching voice, sang a group of American songs—including "Penny Candy" from *No for an Answer*—on an American-Soviet Music Society program at a packed Times Hall in February 1947. The Fine Arts Quartet from Chicago made its first New York appearance at this concert, performing a Walter Piston string quartet and the Shostakovich Second, in its first New York performance. As a bonus for its members, a few days later the society offered a special preview showing of the film *Ivan the Terrible,* with Prokofiev's score. The following month the society held a huge program in Town Hall devoted to "Songs of Two Lands"—folk and choral music of the U.S. and the USSR. Armenian soloists played a variety of instruments from the Caucasus. Pete Seeger on banjo, Hally Wood on guitar, and Sonny Terry on harmonica joined the Peoples' Philharmonic Choir under Max Helfman, the American Choral Singers under Morris Levine, the American Folk-Song Group of Harold Aks, the Margo Mayo Folk Singers and the Byzantine Singers under Christos Vrionides. An ensemble of black singers drawn from a number of current Broadway shows sang the premiere of Alex North's cantata *Negro Mother* to words by Langston Hughes. William Schuman's *Prelude for Voices* and excerpts from Dzerzhinsky's 1935 opera based on the Sholokhov novel *Quiet Flows the Don* both received a hearing. Choruses from Prokofiev's *War and Peace* were heard for the first time in America on this program.

In late April, Fisk University in Nashville, Tennessee, dedicated its George Gershwin Memorial Collection of Music and Books on Music, the gift of music critic, novelist, and photographer Carl Van Vechten. The opening of the collection coincided with the university's annual festival of music, to which they invited Blitzstein. He and Van Vechten both went to Nashville, and at the final concert the men of the Fisk University Choir, joined by a speaker and two soloists, presented four long excerpts from the *Airborne* Symphony.

Blitzstein supervised the next American-Soviet concert at the City Center, a generous offering of "Theatre Music of Two Lands," held May 12. Alfred Drake narrated the production. Leo Smit's ballet *Yerma,* choreographed by Valerie Bettis, reels of two Soviet films, and Walt Disney's *Mickey's Grand Opera* comprised part of the program. Jerome Robbins choreographed Prokofiev's *Summer Day,* which he and Annabelle Lyon danced in its world premiere, with Ray Lev at the piano; this witty piece poking fun at classical ballet scored the biggest success of the evening. Blitzstein also translated a scene from Prokofiev's opera *Betrothal in a Monastery,* which received its American premiere at this concert. Reviewing the evening, Miles Kastendieck spoke of this scene as "a good example of contemporary lyric theatre art. The English adaptation of Marc Blitzstein is a four-star advertisement for more opera in English when handled so expertly."[3]

Gail Kubik's *Mirror for the Sky,* a folk opera based on John James Audubon, to Jessamyn West's libretto, was also part of the show. A few years later as a Prix de Rome winner, Kubik was scheduled to go on a State Department-sponsored tour of several cities in West Germany. At the last minute, the government canceled the tour. Kubik's wife had a close friend in government service, and discreet inquiries into Kubik's dossier in Washington turned up the May 12 concert program as the reason for the cancellation.

At the end of May, RCA released its eight-dollar recording on seven disks of the *Airborne* Symphony. The RCA Victor Chorale listed as the chorus was in fact Robert Shaw's Collegiate Chorale. The last side featured "Dusty Sun," the sharecropper's song from *Native Land,* with baritone Walter Scheff, and Bernstein at the piano. RCA described the set as a "recordrama," "stylishly packed in a Recordstory format" with the complete text and program notes by the composer. In the *RCA Victor Record Review* that June, Blitzstein addressed some of the questions listeners or dealers might have, emphasizing that ideally the work should be heard in the concert hall, where each performer contributes "a kinesthetic value which has its distinct communicative elements." He considered it a part of his work as creator "to achieve completeness on all levels—technical, medial, emotional, coloristic, formal." He also responded to some earlier commentators' complaints about his use of the word *symphony:* "Either that term implies a dynamic and living form, which in the twentieth century is bound to show examples which will differ from those of earlier periods; or it is a dead form, to be scrapped. I am one of those who think it still lives."[4]

Reviews of the recording, far more extensive than those of the original live presentation of the work, appeared in newspapers all over the country. The Indianapolis *Star*'s reviewer was right when he wrote, "It certainly is the most provocative new work brought out on discs in a long time. You'll either like it a lot, or you won't like it at all. . . . This will be one of the most discussed albums of the year."[5] From the engineering standpoint, the recording received universal praise. For Blitzstein's work, however, assessments ran the gamut from the highest of accolades to the basest of attacks, challenging reviewers to new depths of invective. Favorable critics called it "momentous," "in a class by itself," "thrilling," "tremendously effective," "vivid, vigorous, and theatrical," "dynamic," "irresistible," "one of the most original items in contemporary American music," "a Whitman-like poem," "powerful enough to bring any parlor audience to the edge of their chairs." The Springfield (Massachusetts) *Morning Union* thought it "one of the most dramatic works ever put on the records. . . . It must be heard to be appreciated, but in our opinion nothing finer has ever been recorded." The New Orleans *Item:* ". . . makes me feel positive that I am listening to something with the genuine touch of greatness in it. . . . I recommend the album without reservation."[6]

The nay-sayers used words such as "brash, phony, puerile music," "nerve-wracking," "whoop-and-fury," "banal . . . a little too much like Fred Waring," "ill balanced and spotty." From the Toledo *Times:* "It is windy and pretentious and contains little to qualify it for consideration as a serious work of art. Rather, it would be a good score to accompany the sort of pageant you see at state fairs." The Houston *Post:* "None of the performers (least of all Mr. Bernstein) seems to doubt for a moment that he is dealing with a jet-propelled Beethoven Ninth."

The Pittsburgh *Press* reviewer had a field day: Blitzstein's " 'brave new world' lyrics, which sound more like themes more suitable to the soapbox, can be summed up in the four-letter word, 'bore.' At times the monitor and the chorus sound about like collegians cheering at the half. If the war was fought to produce this kind of art, then we lost the war. Musically, Mr. Blitzstein's parachute failed to open." And *Pic* magazine, published in New York, had this to say: "Here is an insignificant score, performed by an inadequate orchestra, under the baton of an immature conductor. Its only effect on the sensitive listener is to cause a slight lifting of the eyebrows."[7]

Few writers dared to contemplate the message of the piece. Wrote Martin Roberts in the Harrisburg *News:* "It might even be dangerous: it may start controversy and might even make you think about the shape of things to come." From London, where the *Airborne* was written, Dyneley Hussey gave his opinion following a BBC broadcast: The work "comes nearer to a true American musical style than the polite essays in European symphony produced by the average transatlantic composer." The song "Emily" is "sentimental; but the sentimentality is handled with a rare delicacy of feeling that raises it to the level of art."[8]

Early in 1947 Blitzstein had written to Koussevitzky saying he would be unable to complete *The Little Foxes* until the summer of 1948. In reply, Koussevitzky offered him the opportunity to go to Tanglewood and work on the opera with the students there—though he declined Blitzstein a formal faculty position because of lack of funds.[9]

Still in need of a place to work that summer, Blitzstein had lunch one day with his neighbors Donald Ogden Stewart and Ella Winter. They offered him their Frazzletop Farm in Upper Jay, New York, whose three-story, rambling white hilltop structure overlooked the Ausable River. It was beautiful country, near Lake Placid, Saranac Lake, and John Brown's farm. While Marc worked on his *Little Foxes* opera, Bill would be there with him, as cook, chauffeur, and companion. They looked forward to a long season beginning the end of May and ending in October.

The house could not have been more ideal. The library contained few books that weren't inscribed first editions. Bill's third-floor room gave access to the attached barn, where Ella Winter kept trunks of her first husband Lincoln Steffens's correspondence. For hours on end, Bill amused himself poring over letters from every famous writer from the first half of the twentieth century. Stewart's Oscar for *The Philadelphia Story* propped open the bathroom door on the second floor. Marc and Bill drove their black Chevy into Upper Jay most evenings for meals at a crossroads Italian restaurant. They reveled in the fresh sweet corn and local produce and a lot of strawberry shortcake that season. Everything promised a delightful and productive summer, and for the most part it turned out that way.

Lina wanted very much to spend her vacation that summer with Marc in Upper Jay, a two-week prospect to which Marc looked forward somewhat dubiously. Her presence could be enchanting. At sixty-seven, she was full of stories told with grace and consummate theatricality. But Marc did not feel he could afford a two-week break from composing: "I keep discovering I'm not up to quota, which is bad for the morale," he wrote to Mordy and Irma Bauman.[10] So Bill happily volunteered to take Lina out on drives every day. One day soon after she arrived, he took her out on a boat ride across Lake Placid to the summer home of Victor Herbert, which she remembered having visited years before when she had been active on the operetta stage. Another day, Bill took her up an elevator to the top of a lookout mountain, where she squealed in wonder. All of a sudden, perceiving the opportunity for a resounding echo, she let out with Brünnhilde's piercing cry of "Ho yo to ho!" She chose to walk the wooden steps down to the base but slipped and sprained her ankle. A park ranger helped Bill get her to the car. Back at the house, a doctor came and bound up her foot, told her to stay off it, and she passed the two weeks sitting there and telling her endless stories as Bill solicitously waited on her.

Once a week, Bill and Marc drove into Ausable to shop for groceries. One day toward the end of June, the left-wing artist Rockwell Kent recognized Marc. His well-kept farm, complete with cows, a horse named Nehru, and a swimming pool fed by clear waters from the Ausable River, was just outside of town, and he invited Marc and Bill to come for a visit and meet his wife Sally.

An artist and book illustrator of firmly established reputation far beyond left-wing political circles, Rockwell Kent had his authoritarian, magisterial side. He had decorated the bar at his home with a huge portrait of Stalin. The young folksinger Lee Hays was working for him as a farmhand that summer, and Bill and Marc could see that Kent treated him like a serf. Sally didn't fare too well, either. In a political discussion, Kent came off as mulish and dogmatic, brooking no disagreement. A local farmer's son had just returned from military service and happened to listen in on the talk one day at the Kents'. The artist was pontificating as usual, blaming all the woes of the Western world on Herbert Hoover and hailing the matchless achievements of the Soviet Union, and the boy began to take exception. Bill, who had known a number of leftists disillusioned with the USSR, voiced his support of the boy's questions when all of a sudden he felt a strong kick under the table. It was Marc. Blitzstein may not have agreed wholly with Rockwell Kent, but he did not like to argue politics with those he considered more knowledgeable on the left. He preferred to direct his proselytizing toward those he considered uninformed.

On the Fourth of July, the Kents organized a picnic for twenty-odd people up on a nearby mountain. As the day wore on, Kent and Lee Hays led the singing of folk songs while everyone got progressively drunker on North Carolina corn liquor. By evening, Hays felt so unhappy about returning to Kent's farm that Marc suggested he go back to Upper Jay with them. There the three of them continued drinking. When Hays rolled himself into bed, Marc tried to climb in with him. Hays rebelled loudly and kicked him out. Marc went upstairs and found Bill in the bathroom.

Bill had heard the noise and knew what had happened. "Can't you find anything better than that?" he rebuked Marc. "Don't you realize you can't get by with things like this?"

Marc must have known Bill was right; there had certainly been incidents before. However, in his drunkenness, and perhaps from his underlying unhappiness that in Bill's fundamental heterosexuality he couldn't be all that Marc wanted him to be, he resented the scolding. Seeing Stewart's Oscar at his feet, he grabbed it and began threatening Bill. Bill escaped from the bathroom, ran downstairs and out onto the lawn. Marc trailed close behind, brandishing the Oscar like a lethal weapon—which one swift, well-aimed blow might well have made it.

"Drop that! Forget it!" Bill yelled.

Eventually Bill was able to push Marc down on the grass. Marc let go of the Oscar and the incident was over. Neither of them mentioned it again.

Someone from Harper's, the publishing firm, had attended the *Airborne* Symphony and had suggested to one of the editors there that the author of such a text might write an interesting book. Blitzstein was approached; he had agreed readily. With a tentative title of "Case Meets History" and an advance of one thousand dollars, Blitzstein had signed a contract with Harper and Brothers early in 1947 for a manuscript of 75,000 to 100,000 words, to be delivered by July 1, 1948. In his working notes he envisioned:

> A full-length book, regulation size, printed on paper; with chapter-headings, covers, margins, copyright credits, and a page for "The End." It will be fiction-non-fiction; comical-serious; about music, about myself, about the art of American lyrics to popular songs, about Why Not To Commit Suicide, about the Refugee and the Expatriate, anything that occurs to me, all of it pitchforked into a more-or-less continuous whole, the individual sections being self-contained. The style will be narration, dramatic dialogue, verse, proverbs, catalogues, diatribes, music criticism. . . .
>
> All I can promise is a relatively readable book; which, now I come to think of it, is quite a promise.

At Frazzletop Farm, he began working at the book the way he worked as a composer: a word or two as a germ, that one appended by another, then attached to a thought, and reworked into an idea. Somehow it would all fit into a framework of sonata form: the Case, himself (Theme I), and History, the world (Theme II), followed by a development section; then a recapitulation of himself, the "second theme in the key of the first"—"World as My Oyster, or possibly My Lemon, or perhaps not quite mine at all"—and a "Resounding Finale and Coda."

He considered possible titles, such as "Mark the Music"—a quote from *The Merchant of Venice*—and even some facetious ones, such as "I Played the Piano (for the CP)" (the Communist Party). He tried to remember the big moments in his life, such as the opening night of *The Cradle Will Rock,* and he wrote to Hallie Flanagan to ask for her recollection of it all (see pages 161–162). He jotted notes of childhood games and memories. "What I remember first is horror," he planned to begin the book, telling the story of his scalding at age three and the innate sense of theatricality that so early in life he had learned to exploit.

In between bouts of composing, Blitzstein poked at the book, but it came hard. Bill read the little Marc wrote, but he found it glib and superficial. Blitzstein could write engagingly and profoundly about his times and about other personalities, but he shied away from introspection. As others on the Communist left, he was suspicious of psychoanalysis and its lessons because so much personal preoccupation would only be an escape from the larger social and political issues. There was also much in his own life he may not have cared to reveal, so he may have felt that any book he wrote about himself and his views would turn out less than honest.

They stayed at the farm until mid-October. Marc composed and wrote. "The new opera is hell-on-wheels in every sense of the word," Blitzstein wrote to the Baumans; "hard as blazes to do, slow in coming, but dynamite when there; and a huge chunk of it is already there."[11] He also made plans for the season. Leonard Bernstein wanted to revive *The Cradle Will Rock* with his New York City Symphony, and in Cleveland, Mordy Bauman arranged to put on an all-Blitzstein concert in January 1948 with Blitzstein and singer Muriel Smith.

Older Communist theory had posited the South as a Black Belt that demanded a Soviet-type solution: Create a black autonomous region in the South, or perhaps even grant it a federated independent status, something similar to one of the constituent Soviet republics. If the Party no longer spoke in those terms, the South still represented for them a kind of "internal colony," similar to some colonial possession in Africa or Latin America complete with its native labor force, a comprador class (the Hubbard family of *The Little Foxes*), and an "imperialist" bourgeoisie (represented in *Foxes* by Mr. Marshall from Chicago).

The Party ceased pushing its Black Belt theory in the postwar period. For one reason, the locus of black political strength had begun to shift during the war, due to mass northward emigration in the search for jobs. In addition, many black servicemen did not return to the somnolent rural South after discharge because nothing there had changed to meet their expanded aspirations in life. In the place of the Black Belt theory, the Party and the CIO encouraged large-scale union organizing in the South. If industry had spread to the southern states, creating a new and in some cases integrated working class, then the organization of workers had to follow. The fusion of capital's and labor's interests would finally make the South an integral part of the nation: No longer could industry pack up and leave one region of the country in order to exploit southern workers with lower, nonunion wages.

Old-style lynchings still occurred in frightening numbers. The Truman administration, deeply beholden to Dixiecrat support, turned a deaf ear on appeals from civil rights organizations and the left to step in with more stringent law enforcement. The pace of uninvestigated crimes against black people in the South grew so shockingly in the postwar years that some black leaders, such as Paul Robeson, went before the United Nations with charges of genocide. There wasn't much difference between the South of the late 1940s and the image from a decade before offered in *Native Land.*

Internally, the Party launched a thorough campaign against white chauvinism that left no one unscathed; it became the obligatory slant on every issue, the cutting edge of every polemic. No matter what the subject under discussion, Party leaders found a way to inject the race question. It seemed in these days that no one measured up to their stringent requirements. In its haste to wrench out chauvinism, the Party often made foolish decisions that misused its members' talents, sending white intellectuals into heavy industry to begin union organizing work, or into black ghettos to sell the Party newspapers. At a time when the Party had come under harsh government attack, it further alienated its own membership with such shortsighted internal discipline. For the most part, however, given the admirable work he was doing for American-Soviet musical cooperation and given the chosen themes of his own work for the theatre, the Party left Blitzstein free from such demands. It was happy with the overall content of his efforts.

Blitzstein remained essentially faithful to Hellman's play about the Hubbard family of Bowden, Alabama. It is cotton country at the turn of the century. The Hubbards are a controlling force in the town. With their sister Regina, Ben and Oscar Hubbard are making a deal with a Mr. Marshall from Chicago to build a cotton plant in Bowden. However, to conclude the arrangement, they need Regina's money, all of which is invested in bonds owned by her sick husband Horace. For her efforts in securing these funds, Regina wants a larger share than her brothers get. Regina sends her daughter Alexandra—Zan—to Baltimore to fetch Horace back from his hospital sickbed. In the meantime, Oscar hopes to marry off his wastrel son Leo to Zan in order to keep the family money intact. Oscar's wife Birdie, a fallen aristocrat now living in a cloud of nostalgic dipsomania, overhears this plan and warns Zan of it.

Regina has called for a ball welcoming Mr. Marshall back to town and celebrating the construction of the plant that is now all but assured. At the party, the guests dance frantically, but the words they sing reveal their contempt for the greedy Hubbard clan. When Horace arrives home wheelchair-bound and clearly unwell, Regina pressures him to use his money for the plant, but he refuses. At Oscar's suggestion, Leo steals the bonds from Horace's safe-deposit box. With this extra money, the two brothers close the deal with Mr. Marshall, leaving their sister out. Unaware of the theft, she is livid with her husband and openly declares she is just waiting for him to die.

The "good" characters assemble the next afternoon for a moment of respite as the healing rain falls—Horace, Zan, Birdie, and the family maid, Addie. Birdie confesses her drinking habit, and Horace asks Addie to save Zan from a similar fate. Horace tells Regina that he will do nothing about the stolen bonds and that furthermore, in his new will, he is leaving her only the bonds. Her ceaseless nagging induces a severe heart attack in Horace, and she refuses to help him reach the medicine that will save him. He dies as Regina confronts her brothers with her knowledge of the theft, saying she will report them to the police unless she gets her more than equal share—75 percent. And so she wins the day, but she loses Zan. Zan has seen her mother's villainy and she will leave Bowden so as not to witness the consequences. The shrewd, shrewish Regina, finally the dominant power in town but condemned to remain alone and unloved forever, ascends the staircase to her rooms. While the Hubbard clan has been depicted as a pack of immature, scrapping children, Regina is now suddenly an old woman.

The Little Foxes touched on questions of race to some extent, though more on changes in the class structure of the South, economics, the oppression of women, and one of Blitzstein's favorite subjects, alcoholism and the false escape it offers. In a world where American power sought to "Marshallize" the global economy for its own aggrandizement, Blitzstein's use of Mr. Marshall from the big industrial center of Chicago served as warning that such uncaring greed could only lead in the end to untold grief. Of course, the opera is not an excuse to orchestrate the Party line for the Broadway public, nor is it merely a musical retelling of Hellman's story. As he had done in *The Cradle Will Rock* and *No for an Answer,* here, too, Blitzstein demonstrated that one of his primary objectives was to say something about American music itself, about its origins and evolution, its forms and influences, its style, and its public.

Musically, Blitzstein illustrates his sympathies by opening and closing the opera with black spirituals, by grafting the good white people's music on to black roots. The very introduction of the Angel Band, a ragtime quintet of trumpet, clarinet, banjo, trombone, and drums that Blitzstein added to the cast of characters in the play, reflects the essentially democratic nature of black music: In an improvisatory collective, each member plays an equal part. While the clarinetist does a solo, the others fill in; then one by one they all take their solo turns in succession. If earlier black protest music had all been couched in the soothing dreams of spiritual freedom "over Jordan," this new, bold secular music dared to demand a better life here on this earth. It figures that Regina would hear it only as a "racket."

The astute Cal, as an older member of the social underclass, instinctively understands the whole system in ways the overlords never do:

If you was like the night
And you could see the things there are,
Then you'd be blue,
Like you ain't never been before, so far.

Jazz, the young trumpet player and leader of the Angel Band who has been to Mobile and New Orleans, sees things more bluntly:

Naught's a naught, figger's a figger.
All for the white man, and none for the nigger.

None of this underlying political view translates into rhetorical music, however, like some of the more wooden choral passages of *No for an Answer.* On the contrary, each scene contains fresh and idiomatic material drawn not only from the black traditions of field songs, spirituals, minstrel, blues, and ragtime but from salon music, dance genres of the late nineteenth century, musical theatre, operetta, and grand opera as well. Some passages he drew from his composer's trunk: Bits of his never-produced *Parabola and Circula* can be found in *Regina,* as the *Little Foxes* opera would eventually be called. By contrast to the sassy Angel Band, he had an onstage trio of piano, violin, and cello performing sleazy, imitation Liszt and Gottschalk for the Hubbards' party guests—music that was already dated by the year 1900 when the play is set but that faithfully symbolizes the hosts' culturally backward musical taste. (Where the pianist plays a saccharine solo tellingly titled "*La cloche au crépuscule* [The Twilight Bell]," the reference to a similar salon scene in Kurt Weill's *Rise and Fall of the City of Mahagonny* must have been conscious.) Blitzstein introduced a little black boy named Chinkypin to dance to a nimble minstrel number sung by Jazz as a sort of scat rap based on overheard comments by the Hubbard guests.*

The composer dotted the score with at least one set piece for each major character. But he surrounded these set pieces, or arias, with underscored dialogue and recitative that most of the time disguised the separateness of the songs: In the context of a basic opera comique format, he still sought fluidity throughout an entire scene. Unlike most composers of Broadway shows, he did not want his audience to stop the action every few minutes with applause at the end of each "number." With a nod toward machine music, he imitated the sound of a train in Regina's aria urging Alexandra to be on her way to fetch Horace. And he put Horace's heartbeat into the orchestra as well.

His producer, Cheryl Crawford, loved what he had done. "You have lifted this piece into the evil of Lucifer," she said to Blitzstein, "way beyond the evil of the characters and the story." But his efforts to create a more through-composed musical effect unsettled her; for the sake of the show's commercial viability, she wanted more straight songs.

In his text, Blitzstein followed Hellman closely, reshaping her thoughts and words into arias, avoiding the stilted poetry of Librettoland. His integration of word and song shows the same superb ear for prosody that he had exploited in his earlier operas. The ballroom scene brought in an element of spectacle missing from the play but requisite for a Broadway musical show. And despite the venality of the story with its strongly melodramatic overtones, he preserved and heightened what he saw as the essentially comic aspect, albeit comic in a clubfooted Chekhov mode. Unlike Hellman's own movie adaptation of *The Little Foxes* in which she folded in a strong romance for Zan, Blitzstein followed the original

*In the published score, the Chinkypin number looks discontinuous from thought to thought because the white people's dialogue that it imitates and improvises upon is not printed as a counterpoint to the song.

play—an audacious risk for Broadway, where both critics and the public expected to find a love story.

But Blitzstein did make other changes. He brought in a Brechtian "alienation" effect, remarkable for this period and for this type of work. At various points, for example in the first scene of Act I after the family has decided on the deal with Mr. Marshall, they step out of character momentarily and like their own self-contained Greek chorus abstractly comment upon themselves. Similar to the characters in a much more fanciful opera, Virgil Thomson's *Four Saints in Three Acts,* they sing their own stage directions:

> *The company*
> *Have the table quit,*
> *With poise and affability infinite;*
> *And now, assembled in the living room—*
> *Sit.*
> *(They sit.)*

A few moments later:

> *The talk is small and delicate.*
> *The wine is old and fine.*

And when Ben admits the Hubbards are not aristocratic Southerners, just plain trading folks, the ensemble again break from role to ask:

> *A regrettable lapse*
> *Of taste, perhaps?*

In the ballroom scene, too, the guests openly comment on the Hubbards' grasping qualities. In Blitzstein's use of choruses, the people, both whites and blacks, are healthy. As in *Cradle, No for an Answer,* and the *Airborne,* they represent the main tendency: They do not get lost in self-worship or neurasthenic escapism.

The purpose of these barely noticed excursions from stage reality is to reinforce the sense of comedy. And they also remind the audience that this is something of a *Lehrstück,* a teaching play: The characters exist not to depict a reality to which, unaccountably, in the "fourth wall" scheme of realistic theatre, the audience is privy. Instead, like a throwback to the thirties and *The Cradle Will Rock,* the actors are there to illustrate and comment on the action for the audience. We are *not* to be hypnotized by our emotional engagement; we must remain fully in control, intellectually detached. Blitzstein made only a few fleeting gestures toward this technique, perhaps too few to make his point. Hellman objected strenuously to them, and for the most part he deferred to her judgment. "The whole of the chorus number 'Sing Hubbard,' ought to come out," he wrote, summing up a telephone conversation with her (though he didn't take it out). "She will not let 'anybody' mess up her work like that. Characters may not step aside, and view themselves or each other for the benefit of the audience, in an editorializing way."[12]

Another amusing interpolation Blitzstein made occurs in the ballroom scene. He has two small black boys hiding outside, looking at the festivities through the windows, and imitating the surreptitious flirting by two of the townspeople. It was a cute touch of homoeroticism on Blitzstein's part—one of the many signals he coded into his works—that also involves elements of voyeurism. Hellman, however, had problems with all of Blitzstein's emphasis, musical and otherwise, on the blacks:

> I still feel that the whole approach to the Negro in the play, whether it is the jazz band, or Jabez's singing to Birdie, or the Negroes at the party, is sentimental. I think the original play already had too much of such sentimentality and it was an artistic mistake. But I don't think we should increase the mistake.[13]

At the end, out of the multiple sicknesses of his country to which he points his accusing tunes, Blitzstein draws a sustaining apotheosis of hope. The lead solo field-worker and his sharecropper chorus chant out their call and response in the final scene:

> *Is a new day a-coming?*
> *Certainly, certainly, certainly, Lord.*

Not strangely, the positive "Certainly, Lord" theme is the same spiritual in which Blitzstein had coached his black chorus at Albert Hall in the midst of World War II.* Fused in counterpoint to the chorus, Zan at the same time makes her break with her mother and stands with her beloved Addie. Like *Cradle*'s Moll, her eyes opened to the possibility of struggle, or *No for an Answer*'s Clara, her mind cleared of adolescent innocence, or the bombardier of the *Airborne* Symphony who has become a "sudden man," Zan has all at once grown up.

Blitzstein restated with this conclusion *No for an Answer*'s idea of winning small gains in a period when the larger gains—revolution, socialism—are not on the historical agenda. True, the Hubbards have made a mess of their town, but out of it something has been salvaged: Zan's future, Addie's independence, a certain class consciousness on the part of both black and white townspeople that one day may lead to unity against racism and the sharecropping system. We simply must not believe that Horace has lived and died in vain. In the context of the time, audiences might see Horace in his wheelchair and dead by the end of the opera as a symbol of Franklin D. Roosevelt. The good rain that has passed over the land must have nourished at least some healthy roots.

*Blitzstein must have been aware of Roi Otteley's bestselling book *New World A-Coming,* published in 1943 by Houghton Mifflin and subsequently by other publishers. Otteley hoped for improvement in American attitudes toward blacks in the postwar era.

On the way back to New York from Upper Jay, Bill was driving. When they passed Hyde Park, he turned to go into town.

"Where the hell are you going?" Marc demanded.

"I'm going in to visit FDR's grave and look around," Bill answered, remembering how two years before, everyone in the hospital ward at Maxwell Field had cried when they had heard the news.

"Not on my time, you don't," Marc shot back. And it was Marc's car, so they didn't. Whatever sentimentality Blitzstein may once have cherished for Roosevelt had already begun to dry up in the backlash Truman years. Only that June, the Republican-dominated Eightieth Congress had passed the Taft-Hartley labor laws that threatened, with their anti-Communist provisions, to cripple the trade unions. The Marshall Plan for Western European recovery had already been put into place, too, guaranteeing that the wartime alliance with the Soviets, albeit never without its detractors, would crumble into dust. On civil rights, Truman's administration ignored the left's campaign against lynchings in the South and refused to pass a fair employment practices law. And the attacks on Henry Wallace, FDR's Vice-President and champion of his New Deal policies, had begun in earnest—so much so that by 1948 Wallace broke with Truman and the Democratic Party to run for the presidency on the new, third-party Progressive ticket, which the Communists supported.

That October of 1947, the House Committee on Un-American Activities began well-publicized hearings targeting the left-wing and progressive political associations of Hollywood artists. Immediately, distinguished actors, composers, screenwriters, and other public figures protested loudly against the government's attempts to muzzle free speech, and against the film industry's capitulation to HUAC. They took out newspaper advertisements, sponsored "Hollywood Fights Back" radio shows, spoke through the Arts, Sciences and Professions Council of the Progressive Citizens of America, and hastily gathered a Committee for the First Amendment. Naturally, Blitzstein signed these statements.

But the tormentors and blacklisters soon got their way. Those who failed to break with whatever radicalism they may have endorsed in the past, those who would not name others suspected of Communist leanings, simply would not work in Hollywood, not under their own names, at least. If necessary, to prove its power, HUAC would go so far as to imprison those who refused to talk: Before long, they sent ten motion picture writers and directors to jail.

The attack on free speech intimidated most screenwriters, directors, actors, and agents. If they came forward with proposals to create pictures about fascism, racism, labor, or a more prominent place for women in society, the studios knocked them down or transformed the treatments so severely as to become unrecognizable. The themes began changing, until by the early 1950s Hollywood seemed to spew out mainly domestic comedies and pillow dramas, werewolf stories, teen romances, and beach party frolics—and, of course, anti-Communist tracts.

Though it restricted access to radio and television, often important adjuncts to theatrical and musical careers, the blacklist affected the theatre and classical-music communities far less. But there, too, the dramas and the musicals that had once raised the vital questions of a developing democratic society yielded more and more to frivolity. No one will ever figure out exactly why HUAC waited so long to go after certain well-known left-wingers, nor why some left-wing activists were never called to testify. In any case, those whose fields were limited to the theatre and the concert hall were not considered as dangerous as those with greater media resonance. For the time being, they were largely left alone.

Against this background, though perhaps not explicitly for this reason, Serge Koussevitzky decided in 1947 not to continue in the post of chairman of the American-Soviet Music Society. Aaron Copland took his place, reminding the board that he might not always be available for day-to-day work if he was absent on composing assignments. The society continued to sponsor two or three more concerts during the fall of 1947, but by then they had turned into more intimate gatherings at supporters' homes. The energy to push on with a task so obviously doomed and so clearly damaging to the careers of anyone associated with it simply vanished. The last known program under the society's auspices took place at Times Hall on December 5, a chamber concert of Copland, Leo Smit, and Kabalevsky, and featuring the first performance of Alexander Mosolov's exchange composition, his Sextet on American Folk Themes. The society never had the opportunity to schedule either Quincy Porter's or Burrill Phillips's works on Soviet themes. The Phillips premiere took place at the Eastman School of Music, where he taught, the following May.

When Blitzstein left Upper Jay, he visited Jo for two weeks. At that point he was far behind on the *Little Foxes* opera, and the commitment to Harper's weighed on him as well. With reluctance, he wrote from Philadelphia declining Douglas Moore's offer of a Ditson Foundation grant to write a new opera. He could not see past his current projects and did not wish in the meantime to deprive another deserving composer of the opportunity.

Performances of Blitzstein's music that season began with Ray Lev, a superb pianist and a left-wing sympathizer, playing music from the unproduced ballet *Show* at her Carnegie Hall concert November 7, 1947. Later that month, more Blitzstein music, on a grander scale, made a greater impact. The Fifty-fifth Street City Center sponsored both the New York City Opera and the New York City Symphony, the latter with Leonard Bernstein as its unpaid conductor. It was operated by New York City's former License Commissioner, Paul Moss, the man who had tried to stop the production of *No for an Answer* in this very house. City Center announced in October a further collaboration between Bernstein and Blitzstein: a concert revival, indeed the world premiere of the orchestral version of *The Cradle Will Rock,* at the final performances of the Symphony's season, November 24 and 25. Bernstein used a reduced orchestra of under thirty players. The production honored the twenty-fifth anniversary of the League of Composers.

Shirley Bernstein, Leonard's sister and the Moll of his 1939 Harvard production, served as casting director. For the Moll, she suggested her roommate that year, Estelle Loring, a bright political science major from Cornell who had already worked in radio and sung in a few Broadway choruses. Howard da Silva came East from California to perform the role of Larry Foreman once again and to direct the minimal staging. As Mr. Mister, Will Geer came from the original cast as well. Among the most notable names in this revival were Jack Albertson and Chandler Cowles as Yasha and Dauber, David Thomas as the Druggist, Jo Hurt as Sister Mister, Walter Scheff from the *Airborne* Symphony as Gus, and in a stroke of brilliant casting, Shirley Booth as Mrs. Mister. It fit well Bernstein's recent plea for more opportunities for blacks in music to ask Muriel Smith to sing Ella Hammer's "Joe Worker" song. Press photographs featured her with da Silva and Bernstein.[14] In addition, Bill's brother Edmund Hewitt, who aspired to an acting career, played Professor Mamie.

In advance of the performances, Blitzstein wrote a capsule history of the opera for the *Herald Tribune,* recalling the government's ban "for reasons involving Outspoken Art and Skittish and Timorous Life." And he remembered Bernstein's Harvard version: "I saw him do my part much better than I had ever done." Blitzstein chose not to change the text by so much as a word, just to see whether in this era of Taft-Hartley and HUAC the piece still had any relevance:

> It will be, therefore, a "period piece," without those last-minute emendations or up-to-datenesses which would make it true of neither then nor now. It is a grim and rather bitter thing to reflect that, doing a "period piece," you discover you are still in the middle of the period.[15]

Apropos, Marx had once suggested that history repeats itself, the first time as tragedy, the second time as farce.

"The house was packed and the audience went wild," wrote Olin Downes in the *Times:*

> *The Cradle Will Rock,* so presented, has qualities of genius. . . . [It] does all the things that it should not do and emerges from the crucible as triumphant art. . . . It catches fire, it blazes, it amuses, moves and grips the listener, until with the really masterly, if unconventional structure of the finale—the screaming trumpets in the orchestra, drumbeats, the sounds of fifes and of voices chorusing from far and near—the listener wants to beat his palms and shout as the curtain falls.
>
> Regardless of theory, point of view or propaganda, it strikes home over the footlights. . . .
>
> It was Shirley Booth, "Mrs. Mister," who brought down the house, as well she might, with her simperings, her insufferable affectations, her art of diction and her rhythm in song and in movement.[16]

For Virgil Thomson, *Cradle* remained

> ten years after its first New York success, one of the most charming creations of the American musical theater. It has sweetness, a cutting wit, inexhaustible fancy and faith. One would have to be wholly untouched

> and untouchable (and who is?) by the humanity and the aspirations of union labor to resist it. Last night's audience could not.[17]

Miles Kastendieck said in the *Journal-American* that *Cradle* "stands up as a real biting satire. . . . It is probably the real thing in American opera taking its first steps." Kolodin in the *Sun* wrote, "It remains a strongly original piece of theater music, for which Broadway has no equivalent now."[18]

One notice that truly struck a timely chord appeared in *Musical America. Cradle*

> still has the effect of a pistol shot in gripping people's emotions and making them think because they have been challenged. . . .
>
> Curiously enough, this piece of frank propaganda is also a first-rate work of art—certainly one of the best if not the best of the musical dramas produced in the United States thus far.
>
> In a time when popular sentiment is swinging to the right, the voices of the left should also be clearly heard; that is what makes a healthy democracy.[19]

Not every reviewer chimed in with praise. John Briggs in the *Post,* for instance, called the show "gauche and inept . . . a political essay set to music"; and Cecil Smith in the *New Republic* saw it as "on the whole crude in style and shallow in psychological insight." "The conflict of forces in 1947," he added, concerning the datedness of the vehicle, "has become too grave and too complex to fit into Blitzstein's neatly contrived antithesis."[20]

Perhaps the unique qualities Blitzstein had brought to the piece as its piano accompanist had been lost—some early fans of the piece swore that as a one-man show *Cradle* achieved its highest expression. But those who took note of the "new" orchestral version appreciated the added tone colors, the variety of expression, and the heightening of effects in sound.

"*The Cradle* was a landslide," Blitzstein wrote to the Baumans in Cleveland. "It means a renascence of the whole progressive cultural movement here, I'm told; political cabaret, theatre-groups, etc. It seems we don't pass out so easily."[21]

Adding to the satisfying success of *Cradle,* the Vancouver Symphony Orchestra performed the *Airborne* Symphony on Sunday, November 30, the first Canadian and the first Pacific Coast performance. Jacques Singer conducted, with Juan Root as the Monitor, Karl Norman, tenor, Derek MacDermot, bass-baritone, and the University of British Columbia chorus. The piece was so well received that to meet the large demand for tickets, a second performance had to be scheduled three nights later. Still, the *Airborne* had never really taken off the way Blitzstein had hoped it might in its early stages of composition, and again after its premiere. The release of the recording, given immense publicity in newspapers all over the nation, did nothing to stimulate performances. Where were the democratic choruses to sing it, the right-minded conductors to program it? Where were the audiences across the country clamoring to hear it? Where was the demand for a "people's composer"?

Joan Kahn of Harper's congratulated Blitzstein on the success of *Cradle* in a brief letter that also served as a not so subtle request to see some draft material of his book. Blitzstein wrote back immediately. In his haste, he unconsciously inverted his pronouns, suggesting a mental distancing from the task at hand: "I have masses of notes for the book—the last few days have not cut down on the verbiage. You'll get some kind of ordered script to you soon. In the meantime, bear with me." A month later, he wrote to her again: "Whatever you may think, there *will* be a book from me, although I can't say exactly when."[22]

Perhaps it was John Ball's *Cradle* review in the Brooklyn *Eagle* that prompted the next step: Nothing lacked in this performance except scenery, he said, "to put this opus on the boards."[23] Half a dozen producers asking for the Broadway rights approached Blitzstein after the City Center performances. But the New Theatre, which had originally handled the property ten years before, already planned a late-December revival, to be directed by Alfred Saxe, with sets by Ralph Alswang. Hoping for a more professional production, the composer settled on Michael Myerberg, owner of the Mansfield Theatre, who agreed to co-produce it with the New Theatre. According to Blitzstein's contract, he would receive 6 percent of the gross weekly box office, and 10 percent if the box office exceeded $14,500, plus a royalty of 12½ percent of net profits, a flat payment of one thousand dollars, and a percentage of subsidiary rights. As neither da Silva nor Shirley Booth was free for a long engagement, Myerberg promptly hired Alfred Drake, famous for creating the part of Curly in *Oklahoma!*—for the Larry Foreman role at five hundred dollars a week, Vivian Vance for Mrs. Mister at two hundred and fifty dollars, and made a small number of other cast substitutions. Dennis King, Jr., played Junior Mister at one hundred dollars a week. Will Geer, at three hundred dollars a week, was the only holdover from 1937. Musicians received $138 a week.[24]

Bernstein planned to conduct the first three performances of the revived *Cradle* for a fee of fifteen hundred dollars, then turn the job over to another conductor. By this time, Hugo Weisgall was back in the United States after his Czech sojourn and desperately needed to find work. Of course, he had once heard Blitzstein name Bernstein "the greatest talent that ever lived," and he must have wondered whether he could dare to step into those shoes. But Weisgall buried his doubts and asked Marc if he could conduct after Bernstein.

"I'd love to have you, but you'd have to ask Lenny," Blitzstein answered.

When Weisgall went to Bernstein, Lenny said, "I'd love to have you, but you'd have to ask Marc."

Weisgall concluded it was their way of saying no. "I didn't know if I was Blitzed or Berned," he told his friends.

Amid a flurry of protests against the government's attempt to deport the German émigré composer Hanns Eisler, the show opened at the Mansfield Theatre on Friday, the night after Christmas, for a limited run of five weeks and two days. All that day snow came down heavily. Before it stopped, New York had been smothered by a record twenty-six-inch snowfall—the worst snowstorm in the city's history. Streets were unpassable. As they climbed over waist-high drifts in the eerie silence on their way to the theatre, the actors expected that they might be playing to a house of a dozen people. But the subways continued to run, hurtling to the theatre a well-dressed crowd that ordinarily did not travel by such plebeian means. Miraculously, the cast found a full house, eager to savor the same delightful escapade they had loved a decade before—and now many of them had brought their children as well. Bernstein received the composer's only slightly garbled telegram: IN SPITE OF GLITZSTEINS BLIZZARD MY UNDYING THANKS HIT IT BOY LOVE MARC.

At the conclusion, the audience screamed with love for the work and the performance. In those times, and against such uncooperative weather, the revival was clearly a victory.

The theatre critics for the most part wrote glowingly about the production. According to Brooks Atkinson, Will Geer was "tall, unctuously villainous in a good old-fashioned medicine-man style"; Estelle Loring sang "with a kind of meditative rapture"; Alfred Drake performed with "enormous gusto"; and Muriel Smith was "nothing short of exalting." "When you hear it with the full musical score rather than the original single piano," George Freedley wrote in the New York *Telegraph,* "you have a chance to realize just how important a composer for the theater is Mr. Blitzstein."[25]

Dissenters included *Daily Variety,* which observed that *Cradle*'s appeal was by now "limited to special groups, particularly the left politically. Blitzstein better watch out for super-snooper [HUAC's J. Parnell] Thomas." And the *Wall Street Journal* questioned why anyone should want to revive the work at all, "now that most of Mr. Blitzstein's objectives have been achieved." John Chapman in the *News* blistered red with anger, or anti-red in his case: "If it can get mad I can, too—and it burns me up. To me it is loud, cheap, unfair and pinko; it is a soap-box opera." The conservative George Jean Nathan cared for the work no more now than he had a decade before: a "cantankerous blitz set to indifferent music and offered to popgun intellects as a revolutionary cannon ball."[26]

But in wide areas of the city, Saturday's newspapers did not get distributed because of the snow; and many who might have gone out to buy the paper simply stayed at home to shovel themselves out. As a courtesy, some newspapers reprinted their reviews the next day, but the weather had done its damage.

One reviewer bemoaned the current state of the theatre, citing the reality that no one was writing or producing a show around the incredible talent of Muriel Smith. Estelle Loring as the Moll also received good notices; within days of her appearance, so many agents were calling her that she hardly knew with whom to sign up. But no one was calling Muriel Smith. The two women shared a dressing room, and the night that article appeared, Loring arrived a bit early. She poked her head into the room and found Muriel Smith sitting dazed, stunned into a kind of speechless anguish, staring into the black face in the mirror, the newspaper propped open in front of her. For a white woman the agents flocked. For a black woman, where were they? Where were the parts? What kind of country was this?

On December 28, Alfred Drake had to meet a previous commitment on the radio, so he arrived late for *Cradle.* As an audience warm-up Bernstein, conducting his last night before Howard Shanet took over, played a jazz piano arrangement of "The Honky Tonk Train Blues"; Blitzstein accompanied Muriel Smith in four of his theatre songs; and Gil Huston played several numbers with guitar. From that night on, the producers decided that an extra fifty-minute lagniappe might help attract theatregoers, and so each week they programmed new musical offerings. One olio was José Limón and his dance company in the "Lament for Ignacio Sánchez Mejías," choreographed by Doris Humphrey.

Among the audiences at the Mansfield, Blitzstein proudly received the conductor Ernest Ansermet one night. Completely won over by the show, he talked excitedly about getting a European production under way. A week later he reappeared, explaining that since he knew how enjoyable this show would be, why see anything else? Another night, Paul Robeson turned up, and the cast hailed him backstage as a hero. The conductor Howard Shanet's mother also came, remarking that Blitzstein was like a mezuzah—everyone who went backstage after the performance would kiss him as he stood at the door.

But audiences weren't coming, whether because of the unfavorable reviews they had seen or because the left had already lost so much ground. Only two or three houses could be sold to such organizations as the Anti-Fascist Refugee Committee and the American Labor Party clubs. After twenty-one performances, *Cradle* closed, costing Myerberg close to ten thousand dollars.

Convinced that attendance was principally the fault of the snowstorm and the undelivered newspapers, producer David Lowe hoped for a new round of reviews by reopening the show with the same cast at the nineteen-hundred-seat Broadway Theatre on Wednesday, January 28, 1948; it was still conducted by Howard Shanet. But it wasn't the snowstorm. Even at a modest $4.80 top price, *Cradle* had ceased rocking. The new production lasted only thirteen performances, closing February 7. If it had played in a smaller house, perhaps with a reduced orchestration to save money, *Cradle* might have lasted long enough to overcome the initial snowstorm problem. In a wistful summing up, Harold Clurman called the revival of *The Cradle Will Rock* "labor's only victory in many months."[27]

On the left, of course, the work received its due share of encomiums. The *Cradle* revival and the first hootenanny at Carnegie Hall, sponsored by People's Songs, were hopeful "signs of the cultural spring that will follow the present winter. May it come soon!" prayed *New Masses.* "The class struggle theme looms up as even more true of American life today; for 'Mr. Mister' one needs only to read 'NAM' [National Association of Manufacturers]." O. V. Clyde, writing for the *Daily Worker,* repeated the idea of the timeliness of the themes. "In fact, they are truer in the era of the Marshall Plan deceits as will become evident in the days to come."

But now both reviewers sounded a new note, a tone that suggested some of the old musical philistinism of the Degeyter Club members in the 1930s, those almost illiterate songwriters who reached for the handiest folk tune around. They also began to reflect some of the resuscitated musical conservatism in the Soviet Union, where the bureaucrat Andrei Zhdanov had already launched his campaign against "formalism." For official Soviet culture in the late Stalin years, and for American Communist taste, music of the people—dressed-up folk music—was the order of the day:

> I do not say that Blitzstein's creative audacity has at all times hit the mark. To the captious critic sitting on the sidelines it might appear that there could be a greater working of the native American musical idiom existing in blues traditions of the unknown Negro particularly. The musical style he uses, while highly effective, has something of a cosmopolitan air about it. But these notions are purely personal on my part and may be impudent in face of the undeniable effect of the score as we heard it.[28]

Restating the point a little differently but hinting at the same tentative changes in the political-musical wind, the unsigned *New Masses* review read:

> Analyzing the musical language one finds little in it of the great American folk and people's music, the sweet mountain songs, the poignant blues and exuberant jazz improvisations. Its starting point is the tawdriest of Tin Pan Alley music; the crooner sentimentality, the torch song, the pseudo-swing, even the German cabaret version of an American cabaret jazz. Yet Blitzstein turns them all into pure gold, through knowing exactly what he wants to do and having the modern composer's knowledge.[29]

Such reviews in the American Communist press hardly carried the same weight as Comrade Zhdanov's pronouncements. An artist of Blitzstein's stature enjoyed far more freedom to create in his own style than the average Party member could dream of, and the Communists were proud that he counted himself among them, especially in these times of immense professional risk. But Blitzstein felt the chastising hand of the Party. They could not come down on him too severely for fear of alienating his loyalty; so these gentle but firm words had to serve as comradely guidance toward a preferable new direction. The Party was reacting to popular fears and government claims that American Communists were nothing but pawns of Soviet policy. Their espousal of folk music formed a part of the attempt to show the Party's all-American roots and support, with the South's Leadbelly, the Dust Bowl's Woody Guthrie, and the Kentucky miner balladeers as their chief representatives. But Blitzstein had never liked the idea of "lifting" the folk idiom to any higher place, and he was not about to change his views now. He had nothing against folk music as such, but he recognized it as a vestigial cultural form. The true popular music of this country that he wanted to "lift," the music of the masses, was commercial music. In time, Blitzstein would grow impatient with the guidance.

In this context it is worth noting, however, that Blitzstein did contribute one piano arrangement to *The People's Song Book*—the Kentucky mountain song, "On Top of Old Smoky." Off-center and simply but expertly devised, it makes prominent use of the subdominant fourth chord.

Now courting's a pleasure, but parting is grief,
And a false-hearted lover is worse than a thief.
For a thief will just rob you, and take what you have,
But a false-hearted lover will lead you to the grave.[30]

Shortly following the City Center *Cradle,* on December 12, Muriel Smith gave her first Town Hall recital; she included both "Mamasha Goose" from *Goloopchik* and the "Orpheus Song" from *Julius Caesar.* Only twenty-four years old now, she had made a smashing success during the war in the title role of Oscar Hammerstein and Billy Rose's adaptation of Bizet, the all-black *Carmen Jones.* She also had studied at the Curtis Institute of Music, where the famous German soprano Elisabeth Schumann was her teacher, and where her classmates included both Bernstein and Ned Rorem. Though she had numbed her audiences with the "Joe Worker" song, she was not in any sense a politically minded performer. She liked Marc, however, and her voice perfectly suited his music.

One day before the end of the year, she and Marc went into the recording studio of Dr. Henry Swoboda's Concert Hall Society, a small company that put out esoteric records, and put onto disk five of his theatre songs: "Orpheus"; "In the Clear," Clara's aria from *No for an Answer,* which Olive Deering had not recorded on the original cast album; "Ode to Reason" from *Danton's Death;* and from *Goloopchik,* the war refugee song "Displaced" and "Mamasha Goose." For the "Ode to Reason" and "Orpheus," Blitzstein played a "prepared" piano made to sound like an early keyboard instrument. The ten-inch recording in the new long-playing format showed off the singer's brilliant artistry, though a minuscule edition kept the record from achieving anything near the circulation it deserved. Blitzstein in general was lucky with the quality of his recordings, but this one is a particular gem displaying what a rare voice was Muriel Smith's.*

Concert Hall Society recorded more Blitzstein at this time. In a set entitled "American Composers at the Piano," Swoboda included Blitzstein playing two numbers from the ballet *Show*—"Variation Three" and "Three-Four Dance and Finale." The first is an easy-paced rumination of a mostly dark cast, the second a sometimes raucous evocation of twenties barrelhouse jazz, which in the finale comes back to the delicate chiaroscuro of the first piece.

Blitzstein's Cleveland concert, sponsored by the Progressive Citizens of America, took place on Sunday, January 18, 1948, at Severance Hall. He stayed with Mordy and Irma Bauman for the two or three days it took to put the program in final shape. As both performer and promoter, Bauman had assembled a male chorus of thirty-plus members to sing in the Captain Bristlepunkt scene from

*Accompanying program notes giving the complete lyrics to the songs indicate that Concert Hall Society may not actually have released this record until 1950.

I've Got the Tune and excerpts from the *Airborne* Symphony. Muriel Smith sang all of the songs from her Blitzstein album and two songs from *The Cradle Will Rock,* plus a Blitzstein arrangement of a "Dublin Street Song," which appears not to have survived. In addition, she joined Bauman in the Joe and Francie scene from *No for an Answer.* Bauman added "Penny Candy" from the same opera, and other Cleveland singers did two more scenes from *Cradle.* Blitzstein himself came on to round out the program with a piano suite of four selections from *Show.* It was a sign partly of the minimal extent to which Blitzstein's name was known outside of New York, and partly of the political retrenchment of the time: Financially, the concert resulted in a substantial loss to the sponsoring organization.

In late February, Bernstein, Copland, Diamond, and others sponsored a farewell concert at Town Hall honoring Hanns Eisler. Author of a remarkable book funded by the Rockefeller Foundation and published the year before, *Composing for the Films,* Eisler had not escaped questioning by HUAC witch-hunters. He protested that his mass songs of the twenties and thirties were forgettable ditties. Such were the travails of those who came to be known as "premature antifascists." Eisler soon afterward left the country for Vienna, but he found musical society closed to him there. At Brecht's urging, he returned to Berlin, where he became the acknowledged dean of composers in the German Democratic Republic when it was established the following year. His brother Gerhart, also a refugee in the United States, was sentenced in March to a one-to-three-year prison term for his Communist politics, but he fled the country instead. Performers responded to new HUAC attacks with meetings organized by the Stop Censorship Committee and an "Un-American Hootenanny" led by Pete Seeger and Laura Duncan.

In March, Bernstein resigned as conductor of the New York City Symphony in protest against budget cuts for the forthcoming season. He had served without pay all along, and in his enthusiasm for the best contemporary and standard works had created an ensemble far more adventurous and invigorating than the stodgy Philharmonic. His performances of *Cradle* the previous November turned out to have been his last concerts with the New York City Symphony.

16

THE PARTY'S OVER

Spring 1948–December 1949

"Red but not dictated."

Right after May Day 1948, the press exploded with a typical Cold War-era furor over the loyalty question. According to an inflammatory United Press dispatch from Moscow, an open letter from thirty-two American writers, painters, and composers had appeared in the *Literaturnaya Gazeta,* which seemed to say that the signers aligned themselves with the Soviet Union against the current U.S. leadership and policies. Prominent among the names were numerous Communists and others closely linked to Communist Party positions: Howard Fast, Alvah Bessie (of the Hollywood Ten), the Party's cultural leader V. J. Jerome, artists Raphael Soyer and Philip Evergood, the music writer Sidney Finkelstein, pianist Ray Lev, and Marc Blitzstein.

The New York Times, as well as other newspapers around the country, carried the dispatch on page one, while *PM* printed it just below a photo of heavy tanks moving through Red Square on May Day. The *Daily News* named all the names in its editorial, graced with accompanying pictures of both Fast and Blitzstein:

> These birds were touted in the Moscow paper as big-shot American intellectuals, leaders of U.S. thought, and so on. The fact is that only a handful of Americans have ever heard of most of them. . . .

> Marc Blitzstein a few years ago wrote a little musical comedy on some labor theme, which made a fair amount of money. . . .
> These 32 alleged artists are against their own country in its current differences with Soviet Russia. Where do you suppose they would line up in case the "cold war" turned hot?[1]

It was the Moscow dateline that made the story more than anything else, for the artists' statement had appeared with no fanfare in the previous month's issue of *Masses and Mainstream,* the Party's widely available literary and cultural organ, which none of the American newspaper editors had bothered to read or to compare with the United Press distortions. Neither had the right-wingers who attacked the signers in Congress. The original open letter had said nothing about taking sides against America. The Moscow journal published it with no additional editorial comment, and certainly not with any claim that the artists had sided with the Soviet Union. The letter stood for peace in a world of atomic brinkmanship, against such American policies as arming the fascist governments of Greece and Spain, Chiang Kai-shek's China, and the oil-rich Arab feudal lords against the Jews in Palestine. It reassured the Soviets that at least this group of American artists was prepared to declare themselves against any further suppression of the freedom of thought and expression in America. By contrast, the signers believed it a higher form of patriotism to oppose reaction and war incitement. "Loving our country," they had said, "we will help show our awakening people the true nature and source of their terrible peril."

The *Times* and only a handful of other newspapers printed a response from *Masses and Mainstream* or any of the artists; in any case, it would have been nearly impossible to ascertain all those media that had picked up the U.P. story or published editorials about it. In the sordid atmosphere of blindly anti-Soviet America, the press had played out another scene in its crude global morality drama, unremorsefully leaving in its wake that much further damage to the careers of thirty-two creative artists. "I am waiting for repercussions," Blitzstein wrote to Mina Curtiss about the affair; "maybe yes, maybe no. I feel personally secure inside, and never more the really patriotic American. And I have no taste for martyrdom."[2]

Few Communist Jews got animated by the idea of Israel as a state, though the Soviet Union had sponsored its creation and was the first nation to recognize it. Most of them felt it would become exclusionary and highly nationalistic, placing ethnicity above class in the Marxist pecking order of priorities. Blitzstein rarely thought about his Jewishness and took no pains to explore Jewish themes in his work. He knew almost nothing of Jewish history and had never read the Bible, though occasionally Bill would read passages aloud to him just to savor the language of the King James Version.

On the day in May 1948 that Israel became an independent state, Bernstein conducted. After the performance, he drove Marc and the critic Paul Moor downtown. He dropped Marc off first, but before Bernstein pulled away from the curb, Marc poked his head back in the window, waving his finger at Lenny. "And remember," he said, "the Jews have a homeland!" For Bernstein, who had conducted the Palestine Philharmonic under most trying circumstances and had helped to shape it into a creditable ensemble, Israel needed no embarrassed apology. For Blitzstein, the remark signaled recognition of his friend's loyalties, and a kind of sardonic amusement at himself that in some way he should partake of any nationalistic feeling. In essence, however, Blitzstein sat this one out: Time would tell what Israel would become.

Neither religion nor nationalism satisfied Blitzstein's own sense of purpose. After World War I, the Dada movement mockingly reflected the illogic and cruel stupidity of the real world. Similarly in the postwar era of the late 1940s, art seemed more and more to be dominated by alienating, dehumanized, escapist forms—or *formalism,* the term the committed left used to disparage such an outlook. The new psychological art emphasized neurotic obsession with murder, drink, sex, and horror. Pessimistic, despairing, and cynical at bottom, the new movies and plays rarely even offered a wholesome anger. In painting, the Abstract Expressionists emerged: Those who still practiced representational, figurative art were hopelessly passé. In literature and philosophy, existentialism questioned every belief system with a moral relativism that shrank away from direct action. And in music, the Schoenberg faction of serial music had won over nearly completely. Academics ruled the esthetic world. Could there be a future for art created not to enhance life but to display method, mere technique?

Blitzstein continued sure in his own principles, even though he saw the tide of fashion turning against him. In this sense, his allegiance to the Communist Party coincided with his commitment to—commitment. As he wrote in response to William Saroyan in a letter to *The New York Times,* the composition of his very committed opera *Regina* largely behind him by now: People are "hungry for some, *any,* standard. . . . 'Meaninglessness of life' is not the absence of a point of view—it is a very immoral actual point of view—immoral because it is dedicated to death, decadence, fruitlessness, and in the deepest sense, misery."[3]

In the same period, he signed *New York Times* and *Daily Worker* ads for Henry Wallace's Presidential campaign on the Progressive Party ticket, attended dinners, and contributed material for a cabaret production called *Show Time for Wallace.* He registered to vote with the pro-Communist American Labor Party. But largely he stayed aloof from much active politicking. He had written to Mina Curtiss about Wallace, "If only, in this stinking moment of history, he can be surrounded by enough strength and wisdom, the world may yet not be lost."[4]

Somehow, in a discussion with Paul Moor about the endless forms of escapism, the subject of psychiatry came up. Skeptical, if not hostile toward too much "navel-contemplation," Blitzstein quipped, "An asshole a day keeps the psychiatrist away." He felt, in other words, that the release of tension in sex, a healthy balance of the physical with the mental, a frank acknowledgment of the body's drives, all this could keep a person feeling balanced, not the systematic examination of one's psyche. The Party would have approved of his doubts about psychiatry—they opposed it, among other reasons, for fear that members might leak out sensitive information—though Party doctrine, needless to say, would not have liked Blitzstein's personal alternative.

Blitzstein's ideological avoidance of psychiatry set him distinctly apart from his theatre and music crowd, however, in an era when psychoanalysis had practically become the new religion. Of course, he never had a lot of money, and psychotherapy was costly. But in reality, he might well have benefited from some focused, guided introspection. If the goals of psychiatry are principally to allow the subject to work and to love, making full potential of his intellectual and emotional resources, it might have provided some insight into Blitzstein's perennial problems. Why did it take him so long to complete his major operas? Why did he find it so painful to find a more experienced writer with whom to collaborate? Why could he so rarely form intimate attachments to others? Why were the men to whom he was attracted always unavailable to him in some way? Why did he court danger in the wrong bars, the wrong parks, with the wrong men? Why did he enjoy the role of pauper in his relations to others, mostly women with money? He may have believed that in not subjecting himself to the analyst's couch, he was escaping escapism; but on his own, he never could escape the consequences of his established, and not always productive, patterns.

According to Blitzstein's file at the Veterans Administration, obtained in 1949 by the FBI, he had in fact "been treated for a psychoneurotic condition" in March 1947, though it is unlikely that he could have stayed in treatment for very long. VA doctors made the following clinical assessment:

> A rather detached withdrawn individual with marked depressive features, some of which are relative in character to present and real difficulties, the majority of which, however, are the inevitable outcomes of very severe psycho-neurotic disturbances. He has blocking in his creativeness, marked inhibitions in his inner personal contacts with some suicidal preoccupation.[5]

Bill and his girlfriend Lu Bowles continued their relationship, unopposed by Marc. For some time, actually, Bill had not lived in Marc's apartment at all: Each needed the space apart. At one period, Marc's nephew Kit came to New York to study at the Art Students League, and Bill shared a room with him in the West Seventies. Later on, Bill took a room on West 118th Street, a block away from Lu's apartment. Once Marc visited him there. They went out for drinks and Marc began flirting with three marines in uniform. Bill didn't like their looks or the way Marc was making himself vulnerable. Hoping to avoid trouble, he said, "Marc, let's get out of here." But Marc stayed. Bill left, ran some errands for half an hour or so, then headed back to his room. He did not know that Marc had left the bar, returned to 118th Street himself, and that the marines, having followed him, were now lurking in wait. Before Bill could enter his building, they pounced on him, gave him a few sound whacks that left him bloody and limping, and took off.

Lu finished her studies and landed a position teaching modern dance and physical culture at Madison College, a Christian women's school in Harrisonburg, Virginia. For most of the next year or two, Bill commuted regularly to see her, returning to New York for a week or two at a time for important openings. But in time, the pull of New York and its endless distractions lessened. Perhaps in the relative tranquillity of the Shenandoah Valley, he would be able to complete some of his manuscripts.

After Bill married Lu, Marc chose for the most part to stay out of the way. He dropped an occasional note encouraging Bill's writing. Bill would see Marc from time to time when he passed through New York. Both of them saw, however, that no point would be served by trying to keep alive a relationship that had at times been extremely close, but—as with Eva—ultimately untenable. In so many ways, Bill had been supremely attractive for Marc: young, handsome, masculine, daring, handy, intelligent, politically savvy—but basically he was straight. If Marc needed to have the people he loved nurse him emotionally, he somehow wound up with people such as Eva and Bill who needed nursing more than he did.

"I have that dratted book still to do," Marc wrote to Bill in Harrisonburg on October 15, 1948, "and perhaps I shall make an orchestra-suite out of that Ballet I wrote with Jerry Robbins, in the hope of getting a stage production later."[6] Discussions along these lines with Lincoln Kirstein, general director of the recently inaugurated New York City Ballet, led to Kirstein's commissioning just such a work, for a five-hundred-dollar fee plus twenty-five dollars for each public performance, which Robbins would choreograph. Kirstein scheduled the first performance of *The Guests* very quickly: January 20.

As with *Freedom Morning,* Blitzstein's twenty-minute score to *The Guests*—essentially the music of the unproduced *Show*—reveals a vital influence from Copland's Piano Concerto in its happy, rhythmic bounce. Governed by a populist sensibility, it is full of tuneful episodes and soulful adagios, unfolded organically in graceful, light textures. One thinks of Prokofiev's *Romeo and Juliet* score for comparison. Blitzstein dedicated it to Kirstein. With only a matter of weeks before the premiere, Blitzstein called in Henry Brant to orchestrate the ballet. Brant had served Blitzstein before in this capacity, and many other composers as well, but as he did not seek to establish his reputation as an orchestrator—as Robert Russell Bennett or Hershy Kay did—he claimed no credit for *The Guests.*

The scenario Blitzstein and Robbins devised for this new version of *Show* did away with all vocal accompaniment. They divided the dancers into two groups, one of ten, and the other of six. A host invites them to begin the dancing. The larger group all bear a special caste mark on their foreheads, indicating that they are socially superior, whether for reasons of race, class, or creed. The dancing begins. Then the host distributes masks, which cover the caste marks. One boy and one girl dance together in the central, exquisite pas de deux. But at the end of the dance when all the masks are removed, the tender couple turns out to be mixed—the girl with the mark of favor, the boy without. Both groups reject the pair. They furtively retreat, but it is not even clear whether they slink off apart into loneliness or stay together to face the cold world.

In his choreography, Robbins exploited the freedom of movement for which he had become recognized, expressing the lovers' first tentative, almost instinctive moments of touching, feeling, and finding one another. This evolves into a gloriously emotional, sensuous pas de deux in which the female partner is in the air much of the time. The power of sexual attraction is elevated into romance, and further into knowledge of discrimination and social barriers.

The treatment is a protest, albeit subdued, against prejudice. At the same time, it is another case—in a city where police arrested hundreds of homosexuals every year just for patronizing a bar or "disturbing the peace" by dancing together, and in a society that gave open homosexuals little freedom of action—where two gay artists may well have sublimated their own cries for justice into a slightly more acceptable Romeo and Juliet theme. That at least could be articulated publicly.

Francisco Monción from Santo Domingo played the role of the haughty host. Maria Tallchief, of American Indian background, and Nicholas Magallanes played the mixed couple. Jean Rosenthal, from Blitzstein's old Mercury Theatre days, designed the lighting, and Leon Barzin conducted the orchestra. Robbins recalled that George Balanchine frequently stopped in to watch rehearsals; at one of them, knowing that Robbins would need a set of masks, he personally went out to purchase them.

Walter Terry, the *Herald Tribune*'s dance critic, found the ballet "absorbing," pointing to "new directions for classic dance," though overall not a great work. The two principals, however, were "splendid in every way, technically, stylistically and dramatically." As for the music, Blitzstein was "right at home in the medium. . . . The music is eminently kinetic." Harriett Johnson in the New York *Post* cared less for the choreographic component than for Blitzstein's music. The composer, who had used "ingenious and vital movement and a provocative harmonic background, achieves a consistent vigor and dramatic poignancy . . . which the choreographer does not." Robert Sylvester spoke of "haunting" and "lovely" music in his *Daily News* review. But "When Blitzstein resolutely turns from melody, as he always insists on doing, he can turn out some of the strangest boiler factory sounds this side of bebop."[7]

Henry Cowell's review of the current New York scene in *The Musical Quarterly* carried a somewhat self-contradictory assessment of Blitzstein's ballet score. He felt that in his use of sweet popular music styles, Blitzstein had surrendered to the original saccharine model, though "the popular element is served for the most part with a wonderfully acrid dressing, and to hear it was a pleasure and surprise." His "harmonies sound both wicked and zestful," Cowell wrote. "The music is pungent, suited to the ballet purpose."[8]

"The ballet was fine from my point of view," Marc wrote to Mina Curtiss—Kirstein's sister. "I mean I think I did a good, direct, even beautiful job on the music." But he continued more questioningly about the choreographer's work:

> Jerry Robbins' visual plan was fine, but cloudy, not direct, and not *structural;* he muffed the climax, through prudish avoidance or his own "immaturity" (a totally inadequate word), and concentrated on the *pas de deux,* a truly grand conception and execution. But a *pas de deux* isn't enough, you will grant; it was the crown of a work not sufficiently garbed, like the Emperor's new clothes which didn't exist. I have of course that inestimable "out" granted a composer; a concert suite which I am making of the ballet.[9]

Cheryl Crawford, the producer, had been a founder and director of the Group Theatre in the early 1930s, and had already put on such shows as *Brigadoon, Porgy and Bess,* Kurt Weill's *One Touch of Venus* and *Love Life,* and Hellman's *The Little Foxes* and *Watch on the Rhine.* She was accustomed to taking risks on material her instinct trusted—for which the theatre owes her an incalculable debt. As she wrote in a letter to a friend, defending her adoption of Blitzstein's *Regina* and sketching a kind of artistic credo for herself:

> If I want to stay in the theatre, I have to firmly believe that a sense of truth, coupled with theatrical talent, has an audience, a big one! If you tingle with a sudden awareness of things you only dimly felt before, of evil, of compassion, so that you know more about life after such an experience, that is all I ask.
>
> I'm going to see to it that the audience sitting before *Regina* has an emotional experience they won't forget. That is theatre. That's why I'm in it. Gags and sugarstick romance have a place in a public's entertainment, but I'd like to give them something richer, truer, deeper.
>
> As a play, this must have had a considerable catharsis for an audience or it wouldn't have run so long. I think the music adds bigger values—more emotion, more passion, more tenderness.[10]

At one of the dozens of backers' auditions she hosted in the early months of 1949 where Blitzstein belted through his arias to raise the necessary $140,000 production costs, Clinton Wilder happened to be present. Obviously impressed, he contributed $5,600 toward this somewhat unlikely moneymaker, and Crawford made him her associate producer. Other backers included Dwight Deere Wiman and the owner and operator of the Forty-sixth Street Theatre, Robert W. Dowling and Louis Lotito. The largest investor, at $25,500, was Edward E. Otis. Only as late as August of 1949, less than two months before the first tryouts in New Haven, did the producers announce the final decision on the name of their property: The *Little Foxes* musical would be known as *Regina.*

Robert (Bobby) Lewis, a prominent director who had been part of the Group Theatre in the thirties, had already agreed to direct. For the sets, Crawford engaged Horace Armistead, who designed a revolving stage whereby the angle of vision, and the psychological emphasis, could be changed. For the sumptuous costuming, she recruited the veteran designer Aline Bernstein. To choreograph the ballroom scene, Chinkypin's quick-stepping jig, and assist with general movement, she brought in the well-known dancer of recognized progressive leanings, Anna Sokolow.

Lillian Hellman gave Blitzstein detailed comments on his script. As someone with little understanding of music, or of its use in the theatre, she entertained her doubts all along about this project. But she had given her permission, and indeed saw Blitzstein's attempt at making a great American opera out of her play as a profoundly touching tribute from one artist to another. "It is a job of true stature and true bigness," she wrote to him. "I am grateful for it beyond the words I have to tell you. . . . Please be happy and very proud of yourself."[11]

Blitzstein spent March and part of April of 1949 at Jo's in Philadelphia, avoiding phone calls so he could finish writing *Regina.* Curiously, it took him until then to compose the "Rain Quartet," which became the most memorable scene in the show, partly because of its stunning vocal evocation of the weather, but perhaps also because it contains Horace's credo:

Consider the rain,
The falling of friendly rain—
That serves the earth, then
Moves on again.
Consider the rain.
Some people eat all the earth.
Some stand around and watch while they eat.
And watch while they eat the earth.
Now rain—consider the rain.

As he worked, a favorite wordless tune by Leonard Bernstein kept playing havoc with his brain, until one day the lyrics came to him. He wrote them to Shirley, who passed them on to her brother:

There goes what's-his-name.
Unhappy what's-his-name.
I've been wondering who's to blame?
Who's to blame? Huh?[12]

Lenny never used Marc's lyrics; but he did keep the tune in his trunk for the next several years, until he finally used it for the words, "There's a place for us, Somewhere a place for us. . . ." Three decades after *West Side Story,* neither Shirley nor Lenny could shake from their minds Marc's "There goes what's-his-name"—nor did they care to.

Lillian Hellman was probably the best known of the American organizers and hosts of the Cultural and Scientific Conference for World Peace that opened under the auspices of the National Council of the Arts, Sciences and Professions on March 25 at the Waldorf-Astoria. For months she had struggled with the strange deliberations of the State Department as to which invited guests would be allowed in. The conference split the American intellectual community into opposite sides: those who considered meeting and talking peaceably with representatives from the Soviet Union a valid occupation, and those, organized by Sidney Hook and his ad-hoc committee of anti-Communists, who either picketed the proceedings outside the hotel or called counterdemonstrations protesting the pro-Soviet bias at the conference. Aside from signing on as a sponsor of the conference, Blitzstein's role involved greeting the musicians and writers, shepherding them to conference functions, concerts, and private gatherings.

Among the Soviet guests, Dmitri Shostakovich came, for his first visit to the United States. Addressing the nearly three thousand delegates—artists, writers, and musicians—he asked for their commitment to peace, freedom, and democracy. There was at least one evening when he, Konstantin Simonov, and Ilya Ehrenburg sat around someone's apartment drinking vodka with Marc and Bill Hewitt, who had come up for the occasion. On the last day, Shostakovich played the piano at a Madison Square Garden rally that attracted a capacity house of eighteen thousand. But he had gone through rough times in recent months: Zhdanov's antiformalist campaign amounted to virtual censorship of his music, and that of every other significant Soviet composer. Reporters questioned him mercilessly about the position of artists and the state of intellectual freedom in the Soviet Union; this conference followed shortly on the heels of Stalin's banning all schools of genetics that did not concur with the fraudulent researcher Lysenko's political theories. There was little Shostakovich could say that wouldn't either make him appear foolish in America or get him into serious, perhaps fatal trouble at home. Obliged to tout the official Soviet position—indeed, he had been asked to attend by Stalin personally—he spoke these words to the conference, a statement that differs in no significant way from the position American Communists also held:

> Formalism we call that art that does not know of love for the people, that is anti-democratic, that takes into account only form and denies content; it is a philosophy that is engendered by a pathologically disturbed, pessimistic concept of reality, by lack of faith in the strength and ideals of man. This is a reactionary nihilist philosophy that must lead to the corruption and death of music. The bad features of cosmopolitanism that are profoundly alien to the fate of the nation and of mankind, the decline and emptiness of that pseudo-culture that has no roots in the people, in the nation, manifest themselves in the rejection of the broad audience and in the loss of national features.[13]

Perhaps Shostakovich should not be judged too harshly in hindsight: However little of this speech he may have believed, or however little he trusted in the power of the state to enforce esthetic policy, he pronounced his words in the hangman's shadow.

Bill had returned to Virginia when Marc, back at Jo's, wrote to bring him up to date on the aftermath of the conference:

The Shostakovich saga would make a book. I was prepared to be chairman for an affair here in Philadelphia for him and the other delegates, when the State Dept. came through with its asinine decision to send them all packing. I can't quite make out whether the govt is more afraid of Shostakovich and the others finding out about what the rest of America is like, or of us finding out what they are like—but fear certainly plays the biggest part. And what a windfall of propaganda-opportunity for the "enemies of democracy!"[14]

There were propaganda opportunities for the conservative side, too. In the fall of 1948, significantly just days before the November election, the government had launched a grand show-trial in federal court at New York's Foley Square against twelve leaders of the Communist Party, on a charge of advocating the overthrow of the government by force or violence. Trial proceedings began in January 1949 and lasted until October 15, 1949. With a verdict of guilty against them, Party leaders began being jailed and fined by the government. Charges such as contempt of Congress (for challenging HUAC) and refusing to register as foreign agents landed others in prison. As a matter of course, Blitzstein signed a number of open letters protesting the government's procedures. At one of his last Carnegie Hall concerts before being consigned to commercial oblivion, Paul Robeson made a point of inviting Eugene Dennis, General Secretary of the Party, to occupy a box near the stage. It was just before Dennis began serving his first prison term. Announcing the dedication of his next song to his close friend Eugene Dennis, he sang "The Purest Kind of a Guy" from *No for an Answer* as the spotlight turned on the general secretary.

That May of 1949, the Alger Hiss trial began, that watershed moment in early Cold War history that appeared to reveal high-level treason within the very ranks of the government. The trial contaminated the news for months until its conclusion in 1950. And what a climate for anger about leaks to the Communists: That summer of 1949 the Chinese Communists definitively drove out Chiang Kai-shek's forces from the mainland, assuming complete power by October 1. In September the Soviets exploded their first atomic bomb. Enraged senators and public leaders screamed of disloyal Communist sympathizers in every quarter of American life. The American Legion's Americanism Division released a list of 128 people whose past activities made them unsuitable for Legion sponsorship. Blitzstein was on the list.

The League of Composers paid tribute to Serge Koussevitzky on May 10 that year, honoring him on the silver anniversary of his tenure with the Boston Symphony. As the beneficiary of a Koussevitzky Music Foundation grant, Blitzstein made an appearance at the Waldorf-Astoria dinner and played the piano in a preview performance of several set pieces from *Regina.* Indeed, Blitzstein dedicated the opera to the foundation and to the memory of Natalie Koussevitzky.

By then Blitzstein, Bobby Lewis, Cheryl Crawford, and Lina Abarbanell were struggling with the casting. For the lead role, Blitzstein would have liked to hire

Risë Stevens or Dorothy Kirsten. The part of Regina is exceedingly difficult to perform eight times a week, however: The fact that Stevens refused, saying the piece more properly belonged in the opera house, is easily understood.

The producers ended their search with a choice that, on the face of it, sounded unlikely. Alfred Drake had recommended Jane Pickens, born and brought up in Macon, Georgia, a veteran of the three Pickens Sisters (Patti, Jane, and Helen), a popular radio and stage group in the 1930s. Their father was a cotton broker, and their mother had taught them singing. They performed together for only five years, though by the time they quit in 1936, they had reportedly earned a million dollars from their recordings and studio work.

Both Jane and Patti continued as solo acts. Jane performed with the Ziegfeld Follies in 1936, then spent a year touring with Eddy Duchin's orchestra. By the late 1940s, she had graduated to fancy supper clubs and to a regular radio spot on NBC, where she earned a cool fifteen hundred dollars a week. Yet despite her enviable achievements, she had never given up the aspirations for a career in classical music that she had nurtured ever since studying at the Curtis Institute of Music with Marcella Sembrich. She had also spent a year at Fontainebleau with Camille Decreus, and four years at Juilliard. She might slip an operatic aria or two into her shows, but managers forever pegged her as one of those "three kids who twang their noses imitating Uncle Ned's banjo."

When she got the part of Regina, the syndicated Broadway columnist Earl Wilson conducted an interview in which she described how badly she had wanted the role. "Ah knew, Ah knew Ah would get it," she told him. "Ah used to read in the papers that somebody else had the part, and Ah said, 'Ah don't know much, but Ah know one thing—Ah'm Regina.' "[15]

It wasn't long before Tallulah Bankhead, the famous Regina of the 1939 stage play, heard about the musical version. "Who's playing me?" she inquired. When she heard the role had been offered to Jane Pickens, she growled, "Pickens? I didn't even like her when she was with the Andrews Sisters." However, she graciously offered Pickens her help on delivering the line Regina addresses to Horace at the end of Act II: "I hope you die. I hope you die soon. I'll be waiting for you to die."

"Well, of course," Bobby Lewis reminded her, "she'll be singing the line."

"She's going to sing it? What the hell do you think I did?"

Brenda Lewis, whose given name curiously was Birdie, had sung professionally for more than eight years. She had begun her career at the age of twenty, amazingly enough singing the Marschallin in *Der Rosenkavalier* with the Philadelphia Opera Company. By now a regular with the New York City Opera, she had an impressive thirty-two roles in her repertory. When she heard about Blitzstein's new musical drama, she took an immediate craving for the lead role. She went to each audition dressed in all the flamboyance she imagined Regina would affect. Unspeakably flattened when the producers chose Pickens but not one to give up hope completely, she returned to the auditions—dressed drably now, like the oppressed, crushed Birdie—and applied for the secondary part. "I love her," Blitzstein noted, hearing her anew. "Bobby still thinks she is too far away from the character; too full of guts and stuff; but I love her, and believe she could be trained to it." She got the part.

William Wilderman had auditioned for the New York City Opera several times, but they never took an interest in him. He had a good ear and a huge natural talent, though he was not a good sight reader. Knowing that he would require painstaking coaching from Blitzstein, but also knowing that his was a rich bass voice not to be passed up, the producers accepted him as Horace.

William Warfield, an Eastman graduate with a good command of languages and a bit of previous Broadway experience, auditioned for Lina. "Fine personality," she commented; "fabulous breath control. Voice not the most beautiful. But let Marc hear him."[16] He got the role of Cal, the black butler.

There was unfortunately no solo part Charles Holland, Blitzstein's *Airborne* tenor, could have played in *Regina.* In keeping with his desire to promote black talent, Blitzstein wrote to Koussevitzky early in the summer of 1949, begging him to hear the singer, "to my mind one of the great promising lyric tenors of our day." Purely because of his color, Holland had not won the success he deserved. Koussevitzsky did hear Holland shortly afterward and seemed pleased, but no work came about.[17]

For the role of Jazz, requiring a singing trumpet player, Blitzstein recruited the well-known jazz artist Bill Dillard. A Philadelphian, Dillard had played trumpet at Blitzstein's old alma mater, West Philadelphia High School. Though he had a limited amount of stage experience, the composer prepared him thoroughly in the big "Chinkypin" number. Blitzstein wanted a tone far removed from the operatic—more of a holler or a field call, even a chain-gang style of singing. The other Angel Band members included Buster Bailey, clarinet, and Benny Morton, trombone, both of whom had played with Fletcher Henderson; and Bernard Addison, banjo, and Rudy Nichols, drums. They all considered Blitzstein's music a quite authentic Dixieland sound that recalled Scott Joplin, and they played it note for note without improvisation. None of the blacks in the cast sensed any stereotyping; they all felt comfortable with the essential dignity of their roles.

Russell Nype had arrived in New York from Illinois in 1947. One night he was dining in a modest family-style restaurant by himself when out of the blue an unknown lady at the next table asked him, "What do you want to do?"

"I want to act and sing," he replied.

"Well, then," the lady said, "I want Lina Abarbanell to hear you." And she made the introduction.

"I love your quality," Lina told him. "Keep studying, and keep coming back to me."

A year or so later, by then a dance instructor at Arthur Murray Studios, he went back just as Lina and the producers of *Regina* had become exasperated with finding a tenor to play the dopey Leo. He sang a couple of numbers and they signed him immediately. After his exposure in *Regina,* Nype went on to do *Great to Be Alive* with Vivienne Segal (Marc's former stepsister); he followed that with a two-year stint with Ethel Merman in *Call Me Madam.*

Cheryl Crawford's production of *Brigadoon* was playing on a cross-country tour, with Priscilla Gillette in the lead role of Fiona. Crawford called her back to New York and asked her to take the role of Zan. During the run of the show, Gillette was in her first months of pregnancy; when the baby came the following summer, she named her Alexandra.

For the role of the boorish Oscar, the producers recruited David Thomas; for Ben, they chose George Lipton, who had appeared on Broadway for three years in *Annie Get Your Gun.* Donald Clarke played Mr. Marshall.

Early in 1949, Blitzstein wrote to Maurice Abravanel about the chance of his conducting *Regina.* They had met a decade before through Lina Abarbanell—the similar names denoted a common origin and perhaps a distant relationship in Spain before the expulsion of the Jews in 1492. Abravanel had long been associated with Kurt Weill's works, conducting many premieres dating back to the 1920s in Berlin. As a refugee in America, he had spent a year at the Metropolitan Opera, though few people believed his story that he had told the Met off and left of his own accord because of its low standards. Lina had taken Abravanel to see *The Cradle Will Rock* during its 1938 run at the Windsor Theatre, and he was bowled over by the music, even more by the great drama. Sharing a drink after that performance, Abravanel told Blitzstein how impressed he had been with the libretto. "Now if you could only write a libretto for Kurt Weill," he suggested, hardly realizing how deeply he was insulting the American composer.

After the war, in 1947, Abravanel left New York for Utah to build up a class orchestra in Salt Lake City. By 1949 the Utah Symphony was on the verge of bankruptcy, however, and might not sponsor another season. Against this background, and since Blitzstein had long forgiven his terrible gaffe, the conductor decided to go to see Blitzstein in New York and hear his proposal. In any case, he had always liked being involved in new works by American composers.

Blitzstein considered Abravanel just the right man for *Regina.* "Why not Lenny?" the conductor asked.

"Lenny would be great for a first performance," Blitzstein answered, knowing how Bernstein operated, "but not after that. He couldn't stick to the tempi and keep the show fresh; he'd become unhappy doing it eight times a week."

Abravanel signed for a definite four weeks only, in case a season in Utah materialized after all. As an assistant, who would carry on after Abravanel left the show, the producers engaged Emanuel Balaban, a teacher at Columbia University with an appreciably lesser feel for the theatre.

Only that summer in Brigantine on the Jersey shore did Blitzstein compose the ballad for Zan, "What Will It Be?" It was a concession to Bobby Lewis and the producers, who wanted more memorable tunes, and until then she had no set piece of her own. Though musically it is clothed in an undeniable Broadway sentimentality, it must count as one of Blitzstein's prettiest songs. With more than a hint of Freudian imagery about the loss of virginity, he again manages to capture that ineffable feeling of late adolescence on the verge of maturity. On another level, it is Blitzstein's confession of readiness for love again, now that Bill had left. How could Marc predict what perfect stranger might walk through the door of a bar where he was drinking some night? Just the way Bill had that time at the Yorkminster:

What will it be for me?
Will someone say "I love you"?
What will it be, to be
The one to say "I love you"?
Will it be all real and right?
And how will it feel
To really love a perfect stranger?
Look in his eyes, and look,
And kiss that perfect stranger?
I cannot imagine it quite.
It's like nothing else before,
The opening of a door
To the light.
I stand at the door, and wait,
And wonder who'll come knocking.
Who'll stand outside, and wait,
And wonder—will I open?
Open to what dazzling light?
My life is waiting for me.
*I wonder what will it be?**

Blitzstein composed new songs for *Regina* up to and including the out-of-town tryouts. These new arias were in direct response to his producer and director, as is normal in writing for Broadway. But his overall process of composing the opera resembled nothing like *The Cradle Will Rock,* torn off in a miraculous five weeks, nor like *No for an Answer,* tugged at for almost four years and resulting in a mountain of unused material. The fact that he had a "collaborator," in the form of an already existing book, helped him strike a comfortable working stride. It was a lesson he might well have studied better, for he rarely achieved such a stride again.

Against the background of the violent anti-Communist Peekskill Riots forty miles up the Hudson from New York, Bobby Lewis began rehearsals in August. "In Russia maybe we'd have six months to rehearse this show," he told his cast, "but here we have only six weeks." He had them first read their lines, without music: He would have them *act* this opera, not just sing and go through the standard blocking. Then, when they had seen what the play was all about, he told them something they may never have learned in the conservatory: "Singing is the highest expression of emotion. You *have* to sing when there's that much in you to come out."

Blitzstein held private coaching sessions with all the principals, showing them

*Years later, in remembrance of Blitzstein, Francis Thorne based a passage of his Lyric Variations no. 5 for Orchestra on the theme of "What Will It Be?" It premiered in 1982.

exactly what he had in mind. Most of them visited his tiny flat on East Twelfth Street, but he went up to his leading lady's Park Avenue home regularly to work with her on her difficult role. At rehearsals he would demonstrate to the chorus how savagely the party scene should go—but Lewis found it difficult to get thirty-two choristers to get that feeling into their delivery. Once, when Blitzstein tried to tell Russell Nype how to play Leo, Lewis pointedly told the actor, "You're not to take direction from anyone else but me." Blitzstein respected the work of a professional colleague, and from them on he enjoyed a solid rapport with Lewis.

The director had problems with Jane Pickens. She was beautiful enough for the role, to be sure—the kind of performer of whom it was said she sported such an ample décolletage that people couldn't take their eyes off her voice. The looks helped to disguise the fact that she did not have a truly good vocal quality for opera. This work, after all, called for developed, trained voices, not Blitzstein's typical theatre singers. Already Bobby Lewis had determined that for anyone to hear her small voice in the theatre, the stage would have to be miked. Maybe if she had been able to compensate as an actress, she could have overcome the vocal problems.

Pickens was a lovely, friendly lady, a devout Christian Scientist and completely apolitical, who devoted much of her free time to fundraising for cerebral palsy research. She didn't want to be disliked. She identified with the gracious side of Regina, not with her essential malice. At most she saw Regina as a woman trapped in the South and desperate to get out. She did not care for vulgarity: She walked away from it when she saw it. During a rehearsal break while others enjoyed a smoke or a chocolate bar or coffee, she would sit to one side, study her music, and nibble a box of raisins. Maurice Abravanel recalled that hardly a day would go by when Blitzstein wouldn't refer to his "Slim Pickens"—and he wasn't referring to her figure.

"I could never kill anything, much less my husband," she once said in rehearsal. Bobby Lewis asked her to imagine being in bed trying to sleep with a mosquito buzzing in her ear.

"Think of the satisfaction you would derive from getting up and smacking it dead against the wall," Lewis told her. That helped her a bit.

Chappell published six songs in advance of the premiere: Regina's "Summer Day" and "The Best Thing of All," Ben's "Greedy Girl," the Chinkypin minstrel number, the "Blues," and Zan's ballad, "What Will It Be?" Only the last song could be lifted from the show as a separate number with any chance of commercial success—indeed, its chance seemed so great that it is truly a wonder that no one recorded it. In time, the company would publish a full piano-vocal score as well.

Regina opened with four sold-out performances at the Shubert in New Haven on October 6. Backstage, Lina went around to all the performers' dressing rooms with her good wishes and a plate of fresh pineapple—her cure for phlegm and dry throat. The audience adored nine-year-old Philip Hepburn as Chinkypin, but they felt bewildered by this untraditional score, missing the songs they had a right to expect from a musical. Critics had problems, too, because the program did not list the names of individual musical numbers. They felt disoriented—they hardly knew if the show *had* any musical numbers.

Several writers about the show remarked admiringly on the fact that Blitzstein had orchestrated it himself—most composers left that job to specialists hired to do it. In fact, Henry Brant had thought he could help Blitzstein with the orchestration, but Blitzstein had begun it already, with some specific ideas fairly distant from Brant's. In the end, Brant felt the score lacked sonority, that Blitzstein's truer gift remained in the smaller theatre works. David Diamond also believed Blitzstein's orchestration thin, and criticized it for a deficiency in counterpoint and middle parts. "That's for you," Blitzstein answered, satisfied that what he had done was already highbrow enough for a Broadway score.

Seeing the show on the stage for the first time, Bobby Lewis felt that Cal's "Blues" slowed down the action too much, and he wanted to cut it. Naturally, William Warfield objected—it was his only moment to stand out, his "Ol' Man River." Abravanel wanted to keep it: The show needed a lyrical pause amidst all of the vicious Hubbard sniping. After all, isn't it "Celeste Aïda," not all the jealousy business, that everyone considers the most beautiful passage in Verdi's opera? Crawford deferred to Lewis, compromising as far as to let Warfield sing it at one matinee in New Haven, but the decision was foregone.*

Variety's advance report, based on the New Haven premiere, predicted correctly that *Regina* would require some reworking out of town, but it also primed New York readers for the fact that *Regina* represented something genuinely new in the theatre.

After New Haven, *Regina* moved on to the Colonial Theatre in Boston and opened on October 11. Peggy Doyle's review in *The American* highlighted the controversy over its unusual form: "*Regina* Applauders Outweigh, Silence Critics." Elinor Hughes reported in the Boston *Herald* the next day how Brenda Lewis had been cheered, and how Jane Pickens "covered herself with deserved glory for her fine performance of a difficult and exacting role and had to buck memories of Tallulah Bankhead in addition."[18] Hughes returned to the fray in a Sunday followup:

> There hasn't been as hot an argument around town in years as the one now raging over Marc Blitzstein's musical drama *Regina,* now in its final pre-Broadway week at the Colonial. There are, as I'm sure you know by now, two sharply divided camps, and the battle lines remind me slightly of those drawn at the Battle of Agincourt; now as then, you can't very well be in the middle.[19]

Cheryl Crawford hoped the show might have at least one or two songs that could become popular by themselves and help make *Regina* a hit. "What Will

*A few months later, in March 1950, Warfield made his New York concert debut, the beginning of a distinguished singing career. Irving Kolodin ran into Blitzstein there and told him he should have his head examined for having taken the "Blues" out of Warfield's part in *Regina.* What could Blitzstein reply but to mumble a few feeble words about the producers, the continuity?

It Be?" was intended as one. Also, it seemed that however much Regina stood at the center of attention, the biggest showpiece fell to Birdie. Responding to the demand for a real star turn for Regina, Blitzstein sat down at the piano installed in his suite at the Copley Plaza and wrote "The Best Thing of All," a reflection of Regina's repellent materialism. It helped to reinforce the satanic element in the character that Pickens found hard to convey. Some of its thematic content clearly comes from passages in *Another Part of the Forest.* The composer liked to refer to this aria as Regina's "bullfighter number" or "toreador song." In some ways it summons up the spirit of a stripper's routine, emphasizing Regina's quintessential vulgarity.

Arnold Arnstein, regarded as the best music copyist in the business, traveled with the show to help with such last-minute additions, for all the orchestra parts would have to be copied out virtually overnight. He remembered one performance in Boston when Jane Pickens couldn't find her fan. As she hunted for it all over the stage, she got distracted and stopped singing. Abravanel kept the orchestra going with the same eight bars of music until she finally located it, then continued with her music.

While the show was in Boston, a young composer living there and working as the pianist for the Boston Symphony went to the theatre to show Abravanel and Blitzstein a short opera he had just written. Both of them rejected the work out of hand because the title role never actually appeared. It was Lukas Foss with his opera *The Jumping Frog of Calaveras County,* which after its premiere the following year did indeed go on to become fairly popular.

New York newspapers noted ominously that at least two people at every one of the sixteen performances in Boston walked out demanding a refund, claiming they had been misled into believing *Regina* to be a musical. But in general the out-of-town press had been enthusiastic. New York anticipated a wild success. Interviewed by *Cue* magazine, Hellman admitted that she had seen nothing of *Regina* since Marc had gone over the final script with her some months before. She kept herself completely out of *Regina*'s way, as her own play *Montserrat,* which she was directing, was due to open on Saturday, October 29, only two nights before Blitzstein's work. "Marc has done a really wonderful job," she said. "And it really is an opera, you know, not just a play with a few songs added."[20] That same night, *Regina* played as a benefit preview for the National Council of the Arts, Sciences and Professions, the pro-Wallace organization. Hellman, Blitzstein, and Brenda Lewis, all members, were honored. Interestingly, Kurt Weill's *Lost in the Stars,* a musical drama on a race theme that also featured a small black boy dancer, opened on Sunday, October 30.

That Sunday, Leonard Bernstein did Marc a favor by publishing a "Prelude to a Musical Adaptation" in the *Times.* Citing the unlikely prospect of turning Hellman's tale of vipers into music, he championed the results Blitzstein had achieved. In an apt metaphor, he defined Blitzstein's technique:

> Coating the wormwood with sugar, and scenting with magnolia blossoms the cursed house in which these evils transpire . . .

> With *Regina* we have a kind of apex, a summation of what Blitzstein has been trying to do. The words sing themselves, so to speak. The result is true song—a long, flexible, pragmatic, dramatic song.[21]

The producers, with the composer, perhaps made a mistake by inviting the drama as well as the music critics to the Forty-sixth Street Theatre for *Regina*'s opening night. Inevitably, the critics would compare this work to the original play, still very fresh in their memories. Brooks Atkinson tried to be supportive: "As theatre, this production of *Regina* could hardly be improved upon and must certainly rank with the most enlightened stage performances of operatic works. . . . Even *Street Scene* was not so thoroughly translated into the language of music." But in the end, he concluded—somewhat missing the point, as did other critics—it does not contribute "to the vitality of one of the theatre's keenest dramas."[22] The drama critics could not face the musical as a separate work with its own set of goals, and they couldn't understand Blitzstein's confounding of all the traditional typologies of stagecraft.

George Jean Nathan revealed his tired theatrical canons in his reflections on *Regina,* titled "An Old-Fashioned with Puccini for Me." First, he pointed correctly to one of Blitzstein's problems: his staunch and sometimes self-destructive resistance to going the tried-and-true commercial route. But then he took Blitzstein to task for even attempting something new:

> There is about Blitzstein an obstreperous arbitrariness that discourages sympathy with his ambitions. He remarks, for instance, that "I wanted to find out how daring it would be to write a musical without one love theme or passage." It is less daring than gratuitous. It is an experiment only for experiment's sake and not with the merit of the experiment uppermost in mind. It is that way with Blitzstein's work in general.[23]

The nerve! To deprive George Jean Nathan and all the theatregoers who followed his opinions of their precious love stories!

Still, in that long-gone world of New York media where dozens of reviewers had outlets for their opinions, a good number of sunny, quotable comments saw print: Robert Garland in the *Journal-American* called *Regina* "the only good American grand opera"; William Hawkins, in the *World-Telegram,* thought it "the most exciting musical theatre since *Rosenkavalier.*" *Time* referred to "first-rate showmanship . . . , exhilarating and enjoyable." Marc's friend the columnist Leonard Lyons tried to put the best face on it, dubbing it a "smash hit." He even quoted Blitzstein as reading the more favorable reviews and saying, "At last—maybe I can make a buck."[24]

The music reviewers who saw it turned in a mixed, if not in some cases spiteful judgment as well. Virgil Thomson, long famous for his motto, "Friendship ends at the stage door," wrote a poisonous notice in the *Herald Tribune.* There is "real operatic writing" in *Regina,* Thomson said, and he praised Jane Pickens for a "clarity of singing speech that is in every way admirable." But alas, the work was theatrical, "not very musical . . . raucous in sound, coarse in texture, explosive, obstreperous and strident." The cast was "without musical distinction" and the orchestra "has a splintery sound. It doesn't blend, and it doesn't support. It either drowns the singers or disappears."[25] Blitzstein had looked to Thomson as to no other critic for an incisive review supportive of the new directions in opera that *Regina* pointed out. His friends tried to comfort him, saying that Thomson was only jealous lest anyone other than himself write the first truly great American opera. But Thomson had done his damage: Theatre parties canceled their tickets to the show on reading his blast.

Like Blitzstein, Thomson was friendly with Mina Curtiss, and he went to her somewhat contritely after writing his review. Curtiss felt personally hurt that Thomson should have allowed his own vanity to color his review. "You don't think," Thomson asked Curtiss about *Regina,* "that this may be so new and different that one's prejudices interfere with one's judging of it?"

Curtiss replied, "I'd think about that if I were you."

"He never mentioned it again," she wrote to John Houseman, "but it seems quite clear to me from the piece that I am enclosing where he curls up cozily with *Rigoletto* that his power has made him either conservative or reactionary. I don't know which."[26]

In *Musical America,* Cecil Smith complained that Blitzstein left too many dramatic moments unscored. He seemed to resent whatever box office success *Regina* earned. People go because they understand it's "a good show, and not hard to take. From the point of view of commerce, this is no doubt very pleasant for both Mr. Blitzstein and his producers; but it is not profitable to his reputation as a serious composer." In short, he declared with some petulance, *Regina* is not "much of a contribution to the growth of American opera."[27]

It took the Communist newspaper the *Daily Worker* more than a week to publish its review. Though signed by Barnard Rubin, it betrayed all the earmarks of having gone through a collective editorial process before reaching print. "Let us remember that this is the Time of the Toad period for American culture," Rubin said, enabling his readers to understand why they should not expect to find *Regina* the same hard-hitting "immediate, working class weapon" as *The Cradle Will Rock.* But since the fight against white chauvinism was the Communist Party's order of the day, he felt obliged to smear Blitzstein with a broad polemical brush. He cited several places in Hellman's play where the good characters' problack sentiments had not been set to music. According to Rubin, the composer had settled for a much watered-down indictment of Jim Crow.

Hellman had no Angel Band, of course. But Rubin considered Blitzstein's ragtime ensemble extraneous to the action, never organically tied in, and he felt Blitzstein made "patronizing use of their talents." It was as if an opera about the Deep South had to have a Negro band, "as if the audience was being told, 'Look how colorful, gay, childlike and cute these poor ragged fellows are.' This business is if nothing else certainly contradictory to everything *Regina* has to say."

And if this knuckle-rapping did not suffice to steer Communist theatregoers away from the Forty-sixth Street Theatre and thereby damage the show's chances for a long run, the reviewer summed up with a coda of left-handed (and ungrammatical) praise for the Party's most prominent musician: "To Marc Blitzstein goes the honor and distinction of now being this country's foremost operatic composer. May he use his great talents to go forward from *Cradle* and not backward from *Regina.*"[28] The FBI clipped Rubin's review for its dossier on Blitzstein.

Though the opera had its social reverberations in 1949, they are built into the work for all time. Blitzstein eschewed the spirit of twenties and thirties *Zeitoper*, the *Kleinkunst* revue, the agitprop vehicle. Instead, he made a strong bid for permanence in the American operatic repertory. Rubin, and the Party behind him, had utterly failed to appreciate his aim.

Blitzstein had been unhappy with the Party of late. If in the past he gained from it moral support, ideological orientation, a sense of working for the future in concert with other progressive forces, by now he had come to regard it as only a drain on his resources, a hole into which he poured his energies. Party ignoramuses, who appreciated nothing of the advances in his technique and style, not to mention the considerable risks he was taking in his subject matter and point of view, took public pleasure in deprecating his work. Like Zhdanov in the Soviet Union who attacked Prokofiev, Shostakovich, and the other commanding heights of Russian music, the philistines had similarly gained control in the American party. To Blitzstein it seemed more and more that the only music they liked was the folk-based drivel that corresponded to Stalin's troglodyte taste. Why should he continue to subject himself to their depressing misguidance—and suffer the ever mounting political liabilities attendant to membership?

It is known that Blitzstein quit the Communist Party sometime in late 1949, though whether before or after Barnard Rubin trashed *Regina* is not clear. It would be convenient if we had his resignation letter dated the day Rubin's review appeared. More likely, his leaving the Party consisted of nothing more than discontinuing dues payments. In the midst of the Party's disarray, attacked from without and withered by recriminations from within—many of these coming from secret government agents—they may hardly have noticed Blitzstein's absence. Even most of his closest friends did not specifically know of his Party affiliation—in those days the wiser policy was not to know such things—and thus would not have known of his leaving. But the essential truth of the matter stands: He would no longer allow the Communist Party to strap him down to its lowest level of dated agitprop standards.

Blitzstein was hardly alone in leaving the Party at this time. From its height of sixty to eighty thousand members in the immediate postwar years while the memory of the Soviet-American alliance glowed brightly, the Party steadily declined to about forty-five thousand in 1949, and then ever more sharply down to ten thousand in 1957. Like many former comrades, however, Blitzstein did not give up his basic commitment to a just social order. Nor, when offered the opportunity, did he ever recant the views he so proudly hailed in earlier days. As he once signed off on a letter to Virgil Thomson, "Red but not dictated." At the same time, the Party press provided its readers with an occasional bit of news about Blitzstein's latest work.

CBS television's "Tonight on Broadway," sponsored by Esso Standard Oil, featured scenes from *Regina* filmed in live performance on its November 13 broadcast. Sir Cedric Hardwicke hosted the program, telling his viewers, "This fine play is replete with exciting scenes, colorful dances and an outstanding musical score. . . . You'll find it to be a memorable experience in playgoing."

So the composer Frank Loesser must have found it. Blitzstein attended the show many nights, and when he saw Loesser there for the fourth time, he couldn't resist asking him why. Loesser replied, "I'm studying."

Aaron Copland also attended. According to Leonard Lyons's column, he came out of the theatre so excited that when asked for his opinion, he declared, "With *Regina,* Mr. Blitzstone has created a milestein in the theatre."[29]

Kurt Weill felt as anxious as anyone to write the first truly successful American opera. Perhaps, if one accepts that a single work can be so characterized, he had already written it in *Street Scene.* "What's wrong with *Regina,* it goes, goes, goes," he said to Abravanel before the conductor returned to Utah. From time to time it should stop, come to a plateau, and reflect, then build again—which, in reality, the opera does, even with the "Blues" gone. Weill was just acting typically superior.

While *Regina* continued to play at the Forty-sixth Street Theatre—and while Blitzstein nursed a broken toe caused by a dropped log—the New York City Ballet revived *The Guests* for four performances during its fall season. Robbins reworked the choreography to some extent and played the role of the host himself. Walter Terry returned to see it and declared it "thematically elegant and choreographically stunning, a work of real stature . . . a fine composition and its central Pas de Deux is a miracle of beauty." John Martin in the *Times* recalled the work as not all that impressive when it was done originally, but with Robbins's changes, "what emerges now is a taut and brilliant theatre work with a style all its own. . . . The whole thing is crisp and clean and telling. Mr. Blitzstein's music has both bite and beauty, and manages to convey with a curious poignance the awareness of a sick society. There is nothing polemic about either music or action."[30]

Jane Pickens received New York University's annual award at an All-University Ball at the Waldorf-Astoria in late November for her achievements in the entertainment field, notably in *Regina.* And she appeared as Regina in a Lux soap advertisement in *The New Yorker.* But after the first month of the run, the theatre parties began to drop off. Failure at the box office threatened not only the future of Blitzstein's opera but of almost any bold new stride on Broadway. Attempting to stave off an early closing, twelve leading theatre men took out an ad in the December 13 *Times.* "We Saw *Regina,*" they headed it, lauding the show. The signers hoped that a hesitant public might be drawn in by the strength of their names: Leonard Bernstein, Moss Hart, Jerome Chodorov, George Jessel, Clifford Odets, Michael Kidd, Cole Porter, Jerome Robbins, Harold Rome,

Michael Todd, Tennessee Williams, and Dwight Deere Wiman. But the box office didn't respond.

Toward the end, pickets from unknown quarters appeared under the marquee with signs reading, "REGINA MUST NOT CLOSE," "SAVE THE SHOW," and "REGINA HAS BEEN STABBED—SAVE HER." To no avail. Reluctantly, after fifty-six performances, Cheryl Crawford had to close on December 17. Though she felt disappointed, fifty-six performances are not, in retrospect, all that shameful a record for an opera on Broadway.

As a further disappointment, especially to Blitzstein, who had been a pioneer in the field, no one wanted to issue a cast recording. After *Regina* closed, despairing that no aural document of the opera would be preserved for the future, Crawford gathered one hundred dollars each from her backers to produce a recording. But the musicians' union insisted on exorbitant fees, and further objected that Crawford could not guarantee that no one would try to issue the recording as a commercial release. So the composer asked several of his soloists to go to a Carnegie Hall studio. They stood around a piano and, with Blitzstein accompanying, recorded five excerpts: Birdie's "Lionnet," Zan's "What Will It Be?," Regina's "The Best Thing of All," the Rain Quartet, and the finale between Zan and Regina, with the other singers filling in for the "Certainly, Lord" chorus.

"Though I am not much on fan letters," the *New York Times* critic John Martin wrote to the producer after attending the final matinee, "I cannot help writing you this one about *Regina*":

> I have seen a great many theatres in a great many languages over the past forty years or so, but I have rarely been so completely shattered by a performance. What Blitzstein has done is to give us a theatre of our own with heroic dimensions for perhaps the first time. I have never heard music made so integral an element in the total art of the theatre, so boldly used to heighten and create theatrical values. His figures emerge in larger-than-life proportions in a situation that, for all its specific localization, takes on universal compulsions. It is difficult not to make some comparisons with those suspect creatures, the old Greeks.[31]

The closing seemed proof to Lillian Hellman that no one could add anything to her play without detracting from its power. Ever the master of the imagined slight, she took rimy umbrage at Blitzstein's fleshing out her story with all the black musical subplotting. Much to Blitzstein's bewilderment, for a long time thereafter she would not speak to him.

Arthur Pollock was only one of the critics who lamented *Regina*'s passing. It was "a failure, so to speak, but one of the most important failures the theater has been blessed with in who knows how long. The theater will be helped to live hereafter because of it." Oscar Hammerstein and Richard Rodgers agreed: "The superb and expressive music of Mr. Blitzstein is a landmark in our development."[32]

Within a month, Gian Carlo Menotti's opera *The Consul* went into rehearsal for its Broadway run at the Ethel Barrymore. Blitzstein could not help feeling that his morally uplifting and ultimately optimistic *Regina* had helped pave the way for Menotti's depressing Cold War vehicle—the Soviets would have called it "formalist"—that went on to win the New York Drama Critics Award and a Pulitzer Prize. Suddenly the critics began talking about Menotti as the present-day Puccini, though Blitzstein, for one, never subscribed to that judgment. As he said to the critic Paul Moor, "At the outside, a present-day Wolf-Ferrari."

It's not so much that Blitzstein begrudged a fellow composer his success. But Menotti was still in his thirties, and in March Blitzstein would turn forty-five—the age by which Siloti had predicted he would be a mature composer. He had just invested more than three years' work on a show that ran seven weeks. Would he soon be over the hill and never have been on top? It looked as though Blitzstein would soon retreat to his artist's garret, far from the gleam of Broadway lights, within reach of fame but not in touch.

Shortly after *Regina*'s closing, Moor wrote that "a kind of '*Regina* Underground' has come into being: indignation over its early demise is bitter, and there are many prophecies that a revival in the not too distant future will prove to the general public how wrong they were the first time." In view of just such a prospect, Cheryl Crawford stored the sets and costumes in Clinton Wilder's barn. Impatient with the Broadway audience, she told the press, "I am stubborn enough to keep on giving them more of the same until everybody learns to like it, or I croak!"[33]

17

NEW MÉTIERS

January 1950–December 1953

"*. . . I have been slowly withering on the vine. How one needs these vanity-assuagements!*"

For years after *Regina* closed, frequent inquiries about possible productions came from theatres and opera houses in Europe. Blitzstein or his agents dutifully sent copies of the score and the libretto to producers and theatrical intendants, the accompanying letters full of thoughts about translations into German or Italian, but of all these nibbles nothing came to pass. Fortunately for his mental well-being, Blitzstein had already conceived his next two projects.

The first of them may have sprung from his nephew Stephen, who since the fall of 1949 had been living in New York as a Columbia law student. Trying to find some outlet for himself as a writer, he had gone to Czechoslovakia two years earlier, where a Czech friend of his parents set him up with contacts for jobs. For nine months he lived in Prague, teaching English and writing a few stories. On a visit to Bratislava, he saw Kurt Weill's *Dreigroschenoper.* Once again, the work had stirred into life after a long dormancy enforced by the Nazis. As did thousands of theatregoers since its premiere in 1928, Stephen came out humming its irresistible theme song, the "Moritat." When he had returned to America in the spring of 1948, he had told his uncle Marc about this extraordinary theatre piece, and Marc had related its fascinating history to him. The reminder may have influenced Blitzstein to prepare an American translation, though at the time, engrossed in composing *Regina,* he had not pursued it.

However, a year later, when Maurice Abravanel first came to New York to discuss *Regina,* Blitzstein insisted before playing through the score on showing him his new translations of several songs from the Weill opera. Abravanel told Weill about them. Not only was the translation correct, but the words also sang well, with a composer's sensitivity to the original music. He recommended Blitzstein's version as the kind of translation that would go over big in America.

In the past, Blitzstein had written many unkind words about Weill and, after *Johnny Johnson,* some kind ones. Weill, in any case, counted few composers as friends, much preferring literary people. He had in fact tried to find some way of presenting his *Dreigroschenoper* before the American public in a commercially viable form; but he had certainly read some critics who believed that his German works were far superior to his American ones, and this made him cautious. Weill told Abravanel that he wanted nothing to do with Marc Blitzstein.

Weill's assistant Lys Symonette recalled riding with him in a taxicab one day in October 1949 after a revival of his early work *The Tsar Has His Photograph Taken.* Heading down to a rehearsal for *Lost in the Stars,* they passed the marquee of the Forty-sixth Street Theatre, where *Regina* was about to open.

"I think Marc Blitzstein is a better writer than a composer," Weill said to her. "I wish he would stop imitating me. Now he wants to do a translation of *Dreigroschenoper.*"

Weill did not rate Blitzstein's musical talents highly. But as he cared for Blitzstein's lyrics more than his music, he gradually warmed to a translation in Blitzstein's hands. In January 1950, after *Regina* had collapsed so soon and while *Lost in the Stars* continued to run, Blitzstein telephoned Weill at his New City, New York, home:

"Call it an exercise, Kurt, or call it an act of love. I don't know which: I've made a translation of the 'Pirate Jenny' song from your *Dreigroschenoper.* When can I show it to you?"

"Right now. Sing it to me."

"Over the phone?"

"Why not? Wait. I'll put Lenya on the extension."

Blitzstein began to speak-sing the number, clearly enunciating the words. And when he had finished, Weill spoke.

"I think you've hit it. After all these years! It does work, Lenya?"

"Yes, yes," Lenya said. "That I can sing. When can I have a copy?"

"Marc," Weill said, "Do it all, why don't you? The whole opera. I wish you could read the half-dozen 'versions' and 'translations' people have sent me; pfui! You do it. You're the one for it."[1]

Even with this encouragement from Weill himself, Blitzstein still did not leap to the task. The other project he had set himself after finishing *Regina* absorbed most of his attention: a new opera for Broadway, to be called *Reuben Reuben.* (The FBI called it *"Rubin Rubin."*) While *Regina* was still playing at the Forty-sixth Street Theatre, *Variety* reported Blitzstein at work on it. And by the winter of 1950, he had already begun putting in long days' work on book, music, and lyrics.

The New York City Ballet revived *The Guests* for five performances during its 1950 winter season. It appeared first on the opening-night program, February 21, followed by Balanchine's Symphony in C and the *Firebird*, the latter conducted by Stravinsky himself. Robbins again danced the role of the host, with Tanaquil LeClercq as the lead female and Nicholas Magallanes repeating the lead male part. Later, Melissa Hayden, Nora Kaye, and Frank Hobi danced in the work. The ballet seemed to grow with repetition and earned more consistently favorable reviews. Walter Terry wrote that it "doesn't preach; it looks and it reports and accomplishes its premise masterfully."[2]

The British saw the work that summer when the City Ballet visited Covent Garden. Their critics divided sharply over the work: The snobbish ones absolutely could not appreciate it. Even more than in America, they fled from works with social themes. One sour reviewer said that Blitzstein's music "sounds like Soviet music at its worst combined with American music at its worst; pretentious but well scored." But another wrote that:

> The solos and *pas de deux* are as beautiful and expressive as anything the Americans have given us, full of tender youthful gestures of diffidence and awakening love. . . . Blitzstein's music, which tends to the use of brass and low strings, has some attractive dissonances which help to produce an atmosphere of tension and mystery.[3]

After that tour, the New York City Ballet never programmed the work again, and the score has remained unheard ever since, even as a concert piece.

Perhaps Robbins never revived *The Guests* because his relationship to Blitzstein suddenly cooled in 1951 when Robbins privately cleared his name with Ted Kirkpatrick, ex-FBI agent who spearheaded the anti-Communist newsletter *Counterattack.* And on May 5, 1953, Robbins testified publicly before the House Committee on Un-American Activities, compliantly naming all the names the committee wanted. "It was too miserably revolting to want to believe," Marc wrote to Mina Curtiss.[4] After that watershed moment, Blitzstein would sometimes run into Robbins at social gatherings. Rather than ignore the choreographer completely or create a scene, Blitzstein would simply address him overrespectfully, and contemptuously. "Good evening, *Mister* Robbins," he would sneer, and walk past him into the crowd. Bernstein, for one, did not cut off relations with Robbins; indeed, he went on to collaborate with him on his most successful endeavor, *West Side Story.*

If Bernstein did not hold on to such personal grudges, he nevertheless remained enough on the correct side of the issues for Blitzstein's taste. True, Marc often sought to take charge of his protégé's politics, hectoring him like a pedantic schoolmarm into a more militant posture. But this was a role Bernstein valued: It gave Blitzstein a kind of moral superiority, which the younger man was pleased to grant at a time when his own career had overtaken Blitzstein's in terms of public recognition and commercial triumph.

Whenever he could, Marc went to Lenny's concerts. He was on Bernstein's complimentary ticket list. He loved Lenny's success—had he not predicted it, encouraged it? Had it not begun, in a sense, with *The Cradle Will Rock* at Harvard? "I don't know when I have been so shattered by the concatenation of piece, orchestra and conductor," he wrote to Lenny the day after a Berlioz performance. "It was that subterranean delight that should underpin a big spiritual experience, but so rarely does. . . . I took it to my heart, and I took you to my heart. Thank you, baby."[5]

At the same time, Blitzstein was not blind to "all his neurotic compulsions and vanities," as he told Mina Curtiss.[6] There were times, too, when friends would see Marc walk into the Russian Tea Room after a concert, his face a mask of dejection as he traipsed in at the end of a long line led by Lenny and his followers, the master overtaken by the protégé.

On April 3, 1950, Kurt Weill died, only fifty years old. *Lost in the Stars* was still playing at the Music Box Theatre. Maurice Abravanel, Blitzstein, and Morris Stonzek, Kurt Weill's longtime musical contractor, rode to Weill's funeral together. On the way home, the "Solomon Song" from *Dreigroschenoper* began haunting Blitzstein, and he stayed up with it all night trying to devise English words. From then on, he was hooked: He had to do the whole thing. Perhaps there was a kind of inevitability to his translating the work and having his name forever associated with it. Eva Goldbeck had translated important poems by Brecht and had wanted to do his *Threepenny Novel.* And as Marc wrote to Mordecai Bauman (whose March 2 birthday he shared), March 2 "also happens to be the late Kurt Weill's, which is why the astrologers still make money."[7]

Blitzstein wrote about Weill's opera:

> Wry ironical-sweet tunes, troubled searching tunes, tunes gasping and agonized or blatant and cock-sure—each is a complete entity, each says one thing completely. I believe the "Moritat" to be one of the great songs of the century. Insistent, unavoidable, it has a relaxed grandeur, a terrifying simplicity. . . . The drive and appeal of the whole work are immediate, local-topical; we hear the world-weariness of, and a bitter compassion for, a defeated and demoralized people, the Germans of the twenties. . . . Immediacy gets alchemized into a general and universal expressivity.[8]

The Cradle Will Rock was a period piece in the 1930s, and ten years later under different but comparable circumstances, it still remained up to date. Similarly, Weill's work had both its historical and its present levels of meaning. "The jokes and the tunes were on everybody's lips," Blitzstein recalled of his time in Europe a score of years before:

> I would walk along a street in Munich, and suddenly there would be some one imitating Lenya's precise sinister gesture as she betrays Macheath to the police; urban Europe made of this moment a pantomimic betrayal.[9]

And now, once again, in the McCarthy "time of the toad," informing and betrayal were the watchwords of the day.

For his translation, Blitzstein consulted the original French verses of the troubadour François Villon, which Brecht had mined himself; and he sought out people such as his music copyist Arnold Arnstein and the set designer Wolfgang Roth, who had done *Androcles and the Lion* with Blitzstein. Both of them possessed an especially refined sensibility about Brecht's colloquial language—the multitalented Roth had known Brecht well, in fact, and had at times acted in the Berlin cabaret. Blitzstein had a basic knowledge of German: He could certainly make his wants known. But he would interrogate his experts closely as to the exact nuances suggested by Brecht's highly idiosyncratic text. For research on Victorian idioms, he consulted John Camden Hotten's *Dictionary of Modern Slang,* published in London in 1865. As an ironic commentary on his own family background, Blitzstein must have found Macheath's line amusing: "What is the robbing of a bank compared to the *founding* of a bank?"

In an attempt to keep the memory of *Regina* alive, Blitzstein accompanied Brenda Lewis at Philadelphia's Academy of Music that April. Aside from Birdie's big drinking scena, she sang Marc's "Orpheus" from *Julius Caesar.* More historic memories of *Regina* were revived that April when the Tony awards were announced: Maurice Abravanel had won as the outstanding musical director, and Aline Bernstein as costume designer.

Blitzstein put some time in helping the producers of *Peter Pan,* for which Bernstein had written the music. Marc rewrote the lyrics to Wendy's song "Dream with Me," supplied words to the final reprise of "Who Am I?" and provided additional lines for the mermaids' song. "At this moment, two days before the first preview," he wrote to Lenny, "the production seems generically right (if you like *Peter Pan* at all), but specifically right almost nowhere."[10] For his labors, he received payment of two hundred dollars, taken, over his objections, from Bernstein's royalties.

A few days later, on the twenty-sixth, he took off for two weeks in Bermuda. There he met Morris Golde, an energetic young executive in the printing-machinery business, who had already embarked on a long avocational career of supporting the arts with his timely patronage. Moish, as Blitzstein liked to call him, had gone to Bermuda with a friend who preferred a restful, sleep-filled vacation. In Marc, who shared his energy, he found a good companion for bicycle rides and more zestful activity. The friendship they formed then would endure permanently.

When he returned, Blitzstein wrote to Bernstein again. "I'm furiously working; Bermuda was fine for me, giving that patina of copper-coloured skin which turns out to be so useful for my psychological morale. I am not in love, and I need to be; that's a perilous state."[11]

He gave a lecture-recital on "The New Lyric Theatre" at the two-year-old Brandeis University that May, including the "Pirate Jenny" number from *The Threepenny Opera,* "the masterpiece of a man whose recent death was an incalculable loss, although his career shows clearly the tragedy of Displacement." "This one is the true Weill," he offered.

Bernstein had introduced Marc to Tally Brown, a talented cabaret singer he had met at Tanglewood. Of a decided progressive political bent, she had loved *Cradle* at the City Center in 1947. Now, for the third week in May, she proposed to Marc a production in Miami. Her parents owned a small hotel on Collins Avenue in strictly segregated Miami Beach, where she auditioned both black and white actors. Brown herself produced, directed, and played Mrs. Mister, and Joe Harnell was the music director. As part of the promotion for the show, Brown prepared stacks of fliers boldly announcing "THIS LEAFLET IS DEADLY," which neighborhood people grabbed up with intense curiosity. Presented under the auspices of the Freedom Players, the production played in several locales—a former restaurant, a Unitarian church in Coconut Grove, a black Episcopal church in the ghetto—under threats that the Ku Klux Klan would "ride" on the play. For aside from the union theme—anathema in a town where the major industry, tourism, remained almost entirely unorganized—this *Cradle* was, by all accounts, the first racially integrated cast and audience anywhere in the South. After the show concluded, Brown and her company proceeded to found an interracial conservatory in Miami, out of which they produced at least one major show a year—the next year's was Brecht's *Caucasian Chalk Circle.*

In a letter inviting him to contribute an article on the new musical theatre for its June issue, *Theatre Arts* magazine asked Blitzstein to use *The Consul* as a starting-off place. "I would also recommend," the editor cautioned, "that you rise above the tempting opportunity to take a whack at the critics who do not realize that *Regina* made it possible for them to accept and understand *The Consul.*"[12] Blitzstein called for a theatre of truth and substance against prettiness and standard, antiquated forms. And if new means are to be used, they must be used to say something—otherwise, methods are merely "a perversion of tools." Perhaps he had *Four Saints in Three Acts* on his mind: "an amiable confection, in which an entirely irrelevant production was plastered upon an abstract script and score and provided a theatrical treat which served as a dessert for no perceivable meal." As for *The Consul,* a "displaced, or uprooted work," he said, "the music is largely punctuation and reinforcement." Though dramatically shrewd and unquestionably "our kind of opera, opera of this place and this time," "there is a political equivocation and safeness about it which I personally deplore":

> What [Menotti] needs is more intellectual vigilance, more ruthlessness in matters of taste, a firmer and more personal musical fibre. I feel confident about him.[13]

In June 1950 Richard Flusser had gotten hold of Blitzstein's 1928 creation *Triple-Sec* and decided to give the piece its first revival in twenty years with his After Dinner Opera Company. The composer allowed him to use a score for solo piano, for a royalty fee of five dollars per performance. The company first presented the work in New York on a program at the Roerich Museum's theatre, along with Bach's *Coffee Cantata* (staged as *Grounds for Marriage*) and Lukas Foss's *Jumping Frog of Calaveras County*—the piece Blitzstein and Maurice Abravanel had found such an impossible conceit less than a year before. Critics found Blitzstein's first opera still fresh and teeming with bright invention, concise and "unprincipled," that is, without any political position. Arthur Berger observed in the *Herald Tribune* that the opera "certainly predicted he would have a career in this medium."[14] Flusser subsequently took the work on a series of college engagements. When Blitzstein later sought to have the Schott score republished, he discovered that all the materials at the Mainz music publishing firm and all remaining stock had been destroyed by fire during the war. Still, despite the difficulty in securing parts and scores, *Triple-Sec* has occasionally cropped up, especially on college opera-workshop programs. It remains a witty example of musical surrealism in America.

After the *Triple-Sec* performance, Blitzstein felt that he had not quite exhausted his affection for the slow benevolence of Bermuda. He returned there and stayed a month this time, renting Cavello Cliff, a house in Somerset with a piano, to finish the Brecht translation and continue with *Reuben Reuben.* His cottage surrounded by tropical vegetation and perched high above the water had its own private cove down the cliff. "It looks like a session of fine work," he told Mina Curtiss, "but there will also be some fun. I like the funny pubs around here; British Navy, colored folks (I don't yet know the *mores,* and will probably stub my toe before long.)"[15]

While Blitzstein worked in Bermuda that June, just as the Korean War broke out, a small group of anti-Communist smear specialists operating under the name of American Business Consultants released a book of 151 names. Following each of them, *Red Channels: The Report of Communist Influence in Radio and Television* listed as many left-wing affiliations as could be uncovered. Priced at one dollar, this 213-page book never achieved a mass circulation; but to producers and agents then under attack for hiring anyone with a "red" past, it became a kind of Bible. Almost everyone listed suffered. Dozens of Blitzstein's friends and colleagues turned up in the book—among the composers, Aaron Copland, Earl Robinson, Harold Rome, and Leonard Bernstein—but of all those named, only the black poet Langston Hughes's listing rivaled in length the four-page dossier on Marc Blitzstein. Recalled were concerts at which he had entertained, petitions and protests he had signed, benefit auctions to which he had contributed, articles he had written, people's committees he had endorsed, professional conferences he had sponsored, organizational letterheads on which his name had appeared, even a 1939 summer milk drive he had helped to promote for International Labor Defense. The earliest reference in *Red Channels* went back to September 1936, when Blitzstein's name appeared on the letterhead of a Committee of Professional Groups for Browder and Ford, the Communist Party's presidential and vice-presidential electoral slate that year. The most recent listing was a year old—a June 21, 1949, performance of *I've Got the Tune* at Carnegie Hall on a benefit program for the National Council of the Arts, Sciences and Professions.

As an inveterate theatre man, Blitzstein's career depended little on the mass media, though occasionally he had branched out into radio and noncommercial film work. Listing in *Red Channels* almost completely guaranteed that he would stay in the theatre. For of all the professional groups in American society, Actors' Equity defended its members' First Amendment rights perhaps not with unqualified resistance, but more than any other group did: In this way the theatre community challenged the age-old legacy of regarding actors as derelicts and outcasts. One witch-hunter of the era, unable to crack the theatre world's protective shield, described Broadway as "New York's Great Red Way." Even in the theatre, however, only the most courageous producers would approach Blitzstein. His work, already on the edge of respectability in style and subject, would have to be overwhelmingly effective to be received well.

Still in Bermuda, Blitzstein received a telegram from Peter Lawrence, a co-producer of *Peter Pan,* asking if he would like to try his hand at a new métier: directing.

Eric Crozier provided a book and lyrics based on William Blake's poem "The Chimney Sweeper" for Benjamin Britten, and the composer wrote the music in two weeks. A group of schoolchildren working with a few adults decide to write an opera, *The Little Sweep.* Together with the play that precedes the opera they create, the work is called *Let's Make an Opera.* Basically a rescue opera, its beguiling setting treats a pitiful, serious subject, the exploitation of children as chimney sweeps in early nineteenth-century England. Britten provided eighteen musical numbers for the opera, with some incidental music in the play. One of his most effective innovations was the distribution of a lyrics sheet to the audience, with four notated songs on which they joined in.

Let's Make an Opera saw its first production at the June 1949 Aldeburgh Festival, with Norman Del Mar as the conductor. It then moved into the Lyric Theatre in London. In the next few years, it rapidly became Britten's most produced opera (though equally rapidly it seems in later years to have faded from view). With no recitative, only spoken dialogue and the songs suited to amateur singers, it was a fairly easy work to stage. In part, its popularity can be ascribed to its easily assembled orchestra: solo string quartet, piano four hands, and percussion.

By the time Peter Lawrence made plans to produce it in New York under the auspices of his Show-of-the-Month Club—just a year after its premiere—*Let's Make an Opera* had already been seen in five different stagings in the United States. Blitzstein asked to see the script and score, and then agreed to direct it. He would supervise the cast, stage manager, costume designer, scenic designer, conductor, and orchestra, and would receive a fee of three thousand dollars plus a small percentage of the weekly box office. With a reported thirteen thousand members, a guaranteed advance sale of seventy-five thousand dollars, and a million-dollar-a-year budget, the Show-of-the-Month Club appeared to assure Blitzstein a substantial run on Broadway. Furthermore, the club had been founded by two reliable musical comrades from the past—the composer Lou Cooper and Sylvia Siegler, an organizer of theatre parties for the left-wing movement. If *Let's Make an Opera* turned into the commercial success in New York that it had been everywhere else, and if it was promoted as "Entire Production Staged by Marc Blitzstein," he might begin to recoup some of the damages he had sustained with *Regina.* And he wouldn't lose too much time from his composing: His term of engagement would extend only from the middle of October until the New York opening in December.

Blitzstein made slight changes in Britten's *Let's Make an Opera.* He merged the first two acts into one, leaving only one intermission, and for obvious reasons he changed the name of the bully master of the little sweeps from Black Bob to Big Bob. Together with his casting director, Lina Abarbanell, he chose the cast of seven children, which included Jo Sullivan, because she was so small, as Juliet, the oldest. She had previously been in the choruses of three Broadway shows.

Lys Symonette, who had worked closely with Kurt Weill, played piano for the auditions. At the end of one day, they still had not found anyone to play Big Bob, a bass-baritone part. Lys's husband Randolph, then singing in Menotti's *The Consul,* came to pick her up, and Blitzstein asked to hear him. He sang Mussorgsky's "Song of the Flea," and Blitzstein jumped out of his seat exclaiming, "That's it! That's what we're looking for!" As *The Consul* was to close shortly thereafter, Symonette was available.

The producer recruited the original conductor, Norman Del Mar, a former assistant conductor to Sir Thomas Beecham, to lead the work in New York. For the most part, Del Mar told Blitzstein what had been done in the first British production, and the director conformed. A kindly gentleman, Del Mar conducted and acted, as part of the mise-en-scène, with a coy demeanor. Energetic and obsequiously kind to the children, but unaccustomed to the strength required of a good director, Blitzstein found himself unable to tone down Del Mar's mugging to the audience. Aline Bernstein provided costumes in bright pastel colors, and Ralph Alswang designed a toylike set. In Del Mar's orchestra was William Kraft as percussionist; he was later to become a prominent composer.

On October 10, Blitzstein appeared on the "Faye Emerson Show" to promote his new venture on Broadway to television audiences; his listing in *Red Channels* had apparently not caught up with him yet. He took along Jo Sullivan, who sang "Why Do You Weep?" from the show, and Pepsi Cola paid $250 for Blitzstein's performance.

Let's Make an Opera played at the Shubert in New Haven from November 22 to 25. The audience received a six-page printed handout containing the music they were supposed to sing. Based on a performance seen there, *Variety* questioned how well it would do in America—it had too much the flavor of an overblown community chorus.

When it moved on to the Wilbur in Boston, Elinor Hughes interviewed Blitzstein for the *Herald.* "I sincerely feel it is the best opera Britten has written," he told her, explaining how he came to be directing it. Aside from composing *Reuben Reuben* and the incidental music to a production of *King Lear* that would open in New York on Christmas night, he mentioned a third project on which he had been working in Bermuda, but which for the time being he had to keep a secret. It was, of course, the *Threepenny Opera* translation.[16]

At Boston's first night, the entire cast of Cole Porter's new musical *Out of This World* joined the audience, as a dress rehearsal of their show had been canceled. But their added voices hardly helped. Though offering benign compliments to Blitzstein's know-how as a director, the critics generally panned the work. For one thing, they found Britten's tunes not the easiest to sing. An emphatic Elliot Norton reported that Norman Del Mar behaved "like a completely silly ass."[17]

Peter Lawrence had invited the drama critics, not the music critics, to review the New York opening at the John Golden Theatre on December 13, though the music critics might have found more interest in Britten. A few reviewers found the piece zestful and captivating, and timely for the Christmas season; but most thought it juvenile, self-conscious, pretentious, and thin. "The rehearsal scenes, which seem to have been staged by Marc Blitzstein," wrote Brooks Atkinson in the *Times*, "are about as spontaneous as a subway rush hour—the children painfully rehearsed to simulate childishness and the adults looking as al fresco as they can. Improvising in the theatre never has been so laboriously planned." Howard Barnes, reviewer for the *Herald Tribune*, criticized the odd turn of the music and cited cumbersome lyrics, such as "through thickets of rushes and tussocks of reeds." He summed up the audience's reaction succinctly: "Let's make an opera? Let's not." If Blitzstein had referred to the work as Britten's best, he confided otherwise to Mina Curtiss: "I am content, no matter what happens. I have done an honorable, even imaginative job, with something less than slight material."[18]

After five performances, the work closed. Broadway was probably the wrong place for it in any case. It would have been much better received in a more family-oriented space—the City Center, or a college playhouse where parents could have comfortably taken their children. A year later, Peter Lawrence went bankrupt, still owing Blitzstein nine hundred dollars.

The early closing of Britten's piece, which might have been predicted from the out-of-town reviews, meant that Blitzstein would not have two shows running simultaneously at the end of the year, but only the *King Lear* that opened on Christmas night. Co-produced by Robert L. Joseph and Alexander H. Cohen, this *Lear* starred Louis Calhern as the king, with a prominent cast of supporting actors that brought back strong reverberations of the old Mercury Theatre days: Martin Gabel, Arnold Moss, Joseph Wiseman, Wesley Addy, and Edith Atwater, Jo Van Fleet, and Nina Foch as the three daughters. Norman Lloyd played the Fool. John Houseman directed. Ralph Alswang, late of *Let's Make an Opera*, provided the sets—a blood-red floor, ramps, traps, and vertical lighting recalling Orson Welles's Mercury style. Dorothy Jenkins, an Academy Award-winning Hollywood designer, created the costumes. The leftish tinge to the cast—besides Blitzstein, Martin Gabel and Edith Atwater were both listed in *Red Channels*—lent a whiff of political daring to the production.

Blitzstein scored his music to *King Lear* for flute, trumpet, French horn, and percussion. The conductor, Max Marlin, himself a former Communist, would also play Hammond organ, piano, celesta, and the electronic solovox. The only real vocal music was for Norman Lloyd, the Fool. For his work, totaling no more than fifteen minutes' worth of music, Blitzstein received a fee of one thousand dollars, plus one-half of 1 percent of the gross weekly box office receipts.

On opening night, Alex Cohen promised his co-producer that if the play was successful with the critics, he would finally get around to reading it. He must have read it, for the reviewers did favor the new staging. As for the music, it had an agelessness about it that helped situate the drama in no particular time. In the storm scene, the little orchestra managed to produce a veritable roar, leading Brooks Atkinson to comment, "Mr. Blitzstein's score is one of his best pieces of work, although it could still be subordinated to the speaking now and then."[19]

Cohen and Joseph presented Blitzstein with an additional gift in appreciation for his work, and the composer duly responded with thanks for

> one of the beautiful watches of all time. . . . Working on the music for *King Lear* under your joint auspices has been an unfailing challenge and an exhilarating experience . . . ; I shall use the new Bulova assiduously in the timing of the orchestra-piece I shall make out of the incidental score.[20]

It would be another seven years before Blitzstein's orchestra piece based on *King Lear* took form. And before that, he would write the music for a second production of the play. In the meantime, the Louis Calhern *Lear* ran for forty-eight performances before it closed.[21]

Now Blitzstein could return to *Reuben Reuben.* He probably had on his mind his most recent bouts with its libretto when he described in a magazine article the variants of work styles—words first, then music; and vice versa. He continued:

> The third, or running-relay procedure, is beloved of many Tin Pan Alley song-writers, as well as the schiz-or Narcissist theatre man. (This last is both lyric-writer and composer, each wildly in love with the other; and here I include myself.) One typical chronology is: title; tune for title, often repeated several times during the course of a "pop" song; rest of tune; rest of words.[22]

Though he expressed himself jovially for the public, his work on *Reuben Reuben* troubled him deeply. "Why the hell can't I have a collaborator at this point," he mused to Mina Curtiss,

> whom I could beat up and persecute? Because the problem and the impasse (and the possible solution) are all dramatic, not musical. The music sits around like a patient friend, waiting to step in at the right time with comfort and a dish of cream. Being both words and music is like being a conscious schizoid, or an unhappy Narcissus whose love-affair isn't working out.[23]

Perhaps it was irresponsible of Blitzstein to begin writing a new opera while the long-outstanding project of his book for Harper's still hung over his head. He had received his one-thousand-dollar advance back in 1947, and over and over again since then he had assured his editor that he was making progress. More probably, he had already lost heart for the assignment. He just couldn't bring himself to admit it. If he was ever to write the book, the right moment would have been after finishing *Regina.*

The last trace of it turns up in an internal Harper's memorandum dated November 15, 1950, from Joan Kahn to Blitzstein's editor, John Fischer. She had run into Blitzstein socially and he told her "he has done part of the manuscript, and is still very much interested in finishing it. . . . So I guess we ride along a little further. And I think I'll drop Blitzstein a prodding note. He says he feels very guilty about no finished book yet."[24] Characteristically, Blitzstein saved all his work. The fact that only a very few pages' worth of notes for the book survive, and the absence of comment on it in correspondence, diaries, and notebooks, and in the memory of his friends, strongly suggest that all along he had misrepresented the amount of work he had done.

In February, Ernst Josef Aufricht, who had originally produced Kurt Weill's *Dreigroschenoper* back in 1928, put on a Weill memorial concert at Town Hall that featured a truncated version of the piece. Lotte Lenya sang the role of Polly—not Lucy, for which she had been known. The reception New York audiences gave the work—many German refugees were present—forced Aufricht to repeat the evening twice. The occasion proved that Blitzstein was on the right track to make a new translation: This work would not die. It would live far longer than the American works Weill died believing to be his lasting legacy.

At the time of *Regina,* Blitzstein quit the Communist movement, though as late as February 1951 the *Daily Worker* listed his name as a petitioner to the Attorney General urging a halt to HUAC's contempt proceedings against Communist leaders. In many ways *Reuben Reuben* is the composer's reaction against the esthetic literalism demanded by Party canons. He resolved to write something lighter in tone—comic but not burlesque or sentimental—that would yet address society and its problems. At bottom, of course, he had no intention of discarding the basic social outlook it had taken him decades to develop. He would not change directions and go the route of the abstract; nor would he make over his musical language into an academic formalist mold. After all, he was still trying to reach a mass audience through the popular stage. But this opera for Broadway would not deal with social issues in the old terms of class conflict. Instead, Blitzstein found his critique of society more in the punditry of sociologists and psychologists who saw society's woes as a breakdown of communication.

But who failed to communicate what? The mainstream sociologists and psychologists mostly wrung their hands. Only a few on the left recognized with Blitzstein that the increasing banality of American public life had to do with the Bomb, its threat hanging hourly over every citizen's head. It also had to do with the restricted scope of public discourse brought on by the anti-Communist craze engulfing the country. In other words, Americans were plagued on the one hand by fears for the future, by a numbing kind of hopelessness and an attendant imperial recklessness; and on the other by a political régime that considered the open expression of such fears, and debate over our future, acts of such serious affront to patriotic loyalty that a person could be jailed or harassed into a kind of internal exile for voicing them. The country was like a man with a speech block.

And that is the very metaphor Blitzstein chose for his opera. Reuben is a recently discharged army veteran with a psychological condition known as functional aphonia. When there is fighting around him or when he is fearful or flustered, he is unable to speak; but when approached by feelings of warmth, comfort, and love, he is fine. The action of the play takes place entirely within one night in New York City. Reuben is contemplating suicide. His father, a circus performer known as "The Human Dart," killed himself and Reuben figures it an honorable way out of life's problems. In a bar on the Bowery, the mafioso-type proprietor Bart takes a strong interest in Reuben's suicide and places a large bet that he will go through with it. No doubt Reuben would have done just that, but early on in the night he meets Nina, a wholesome, no-nonsense girl with an animal instinct for survival. In the course of the night, which brings adventures set in such places as the Manhattan Bridge, the San Gennaro street fair, a sleazy nightclub, an insane asylum ward, and the girl's bedroom, Nina persuades Reuben that he is loved and that there is reason to live. As dawn breaks, we are confident that Reuben has rebounded and will survive.

The whole opera turns around the theme of death—and the opposing force of life. And how many deaths Blitzstein had already treated in his operas! No one merely passes away: His deaths are deaths by execution, by persecution, by chance, by treachery and violence, by jealousy and malice; deaths from electric chairs and explosions, from deprivation, from hate, and from war—premeditated death, unjust death. Now a whole theatre piece about death by suicide—"How Not to Commit Suicide," he had considered calling his book for Harper's.

As he had done in the past, in *I've Got the Tune,* for example, but here much more probingly, Blitzstein reached into his own life experience for the raw materials of his work. Reuben's plight is related to all the plans and hopes the left had entertained for the postwar reconstruction of the country—a true democratic overhaul based on the ideals of the antifascist struggle. No more racism, no more economic piracy, no more putting the accumulation of private wealth above the public weal—in short, a deepening of the New Deal process. More than that, Reuben is a partial stage incarnation of Marc's buddy Bill Hewitt, of his inability to communicate with the world, his block against completing and publishing his stories. Blitzstein's biographical notes on the character confirm this: "Enlisted AirForce; radio-gunner, end of war; occupation-troops in Germany when receives word of Pop's suicide, day after Bikini-bomb. Maxwell Field Hospital, Alabama(?). Major, psych. Medical discharge, with 75% disability. . . ."[25] At the same time, mixed in is the death of Marc's own father just at the end of the war, making *Reuben Reuben* the tribute to Sam Blitzstein that *Goloopchik* never turned out to be.

The character of Nina recalls Bill's girlfriend and later wife Lu, a likewise patient and unaffected woman with enough room in her heart to welcome in a suffering soul such as Reuben. Though he didn't need the constant attention himself, Jo, with her animal strength, played a similarly supportive role in Marc's life. By the time he began writing *Reuben Reuben,* Bill had already left Marc to live in Virginia. Just as *The Cradle Will Rock* was Marc's mourning piece and victory over Eva's death, the plea for love and understanding in his new opera can be seen as his will to conquer his personal despair over his inability to form lasting romantic relationships.

It was not that Bill didn't turn up from time to time, like a ghost from the past. One morning, he showed up at Marc's apartment, and Marc told Mina Curtiss how it went:

> I believe I did the right things; was casual, chattered away, listened with half an ear. He still has the capacity to get somewhat under my skin, with his outright plea for friendship, his "need" for me, the "confidence" I inspire in him, etc. It was more boring than usual. He is still a tormented soul, and somewhere valuable—but I can't bother any more to locate the value. . . . it is all finished; and we parted amicably, and lightly, with no plans for a re-meeting.[26]

Even if he had wanted to, Blitzstein was hardly free in the early fifties to speak his plea in homosexual terms. But in his notes for *Reuben Reuben* (not in the finished script), he repeatedly referred to the Mephistophelian character Bart as a repressed or subliminal homosexual, along the same order as Claggart in Benjamin Britten's 1951 opera *Billy Budd* (whose composition immediately followed *Let's Make an Opera*); or Iago in *Othello,* as psychoanalytically oriented critics might find. Closer to home, Bart is a close cousin to Applegate, the devil figure in *Damn Yankees;* or to Eddie Fuseli, a homosexual gambler and gunman, played by Elia Kazan in Clifford Odets's *Golden Boy.*

Why choose a homosexual to represent the dark, violent, life-denying forces? Was this some kind of prescient insight into the true nature of the nation's three most renowned Commie-hunters—J. Edgar Hoover, Joseph McCarthy, and Roy Cohn? Was it Blitzstein's internal absorption of society's judgment? Was it a natural association to make with the seedy baths and wharves and dives where he found his sex partners so often? Or, if Bart's evil and Nina's goodness serve as mirrors of the conflict within Reuben's mind, perhaps Blitzstein is pointing to the homosexual component in Reuben; in which case, Bart is a stand-in for Blitzstein himself, drawing Reuben (Bill) away from Nina (Lu) and heterosexuality. That Reuben should be afflicted with aphonia can hardly be an accidental choice of medical condition on Blitzstein's part—for was not homosexuality known as "the love that dared not speak its name"?

None of this comes to the surface in Blitzstein's final libretto. In the five years it took him to write and compose the opera, he came up with a huge cast of nearly fifty characters, a score with thirty different musical numbers, and a scenario that required eight different stage sets. But he was unable to produce a simple, sufficient reason for Bart to want Reuben's death so badly, and therein lay a pivotal flaw in the work.

Mordy and Irma Bauman had asked for Blitzstein's sponsorship for their Indian Hill summer arts camp in Stockbridge, Massachusetts. Misinterpreting their request as a bid for money, he responded in a fit of displeasure: "Whatever gave you the notion that I am solvent?" It was an old theme with Blitzstein, the result of the decision he had made back in 1928 not to take the well-paying job with sound pictures:

> For the past twenty years (aside from the war) I have been skating on the thin edge of pauperism, with a subsidy or fellowship here, an advance there. I have exhausted (about) the supply-source at this point, and am looking around, with as little desperation as possible, to try to find someway to keep alive in order to complete *Reuben Reuben.*
>
> *Reuben* goes well, or would go well if I didn't have the blasted Damocles sword hanging over me. It's a very hard job, and needs relative peace of mind, which I don't have a great deal of.[27]

The Baumans named Blitzstein on their roster of prestigious sponsors. But the truth is that Blitzstein made little money from his music. He refused to go the commercial route, forever hoping against hope that public taste would come up to *his* standards. His annual payments from ASCAP ranged from one thousand dollars in the late 1940s to two thousand dollars a decade later, the single most dependable source of income he had from his music.

Maybe his translations, more than his music, would pay off, for by this time news of his *Threepenny Opera* translation had spread. He only awaited a suitable production. The critic Eric Bentley, who at the time was very close to Brecht in his European projects, wrote to Blitzstein:

> I should like you to know that I am by no means unfriendly to the idea, even though I collaborated on a literal version made for the British public by Desmond Vesey. In all probability your version is the one for the American public, and this I said to Brecht, who replied that he also was well-disposed to you and would only wish to read your script to be finally convinced.
>
> It seems that there are now possibilities of production, and I hope you can forgive my proposing my own name as a possible director; I do not like to do such things, yet, fighting for my existence in the theatre, I see very little alternative. I should like to add that if no New York production comes off I could probably arrange one in Philadelphia at the Hedgerow Theatre. Would this interest you?[28]

Blitzstein answered at once. Frankly, he was looking for more of a name director than Bentley. He had also examined the Bentley-Vesey translation, agreeing with it "as to general tone, but not at all as to language," he wrote Bentley; "and I don't feel that your lyrics really sing or work with the tunes. I hope you will not be offended at my gratuitous criticism."[29]

Just before Thanksgiving, Blitzstein flew to Bermuda to spend six weeks at Landmark—Dwight Deere Wiman's splendid estate in Southampton—which was situated on twelve acres and fully staffed for the visitor's convenience and comfort. The studio he occupied looked out in three directions over land and sea. Perhaps the most memorable feature of the home was a shortwave receiver filling an entire wall; it was capable of pulling in stations from all over the world. He swam, he worked, he socialized, he drank. Even a bed partner or two turned up. Blitzstein noted in Bermuda "an enormous amount of homosexuality among the married upper classes," as he said to Mina Curtiss:

> a rather new thing for me, and I find I don't fancy it much. My old rigidities, I guess; but really, the natives, both colored and Portuguese, are enchanting, both physically and in terms of nature.
>
> What a typically colonial-tourist letter! Forgive it.[30]

Wiman had died at fifty-five in January of that year, leaving the business to his daughter Anna Wiman. After his death, Lina never had any money to speak of, though she continued to rent office space from Anna at the Alvin Theatre and tried to scare up a little casting work now and then. Marc would turn up there at least once or twice a week to pick her up for dinner. Wiman had a reputation for stinginess, but he had been as fond of Lina as he could be of anyone. He had left her an assortment of lighting equipment stored in a warehouse in one of the outer boroughs, believing its sale would bring her some much needed money. On inspection, it turned out to be grossly antiquated, utterly worthless for modern theatrical needs. Her friends were too heartbroken to tell her. They raised money among themselves and gave it to Lina, who believed until she died that it had come from the sale of Wiman's equipment. An alcoholic like her father, Anna Wiman treated Lina erratically: At times she felt extremely close and at other times she pushed Lina aside ungratefully. She wavered between seeing Lina as her surrogate mother and her employee; but more and more, she conducted her theatrical production business in London and rarely came to New York.

When Blitzstein returned from Bermuda, he spent only a week in New York before installing himself at Yaddo for a long session with *Reuben Reuben,* lasting until the end of February 1952. He put the piano in the middle of room no. 6 in the West House, and surrounded it with tables, forming a little studio inside his room. Among the other residents at Yaddo that winter were the playwright David Rayfiel, the artists Peter Takal and Hyde Solomon, and the writers William Slater Brown and Paolo Milano. Also the political philosopher Hannah Arendt, who said after Blitzstein played through *The Threepenny Opera* one evening for all the guests—always with that cigarette hung from his lower lip—

that the tone he struck was just what she had remembered from her youth in Germany. Blitzstein gained a certain fame for his dangerous martinis, mixed twelve parts to one. After dinner, Blitzstein generally trounced his fellow guests at Botticelli and other word games.

Among those who bit at the chance of producing the Blitzstein *Threepenny* was the New York City Opera, which went so far as to announce it for the spring season. Brecht wrote a letter to Blitzstein authorizing the production. The Vienna-born critic Kurt List, a failed composer of two never-performed operas in Straussian style, showed his McCarthyite political colors in "A Musical Brief for Gangsterism," published in the staunchly anti-Communist magazine *The New Leader.* Why provide public support of political propaganda when there are so many other operas "free of an odious political stigma" available? "The morality of the *Dreigroschenoper* is completely out of place in our America of today." It "exalts anarchical gangsterism and prostitution over democratic law and order." Letters of protest poured in to the magazine. One, from Lewis A. Coser, a Brandeis historian noted for his criticism of the Communist Party, remarked that Mr. List had apparently not yet learned in the United States that theatregoers can be trusted without nurses. Dwight Macdonald also sardonically suggested that List hardly went far enough in his proposal to cancel the City Opera production; he should take a lesson from the late Comrade Zhdanov in the Soviet Union and ban everything with a tint of immorality—Shakespeare, O'Neill! In self-defense, List assured his readers that *The Threepenny Opera* would be forgotten, never to live as a work of art.[31]

By this time, David Diamond had been appointed Fulbright professor at the University of Rome. He invited Marc to come spend some time with him there, but Blitzstein demurred. For one thing, he had not tried to obtain a passport since the war. In the current political climate, the State Department had denied passports to current, suspected, or former Communists—Paul Robeson's case was the most famous, but there were many more—and he felt timid about applying for one.

"Cheryl [Crawford] is a rock of strength and a lamb at the same time," he wrote to Diamond from Yaddo on Valentine's Day about his producer's patience with *Reuben Reuben.* "She only wants it 'right'; it can take forever."

> And now interest has picked up all over the place for my version of the Brecht-Weill *Dreigroschenoper.* ANTA had it, gave it up; City Center scheduled it, but I didn't like any stage-director, and couldn't get the one, or ones, I want. Now a private producer, with money, is after it. Perhaps it will get done after all.
>
> My love-life is non-existent; I am withering on the vine, and smile sourly at the thought. But some impish juvenile impulse keeps saying all is not yet lost.[32]

"Lenny has been coming regularly to me with his one-act opera," Marc wrote to David. "It is lively musically, but dreary in subject."[33] In the early months of

1952, Bernstein worked on *Trouble in Tahiti,* which he dedicated to his mentor Blitzstein. Indeed, just after the elder composer left Yaddo, Bernstein got there and occupied the same rooms for six weeks. Though the piece is seen principally as a tragic satire on the settled domestic life of suburban couples—as a protest against the depressing sexual division of labor that feminists would later criticize—there is also in the opera's centerpiece, the hat shop scene, a sharp rejoinder to the Cold War-period fantasy of American soldiers running free anywhere on earth to protect the interests of democracy. In this case it's a South Sea locale, similar to the Honolulu of *The Cradle Will Rock;* but it could be anywhere—Korea, perhaps, Lebanon, or Cuba.

In its aspect of social protest, *Trouble in Tahiti* is definitely a child of *Cradle.* But Bernstein folded in a more literal tribute in a private joke imbedded into the scat lyrics of his radio commercial-style Greek chorus. "Skid a lit day. Skid a lit Ada Abarbanel: who but Abarbanel buys a visa." How many people ever understood this reference (minus a final *l*) to Lina Abarbanell, Marc's mother-in-law?

Maurice Levine (then known as Morris Levine) had coached the chorus in the 1947 revival of *The Cradle Will Rock.* He also knew Blitzstein from Tanglewood. Blitzstein had attended Levine's concert version of Kurt Weill's *Street Scene* at the Ninety-second Street Y, where Levine led a symphonic workshop for students, trained amateurs, and semiprofessionals. Why not give *Regina* the same way? Cheryl Crawford believed the new exposure to the piece might convince critics and the public that they had been wrong three years before.

Levine assembled most of the original cast for a single performance on Sunday, June 1, 1952. For the chorus, he used cast members of the revival he was then conducting on Broadway of Gershwin's *Of Thee I Sing.* Randolph Symonette, who had appeared in *Let's Make an Opera,* sang the role of Ben with all the savagery Blitzstein intended. Bobby Lewis assisted with the staging, and Michael Wager, the son of the Zionist fundraiser and philanthropist Meyer Weisgal, helped Lewis.

For the concert version of the opera, the soloists sat stage front, the orchestra behind them, and in the rear sat the chorus. Lillian Hellman wrote a narration with which, from a red plush upholstered armchair off to one side of the stage, she would introduce each musical number. A few days before the performance, she met Marc at the Russian Tea Room to tell him she had to cancel her appearance. She had been summoned to another appearance: before the House Committee on Un-American Activities. And she could not go onstage and face the hisses she would undoubtedly receive after the attendant publicity.

"I don't think they will hiss you," Marc assured her. "And if they do, I won't have it. I'll just come out and say I don't want my music played before such people, and we'll give them their money back and send them home."[34]

Hellman's longtime companion, the writer Dashiell Hammett, had been jailed the year before for refusing to turn over to the government a list of contributors to the Civil Rights Congress. Now it was Hellman's turn. She testified in Washington, wearing the expensive Balmain dress she had bought just for the occasion.

"I am most willing to answer all questions about myself," she told her inquisitors, the glare of the world upon her.

> But . . . I am not willing, now or in the future, to bring bad trouble to people who, in my past association with them, were completely innocent of any talk or any action that was disloyal or subversive. . . .
>
> I cannot and will not cut my conscience to fit this year's fashions. . . .[35]

Overnight, the movie producers who had rewarded her so generously for her scripts in the past refused to touch her. Under the blacklist, her income plummeted from an average $150,000 a year to almost nothing. For a time she even worked under an assumed name as a department store salesclerk.

On the night of June 1, crossing the Ninety-second Street Y stage to her armchair, Hellman heard a deafening applause from the packed house—meant, she thought, for someone else. She stopped midway on her path and looked upstage in wonderment. The audience found this funny and began to laugh. When she turned around to face them, the concertgoers stood to their feet and with their sustained clapping continued to welcome her home to the safety of a New York theatre. Once again wearing her Balmain dress, she sat down. Her first words to the audience guaranteed the success of the evening. "Well," she said, "this chair is a lot more comfortable than the one I've been sitting on all week."

Blitzstein thought the performance superlative and thanked the participants profusely. Francis D. Perkins in the *Herald Tribune* said, "There was particular vividness in the Regina of Miss Pickens, who could set forth a fusillade of rapid syllables with notable intelligibility." Douglas Watt in the *Daily News* thought Brenda Lewis the outstanding voice of the evening, and he more or less made amends for all the critics who failed to appreciate the work the first time around:

> *Regina* is, in a sense, a masterpiece; an American opera to the core, with a good libretto, dramatic music and great sincerity. It should have been on Broadway, for it is an extension, a glorification of our popular musical forms and owes very little to the European musical tradition.

William Hawkins, writing in the amalgamated New York *World-Telegram and Sun,* said, "The work has more blood and thunder, and more complex dramatic excitement than many works done by the Metropolitan." Citing the one-night revival as "one of the most exciting events of the season," Arthur Bronson in *Variety* recommended that the work be incorporated into the repertory of an established opera company, such as the New York City Opera.[36]

Within days, Cheryl Crawford put together a promotional sheet with four of the revival's most approving notices and sent them out to friends and associates in the theatre world. "I thought you might like to see these reviews," she said on the flyer. "Perhaps we *weren't* crazy." In the audience that night at the Y sat

Julius Rudel, director of the New York City Opera. He needed prompting neither from *Variety* nor from Crawford: He fell in love with the work, and less than a year later he would do *Regina* with his own company.[37]

Leonard Bernstein's position as professor of music and director of the School of the Creative Arts at the then recently established Brandeis University in Waltham, Massachusetts, provided Blitzstein with a good launching pad for his *Threepenny* translation. Brandeis offered him a five-hundred-dollar honorarium plus travel and living expenses in Boston. In the first days of June, workmen rushed to finish constructing the open-air Adolph Ullman Auditorium in time for the first weekend-long Festival of the Creative Arts, to be held June 12–15. Bernstein included jazz, dance, poetry, opera, and theatre. He premiered his own *Trouble in Tahiti* on Thursday the twelfth, and conducted the Weill work on the Saturday-night program. According to press reports, Bernstein regarded *The Threepenny Opera* as a twentieth-century masterpiece, which he was prepared to conduct on Broadway the coming season. On Sunday, the final day of the festival, Bernstein conducted a concert in memory of Serge Koussevitzky.

An audience of five thousand gathered that Saturday night to hear Hans W. Heinsheimer, who had worked for Weill's publisher Universal Edition in Vienna during the *Dreigroschenoper* time, recall the atmosphere surrounding the premiere twenty-four years before and to say how remarkably Blitzstein had captured the Brecht essence. The music for the evening began with the first public performance of *musique concrète* in America, Pierre Schaeffer's *Symphonie pour un homme seul,* choreographed by Merce Cunningham; Stravinsky's *Les Noces,* also staged by Cunningham, with Howard Bay's sets and costumes; followed by all twenty-one numbers from *The Threepenny Opera.* Irving Fine, a composer at Brandeis and the man who performed most of the legwork for the festival, had coached members of the Brandeis University Glee Club for the opera's choruses of gangsters, beggars, policemen, and prostitutes.

For his casting, Blitzstein asked David Brooks to sing Macheath. Brooks had been at Curtis with Bernstein and knew Blitzstein from his appearances in Philadelphia for liberal causes. He later went on to direct and produce *Trouble in Tahiti* on Broadway. George Mathews sang Tiger Brown and Anita Ellis sang Lucy. A singer of superb talent, Ellis never considered herself a theatre performer and never sought to appear in the stage production of *Threepenny* that might eventually occur; but she had known all about the work from her former lover Hans Viertel, son of the actress Salka Viertel. And, in a coincidental bond with Blitzstein, she had also taken classes with Arnold Schoenberg—at UCLA.

David Thomas sang Peachum, and Mary Kreste, Mrs. Peachum. As her big number, she sang the "Ballad of Dependency," the single most bawdy number in Brecht's script, which not even the original Mrs. Peachum in Berlin had had the gumption to sing, nor Yvette Guilbert in the Parisian production. The role of Polly Peachum went to Jo Sullivan, who had performed to Blitzstein's great satisfaction in *Let's Make an Opera.*

The Jenny of the evening was Lotte Lenya. Creator of the role in 1928, she now sang it in English. Her right to the part had recently been confirmed in America when Capitol rereleased her early Telefunken recordings in the new long-play format. Now she had the chance to introduce not only her vision of the character to a much wider public, but her vision of the work as a whole, for both Blitzstein and the other singers in the cast consistently deferred to her memory of how things had been done in the beginning.

Bernstein and his orchestra were placed at stage left; the singers on the right, with Blitzstein, who read a narrative connecting the musical numbers. Bernstein performed from Kurt Weill's original manuscript. The evening went well, tension heightened by the fact that critics from most of the major newspapers had gone to Brandeis above all to hear this translation. Producers had also gone to see what present-day commercial potential lay in this fabled work, virtually unknown in America since a mangled, incomprehensible production lasting only twelve performances had embarrassed the New York stage back in 1933.

Trouble in Tahiti received generally poor reviews, though in its finished, revised form it later proved fairly popular. For the *Threepenny,* however, the critics rang in with a tumult of praise. "Mr. Blitzstein has set his version of the piece in New York City in the 1870's," wrote Harold Rogers in the *Christian Science Monitor.* "His lyrics capture the spirit of the times in vernacular and meter. They have punch; they are exactly suited to the music." Lotte Lenya sang "with the same provocative charm" as of old. In short, it was "a captivating performance." Howard Taubman, reviewing for *The New York Times,* called it "a truly creative job. . . . If the rest is as good as what was heard last night, *The Threepenny Opera* in this version is a sure shot to enliven the coming season."[38]

The composer and critic Arthur Berger considered the event "particularly newsworthy." "It offered many delights, and it was clear, as one had anticipated, that a better man for the translation would be hard to find indeed." "His translation was made with a devotion that runs deep. It is rare, too, to have for translator of a libretto some one who is a librettist in his own right. . . . It will be something to regret if New York does not have a stage production of it soon."[39] "If the Festival had produced this work alone," wrote Elinor Hughes in the Boston *Sunday Herald* a week later, "the occasion would have been memorable."[40]

Back in the fall, Bernstein had finally married Felicia Montealegre, the Chilean woman who had been so desperate to win him. As one of Bernstein's closest friends, Blitzstein knew her from Tanglewood and many other contexts and genuinely liked her. At the time of the marriage, however, Blitzstein entertained his doubts and shared them with Mina Curtiss:

> Good or bad, the thing has been simmering for so long a time, I am relieved; let it happen, let him hurt her, her hurt him (it sounds like a perverted lyric, except that the aitches won't sing), let them part or not. Hitched or unhitched, they will be through and un-itched, as Cole Porter might have written.[41]

A few weeks after the Brandeis premiere, Marc stayed with the Bernsteins at Tanglewood. Thanking them for their hospitality, he wrote from New Canaan, Connecticut:

> Sitting in the kitchen with Cheryl and Ruth, eating raspberries for breakfast, it comes all over me what a fine time I have been having recently. The *Regina* concert started, really sparked, the sense of well-being; then Brandeis and the *Threepenny;* then Mina's; then Tanglewood and you-all. Not a great deal of work to show for it; maybe something just as good for me now, and for which I have apparently been hungry: well-being, that says it. It comes over me that for a long time since the Broadway *debacle* of *Regina* I have been slowly withering on the vine. How one needs these vanity-assuagements![42]

From Jo's place in Brigantine, Marc took up with Lenny the matter of an opera about Evita Perón that Bernstein had considered writing, maybe with Hellman as librettist:

> Once the Latin color is snagged, and the expanded picture of power-area registered, will she (L) not find herself treading well-worn paths? Then you could call the opera "The Bigger Foxes" or "The Same Old Part of Another Forest."
>
> *Reuben* really goes well. More later.[43]

After the Brandeis performance, Blitzstein heard from Samuel Matlovsky, then on tour in Chicago as conductor of a revival of *Porgy and Bess* starring Leontyne Price and William Warfield. He knew Blitzstein through his filmmaker friend Leo Hurwitz; he knew *The Threepenny Opera* from his years in Europe after the war; and he had once directed a production of *The Cradle Will Rock* at Green Mansions, a summer camp in upstate New York. He had suggested *The Threepenny Opera* to *Porgy*'s producer Robert Breen as a possible next project for the *Porgy* cast, and Breen flew Blitzstein to Chicago to play through the score. An all-black *Threepenny Opera* did not result; but Samuel Matlovsky would eventually conduct Blitzstein's adaptation.

Other producers looked at the translation as well, but in every case they wanted to see such drastic changes in the book, the lyrics, the orchestration, and the style of presentation that neither Blitzstein nor Lenya could countenance a production on such terms. "I feel strongly that *The Threepenny Opera* in English, properly adapted, can play for the rest of our lives—and beyond," Billy Rose said to Blitzstein. Recommending that the translator reconcile the time setting of the work with the language employed, he pointed out the discrepancy between the nineteenth-century setting and Blitzstein's up-to-date slang usages. Further, he argued, Blitzstein should feel free to adapt Brecht's text much more freely if that would produce an even more singable lyric. "In my opinion," Rose stated, "you owe no more allegiance to the German librettist than he did to Gay," suggesting as an apt parallel what Oscar Hammerstein did when he rewrote the Bizet opera into *Carmen Jones.* Finally, Rose offered:

> I am not too taken with the happy ending in the final scene. It seems to me that the John Gay concept, with the ending left up in the air, is more valid and believable—and equally satiric. . . .
>
> If you're willing to work with me as producer in the old-time sense, and not relegate me to the present-day role of the emotional janitor who merely raises the money, I'm prepared to make an immediate, dollar-down, washed-in-the-blood-of-the-lamb deal with you.[44]

Blitzstein would not make such a deal with Rose. Their relations remained friendly, however. At this time, the beginning of 1953, Rose announced a full-dress opera season at his Ziegfeld Theatre, featuring operatic classics as "shows" in English translation. Blitzstein very much figured into his plans: Existing translations of *La Traviata,* one of the first projects under discussion, were in Blitzstein's view "low in passion and low in wit." In his libretto, which he had begun already, he aimed to recreate the decadent world of Chopin and George Sand's Paris of the 1850s, and "the philosophy of hedonism of the demi-mondaine, with a heart-of-gold." Rose offered a contract of a one-thousand-dollar fee, 2 percent royalty on performances, and 20 percent of subsidiary returns, but Blitzstein, hoping to better his weak financial position, held out for more, and further stipulated "no concessions because of politics." In the end, they did not agree on terms and signed no contract.

If Blitzstein stayed up to date with popular culture, it was more through his love of movies and theatre than poetry or fiction. One thing that he did read that summer was Ernest Hemingway's *The Old Man and the Sea,* first published in the September 1, 1952, issue of *Life.* With a devastating, rapier archness that no one could appreciate, other than perhaps members of Jo's family who might pick up the magazine after he did, he recorded on the title page his reaction to this latest sign of life from the old macho expatriate:

> *Ave,* Sportsmanship! *And* Anglo-Saxon-Dreamboat-Mysticism, and Ultimate Male Challenge! By all means, let us build up the *fish,* to be a worthy challenger! As man to fish, and true brother to true brother, and breakfast to supper, let's have a drink!

After the success of *Threepenny* at Brandeis, while waiting for a producer to come along who would respect the integrity of the work, Blitzstein turned his renown into a traveling public relations show. In mid-December 1952 he appeared in Boston again, where the Friends of the School of Creative Arts of Brandeis University had organized a reception and musicale featuring Blitzstein as a speaker and pianist, and Lenya repeating Weill's songs in Blitzstein's translations. A month later they appeared at the Hartt College of Music in Hartford. Blitzstein spoke on "The Composer as Librettist." Hartt students performed excerpts from his works and Lenya sang two numbers.

An amusing flurry of internal FBI correspondence extending from October 1952 to August 1955 related to an unconfirmed report that Blitzstein had traveled to Vienna, Austria. U.S. officials there were asked if they could determine his activities; of course they turned up nothing, as Blitzstein did not make the trip. The investigation into Blitzstein's passport status must have confused the FBI, as his last passport had been issued in 1934.

The themes of American opera and opera in English dominated Blitzstein's consciousness. He worked up some of his thoughts into an article intended for *The New York Times* but never published. Approving of Rudolf Bing's innovations at the Metropolitan—translations, competent directors, more integrated casts—he cited the needs for opera both in the original language and in translation, and for both opera and lighter musical theatre works. With a New York City Opera revival of *Regina* about to take place, he joshed, "Perhaps since there have been protests in certain quarters about the inadequacy of opera-in-English, the proposed City Center revival this spring should be in Italian!" Finally, he objected to the production of American opera if technique "dominated, and not at all concealed, trivial and hollow ideas. Is it too much to ask that 'know-how' be preceded and pervaded by 'know-what?' " The implication suggested Menotti above all, his theatrical trickery outshining what Blitzstein considered his undeveloped political and social outlook. Since his article did not see print, he took the opportunity to address the same subject at a panel discussion called "The Music and the Libretto" at the City Center in May of 1953.

If Blitzstein had come to recognize Leonard Bernstein's vanity as an inescapable adjunct to his genius, he considered Bernstein's methods suspect. *Wonderful Town* opened at the end of February 1953. "It's not my cup of tea," Blitzstein wrote to Mina Curtiss:

> He has been this time rather exorbitant in his demand for lenience in the matter of borrowing. I don't seriously mind when he swipes from me (he has a number, "Quiet Girl," which title I used years ago; but instead of writing *that* song, he has written another of mine: a lullaby I wrote for *No for an Answer*)—but, when he calmly grabs the Brahms *2nd Piano Concerto* for his "hit," called "Why-oh-why-oh-why-oh, Why-did-I-ever-leave-Ohio?", I gaga. (I mean gag.)[45]

Bernstein had, of course, already borrowed a major theme from *Freedom Morning* for *On the Town.* Now he had done it again. And it wouldn't be the last time.

By now somewhat skeptical of his earlier confidence in Broadway as the home of an emergent American opera, Blitzstein prepared *Regina* for the opera house. For such presentation, he further eliminated some of the small plotting from the original play, cut some of the spoken dialogue, and composed recitative for much of the rest, leaving an estimated 8 percent as unaccompanied speech. He divided the action into three acts instead of two and restored three substantial pieces of music cut in tryouts because Bobby Lewis had felt they slowed down the action. William Warfield as Cal was to have sung the "Blues" number to Birdie in 1949; in this revised production, while Regina ranted and raved in near apoplexy, the servant woman Addie sang the "Blues" and brought the house down. In the words of an Addie from a later production, "the audience needed a moment of respite and quietude in the midst of all that dissonance, controversy and confusion."[46]

Surviving from the original production were Priscilla Gillette as Zan, William Wilderman as Horace, William Dillard as Jazz, all making their City Center debuts, and Brenda Lewis, who now switched roles from Birdie to Regina. Ellen Faull, a regular member of the City Opera company, sang Birdie, and Lucretia West sang Addie. Veteran jazz clarinetist Eddie Barefield joined the Angel Band quintet, and Julius Rudel conducted. Bobby Lewis directed: This in itself proved a reeducation for the City Opera company, for Lewis tolerated no mere singing out into space. Instead, he demanded the kind of sustained contact with the other actors on the stage that he was used to getting in his regular dramatic plays, and he did not shrink from giving lengthy notes after each rehearsal. Jean Rosenthal, of the old Mercury Theatre days but by now much better known, designed the lighting.

Also surviving from the Broadway production were the Horace Armistead sets and Aline Bernstein's costumes, which Crawford and Clinton Wilder had wisely stored in Wilder's barn. Otherwise, the City Opera would not have been able to afford a new production.

Blitzstein could count on a better orchestra at the City Opera than he had on Broadway. Nevertheless, he complained of very paltry rehearsal time—only five weeks—during which he had to play the piano himself, since no one on the City Center staff was capable of sight-reading the score. During that time, Lincoln Kirstein and Blitzstein had a falling out over the opera: Kirstein hated it, considering it middlebrow pandering, and tried to disrupt the rehearsals. The root cause may have lain in jealousy over the closeness of Marc's relationship to Lincoln's sister—a timely check from Mina helped to pay for an additional orchestra rehearsal. In any case, the two men never repaired the friendship in subsequent years.

Howard Taubman summed up for readers of *The New York Times* the overwhelmingly favorable press reviews. The production "so lavish and so right," the orchestration "transparent, economical and immensely dramatic," "*Regina* is one of the best operas any American has written":

> There was electricity on the stage and in the pit, and there was electricity in the audience. With this achievement, the Center's opera company not only did itself proud but, even more important, restored a notable American lyric work to the stage. . . .
>
> Mr. Blitzstein has had to wait three years and a few months to see his opera back on the stage—not a long time as epochs are measured but long enough for any creator's morale. The applause that greeted the performers all during the show and that caressed the composer—and his colleagues—at the end must have sounded sweet, indeed. Every bit of it was deserved.[47]

Richard RePass topped that praise with his remarks about *Regina* in *The Music Review:* this "stunning work" "left little room for doubt that Blitzstein is the most important native opera composer in America to-day. Whatever its weaknesses, *Regina* has swept the field clear—for the moment, at least." The *Musical Courier* chimed in, saying that the opera deserved to be staged "season after season as a valuable addition to the growing list of modern music dramas."[48]

"Lillian Hellman may someday best be remembered as the librettist of *Regina,*" said Douglas Watt in his *Daily News* review, words calculated to rub the playwright just the wrong way. *Variety* picked up the same thread: "Opus has bite, drive, drama and ear-appeal . . . the music in many ways enhancing the story." The *Musical Courier* went even further:

> The music of Mr. Blitzstein not only does not detract from the fascinating dramatic content of the play but adds to it greatly, employing a language which (based on music's emotional projection) is superior to the purely spoken word.[49]

As Regina, Brenda Lewis scored perhaps the greatest sensation of her career. Though she had been a touching Birdie before, now her every note shot flaming venom. She also had the requisite sense of humor about the role. Here, at last, was the Regina Blitzstein had wanted all along.

The Cleveland Play House also produced *Regina* that spring, performed to a two-piano accompaniment. Adele Khoury, a contralto, sang the title role, and Beverly Dame—a veteran of Menotti's *The Medium*—portrayed Birdie. Benno Frank directed. A team from Cleveland went to New York to see the City Opera's presentation, but they decided to use the original 1949 Broadway version, not the new one. At least one reviewer, Omar Ranney in the Cleveland *Press,* preferred the Ohio production to the Broadway original, which he had seen. For one thing, he liked the sets better. Blitzstein did not attend: His doctor, Sam Standard, had performed a second hernia operation on him just after the City Center *Regina* opened.

Julius Rudel programmed *Regina* at the City Center again in the fall season, with only two cast substitutions: Dorothy MacNeil as Zan (Priscilla Gillette was away on tour in Hellman's *The Children's Hour*), and Willabelle Underwood as Birdie.

Skitch Henderson had flown in the Eighth Army Air Force in World War II and remained active in the Air Force Reserves. Schuyler Chapin was also a former air force pilot, and both were now in the employ of NBC. Together they decided to organize a pops series to give the New York Philharmonic players more employment.* Remembering the enthralling power of the *Airborne* Symphony when the records came out, the producers determined to present it at Carnegie Hall. The performance took place on May 4—it was actually the second perfor-

*Two years before, on the "Faye Emerson Show," Henderson had conducted an excerpt from *Regina* with Jane Pickens as a salute to the city of Atlanta; Henderson was married to Emerson at the time.

mance of the work that week, for Lehigh University in Bethlehem, Pennsylvania, did it on April 27 as well.

Henderson conducted, in his debut with a serious work. Tyrone Power, who had served in the Second World War as a marine aviator and who had owned an ice cream business with Henderson in Hollywood after the war, spoke the role of the Monitor most convincingly. Rawn Spearman was the tenor soloist, and Norman Clayton the baritone. The Lehigh University Glee Club repeated their work from the week before, and the United States Air Force volunteered the Singing Sergeants to join them.

When the American Legion got wind of the performance, they let Henderson know that they very much wanted the politically questionable section calling for the second front to be omitted. In deference to their wishes—a veiled threat of pickets and leaflets outside the hall—he excised the passage, and the Legion made him an honorary member. They did not, however, promote the concert to their membership.

Blitzstein may have gotten exercised at the deletion, or he may have lacked confidence in Henderson's abilities. At the dress rehearsal, he screamed so much about nothing being right that Henderson despaired of getting through the piece. The composer did appreciate the timbre of college-age voices, rather than the professional, older chorus sound. And he liked the way Tyrone Power talked, like a marine pilot, not like an actor, and certainly not like the great pontificator Welles.

The hall was half-full—with a pops crowd, not the regular concertgoing audience, and with a healthy contingent of VIPs from Washington. Blitzstein may not have been pleased by the performance, but he certainly couldn't have minded the cheering that followed it. Ross Parmenter of the *Times* said the reading had "dramatic intensity, drive, an agreeable degree of variety and a mounting excitement." Jay S. Harrison reviewed for the *Herald Tribune:* "Despite the occasional banalities of word and sound which scurry through the symphony, there is no denying that its character provides an hour of drama in which speech, song and choral interludes combine to make the history of flight a throbbing and vibrant experience." Harriett Johnson said in the New York *Post* that "much of it seemed verbose and musically obvious."[50]

For another reach back into Blitzstein's catalogue, Hugh Ross, who had conducted Marc's film score to Ralph Steiner's *Surf and Seaweed* back in 1931, expressed interest in *The Harpies,* the short opera Blitzstein had written later in 1931 for the League of Composers. The performance had been canceled at the time for lack of funds. Since he changed his style not long afterward, Blitzstein never promoted the work; it had remained unperformed for twenty-two years. Ross conducted it with a student cast at the Manhattan School of Music on May 25, 1953, on a bill with Haydn's *The Songstress* and Martinů's *Comedy on the Bridge.* "I have no great hopes for an efficient performance," the composer wrote to the Baumans.[51]

Most of the critical interest in the program focused on the Blitzstein work, staged with the Harpies in modified flapper outfits in a stylized Greek mode. Robert Sabin in *Musical America* found the opera "thoroughly entertaining," praising the "extremely rich and sonorously beguiling" finale.[52] Other critics, in the *Herald Tribune* and the *Times,* found the work effective, if not particularly memorable, only a precursor to Blitzstein's later creations.

During the summer of 1953, Blitzstein came to an agreement with Albert Sirmay, his Chappell publisher, granting the composer an automatic yearly advance on royalties of two thousand dollars. The money would come to represent a healthy component of his income because the agreement was always renewed upon expiration; but in no year from 1953 until the time of Blitzstein's death would Chappell ever be obliged to pay additional royalties. Financially, their adoption of Marc Blitzstein never paid off.

Blitzstein often endeared himself to his friends by composing occasional pieces, tunes tossed off to mark a celebration, a birth, a marriage. For his nephew Kit's wedding in June of 1953, he wrote a little piano piece. On the birth of the Bernstein's first child, Jamie, for whom they named Blitzstein as godfather, he composed a one-page "Innocent Psalm," a slow, almost holy-sounding piece to which one can easily imagine setting a religious text. Undoubtedly, he meant to evoke the Hebrew texts that Bernstein frequently set. This was the kind of piece he would save for what the Bernsteins called a "glee," an afterdinner entertainment involving words or music or both, supplied by hosts and guests as continuing affirmation of love and mutual respect.

Engrossed with *Reuben Reuben,* Blitzstein spent the entire month of June and part of July with Mina Curtiss. He was there in the Berkshires when news came of the execution of Julius and Ethel Rosenberg on charges of spying for the Soviet Union. All the appeals and protests, the marches and petitions had been useless. Right up until June 19, the left, and with them decent people all around the world, had hoped for a last-minute clemency. None came. It was the darkest moment of the government's war on American Communism.

The French poet Saint-Jean Perse also spent a week with Mina Curtiss that summer; he and Blitzstein got on famously. Work went well for Blitzstein. He felt rejuvenated and expected to finish *Reuben Reuben* in a matter of weeks. Cheryl Crawford planned to begin rehearsals in November. At the same time, he helped Mina with her biography of Georges Bizet, playing through scores for her and analyzing music, for which she had no expertise. In fact, though the publisher inadvertently omitted the dedication page—much to her chagrin—she assured Marc that she had dedicated the book to him.

Mina's relationship to her brother Lincoln Kirstein had long ago gone sour. He could barely stand to be in the same room with her; and in the intensity of his dislike for her, he took out his hostility against her friends—Marc, in particular. Mina and Marc shared a warm love for one another based on profound civility and mutual respect for intellectual creation, something similar to what Marc had wanted with Eva, but without all the attendant neurotic drives. "I have great faith in him," Curtiss told John Houseman. "I love him dearly and he has shown a kind of consistently generous, devoted and considerate affection for me that alone has compensated me for the loss of Lincoln."[53] From time to time, she gave him a much needed check to help him keep working, as well as making other presents to him. He overcame the embarrassment about accepting this unearned support only by reassuring himself that she simply made available to him a tiny portion of the large fortune she controlled. If the economic system was grossly unfair, this was but a small corrective.

What Marc did not anticipate was Mina's proposal of marriage. She certainly understood that Marc could hardly have been interested in her sexually. Aside from her imposing physical appearance as a walking monument, she was almost ten years older than Marc. She offered him complete independence and separate sleeping quarters. The proposal would simply guarantee a certain degree of companionship; undeniably, they did get on extremely well together, and whatever Marc's political sympathies may have been, he shared with Mina a taste for fine things: crystal, caviar, cuisine, flowers, furnishings, and clothing. The marriage would also offer Marc the financial security that had always eluded him in life—or that he had always thwarted.

He declined the offer. He enjoyed the attention of women in general, especially those with money who were willing to play out subtle adult versions of the Prince and the Pauper game he had shared with Jo as a child. But marriage, with all its evocations of Eva, might be altogether too difficult an arrangement to explain honorably. He would feel guilty about the unearned financial comfort, and he might have to surrender his precious time alone. No, better to continue struggling on, emotionally alone, fearing as he reached the age of fifty and scarred from his hernia operations that no one would ever want him again.

Summers, Jo always went to the Jersey shore. It was when she could look forward to spending the most time with Marc, who loved the ocean, the sun, and the quiet. Her new house in Brigantine had a studio on top of the two-car garage, reachable by an outside staircase; it had a piano, of course, and wide windows facing directly out to sea. He could be up before seven in the morning, work, swim, sleep, and eat with as much or as little contact with the world as he desired. And Jo protected him against all unwelcome interference. The normal routine included a long morning work session, followed by lunch and a swim, then another bout with words and notes until cocktail time. To relax, Marc would dash through a crossword puzzle. Or if he wanted to share an hour's diversion, he would lie back on a deck chair, his arms folded behind his head, while Jo read off the clues to a double-crostic and he would suggest the answers. These were golden days, that July and August of 1953, and Marc loved returning there year after year.

"*Reuben,* the rummy rogue, is finished," Marc wrote to Bernstein in Israel,

> or *about* finished, which means I shall finish him off weeks after the first-night. We have found nobody to play him, which is just ducky. . . . I will take a star, I will take an unknown; where the hell is he? . . . I feel debauched by the effort. The summer was a long love-scene with

> myself, doing the work, loving every virtuous abstinence, moving in the grandest compulsion of my life. What's not yet right is quite apparent; I know where I must emphasize, where let go, where excise. I think it is a sublime "lightweight"; so sublime it may not be lightweight at all: have I got into a Mozartean groove?[54]

But after he had "finished or *about* finished" *Reuben Reuben,* it would still be another two years before he considered it ready to put on the stage.

December 17, 1953, marked the fiftieth anniversary of the Wright Brothers' experiment in powered flight at Kitty Hawk, North Carolina. To celebrate the occasion, the city of San Antonio, Texas—which locals liked to call "the World's Flyingest City"—sponsored a series of events capped by the San Antonio Symphony Orchestra playing the *Airborne* Symphony. Victor Alessandro conducted seventy-five voices from nearby Lackland Air Force Base, and the film star Zachary Scott, a native of Austin, narrated. Norman Clayton repeated his baritone solo from the Skitch Henderson performance in May. As the tenor soloist, Blitzstein recommended Russell Nype, the Leo from the original *Regina.* Sarah Churchill, daughter of Sir Winston and the starring actress of NBC's Hallmark Hall of Fame, gave the welcoming speech. Two performances were scheduled at the Municipal Auditorium, December 17 and 18, with a delayed NBC coast-to-coast broadcast on Sunday the twentieth.

The Korean War had ended with a stalemate only that July. Estimates of the total number of dead, wounded, and missing reached over two million. Yet Blitzstein was pleased to go to Texas and acknowledge the applause of a whole crop of Cold Warriors—state and military officials—who turned out for the occasion. From Alabama's Maxwell Field, where Marc's buddy Bill Hewitt had been hospitalized after his term of service, Lieutenant General Laurence Kuter represented General Nathan F. Twining, air force chief of staff. If they were willing to listen to his music, Blitzstein was willing to have them hear it. Maybe his warning against the uselessness of war might yet affect someone in the audience, even if for the generals the score was little more than a nostalgia trip for the comraderie of World War II.

The composer traveled to Texas a few days early to hear the final rehearsals. On December 16 the San Antonio *Express* carried a publicity photo of him with the pilot in the control room of the plane that took him to San Antonio. Just as during his old army days, he rode out to Lackland to rehearse the chorus. "Those boys sing like angels," he told the San Antonio *Light.*[55] These were two very commendable performances: Russell Nype particularly distinguished himself with a supple, folksy delivery of the "Ballad of History and Mythology."

In this heyday of Senator Joseph McCarthy, Blitzstein might have encountered quite a rude reception if his past political affiliations had been known to this audience in San Antonio. Indeed, it seems unlikely that his work would have been programmed for such an occasion. But so far, except for his listing in *Red Channels* and a passing newspaper reference or two, his name had not been brought before the public. He went onto the stage at the end of his piece to congratulate the principals and make his bows to the audience.

CONCERTS UNMITIGATED WOW ROYAL RECEPTION FEEL LIKE A KING, he wired to Jo.[56]

It was the last performance of the *Airborne* Symphony that Blitzstein would ever hear.

18

A SMASH, A FLOP

Winter 1954–October 1955

"... how much completion is there in this life?"

Carmen Capalbo had studied at the Yale Drama School after his wartime service in the army. He knew Kurt Weill's American works well; indeed, the first musical he had ever seen was *Lady in the Dark.* He also owned recordings of Blitzstein's *The Cradle Will Rock* and the *Airborne* Symphony. In 1946, as an indication of the socially relevant drama he liked, he had given Sean O'Casey's *Juno and the Paycock* an Off-Broadway production at the Cherry Lane Theatre in New York. At that time he lived at 28 West Tenth Street in a sublet from Jane Bowles, whose husband, the composer and novelist Paul Bowles, lived on the top floor, adjacent to Leonard Bernstein's apartment in the next building. In summer, Bowles and Bernstein liked to play two-piano music together in their separate studios with the windows open, which the other tenants in Capalbo's building appreciated—they included the writer Dashiell Hammett and the stage designer Oliver Smith. Capalbo's roommate had somehow gotten hold of the original Telefunken records of the *Dreigroschenoper* songs and he played them over and over again. Profoundly affected by the music and curious to know something about the work from which it came, Capalbo went to the New York Public Library and consulted a copy of the promptbook from the disastrous 1933 production. It made very little sense; but he vowed that one day, somehow, he was going to produce that show.

Some years later, Capalbo and a fellow CBS employee, Stanley Chase, decided to form a production team together. They took out a twelve-week lease on the Theater de Lys, a tiny converted movie house on Christopher Street, a Greenwich Village byway that was little more than a slum. A failed playwright and producer named William de Lys had taken over the theatre, then skipped town when his first play flopped, leaving the house in the hands of his principal creditor.

Capalbo and Chase planned to stage Capalbo's own translation of Albert Camus's *State of Siege* in March 1954, with Marlon Brando, Claude Rains, and Vera Zorina. But Brando withdrew, making the production far less attractive if not impossible to mount. In October of 1953, they had a rented theatre and no show.

Neither Capalbo nor Chase had attended *The Threepenny Opera* at Brandeis, but they had read the enthusiastic reports. They also knew that a year and a half had passed, and so far no one had come forward to produce it, at least not in anything like an authentic version. Why not make a bid for this property that had fascinated Capalbo for so long?

Capalbo telephoned Blitzstein to make his proposal.

"You're one day too late," Blitzstein told him. "I just made a deal with a producer yesterday." It was the Phoenix Theatre.

"Is it definite?" Capalbo asked.

"Yes, it's definite."

"But just in case anything happens, can I call you back?" Capalbo pleaded. And every day for ten days running, Capalbo put in a call to Blitzstein, until Blitzstein began to get annoyed.

"Look," he said, "I admire your persistence, but please don't call me again. Forget about it."

The next morning, Blitzstein called Capalbo. "Are you still interested?" he asked. The Phoenix had fallen through. He asked Capalbo and his partner to meet him and Lenya at his apartment the next day.

Approaching the fateful meeting, Capalbo and Chase worried that the Theater de Lys would not be respectable enough. Capalbo also wondered what the reaction would be when he proposed himself as the director.

Based on their experience with other would-be producers who wanted to change the locale of the opera, alter the text and the orchestration, and otherwise update the property, Lenya and Blitzstein figured they would talk Capalbo into a losing position. "How would you like to do this work?" they asked him.

"Exactly as written," Capalbo answered, passing the first test.

Eyes gleamed as he elaborated on his approach to the play. Then Blitzstein went to the piano and invited Capalbo to sing "Mack the Knife" and a few other songs, reading the Blitzstein translation at sight. He wanted to get a sense of what vocal technique Capalbo had in mind.

"Where did you learn to sing like that?" Lenya inquired.

"From you!"

And Lenya pointed to him, saying, "That's the man to direct *Threepenny Opera.*"

The producers took the script home, read it through carefully, and the following day gave their decision to proceed with it. Capalbo asked for only one word change: In the final "Death Message" where Blitzstein had written, "May heavy hammers hit their faces," Capalbo suggested "hatchets" to avoid the hammer and sickle imagery. Marc agreed.

Blitzstein and Lenya went to see the Theater de Lys. Far from seeming inappropriate for *Threepenny,* it reminded Lenya of the out-of-the-way Theater am Schiffbauerdamm in Berlin where the original had been offered in 1928.

Carmen Capalbo basically cast the show, following Lenya's preference that he use mostly young people. Gerald Price played the Streetsinger. Charlotte Rae, a delicious comedienne, portrayed Mrs. Peachum; she had, in fact, played the role before—at Northwestern University in 1948 in the Bentley-Vesey translation—except that at that time she appeared under the name Charlotte Lubotsky. Leon Lishner, a City Opera singer who had sung Ben in *Regina,* was Peachum. Jo Sullivan, a holdover from the Brandeis performance but by now a much more familiar face on both the supper-club circuit and on television, sang Polly. Scott Merrill, famous more for his dancing than his acting, portrayed Macheath. George Tyne did Tiger Brown. Known in his old radical theatre days as Buddy Yarus, he had recently returned from Europe, where he had been evading the blacklist.

Capalbo thought the ideal Jenny would be Lenya herself. Why not recreate on the American stage her most famous role? Marc loved the idea, knowing what cachet her name would lend to the production. Together with Stanley Chase and Lenya's husband George Davis, he encouraged her. She objected strenuously: At fifty-five, she was too old and too out of practice. Furthermore, she had never gained much favorable critical attention in America. After weeks of persuasive effort, she agreed to perform the part, though she utterly fulfilled her predictions by behaving insecurely during the rehearsals. By opening night, she was a jangle of nerves.

Samuel Matlovsky conducted an eight-man orchestra that included himself at the keyboard. The theatre had a thrust stage because there was no room at the rear of the house into which to expand; the orchestra sat at stage left. Lenya recognized that this would not be simply a recreation of the Berlin production; she allowed Capalbo the independence he needed, though her recollections were often useful. William Pitkin provided the seedy settings, and Saul Bolasni designed the ragged costumes. A hallway with a curtain down the middle to separate men from women served as a dressing room.

Off-Broadway shows could sometimes be done for one thousand dollars. Capalbo and Chase spent close to ten thousand dollars on *The Threepenny Opera,* then considered an astronomical sum. At the time, Off-Broadway rules mandated that a show could not gross over forty-five hundred dollars. Capalbo argued with

Actors' Equity that *Threepenny* had to gross more in order to pay twenty-five actors, eight musicians, and stagehands. He proposed a sliding scale, with twenty-five dollars a week minimum pay plus increments according to the gross box office receipts. Equity agreed to the arrangement, which became the basis for future Off-Broadway contracts. In actuality, the actors earned fifty-five dollars a week because the show did so well—and Lenya took home the same as everyone else.

Even though Lenya could not read music, Blitzstein trusted her judgment completely. She knew the work in the most intimate possible way and he respected her authority. Lenya was well aware of her position. She may have felt insecure as a performer at this stage of her life, but she showed a ferocious temper whenever she perceived anyone tampering with Weill's music. Once, before the show opened and before Matlovsky had been contracted, Blitzstein mentioned, without particularly recommending, a possible conductor. The man went to Blitzstein's apartment and played the score as though it was Mozart. As soon as he left, Lenya turned on Blitzstein with a coruscating fifteen-minute diatribe. Both Capalbo and Chase were present.

"You're not a composer," she lashed out at Blitzstein. "You have no respect for this work. You know nothing." She kept up in that vein, and Blitzstein took it all in. By the end of her performance, he was drooping from shame.

At other times, auditioning a new singer, Blitzstein might play too fast. "You see," Lenya screamed to the producers, "he rushes everything, he doesn't understand this work."

When the show was ready to be announced, Capalbo and Chase worked out with Blitzstein and Lenya a carefully worded press release. Everyone approved it, and Sam Zolotow wrote the article for the *Times.* The show would open on March 2, Weill's and Blitzstein's birthday. If Lenya harbored a fundamental mistrust of other people's appropriation of her husband's work, she became enraged when she saw Zolotow's article on the morning of January 4, 1954. An editor had headlined it "Blitzstein Work Due Here March 2." Here was Blitzstein seemingly claiming credit for *both Weill and Brecht!*

Lenya called up Carmen Capalbo in a fury. "He's just a little Jewish tailor, not a composer," she yelled through the phone, threatening to withdraw the property entirely. Capalbo objected that the fault lay exclusively with the newspaper and that the subhead to the article did mention the Weill music. Only after many days' worth of cajoling reassurance did she calm down enough to proceed with the production.

In the Brandeis version, Blitzstein had set the opera on the docks of New York in Boss Tweed's era. His point was to offer a vernacular American, not a "correct" British translation. Not persuaded himself of the rightness of this choice, he toyed with other settings—Philadelphia, San Francisco, and New Orleans—in order to grasp the roughness of Brecht's language. In the end, he returned to the Victorian England of the original but used American colloquialisms in place of Cockney pretensions that would only have made the opera that much more alien to the public.

Before putting the work into final form, Blitzstein made a few other alterations, some based on Capalbo's preferences and some on Lenya's. Brecht had given Lenya authority to negotiate such changes; he turned out to be less rigorous in staying exactly to the script than one might suppose. Lucy, slated to be sung by Beatrice Arthur, veteran of many Off-Broadway shows and of a solo nightclub act, got Polly's "Barbara Song"—for which there was precedent in the original German production. And Jenny got "Pirate Jenny," Polly's wedding song, for which there was also ample precedent: Lenya had recorded it in Berlin and also had sung it in the 1931 movie. It had long been identified as her signature tune, and it would have been crazy in this production not to assign it to Lenya. But now Polly needed a new song for her wedding scene. At Lenya's suggestion, Blitzstein took the "Bilbao Song" from Weill and Brecht's *Happy End* and translated it as "Bide-A-Wee in Soho" for Polly. Restored to the opera were Jenny's "Solomon Song" and Mrs. Peachum's "Ballad of Dependency"—both cut from the Berlin production at the last minute. Blitzstein also changed the order of certain scenes.

Beatrice Arthur, practically a baritone, could not possibly have handled the high soprano tessitura of Weill's score. Blitzstein lowered her music, as he did for Lenya. In places, Weill's timbre suffered somewhat: The Lucy-Polly "Jealousy Duet" was intended as a scrap between two equally matched sopranos, satirizing operatic convention. In Blitzstein's version, it occurs between a soprano and a smoky-throated torch singer, a contrast that Capalbo thought would work better. Finally, this production ended with a reprise of "Mack the Knife," whereas Weill had ended with his "Third Finale."

Concerning the scoring, Weill had called for twenty-one different instruments plus percussion to be played by seven performers. Incredibly, Weill had called for one man to strum the banjo, guitar, Hawaiian guitar, and mandolin, and also play the bandoneon and the cello! He had used the Lewis Ruth Band, an eight-member ensemble under Theo Mackeben, which no doubt was able to provide such a curious range of expertise. But such ensembles might well be difficult to assemble under ordinary theatrical circumstances. Blitzstein made his an eight-man orchestra, adjusting the scoring in places by reassigning some parts to other players.

Because of these musical and textual differences from *Die Dreigroschenoper,* Blitzstein referred to his work as more an adaptation than simply a translation. All things taken into account, in the adaptation of the work for an American public a whole generation later, these changes were relatively minor. As a practical theatre person, Lenya raised no objection. These were the kinds of changes that any musical show undergoes. "Marc Blitzstein has come closest to capturing the power of Brecht's book and lyrics. He has kept the slang and the sting," she told one reporter. And in the German-language press, she told an interviewer shortly before the stage premiere:

> *Das ist eben ein rührenden Akt der Uneigennützigkeit und der Verehrung für Kurt Weill: Blitzstein hat sehr akkurat den Text und die Songs von Brecht übertragen und nichts hinzugefügt, und er hat überhaupt nichts*

> *von der Musik von Kurt Weill geändert oder neu instrumentiert.* [It is truly a moving act of unselfishness and honor to Kurt Weill: Blitzstein has rendered Brecht's text and lyrics very accurately, adding nothing to them, and above all he has not changed nor given new scoring to any of Kurt Weill's music.][1]

Clearly, she was reaching out to attract to the theatre the sizable audience of German refugees nostalgic for the 1920s—a period most of them had not much liked at the time.

As director, Capalbo used a nonrealistic technique absent from the American stage since the thirties. His actors, particularly the younger ones, didn't know the style. They couldn't understand talking to the audience directly; they had trouble with the absence of the "fourth wall." At rehearsals, Blitzstein would sometimes share his knowledge of Brechtian technique with the actors, going over Capalbo's head to suggest a mode of delivery or a bit of stage business. His intervention made the actors uncomfortable, however; ultimately Capalbo had to ask him not to go to rehearsals.

After only four weeks of rehearsal, the show opened with two preview performances. At nearly four hours in length and with an 8:40 curtain, it lasted well past midnight. Blitzstein had resisted making cuts up to the first preview, which Bernstein and other friends attended. With their suggestions and with Lenya's approval, Marc returned to Capalbo's apartment that night to relieve the script of its repetitiveness. About forty minutes went by the way, though none of the songs. Between director and adapter, they found it easy to cut back on many of Peachum's speeches, especially since it had become gratingly obvious that Leon Lishner was no actor. His problem was that he sang too operatically for the singing-actor style Capalbo wanted. With two intermissions, the show now ended at 11:20. Top ticket price was $3.30; other seats went for $2.20 and $1.20, the going Off-Broadway rate.

Before opening night, Wednesday, March 10, 1954—they had missed the Weill-Blitzstein birthday by eight days—everyone was convinced that the FBI would close down the show and everyone would be blacklisted. If it managed to whimper along for a few performances, there would surely be right-wing pickets outside the door to discourage ticket buyers. Before the curtain went up, Carmen Capalbo said to the company, "This thing will either run one night or a year." He didn't know how far off his prognosis would be.

The performance went without a hitch. Each musical number got hearty applause, and the laughs all came in the right places. At the end there were shouts of "Bravo!"

The cast party took place at Oliver Smith's apartment at 28 West Tenth Street. By fluke, it was the same building but just a floor above the apartment where Capalbo had first heard the Telefunken recordings eight years before. Lenya considered it a good omen, a circle completed. Actors and friends stood around the piano and belted out "Mack the Knife," making up new verses as the night wore on, hypnotized by the haunting melody. The song had become its antithesis through repetition—a narcotic. The merrymaking came to a halt sometime around two A.M. when the press agent phoned in and then took over the newspaper reviews.

Though it seems surprising from the subsequent history of the production, these first reviews were not, in the main, so positive. The sets were tawdry, the staging was poor, the score dated, the orchestra thin, the translation inadequate, and there was still too much dialogue, and too much of it politically objectionable. "For instance," said Robert Coleman in the *Daily Mirror,* "the Bible is cited as a first-rate source for commercial slogans. That joke just isn't funny . . . falls on its face. . . . Perhaps we have it too good over here to find heavy-handed swipes at the industrial system very amusing." John Chapman in the *Daily News* couldn't "see that Blitzstein has done anything remarkable in reworking a libretto which, under the authorship of John Gay, had its first performance in 1728." On top of which, according to Olin Downes, the de Lys was a "crowded, smelly little theatre."[2]

But Lewis Funke's *New York Times* review contrasted sharply, praising "words that fit the music, words that retain the bite, the savage satire, the overwhelming bitterness underlying this work," and drawing special attention to the wily performances, especially of the women. "To Mr. Blitzstein this morning this department extends heartfelt thanks." Brooks Atkinson also saw *Threepenny,* and discussed it in the *Times* alongside the Jerome Moross-John Latouche musical *The Golden Apple* playing at the Phoenix. Citing Harold Rome's *Wish You Were Here* by contrast, Atkinson attacked "Broadway's current passion for the tasteless, the hackneyed and the dull. . . . Banality has assumed the proportions of a cult. Stupidity is back in the market, earning a cozy profit. The music comes out of the filing case and the lyrics out of the foundry. . . . The brains, taste and inventiveness of the musical theatre have moved off-Broadway this season," Atkinson wrote.[3]

Jay Harrison's first-night review in the *Herald Tribune* did nothing to pull in business, but when Virgil Thomson approached the work in a Sunday follow-up, he claimed that "Marc Blitzstein's translation of the Brecht text is, to my guess, the finest thing of its kind in existence. He has got the spirit of the play and rendered it powerfully, colloquially, compactly." As for his prosodically apt lyrics, "one can scarcely believe them to be translations at all." The *Saturday Review*'s critic Henry Hewes found "a trip to Christopher Street the most rewarding of the season."[4]

Eric Bentley felt that in an attempt to "revive" a work that still possessed a healthy grasp on life, Blitzstein had killed it by altering its style and betraying its meaning—though Bentley's judgment at that time must surely have been colored by Blitzstein's cool rejection of Bentley as a director. Also, within the month after *Threepenny* opened at the de Lys, Lotte Lenya had a staging of the more exact but far less singable and theatrical Eric Bentley-Desmond Vesey version stopped in Chicago because the Capalbo-Chase production was the only one she and Brecht had authorized for the United States and Canada.[5] Brecht himself, however, did not share Bentley's disappointment. To the contrary, he wrote most appreciatively to Blitzstein from East Berlin, admiring both the adaptation and the adapter.[6]

Always one to value his own contributions over those of his collaborators, Brecht had demanded 60 percent of the royalties from German-language productions, to Weill's 25 percent (other co-contributors divided the remaining 15 percent). He reduced his own share to 40 percent for this production but insisted that Lenya as Weill's heir still not receive more than 25 percent. Lenya and Blitzstein then signed a side agreement to share the royalties equally after Brecht's 40 percent. According to the standard producers' contract, the authors (Brecht, Weill, and Blitzstein) together received 6 percent of the gross weekly box office.

Based largely on spectacular notices in the two most prominent newspapers in town, *The Threepenny Opera* was a hit from the first minute. The morning the reviews appeared, a line formed at the box office and reappeared every day, an absolutely unprecedented response to an Off-Broadway production. In six weeks, Capalbo and Chase paid off their expenses—equally unheard of for Off-Broadway. Somehow the show blew the lid off, let loose some of the pent-up tension of those repressive years, gave the left a bona fide success, a safe haven for all its battered warriors. The irony is that politically no one ever bothered the show and it was never picketed. Tired and relieved, Blitzstein flew to Bermuda for a week's rest at Landmark.

Amidst the nationally televised army McCarthy hearings taking place that April, Blitzstein wrote to David Diamond in Italy:

> I am valiantly trying to remember and hold on to the residue of decency, blunt honesty and humor I know exists in our people—it is more than easy to grow cynical in order not to become enraged or fear-paralyzed. Running to work is always possible; you know how I have tried to make my composing not a running-*from,* but a hand-in-hand walk-*with,* my times and tribulations. One can get so windy and pompous on the subject.
>
> *The Threepenny Opera* is a nondescript production of a masterpiece; and the masterpiece comes through.[7]

That week, he told Diamond, MGM would record the show. Since the opening, Martin Wolfson—the Nick Kyriakos of *No for an Answer*—replaced the operatic Leon Lishner as Peachum. Blacklisted at the time, Wolfson appreciated the opportunity to work. However, his appreciation did not stop him from reacting like a habitual left-wing organizer: On the very first day he went into the show, he raised his voice in loud, threatening protest, citing Equity rules, because the toilet backstage wasn't working properly. Even on the *Threepenny* set, it was the workers versus the bosses all over again.

Carmen Capalbo had tried to sell the idea of a cast album to various companies and was laughed out of their offices. Recording Off-Broadway shows simply was not done. Lenya convinced herself that no one would record it. Not wanting to jeopardize her personal friendship with CBS's Goddard Lieberson, she instructed Capalbo not to ask him: She could not have faced the rejection. (Later on, Lieberson said he would have leapt at the chance to record the show, had he only been asked.)

MGM Records was known at that time mostly for film scores and popular music, as an adjunct to the Metro-Goldwyn-Mayer movie business—Eva Goldbeck's old employer. Edward Cole agreed to record *Threepenny* as MGM's first cast album, offering a contract whereby the show would get 10 percent of the retail record price. Out of her insecurity and gratitude for Cole's enthusiasm, Lenya cut the show's percentage down to half that amount. The producers and Blitzstein felt like wringing her neck for her modesty, but she claimed that as an artist she possessed no business sense whatsoever. In fact, it was unusual for her to give up income such as that.

The recording took place at RCA studios. Ed Cole appeared there that morning accompanied by a contingent of MGM officers who had taken the precaution the night before of seeing the show their colleague had committed the company to record. They presented a long list of cuts—obscene or otherwise crude material they would absolutely not release to the public. If these cuts had been respected, there would hardly have been a show left—whole songs would have had to go. The producers were ready to walk out, but it was Marc—curiously enough, as he was not a compromiser by nature—who volunteered, "Hold on, let me see what I can do." And on the spot, while the cast and orchestra waited, Blitzstein drafted the new lyrics he needed to pass the MGM censors.

In other ways, the recording does not quite represent what playgoers experienced: Everyone agreed that the theatrical vocal style, so effective coming from the mouths of actors on the stage, would only be heard as bad singing on a recording. The cast therefore recorded a much more "sung" version. And the songs occur slightly out of order because the recording corresponds to the original work, not to the New York show where a few shifts had been made. For the sake of time, some reprises and intermediate verses were omitted.

By August 1954, sales of the MGM cast album approached thirty thousand copies—an average of more than one for each person who had seen the show. The music spread like wildfire.

After ninety-six sold-out performances, *The Threepenny Opera* closed. It seemed like such a shocking, demented thing to do—close a smash hit? But the producers' lease expired after twelve weeks. The Theater de Lys was operated by a self-important press agent who would only book shows he could promote, and Capalbo and Chase had refused to hire him as their agent. Now he chose to throw *Threepenny* out and open a new show of his own.

In the interim, Capalbo stored the sets and costumes in the basement of his house on Gay Street. He and Chase turned down offers to transfer the show to Broadway, feeling that a move to a larger house would kill the work. As no other Off-Broadway theatre was available, they simply had to wait until the de Lys was free again—or until they could buy it.

The play that replaced the Weill opera lasted one night. Flop after flop followed in endless procession. Not one lasted a week despite the press agent's efforts. Brooks Atkinson, a strong supporter of the Off-Broadway movement and a powerful fan of Weill's work who understood the abnormal arrangement at the theatre, helped to create a groundswell for *Threepenny*'s return, an unusual stance for a critic to assume. He would conclude each of his damning reviews of shows at the de Lys with lines such as, "Bring back *The Threepenny Opera.* The Theater de Lys never had it so good."

While Blitzstein and his *Threepenny* producers awaited the availability of the de Lys, other requests from around the country came in for rights to present the work elsewhere. Most of them Blitzstein turned down, hoping for someone of Bernstein's attention-getting calibre to lead an important West Coast production. He did allow a production at Harvard. Tally Brown asked whether she could do the work in Miami with her interracial Freedom Players. She did not have the resources to produce the whole work, but she did the main songs with spoken connectives. The YMCA in Liberty City lent her rehearsal facilities, and the production itself took place in the Baptist church next door. Apparently no one objected when Brown, playing the role of Jenny herself, performed her big numbers circling around the baptismal font.

Blitzstein reported to Bernstein, then conducting in Milan, about one further authorized production at Cleveland's Karamu Theatre: "*3d* was great—fresh, charmingly conceived in true Brechtian-Epic-Theatre style, and full of values we never began to get in the NY production."[8]

But in New York there was nothing to do but wait.

The *Threepenny Opera* program had carried news of Blitzstein's forthcoming translations not only of *La Traviata*—as discussed with Billy Rose and then abandoned—but of several short Offenbach operas as well. When John Gutman of the Metropolitan Opera asked to see the *Traviata,* Blitzstein answered that only one and a half acts had been done, and even that much was still in rough draft. He sounded less than enthusiastic about the possibility of a Met production; perhaps he still envisioned more lucrative commercial opportunities for the property on Broadway.

As for the Offenbach works, Blitzstein had examined songs from a little-known operetta by Offenbach, *Tulipatan,* or *Tulip Island,* written in the 1870s to words by Henri Chivot and Alfred Duru. The work concerned the amorous adventures of a native Amazon lady with a European. The songs, which Blitzstein made somewhat ribald in his English adaptation, were a "Canary Song" *("Couplets de Colibri"),* "Hermosa's Song" *("Couplets du Canard"),* and a *"Duettino."* He dedicated the songs to Jennie Tourel, who first performed them at Town Hall on March 5, 1955, and Chappell published the sixteen-page score that year as "Three Offenbach Songs." Two reviewers in the *Musical Courier* found them "excellent" and "superbly versioned into English," but few other singers seem to have discovered them.[9]

Waiting for *Threepenny* to reopen, Blitzstein pushed on with *Reuben Reuben.* By then it had reached something close to its final form. The musical opens with a circuslike overture—big, *Pagliacci*-like climaxes doused with tragic overtones. The action begins on the street—near a subway station at Third Avenue near the Bowery—about 9:30 on a warm night in September. Two comic lumpen types are pantomiming their pickpocket technique; already we are to read this as an introduction to the kind of America we are in. Reuben enters, juggling and singing. His theme, taken from the folk song, shows that Reuben is not all there; but if he is like any seriocomic Fool, he still has something to say about our fragile existence:

Reuben Reuben I been thinking
If this world were made of glass
All the people in creation
Would be sliding on their
Reuben Reuben I been thinking. . . .

He tries to give away everything in his possession, joyously expounding in song on the graciousness of the simple phrase "Thank you." The pickpockets do their number on him, but out of compassion for a newcomer to the big city they give everything back (except a dollar bill). A girl looking for the BMT subway loses her way as an argumentative couple pass by. They steer her in the right direction, and the quartet sing "Never Get Lost" in madrigal style:

Never get lost. Never get lost.
Try to know which way you're going.
Places get so vast. You can get lost so fast.
But don't be afraid. Don't be dismayed.
Try to keep your fears from growing.
Summon help, or calmly let
Someone help. Or better yet,
Just don't ever get lost.

Buried in this lushly voiced number is Blitzstein's Aesopian message to his listeners: Don't allow the perversities of the McCarthy era to distort your basic values or sway you from your true course. Remembering his Pop's suicide, and feeling perhaps that he may need the strength to decide on his own course of action, Reuben decides he needs a drink.

As Bart and the Countess flip nickels for drinks at the bar, four barflies sing "Tell It to Bart," a catalogue of their problems (one of them has a backache, a reminder of Bill Hewitt). Bart's luck is bad tonight, but in a song called "It's in the Cards" he trusts that a sign of fortune will appear tonight to ward off the harm with which someone named Malatesta has threatened him. Just as he superstitiously imagines that the sign could walk right through the bar door, Reuben appears. With his condition of aphonia, Reuben cannot talk, so he writes messages. He wants a double and signs his name. Bart muses, "Reuben Reuben"—thus the title (without comma), expressing the protagonist's essential dualism. When Bart calls him "sonny," Reuben produces a newspaper clipping about his father who killed himself two months before, blaming world tension. Reuben asks where he can find a high place, and a barfly suggests the Manhattan Bridge. When Reuben leaves, Bart sadistically telephones Malatesta asking for odds on Reuben's killing himself by daybreak.

The third scene takes place at the bridge. It is now 10:30. Nina is there, lustily spitting into the water, celebrating her new job as a chorus girl with a coloratura song about escaping like a bird. Independent in spirit, she is very explicit about not wishing to be bothered by male company: "My femininity is quite content without a need for any masculinity," she sings. As she leans over to watch her spit land, Reuben enters; he has come to jump off. He "saves" her from what he perceives as *her* attempt to jump. They tussle, then discover she has cut her little finger. An Irish cop comes along and grabs Reuben, who he thinks has tried to molest the girl. However mystified she is by the silent Reuben, she hates cops more—shades of the Moll in *The Cradle Will Rock*—and pretends that she and Reuben were kissing. She takes Reuben's arm and they walk off, leaving the cop to sing a pathetic lament.

Back at the bar, Bart is on the phone again with Malatesta. He proposes that if Reuben does kill himself, Malatesta can write out a phony, back-dated insurance policy and collect the proceeds. Reuben and Nina walk in and they introduce themselves to one another more formally, Reuben mostly writing notes. She mentions a street carnival Reuben might like to see. While she steps away to go to the ladies' room, Bart goes to their booth and urges Reuben to "Have Yourself a Night," then kill himself just like his Pop. Nina senses Bart's evil intentions, then follows Reuben out to the carnival.

The San Gennaro fair is in full progress on Mulberry Street: The stage is colorfully populated with vendors, neighborhood residents, and tourists. In the middle of a festive chorus telling the story of the Neapolitan patron saint, a small group from the church passes by with his effigy. A pasta seller sings "With a Woman to Be" to Reuben. A male quartet serenades Nina with "The Hills of Amalfi," then the crowd gradually disappears. Left on stage are Reuben and Nina, and a pair of punk teenagers, a gutter Romeo and Juliet who taunt each other with slurs. Reuben delivers a poignant "Rose Song" (the first number Blitzstein wrote for this opera, dedicated to Mina Curtiss in February 1950). He tells Nina to watch what happens as he sings: As if by magic, the punks suddenly lose all their vulgarity and dance an exquisitely melting pas de deux. When the song is over, the punks depart and the crowd wanders back on. For their entertainment, Reuben begins a series of circus tricks. Bart has joined the crowd. Seeing how popular Reuben is, he calls for a speech, in which he expects Reuben will recall his father's farewell to the world. Instead, Reuben launches into the "Miracle Song," a tribute to his fortuitous meeting with Nina, who is thankfully of "the right gender." Bart starts a brawl and Nina takes Reuben away. The Countess appears, asking what Bart is doing here leaving his bar unattended, his customers helping themselves to his liquor. The scene ends with the brawl still on.

After a musical interlude, the lights come up on Nina and Reuben seated on a bench a block away. It is now 12:30 in the morning. Exhausted, Reuben falls asleep. She sings a lullaby as he mumbles memories of his father. When he wakes, they declare their love for one another. Significantly, with autobiographical insight into his relationships with both Eva and Bill, Blitzstein has Nina say, "I think it's why I love you. Your trouble." Bart turns up with the Countess, who invites Reuben and Nina to The Spot, the nightclub Bart owns and where the Countess entertains. Her song about the place recalls Blitzstein's cabaret numbers from the thirties.

The stage is transformed into the sleazy club setting for Scene Seven. Overhead a mobile decorates the ceiling. The Countess continues singing, but now it is her lecherous routine, "Mystery of the Flesh," recalling the nightclub act in *No for an Answer.* Three Spot girls do a leggy dance routine and another suggestive musical number. Here Blitzstein inserts a vaudeville turn with ironic social implications in which a black waiter named Smith and a wealthy customer named Smythe, both wearing identical tuxedos, switch roles. Somehow they become enmeshed in the sleeves of each other's jackets and begin waltzing around together. The Countess reveals Bart's sinister plan. Nina comprehends it fully and wants to take Reuben away, but just then Reuben climbs up to the mobile hanging from the ceiling. There he feels free and comfortable, thinking of himself at the circus, especially when Nina reassures him of her love. But Bart taunts him. Part of the crowd debates whether or not Reuben will make a high jump, while the other part believes he and Nina are both crazy. Attendants from the insane asylum arrive to seize the two; also, the Countess has summoned men from the fire department with a net to catch Reuben if he jumps. As people alternately tell him to jump and not to jump, Reuben yells out, "Make way for the Human Dart." He jumps, to a quick blackout and the first-act curtain.

Act Two opens in the Wards. It is 2:30 A.M. A divider down the middle of the stage separates the men's and the women's wards. Reuben and Nina have been taken there. This is, in the Faust metaphor, the Walpurgisnacht scene, which Blitzstein originally conceived in the setting of a dope hangout. The ensemble, looking like characters out of drawings by Käthe Kollwitz, sings "Moment of Love," capturing the sense of a drugged marijuana haze:

The very moment of love
Is never the moment remembered ever any other
Never any other of.
The very moment of love
Is not forgotten ever
Never remembered or other. Or other
With without. With without.
Ever without with never without.
The wordless of mindless
The dreamless of nothing
Moment of love.

Nina says, "I gotta get us out of here," as the macabre ballet commences. It is a study in frustration—men dancing with men, women with women, though from each side of the stage people reach toward the other, fantasizing that they can connect. Reuben remembers something about the last scene in the nightclub; "I musta been crazy," he says. Both Nina and Reuben show helpfulness to the other inmates, then break into a duet, "There Goes My Love." An inmate cuts his wrists with a spike, an actual suicide that Reuben tries unsuccessfully to prevent—a sign that Reuben is back on the road to recovery, as he values life. An attendant and a matron appear to announce that Bart's emissary Harry has come to release Reuben and Nina.

At three o'clock, we are in Nina's modest studio apartment, where she and Reuben try to discuss what happened at the nightclub. With the jump into the firemen's net, Reuben symbolically died and is now free of the deathwish. They kiss and Reuben asks her to "Be with Me," to help him assemble the pieces of a man all mixed up inside. Harry is waiting outside for them, asking them to come to Bart's party. Reuben is confident now that he can confront Bart without fear, and they decide to go. First Nina sings to him the "Mother of the Bridegroom," an old family tune passed on from mother to daughter that, sung by Nina, fuses mother and lover into one:

> *Push everything out and make room.*
> *This is the night my son's a bridegroom.*
> *Dressed in his fine linen shirt I wove on my loom—*
> *Shirt that is only for the bridegroom.*
> *Push everything out and make room for the sight.*
> *Here comes my darling, and walks into the light.*
> *Fathers, what a sight. Joyful, joyful,*
> *Oh the joyful night.*
> *Soon we will notice a new home.*
> *Now they must have my own room.*
> *This is the night my son's a bridegroom.*

Back at Bart's bar and grill, the party is in full swing. The Countess sings a sexy baby-talk lullaby to one of the sleeping barflies. Following that comes a drinking song by the barfly and the Irish cop—making a reappearance from the bridge in Act One—in which they say "Musky [muscatel] and whisky do not mix." Reuben and Nina enter, and the Countess begs them to get out for their own good. A euphoric Reuben begins talking a blue streak now that he has overcome his block, and he gives a confused little sermon on communication and the misunderstandings it sometimes brings. He sums up its moral this way:

> *If you're not gonna listen to what you hear,*
> *And you only hear what you* wanna *hear,*
> *The space between the mouth and the ear*
> *Gets wider every year.*

Bart tries one last time to persuade Reuben into following his father's example. But by now Reuben has won out over the dead hand of his past. He has arrived at that portal of mature understanding of life, as Clara did in *No for an Answer* or Alexandra in *Regina,* a delicate moment the composer constantly felt drawn to depicting in his works. Reuben has learned that his Pop was wrong, and says so to Bart:

> *He was like you.*
> *Nothing, no one ever reached him.*
> *He never wanted to hear.*
> *When he had to hear, he shut it all up.*
> *He walked out. He walked out. He was a coward.*
> *That's what I found out tonight.*
> *It nearly killed me.*
> *I guess it did.*
> *I guess you have to die at least once*
> *To find out anything.*

As dawn approaches, Bart is furious that he is losing his bet with Malatesta. He takes his lucky horseshoe off the wall and hurls it at a mirrored wall, breaking it to splinters. The spell is broken, and Reuben hauls off with a solid fist to Bart's neck. The party breaks up; the Countess takes care of Bart; and Reuben and Nina leave—for the bridge and the final scene.

Now it is almost dawn, and we find a tipsy, fatigued gob heading back over the bridge toward the Brooklyn Navy Yards, singing his "Monday Morning Blues," a wistful good-bye to a weekend of carousing with the girls.* It is the same melody Blitzstein had emphasized in a brassier circus mode in the overture. Blitzstein specifically identifies the sailor as Henry Lippincott, a young Southerner with a distinguished-sounding name, once more recalling Bill Hewitt and his enchanting Tidewater accent. Although it may seem unwieldy to introduce a new character at this point, he represents all the people who still live unexamined lives, all those who face future existential crises such as the one Reuben has pulled himself through. As they affirm their new life together, Reuben and Nina wave a long farewell to the charming sailor across the bridge that has now become a symbol of communication. Suggesting the concluding chorus of *Regina*—"Is a new day a-coming?"—the sun comes up as the final curtain descends.

At the very end of the work, according to an earlier line in Blitzstein's notes, Reuben was to have said, "Here we are all changed, and together. But the world hasn't changed any since last night." "The apprehensiveness mixed with the *love,* as they wave," Blitzstein commented, wanting to throw the lessons of the opera into the laps of his listeners. Another note has Reuben seeing the answer "not in 'adjusting,' but in fighting, protesting, helping to clear the way for a better life."[10] But he cut these thoughts, as he did many others.

In the course of his thinking about what he wanted to say with *Reuben Reuben,* Blitzstein free-associated this train of thought:

*Gershwin's early opera *Blue Monday* has a "Blue Monday Blues" that Blitzstein probably knew.

Who did this to us? What is it, this unceasing barrage of pin-up pictures, radio-innuendo, movie fade-outs violent murderous comic-strips, all wrist-slapped by the Trinity-of-Church-School-and-Home homilies, has done to us (naked-girl-night-shows, columnists, peek-a-boo)—what is this intricate pulling on our debilitations, fostering our weakness of spirit, this web, so seemingly airy, so "free" of conspiracy, so actually conspiratorial? There *is* a conspiracy—to rob us of our strength, our independence, to break our spirit—but it isn't always personal villainy, it is the daily functioning of a system, and the virulent maintenance of it.[11]

"Make this work *dangerous,*" Blitzstein remarked to himself in terms that summon up an image of Larry Foreman in *Cradle:*

It's nothing if it's not dangerous. I mean it must threaten and challenge every lopsided sick notion of our society, and the bulldoggish grip that the lunks have of keeping our society sick and cruel and murderous—it must threaten them and come out swinging and smiling.[12]

But McCarthyism was in the air—former comrades "singing" to HUAC, blacklists, stigma, and isolation. The atmosphere constantly filtered into Blitzstein's work on *Reuben Reuben.* Could he place this story about communication in a context people would recognize? Could he say as much as he wanted to say? Could he "come out swinging" and would anyone want to watch? "No middle ground between the surrender of one's principles (death) and the clear firm stand (life)," he wrote as the Committee proceeded with its business. "Larry Parks tries to do both, have his cake and eat it too; both sides reject him. Sterling Hayden informs; Geer, etc., refuse to state."[13] Indeed, in one note to himself, Blitzstein projected that the last scene of the first act

should go like a McCarthy Inquisition: R innocent but suspicious (up there on the chandelier) . . . the CROWD yelling for his blood . . . should grow . . . from alarm to suspicion to hostility to "prejudged guilty" and utter condemnation—all the steps of UnAmer. Act. Comm.[14]

In one draft, Reuben makes a speech to the assembled party crowd in Act Two: "Sure we all want peace, or we think so. Sure we don't want bombs. But are we willing to listen and then talk? Would we earn a peaceful world?" And later in the same speech: "I just found out something for myself tonight. You always want leaders, you don't even pick them, you sit down and let them lead. You corrupt them." But Blitzstein cut both of these passages. He also cut all specific references to Hiroshima and to the 1946 bomb test at Bikini that so disillusioned Reuben's father because it proved that the government was preparing to use atomic power for war, not for peace. He cut mention of the Las Vegas atomic tests in early 1951 that took place at dawn—which conditions Reuben's original choice of a time to die. "We don't have to *explain* why R is what he is, does what he does," the librettist jotted to himself early on. "We have to *show* him *being, doing*—(No novel, this)."[15] In another note to himself, he said, "All the detail that can pile up in plot (*re* R's father, for example): use only what is indispensable (for understanding) or what is theatrically arresting. Remember this is a musical! Not ideas, but action-and-emotion from ideas!"[16]

But in his reticence to explain, the composer cast his characters and their predicament into such a blurry motivational half-light that no audience could rightly be expected to know what the show is fundamentally about.

If Blitzstein shrank from giving Reuben too much political motivation, he imagined in one sketch letting one of Bart's barflies speak for the Revolution:

> *Bart, when you kill,*
> *That ain't the way.*
> *That's how we all*
> *First went astray.*
> *Change the whole system now, I say.*
> *We got leaders that don't know*
> *Their biological ass*
> *From their political elbow. . . .*
> *Another war will kill every last soul on earth here,*
> *So let's boot them out, one and all.*

Bart is unimpressed. "Take your revolution somewhere else," he replies, "tonight I'm busy."[17] This exchange Blitzstein cut as well, perhaps for fear that the critics might echo Bart's reaction. Or perhaps he cut it because it violated the guidelines he had set for this work: "Now, for Christ's sake," he told himself, "don't get loaded down by the *seriousness* of this thing. All the writing is to be in the comic vein."[18] Which amazingly, considering that the central figure is a candidate for suicide, much of it is—not burlesque or satire, certainly, but comedy like *Don Giovanni,* whose humor interpenetrates with the tragic and surrounds it.

Though Blitzstein meant to write a modern Faust story wherein Bart represented Mephistopheles, Reuben Faust, and Nina Gretchen, the essay must be counted as largely unsuccessful. A metaphor must work on both the archetypal and the articulated levels. It may be sufficient for the myth that Mephistopheles acts the way he does because he is Mephistopheles, but on the stage there must be greater reasons. As late as February 1955, Blitzstein had still not answered the question as to why Bart needs Reuben's death; perhaps because a body was needed to claim some shady insurance policy, or because Bart owes something big to Malatesta and the deadline is tonight. On his fiftieth birthday—March 2, 1955—Blitzstein worked on this problem. Lady Luck "has *sent* R to B for a purpose (this kid is odd, strange, *special*)—but what *is* the purpose?" the librettist asked.

Then, too, if Bart promises Reuben a grand night of partying, drinking, and sex (with the Countess) before dying in the morning, somehow this scenario falls far short of equaling the recapture of youth and romance that Mephistopheles promised Faust. Bart's ability to influence Reuben is not adequately explained. About the best Blitzstein came up with is that Bart reminds Reuben of his Pop, and that is the hold he exerts on him.

Nor, for that matter, does Nina's falling in love with Reuben ring true. She is a strong, healthy girl with a job and a loving community to give her support. In one abandoned thought, Blitzstein considered making her the victim of an earlier rape, so that she needs Reuben to help her get over her block against men and sex, and further, that she had been harassed by the police after she reported the rape, which makes her hate cops. As a vestige of that notion, Nina says she has no need for men in her life; but even if she does, her good looks, talent, and warm personality could land her a far more attractive mate than Reuben. If she takes a kindly interest in a veteran with some serious emotional problems, Blitzstein doesn't convince us that this is truly the stuff of love. The prospects for this relationship somehow do not appear bright. It seems that Blitzstein's own past relationships, with all the mutual insecurities they entailed, so intrinsically stamped his thinking about *Reuben Reuben* that he could not rise above the material long enough to assess its plausibility.

Blitzstein's working process on *Reuben Reuben* recalled his painfully protracted tugging and pulling at *No for an Answer.* If composing music came naturally to him, writing a libretto did not. In the earlier case, a comparatively well organized left-wing movement existed to support a Blitzstein opus once it arrived on the stage, or so he believed when writing it. In this case, his producer Cheryl Crawford had given him the permission to take his time until he got the work just right. And so, with no special sense of urgency about his task, he managed to find hundreds of places where revisions could be made, characters expanded, new scenes introduced and then eliminated. Without a collaborator to keep him on course, he had trouble zeroing in on the point: Extraneous characters and situations that lead nowhere waylaid the action, and he interpolated clever songs for insufficient reason.

The music to which Blitzstein set this most vexatious libretto turned out to be the most seductive, ecstatic, lush, and lyrical score he ever wrote. While less operatic than *Regina,* it is also less tied to standard commercial forms than the songs of *Cradle.* Its music, though hardly its book, is best described as quintessentially American "Broadway opera." As a whole, *Reuben Reuben* is arguably Blitzstein's best synthesis of "art" and "popular" music styles. At first glance, many of his songs appear superficial; but often there are hidden ambiguities, unresolved or delayed chords, that make his music of far more than passing interest. The few songs Chappell published in sheet music before the show opened belie the pungency in his orchestration, where he achieved a light, rippling timbre, as opposed to the big effects he was more accustomed to producing. The composer also incorporated a traditional Blitzstein family whistle into the score, as well as a signal call that Marc and Eva had once developed. He did not resort to traditional compositional devices or intricate contrapuntal elaboration. "As to the music," he explained to David Diamond, "I have whittled myself down-to-size. I have surgically cut out all self-indulgence. I shall be simple and forthright and diatonic and I shall not let myself produce technical virtuosities to prove anything."[19]

As with *Regina,* Cheryl Crawford once again chose Bobby Lewis to direct. Blitzstein himself orchestrated large chunks of the through-composed work; for the rest, they hired Hershy Kay and, for a few numbers, Bill Stegmeyer. From the beginning they worried about who would play Blitzstein's difficult roles; by mid-1954, while he was still putting in thirteen-hour days on the opera, writing, revising, orchestrating, some of the casting began falling into place. For the title role, they decided on Eddie Albert, though Marc wrote to Bernstein that summer from Brigantine:

> I worry more and more about Eddie Albert as being too old, too settled. He can make it, because he is a superb actor; but he runs the danger of seeming cute, in personating [*sic*] a youngster looking forward. Maybe we've all grown too crotchety and demanding over the months, in the matter of casting.[20]

Albert prepared energetically for the part. He took lessons in magic and tumbling; and for the jump scene at the end of Act One where his life was to be on the line every night, he practiced with his local fire department in California, first with five- and six-foot jumps, gradually working his way up to thirty feet.

For the name value, the producers auditioned Patrice Munsel, who actually began learning some of Nina's music. Blitzstein had written a part that he felt would not harm an operatic voice even if performed eight times a week. They also considered Anna Maria Alberghetti; but in the end they chose neither.

The young baritone Thomas Stewart auditioned one day for a role in *Reuben Reuben* and took along his wife, the Juilliard graduate Evelyn Lear, for encouragement. Samuel Krachmalnick, a pianist and conductor, came in as his accompanist. The producers accepted Stewart as a chorus member, and then he introduced his wife. They asked whether they could hear her too, as long as she was there, and she sang several operatic arias. They asked for something in English and she did Britten's "The Ash Grove." Bobby Lewis asked her to do it again but this time to sing as if they were all five-year-olds who could not understand the words well. They loved her and before long hired her, a complete unknown in her first major role. She herself devised her own cadenza on the "Song of the Arrow," her spitting song in the first act. Blitzstein liked it and wrote it in. He became more and more impressed with her voice throughout the rehearsals; she could go higher and higher and produce almost any effect she wanted with it. The composer wrote rapturously to David Diamond about his discovery: "so beautiful of voice, so human of face, so brilliant a theatre-person (Bobby Lewis almost cried at her big Imperial-Theatre audition, saying 'I don't know when I have seen or heard anyone so made for the stage') that I am beside myself with pleasure and gratitude."[21]

From that first meeting with Samuel Krachmalnick Blitzstein also had found a conductor for the show. Krachmalnick had taken over the baton for Menotti's opera *The Saint of Bleecker Street,* but *Reuben Reuben* would be the first Broadway show he had led from the outset.

Once the two leads had been chosen, they and some other pickup singers recorded several songs from the show for fundraising purposes. The press carried regular notices of the show's progress; the Sunday *Times* crossword puzzle for February 6, 1955, titled "Double Feature," gave "Marc Blitzstein's latest opus" as a clue for a twelve-letter word. To David Diamond on the eve of Valentine's Day, Blitzstein talked about *Reuben Reuben* and also reiterated an old theme: "I need love, of course. It is too long—and active pain gives way to general sadness."[22] On April 20, the producers held the last of a series of backers' auditions. "It has been so much too long on this thing," Marc wrote to Bernstein:

> where will I ever get the freshness I need for this session? I am tired and nervous, with auditions, no real consecutive work by myself, and the pulling-about of various minds and authorities. . . . I am only eternally cross; what you call quarrelsome.[23]

As actual production loomed closer and closer, Blitzstein's earlier doubts about his forty-seven-year-old star vanished. "We go into rehearsal with *Reuben* the middle of August," he reported to Bernstein:

> An overpowering amount of work still remains to be done. The piece works like a play, and has to meet demands which are both textual and musical, theatrically speaking. . . . I can only admit to being a tyro in the matter of construction, as witness the twelve different versions of one scene. But it keeps coming righter, and will be ready on time. Eddie Albert will be immense; I have three tapes of him ("Rose Song," "Thank You," "There Goes My Love"), and although they were done when he was dead after a "spectacular" telecast of *Connecticut Yankee,* they show all the qualities I hoped for. He is ready to kill himself on the jump that curtains Act I; he has learned juggling, jitterbug, back-flips (*not* somersaults; flips), and all types of sleight-of-hand. He threatens to eat flaming chestnuts as well in the Carnival scene.[24]

A number of months previously, Blitzstein had received from Dr. Antonio Ghiringhelli, the *Sovrintendente* of La Scala, a request for the Chappell piano-vocal score to *Regina,* with a view toward producing it in Milan. Within weeks, a prospective translator submitted *"Il vero gran ben,"* the Italian of Regina's "toreador song," "The Best Thing of All." Menotti looked it over and pronounced it only fair, so the translation might be a problem. But as of November 1954 Ghiringhelli assured Leonard Bernstein that he should be prepared to conduct the work at La Scala during the 1955–1956 season. Blitzstein could hardly have heard sweeter news.

Bernstein thought Maria Callas had the voice for a great Regina. If a proper translation could not be made, then she might sing the role in English, which after all was her native language. Blitzstein offered to set to music every bit of spoken dialogue if that would please La Scala; and he considered a linguistic compromise whereby the black music, the jazz, hymns, and spirituals, would remain in English, while the white characters would sing in Italian.

As the months passed, Bernstein sent no word as to the prospects for a production. The anxiety upset Blitzstein's work routine. A sharp note from Blitzstein elicited a vaguely hopeful response, but so far nothing was certain:

> Ghiringhelli seems to take it for granted that the work will be done next year, every time I mention it: but it is really up to DeSabata. The latter, a very fine gent, loves the piece, and readily quotes and sings from it (especially "Watching my gal watch me," which he performs by heart at the piano) but he has worries about the translation.[25]

Victor de Sabata, the musical director of La Scala, had wanted to read the complete libretto of *Regina* before he committed himself. Finally, he wrote directly to Blitzstein:

> I have the big surprise to realize that it does not combine with La Scala's atmosphere, tradition, public, stage's magnitude, taste and phisiognomy. Strictly between us, it would be a great mistake to risk a production of *Regina* at "La Scala."[26]

For some reason, de Sabata could not accept certain themes as legitimate for the operatic stage: wrangling over money, compulsory marriage, or the idea of a woman allowing her husband to die. He proposed instead some other work by Blitzstein, perhaps his ballet *The Guests.* "Where has he learned about operatexts?" a disappointed Blitzstein asked Bernstein. "Lillian [Hellman]'s explanation is probably correct: that the Italians just don't go for satire. A straight emotional bath and a minimum of creative indignation is apparently the desideratum."[27]

Trying to console his friend, Bernstein promised that he would promote the opera to both the Florence and the Holland Festivals. "I am a dill prickle if it won't be seen SOMEWHERE in Europe next year."[28] But all efforts failed. Bernstein was a dill prickle.

Marc's nephew Stephen had met his wife Joyce when he was a law student at Columbia some years earlier. She had a winning sunniness about her, cooked superbly, and had studied in Brussels on a Fulbright scholarship. Long before imagining any future relation to its composer, she had seen *Regina* during its Broadway run. For their wedding on July 30, 1955, Blitzstein composed a gentle, stately march, which he played as the bride descended the stairs of her parents' home. Although Joyce had a liberal mind, she soon found one point on which she and Marc crossed swords. Casually one day she mentioned liking a piece of music by Carl Orff. As though by knee-jerk reaction, Blitzstein lit into Orff as a Nazi sympathizer who stayed in Germany throughout Hitler's régime and premiered his works under those conditions. Still, she defended his work. "Don't you see you're using the same argument as Hitler banning Mendelssohn?" Joyce said. So from then on, whenever the family broke into argumentation over any esthetic question, Marc always nodded to Joyce as the upholder of "art for art's sake."

Earlier in 1955, a young producer named Ben Bagley had put on the *Shoestring Review,* with Blitzstein's *Threepenny* actress Beatrice Arthur. At a party given by John Latouche, Blitzstein heard Bagley mention that he was always on the lookout for suitable novelty material. Blitzstein recalled a song written for Beatrice Lillie during the war that was never used. He ran home to fetch it, returning with "Modest Maid," which he performed on the spot to the delight of all the guests.

Marked *allegretto grazioso,* the number is of the British music-hall type and relates the fantasies of a lecherous young lady not averse to late-night dalliances in the park. At the time he wrote it, Blitzstein must have been thinking of the sexual free-for-all that enlivened nighttime London during the blackouts. In the original version, loaded with one double entendre after another in a Noël Coward vein, the song concluded with these lyrics:

> *So behold me bonneted and cloaked.*
> *Never kissed, caressed, betrothed nor yoked.*
> *And all I ask is to be mauled and pumped*
> *and kicked and choked.*

Knowing that Charlotte Rae, another of the *Threepenny* cast, was about to appear in her own nightclub act at the Blue Angel, Blitzstein showed her the song. She adopted it as her opening number, though for her use the composer dropped the shocking masochism in the final lines, which extended far beyond the usual torch song blues, and substituted a phrase about "how to get this rampant little maid allayed." Rae performed the number dressed in a full nun's habit, a costume she retained when she used the song later in Bagley's next production, *The Littlest Revue,* at the Phoenix Theatre. Audiences roared just seeing her enter the stage all decked out as a sex-bedeviled sister.

In August 1955 Rae recorded an album on the Vanguard label called *Songs I Taught My Mother,* and included both "Modest Maid" and "Fraught" from *No for an Answer,* with her husband John Strauss and his Baroque Bearcats in a small backup combo. Blitzstein's royalty came to one hundred dollars. With a certain degree of license, Nat Shapiro's jacket notes called "Modest Maid" "a wild concoction conjured up especially for Charlotte by Mark Blitzstein"—misspelling his name four times on the album. In many ways, Rae's rendition of "Fraught," happily relieved of the silly "Dimples" routine joined to it in the original opera, is superior to Carol Channing's original. *Playboy* reviewed the record in March of the next year, calling "Modest Maid" the "plum" of Rae's repertoire. Why Vanguard never rereleased this preciously wicked record is anybody's guess.

Sometime during the summer of 1955, Carmen Capalbo and Stanley Chase ran into Louis Schweitzer, whose fortune came from a chemical process for making cigarette paper. He offered to buy the Theater de Lys as a twenty-fourth anniversary present to his wife, the former actress Lucille Lortel. She already owned the

White Barn in Westport, Connecticut, where she presented plays. The conditions of Schweitzer's purchase, however, were that Capalbo and Chase return *The Threepenny Opera* to the de Lys—exactly what they had wanted all along—and that Lortel be named an associate producer. By this time the owner had come to see that the house press agent who dreamed of being a producer was incapable of turning a profit, and he sold the theatre to Schweitzer for around $150,000. On Monday nights when there was no show, Lortel could try out new scripts; otherwise, if she had no active role to play in her theatre, what was the point of owning it?

For the second production, Schweitzer installed new seats and an air-conditioning system. But the production itself remained unchanged: Capalbo merely brought out the sets and costumes he had placed in storage. *The Threepenny Opera* opened again on September 20, 1955, now to universally rave reviews, just as *Reuben Reuben* entered its final weeks of rehearsal. The program still carried news of Blitzstein's adaptation of *La Traviata* and the Offenbach operas. For years, despite other changes and updates in his bio, this information remained, though there is no evidence that Blitzstein had continued working on these translations since his initial efforts in 1953. He had obviously lost interest but failed to notify the press department.

When the show had first opened fifteen months before, Capalbo predicted it would run either a night or a year. Events proved him wrong on both counts. After opening this second time, *Threepenny* recouped its production costs again after six weeks. And then to universal amazement, the show continued to run for more than six years! In that time, it would rack up 2,611 performances seen by three-quarters of a million people. From an original investment of under ten thousand dollars, the show took in an estimated three million dollars.

As the owner of the theatre and as an enterprising producer, Lucille Lortel actually would have preferred the show to leave. As soon as it closed—in a few months, probably—she planned to introduce an average of five or six new plays and playwrights a year. According to contract, however, if the show did well enough in filling the house for the current thirteen-week period, she was obliged to renew *Threepenny*'s lease. And it always did do that well. Aside from the Monday-night readings, she added a Tuesday matinee series for new works. But the rest of the week, *Threepenny* ran and ran and ran.

Matlovsky conducted again with largely the same cast as the year before. In April of 1956, the work won a special Tony award, and Lenya captured the Tony prize as best featured musical actress. After she formally left the show that April, she sometimes went back when needed. One night, when Tige Andrews fell ill and no replacement could be found, Lenya played both Jenny and the Streetsinger.

Over the years, a total of 709 actors performed in the twenty-two roles, many of them graduating from role to role: Jerry Orbach was in the show for more than three years and played seven different roles before becoming the Streetsinger. Nancy Andrews, Georgia Brown, Jane Connell, Grete Mosheim, Jo Wilder, Frederic Downs, Emile Renan, Edward (Ed) Asner, John Astin, Paul Dooley,

Tony Lo Bianco, and Valerie Bettis are only a few of those who appeared. It became a veritable factory of Off-Broadway talent. Jo Sullivan stayed in the show for the better part of a year, long enough for Frank Loesser to see it. Though he hated the show, he liked her and put her into *The Most Happy Fella* in 1956. He also married her. Two actors, William Duell as the Messenger and Marion Selee as Molly, one of the bordello girls, stayed with the show from the beginning. After Matlovsky, the black conductor Kelly Wyatt took over for half a year or so, followed by Abba Bogin and later Mordechai Scheinkman, who conducted longer than anyone else. Blitzstein, who would go around to help audition for important cast changes, occasionally stepped into the pit himself as a relief conductor.

With all these actors passing through the show, the sight of producers in the audience soon became a common one. Capalbo hated spotting them: It only meant they had come to raid the show of its newest talents. In time, however, actors could no longer appear in *Threepenny* and expect to be seen, because the agents and producers had seen the show so many times they refused to go anymore. Under the reigning Off-Broadway Equity terms, actors could leave the show on only five days' notice, and many of them did as soon as more lucrative offers came along. (Though at seventy-five dollars a week, *Threepenny* was the best-paying show Off-Broadway.) Then new actors would have to be found and rehearsed. If no one could be found right away or if someone got sick, the producers would call back some former player and ask him or her to step in for the night. Almost always, the program carried inserted slips of paper announcing cast changes.

Something totally unexpected came up a few weeks after *The Threepenny Opera* reopened: a lawsuit against Blitzstein and the producers. It seems that back in 1933 when the property had first been offered in America, Edmond Pauker had bought the translation and production rights from Universal Edition, the work's publisher in Vienna. Pauker had assigned his rights to John Krimsky and Clifford Cochran, who had produced the show. Though now, twenty-two years later, Cochran waived his license to the property, Pauker, Krimsky, and Universal claimed that Blitzstein and his producers had no legal rights to the opera. They sought a court injunction to halt the production, which a federal court judge refused to grant because he did not like the prospect of throwing all those actors out of work.

If the show looked as though it might finally bring Blitzstein some long-deferred income, the lawsuit could wipe it out in a stroke. Lenya had in the meantime delayed signing a contract for this second production so she could claim that she hadn't assigned Weill's rights to the producers—an absurd claim, of course, because of the precedent of the first production and because she was still appearing in the second! The producers could also assert the legal principle of laches: Why had Krimsky and Pauker not said anything at the time of the first production? Their failure to assert their rights then would probably disqualify them in a court of law from making their present argument.

Advised by their lawyers that litigation would be very costly and time-consuming, Capalbo, Chase, and Blitzstein settled out of court. The plaintiffs secured a settlement providing for an initial payment of thirty-five hundred dollars, plus a weekly sum, at least until Universal's copyright ran out in 1957. The forfeiture of income and the legal fees had to come from the producers and Blitzstein. As Blitzstein expressed it to David Diamond with some hyperbole, "It will probably cost me more in the end than I have made on the work."[29]

More than forty different recordings of "Mack the Knife" came out by the biggest names in show business. Sometime after the second opening, Lenya and her second husband George Davis happened to be dining with George Avakian, producer for Columbia Records. Louis Armstrong was flying in later that night to make some recordings, and Avakian invited his dinner companions to ride out to the airport to pick him up. In the car on the way back into town, they worked out the idea of recording "Mack the Knife" in a session scheduled that very night. Lenya and Armstrong sang together in one take, which was never released, and Armstrong sang it as a solo.

After the song began to be heard on radio, broadcasters banned it because it appeared to glorify criminals and immorality, though the record stores could hardly keep it in stock. To get around this ticklish dilemma, MGM released an instrumental version with Dick Hyman and a whistler. This the radio stations could play. The music stores in New York used to have speakers over the door playing the number-one hit song. For six months, people walked for blocks in the West Fifties where the stores were concentrated, and it was Louis Armstrong's "Mack the Knife" that they heard all day long. Responding to popular demand, radio started broadcasting it again. The Columbia movie *Satchmo the Great* included the song, for which they paid Blitzstein twenty-five hundred dollars.

To be sure, not everyone was enthralled by the song. "Exposed," shrieked a cover teaser on *Top Secret* magazine, "The Hit Song that Makes $$$ for the Reds!" "Every time you play 'Mack the Knife,' " reporter John Lewis Carver told his scandal-seeking readers, "you're sending money behind the Iron Curtain." A confirmed Communist, Brecht "posed as a victim of the Nazis, a refugee from persecution, and we swallowed his tale hook, line and sinker." People "should bear in mind that the knife in that song is really a dagger with which Brecht is stabbing them in the back."[30]

But the fascination with the song never ceased. After Louis Armstrong and Dick Hyman's versions came others by Ella Fitzgerald, Eartha Kitt, Frank Sinatra, Les Paul, and Mary Ford—even Lawrence Welk. It was recorded abroad in other languages; it is no exaggeration to say that its worldwide popularity is a direct by-product of Blitzstein's adaptation. In the fourth year of the show, Bobby Darin's recording came out, and the song went right back up to the top of the charts. It appealed to a new audience of teenagers, many of whom, curious to see the show from which the song had sprung, stepped into a legitimate theatre for the first time in their lives. With each new version topping the national hit parade, the legend spread. *Threepenny* became the one show out-of-towners always wanted to see in New York. The office handled 100 to 125 ticket orders that came through the mail a day. Advance sales booked the theatre solid four and five months ahead, and there was always a line in front of the box office. "Why did you come to see *The Threepenny Opera?*" Carmen Capalbo often asked patrons during the intermission—people who had come in from Nebraska, Idaho, Texas. They all answered the same way, citing some recent incident of corruption in their hometowns. The message was indeed universal.

The show helped to transform both Greenwich Village and the Off-Broadway theatre scene. At the beginning, telephone callers asked how to get to Christopher Street, for at that time few people knew of its existence. The gay crowd had not yet adopted the street as its own preserve—their Village bars were mostly along Eighth Street between Fifth and Sixth Avenues. People arrived at the theatre with maps in their hands. Sailors who hung out at a bar on the corner of Bedford and Christopher streets soon lost their surprise at seeing *Threepenny* cast members join them. Before long the cast dubbed the bar their own New York "Bide-A-Wee." New restaurants sprang up to accommodate the nightly invasion of theatregoers. The street began to upgrade itself.

As for the Off-Broadway phenomenon, in 1954 there were seven Off-Broadway theatres. Within seven years their number had grown to thirty-eight, many of them in Greenwich Village. The shows that played there did not always aspire to Broadway; a new readiness had set in to let these low-budget productions stay and flourish—or not—where they were. The developing sense of *Kleinkunst* implicitly rejected the bourgeois success ethic.

By the summer of 1956, MGM reported over 150,000 copies of the cast recording sold. After five years, it had outsold any show on Broadway with the exception of *My Fair Lady.* Royalties from the sale of over half a million albums flowed in to the lyricist. And these royalties, not derived from the stage production per se, Krimsky and Pauker could not touch. As a result, in the latter half of the fifties, Blitzstein began to dress better, take more expensive vacations, and drive a fancier car. By the beginning of the sixties, his ASCAP earnings yielded more than ten thousand dollars a year, almost all of it from "Mack the Knife." Though his chronic money woes subsided, Blitzstein's newfound wealth was great only relative to his own past; he never earned more than about fifteen thousand dollars a year and he never moved out of his tiny third-floor studio on East Twelfth Street.

At the same time, the renown of this show led to an intense interest in both Weill's other works and in Brecht's oeuvre. In Europe, interest in the Weill-Brecht canon remained strong. For one thing, Brecht's successes in East Berlin with his own company, the Berliner Ensemble, had profoundly impressed those who saw its productions. For another, the Europeans sought to revive the best qualities of Weimar German experimental art, and no McCarthyism restricted their freedom to explore. Lenya herself, having begun the second and far more stunning phase of her performing and recording career, became the standard-bearer of Weill's art for another generation; she was internationally regarded as the single most authentic interpreter of her husband's material. In America, Brecht and Weill and their entire generation stood for something forbidden and magnetically attractive; through the arts, at least, those who felt constricted might possibly transcend the crushing social conservatism of the interminable Eisenhower years. Importantly for the future of American theatre, this interest centered on college campuses, in regional theatres, and on the Off-Broadway stage, where theatre artists of every kind tried flapping their anti-Establishment wings. The face of theatre, the way people looked at theatre, the expectations audiences brought to the theatre, all changed.

But all this was yet to come. Of *Threepenny*'s enduring power, no one had any inkling in September 1955. As for himself, Blitzstein was more concerned about getting *Reuben Reuben* launched.

George Gaynes, a lead player in Bernstein's *Wonderful Town* in 1953, was signed on to portray Bart. A natural white blond, he dyed his hair black for the Mephistopheles role. Kaye Ballard, a whisky-voiced comic talent of immense resourcefulness who had appeared in the Spike Jones Band as a tuba player, as well as in *The Golden Apple, Touch and Go, Top Banana,* and *Three to Make Ready,* played the part of the Countess.

For the role of Fez the pickpocket—a minor character but the first one onstage—Bobby Lewis hired Will Lee. Lee had worked with Lewis back in the Group Theatre days and had succeeded John Garfield as the lead in *Golden Boy.* A committed progressive, he had once appeared in *I've Got the Tune.* Blacklisted from film work by the Tenney Committee in California, he returned to the East Coast to work in theatre. Later in life, he would gain further recognition as Mr. Hooper on "Sesame Street."

As the gutter Romeo and Juliet dancers, Sondra Lee and Timmy Everett joined the show. Others appearing included Tony Gardell, Karen Anders, Anita Darian, Emile Renan, and, as a chorus member and Attilio the pasta salesman at the San Gennaro carnival, an unknown Enzo Stuarti. Abba Bogin rehearsed the chorus and played piano in the orchestra. In all, some seventy people were hired for the cast. A number of them made personal financial investments in the show.

As choreographer, Hanya Holm worked mainly on the punk Romeo and Juliet pas de deux, the festive, expansive San Gennaro scene, and the insane asylum scene. Casting the dancers herself, Holm went down to Little Italy to extract the gist of its spirit in movement. Eventually, choreography, acting, and direction ended up so well coordinated that it would be hard to say where one left off and the other took up.

The team of William and Jean Eckart came in to design the sets, costumes, and lighting. The Eckarts represented a kind of mutual support system, a collaboration team that Blitzstein shortly came to envy. Though thrilled to have on his show the pair that had designed the previous year's hit *Damn Yankees*—also based on the Faust legend—Blitzstein let them know how appalled he had been at the open depiction of its devil figure Applegate as a homosexual.

Blitzstein had worked on *Reuben Reuben* since November 1949; now others would hold it in their hands, molding it into something that at one and the same time both fulfilled and distorted his original conception. "This work has been mine, and only mine for so long," he admitted to Mina Curtiss, "I find it intolerable to give it the light of 'day' (in this case the booms and the floods and the follow-spots)."[31]

Rehearsals began on Thursday, September eighth at Schumer's Warehouse on West Sixty-fifth Street, the trucking company that transported theatre props. Bobby Lewis read the script to the cast all that first day. As the show began taking shape, it seemed brilliant, refreshingly unlike anything ever seen before. The cast believed in it deeply; they fantasized about the extraordinary gifts the world was about to receive. It would open in Boston, go through the usual process of fine-tuning, then begin its New York run at the ANTA Theatre beginning November eighth. Ticket sales for the $200,000 show extended into January 1956.

As the star, Eddie Albert was everything that could be desired. At forty-seven, he acted and danced and sang with the vigor of a man half his age. And Evelyn Lear fully justified the faith Blitzstein and his producers had placed in her. During lulls in rehearsals, she and the composer played Scrabble; he would always try to find an opportunity to spell the word *leer.* A first complete run-through took place on Sunday, September 25. Samuel Krachmalnick began rehearsing with a core group of New York musicians who would travel with the show up to Boston; the rest of the orchestra would be hired by a local contractor there. With *Threepenny* reopening and the expectation that it might last at least a few months, Blitzstein would soon have two shows playing in New York.

The audience in Boston's Shubert Theatre was ill-prepared for what they saw on October tenth, opening night. The show had been billed as "a new musical." It had a fanciful title and starred Eddie Albert. It featured a Barnum-like atmosphere, fleshed out with splendid sets and colorful costumes. But what was it? A confused, incomprehensible, only intermittently fascinating psychological drama set to unreassuringly dissonant music—a bizarre urban folk opera pitched way over the heads of an average Broadway theatre crowd.

Bravely, after the fact, Blitzstein reported the scene to Mina Curtiss:

> Up until five minutes after *opening-night* curtain in Boston, there was not one person connected with the production who wasn't sure we were wonderful. And a moment later, we were ashes. We all knew it. The actors onstage went berserk, forgot lines, gave dizzily unreal performances that made my poor conductor in the pit try desperately to meet them at least in terms of musical bars.[32]

In the last scene of the first act when its sympathies are supposed to be with Reuben, not with Bart, the audience joined in yelling "Jump!" to Eddie Albert. After the first act, a substantial number decided not to return for the rest. Others believed the second act could not possibly be as obtuse as the first, and went back to their seats. The second act opens in the insane asylum wards, though the murky stage populated by a motley collection of weirdos doesn't make this immediately clear to an audience. Once the spotlight has picked Reuben out from the haze, he has the lines:

This is one helluva place, isn't it?
A man could go crazy in here.
It's a nuthouse, I know.
I musta been crazy at that.

A man leapt from his seat in the house and in a stentorian voice shouted, "No, Eddie. We're crazy." With twenty others in his trail, he stalked out of the theatre.

Toward the end in the final confrontation scene between Bart and Reuben, after Reuben has punched Bart out, Bart tells his henchman Harry to send everyone home. "Party's over," Harry says. "Go home. Everybody out. Out. Out. Out." At this cue, another good chunk of audience, already waiting for an excuse to leave, got up as if ordered to do so. Cheryl Crawford and Bobby Lewis ran down the aisles saying, "Everybody back. The show's not over yet."

Some three hundred people walked out that first night. Similar scenes punctuated by catcalls and discontented chatter were repeated at subsequent performances. When people got up to leave, they found Cheryl Crawford standing in the aisle with her arms folded like an Indian chieftain, forcing them to walk around her and excuse themselves as they edged past. At one performance, a man in the audience found Blitzstein standing at the rear of the house. He grabbed him by the tie, held a threatening fist in his face, and said, "I wish I could make you suffer the way you've made me suffer."

Yet according to one or two of the reviews and to the memories of people in the show, a few who remained till the end shouted "Bravo!" and went wild with enthusiasm. These were decidedly in the minority, however.

Elinor Hughes, reviewing for the Boston *Herald,* wrote:

> *Reuben Reuben* provided one of the most bewildering evenings I have ever spent in the theatre, and I am reasonably sure that goes for the big audience present. . . .
>
> There must be a parallel here about modern man's confusion and Reuben's search for his identity, but it is never really personalized and the audience last night grew increasingly restive and disturbed as a result. . . .
>
> The talent was there, in the performers and designers and director, and no one can deny Mr. Blitzstein's gifts as a composer and lyric writer. But he should have let someone else write that libretto.[33]

Cyrus Durgin in the Boston *Globe* called the show "obscure, unfunny, musically dry, pretentious, solemnly nonsensical and boring. . . . What's it all about? Brother, you've got me." L. G. Gaffney, writing in the Boston *Record,* lamented, "Sad to say, the whole thing looks like a total loss. How do these things happen? Nobody knows."[34]

A few kind words poked through the muck. In George E. Ryan's assessment, "Musically, *Reuben* struck us as being uncommonly beautiful in all but the recitative portions." Elliot Norton referred to Blitzstein's "occasional moments of grandeur and exaltation," and to Evelyn Lear as "an extraordinary young actress and singer. . . . Dark, slender and pretty, she has a sweet personality and a free, natural voice of enormous range." Eddie Albert, said Hollywood *Daily Variety,* "is called upon to perform handstands, eat fire, do gymnastics on a swinging ladder, jump from a trapeze into a fire net, and sing and dance. He gives a great performance in the difficult role." And Elinor Hughes had written of "a handsome production with some scenes that are really lovely to look at and others that are astonishing—the nightclub—or frightening—the ward of a lunatic asylum."[35]

In his Sunday thought-piece, Elliot Norton returned to *Reuben Reuben* and its creator:

> He fails, first, because he has neglected some of the simple fundamentals of playmaking. An audience has to know quickly who the central characters are and what they are up to, and must then be able to follow them through a coherent series of incidents. . . . The music is neither melodious nor meaningful. Mr. Blitzstein shuns melody and embraces dissonance. Some of us would be willing to accept the harsh sounds if they seemed justifiable in the dramatic sense, if they gave some significance or new intensity to the play. But this rarely happens.

Revisions, he added, "will have to be drastic and daring. The theatre is no place for private experiments; the public has a primary claim."[36]

Before the first week was out, George Clarke reported in the Boston *Record,* that:

> (1) Marc Blitzstein, the author and composer of *Reuben Reuben,* has locked himself in his room at the Ritz and is furiously rewriting the script; (2) that four, no more, no less, experts are up from New York to do what they can with the show, and (3) that 20 minutes have already been cut from the first act, and 16 minutes from the second . . . maybe a miracle might save it.[37]

The show was in deep trouble, but for the press Cheryl Crawford put the best possible face on it. "We have already cut eight minutes, and more will be cut," she told a newspaper interviewer. "By the third week the new material—a lot of it—will go in. . . . Fundamentally, this show has the makings of a hit. The story is good and will be better; and no one has found any fault with the actors or the voices."[38]

Where Blitzstein had written recitative, he substituted straight dialogue in places to save time. But beyond that, faced with the necessity to make speedy and drastic changes, he nearly froze with panic. He became testy and obstinate, intractable. His open fights with Bobby Lewis shook the company morale badly. Krachmalnick, the conductor, sensing that time was running out, could also turn argumentative, impatient, obdurate at times. One day someone referred to "our show." Blitzstein stiffened and said, "No, it's *my* show."

"Marc, you're wrong," they replied. "It becomes all of our show."

The only major piece of music put into the show in Boston was a stretch of dance music for the asylum scene. "Now I got a present for you," he said to the orchestrator Hershy Kay, who was traveling with the show. "Do it weird." When Kay handed him the complete scoring the next day, Blitzstein remarked—approvingly but not without a touch of doubtfulness—"I just wanted to see if you were able to do it or not." Cheryl Crawford was not afraid to spend money on the improvements: Instead of buying cheap pajamas for the inmates in the asylum, she ordered custom-made costumes. For the scene in The Spot with the patrician Mr. Smythe, nothing less than a cashmere sweater would do.

Blitzstein called his old wartime friend Garson Kanin to ask whether he would come up to Boston to help the show. Kanin was not free to travel at the time but volunteered to read the script. He looked at it for a few days, then telephoned Boston.

"I would love to help you, Marc, in any way I possibly could. But I don't know what you are trying to do or say with this piece. I don't understand it at all." At this, Marc emitted a hearty guffaw and thanked him.

Invited in by Bobby Lewis, Norman Rosten attempted some revisions; as did N. Richard Nash, author of *The Rainmaker,* who wanted to remake *Reuben Reuben* into a more standard musical. Robert Anderson, author of *Tea and Sympathy,* gave Blitzstein extensive notes on October 12. He asked Blitzstein to resolve simple, basic questions. "Audience must know clearly what Reuben wants," he told the librettist. "Whole concept of Father and his meaning and influence must be clarified." And "Who is Malatesta and why is he being called—why must Bart win this time? What does he have at stake?" Anderson also faulted many of the composer's songs, which failed to move the action along; and he found the central love relationship static.[39]

At heart, however, the composer resented anyone's breaking into his work. As a defense, he retreated into details. Asked for major revisions, he would emerge from hours of solitary confinement in his hotel room with a few note changes or a few passages he felt he could sacrifice to speed up the action. But as composer, lyricist, and book writer, all of them under severe pressure, he had neither the time nor the skill to rethink the whole opera so quickly.

Arnold Arnstein, the music copyist with the show, had already worked with Blitzstein on the *Airborne* Symphony, *The Guests,* and *Regina.* He had given Blitzstein ample advice on the translation of *The Threepenny Opera.* They considered themselves close friends. Once, in Boston, Marc asked Arnstein to assign a flute passage to the oboe. Arnstein asked him to repeat what he had said, and Marc snarled back, "Shut up!"

"Look, Marc, I got my plane ticket right here. I don't have to listen to 'shut up!' from you."

"When I say 'shut up' I don't mean 'shut up,' " Blitzstein answered. Arnstein patiently waited out the inevitable end of this sorry trial.

On October 18, the Boston press announced that Crawford had decided to close. She canceled the New York opening with a telegram saying, YOU HAVE NOT SEEN THE LAST OF REUBEN REUBEN. In the meantime, Blitzstein would make the necessary revisions. "I don't know how long it will take," she stated,

> a month, two months, three months, a year—but we're going to make it right. I realize now that when you have been with a production as long as I have with this one you can persuade yourself that your audience will see it through your eyes. Opening night here I learned that wasn't always so. The show didn't confuse me because I'd been with it so long and known it so well, but the customers were bewildered and annoyed. I came to Boston to find out what I had and how it would look on the stage with an audience. I found out, and now we're going to work harder than ever. But I still believe there's a fine show here and that we can make it right. And you haven't seen the last of me this year either. I'll be back later with my next production, *Mr. Johnson,* based on the best-selling novel.[40]

At the farewell, Eddie Albert said to the assembled company, "If it had closed after one day I would still consider it a privilege to have worked in it." Privately, he was somewhat more bitter. "I put forty thousand bucks into this show," he complained about Marc to Arnold Arnstein. "He promised to make all kinds of changes and he didn't make one."

Marc felt apologetic about the show; if he had been prepared to claim all the credit for its triumph, he also acknowledged its failure as his own. "I've let you down," he said over and over. Perhaps in his soul he preferred to be thought of as a flawed genius than as a success. Alexander Siloti had predicted that Blitzstein would come into his own as a composer only in his forties. Now he was fifty, and his biggest commercial success had been with another composer's work.

In only forty minutes, workmen struck the set, leaving the Shubert stage totally bare, where five years' work had been witnessed by dwindling audiences at barely a dozen performances.

On the train back to New York, the cast talked about nothing else but trying to mount the show somehow, perhaps more modestly, Off-Broadway, if need be. Indeed, if *Reuben Reuben* had been a success of any kind in New York, Evelyn Lear's entire future might easily have been on Broadway rather than in the opera house.

The show closed on the twenty-second, but Blitzstein flew back home four days before, writing in his notebook before the flight:

> Oct 18—at the Airport, Boston, *en route* to NYC after the "débacle." I don't imagine I will be believed—but it turns out the work—I mean the *working* was worth it for its own sake. I don't mean that the "act" has been completed—it takes an audience, greeting a work, to do that—but how much completion is there in this life? In a sense, the work is once again mine, *to make,* to fix, to correct, & do right by. If I am not happy, I am comforted; and in a way, ready. In short, I'm all right.

Mutual recriminations followed. Blitzstein blamed Bobby Lewis for suddenly losing interest after the first night, for not continuing to convey enthusiasm to the cast. If Lewis did not want to discuss the matter, Marc wrote to him that same October 18—if this was to be the end of their good professional relationship, that is—"then you have my wishes for what is obviously going to be a long and highly successful career."

Lewis answered Marc by return mail:

> Your note was no surprise to me. All of us who have knocked ourselves out on the show; Hanya, Eddie, myself, etc. have been waiting for you to turn on us and blame us, because we have all, at one time or another, been witness to your ingratitude. The simple fact of the matter is that you were unable to do the job required to put the show over. Of course I could work with enthusiasm on *Regina* after the opening since all that was needed was fixings on a solid foundation originally built by Lillian Hellman. In this case what was required was either a new format with an additional writer writing dialogue scenes which you could and should not accept as it would change the piece into a regulation musical, or, a re-write in your own form by yourself which I think will take you months or years. The piddling things that you could only do now in the time given, always avoiding the central problem, were too embarrassing to present to the cast at all—much less with enthusiasm. In spite of your analysis of my remarks, I do still love the show that opened and played in Boston and I am proud of the production. It is however, ironic that your play about non-communication was not communicated to the audience. You will probably go on feeling that only you are right and that I am wrong, the Eckarts are wrong, Eddie Albert is wrong, Kaye Ballard and all the other actors are wrong, the entire public, the insensitive ones and the sensitive well-wishers from both Boston and New York are wrong, and the entire press is wrong. . . . [L]et me end on a happier note. We all agreed that giving you back your baby now, still alive and kicking, was the only way that you could ultimately have a success with it, and that is what we all wanted for you.[41]

Blitzstein denied Lewis's points. He did take responsibility for the failure of *Reuben Reuben.* "I see quite clearly my limitations as a writer and play-constructor (of this story, anyway); and I am prepared to ask for expert help." But why couldn't the help have come in time?

Why not? Lewis answered, in the final round of letters: because "the fact is that the kind of re-write demanded by the audience, with or without help of any kind, could not be made 'in time.' "[42]

Cheryl Crawford had advanced Blitzstein at least four thousand dollars on his future royalties during the writing stage. And she had paid him another four thousand for his orchestrations. This money, of course, she would never see again. As a question of personal honor, however, she promised to repay her investors out of the profits from future productions; she managed to hand back only some thirty thousand dollars.

The Boston *Post* critic Elliot Norton later wrote to Crawford privately: "The failure of any show is unpleasant, but this one had so much talent and ingenuity and adventurous spirit behind it that it is particularly distressing. I hope your faith will be justified eventually—that Blitzstein will be able to clarify and improve it."[43] It had taken four years for *Regina* to make good on its promise—artistically, at least, if not commercially. With luck and more hard work by its composer, *Reuben Reuben* might also spring back to success.

In the weeks following the closing, Blitzstein showed the opera to the playwright William Inge for another opinion. Inge confused matters for Blitzstein in that he recognized *Reuben Reuben* as an opera so closely integrated, text and plot and lyrics and music, that a rewrite hardly seemed possible. If that were so, then what could be its future? Blitzstein had his baby back; but the chance that he had sired a malformed creature that no one wanted to nurture into normal life left him staggering in a gloomy, self-deprecating numbness. When friends would ask as gently as they could what had happened to *Reuben Reuben,* Blitzstein almost gloated. "They hated me," he would tell them cheerfully.

Lenny and Felicia Bernstein remained loyal to Marc. They had already made their first child Jamie Marc's godchild. Their son Alexander's name is the male form of Alexandra from *Regina.* And their third child they named for Marc's heroine in *Reuben Reuben*—Nina.

Songs Chappell published from *Reuben Reuben,* so they would be available for sale in the lobby and in music stores once the show opened, included "Monday Morning Blues," "Miracle Song," "Never Get Lost," "Be with Me," and "The Hills of Amalfi." (The press had also reported that ABC-Paramount planned to release the cast album.) The publisher paid Blitzstein a quarterly five-hundred-dollar advance on royalties as one of its exclusive house composers. In the middle two quarters of 1956, Chappell sold four copies of songs from *Reuben Reuben* and dutifully reported the sales. At six cents apiece, Blitzstein had earned twenty-four cents.

PART
Four

19

TIME OF THE FRIGHT

Fall 1955–May 1957

"Not me, not this time, not me."

In late 1955, Orson Welles returned to America with the idea of reviving the classical theatre. Now forty years old, he had not been seen in New York since his musical comedy *Around the World,* set to a tired Cole Porter score, ground to an early closing in 1946. In October, he proposed that Blitzstein write the incidental music for two plays he would star in and direct at the City Center: *King Lear* and *Volpone.*

The City Center had been established during the war as a municipally administered performing arts entity located in the Mecca Temple on West Fifty-fifth Street, site of the three performances of *No for an Answer.* Bernstein had revived *The Cradle Will Rock* there; the New York City Ballet had premiered *The Guests;* and the City Opera had offered *Regina* there as well. Though Welles, along with the other actors, would assume a substantial cut in income by accepting the City Center's maximum of eighty-five dollars a week, he saw the venture as reminiscent of his old Federal Theatre days and worthy of his return. *Lear* would go out on tour after its run in New York, and the proceeds from the tour would contribute toward the opera and ballet seasons at the house. Mayor Wagner greeted him at City Hall to thank him for his plans. Martin Gabel and Henry M. Margolis signed on as producers.

For the Shakespeare, Welles wanted a new kind of score with "symbolic abstract effects," as he put it to Blitzstein, "not Wagnerian heroic." For the Ben Jonson play, the composer and director agreed on "really a kind of 'musical,' with songs, numbers, dances, production-pieces. The Harpsichord is the center of the instrumental ensemble." Noting possible comparisons to Poulenc's *Les Mamelles de Tirésias,* Stravinsky's *L'Histoire du Soldat* and *Renard,* and to Weill's *Silbersee,* Blitzstein conceived "gay, tart, heartless, brilliant, juicy, stylish, popular-venetio-serenadeo pieces."[1]

Volpone soon dropped out of Welles's plans as, in typical fashion, his production costs for *King Lear* began to mount. In December, he announced it as a future Broadway show starring himself and Jackie Gleason, but this project also failed to materialize. The harpsichord remained the centerpiece of the orchestra for *Lear,* however. Blitzstein had the harpsichordist Ralph Kirkpatrick test an instrument offered for $750, and on his recommendation it was purchased for the show. Blitzstein's score for *Lear* also included a flute, clarinet, trumpet, French horn, timpani, and percussion. As his fee he received seven hundred dollars.

The score for Welles included more than forty sound cues tape-recorded by the team of Otto Luening and Vladimir Ussachevsky. Well acquainted with their work, having attended their concerts at the Museum of Modern Art and elsewhere, Blitzstein had recommended them. He had known Luening years before as the chairman of the music department at Bennington College, where in the thirties he had played and sung his operas for Luening's classes.

In late November, Blitzstein visited the Columbia University laboratory and studios of the two electronic composers. He heard their tape loops, flutters, wind effects, and what he described as "rhapsodic whizz I and II," and was satisfied that they were right for the job Welles wanted. Blitzstein had to verify the musicians' union position on the use of such sounds, as electronic scoring had never been used in such a large commercial production. Privately, Ussachevsky felt that their contribution to the *King Lear* score was the more important and that Blitzstein and his five-man ensemble were present, effectively, to placate the union.

At first, Welles expressed skepticism about "the recorded abstract musical boys," finding them "tiresome" and "excessive" in their demands for payment in advance of the opening. "This really has turned into a city entirely ruled over by lawyers. I would have thought my own name to say nothing of yours, and our mutual enthusiasm would have represented enough credit to get those gentlemen started at least on a project which would result in good publicity for them."[2] In time, Welles and the electronic "boys" did find a mode of mutual accommodation. He made frequent trips to the recording studio to hear and approve their work.

Rehearsals often stretched on until five in the morning. Cueing the sound perfectly to the script turned out to be an excruciating task, and expensive time was lost in countless subtle adjustments. In the end, the sound cues rarely did work properly because Welles delivered his lines at a varying pace from night to night. Having spent forty hours on cues to the "Blow, wind, blow" soliloquy, Ussachevsky often heard his sounds punctuate Welles's speech at the wrong places.

Unable to delegate authority to others, Welles took on every job he possibly could. It was he, despite the program credits, who actually designed the twenty-five-thousand-dollar set, an interlocking system of ramps, steps, and platforms. Backdrops based on Piranesi prints and painted on black velour allowed the lurid colors of the scenery to emerge from the surrounding pitch darkness. It was Welles himself who climbed ladders to fix the lighting system while the entire crew of electrical engineers and carpenters sat around playing poker at time-and-a-half. Production costs rose in other ways, too, for all through rehearsals Ussachevsky could not directly communicate with the operator of the tape recorder: Such instructions had to go through a union representative.

When the play opened on Thursday, January 12, 1956, it was billed promisingly as "A New Mercury Theatre Production." Welles had originally thought of using some of the Abbey Theatre actors he had known in Ireland, but American union regulations forced him to change this plan. A late call for actors yielded Geraldine Fitzgerald as Goneril, Viveca Lindfors as Cordelia, and in his first American acting role, Alvin Epstein as the Fool, a part he had recently performed in Hebrew during a three-year residency in Israel. To Epstein fell all of the vocal music. Once again the composer returned to an Elizabethan style for the Fool's ditties, writing little tunes that barely stand apart as separate musical numbers.

Welles was drinking heavily again. Shortly before opening night he tripped on his platforms and broke his ankle. He played the first night with one leg in a cast, supporting himself on crutches. By the second night, Friday the thirteenth, he had sprained the other ankle and was now reduced to a wheelchair. On this occasion, not yet having resolved the logistical problems of negotiating the platforms in a wheelchair, he gave not *King Lear* but "An Evening with Orson Welles," reciting favorite Shakespearean monologues and later opening up the session to a question and answer period with the audience. Most of the cast, by now thoroughly unhappy with the progress of the production, left the theatre and went home for the night. On successive nights until the twentieth and last performance of *Lear* on January 29, Epstein wheeled the great actor around in his chair while the ambulance Welles had ordered sat stationed at the stage door.

Blitzstein played the harpsichord for the length of the run, leading the ensemble in the pit. He received additional payment of $541.26 in his capacity as union musician, money he sorely needed now to pay off the *Threepenny Opera* lawsuit. Wind man Harvey Estrin had played in the *Reuben Reuben* orchestra and before that had played in the *Threepenny* band. Now he joined the composer again on the flute and clarinet. In the long waits during the rehearsal period, the two musicians happily played through Bach sonatas while Welles finished with his actors. Another of Blitzstein's men, Frank Weisberg, on timpani and percussion, had also played in the 1950 *Lear.*

Reviews were almost entirely damaging. They cited Welles's grand theatrical effects but monotonous and cold dramatic results. Some writers found the performance too much to sit through, as Welles staged *Lear* in one continuous act of two hours and twenty minutes. Some commentators found the music effective, though unremarkable; others felt it overwhelmed the play. In a long review article in *The New Republic,* Eric Bentley worshiped Welles as a director, but faulted him for taking on too many roles. Principally he criticized the coordination with other members of the cast whom Welles had directed excellently but never played with as fellow actor until the actual performance. Bentley wrote what everyone knew: that Welles was self-destructive in his attempt to reemerge on the American stage.

King Lear was the City Center's most expensive dramatic production to date and resulted in a sixty-thousand-dollar loss. Received badly, it did not go on the expected tour, thus severely crimping the City Center's artistic program for the rest of the season. It was the last time Orson Welles acted on the New York stage. His hopes for an American classical repertory theatre had met with complete disaster. He fled to the West Coast, where he engaged the sympathies of Lucille Ball and Desi Arnaz in a classic theatre project for television. Still considering *Volpone,* he asked for Blitzstein's cooperation. Blitzstein sent him his songs for the play, with texts adapted from Jonson, including the "Glove Song" and a "jazzed waltz" called "Come, My Celia." Nothing happened.

Ussachevsky and Luening used the material they had produced for City Center in their *King Lear* Suite. In addition, they made the forty-five cues of their "all-electronic score (no performing musicians)" available to theatrical producers on a rental basis.[3] Blitzstein, too, eventually returned to his music for *King Lear,* as Dimitri Mitropoulos, conductor of the New York Philharmonic, had been asking Blitzstein for an orchestra piece since the first *Lear* five years before.

Perhaps Blitzstein believed that for a time he would be occupied with Orson Welles and his classical theatre repertory venture. He had little else planned. He spent a week "translating" into English Ned Rorem's text for *The Robbers,* an opera based on Chaucer from Rorem's fussy Librettoland original. He typed it up himself, signing it with only the initials "M.B." He refused to take any credit for this assistance. In gratitude, and also in recognition of many other sessions of mutual music criticism, Rorem dedicated to Blitzstein one of his strongest songs, "Such Beauty as Hurts to Behold." Small comfort came from such sources, from Charlotte Rae's album, and from the 140 performances of *The Threepenny Opera* at London's Royal Court Theatre.

At the beginning of February, however, he received a letter that lifted his spirits somewhat. As the first in a series of such releases, Arthur Luce Klein, producer of Spoken Arts recordings, proposed an entire album of Blitzstein's music accompanied by spoken recollections and explanations by the composer. Immediately, Blitzstein set himself to the challenge of selecting the repertoire for the album. In his initial fantasies he named almost all of his theatre works and numerous instrumental pieces—the Sonata, the Serenade, the Piano Concerto, *Cain,* the Cummings songs, and the Whitman settings with William Warfield. But shortly he reduced the list to excerpts from three operas: *Cradle, No for an Answer* and *Regina.* In the following weeks he wrote out the spoken passages and selected his performers, rehearsing them in his apartment with meticulous attention to note values. The recording took place in New York on May 7 and 8.

Side one begins with Evelyn Lear singing "Nickel Under the Foot," with Blitzstein at the piano. Curiously, he chose a deliberate, ponderous tempo. Lear renders little of the inherent cynicism of the number. He might have chosen another performer for the song, but he doubtless felt that in this small way he could repay her for *Reuben Reuben.* Limits in radio broadcasting obliged a textual change in "Nickel": The Moll's guy turns out not to be a "bastard" but a "stinker."

Then Blitzstein is heard telling the story of *Cradle*'s opening night, in which he tries to sort out the "many embellished and apochryphal versions." Blitzstein's was a measured, clipped voice, almost British in its punctilious attention to consonants and with no particular regional inflection, similar to a standard radio voice. (It complemented his equally distinct handwriting: Few elisions of letters ever obscured his words. In writing music, he was similarly clear and scrupulous.) Sure of his words, he adopted the tone of an announcer and pitched his voice high. His voice on the recording shows obvious delight and little modesty in the recitation, especially when he recalls his preparedness to sing and play the whole opera through all alone at the piano: "Myself, produced by John Houseman, directed by Orson Welles, lit by Abe Feder, and conducted by Lehman Engel." Fresh from the debacle of *King Lear* when he recorded his story of *Cradle,* Blitzstein bubbled with tribute to Welles's extraordinary energy and problem-solving capabilities. However aggravating Welles had become in more recent years, nothing could ever remove Blitzstein's awe of the young genius.

He reminded his listeners of the positive role played by the Federal Theatre Project, where so many of the biggest names in theatre received their early training. He went further, saying that *Cradle*'s banning itself symbolized the very prostitution of the professions to which the opera points. In 1956 this was hardly a fashionable view to assume, but Blitzstein must have felt that once the current era of cowardice had passed, his words would remain for posterity. In the same talk he took the opportunity to poke sly fun at Archibald MacLeish for his pomposity that night at the Venice.

Rounding out his recollections of the work, Blitzstein cited the twenty-five productions of *Cradle* to date in the United States and England. With special pride, he mentioned the revived orchestral version conducted by Bernstein back in 1947. Still, he added his hope that one day, perhaps in another ten years, he might see the work performed again as he had originally written it, fully orchestrated and fully staged. His wish was to be granted, sooner than he imagined.

Completing the first side is the Hotel Lobby scene, with Alvin Epstein as Yasha and Roddy McDowall as Dauber. Jane Connell, who had performed the role of Mrs. Peachum at intermittent periods, was Mrs. Mister. This is a lively reading of the scene with a flexible, appropriately zany characterization on Connell's part. Both men are more than competent singing actors. Again, words were changed for public consumption: "For there's something so blamed low about the rich," the painter and the violinist sing, not "damned." A "hell" is altered to "oh."

On the reverse side of the record, Blitzstein explained the differences between the two-dimensional figures in *The Cradle Will Rock* and the fuller characterizations in *No for an Answer.* He also explained his method of writing music and words as a push-and-pull process of fitting thoughts to words to scenes to the entire work, all the while thinking of notes, intervals, tunes, songs, and the overall musical form. He may have been reflecting on his recent failure with *Reuben Reuben* as much as on the truncated history of *No for an Answer* when he defined the disadvantage of a composer's being his own librettist: "You lack the fresh perspective of another mind working with you, and you have to dig up that perspective within yourself—be two people, as it were, in constant battle and agreement."

Joshua Shelley, with the rich accents of a streetwise New Yorker, performs "Penny Candy," followed by Evelyn Lear and George Gaynes in the "Francie" scene. Lear is at her best here, blushing with fresh naïveté as she tries to interest Joe in the developments of the union struggle now that he is home again. Gaynes's huge "placed" voice with its operatic resonance so suited to *Reuben Reuben* seems out of character.

A speech remarkable for its candor follows the two excerpts from *No for an Answer.* In this "message to the world," the old materialist Marxist interpretation of music history shows through clearly as Blitzstein touches on the socially committed themes predominant in his output. Again he emphasizes how much the music of any composer and the creation of any artist show a close relation to the life about them. Some artists more than others attempt to fix this relation clearly in their subject matter, leaving as little as possible in the creation that is not conscious to the artist or that would be open to later re- or misinterpretation. He cites "Zola, Mussorgsky, and Ben Shahn, in whose camp I find myself."

This discussion leads into an aria from *Regina,* Birdie's scena from the third act. As sung by Brenda Lewis, this had been among the most riveting moments in all of Blitzstein's music, and it was certainly a sensible inclusion on this recording. It appears also because Blitzstein wanted to show his formal operatic side along with his "popular" music style. Lewis dramatically captures the pathos of the shifting moods in Birdie's scene. To those familiar with the opera as later recorded with full orchestra, the piece comes off flatly with just the piano as accompaniment; but this was the first music from *Regina* released to the public. From the composer's jottings at a playback session on May 31, it seems as though the "Rain Quartet" had also been taped in case room remained on the record.

Blitzstein's agreement with Spoken Arts, signed in April, entitled him to a three-hundred-dollar advance to be deducted from future royalties, plus twenty cents per record sold. By the end of 1956, he had not exceeded his advance. The singers were not paid. The Spoken Arts record was Evelyn Lear's first appearance on disk. Within a few weeks, certainly on Blitzstein's recommendation, she also recorded Kurt Weill's *Johnny Johnson* on an MGM album produced by Edward Cole, along with other veterans of Blitzstein shows: Thomas Stewart, Hiram

Sherman, Jane Connell, Scott Merrill, Burgess Meredith, and of course Lenya. Samuel Matlovsky conducted, and Joseph Liebling served as choral director.

In correspondence extending from the summer through the fall of 1956, Edward Cole expressed interest in an all-Blitzstein recording with orchestral forces on MGM. Again Blitzstein thought of the Serenade for Strings, and of *Triple-Sec.* Within a few weeks, he pared down the choices to two suites, from *Cradle* and *Regina.* "I think that we might have something fairly big commercially in these suites and I hope that the specific project under discussion now will be the first of many involving your theater scores," Cole wrote to the composer.[4] As the fall progressed, Blitzstein determined the exact timings of the suites, and recording dates were set: the *Cradle* suite on November 12, and *Regina* on the nineteenth, to be conducted by Carlos Surinach. Further plans were set for recording a suite from *No for an Answer, I've Got the Tune,* and *The Guests.* Unexplained delays and perhaps reassessment of these records' commercial viability eventually turned into their complete abandonment.

Little of this retrospective activity—nor his name in the March 26 *New York Times* crossword puzzle—made up for the still painful defeat of *Reuben Reuben.* Significantly, none of its music appears in Blitzstein's ideas for recording. The memories were too recent and too bitter. In a Ford Hall Forum address given in Boston's Jordan Hall on April 22 and broadcast the same night on WCOP AM and FM stations, he flagellated himself publicly for his sins:

> I don't know if any of you present or listening tonight were witnesses of a musical-stage-work of mine which was born and which died a scurvy death here in Boston earlier this season. It was called *Reuben Reuben*—and it was a first-class, A-one disaster; a really rather spectacular disaster in its way, with threatening fists pushed in my face, and actual brawls in the Shubert theatre lobby. You may therefore wonder where I get the audacity to address you now on the subject of American Opera Today. Let me say at once that I shoulder most of the blame for the miscalculations that caused that disaster (I can only hope they were miscalculations, and not more serious crimes); and that I have a valiant fighting producer, with whom I am still on admiring and loyal terms, and who insists she will re-present the work, as soon as I have completed extensive and drastic revisions.

In the course of his speech, he attacked the smugness, the lack of courage and protest in American arts. "The time is the time of The Fright," he warned, "the time of The Bomb. In a moment of great world-tension and friction, we are looking, not at the world, but under the bed." In a reference that all too closely suggests many of *Reuben Reuben*'s problems, Blitzstein lamented that so much of our art had become "super-personalized, neurasthenic, fantasy-ridden, exotic, wandering down psychological and sometimes pathological by-ways." In what he explained as possibly a "sour interpolation" to the main theme of his talk, he summoned the protest spirit of the thirties and urged "a little adventure, please, a little air, a little gut."

A few months later in a letter to the *Times* responding to Norris Houghton's article about the new Off-Broadway scene, Blitzstein once again mentioned the Federal Theatre Project and the activist theatre groups of the 1930s as precursors of the revived alternative stage. Houghton had failed to note the existence of any earlier expressions in the Off-Broadway movement. In an implied criticism of McCarthyist revisionism, Blitzstein asked, "Let us please not erase these groups, which also added 'another chapter of theatrical history.' "[5]

During these directionless months of 1956, Blitzstein marked time. He wrote reviews of published opera scores for the Music Library Association's *Notes.* In a lukewarm notice on Richard Mohaupt's *Double-Trouble,* he recommended its use for college opera workshops. In a longer piece on *The Saint of Bleecker Street,* Blitzstein remarked that "Menotti is a fiendishly talented music-theater man. But he rarely, if ever, writes about themes which have been his life-long convictions; the convictions grow with the actual working, and may quite possibly fade with a work's completion. This means he has not much in reserve; and it often means ultimate shallowness." At the premiere performance in 1954, he recalled, "I got the feeling I was hearing a translation from the Italian"—at La Scala the text "sat" better.[6] He did not put into his review the opening-night remark he made to Lenny and Felicia Bernstein when he could see how well Menotti's audience liked the work—"It's a tough night for the Jews!"

In early June 1956 Blitzstein participated in a convocation entitled "What Mozart Means to Modern Music." Held at the Stratford Festival Theatre in Connecticut, the symposium honored Mozart on his bicentennial. Virgil Thomson chaired the Saturday panel on which Blitzstein served along with Erich Leinsdorf and Chester Kallman. In his remarks, Blitzstein stressed the point, which can be taken as the principal lesson he derived from Mozart, that Mozart's grandeur lay in his slightly understating the size of his theme. In these various ways, Blitzstein kept restating and rethinking the purpose of theatre.

Following the Mozart symposium, Blitzstein traveled to Martha's Vineyard for a few days, consulting with Bernstein and Hellman on *Candide* and moving back and forth between their two houses. On his return trip, he stopped in Ashfield for a visit with Mina Curtiss. By the end of June, he had ensconced himself in Brigantine for the rest of the summer.

The team of Capalbo and Chase had approached him concerning a production of William Saroyan's play about homeless people, *The Cave Dwellers,* for which they wanted a musical score. Admiring of Saroyan's "never overstated, always clean" way with words, Blitzstein nevertheless refused their proposal with an extended critique of the work:

> It is the ideas themselves, the philosophy itself which alienate me: something between moral masochism and Mary Baker Eddy. In a setting which symbolizes an atom-world on the brink of total catastrophe, mere sweetness (and mere, yes mere individual brotherhoodism) seems almost an affront. We all love a good cry; but it ought to be worth something, it ought to leave us stimulated by the purging, not debilitated.[7]

Blitzstein's interest in translating Brecht's *Mother Courage* dates to this summer, shortly before the playwright's unexpected death in August. With hope of recognition as a composer seemingly growing fainter with each passing year, he trusted that he might repeat his success as a translator. *Mother Courage* dates from 1938 to 1939. H. R. Hays had made the first English translation as early as 1941. Eric Bentley provided another in 1955, publishing it with Doubleday. This was the translation used in the first United States staging of the play in San Francisco in early 1956.

Mother Courage is a camp follower, selling comestibles and equipment alternately to the Protestant and Catholic troops. During the twelve-year chronicle covered in the play, she loses her three children to war. A hard-bitten materialist who nevertheless suffers deeply over her losses, she resolves above all to maintain herself in business. At the end, she has only her wagon and her wits to console her.

As always, Blitzstein researched his subject in detail, noting the names and dates of towns and battles in the Thirty Years' War of the early seventeenth century, the setting of the play. He prepared rough-draft translations of Paul Dessau's songs, using as a reference the recording by Germaine Montero of music from the French production.

A break from his theatre concerns and from his career as a translator came along through Mordecai Bauman. Worried over his friend's obviously depressed state, Mordy felt that a fresh commission for him involving a Carnegie Hall premiere with large chorus and orchestra might give him a needed lift. He suggested Blitzstein's name to Harold Aks, conductor of the Interracial Fellowship Chorus, who had previously commissioned works from such men as Wallingford Riegger, Robert Starer, Andrew Imbrie, and Ulysses Kay. Aks wondered whether Blitzstein's satirical style would be suited to choral music; he also feared that a composer of Blitzstein's stature might not be interested in writing for an amateur chorus.

Aks did make the offer, for a five-hundred-dollar fee, and Blitzstein accepted the challenge. He knew Aks as the man who had once prepared the ensemble and played the Chorus Director in a staging of *I've Got the Tune;* and he knew the reputation of the chorus, famous in New York for performing the seldom heard Haydn masses. Aks conducted the group from its founding in 1947 until its demise almost twenty years later. The associate director of the chorus, David Labovitz, originally from Philadelphia, had worked with Dr. Leof in the Russian War Relief movement during the first years of the war.

Blitzstein also knew that in its own way the chorus played a progressive social role. Originally sponsored by the Interracial Fellowship Council, a Protestant brotherhood organization with honorary sponsors such as Eleanor Roosevelt, Jacob Javits, and Mayor Wagner, the chorus had long grown apart as an independent body. All who wished to sing were accepted, even if they did not know how to read music—*Gebrauchsmusik* at work—and in the mid-1950s the chorus boasted a membership of 150 singers. Occasionally they would be invited by ministers of churches in New England to give concerts, and the singers would be housed by members of the community. In many cases it was the first time a black visitor had ever stayed overnight in their homes.

Once Blitzstein threw himself into work on the choral piece, he put aside the translation of *Mother Courage* for the time being, poking at it only intermittently. However, he remained mesmerized by its tremendous power, even a heightened power in the atomic age, and he committed himself to return to it.

Blitzstein began writing his texts in July, choosing to portray six vignettes of New York City life. Not aimed to be a complete portrait of the city—"still other 'New York Cantatas' may follow," he announced in the program notes—the themes and moods of the piece touch a wide base. As he stops in to visit a number of ethnic neighborhoods, he encompasses work and play, birth and death, day and night, public and private, the solemn and festive. He uses the chorus as both the crowd and the individual, a child and a whole neighborhood, with personal as well as collective feelings and responses articulated—all without solos. Each scene is set outside, "but the work is no travelogue," Blitzstein wrote—no glitter, no tourist attractions, just genre scenes of the extraordinary ordinary life of the city. *This Is the Garden: A Cantata of New York* became the title of the work, its name derived from a 1925 poem by E. E. Cummings: "This is the garden. Colours come and go. . . ." Blitzstein had heard William Schuman's 1940 cantata *This Is Our Time,* a celebration of proletarian joys set to a text by Genevieve Taggard that was well received in its day. He may also have known Busoni's comparison of music to a garden, where the composer can "survey, handle, and display only a fraction of the complete flora of the earth, a tiny fragment of that paradise-garden which covers the planets."[8]

"The Lex Express" opens up the day and the piece. Here is the composer in a familiar populist vein. The subway ride recalls much of his previous machine music. As in the song "American Day" from *Native Land,* the worker going to his job is in a good mood: "wake up humming," "feel what a fine big high-stepping day," "Your feet do a jiggling step." Until the "unbelievable hell" of the train: "the sweat, the noise, and the people. These are no longer people—scratching, clawing. A milling jamming pawing mess of cattle." Mass society strikes against the individual human spirit.

Need it be like this? we wonder. The rider gets off at "Union Square! My stop," the chorus singing as one voice. As if to suggest that rush-hour crowding on the subway system is not worth taking too much to heart, the text ends, "Save yourself. Lose your temper. Save yourself, save yourself. Swear. Give way. Then laugh. That helpless, helpless laugh."

In "I'm Ten and You'll See," the chorus personifies a youngster and his visions of happiness. From the point of view of this ten-year-old, human needs are relatively simple: freedom of expression, satisfaction of hunger, respect, acceptance, and warmth.

The child's horizons are for now limited to a gang-dominated neighborhood of the city, but his imagination is broad. In prepubescent dreamlike fantasies, he wants to "fly solo over Washington Square," and "be in China tomorrow, or any place," "fly back, and land smack on my own roof. And the crowd will be cheering me on." Having stolen "all the money in the world," he will buy his mother a fur coat, a box of good cigars for his father, and for himself a manly "wool-lined leather jacket, good and warm, shining with silver clips all over"—a throwback to the bombardier's costume in the *Airborne* Symphony. Most important of all, the heroic mock patriotism of the music underlines this theme: "I am proud and ready and worthy to be part of their gang." At the time Blitzstein was writing *This Is the Garden,* Bernstein was writing *West Side Story.* Like the "Officer Krupke" number that also depicts the world of juvenile delinquents, the episode is essentially humorous. It reflects the "helpless laugh" of Blitzstein the composer: The child may be "dirty and dirty forever and ever," and he may "write all the four-letter words I can write on the wall of the store." Still he wants to "show them that I am as good as they are, and even better." Blitzstein's failures stand as the very emblem of his success; if he had all the money and the power to be Czar or Commissar of American Music, his status in "the gang" would be just the reverse of its current depths.

Sudden death is the topic of the following segment, titled, as if a newspaper headline, "Harlan Brown, Killed in the Street." The incident leading to the fact of "a body: slung back against the curb, this pile of rags" is not described. The text instead recounts the reaction of the neighborhood on discovering the corpse. First is the urge to revive him somehow: "One linking moment linked us" in the need to bring him back to the community of the living. Then come repulsion and denial: "Just this hateful glee, to think: Not me, not this time, not me." Finally, the casual thought occurs: "Who were you?," and off running, late, to the business of the day. The incident has already become a discrete event in the collective memory.

In form, this is a simple A-B-A, with a persistent use of fourths that again recalls the language of the *Airborne.* Marked *grave,* "Harlan Brown" is at center a mourning dirge for humanity conditioned to the disposability of life.

In delicious contrast comes a Latin number called "Hymie Is a Poop" that inevitably recalls the setting of *West Side Story.* To a gently syncopated tropical rhythm marked *alla conga,* the whole neighborhood retells the story of Pepita, who gave birth to her baby right on the front stoop of her building. She woke her husband Hymie (Jaime in Blitzstein's earlier drafts) so late in her labor that there was no time to get to the hospital.

When one voice in the neighborhood claims, "Pepita she is young, and she don't know no better," it is answered by another saying, "Pepita she is smart, she knows her way around." "She still can't talk good English" is answered by "She don't have to." The *Daily Mirror* reported the story with pictures of the mother, baby, and Hymie, and from all over the city came baby presents—a silver go-cart ("it looks like silver, anyway"), "one dozen woolen play-suits, two dozen silken dresses, and more nice things than you could count," including, not the least of it all, "in the bank a nice amount."

Later on, "skinny, mad and helpless," Hymie cares for the baby while Pepita tries to sleep. He keeps asking his wife why she waited so long. "It had to get printed in the paper," she replies. "It's because we need the money." She has taken the support of her family into her own hands, shrewd beyond her neighbors' ken to the ways of modern media and to the patterns of popular charity.

One of Blitzstein's few love songs—again, a thwarted love—is the fifth vignette in *This Is the Garden.* "In Twos" shows us a pair of lovers in the big city walking in the park, sitting on benches, lying on the grass, seeing hospitable "lighted windows as they pass." "And when at last they go, they won't go home," for there "it's hard to stay in twos." As in *The Guests,* the composer might be suggesting an interracial couple whose families will not accept this love—an appropriate theme for this chorus to sing. Another possibility is clearly coded into the text by the careful omission of any reference to gender. "For lovers feel that they are cheating time, as long as they remain in twos." The *andante cantando* pace of "In Twos" recalls the aching yearning of Marc's song to Eva more than twenty years before, "Stay in My Arms." This, too, saw love as a refuge in the city.

The cantata concludes with an overlong transplant of the San Gennaro chorus from *Reuben Reuben.* Boisterous and rollicking with its childlike piety and its evocation of Southern Italian folk tunes, it serves in this work to bring the New York day to a festive close.

Having begun work on *This Is the Garden* in Brigantine, Blitzstein continued his writing and composition on a trip to Mexico during most of September and October. David Diamond occupied Marc's East Twelfth Street apartment, supporting himself after his return from Italy by playing the violin in the orchestra for Bernstein's *Candide.* From Mexico City, Blitzstein wrote to David: "Of course one falls in love with Mexicans and their city—patience, brooding, attachment seem their best qualities. I have been doing some 'night-flying' with native friends. It all adds up to a change of pace, good for me."[9]

In Cuernavaca he rented a house with a swimming pool, garden, and cook, and with a tower from which he could view Popocatépetl. Aside from *This Is the Garden,* he thought more about the *Lear* piece for Mitropoulos. He visited several pre-Columbian archeological sites and socialized with other members of the American colony at the cafés on the square.

On his return to the United States, he immediately headed for Boston to see *Candide,* which had opened on October 29 and would begin at New York's Martin Beck Theater on December 1. Running only seventy-three performances, the show and its failure must have given Bernstein for the first time in his theatrical career a clear sense of empathy with Marc's more consistent record of disappointment.

Shortly after the beginning of the year, Blitzstein entered a hospital for yet another hernia operation. His doctor Sam Standard predicted a slow recovery. Even then, Blitzstein was a man of imperfect health: For years he suffered from debilitating bouts of recurrent hepatitis certainly exacerbated by drinking. His liver was weak. Jo picked him up and took him home to recuperate in Philadelphia. "I've emerged as good as second-hand new," he wrote to Irma Bauman,

> Which is to say that I feel old. Now the good doctor is pressing me to go South for sun and sea, and I'll take his advice, since I do seem to need it. If only this mental depression would go—I can take care of knees-like-water, etc.[10]

Both Blitzstein and Bernstein needed consoling: the former for his health, the latter for *Candide.* They did so with a two-week trip to Cuba beginning at the end of January. Felicia accompanied Lenny, and Jo and Ed joined Marc. In those dying years of the Batista régime—Fidel Castro had already begun his final assault in the mountains—they noted large numbers of army and police about. Their families lavished affection on the two composers: Whatever they said and did, they were scintillating, surprising, maybe moody at times, but fun. Marc and Lenny played word games that got so boring in English that they incorporated French, German, Italian, and Latin to make it more stimulating—that drove everyone else out. And they would take a tune from Copland's *Billy the Kid* and sing their own words to it: "Bernstein and Blitzstein and Blitzstein and Bern, Blitzstein and Bernstein and Blitzstein and Bernstein AND BLITZSTEIN!" Of course, when Lenny sang it, he reversed the order in the last line. Those two names together: Sometimes, hypnotically, it seemed that's all there was in the world.

In the early months of 1957, while the chorus began rehearsing, Blitzstein orchestrated *This Is the Garden.* In the composition stage, he had noted to himself, "Remember, it's not a stage work—watch lyrics, etc. Make it available for all choruses—not too much story!!" In places he failed to follow his own precaution, but at least with the orchestration he made the piece accessible to almost any group of amateurs, and certainly to professional singers, by doubling much of the chorus part. He also doubled the altos with the tenors in numerous passages, since the chorus had more women than men.

At rehearsals, Blitzstein emphasized the importance of clear diction over and over again. Aks brought in an oboist and a bassoonist to sit in sections of the chorus and play notes. Still, some in the chorus found the writing too difficult, especially rhythmically. A week before the premiere, John Briggs reported in the *Times* that "the chorus held a formal open debate on the question: to perform, or not to perform. Partisan feeling ran high, but the Blitzstein work eventually won out and will be performed as scheduled."[11]

As rehearsals proceeded, political harassment arrived in the music world, once again striking a number of Blitzstein's associates, as well as Aks's former father-in-law. A HUAC subcommittee began four days of well-publicized hearings on "Communist infiltration" at the United States Court House at Foley Square. Beginning on April 9, three congressmen from the committee, Representatives Bernard W. Kearney of New York, Clyde Doyle of California, and Morgan M. Moulder of Missouri, heard testimony concerning the Metropolitan Music School—successor to the Downtown Music School—Local 802 of the musicians' union, and other musical organizations. Eleven witnesses from the school refused to answer questions concerning alleged past or present Party membership. Lilly Popper, director of the school, invoked both the First and the Fifth amendments. The most prominent witness called to testify was Wallingford Riegger, president emeritus of the school. Harold Aks had been married to Riegger's daughter Mary Rose; they had two children. Among all the witnesses, only Riegger, almost seventy-two, pleaded the First Amendment alone, and he was promptly threatened with a citation for contempt of Congress.

The hearings brought out the usual range of cooperative witnesses. A former Communist functionary, John Lautner, identified Riegger as a Party branch organizer on the West Side between 1933 and 1936, a charge Riegger refused to confirm or deny. Abram Chasins, music director of WQXR and a onetime member of the musical board of the school—only, he hastened to assert, because its stated objectives appeared worthy—had since resigned from the board. When the director asked him to support the school against the committee's attacks, he wrote to HUAC braying that he stood "unequivocally opposed to every aspect of Communist ideology." In a letter to Popper, he also defended HUAC's right to investigate the school, gratuitously adding a warning about instructors who abused their privileges being "unfit to teach."[12]

Max Marlin, a friendly witness and the conductor of Blitzstein's music in the 1950 *King Lear* with Louis Calhern, testified that he was forced to join the Party in 1936 in order to get jobs. As a band leader, he was then obligated to hire other Party members even when he would have preferred to take on more qualified players. The pianist Seymour Levitan also talked about his days as a Party cell member within the ranks of Local 802.

During the four days, thirty-seven witnesses "took the Fifth." They included Sidney Finkelstein, the Party's leading historian and theoretician on musical subjects, who also worked for Vanguard Records; Max Polikoff; jazz pianist John Mehegan; David Walter, former chairman of the board of the Symphony of the Air; Earl Robinson; and Max Goberman, conductor and former musical director of the Ballet Theatre.

Against the background of these new assaults on the Bill of Rights, the tenth anniversary concert of the Interracial Fellowship Chorus, featuring the premiere of Blitzstein's new work, took place in Carnegie Hall on Sunday, May 5, 1957. In the light of the HUAC hearings, Blitzstein's lyrics for the love song "In Twos" assumed a new meaning:

And lovers have to be in twos.
How else are they to fight off moulder?

The composer may be slyly injecting a message in the form of a pun for unity against the likes of the Hon. Morgan M. Moulder, Democrat of Missouri. Why else such a strange noun, and in its nonpreferred spelling?

On the same program, Haydn's *Creation* Mass, given its first full presentation in America, included the soloists Arabella Hong, Charles Bressler, Carol Brice, and her brother Eugene Brice. Instrumentalists were drawn from the ranks of the

New York Philharmonic. The performance of *This Is the Garden* was raw and energetic, in many respects amateurish but wholesome, though the composer felt that Aks had speeded up the tempo in places.

After the concert, members of the cast of *Reuben Reuben* turned up backstage, greeting Blitzstein with tears in their eyes. They knew that with this relatively unimpressive recycling of the San Gennaro music, their show, far from being revised for representation, had finally dropped into its composer's trunk.

The after-concert reception was held in the mobbed Park Avenue living room of Dr. and Mrs. Samuel Gaines, whose daughter sang in the chorus. Lenny's intimate embrace of Marc upset certain of the guests. Despite his ostensible warmth, Bernstein must surely have recognized *This Is the Garden*—barely twenty minutes' worth of music—as a minor accomplishment and a certain defeat for *Reuben Reuben.*

Appreciative, if hardly rousing reviews appeared in Monday's papers. Harriett Johnson referred in the *Post* to the "pulsating, verbal vigor" of the piece. Jay Harrison, in the *Herald Tribune,* called it "an unpretentious and touching work." The *Times*'s Howard Taubman cited Blitzstein's "somewhat prosy poems, like so much that happens in New York. His music is not complicated, as though carefully designed for amateur chorus. It harks back in its simplicity to the style Mr. Blitzstein used two decades ago. . . . The music has a disingenuous air. It is all genre stuff—jaunty, sentimental, mocking, pathetic and not very deep."[13]

Within a year, Chappell released the piano-vocal score to *This Is the Garden,* its ninety-two pages priced at $2.50. The dedication read, "For my mother." Robert Sabin reviewed the edition in *Musical America,* admiring Blitzstein's "many shrewd touches of psychology." He found the cantata "readily singable, even catchy. . . . What a relief, after the Victorian stuff that many of our choral composers are still turning out!"[14]

Despite the fact that the score was available in print, no evidence survives of another performance of *This Is the Garden* for another thirty years. Eventually, the publisher destroyed the remaining stock.

20

BIRD UPON THE TREE

Spring 1957–Spring 1958

". . . 'twas the storm itself that did free . . ."

The playwright Joseph Stein, a client of the William Morris Agency, had been responsible with Will Glickman for the books of three musicals, *Plain and Fancy, Mr. Wonderful,* and *The Body Beautiful.* Stein conceived the idea of making a musical version of Sean O'Casey's 1924 play *Juno and the Paycock;* out of consideration for their past collaborations, he invited Glickman to come into the project.

In July 1956 Stein and his wife had paid a visit to O'Casey at his home in Devon. Over the course of a long luncheon and an afternoon on the lawn, Stein discovered that O'Casey really had no familiarity with the American musical. "I wish I had," said O'Casey, "for playwrights should be well up in all forms done in the theatre; but circumstance forced me to begin late, and I had no time, no time, no time."[1] He had known about some of the Rodgers and Hammerstein works, and he knew that Lerner and Loewe had not long before made an adaptation of Shaw, calling it *My Fair Lady.* The Steins had, in fact, brought with them a copy of the cast album, but the O'Caseys did not own a phonograph. Nevertheless, Stein was able to demonstrate how *Juno* could be put on the musical stage, with a sense of space expanded beyond the Boyles' living room, with choruses, soloists, and dance. O'Casey gradually warmed to the notion. By the end of an evening filled with talk of theatre and politics, he extended his blessing over the project.*

On his return to the States, Stein and Glickman began thinking about the music. For this show they sought not just a tunesmith who would produce a typical Broadway sound but a composer of weight and substance. Such a composer would have to possess an understanding of both the comic and the tragic sides of the play and be willing to write a serious score. Stein already knew some of Blitzstein's work; and as a budding writer back in 1946, he had scripted some dialogue for Blitzstein to exchange with Hildegarde when she sang "Emily" on the radio. But it was Helen Harvey of the play department at the William Morris Agency who, shortly before the premiere of *This Is the Garden,* had suggested Blitzstein's name.

The formal approach came in April 1957. Stein could not have been aware how vital his timing turned out to be, just the moment to rouse Blitzstein from his anomie, to slake his thirst for creation. To be remembered, to be wanted, to be useful! And to be rescued from being his own collaborator! By May they had begun work as a team.

In some ways, Blitzstein's quick decision to work on the new musical showed how vital he remained, even as he entered late middle age. He wouldn't become stodgy, settled, complacent. In spirit he stayed quarrelsome, ready for impassioned battle. With no troublesome deliberation, he would write a letter to the editor, give a lecture or participate in a public forum, travel to other cities and abroad, review the occasional book or record. Life had to be multicolored, a quilt of variegated activity, to satisfy. Mere existence, a single job, the marking of deadly time—that he could not take.

O'Casey's play takes place in 1922, just after the Irish Free State had been established. Former allies in the struggle for independence are now engaged in bitter civil war. For the purposes of the musical, the story is set back a year, so that the political question is simplified: The Irish people against British rule. At the center of the story is the Boyle family. "Captain" Jack Boyle is a Falstaffian figure, despising an honest day's work. Strutting about the house and the neighborhood like a peacock, he lives parasitically off his wife Juno's labor and sympathy. His lumpen sidekick Joxer Daly is his drinking buddy and collaborator in sloth. The two Boyle children are Mary, who works in a factory and has vague aspirations of a better life; and Johnny, once active in the independence cause, now a chronic hysteric and virtual recluse. Jerry Devine is a sweet and thoughtful but dull fellow wooing Mary. She rejects him in favor of Charlie Bentham, more of a man about town who flaunts his middle-class pretensions. Various neighbors,

*The composer Hugo Weisgall wanted to set O'Casey's play *The Plough and the Stars* as an opera, and in April 1956 visited O'Casey to ask for the rights. O'Casey refused but, according to Weisgall, begged him to do *Juno and the Paycock.* "Do *Juno*—it's a great opera," O'Casey said, the conversation extending even to what kinds of voices would be appropriate for each character. Stein knew nothing of Weisgall's earlier visit. O'Casey's initial resistance to Stein's notion of setting *Juno and the Paycock* as a musical may substantiate his preference for the idea of an opera made from the same material. Elie Siegmeister later made an opera of *The Plough and the Stars.*

especially women of the tenement, Boyle's pub companions, and young men united in the anti-British movement, fill out the cast.

Bentham presents the news that the Boyles have been left a sizable legacy by a wealthy relative. Right away they go out shopping on credit, buying new furnishings for the house and a gramophone. They host a grand musical party to celebrate their new richesse. The evening is interrupted by the passing funeral of Robbie Tancred, shot by the British. As it becomes clear that the legacy is not going to materialize after all, Bentham ceases to come around, though he has left Mary pregnant. Boyle repudiates Mary for her indiscretions. Men sent by the creditors come and remove all the furniture and the gramophone. Finally, Johnny himself is taken away by men from the Irregular forces and shot. As Boyle and Joxer sink ever deeper into the mire of drink, Juno and Mary resolve to leave and start life over again by themselves. The baby will have two mothers.

Juno fascinated Blitzstein. Here was a powerful story—already proven stage-worthy—by a playwright of renown, with so many appealing elements. Against the background of the Irish struggle for freedom in the early 1920s, he could exercise his musical muscle with tuneful comment on so many themes: British imperialism, the position of women in society, the nature of political commitment, the place of music and media in ordinary life, the flight from responsibility through alcoholic addiction, violence in the struggle for rights and ideas. And he had a ready musical hook—the ancient Irish tradition of song—to exploit and adapt to his purposes.

Ideologically, he felt right at home with O'Casey's Marxist humanism and with his tragic, ironic vision of life. As Brecht and Hellman did, O'Casey placed his characters confidently within the frame of a specific time and place, knowing that they, and the types of social relations he created among them, would survive beyond the moment as telling archetypes for future audiences. Blitzstein found the adapter wholly compatible as well: "We were on the same wavelength," says Stein.

Will Glickman wanted to end the musical happily with a good marriage for Mary, but O'Casey insisted on keeping the mostly pessimistic original ending. Glickman also was not convinced that a "long-hair" composer like Blitzstein was right for *Juno.* Within a few weeks he bowed out of the project. Unencumbered by the additional partner, composer and book writer immediately set about brainstorming, compiling lists of possible producers, directors, costume, lighting, and set designers, conductors, contractors, and actors.

As with the writing of *The Cradle Will Rock,* Blitzstein worked "at white heat" on the music for *Juno,* or *Daarlin' Man,* as they thought of calling it. During that summer, he stayed with Mina Curtiss at Chapelbrook and composed two dozen songs and lyrics. For two numbers, "What Is the Stars?" and "Song of the Ma," O'Casey himself provided lyrics, which Blitzstein only slightly modified. A few of the songs from the summer of 1957 would later be cut in production, or even before. And as the show ran its course through out-of-town tryouts, more numbers would be added. But most of the music that found its way into the final show was written at this time.

Ever attentive to language and precise usage, Blitzstein sought out a number of Irish informants. From them he garnered a clear picture of the working-class residential and commercial areas fronting on Dublin's River Liffey.

He also researched Irish musical history, and incorporated dozens of authentic tunes, rhythms, cadences, and verses into his score. From Thomas Moore's "Molly, My Dear" went some lines into "I Wish It So." "Hills of Donegal" crept into "What Is the Stars?" "Lady Nelson's Reel" he used in the song "Daarlin' Man." The slip-jigs "Rocky Road to Dublin" and "Ride a Mile" found their way into the dance segment of "On a Day Like This." Geraldine Fitzgerald sang the Irish fling "Molly Brannigan" to Blitzstein one day in October, and he used that, too, in "On a Day Like This." Liking to date his music precisely, almost archaeologically, he imitated routines such as Billy Rose's "Barney Google" (ca. 1922) in the patter songs involving Captain Boyle and Joxer.

By the middle of June, Blitzstein had recorded his first songs on a tape for Stein's opinion. "I've been listening to your music," wrote a pleased bookwriter to composer, "and have fallen madly in love with it, number after number."[2]

While O'Casey's play itself suggested the themes and something of the vocabulary for the lyrics, nevertheless Blitzstein's contributions integrated into the songs cannot be overlooked. In the ensemble number "On a Day Like This," when the entire cast assembles to voice their hopes from the new sudden legacy, two main desires emerge: for wealth and for love. Could it be that *Juno* might finally bring Blitzstein the former, if not the latter? When Boyle speaks his desires, he rises, to everyone's surprise, to unfamiliar heights. For he wishes above all respect and a responsible status in the community:

I hope the neighborhood will come to me
For simple sound advice, a loan or so.
I'll want a fountain-pen, a small portfolio. . . .
I'll order spectacles, the kind that pinch.
A narrow ribbon runnin', quarter-inch.
I'll read those thick newspapers, take my time,
An' study poems that don't even rhyme.

Unmistakably, Boyle serves as a model for Tevye the Milkman's "If I Were a Rich Man" in *Fiddler on the Roof,* which Stein brought to Broadway seven years later.

In Mary's songs, a yearning for love comes through that can be seen as the composer's own. Early in the show, her "I Wish It So," sung to Juno in the realization that Jerry Devine is not the right kind of man, describes her feelings of unrest, wanting something, not knowing what, but hoping "it" will come soon:

And my heart clamors and prays it will not come too late!
But when come it does, in the shape of love or life,
I will give my life, and my love, I know.

In "My True Heart," which Mary sings to Charlie Bentham, she reveals her love:

Will you care, or be sorry I know you,
If once I show you my true heart?
Oh, let me live by my love,
Or I die by my love;
And my love it will endure
Till death do us part.

Both play and musical emphasize Ireland's divided society—the pragmatic unmarried to the lyrical; the rebellious impulse vitiated by the lack of revolutionary discipline; alcohol, religion, blarney, and sloth draining the country's human resources. Nowhere is the symbolism of dividedness more apparent than in the separate worlds men and women inhabit. In the duet "What Is the Stars?" between the two "butties" Joxer and Boyle, Captain Boyle fantasizes about his fictitious oceanic days:

The life on the sea is the life that's for me;
I'm me own man at work an' at play.
With no rent, no children, no females—
Thinkin' nothin' but thoughts all the day;
The life on the brine is the life full o' wine,
Full o' song, but no women—hurray!
Where the only dainty curve is the curve o' the ship.
There is me, *there is* me,
An' one she, *just one* she—
It's Venus, a million miles away.
The sea, the sea—
There's no other she *on the sea—God bless me!*
Let me go, let me go, where the winds they do blow,
Where the whiskey can flow, where the whiskers can grow.
For I know—yes, I know—
That a man is a he *on the sea.*

Whatever pleasures Boyle may find in women, Blitzstein's lyrics leave it to the listener to imagine what it takes to satisfy the male need for company.

At the same time, the women have their own society apart from men but dependent on and unequal to them. In a humorous number called "Poor Thing," the crones of the tenement lament their sad fates. With their undiagnosable diseases and nameless woes, they appeal for each other's sympathies. But especially their misery comes from men—from being either widowed or single, or from having men hardly worth having. Mrs. Coyne moans:

Ev'ryone has troubles, dear—
But mine is one you'll hate to hear.
Paddy, he beats me. 'Tis his love that speaks.

Then he's charmin';—but of late, alarmin',
The way he treats me.
My darlin' Paddy hasn't laid a hand on me for weeks.

Violence in love, remarkably similar to the composer's "Modest Maid" fantasies, and Oscar's beating his wife Birdie, reappears in his *Juno* lyrics.

For Juno's "Lament," taken almost verbatim from the closing moments of the play, Blitzstein called upon the same spirit Brecht and Eisler summoned in their "Song of a German Mother" written in 1942. The mood is similar: What use are principles and politics, even faith, when all that is left is a poor dead son "riddled with bullets an' pain"? "Take away our hearts o' stone," Juno moans, "Oh, give us hearts of flesh." Blitzstein had turned 180 degrees from his 1939 text in "Invitation to Bitterness": "Make the mind be fire. Make the heart be stone."

The winds on Captain Boyle's oceans may have "blowed and blowed," but all his bluster comes to naught in the crucible of his sodden brain. Ireland's troubles can never be resolved through his kind of boastful posturing, nor through the bloated masculine bravado posing within every political faction as unshakable principle. Juno is less prone to indulge her imaginative powers. But in the end, she and her daughter Mary do begin their assault on the monument of Irish futility, ever so simply rendering in the party scene and reprising at the end the one truly revolutionary song of the evening, "Bird Upon the Tree":

There was a bird upon a tree.
Its foot was caught within its own nest.
It pulled and pulled, could not be free,
Although it pulled with all zest.
There came a wind and rushing rain,
That swayed the nest again and again.
All beaten back, its feathers wet,
The bird was truly sore beset.
The rain was still, the wind died down.
The nest remained upon the tree.
And then a strange miracle did happen:
The bird looked down and was free.
Ah, yes, 'twas the storm itself that did free
The bird upon the tree.

Blitzstein contrasted Jack Boyle and Juno's storm songs to show that struggle is a surer means than bluster as a way out of the Irish dilemma. Significantly, the composer once again returned to the storm symbolism of *The Cradle Will Rock.* Economic recovery and war and the unpreparedness of the American working class had compromised and diverted the revolutionary movement in the thirties, just as the emergence of the Irish Free State in the twenties had thwarted the independent labor movement that O'Casey had so long urged on.

By the fall of 1957, news of the rialto throbbed with O'Casey's name. Aside from the stage adaptations of his autobiographical writings that had appeared the previous season, forthcoming productions of at least three of his plays had been announced, including *Juno.* O'Casey had last been in New York in 1934 at the time his play *Within the Gates,* with incidental music by Lehman Engel, played on Broadway. Alfred Hitchcock had made a film of *Juno and the Paycock* in the early 1930s. Then for two decades, both in the United States and at home, O'Casey's name virtually disappeared. The revival of interest in his work can be seen as part of the breakdown of 1950s quietism. "I'm neither perturbed nor enthusiastic," he said to *The New York Times* about the musical, while his wife Eileen traveled to New York to investigate all this O'Casey activity. "It will all depend on the point of view of those who are doing it. It will be the first O'Casey musical—and I hope it won't be the last."[3]

In letters addressed to Joseph Stein, the O'Caseys each gave enthusiastic approval to the songs tape-recorded by Blitzstein in a delicious brogue that might have been the envy of any actor. "I have played them over and over and like it all very very much," wrote Mrs. O'Casey. The playwright considered himself no musician, and could not "give a safe or a convinced opinion about the music." But he wrote, "I listened the other night to the BBC Third Program giving Poulenc's 'Chansons Françaises,' and when they ended, I ejaculated, 'Well, the music of *Juno* is as good as that.' Eileen, who was listening too, adding, 'Better; a lot better.' So there I'll leave it."[4]

In September the *Times* reported that the show was written and ready to be produced. Armed with Blitzstein's tape, Stein now occupied himself with the job of interesting a producer.

While *Juno* traveled the circuit of potential producers, Blitzstein could do little, so he turned back to his translation of *Mother Courage.* During the months of September and October 1957, he completed the major part of his work. Taking his cue from the elevated vulgarity of Brecht's German, he adopted a tough, urbane, street-smart dialect for the prose. He never felt entirely satisfied with the lyrics to the songs, however, and made repeated alterations.

Stuart Scheftel, husband of Geraldine Fitzgerald, had acquired the American rights to the play from Lars Schmidt, London agent for the Brecht estate. Scheftel felt confident that proper permissions for the staging would come through and that the new translation would be completed on time. He announced to the press in September that the Blitzstein version would appear on Broadway in January, directed by Orson Welles and starring Geraldine Fitzgerald. As prospective producer he paid Blitzstein $1,750 for the translation, according to a contract signed that fall, with a built-in percentage of box office.

Blitzstein sent drafts of his translation to Elisabeth Hauptmann, Brecht's collaborator, and to Helene Weigel, Brecht's widow and herself one of the great interpreters of the title role. He received from Lars Schmidt a large packet of materials from the Berliner Ensemble production, including scores, instrumental and vocal parts. (In Paul Dessau's scoring, which Blitzstein intended to retain, the play requires seven musicians.) Plans for *Mother Courage* appeared to progress, but everything hinged on final approval from the Brecht heirs. As the weeks passed, the delays accumulated.

That Blitzstein was not an unerring judge of commercial theatre can be seen from this assessment that he rendered to David Diamond:

> I did get to see Lenny's *West Side Story:* full of talent, remarkable in many ways, in the end a wrong 'un, and I'm not sure why. I don't find it a "phony," as Clurman does; but it does go condescending at times ("Ah-the-poor-workers" mood of some of the stuff of the thirties), and uncomfortably affectionate. The music has drive but little poetry; the text has craft but *no* poetry (very needed in this work), which he seems afraid of, and covers up regularly, with bounce, violence, what-not.[5]

Some of Blitzstein's sense of pique can be explained by the fact that once again Bernstein had transparently "borrowed" a musical theme of his, from *Regina* this time, and transformed it into one of the musical theatre's greatest money-makers of all time: the song "Maria."

Among potential producers for *Juno,* Joseph Stein approached Roger L. Stevens, a millionaire many times over from his New York real estate investments who had by now, as president of the Playwrights Company, become one of Broadway's most daring producers. The Company had produced *Knickerbocker Holiday, Street Scene,* and *Lost in the Stars* for Kurt Weill, and about sixty other plays. Separately Stevens had produced Bernstein's *Peter Pan* and *West Side Story.* By the end of November, *Juno* had become the property of the Playwrights Company. Oliver Smith, the set designer for the show, also joined as a producer. Creator of the decor for ballets, films, operas, and musicals, and active as a producer on the stage and for film, Smith was represented on Broadway during the 1958–1959 season by no fewer than five productions aside from *Juno: Flower Drum Song, West Side Story, My Fair Lady, Jamaica,* and *Say, Darling.* His work also appeared in the new staging of *La Traviata* at the Metropolitan Opera. Oliver Rea, a book editor, public relations man, and sometime play producer, joined the company as well. Among the investors in the show, budgeted at $300,000, were Carol Channing and her husband Charles F. Lowe.

Terms of the Playwrights Company contract with the authors granted 3 percent of royalties from the weekly box office to Stein, and 5 percent to Blitzstein. O'Casey had already received twenty-five hundred dollars for the rights, and an agreement to receive a further 1½ percent of the gross weekly box office.

Now the Playwrights Company set about its job: to interest a group of compatible professionals and the right cast in putting the show on the stage.

The company decided on the British director Tony Richardson for *Juno.* At the height of his career, he directed regularly at the Royal Court Theatre and at the Shakespeare Memorial Theatre in Stratford-on-Avon. He had just directed the stage adaptation of William Faulkner's *Requiem for a Nun,* with Ruth Ford and Zachary Scott, as well as John Osborne's *Look Back in Anger.* Both shows went to Broadway.

It was Oliver Smith who took Blitzstein to Agnes de Mille one day toward the end of 1957 to play through the songs and to interest her in creating the dances for the show. She had known Lina since her childhood in Baltimore, where she had served as Mme. Abarbanell's dresser for musical comedies such as *Fata Morgana.* She knew Blitzstein slightly, too, going back to soirées at Kirk and Constance Askew's home in the 1930s. She accepted, thinking it a project as straightforward as *Brigadoon,* for a five-thousand-dollar fee, plus 2 percent of gross, 2½ percent of profits, and 5 percent of subsidiary rights.

Irene Sharaff, one of the most experienced costume designers in the field, was hired for five thousand dollars. Peggy Clark, veteran of sixty-one Broadway productions including the then current *Flower Drum Song* and *Bells Are Ringing,* came in as lighting designer at fifteen hundred dollars. In his capacity as stage designer, Oliver Smith earned five thousand dollars.

As could be expected, the January production of *Mother Courage* fell through. Now Stuart Scheftel announced it for the fall. Blitzstein reported the delay to the composer Paul Dessau in East Berlin, who was naturally disappointed but expressed complete confidence in Blitzstein's handling of the music. He suggested no musical cuts; to the contrary, he seemed anxious in view of an eventual recording to include as many musical numbers as possible from various productions of the work. "Thank you very much for taking care of the little score which in spite of that is very dear to me," he wrote to Blitzstein.[6]

Blitzstein also corresponded with the British expert on Brecht, John Willett, and sent him a typescript of the translation. Willett wrote, "I have now read it, and shall certainly advise Methuen's, the potential publishers, that it is the best available. The songs remain a problem, as you say, but otherwise I enjoyed it a lot." Blitzstein later returned the compliment with a highly favorable thought-piece in *The Nation* centered around Willett's interpretive book, *The Theatre of Bertolt Brecht.* Blitzstein recommended Willett's "inestimable service in giving us a first total picture."[7]

Dimitri Mitropoulos, musical director of the New York Philharmonic, had commissioned an orchestral piece from Blitzstein for a Carnegie Hall premiere on Thursday, February 27, and on the afternoon of Friday the twenty-eighth. It was to be based on the music for *King Lear*—both the 1950 Louis Calhern score and the Orson Welles score for City Center five years later. Though Blitzstein had initially considered such a work at the time of the first *Lear,* he concentrated on it in December 1957 and January 1958. For *Lear: A Study* Blitzstein typically researched his subject, finding recordings of the Berlioz overture on the same theme and reading the French composer's *Memoirs* for background on the 1831 work. "I'm laboring on the last stages of *Lear,*" he told David Diamond, "hoping to deliver the final score to D.M. next Monday. All sorts of obstacles, ptomaine, back-collapse, etc.—every one, I'm sure, part of my beastly unconscious—are trying to keep me from finishing. I'll get it done."[8]

Once again, Blitzstein shows his fascination with the storm metaphor. In the program note for the piece, he wrote:

> Shakespeare's *King Lear* has been with me for a long time. For me it is his most compelling tragedy; of all his works it seems the one which announces the modern epoch. The hero Lear *attains* tragic dimension as the play proceeds. He is quite unlike the heroes of Greek tragedy, who are fully-realized characters in conflict with unyielding fates. Lear is a king; but a boastful barbaric king, a playboy, a carouser and hunter with his knights. He receives the true and false loyalties of his three daughters with little or no sensitiveness or differentiation. When friction, ingratitude, insubordination develop, he meets them with lordly petulance; later with irresponsible fury and explosiveness. It is only through the ravages of trial-by-storm, of pain to the point of madness, that the bullying child at last comes into his own as full protagonist, strong and beautiful in self-knowledge. And by a stroke of irony which is pure Shakespeare, it happens too late, at the moment of death itself.

Lear: A Study is in three sections without pause, representing, in his words, "a) the stripe of man and king; b) the nature-storm and the inner-storm; and c) growth, serenity and death." In at least two sections of the work, a breather in the storm and a climactic passage, Blitzstein dipped into his 1929 *Parabola and Circula* music. The scoring is for large orchestra, with two cornets added to the brass, and expanded percussion. Luening and Ussachevsky's electronic contributions to the Orson Welles *Lear* play no part in Blitzstein's piece.

The premiere was almost postponed, for just as he was completing work on the piece, Blitzstein suffered an extremely painful attack of kidney stones and was hospitalized for several days. (As late as January 30, Mitropoulos wrote to the recuperating Blitzstein that the work could be rescheduled the following season.) Also on the program were Schoenberg's *Verklärte Nacht* and his orchestration of Two Chorale-Preludes by Bach, and the New York premiere of Mendelssohn's Concerto for Two Pianos, with the duo-piano team of Gold and Fizdale.

The next morning's reviews gave the new work a wide-ranging reception. Harold C. Schonberg of the *Times* pronounced that *Lear* "does not seem to be a repertory item." Jay Harrison in the *Herald Tribune,* however, found it "masterful," "compelling," a "first-rate piece of music." In Harriett Johnson's summation in the *Post,* "The early part of the work is dissonant without convincing us of the emotional gamut which this 'psychological study' runs. In the final *adagietto,* however, Blitzstein achieves an eery, mysterious beauty which arrests the attention."[9]

Among the telegrams and letters Blitzstein received, his mother's postcard struck an appropriate chord for a work in part about parent-child conflict: "I'm so proud and grateful that you are *my son,*" she wrote. "Really *hearing* Lear was my most exciting experience."[10]

The composer reported to David Diamond: "All the composers love it: Haieff, Chávez, Lenny, Bill Schuman. . . . It sounds; very big, clear, short, with a spread serene finish, which was the only thing Mitropoulos had trouble with. In general, he played it beautifully, particularly on the Friday afternoon, when it had a real audience success."[11] But despite a reasonably auspicious premiere, *Lear: A Study* has never been played since.

The year 1958 was turning out to be a busy one for Blitzstein. In an interview granted to a reporter for *Entertainment Off Broadway,* he touched on the history behind the translation of *Threepenny,* playing forever at the Theater de Lys; on Bernstein's television talks on music and his affinity for *Cradle;* on the *Mother Courage* translation, ever hopefully scheduled for production with Geraldine Fitzgerald; and on *Juno* and his association with Joseph Stein. Comparing this project to others in the past, he admitted to "no Wagnerian dreams, just couldn't find anyone to work with before. Who knows? I might even be able to collaborate on an opera next." Finally, he discussed the forthcoming New York City Opera revival of *Regina.*[12]

In line with the City Center's endeavor to present opera with greater dramatic impact, the New York City Opera announced early in the year that the well-known Broadway director Herman Shumlin would restage *Regina* in its spring season. The company also brought in José Quintero to direct Weill's *Lost in the Stars.* Together with eight other American operas, they comprised a five-week season of contemporary works funded by a $105,000 grant from the Ford Foundation.

Julius Rudel regarded the choice of Shumlin as a coup for the City Opera, as he had directed *The Little Foxes* originally in 1939. The designer Howard Bay, also responsible for the original play, would remount the upcoming production of the opera with all new scenery. Both Shumlin and Bay had worked with Blitzstein before on *No for an Answer*—Bay as designer, and Shumlin as one of the committee of producers for that show. Samuel Krachmalnick conducted; Robert Joffrey provided choreography; and Aline Bernstein, brought out of retirement, designed the costumes.

Three performances were scheduled, the first on April 17. Only Brenda Lewis as Regina and Emile Renan as Oscar repeated their roles from the 1953 production. Renan had more recently sung Blitzstein's music in *Reuben Reuben.* Joshua Hecht sang Horace, Andrew Frierson was Cal, George S. Irving sang Ben, and Loren Driscoll played Leo. Blitzstein had found Helen Strine, a newcomer, for the role of Zan. Rudel asked a member of the company, Elisabeth Carron, to sing the part of Birdie, though it took a visit to Blitzstein, a thorough marking of Birdie's big scena, and considerable coaxing before she accepted the role. Carol Brice, whom Blitzstein had heard in the Haydn *Creation* Mass with the Interracial Fellowship Chorus, sang the role of Addie. Just two months before at her Town Hall recital, she had included the "Orpheus" song from *Julius Caesar,* which Blitzstein had thought suited to her voice.

For the new production, Blitzstein again revised the score, this time even more drastically. The main change was the omission of Chinkypin, Jazz and his Angel Band and all its music. For public consumption in interviews given to the press, Blitzstein accounted for his new version by citing the stringent economic position of the City Opera and the expense of hiring additional jazz musicians from outside the regular company. In this light, he justified cutting the band as a composer's self-indulgence.

Expense, however, did not entirely explain Blitzstein's radical change of mind about the scoring of the opera. Shumlin and Hellman, once lovers, remained close friends; he could hardly have been unaware of Hellman's continued reservations about the making of an opera from *The Little Foxes.* And if there was any aspect of Blitzstein's work that she had found particularly inappropriate, it was precisely the black music in the piece. Furthermore, as Rudel and the company soon discovered to their dismay, Shumlin had never directed a musical show before and had little appreciation for jazz. As complicated as it was for him to coordinate the activity on the stage with an orchestra, he found the presence of an additional musical ensemble on stage a completely unmanageable proposition. Rudel fought Shumlin's decision to eliminate the Angel Band, but to no avail. In his desire to see *Regina* restaged, and with such a prominent slate of co-workers, Blitzstein agreed to the changes.

Wearing his hat for good luck as always, Shumlin gathered the entire cast together on the first day of rehearsal. To everyone's surprise, he told them, "Open your scores." And when they had done so, he commanded, "Read." Upon which, they declaimed the entire script. Unaccustomed to working in the musical field, not to mention in a repertory season where singers and dancers might have other responsibilities than *Regina,* he never could understand why in subsequent cast calls singers would often be absent, attending musical rehearsals or receiving costume fittings.

At the dress rehearsal on April 14, a fire broke out, threatening to destroy the show. Most of the damage came from water, however, and by the time of the opening curtain, the scenery and costumes had dried out.

Critics had never unified behind *Regina,* but at least now in the context of an all-American season, they could judge Blitzstein's opera alongside ones by Menotti, Floyd, Weill, Kurka, and others. The production proved that *Regina* had become a repertory piece, secure in its place on any roster of worthy American operas.

In his review of the new version in the *Daily Mirror,* Robert Coleman, an early champion of the work, hailed the score that "brought a first-night audience to its feet last evening. It was spellbound by the conciseness, dramatic urge and musical power of the revival. Brenda Lewis was nothing less than magnificent as the domineering, ruthless Regina Giddens. She sang and acted the role to the hilt, under Herman Shumlin's driving direction." Perhaps the revised opera became tauter drama, but most critics seemed not to notice the changes. Howard Taubman, for one, missed the Angel Band. Thomas R. Dash, writing for *Women's Wear Daily,* hoped that the City Opera would take *Regina* to the Brussels World Fair with Floyd's *Susannah,* though this did not happen. *Variety*'s reviewer concluded, "It may be the finest compliment of all to say that the audience frequently forgets it's an opera, so engulfing is the sheer story unfoldment."[13]

Ever since 1949, Blitzstein had wanted *Regina* recorded. As a Broadway score, it would have been a one-disk cast album, but none was made. In 1956 he came near to recording a suite from the opera for MGM. Now an opportunity seemed possible for a complete recording of the opera—albeit in a truncated version—and he exerted himself mightily to see it happen. CBS offered to produce the recording, but only with funds he could personally raise. The Koussevitzky Music Foundation helped with four thousand dollars, half of the required amount. Blitzstein arranged a series of dinners and cocktail meetings with potential patrons for the recording, and gathered the rest. Mina Curtiss contributed one thousand dollars, Roger Stevens five hundred dollars. Morris Golde, Irene Diamond, William Morris, and other friends gave smaller amounts.

Late at night after the second performance on April 27, the entire cast and orchestra reassembled in a CBS studio. From beginning to end, without pause for correcting mistakes, they recorded the entire opera. Already worn out from the performance, the singers stayed awake with coffee and adrenaline, fearing the worst results on tape.

Almost miraculously, a fine recording emerged in a few months' time, in stereo and monaural versions on three disks. "Technically the Columbia production is beyond reproach," wrote the *Atlantic Monthly* reviewer. "The stage atmosphere is very real." Virgil Thomson, writing in the *Saturday Review* about *Regina,* showed a greater enthusiasm than he had originally voiced in 1949, though he remained levelheaded: "Here is a work that fills an operatic stage and fulfills the listener. Not a perfect piece, perhaps, but a machine that runs—that runs, moreover, as an opera must, on music, not on words or situational drama." Elisabeth Carron's Birdie received special notice from several reviewers.[14]

As part of the packaging, CBS included the complete libretto, with photographs of Blitzstein and the principals. Short articles by Bernstein, Frank Loesser, and Hellman fill out the booklet. Hellman's five paragraphs are a model of evasion passing for confession, for she admits that she was wary of the opera from the beginning, even jealous that Blitzstein had perhaps improved upon her play. "It was only in 1958, at the City Center, in its latest and I think best interpretation—perhaps because it was directed by Herman Shumlin and designed by Howard Bay, both of whom had done the original play—that I fully appreciated *Regina.*" She omits any reference to the excised Angel Band.

Because it is the version commercially available on disk, at least when CBS rereleases it from time to time, and because it is the version subsequently rented out to producers, the 1958 City Opera *Regina* has wrongly come to be regarded as Blitzstein's definitive edition of the work.

During the winter and spring months, the producers of *Juno,* still known as *Daarlin' Man,* busily engaged themselves in finding principal actors. Blitzstein paid numerous social calls and invited many a performer to dinner and drinks to sound them out on their availability.

In the search for a Captain Jack Boyle, a meeting between Blitzstein and James Cagney on Martha's Vineyard had yielded valuable criticisms of some inapt phrases but no interest in doing the stage show. Perhaps later on, if the show was successful, he might want to play in the film.

Melvyn Douglas was another early consideration for the lead male role. He had turned from matinee-idol roles and had taken on character parts. His liberalism and intellect were well known in political circles. His wife, Helen Gahagan Douglas, had served as a California congresswoman for three terms in the late 1940s; it was against her in 1950 that Richard Nixon conducted a successful anti-Communist campaign of innuendo to capture her seat. In addition, Melvyn Douglas had co-produced Harold Rome's postwar musical *Call Me Mister,* a cheerful spoof of army life. Long before, in fact, he had even directed the New York production of O'Casey's play *Within the Gates,* with O'Casey present to supervise. Blitzstein met with Douglas in the spring of 1958. The actor objected that he was no song and dance man by any stretch of the imagination. "I'll worry about the song end of the business," the composer countered, knowing that Agnes de Mille could also work within his limitations.[15] Douglas signed in May, at a salary of $2,500 per week before the New York opening and $3,000 thereafter, with a further raise once production costs had been recouped.

Blitzstein met with Rosalind Russell and Eileen Herlie about the lead female role, but neither was interested. For the first time in his life, when he heard Claire Bloom, Blitzstein retreated from his long-held conviction that "anybody can sing."

Shirley Booth was a logical and an early favorite choice for the lead. A name actress, she had at least a bit of singing experience in summer stock and on Broadway in the musical version of *A Tree Grows in Brooklyn.* Blitzstein had worked with her before in *I've Got the Tune* and in 1947 when she played Mrs. Mister in the *Cradle* revival. He knew that she could handle the narrow musical range of his songs for Juno. Called on the phone in Jamaica during the fall of 1957 while recuperating from a bout with bronchitis, she hesitated for months before accepting the offer. Her truest feelings told her she was not right for the part—that in her early fifties, when most actresses began settling into character parts, she could not perform the title role in a serious, all-singing, all-dancing Broadway tragicomedy. But the producers saw her as a key draw, and eventually in June 1958, she agreed to be Juno, for three thousand dollars a week for the first sixteen weeks and the promise of more later.

For the critical supporting role of Joxer Daley, O'Casey's suggestion of Jack MacGowran, an Abbey Theatre actor, proved a stroke of genius and good fortune, maybe even too much so. For as an authentic Dubliner, he showed up the rest of the cast as something less than genuine. His pay was $650 a week.

In May MCA Artists sent the conductor Robert Emmett Dolan's résumé to Blitzstein. On the basis of his extensive credits as film composer, producer of two

Academy Award shows, and musical director of at least a dozen Broadway ventures, the company took him on, at five hundred dollars a week. Lesser acting roles would be signed up later in the summer, once the casting call had been published.

21

WE'RE ALIVE

Spring 1958–March 1959

". . . such sweet thunder"

In April, just as the City Opera was putting the finishing touches on its *Regina* revival, an announcement went to the press from the American Shakespeare Festival in Stratford, Connecticut, saying that Marc Blitzstein had been contracted to write incidental music for two of its 1958 summer productions. The first, *A Midsummer Night's Dream,* would open June 20, with *The Winter's Tale* to follow a month later. The other production of the season, *Hamlet,* featured music by Virgil Thomson from a production John Houseman had directed some twenty years before.

As artistic director and administrator of the festival, Houseman had recruited, for his longest season and largest company to date, a solid repertory ensemble impressive for its quality. Among the season's players were Geraldine Fitzgerald, June Ericson, June Havoc, Nancy Wickwire, Nancy Marchand, Morris Carnovsky, Hiram Sherman, Will Geer, Fritz Weaver, John Colicos, Ellis Rabb, and Severn Darden. George Balanchine came in to provide dances for the productions. Both Houseman and Jack Landau would direct. Jean Rosenthal acted as technical director, though claiming credit only for lighting design. Set designs for all three productions were by David Hays, who three years before had designed a production of *The Threepenny Opera* at Boston University, the Blitzstein adaptation directed by Sarah Caldwell. Bernard Gersten served as production stage manager.

Houseman asked the composer not to write "psychological" music for these productions. Blitzstein complied with music he called "not coy, not arch, but still neo-Elizabethan." His orchestra consisted of a lute, harp, violin and cello, flute, brasses, and percussion, including glockenspiel. He distributed snippets of tunes among various characters, but the countertenor Russell Oberlin carried most of the true songs. For *A Midsummer Night's Dream,* staged in three acts, Blitzstein provided thirty-six musical cues. For his work that summer, he received $1,200 in payment, with additional royalties of $25 for each performance of either work after the close of the season, half that amount for school performances.

Against the background of reportage on Vice-President Nixon's stormy Latin American tour, rehearsals began in New York in early May and advertisements for the season started appearing in the press. As the players started learning their parts, along with Blitzstein's music, he continued writing the *Winter's Tale* score. Just then, the bomb that Blitzstein had been awaiting dropped. The House Committee on Un-American Activities had fairly well exhausted its supply of name-namers by 1958. It hung on, however, still desperate in its last phase to justify its continued life by producing some fortuitous revelations, recantations, and embarrassments. Its investigations of Wallingford Riegger, the Metropolitan Music School, and Local 802 the year before drooped with insignificance. In Riegger's case, favorable national recognition increased, if anything, in the four years of life remaining to him. Still, Blitzstein must indeed have wondered how they could have overlooked him this long. Now they came.

The subpoena ordered Blitzstein to appear on Thursday, May 8 for a closed "executive session" chaired by Rep. Moulder of Missouri. Once more, the Federal Court House at Foley Square served as the venue for the two-day proceedings, involving more than twenty witnesses in the music industry and allied fields. Blitzstein chose as his counsel the distinguished lawyer Telford Taylor, who had made a name for himself as a member of the prosecuting team during the Nuremberg Trials.

Blitzstein did not invoke the Fifth Amendment. First he read a prepared statement challenging the propriety of HUAC's mandate to question him at all. Voluntarily, then, he spoke as one with nothing to hide or explain or apologize for. He claimed complete innocence of all legal or moral crime, and unsettled his questioners by refusing to "return to the fold" or inform. He admitted to Communist Party membership from the spring of 1938 to late 1949, confirming the report on his membership given to HUAC in 1954 by a previous informer, Gwen Anderson, who had known him in the postwar period. He affirmed his support at different times for a large number of organizations cited on the Attorney General's list. He explained that he dropped out of the Party because of policy disagreements and because he resented the Party's interference with his intellectual life. He would not, to the disappointment of the committee, give further details about his or anyone's activities in the Party.

Unsatisfied with the minimal cooperation on the part of their witnesses, the congressmen called Blitzstein and the others back for a second round of testimony, this time in a public hearing set for the third week of June. Rep. Francis E. Walter, Democrat of Pennsylvania and chairman of HUAC, claimed to be seeking more information on those who, having broken with the Party, were "nevertheless continuing to put a substantial part of their large incomes at the service of the Communist operation in the United States."[1]

Despite the considerable damage they could still inflict, the committee and its allies faced greater and greater opposition. An Actors' Equity meeting had recently sponsored a meeting at which Bernard Gersten, now stage manager for the Shakespeare Festival, had spoken in favor of granting a passport to Paul Robeson; indeed, on June 16 the Supreme Court, in a long-awaited 5 to 4 decision, overturned the State Department's policy of denying passports to suspected Communists. A public meeting called by the Emergency Civil Liberties Committee for June 18 at the Hotel New Yorker featured the barely known folksinger Joan Baez and longtime civil liberties defenders Alexander Meiklejohn and the New Haven rabbi Robert E. Goldburg speaking against the new HUAC hearings—"still another disgraceful public spectacle."[2] (Just that week, too, Bernstein and Mitropoulos returned with the entire New York Philharmonic from their seven-week tour of Latin America, a sharp contrast in its peaceful and welcome reception to Nixon's debacle.)

The page-one story in the *Times* on June 19 achieved some of the committee's purpose: to win publicity with the biggest names it could dredge up. The article related the refusals to talk by Arthur Lief, American guest conductor of the Moiseyev Russian Ballet presently on tour under Sol Hurok sponsorship; actors Adelaide Klein, Paul Mann, Earl Jones, and Will Lee; pianist Carroll Hollister; Charles S. Dubin, television director, promptly fired by NBC; Israel (Swifty) Lazar, who would not say whether he had been head of the Party's cultural division; and Bernard Gersten.

The following day, the *Times* continued its front-page reportage, listing the final day's witnesses, for a total of seventeen who refused to cooperate. Among them were Irwin Silber; James D. Proctor, press agent for Kermit Bloomgarden and chairman of the old *No for an Answer* committee; Horace Grennell, president of Young People's Records; Benjamin Steinberg, a violinist in *The Music Man* orchestra; Clifford Carpenter, an actor in *Sunrise at Campobello;* and Joseph Papp, immediately fired by CBS from his position as a television stage manager.

The Hellman position had been to talk openly about herself but to rely on the Fifth Amendment if asked about others. Wallingford Riegger had relied exclusively on the First Amendment, the approach that led to imprisonment for the Hollywood Ten. As Blitzstein's counsel, Telford Taylor never knew what approach his client intended to use. Blitzstein appeared at the June 18 and 19 hearings, and waited. But for reasons likely never to be known, perhaps simply that they ran out of time, the committee did not summon him to the stand. His name never appeared in the press in connection with having been subpoenaed to testify. So the greatly feared ordeal involving a possible storm of innuendo in the press about his political subversiveness came to little in the end.

The most primitive forms of McCarthyism were receding at last. The blacklist was shortly to become a thing of the past. Students and civil rights activists were advancing the good fight in fresh, creative ways. The Supreme Court was busy knocking down laws about segregation, passports, and the right of political affiliation. The Soviets had launched Sputnik—clearly, Communism meant something more than godless atheism and slave labor camps. Few but the fanatical know-nothings in Congress and the right-wing newspaper columnists who had built their reputations together on a foundation of witch-hunting now bothered to care about composers who signed petitions.

It was as if Blitzstein had just taken a terrifying ride in a small plane in the middle of a tornado. Suddenly his life had been thrown into a dizzy spin without his knowing how he might emerge. And now, just as suddenly, all returned to normal. He felt almost cheated when the committee declined to finger him publicly.

As planned, Blitzstein moved up to Connecticut for the summer, remaining within easy driving distance of the city for ongoing work on *Juno* when required. But the HUAC episode was not quite over. In the light of HUAC's attentions focused on Stratford personnel, frightened members of the festival board sought Bernard Gersten's dismissal. No doubt, they would have sought Blitzstein's replacement as well had he been mentioned in the press as a noncooperator. Their concerns rose when local anti-Communists took to picketing performances at the theatre, accusing Gersten of red ties. Likely as not, the pickets were unaware just how many people in Stratford that summer had "taken the Fifth"—five, at least, by Houseman's count—and how many more, such as Blitzstein or Houseman himself, could be cited on any number of counts for "un-American" behavior. Houseman refused to fire Gersten or anyone else, assuring his board that if he did so, others in the company would resign in protest and the entire season would have to be canceled. After a few days, the pickets tired of their harassment and stayed home. The nervous board members, however, sought to protect their future political and banking connections, and several of them resigned. In their wake, they left a financial hole the festival would struggle for years to fill.

Artistically, the season shone brightly. The three productions won over critics who had until now reserved their enthusiasm. Harold Clurman in *The Nation* found *A Midsummer Night's Dream* "the pleasantest performance I remember seeing at the festival since its inception four years ago." Blitzstein's music—which incorporated the piece written for Kit and Sonia's wedding five years before—was infectious: No one printed a sour note about it. John Chapman judged it in the *Daily News* "far more impressive and enjoyable than the run-of-the-mill stuff one usually associates with Shakespearean productions." The *Herald Tribune* found in Russell Oberlin "a tenor of true Elizabethan pitch and sweetness." For *The Winter's Tale,* wrote Brooks Atkinson, Blitzstein had put "a modern edge on some traditional and well-loved forms."[3]

"Blitzstein's Music in *Dream* Proves 'Such Sweet Thunder,' " Harriett Johnson titled her feature article in the *Post.* She fairly exhausted herself singing Blitzstein's praises. His music added

> enchantment to enchantment as the play proceeds. . . . We occasionally wish for a repetition of a tuneful bit, whether humorous or poignant, knowing, of course, that our desire is futile, as "the play must go on." . . . Blitzstein has achieved a mildly archaic flavor by definitive musical means, easily understandable to the musician, but it all sounds so natural and pleasant that the layman should enjoy its appropriateness without worrying about from whence it comes or what produces it. . . . By the alchemy of music, we have dreamed more happily.[4]

Aside from composing for the two plays, Blitzstein also served as coordinator of all musical activities for the festival, including preparing and directing Thomson's *Hamlet* score. It was a charmed time for him—away from the city's heat, a proud and unbowed and only slightly bloodied victim of politics, together with old friends and new ones who shared his sympathies; busy, productive, acclaimed for his special talents; and looking forward excitedly to a big Broadway show.

Among his new friends, he counted the designer for all three productions that summer, David Hays. Blitzstein also became friendly with David's wife Leonora, and in time with their two children. Even more than Marc, Lina Abarbanell became a devoted friend of the Hays family, always having a pocketful of honey candies for the kids. They exchanged visits at least weekly, and Lina attended all of David's openings.

The summer of 1958 did not end with his work in Stratford. *The Winter's Tale* opened on July 20. On the twenty-fifth Gustav Meier led an all-Blitzstein concert at an afternoon seminar in contemporary music at Tanglewood, featuring a revival of *Triple-Sec* for which the composer had sent large packets of newly copied musical materials. In the course of his glance back at past creations, he realized that he had allowed certain of his copyrights to lapse and he moved to correct his oversight. In general, however, Blitzstein did not encourage performances of his early works, even when asked. He refused Richard Flusser of the After Dinner Opera Company a look at *Parabola and Circula,* explaining that as part of his composer's trunk he had pilfered from it for *Native Land,* the *Airborne* Symphony, and *Regina.* When David Diamond wrote him from Florence saying that the Italian pianist Pietro Scarpini, a well-known proponent of twentieth-century music, wanted to consider Blitzstein's 1931 Piano Concerto, the composer wrote that he didn't want it done.

Returning from Massachusetts, Blitzstein headed to New York, where Samuel Matlovsky had programmed an all-American concert at Lewisohn Stadium on the twenty-ninth. Scheduling music by Bernstein, Barber, Gould, Copland, and Harold Arlen, he included the *Native Land* Suite in his plans, which Blitzstein might well have suggested as the most direct statement on Americanism that he could offer to the federal witch-hunters. From the seven-movement suite that Laszlo Halasz had led in 1946—also at the Lewisohn Stadium—Blitzstein deleted five sections and then added three other sections, to constitute a definitive arrangement for symphonic presentation. The five movements now included: "Statue of Liberty," "Mulberry Street," "American Day," "Chase," and

"Funeral and Finale." Rain on the night of the twenty-eighth canceled an all-Verdi program, however, which was rescheduled for the twenty-ninth. On the thirtieth, Matlovsky fused most of the all-American concert with the previously announced program of Mozart and Schumann, dropping the Blitzstein suite.

Matlovsky again conducted at Lewisohn Stadium on August 1, this time in an all-Weill program with Lenya performing songs from the theatre in the first half and returning with Charlotte Rae, Betty Kent, Scott Merrill, and Maurice Edwards in a concert version of *Threepenny.*

As for Blitzstein's music for Stratford, he arranged Six Elizabethan Songs for tenor or soprano and piano. One, the "Song of the Glove," carries the distinct flavor of a Leonard Bernstein melody; not surprisingly, Blitzstein dedicated the suite to Bernstein. In addition, in the "Vendor's Song," Shakespeare's text twice refers to amber, which is what the word *Bernstein* means. Chappell published the songs the following year. Perhaps they have been performed somewhere, but no specific evidence exists in Blitzstein's papers.

Daarlin' Man now picked up its pace rapidly. The Playwrights Company brought Tony Richardson from England in early August 1958 to talk with the producers and to participate in the next stage of auditions. In a series of detailed meetings concerning the staging of the show, they agreed on a number of decisions: to shorten "What Is the Stars?" and to cut "You're the Girl," an inappropriate rumbalike tune recalling the Weill idiom that Charlie Bentham sings to Mary. Richardson demanded a huge revolving stage set that allowed the street scenes to turn into the bar scenes and around again to the Boyles' flat, a concept that Oliver Smith faithfully reproduced. After a week, he returned to England, where he was finishing the film of *Look Back in Anger.* During a two-week series of backers' auditions, the company attracted enough investments to guarantee an opening. Rehearsals were now scheduled to begin on November 15, with first tryouts around Christmas.

The cast call went out in mid-summer 1958, and the first casting sessions were set for July 31 through August 8. Blitzstein asked that Lina be taken on as casting consultant, and she was. At the age of seventy-nine, ever cheery, sparkling, and smelling of Nina Ricci perfume, she heard dozens of singers try out for parts and she took copious notes all the while. Carroll O'Connor auditioned on the first day as understudy for Boyle and Joxer and for the ensemble. Blitzstein found him a "fine all-around Irish male type. . . . Light, true baritone, not much volume. Good actor." O'Connor did not join the company, however. Further casting sessions took place in October and November.

A shock from which the show would never recover came in the form of a 7:45 A.M. transatlantic phone call to Blitzstein on October 22. It was from Tony Richardson. A previous commitment to direct *Othello* in Stratford now forced him to remain in England; he was bowing out of the show. Further, though he omitted to mention this at the time, his production of *Requiem for a Nun* was to open in its American premiere at the John Golden Theatre on January 30 of the coming year, and he would have to make himself available for that as well.

"I want to do *Juno* more than anything," he told Blitzstein, who afterward jotted down the exchange of conversation.

"Then you will," the composer urged.

"But I can't."

"Is that your final answer?"

"I'm afraid so."

"Then goodbye, Tony Richardson."

In a letter dated the same day, the director confirmed his devastating news. "I believe in your wonderful, original and daring work more than I can say, and it really is the greatest disappointment in the theatre that I have ever had that I can't do it. I was so thrilled and delighted when you asked me to, and so much loved working with you when I was last in New York."[5] Meager compensation, these kind words. Now to find a new director.

The producers named Vincent J. Donehue. He had directed Horton Foote's *The Traveling Lady* for the Playwrights Company. He had also staged Dore Schary's successful play *Sunrise at Campobello* for both Broadway and the touring companies, and he had done a fair amount of television work. Neither Stein nor Blitzstein had heard of him; but *Juno* needed a director fast, and they thought that if he had created one hit on Broadway, he might be able to create another.

The part of Mary turned out to be the most elusive to cast. Donehue wanted to bring over an actress from the Abbey Theatre, but the others could not agree on just what they were seeking. A voice to render Mary's arias like *Misuk?* A singer first, also an actress? An actress who sings? And what mood to strike in this character? Sweetness? Grit?

Benita Valente auditioned but looked too Italian. Anne Fielding sang "I Wish It So" "enchantingly" on August 1, and she was strongly considered; hired as a member of the chorus, she served as understudy for Mary. Well into November as the secondary roles and the chorus were being signed, the role of Mary remained unfilled. The producers saw a reported six hundred aspirants.

Monte Amundsen auditioned a number of times. She impressed Blitzstein at once with her clear, unforced soprano. After one audition, frustrated with Donehue's indecision, Blitzstein shouted from the back of the house, "If you keep insisting on an actress, who's going to sing my music?" He approached the stage after she sang and asked where she had been. "In California," she answered.

"Our director is very concerned about having a 'singer' doing a part of this magnitude," he prompted. "So may I ask you if you have had any dramatic experience at all." Most recently, Amundsen told him, she had done two shows with Leo Fuchs in the Yiddish theatre in Los Angeles.

"Monte, what were you doing in Yiddish theatre?"

"Making a living!"

In actuality, her experience had been broader than that. In October while auditioning for Mary, she appeared with the New York City Opera as Adele in *Die Fledermaus,* which must certainly have pleased Lina to know. Still, it was December before she finally got the part. By now she had utterly endeared herself to Blitzstein, particularly with her singing of the romantic ballad of the show,

"My True Heart." "Monte," he told her one day, "if for some reason they don't cast you for this, you are to come to Santa Fe and do Alexandra in *Regina* with me." By this time, a revival in New Mexico had been announced for the summer of 1959. No one could fail to note the obvious similarities between the two roles, set for the same kind of voice and filled with unformulated youthful yearnings.

Other cast members included Jean Stapleton, Sada Thompson, Nancy Andrews, and Beulah Garrick as the neighborhood crones, Loren Driscoll, who had just sung Leo at the City Opera, as Jerry Devine, and Earl Hammond as Charlie Bentham.

From the start, Stein, Blitzstein, and de Mille despaired over Vincent Donehue. He particularly mishandled Shirley Booth. Not an overly original actress, she required strong direction. Instead, Donehue coddled her, waited on her, and gave in to her whims. He emphasized softness and vulnerability in Juno as opposed to the toughness for which the role calls. Moreover, Donehue did nothing to restrain the idiotic attention she paid to her two toy poodles Grazie and Prego, to the intense annoyance of the other cast members.

At the same time, Donehue never seemed to accept Jack MacGowran. Mercilessly he picked on the only Irishman in the show; and the pettier Donehue became, the more MacGowran yielded to his tendencies toward the bottle. One day as the show moved into rehearsals, MacGowran exploded. "Hold it just one fuckin' moment!" he yelled. Melvyn Douglas remembered:

> Dead silence ensued from the astounded cast while MacGowran let go a fusillade of abuse for director, company and producing organization such as I have rarely heard in many decades of performance work. His invective ended with, "No one here knows a fuckin' thing about O'Casey or this fuckin' play and you don't have the slightest notion of what the fuckin' playwright is saying, or what the fuckin' actors are saying or what any of you fuckin' people are trying to do!" Drunk or sober, there was a good deal of truth to what he said.[6]

During the run of the show, MacGowran never missed a line, but by the time the cast came out for the curtain calls, this gifted drinker would often be obliged to lean on Melvyn Douglas's arm for support.

Typically, in his exacting manner, Blitzstein taught the performers his music and lyrics. In the absence of any firmer direction, it was he who defined the Irish accent for the cast and instructed them on the inflection he wanted. After dozens of coaching sessions with the principals in his Greenwich Village apartment, he achieved from the actors an accent and inflection uncannily close to the sound of his own voice.

Agnes de Mille devised choreography that those who saw the show remember as among the very best of her theatrical career. Consistent with dance styles of the British Isles, movement of the arms took second place to fancy legwork. She fused Irish jigs with kicks and hip swivels suggesting American jazz ballet. She particularly reveled in special effects with the rhythms of the men's boots, both in the angry crowd scenes and the more festive outbursts.

27. Marc with Kenneth Cantril *(l)* and Hugo Weisgall

28. Ca. 1943

29. *Freedom Morning,* Royal Albert Hall, September 28, 1943

30. With Bill Hewitt and Aaron Copland *(Victor Kraft)*

31. Bill Hewitt

32. Bill and Marc at Marie's Crisis, New York bar, October 1945

3. Robert Shaw, Leonard Bernstein, Marc, recording the *Airborne* Symphony,)46

:4. The American-Soviet Music Society *(l to r):* Mordecai Bauman, Morton Gould, Betty Bean, Serge Koussevitzky, Elie Siegmeister, Margaret Grant, Aaron Copland, Marc Blitzstein *(Alton Taube)*

35. Morris Golde *(Ted Tessler)*

36. Mina Curtiss

37. *Regina (l to r):* Robert Lewis, Cheryl Crawford, Marc Blitzstein, Jane Pickens, Clinton Wilder

2,611 performances *(Friedman-Abeles)*

. Marc and Lotte Lenya, with producers Stanley Chase *(l)* and Carmen Capalbo

40. *Juno:* With *(l to r)* Joseph Stein, Shirley Booth, Melvyn Douglas

41. Mama

42. Jo and Marc

43. With Leonard Bernstein, Cuba, 1957

45. *The Dying Gaul* at the Capitoline Museum, Rome

44. In Rome, 1961 *(Janet McDevitt)*

. Early 1960s *(Mara Weissman)*

47. Early 1960s

48. Marc with grandnephew Owen Davis, 1963 *(Stephen Davis)*

49. At the United States Information Agency office in Fort-de-France, Martinique, 1963

50. On the beach Martinique, 1964

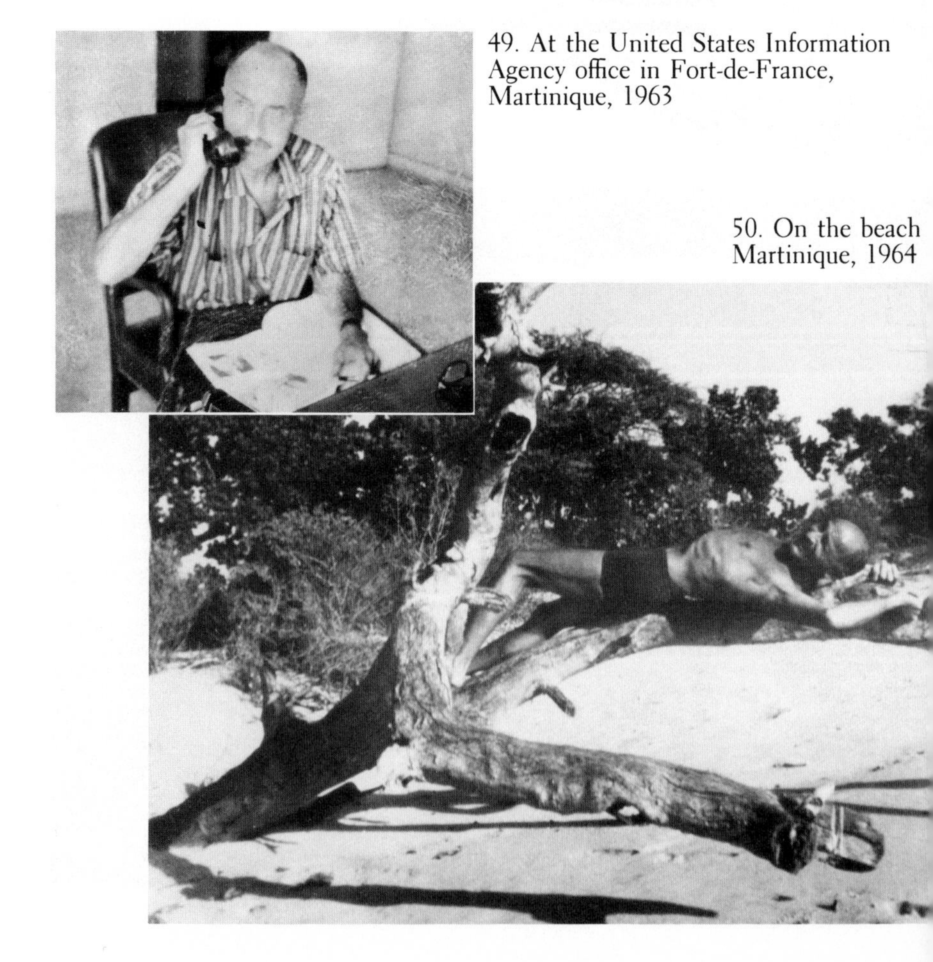

Tommy Rall, dancing the part of Mary's brother Johnny, was a perfectionist who held de Mille in deepest esteem. Knowing how much she could expect, de Mille came up with her most spectacular, acrobatic choreography for him. For his anguished solo, she had him pounding the floor like a wounded bear. Since Johnny had lost the use of an arm in the Easter Uprising of 1916, she created a mostly one-armed partnering sequence with Gemze de Lappe—the principal female dancer—featuring extravagant flips that stunned viewers. Rall's exacting personality, however, grated on the rest of the cast. Monte Amundsen fell completely in love with his talent, mistaking it as love for him, and they wed within a year. The marriage lasted less than five years, and she subsequently married the singer Giorgio Tozzi.

For the principals, de Mille kept the choreography to a minimum: the dance equivalent to Blitzstein's *Misuk.* At fifty-seven, Melvyn Douglas told the press, "I'd be the last to say I sing in *Juno.* I speak with a certain rhythm and meter. I'm involved—that's the word I like—in five numbers. And I do some dance steps. Nothing too complicated." "The trick is to *sound* like an Irishman," he confided to *Cue* magazine, "and to seem to sing, and let it go even if your voice sounds like a crow."[7]

Booth's story was not too different: "I always thought when you danced you were supposed to move. But this was an Irish step dance and only your feet move. And my feet are the only part of me that aren't educated!" Unenthusiastic about the role, Booth afterward claimed, "I tried to make it as plaintive as I could. I thought they should have had someone more heroic. I wasn't in any position to tell them I wasn't any good, and why should I do it? It should have been an Irish Judith Anderson."

With those he judged to be his equals in talent, Blitzstein acted the perfect gentleman. But with others who appeared to be grinding out their work, he could show a wicked temper, snapping defensively. Even de Mille at times saw Blitzstein undercutting her work. She would teach her steps to the dancers, and Blitzstein would casually remark, "You'll want to change all of that in Washington, of course."

Two of the best men in the field worked on orchestrations for *Juno.* Robert Russell Bennett, whom Blitzstein had known as far back as the days of Boulanger's salon in the late 1920s, scored most of the show. One inspiration that Blitzstein especially appreciated was the use of an unexpected banjo in the dance numbers. The other orchestrator was Hershy Kay, called in during the tryouts to help score the latest numbers rushed into the show. The sound Blitzstein aimed for encompassed a range of twentieth-century harmonies quite rare in a Broadway score, with noticeable influences from Benjamin Britten. In the dramatic scenes and in the underscoring, tension rose to heights audiences found unfamiliar and unsettling.

In advance of the opening, Chappell published three songs from *Juno:* Jerry Devine's "One Kind Word," as a solo, without Mary's interpolations; "My True Heart"; and "The Liffey Waltz," one of the poorer numbers from the second-act party scene, with no fewer than five forced rhymes to the word *Liffey.* Chappell later published "I Wish It So" in a collection of Broadway songs: It has become a frequently heard audition piece by young singers who otherwise know neither Blitzstein's name nor the work from which the song comes.

January 7, 1959, was the dress parade, and on the ninth the show began hauling out to Washington. Blitzstein and the musicians arrived there on Monday the twelfth, the cast the following day. Everyone stayed at the Hotel Willard.

Once in Washington, de Mille became more desperate and angry every day, particularly about the music for her big numbers. When she asked for extended pieces of music, Blitzstein handed her loose scraps of antique Irish tunes taken from library books. One night shortly before opening, she left a run-through and walked around the White House three times deciding what to do. The next day she announced that unless her longtime collaborator, the composer and arranger Trude Rittmann, were brought in, she would resign. De Mille won, and Rittmann was engaged immediately, at $350 a week.

Blitzstein felt no animosity toward Trude Rittmann, for they had known one another since 1934 and had worked together successfully on *No for an Answer.* He simply felt that his composing abilities were considered less than adequate, a hard admission for him to make. Using material Blitzstein had gathered, including the oldest-known Irish tune, "Callino Casturame" (My Treasured Colleen), first published in 1584, Rittmann wrote the music for the ballet "Dublin Night" in the first act, to which Blitzstein added rhythmic accents and spicy effects.

Shirley Booth kept saying she didn't feel right for her part. Night after night, Oliver Rea would take her out to dinner to buoy her spirits, but she remained joyless. As opening night approached, she stayed away from the orchestra rehearsals for reasons of illness. Her understudy filled in, fully expecting to open the show. On the night of the dress rehearsal, Booth reappeared. Almost as soon as the music began, she stopped the rehearsal and demanded real sausages on the kitchen table for her first number. The entire cast and crew sat on their hands while caterers from the restaurant next door prepared her props. Donehue proved incapable of disciplining her. De Mille and others in the company would have liked to have seen her replaced immediately.

Bewildered, helpless, Blitzstein stood by, watching as his show fell victim to aggravated incompetence. Collaboration!

Dress rehearsals took place on the fifteenth and sixteenth. The official opening at the National Theatre was January 17. Invited down by Oliver Smith, both Hellman and Bernstein saw the show in Washington. The next morning de Mille asked Blitzstein what they felt about the show. "What they said was so terrible for me, I can't tell you," he replied. "It would be too embarrassing."

Hellman spoke her criticisms of the show in her characteristically opinionated fashion. She pointed out that two telling points had been excised from the musical: the fact that Mary was on strike as the play opens, and that her suitor Jerry Devine is a minor labor organizer. The end of the play has Juno and Mary leaving for a spare room at Juno's sister's place, presumably an apartment not unlike the Boyles'. In the musical, the sister has a farm to which they can go. Blitzstein quoted Hellman in his daybook: "That's a real, if unconscious betrayal of O'Casey. Point is they have really nowhere to go, but are still undaunted in spirit. That's what makes it daring, and true. So pat, so sentimental, the farm."

Blitzstein prepared a two-page memorandum based on her comments, "Notes from L. Hellman, advisor to Kings":

> The play has lost too much Irishness: there isn't enough fun, enough bite, enough of the classic combination of warmth and malice. . . . Lennie and I both had idea of opening with funeral. . . . I don't like Mary. She comes out as nothing for me and isn't pretty. Forgive, but I think you ought to change her. . . . Ma song shouldn't be: Juno has been too sentimentalized. . . . Peculiar Charm is wrong for Juno. Charm is not a conception she could ever have, nor could she ever have been held to a man by a torch. PLEASE CHANGE. . . .

Lina found objections, too, in "Marc's show," as she felt entitled to call it. "The ensemble seems to just sneak on at all times. There's never a clear motivation why they are there," she wrote watching a run-through. "This Is My Day" should be Juno's song, Lina felt, but "in this number, as in so many others, the dancers immediately take over to the detriment of the story line." Inadequate differentiation of tone between one actor and another led to monotony. "Bentham at the moment is just impossible. He does not seem to be interested in Mary at all—and one of the most vital aspects of the story is completely missing. Through his listlessness and lack of interest in Mary the whole suspense is lost." At points she disliked the "jazzy orchestration."[8]

Washington reviewers set the tone for all the later criticisms of the show: Acknowledging in theory the challenge of turning O'Casey's play into a musical, at the core they could not justify the project. "The singing *Juno* is prosier than its source," wrote Tom Donnelly in the Washington *Daily News:* "The show is largely a matter of pretty decorations, the fuss and feathers of Broadway experts, with no paycock underneath." "An awkward hybrid" with "grand moments," Richard L. Coe said in the Washington *Post and Times Herald.* "It is more of a jigsaw operation than a creative one." Jay Carmody's review in the Washington *Evening Star* called the show "a merely sprawling, fugitively promising musical," citing problems with Oliver Smith's "fascinatingly mobile set . . . , a machine whose complicated operation did nothing to make the opening performance smooth." *Variety* called the show "a play which takes time out for a song or dance here and there." With a first act running over 100 minutes, Donehue must "integrate, tighten and trim."[9]

De Mille's work received mixed praise. The dances "do not reflect her best effort," said *Variety.* Coe thought the production "has that curious air of offering something about to happen which never quite does. We get keyed up for a rollicking dance or a programmed jig and we don't quite get it. Miss de Mille scorns the evidently easy way of clickety-clacks in jigs." But Tom Donnelly considered Johnny's dance "one of Agnes de Mille's finest creations, passionate, stinging, a point of fire. It is brilliantly performed by Tommy Rall and Gemze de Lappe."[10]

Concerning the score, the critics could not bring themselves to offer wholly positive notices. Coe thought it "fuller than his work for *Regina* and *The Cradle Will Rock.* He's clearly strived for melody in the pleasantly old-fashioned Balfe-Kern manner. But just as a melody seems about to soar, it doesn't. The composer wrote his own lyrics and they either get in the way or his belief in the rounded phrase does." "Marc Blitzstein's songs are often agreeable," Donnelly felt, "but they do not fill in the emotional gaps."[11]

In his initial review, Carmody called Blitzstein's music "more melodic than in earlier works," "with flashes of downright brilliance," though "it slips neither easily, comfortably nor truly dramatically over Mr. Stein's uneasy book." In the Sunday arts section at the end of the first week, he gave his opinions more ample space. Saying that Stein and Blitzstein's work represented "an act of courage above and beyond any duty the two owe to the theater," he felt that the music was the strongest element. The major problems remained the book and Donehue's direction. "Through the clutter of music, book and dance, one could perceive that with time a cohesive, attractive musical treatment of O'Casey's play might be attained. Expediently, yet wisely, the producers quickly added another week to its road booking which will delay its Broadway arrival now until the first week in March."[12]

Blitzstein felt pulled in a number of directions at once, caught within the nest of collaborative work. Should the show be more Irish or less? Sentimental or sharp-witted? A bursting Broadway production or a play with songs? His music "composed" or "arranged"? Sung in tune or as a kind of *Misuk?* And should everyone in the cast sing in the same style or just certain characters? At one point in the production, a wag with a cartooning bent drew Blitzstein, mustache, cigarette, and monogrammed briefcase, complaining, "I'm sorry, Oliver, but I refuse to turn 'Music in the House' into a rock & roll number. I think it's very commercial as it is."

Juno played through January 31, then moved to Boston's Shubert Theatre for a February 4 opening.

In an overall friendly review in the *Christian Science Monitor* on February 5, Melvin Maddocks called Shirley Booth's contributions "persuasively moving." But most other critics failed to agree. "Miss Booth is a miscast," wrote Peggy Doyle in the Boston *Evening American,* echoing Booth's own fears. "Juno is something of a lioness, somnolent most of the time but ready to spring into action when need be. Miss Booth plays her with genuine warmth and with tart humor but not with the mother-of-men depth of compassion inherent in the character."[13]

The powerful *Daily Record* critic, Elliot Norton, who had so thoroughly smashed *Reuben Reuben* less than four years before, now saw *Juno.* Though he admitted the possibility of improvement over the next four weeks in Boston, he found "little life in it, and not much truth or beauty." His inability to appreciate the freshness and originality of the scoring is reflected in the range he heard "from more or less conventional musical comedy tunes to gloomily dissonant dirges"; as if to confirm the standard criteria for musical entertainment—no gloom, no dissonance, and no dirges on our Broadway stage, please! Correctly, he pointed out that Douglas "doesn't sing very well" and that Booth made "a mild Juno." Only in de Mille's dances and in Jack MacGowran did Norton find the true spirit of the play captured. He "is all guile and gaiety and furtive grace. To describe this actor from Ireland as a leprechaun is to hew hard to something like the literal truth. They could never have found him in a casting office; he is the living lying image of Joxer Daly, merry and malicious."[14]

Had Blitzstein at any time speculated that as a musical *Juno* was an unfortunate miscalculation? Elinor Hughes, writing in the Boston *Herald,* both in a review and in a Sunday thought-piece, suggested that the play might make a better opera: "In that medium its essentially serious subject matter and strong dramatic characters could have been translated into powerful musical terms that would have paralleled its effectiveness as a drama." As it stood, *Juno* amounted to little more than "a play with musical embellishments." Once again, Blitzstein may have thought, his work had come to Broadway ten or fifteen years too soon. Perhaps, too, he would have been more pleased if, as with *The Little Foxes,* he had made his own adaptation of *Juno and the Paycock.*[15]

The time had come for the Playwrights Company to fire Vincent Donehue. Whatever changes the show required, they were drastic and required immediately. On Thursday the fifth the company dismissed him, though he remained in his hotel room, refusing on his lawyer's advice to leave the show. On Saturday José Ferrer arrived in Boston from the West Coast to see the production and discuss taking it over. The company offered him a contract of five thousand dollars plus 3 percent of box office.

In an entirely new opening prologue, "We're Alive," Tancred is shown being shot by British soldiers who recognize Johnny with a friendly salute: Thus the audience knows Johnny as a traitor from the beginning. Whether based on the Hellman-Bernstein idea of opening with a funeral or on an original concept of Ferrer, the scene strengthened the political background of the story with a glimpse of the genuine terror in the city. The chorus emphasizes the vitality and continuity of the Irish people despite all manner of oppression. Blitzstein composed this number on February 10.

Several more new songs went in. The song Hellman disliked so much, Juno's "His Own Peculiar Charm," an unpersuasive recounting of the ways Boyle is attractive to her, was substituted by the clever repartee of "Old Sayin's." In wording recalling *My Fair Lady*'s "Why Can't a Woman Be More Like a Man?" Boyle falls back on standard clichés to defend his male privilege, while she retorts with aspersions on his usefulness as a man:

Boyle: Why can't you be like a woman ought to be?
Spoilin' her man, an' she does it willin'ly.
Juno: There's mighty little left to spoil,
Spoiled you are already, Boyle. . . .
Boyle: Why can't you be like Missus Madigan, at least?
One word from her an' me self-respect's increased.
Juno: You know that she's a widow now.
Let that *be arranged somehow.*

Once again, the theme of the separate worlds of men and women is restated.

Blitzstein now wrote "It's Not Irish," an ode to motherhood recorded by Arthur Rubin. Played on the gramophone in the party scene, recalling a similar use of the gramophone at the climax of Kurt Weill's *Der Zar lässt sich photographieren,* it is similar to dozens of such sentimental numbers popularized by soaring tenors like John McCormack. And instead of a reprise of Mary's "I Wish It So," Blitzstein came up with "For Love," conceived for Monte Amundsen's silvery timbre.

Once Ferrer took charge of the show, he asked Shirley Booth to reconstruct her performance thoroughly, to abandon the docility Donehue had sought, and give the role the asperity it lacked. She could hardly defend the ineffectual Donehue; but at the same time she found Ferrer autocratic and only begrudgingly accepted his changes.

At the end of February 1959 with the show still in a state of suspended disaster in Boston, both Stein and Blitzstein agreed to substantial cuts in royalties. And neither Donehue nor Ferrer had yet been paid: Two weeks after coming to Boston, the new director had his lawyer writing the company to demand payment, on threat of returning home.

On March 9, five weeks after its Boston opening, *Juno* opened at the Winter Palace in New York. The Playwrights Company production of *Look After Lulu* had opened the week before. *Sweet Bird of Youth, A Raisin in the Sun* and *First Impressions* would immediately follow. *My Fair Lady, West Side Story, The Music Man* and *Sunrise at Campobello* were still running.

The New York critics pounced. In Brooks Atkinson's examination of "the season's first musical with a high purpose," he regretted that "*Juno* as a whole does not have the strength, the rhythm and the sustained personality of an independent theatre work. It does not quite hang together." He called the music "melodic," "gay," "poignant and melancholy." " 'We're Alive' recaptures the angry mood of rebellion. Whatever Mr. Blitzstein writes shows the taste of a professional musician," he concluded, but "as a musical work, it does not have the drive, the scorn and the fury of the play."[16]

"An immensely honorable failure" was Kenneth Tynan's summation in *The New Yorker.* "Mr. Blitzstein's music is about ten times as good as his lyrics," he said, but little could save *Juno* from its principal weakness, "its habit of bringing into the foreground what O'Casey kept in the background—of stating what he implied and of underscoring what he stated."[17]

Some critics seemed to take special glee in castigating the show. John McClain in the *Journal-American* thought Johnny's dance "almost worth the whole evening," but had little else to commend. "Expensive and pretentious," he wrote, "the evening will not be long remembered." "Shirley Booth and Melvyn Douglas have a tough time doing anything wrong, but here they have succeeded. . . . This is entertainment? . . . So much talent, so much money, and so little fun."[18]

The most supportive notice came from John Chapman of the *Daily News.* It must have pleased the creators of the show to read his respect for their "bold and intelligent step away from Broadway formula." To Melvyn Douglas he gave a high score for "the most impressive performance of his career as the Paycock." Shirley Booth provided "a finely outlined characterization," while MacGowran came forth with "the season's most splendid character performance." "Musically it is modern enough to be interesting, with some fine instrumental and vocal expressions by Marc Blitzstein which bear the mark of an individualist among composers." Chapman's reservations lay primarily with the lyrics. "All I wish," he concurred finally with the mainstream criticism, "is that O'Casey could have written the book, lyrics and music of *Juno.*"[19]

As they had with *Regina,* many critics could not escape comparing the musical to the original play. They failed to see the new work as a freestanding creation to be judged on its own terms. And for all the love they claimed for O'Casey's inherently musical language, they chose to ignore the fact that it had been nearly two decades since Barry Fitzgerald and Sarah Allgood from the original Abbey Theatre production had given the play its last staging in the city.

On March 16, Victor Samrock, business manager for the Daarlin' Man Company, reported to Roger L. Stevens and Oliver Rea the estimated box office take it would require to keep *Juno* on the boards. Even were the two leads to take a 50 percent salary cut, the principal creative talents to waive their royalty rights completely, and the theatre guarantees to be reduced by fifteen hundred dollars, the show might still stand to lose up to fifteen thousand dollars. "On the basis of the above figures and facts, I cannot see any recourse except to put the notice up tonight to close at the end of this week."[20] Perhaps Stevens might have pumped up the publicity. Perhaps he could have given the box office more of a chance. But he decided to cut his losses without delay. After sixteen performances on Broadway, *Juno* closed.

Blitzstein did not hang around to witness the end. He followed Hellman's advice and got out of town. On March 12 he fled with Morris Golde for Acapulco, whose sun warmed Blitzstein's spirits for the next ten days. Aaron Copland met them there, and the three men visited a series of bars in the red light district where both boys and girls made themselves available. At one establishment, policemen suddenly came in chasing their quarry; Aaron and Marc jumped behind the jukebox and hid.

Months later, in their summations of the Broadway season, more than one columnist cited *Juno* among the year's best offerings despite its problems. Stein recalled O'Casey's saying, not bitterly but with bemusement, "The critics always loved my plays after they closed."

Goddard Lieberson, president of Columbia Records, might have chosen not to issue the cast album, given the brevity of the run and the certain unprofitability of such a release. But out of respect for Blitzstein's music, he felt an obligation to preserve this unusually sophisticated, astringent score. CBS issued both mono and stereo versions of the show. The writer for the July issue of *Hi Fi Review* also wondered whether Blitzstein shouldn't have written an opera from O'Casey's play. Given the limitations of Booth's and Douglas's voices, he pointed out, most of the demanding music fell to Monte Amundsen alone. In particular, he found the stereo version "the most effective I have heard so far of an original Broadway cast," and praised the illusion of movement and action created on disk.[21]

Perhaps if Ferrer had come into the show once Richardson resigned or even a month earlier than he did, *Juno*'s problems might have been resolved—the lumbering sets simplified and toned down, the shaping of the characters firmed up, the dances shortened and better integrated into the action, maybe even a replacement or two made. The story of *Juno* is a case study of the difficulties and grief inherent in the Broadway system. The show might have fared better playing first in a more modest workshop form in New York, then expanding into a full Broadway production once it had taken final shape. On the road—with theatres booked, hotels and salaries to be paid, the critics hovering like carrion crows—the pressure to doctor such an immense machine into perfect health overwhelmed the creators, and there was no time.

From Devon, Eileen O'Casey wrote, "Isn't it a shame about *Juno.* Poor Joe and Marc and everyone after all that work, and I am sure it really might have made it, if the director had been right from the start. . . . We just don't seem to be meant to have this large fortune yet."[22] The Playwrights Company had yet to hear from Vincent Donehue, who sued for unpaid wages of thirty-five hundred dollars. By January 1960, they settled.

On his return home to California, the music director Robert Emmett Dolan wrote to Marc thanking him for the opportunity of conducting *Juno.* He filled a two-page typed letter with criticisms of the set, the cast, the producers, and especially the critics. They "displayed a new-found reverence for O'Casey—a man who, at their hands, has lived these past thirty years one foot this side of abject poverty—that carried as much sincerity as Nixon's TV apologia in 1952 with his wife by his side." Among the sweetest words Blitzstein ever read was Dolan's consolation:

> The only people in any art who are worth a hoot are those who have something to say that hasn't been said before. You are one of those. For that reason alone—if for no other—I urge you to keep your voice ringing in the theater, no matter how discouraging *Juno* turned out to be. . . . I hope you will never be benign about *Juno*'s fate. I could never forgive that. This score was written with deep conviction. If you dismiss your convictions you have nothing left. God bless you.[23]

Nowhere in Blitzstein's FBI file is *Juno* mentioned. The absence even of newspaper clippings about the show indicates that the FBI was rather less than thorough in its investigation. But since December of the previous year, agents had placed him under surveillance to determine his patterns of activity. They wanted to see when might be the optimal time to interview him. "There is no information of CP activity on the part of the subject since 1951," wrote the New York special agent in charge to the director of the FBI. And since Blitzstein had not been wholly uncooperative with HUAC, the FBI hoped that he might be ready to yield more.

> An interview of this subject is expected to result in clarification of the subject's present status and attitude towards subversive groups in which he was a member or affiliated. . . .
>
> If this subject is co-operative, no affirmative steps will be taken during the initial interview to direct his activities but a separate communication will be directed to the Bureau setting forth the results of the interview and requesting authority to recontact the subject as a PSI [Potential Security Informant].

Referring back to Blitzstein's psychiatric sessions at the Veterans Administration in 1947, the director answered, "In view of subject's history of psychoneurosis, the Bureau is of the opinion that he should be interviewed by two mature and experienced Agents and that every caution should be exercised in order to preclude embarrassment to the Bureau."[24]

The FBI seems not to have known about Blitzstein's trip to Mexico. Two agents found him at home on March 25, and described him in their reports: "Build—Small; Complexion—Dark olive; Hair—Black, bald on top; Eyes—Dark, deep set; Characteristics—Wears mustache, Horn rimmed glasses, Elongated slightly hooked nose, soft spoken, theatrical mannerisms."

> The subject stated . . . that he had nothing further to add to his testimony before the government committee, . . . and that he resented the attempts of the FBI to interview him as he considered it an invasion of his privacy. The subject was cold in his manner toward the agents and exhibited no inclination to cooperate. In view of the above, no further efforts are warranted to interview him again. . . . NY will remain alert for any information of subversive activity on the part of the subject and will reopen investigation if warranted in the future.[25]

22

PART OF THE GANG

Spring 1959–Winter 1960

". . . there are enough beasts in the American business-jungle; I like to feel that I am not a part of that wolf-pack."

Once *Juno* had closed, Blitzstein returned to the long-delayed *Mother Courage.* Stefan Brecht, the playwright's son, told Blitzstein in March 1959 that no definite translation had been decided upon for a proposed production at the Circle in the Square, but that with revised lyrics for the songs, Blitzstein's version might well be the one used. The Brecht heir further teased Blitzstein by mentioning W. H. Auden and Richard Wilbur for the lyrics. In any case, neither Stefan Brecht nor his mother Helene Weigel seemed to be in any rush to see *Mother Courage* on the New York stage.[1]

Blitzstein had also begun a translation of Weill and Brecht's *Aufstieg und Fall der Stadt Mahagonny* as early as the summer of 1956, just around the time he began looking at *Mother Courage.* By early 1958 the full-length recording with Lenya had been released, which he reviewed ecstatically in the May 31 issue of the *Saturday Review.* He described Lenya's voice as "a cross between a choir-boy and Duse. . . . In this, her most ambitious attempt, she emerges as a singing and acting star of the very first rank." "I came upon *Mahagonny* late," he said. "It was not one of the works which influenced my youth, as had *Dreigroschenoper.*" He called it "the crowning achievement of the Weill-Brecht collaboration," "bigger and broader" than *Threepenny.* "Brecht's libretto offers no rostrum, no facile remedy for the chaos and disaster it excoriates. It is of an extreme moral bitterness, which at times mounts to a poetic paean of rage; and with the rage, it has had its say."

As expected, the Nazis had cited it as an example of *Kultur-Bolschewismus.* But in words foreshadowing the changed relation between political ideas and his own art in the years to come, Blitzstein added that "the Communists blasted it too, as anarchistic, even nihilistic. It is neither, being a tragedy of real pity and terror. One can see that it lends itself to no specific social or political sponsorship."[2]

Negotiations on the rights to *Mahagonny* proceeded no more smoothly than those for *Mother Courage.* The Capalbo and Chase team originally had wanted to produce the work and open it in the fall of 1958, but clearance had not yet come through for the translation. While Stefan Brecht had encouraged Blitzstein in the translation, Brecht had also approached W. H. Auden and Chester Kallman, commissioning a translation from them. Others eventually came about as well. (The CBS recording Blitzstein reviewed contained a complete, literal translation, not intended for performance, by Guy Stern.)

Helene Weigel expressed some worry about the *Mahagonny* translation. In Stefan's presence, Blitzstein wrote to her in East Berlin to allay her concerns: "Heaven knows there are enough beasts in the American business-jungle; I like to feel that I am not a part of that wolf-pack." Promising to deal honorably with "whoever is the accredited executor of Brecht's estate" and to "listen to any suggestions Stefan might have to offer, in the way of making a rendering of Brecht's words and meanings closer to the original," Blitzstein wished above all that Weigel should see him as "a man of some moral fibre."[3] Such was Blitzstein's naïveté as a businessman, however, that he failed to secure an ironclad contractual agreement about the translation rights.

The music of *Mahagonny* is so strongly accented and the text is in a German that so often imitates American rhythms and prosody that a translation almost naturally fell into place in Blitzstein's hands. Still, he toyed with many possible versions of the lyrics. While awaiting the elusive production, he continued to revise, not settling on a definitive English text. Not even his title had been set, though he felt attracted to the word *magnet* and intended to use it somehow: "Magnet City," "Magnet Was a City," "Birth and Death of Magnet City." As the translation stands, it remains somewhat short of a final performing version and would require a thorough revision and modernization if ever brought to the stage.

Toward the end of 1958, Virgil Thomson had nominated Blitzstein for membership in the National Institute of Arts and Letters. Aaron Copland and Douglas Moore had seconded. Thomson had cited Blitzstein's "remarkable gift for parody and a humane tenderness" characterizing "some of the most powerful works of our time." On the setting of words to music, he said of Blitzstein, "Nobody fits them better."[4] At the annual meeting of the institute held January 28, 1959, while *Juno* was winding up its Washington run, Blitzstein was elected.

Even before the formal induction ceremony on May 20, he volunteered to serve on the Grants Committee for Music, recommending small awards to deserving and needy composers during his three-year term. He clearly savored the role; Lester Trimble and Ramiro Cortés were two of the first composers for whom he facilitated grants. Later on, he recommended William Flanagan, Ned Rorem, Frederic Myrow, Ernst Bacon, William Sydeman, and Mel Powell. After the spring dinner meeting at the Harvard Club, still before his induction, he thanked president Glenway Wescott—Eva's old friend—for the hospitality. "It was good to meet old friends in a new setting, and to talk to men and women I have wanted to know for years. I look forward to my duties and privileges as a member of the Institute with considerable pleasure."[5]

Membership in the institute confirmed for Blitzstein his status among the nation's leading composers. Few other honors or distinctions, not even commercial success, could match his satisfaction to be numbered in the company of his rightful peers in American culture. As he had announced in *This Is the Garden*, "I am proud and ready and worthy to be part of their gang." Too, membership represented his profession's best answer to the snoopers and blacklisters.

For an exhibition that ran from May 20 through June 14 at the Academy Museum featuring works by all the new inductees, Blitzstein supplied material from *Regina*. The recording had appeared only shortly before, and the City Opera had included two performances of its production once again in its spring season. Krachmalnick conducted the same cast as the year before with only one exception: Margot Moser, making her debut with the company, took over the role of Alexandra. These turned out to be the last performances of the opera by the company.

Regina also received its first productions out West. One was in San José, conducted by Fred Coradetti, with Meg Broughton as Regina. The other, at Santa Fe in late July, was under the musical direction of Margaret Hillis. The mezzo soprano Elaine Bonazzi as Regina headed the cast of young singers, scoring a well-noted triumph. Earlier that spring, she had gone to Blitzstein's apartment several times for coaching sessions. In reality, he had originally conceived the role for a mezzo voice such as Carmen. So impressed with her vocal quality was he that he made changes in her music to avoid some of the higher tessituras. (*Juno*'s Monte Amundsen, whom Blitzstein had imagined in the role of Alexandra, did not sing.) Henry Heyman designed the set, Robert Benson the lighting, and Bliss Hebert directed. Laurence Pawell of the *New Mexican* found the opera "right-wing contemporary music resorting freely to jazz and Negro idioms. . . . This opera is more than Puccini à la Dixie, but it could easily be pigeonholed as 'verismo' opera."[6] It was probably the first and only time anything connected to Marc Blitzstein had been called "right-wing!"

Blitzstein had not wished to test the State Department's ban on issuing passports to suspected Communists. In the years since the war, he had limited his foreign travels to Mexico, Bermuda, and Cuba—Western Hemisphere countries where passports were not required. But after the Supreme Court banned the government from exercising such punitive control, he decided on a five-country European tour for six weeks beginning in mid-June. It was the first of a new series of trips abroad that inevitably summoned to mind his travels in the 1920s and 1930s. From *Juno* he had managed to eke out almost nine thousand dollars, and he budgeted a portion of his earnings to pay for the trip. For the first two weeks he traveled with Irene Lee Diamond, his friend from the 1930s. The FBI, learning of the issuance of a passport to Blitzstein, alerted the Department of State, the Central Intelligence Agency, and the United States legal attachés in Bonn, London, Paris, Rome, and Madrid.

In essence, Blitzstein boiled down the purpose of his trip to these motivations: "1) Make money, 2) Try to be your wish-fulfillment homosexual self, 3) Combine the two." He made lists of musical contacts in Italy, France, Germany, England, and Ireland, and in his notebook he gathered information on the locales in Rome, and perhaps elsewhere as well, where contacts of a different nature could be made: "Hey, for Christ's sake! The Grand Hotel, and the Piazza della Repubblica! (Ruins of the Diocletian baths—superb!) Other Baths: Giovanni Amendola and via d'Azeglio; left of the RR station, after Piazza Cinque Cento—whores too."

Blitzstein kept a detailed diary of his European trip, beginning it after visiting Rome and Florence. He had a letter of introduction from Bernstein to Luchino Visconti in Rome, but Visconti was not in town at the time. He and Irene visited the artist Beverly Pepper and her husband William Pepper, a *Newsweek* reporter. They had dinner one evening in Ostia at the home of film director Martin Ritt and his wife. Blitzstein saw the composer Alexei Haieff at the American Academy in Rome. Otherwise, they went sightseeing as any tourists.

Among those he met in Rome, the music critic Fedele D'Amico happened to remember Blitzstein's choral opera *The Condemned,* and he presented him with a curiosity item: a fifty-page pamphlet by the longtime anarchist propagandist Augustin Souchy, published by "Der Syndikalist" in Berlin some thirty years before, just when Blitzstein had lived in the city. The title was *Sacco und Vanzetti: Zwei Opfer Amerikanischer Dollarjustiz* (Two Victims of American Dollar-Justice).

In Florence the principal attraction was his old friend, the composer David Diamond—no relation to Irene and Aaron Diamond—with whom he stayed. There, he mentions in his diary, he frequented Harry's Bar, very often in David's company.

David took Marc to the home of the American composer Francis Thorne, then living in Florence with his family, studying with Diamond, and writing pop songs for Italian bands. It was June 23, Thorne's birthday, and thirty-odd friends, mostly Americans, had gathered for the occasion. In the course of the party, Thorne sat at the piano and played through half a dozen of his tunes, asking Blitzstein's advice, which he gladly gave. When Blitzstein sat down to play, the guests requested "Mack the Knife," "Pirate Jenny," and the other hits from *Threepenny Opera.* Though happy to oblige, it was not the first time he felt his own music slighted. Sensitive to his friend's growing annoyance, Diamond gently guided him toward "Nickel Under the Foot," but with that one number of his own, he stopped.

In Paris, Blitzstein spent no time trying to interest the French in his works. Still with Irene and now joined by her husband Aaron, Blitzstein saw Virgil Thomson—newly installed in his apartment at 17 quai Voltaire—Georges Auric, Jules Dassin, and Janet Flanner; met Nelson Aldredge of the *Paris Review;* saw the film *Black Orpheus;* and watched Yul Brynner shoot the last scene of *Once More with Feeling.* One day sitting at an outdoor café, he and Irene spotted the pianists Gold and Fizdale and invited them to sit down for a chat.

On July 4 he flew to Frankfurt, Irene and Aaron taking off in another direction. The first night there he visited some striptease parlors—"poor and sickening," Blitzstein called them—then drifted alone over to the Hillbilly bar near the train station. There he found "sad GI's making time with the whores." On Monday the sixth, he began serious promotional work on his own behalf. Inge Borkh, deep in rehearsals for *Elektra,* showed great interest in *Regina* if a German translation could be made. She hoped for productions in Berlin and maybe Munich and Stuttgart. Blitzstein also thought he found interest in Frankfurt in *Cradle* and *The Guests.*

On the seventh, he continued on to Berlin, which he had last seen more than twenty-five years before. "Laid waste! (East *and* West B.). The old 'spaciousness' has become a desert; new buildings seem garish and un-surrounded." On the first night he dined with Paul Moor, the American music critic and student of psychoanalysis living there, and he continued to share Moor's company on successive days. He managed to hit Berlin two years before the city divided permanently: Travel between the western and eastern sectors held none of the inconveniences of later years.

> July 8. By taxi to E. Berlin, Theater am Schiffbauerdamm, and Helene Weigl [*sic*], whom I like enormously. Two hours of talk (E. Hauptmann too); a *probe* of the wedding-scene of *DGO*—only pretty good—not ready yet. H. Eisler sends for me in his car (with chauffeur yet) for lunch at his "dacha"—Viennese wife-and-grown-daughter. And then driven back across to W. Berlin (*no* telephonic communication!). . . . Then El Dorado . . . Martin-Luther-Strasse, where the bar-tenderins (in travesti) made up to me—astonishing boys so like girls even I am fooled. By foot to "Charly's Night Club" on the Wittenbergplatz = Versailles-in-a-matchbox—and full of astonishing by-play of sex (male whore, bar-man and client, two fellas at bar *in mitte eine* affair, groping each other) covered by heterosexual types dancing, and a stern boarding-house-mistress-type manageress. Home by taxi at 2 AM.

It appears that Hanns Eisler had forgiven Blitzstein's political denunciation during the war. He had now become East Germany's leading composer, though not without his own share of troubles from Stalin's super-loyal sycophants. Blitzstein had long since quit the Communist Party, but would continue to pay the price for his earlier sins.

On the ninth, Weigel sent for Blitzstein in her car for another *Dreigros-*

chenoper rehearsal; then he returned to West Berlin to see the composer Boris Blacher, who gave him a "lovely warm cordial greeting in his very new modern house."

Paul Dessau came over for lunch with Blitzstein on the tenth to discuss the music and lyrics of *Mother Courage.* In the afternoon, Blitzstein visited Hans Stuckenschmidt, the German critic and writer—"he has got very stuffy, precise, finicky and formal." Stuckenschmidt phoned Dr. von Westermann, head of the Berlin Festspiele, setting up an appointment with Blitzstein the following day.

In the evening, he went out again to the bars with Paul Moor. At one place, they met an old prizefighter who had known Brecht. Blitzstein found himself deeply discomfited by the lingering anti-Semitism he found in Berlin, and he behaved cautiously, fearful of ending up in some embarrassing contretemps. Still, he regaled Moor with the tale of a pickup that he had made back in New York not long before. His glee in telling the story filled him with an almost frightening thrill: Moor frankly wondered what good could ever come to Marc, who was attracted to men who could only make him miserable.

The next day, von Westermann discussed a possible Rolf Liebermann production of *Regina* with Borkh, to be directed by Günther Rennert in Hamburg, then brought to Berlin for the 1960 Festspiele. Later at the British Officers Club, Blitzstein met Daniel Schorr, a former CBS correspondent in Moscow—"nice guy who treasures a copy of my *No for an Answer* in his Moscow home." Again, he went out on the town with Moor that night. The new bar they visited was the Schnurrbart-Diele, "a 'private club' of old bourgeois business-men, all homos. We, P & I, are a great success, but it is, finally, a melancholy experience. But in Elly's bar there is a dream of a type (the *expanse* of every feature!) whom we are warned off: 'Watch out. He is not from us.' A life-guard at a neighboring public-pool. . . . Home by 4 A.M."

On Sunday the twelfth, he saw Brecht's *Arturo Ui* in East Berlin, then had supper with the entire company afterward at the adjoining restaurant, Ganymed. There he met Götz Friedrich, twenty-eight-year-old protégé of the Komische Oper's director Walter Felsenstein—"a charming guy, full of beans," Blitzstein wrote of Friedrich. He also encountered a young Polish conductor named Satanowski and promised to send the score to *Lear: A Study.* Later on with Moor, "one last fling at Kleist Casino," where he records that the night before he had been stood up by Kurt, the ticket taker, after they had arranged a rendezvous.

On the thirteenth, he bought copies of two Weill scores, *Dreigroschenoper* and *Mahagonny.* In the evening Eisler's car came around again and he was driven to the Eastern Section for a chat with Eisler and the general secretary of the composers' guild. Then he saw Weigel in *Die Mutter* at the Schiffbauerdamm. "She is wonderful, a totally quiet performer in an austere deliberately un-flowing production."

Just before he left Berlin on the fourteenth, he discovered to his surprise that the magazine *Monat* featured his nephew Kit's story "Man of Affairs," translated as "*Sprachunterricht.*" He projected a return to the city if *Regina* materialized there the next year.

London: "So devastatingly *square,* so doggedly old-fashioned." With Eddie and Rosemary Chodorov, he dined at Isow's Yiddish restaurant "off Wardour St., my old war-time hang-out." Others he saw, including a few American blacklist refugees, were Wolf Mankowitz, Don and Ella Stewart, Lester Cole, Sam Wanamaker, Max Kester, Oliver Rea, David Drew, and Oscar Lewenstein, "who's interested in co-producing *Juno* here." "I meet John Willett, a good earnest (*re* Brecht) and knowledgeable man. He doesn't like my version of *Threepenny Opera,* and says so flatly (with some good points). He *does* like my *Mother Courage* and will push it, for Methuen publication." Blitzstein called on the publishing house himself and was indeed assured of their interest. He ran into Earle Hyman, who "sang badly" in *The Winter's Tale* the year before. He also met with Anna Wiman—"still a drinker, then her play *The Grass Is Greener,* dinner at her house afterwards." Anna repeated her standing offer of the use of Landmark, her Bermuda house, whenever Marc wished.

"Remember Regina Resnik who auditioned for *Regina* in Brigantine in 1948?" Blitzstein wrote on a postcard to Jo in Brigantine. "She's a big star at Covent Garden Opera (Carmen, Amneris, etc.) now—and wants to do *Regina* here. So the wheel comes full circle. Oh, to stay in London!"[7]

"I have held off writing about the phone-call with Sean O'Casey in Torquay," Blitzstein wrote in the diary. "Eileen was away; he was crotchety, petulant, and blames Jo [Stein] and me for the *Juno* failure ('I told him and told him *Juno* was not the play for a musical; it doesn't make one. I hate the thing myself, but people have taken it so to their hearts, it mustn't be tampered with—still, go and do it in London if you can; heaven knows I need the success as much as you do.')." Blitzstein offered to go down to Devon to see O'Casey, but he was told not to. The chagrin, to speak with the venerable author himself and hear not one kind word! And just before embarking on the final leg of his trip, to O'Casey's homeland.

Tony Guthrie met Blitzstein at the Dublin airport on July 21. On the following day, they played through the recording of *Juno.* "He is impressed by the melodic gift, loves the treatment of the women, carps at Boyle & Joxer (says I haven't plumbed *their* depths; too American and music-hall in treatment)—I think he likes it—I'll find out (tomorrow?) whether he will do it. Much talk of Lenny—I teach them all the word game of Lenny and me. Evening spent singing English folk songs and art songs."

For the next two days Blitzstein's companion was the actor Micheal MacLiammoir, a 1928 founder of the Gate Theatre, whom Guthrie had asked to show the American the city. He was duly forewarned—"Watch your step, there, Blitzstein: This one is said to make passes!" After an afternoon of pub-hopping, where the generous denizens offered them drinks, they found they could not locate the "nite-spots"—Blitzstein must have meant the bars that catered to homosexuals. But he did walk around Mountjoy Square and Gardiner Street, scene of *Juno and the Paycock.* The next night they resolved to try again.

> At 11.10 P.M. Michael McLiammoir [*sic*] by appointment appears in my room. He makes no effort to leave; so we have drinks there—too many vodkas for me, gin for him. He is loaded already; a preposterous non-man,

> an invention, who gets briskly down to brass-tacks—i.e., sex—confiding in me that Ireland *is* Kathleen O'Hounihan, a woman, and that any footballer or boxer or guardsman can be had by an enterprising homosexual. He himself had as lover the Chief of Police of Dublin for six years, etc. . . . He avoids much mention of Hilton Edwards, his present ménage, and director/producer whom I wanted to meet; and it is all a bit like Boyle and Joxer, winding up miles away from the original topic, which was that McL show me Dublin. . . . He is a brilliant old auntie.

After he had gone, Blitzstein vomited up the too many vodkas. Now at the end of his five-nation tour, he probably never stopped to reckon how much of his "wish-fulfillment homosexual self" he had poured down his throat in the bars and clubs and dives of Europe.

Blitzstein spent his last day in Dublin with Stuart Scheftel and Geraldine Fitzgerald and flew home that evening, the twenty-fifth. Within days he was back in his studio in Brigantine. From there he wrote to Ned Rorem: "It was a glorious trip, from all points of view—including *amours* and the business aspect."[8] But in the end, he made no money from it. Not a single note of his music got played as a result of it, not in Italy or France, where he hardly promoted it; not in Germany, West or East; not in England, nor in Ireland, nor in Poland.

Still, the trip turned out to yield an entirely unforeseen result. Not long after his return, he glanced once again at the Sacco and Vanzetti pamphlet given to him in Rome. He had long ago pilfered sections of *The Condemned* for *Cradle* and *Regina,* abandoning any performance prospects for this unwieldy oratorio. But now the idea struck with an unimagined force: *Now* he could write the full-scale Sacco and Vanzetti opera for which it seemed his whole career had destined him. Now he could probe the simple souls of these two long-suffering innocents against the background of heinous injustice in Judge Thayer's court and Governor Fuller's Commonwealth.

A classic American subject! The magnificent confrontation of two powerless individuals against the state. The occasion for a perfect marriage of politics and art. The moment and the inspiration had come for his greatest and most enduring statement in music.

At once he began studying the history of the case—the famous collection of letters written by the two Italian immigrants in their wrenching, fractured eloquence, the trial transcripts, the newspapers, the eyewitness accounts by journalists and lawyers, the poetry and the creative works generated by the story, Upton Sinclair's novel *Boston,* Maxwell Anderson's play *Winterset,* and more. (He seemed to have forgotten the 1928 Erich Mühsam play *Staatsräson* [For Reasons of State] in which Eva had taken such a strong interest in the mid-1930s, for it remained undisturbed among her dusty papers still in Blitzstein's possession.) And with this story, too, he knew he would be making a statement about more recent political history—the execution twenty-six years later, in 1953, of Julius and Ethel Rosenberg.

Everything he read pointed to the necessity of an opera. On Labor Day he sat down to commit his first ideas to paper.

The necessity of an opera, yes, but what kind of opera? "Watch out for sentimental approach!" he told himself. "Watch out for 'agit-prop' method or plugging!" "No realistic or verismo opera."

At first he thought of moving from the initial arrest in 1920 to the execution in 1927, "dividing the S-V story into 7 years (with some view to '7 stages of hell,' and somewhere along the line, a reference to Dante's *Inferno.*" The literal chronology soon appeared overstated, though he cautioned himself, "Don't avoid the story; tell it!" Further, "Don't tell the story as though that were all. Make sure the[y] grasp the meaning, or *meanings* (better) that accompany the story; but involved in it, in its very texture." He took his questions to Mina Curtiss that September and quoted her reaction: "Think how much S and V grew during those 7 years—and think how Thayer and Fuller both shrank during the same time!" Is that what he should try to say or do?

Only a few weeks later, still wrestling with approaches to the opera, Blitzstein spotted the front-page announcement in *The New York Times,* to the effect that the Ford Foundation had granted $950,000 to four opera companies for the purpose of commissioning and producing as many as eighteen new American operas. They intended to help the companies break out of the cycle of all-European repertory. The companies included both the Metropolitan and the City Opera in New York, the San Francisco Opera, and the Chicago Lyric Opera. Blitzstein clipped the article and red-penciled it: "S-V?" A few phone calls and he was well on his way to finding a path to the Ford Foundation's door.

Two lengthy articles Blitzstein worked on that fall of 1959 failed to see print. The *Saturday Evening Post* asked for a piece on the musical theatre for its "Adventures of the Mind" series. He planned a defense of the public, the audience, whose need for witnessing a spectacle together created the very urge of theatre. He put in a plug for translations. He also wanted to make reference to one of his favorite subjects: how politically aware certain standard operas are, such as *Carmen, The Marriage of Figaro,* and *Louise.* Musical theatre, he confirmed, is above all a collective project, but alas, endangered by money. He must have been thinking about his experience with *Juno* when he wrote that a show has to "mollify the critics and the public, placate them, feed the new thing in small doses, so as to recoup. . . . also with that out-of-town nightmare, the 're-write,' whereby many of the original concepts get lost, and *all* of the form goes to pot."

For *Horizon* magazine he sketched a piece on the Brecht-Weill collaboration. He mentioned Brecht's famous characterization of *Mahagonny* as a "culinary" opera, recalling from his work with Mina Curtiss that Bizet in a letter to his publisher Choudens had used the same word in a musical sense.

A short biography and a catalogue of Blitzstein works appeared that year in the Pan American Union's magazine *Composers of the Americas,* presumably spreading his name around two continents, but no performances seem to have resulted.[9]

For the remainder of the year, aside from his ongoing struggle with the form *Sacco and Vanzetti* should take, there was the usual seminar on contemporary

American opera on which he would serve as panelist, and volunteer work on the National Institute's grants committee. John Houseman wrote him, and Blitzstein answered with his version of the original *Cradle* story for inclusion in Houseman's book of memoirs *Run-through.* Hellman needed music for her new play, *Toys in the Attic,* slated to open the following February; Blitzstein wrote it for her. Charles Schwartz, director of Composers' Showcase—a group dedicated to promoting the cause of living composers—invited Blitzstein to narrate and help prepare two concert performances of *No for an Answer* in April.

That fall he took up Anna Wiman's offer of the house in Bermuda and invited Jo and Ed to go along. Wiman's housekeeper, cook, and chauffeur came with the property. After days of sun and beach and continued reading on Sacco and Vanzetti, Marc, Jo, and Ed would enjoy a gourmet dinner prepared by Wiman's staff, then retire to the upstairs room with the mammoth shortwave receiver and listen to programs from Europe, Latin America, and the USSR.

Blitzstein's biggest excitement that fall was the City Opera's announcement of a revival of *The Cradle Will Rock,* to be given four performances at the City Center beginning February 11, 1960. This was the opportunity he had anticipated in his Spoken Arts recording—when the work could be seen fully staged and heard with its original orchestration. "This is the way I wrote the piece," Blitzstein recalled in his program note,

> how I meant it to be staged. By now, of course, the theme and the treatment—the rise of unionism in America, seen from a brash, exuberant, idealistic viewpoint—make the work something of a period piece. But I still feel as I did about the subject; and I have nothing to apologize for in the music. Let it take its chances, say I; let it prove whether it remains an engrossing and entertaining musical stage piece.

No longer admitting *Cradle*'s potentially active role as agitprop theatre, as he imagined it might have played in 1947 ("a period piece . . . still in the middle of the period"), he now remained content to allow the work to find its natural level in the history of American theatre.

The City Opera had once again decided on an all-American season, in part funded by the Ford Foundation. Its compliant board raised no objections, political or musical, to Julius Rudel's decision to include *Cradle.* Indeed, when Blitzstein mentioned his new opera on Sacco and Vanzetti, Rudel volunteered to produce it sound unheard and to obtain the Ford Foundation grant for Blitzstein to compose it. Despite the assurance—and what could be more assuring to a composer?—Blitzstein tried to get the commission from the more prestigious Met.

Sir Rudolf Bing, general manager of the Metropolitan Opera, often prided himself on his distance from the lower depths of life, not the least of which would be some unsavory bygone of American history. When first approached about Blitzstein's proposal for the Ford Foundation commission, he asked, "Sacco and Vanzetti? Are these two Italian lovers?" But by the time he and the assistant manager John Gutman met with Blitzstein in early January, he had become more receptive to the project. He promised to write to the foundation strongly recommending Blitzstein's opera "for consideration for production" at the Met. He could not give final commitment, however, until 75 percent of the libretto and about 40 percent of the music, or one act, had been seen and approved.* At this point, Blitzstein supposed he could have the opera finished in two years, and the production could take place in January of 1963. Aware of Rudel's unconditional offer, Bing sweetened the projected Ford grant with an additional one thousand dollars as an option, to be kept if the Met decided not to produce the opera, to serve as an advance against royalties if they did produce it.

Most of the Ford Foundation's opera budget would go toward production costs, with only $110,000 going directly to the composers and librettists. The foundation parceled out its grants to composers on the basis of need, not their abstract worth in the cultural marketplace. For each composer and librettist, they estimated a figure of six thousand dollars. Blitzstein met with them to discuss his personal budget; he showed that beyond what he could expect from ASCAP and *The Threepenny Opera,* he would need to earn another seventy-five hundred dollars a year. Of course, he would not reduce the hundred dollars a month he sent Mama, nor the twenty-five hundred dollars a year he gave to Lina, whom he referred to as the "one member of my staff." Since he anticipated two years' work on *Sacco and Vanzetti,* and since he had both libretto and music to write, he was able to persuade the Ford Foundation that fifteen thousand dollars paid out over twenty-four months was a reasonable assessment of his actual need. Happily, the William Morris Agency informed him that it would not take its regular commission on the grant itself, only on the Met's option and on any royalties from the opera.

Writing the foundation, he promised, "Now I can go to work with zest and a free mind, thanks to your fine project. My deep appreciation, both for the grant, and for the tactful and graceful handling of it."[10] It had all come about so fortuitously. He had returned from Europe with no real creative plans other than his Brecht translations, and no secure prospects for his livelihood. Yet within a few months he managed to parlay a brainstorm almost accidentally arrived at into his living for the next two years.

On February 1, Blitzstein called Bing to let him know that he planned to accept the Met's offer; but he asked that for the moment the acceptance be kept off the record, as the City Opera's *Cradle* was then in preparation and a premature announcement could be awkward.

Rudel had invited the composer to take an active part in the casting and preparation of *Cradle.* Blitzstein asked the City Opera to engage the original music director, Lehman Engel, as conductor, and Engel accepted, making his debut with the company. Also making his debut there, Howard da Silva as director resumed a familiar role in the work. David Hays designed the sets; Ruth Morley created the costumes; and Billy Parsons devised the dances.

*The Ford Foundation played no role in selecting composers or librettists engaged by the companies it funded.

Between singers already engaged by the City Opera and a handpicked crew that Blitzstein brought in from the theatre world, a splendid cast emerged. From the company, Jack Harrold played Editor Daily, and Joshua Hecht Dr. Specialist. Philip Bruns played Professor Trixie, and Nancy Dussault played Sister Mister. Future music critic William Zakariasen, then singing with the company under the name William Saxon, played a reporter. Artists making their first appearances with the City Opera included Tammy Grimes as the Moll, Michael Wager and Chandler Cowles as Yasha and Dauber, William Griffis as Harry Druggist, Sophie Ginn as Sadie Polock, and Jane A. Johnston as Ella Hammer. Cowles, of course, was repeating his role from the 1947 production.

Someone had recommended for the role of Mrs. Mister a former burlesque queen "of a certain age," who came to the audition wearing a fox cape and a feather boa, both dripping from the rain. To give her an idea of what he wanted, Blitzstein crowed through her part entirely in character. When he had finished, the lady trotted out, loudly exclaiming, "Why'nt you do it yourself, dearie?"

Wager, an experienced actor and an avid opera buff with a strong devotion to Maria Callas, recounted how Blitzstein approached him for his role. "Do you want to be in my opera?" his friend Marc asked him one day.

"Is my tessitura right?"

"Mendy, I've heard you sing everything from Isolde to Carmen. Your tessitura's right. Call Rudel."

"I'll be in it on one condition—that my name be followed by 'debut.' "

Blitzstein coached many of the singers privately; Tammy Grimes reported to Blitzstein's apartment daily for two weeks of exacting lessons in phrasing, timing, and breathing. He emphasized a naturally produced speaking voice that would drift seamlessly into the sung passages. One day in a rehearsal of the Faculty Room scene, hearing John Macurdy's trained, "placed" voice that sent President Prexy's lines booming into the house, he asked, "Must you talk like that?" To which Macurdy resonantly replied, "We singers have to talk this way." Ruth Kobart, playing Mrs. Mister, once caught Michael Wager vocalizing too operatically and she chided him, "Mendy, this is not Bellini."

Blitzstein also served as adjunct publicity agent, giving radio interviews and converting his Spoken Arts speech into an article for *Opera News.* One of the Jewish newspapers picked up the City Opera's press release and informed its readers about the revival of—in Yiddish characters—"Dhi Kreidel Vil Rok."

He made a few minor changes in the text. He established the time as 1931, several years before the play's most logical period in the mid- or late 1930s, probably to emphasize the naïveté of the work. He had considered but dropped the idea of dating the action at a time "when unions were young." In his instructions to the press on how to "research" Larry Foreman's record, Mr. Mister in the original play says, "And look up his past till at last you've got it on him." Perhaps because the memory of HUAC was too fresh for him—and after all, the committee still dragged on, holding its hearings, however laughable they had become by then—Blitzstein altered the first words of the line to read, "And make up the rest. . . ." From the perspective of almost twenty-five years, he could appreciate that the CIO union struggle had hardly blown into the "final wind"; so in the City Opera version, Larry Foreman sang more weakly that "a certain wind blows." During the course of the season, he had occasion to write to George Freedley of the New York Public Library: "I like the work still, all except the jokes, which I find atrocious. They couldn't have been any better in 1937."[11]

Other references from 1937 were lost, even to the performers. Only three years old when *Cradle* was first presented, Tammy Grimes stopped one day in rehearsal after singing her big number of the show and asked Howard da Silva, "Just what *does* the phrase 'nickel under the foot' mean?"

Da Silva was the first person with whom she had ever worked who had been blacklisted. He looked at her as if she had dropped in from another planet. "Are you serious?" He patiently explained what it would have meant to the Moll to find a nickel in those days, and he asked the twenty-six-year-old, "What would get you excited about finding?"

"A dollar," she replied.

David Hays designed a set with an appropriate industrial motif and framed it with a false proscenium of steel girders. The cast, assembled on a grandstand at the rear of the stage, assumed position in their scenes and then returned to their places. The proscenium lit up brightly for the Hotel Lobby scene and a section of it lowered to form the drugstore countertop. The actors themselves carried the props on and off the central playing area.

The usual opening-night telegrams arrived at the stage door. From Lenny and Felicia came a LOVING MESSAGE OF HOPE AND GLORY FOR TONIGHT, AND THE LONG FUTURE OF THE CRADLE. AND OF SACCO AND ALL THE OTHERS. Later that night at the party Mina Curtiss gave for Marc at her home in the East Seventies, Blitzstein let Rudel know of his decision to give the new opera to the Met. "Very well," Rudel answered gracefully. "Good luck. Try your wings."

As could be expected, reviewers disagreed dramatically as to the inherent worth of the piece and its appropriateness for the New York City Opera. In a damning broadside in the *Herald Tribune,* the editor of *The Musical Quarterly,* Paul Henry Lang, steamed, "The issues are gone, and what we see is a sort of vaudeville, at times of a very low grade . . . and most of it is only once removed from Tin Pan Alley." Miles Kastendieck of the New York *Journal-American* asked, "Where was the opera?" and answered that the choice was "a blight on the record" of the company, "a sophomoric effort, brashly elemental and artistically crude." He admitted da Silva's direction as a "tour de force," wondering, however, whether it was legitimate to call the Grimes, Wager, and Cowles debuts "operatic." In the *Times,* Howard Taubman repeated the opinion that the ideas of *Cradle* no longer held any urgency, though he praised the courage of the City Opera for presenting the work and longed for a return of the passion and commitment of the thirties. The orchestration, he felt, added little to the show.[13]

On the positive side, Douglas Watt of the *Daily News* called *Cradle* "not out of place" at the City Opera. The basic theme of unionism may be dated now, he said, but it "still carries a punch. . . . Corruption and sycophancy are still very much a part of our national life (turn to the news section)." Harriett Johnson in the *Post* referred to the audience's sustained appreciation for the choreography of the Honolulu number. "Only Engel's unbending attitude prevented an encore." She was not alone in savoring Grimes's performance: "languid, sexy and overwhelmingly successful." *Variety* said of her, "Tammy Grimes as the tramp was the closest thing to a new, young Lotte Lenya which in spite of all replacements during the years of *Three Penny Opera* running has as yet never been found!"[14]

The Nation's Harold Clurman reminded his readers that *Cradle* is, after all, no more dated than *La Bohème:*

> one is sentimental about "workers," the other about "artists". . . . What it typifies is a certain permanent American big-city-young-man cockiness, a derisive unwillingness to take any guff—political, social or casual—from anybody. It's the boy in the candy store, the man at the bar, the alert laborer refusing to be hoaxed by any pretension. It is the poor man's Bronx cheer against complacency that we hear on any city street not yet razed by traffic or the police. . . .
>
> If this opera is retained in the repertory of the New York City Opera, don't let the snobs or the fearful prevent you from seeing it.[15]

But for several reasons the opera was not retained: the difficulty of keeping such an uncustomary cast together; the expense of keeping Lehman Engel as conductor. *Cradle* did not go out on the month-long East Coast and midwestern tour in late February and March because Rudel felt it would have less appeal than the other operas. The final performance on February 21, 1960, was (at this writing) the last time *The Cradle Will Rock* has been staged anywhere with full orchestra.

A tape recording of the City Opera production clearly shows how much the audience took the work to heart, despite what any critics said. Its very appearance on the roster in these waning months of the Eisenhower years seemed to spell a certain finish to the blacklist era. Tammy Grimes wrote to Blitzstein at the end of the season: "Would love to do the album." Sadly, none was made. Jack Harrold also wrote, thanking Blitzstein for the opportunity of working with him: "It was the most thrilling evening in the theatre in my life, and the cheers and applause given to you really brought tears to my eyes."[16]

Rudolf Bing attended the performance on February 17 to see for himself what kind of composer the Met had just optioned, but his reactions went unrecorded. Two days later, he met with Gutman and Blitzstein to float possible production ideas for *Sacco and Vanzetti* and to hand over a formal agreement. Blitzstein proposed Bernstein as conductor and Ben Shahn as set designer, both agreeable to Bing. For the Vanzetti, they agreed that the bass Cesare Siepi would be fine. For Sacco, Blitzstein thought of the tenor Cesare Valletti, but Bing felt that Valletti's voice was deteriorating—in fact, 1960 turned out to be his last season at the Met. "But it's all a bit premature anyway," Blitzstein observed.

23

LOYALTY UNDER ATTACK

February 1960–Summer 1960

"1) the courage; *2) the* poetry"

Toys in the Attic opened at the Hudson Theatre on February 25, 1960, produced by Kermit Bloomgarden, designed by Howard Bay, costumed by Ruth Morley, and directed by Arthur Penn. Set in the Berniers' down-at-the-heels New Orleans household, Hellman's Freudian drama revolves around the twisted love two sisters shower on their prodigal younger brother. His daft wife, barely out of her teens, enters the nest unsuspectingly; it seems he has married her for her money. Adultery, miscegenation, and land speculation round out this neurotic tale of misspent emotions.

For a fee of five hundred dollars, Blitzstein wrote the music to two songs with lyrics by Hellman. The first occurs not long into the opening act when the two sisters, played by Maureen Stapleton and Anne Revere, are discussing a possible trip to Europe. In simple mixed French and English—recalling the Russian and English of "Mamasha Goose"—they practice their communication skills, saying the room offered at a French hotel is "Trop Chère" (or "French Lessons in Songs," as the program lists it). With its style imitating a first-level language lesson, the song brings to mind the "Dites-moi" number from Rodgers and Hammerstein's *South Pacific.*

The second song occurs at the beginning of the third act, and is given to the brother, Julian (Jason Robards, Jr.). He celebrates his financial coup in "Big Day" ("Bernier Day"), based in part on a bayou ballad Blitzstein had uncovered called "Tan patate-la t'chuite" (When your potato's done). As it happened, Robards could play the banjo proficiently and, in his first public display of talent with it, he accompanied himself in the number. Maureen Stapleton could not play the piano, however, and an offstage pianist was hired to play "badly" a few seconds' worth of Chopin's *Valse Brillante* in E-Flat.

The play won the Critics' Circle award for best American drama of the season; it proved to be one of Hellman's most highly regarded stage works, racking up 464 performances before it closed. Many later productions of the play continued to use the two Blitzstein songs.

That February and March, in a series of press releases, the Ford Foundation announced support for Samuel Barber's *Antony and Cleopatra,* Douglas Moore's *Wings of the Dove,* Robert Ward's *The Crucible,* Ned Rorem's *Miss Julie,* Jack Beeson's *Lizzie Borden,* Hugo Weisgall's *Nine Rivers from Jordan,* Marvin David Levy's *Mourning Becomes Electra,* and several more operas. But the release announcing Blitzstein's grant found its way into more than the music pages of the nation's newspapers. Neither Reginald Rose's NBC television drama about the Sacco and Vanzetti case to be aired in June, nor the forthcoming Dino De Laurentiis film, nor the two or three new plays inspired by the story carried anywhere near the impact of an opera slated for the holy Metropolitan Opera stage.

All the fresh attention he received piqued Blitzstein's excitement over the commission. With the interviewer from *Time,* he shared his dream of setting Vanzetti's famous words, "If it had not been for these thing," for a singer like Leonard Warren or Giorgio Tozzi. "This is a hell of a noble story. It is a great and noble theme." To *Newsweek,* he explained that his opera would "explore the inside of people in a social context." Smoking his perpetual cigarette during a talk with the *Herald Tribune*'s Don Ross, Blitzstein admitted that at the moment he had not yet written a line of the libretto or a note of the music. Still buried under mountains of literature on the case, he also had not decided on the style he wanted to use. He had "enough material to write not one but six operas on Sacco and Vanzetti," he mused. "But never fear. I will write only one. . . . I hope to high heaven I'm up to the importance and the grandeur of this theme."[1]

Aside from Cesare Siepi, Blitzstein had imagined Leonard Warren or Giorgio Tozzi as a possible Vanzetti. But just as his interview appeared in *Time* on March 4, Warren suddenly collapsed on the Metropolitan stage while singing the role of Don Carlo in *La Forza del Destino.* He died at age forty-eight of a cerebral hemorrhage. Blitzstein had just turned fifty-five.

"It was good of you to write," Rudolf Bing answered Blitzstein's letter of condolence to the Met:

> It is indeed a terrible loss—but who are we to say "senseless." In any case, Leonard Warren can almost be envied: at the height of his career, in the

> midst of one of his triumphant performances and without a moment of fear or suffering. But, as you rightly say, it will be a long time for us trying to fill the gap.[2]

Almost as soon as the Ford Foundation and the Metropolitan had issued the release about the opera, questions arose. The wording had been vague: "On the recommendation of the Metropolitan Opera, the Ford Foundation has commissioned a new opera by Marc Blitzstein." The composer wrote to the *Herald Tribune* to clarify the matter. The choice of subject remained entirely in the composer's hands. The Ford Foundation only provided financial support for the creation of the work and the later production.

Clarifications in the press notwithstanding, certain journalists raised high-pitched voices in protest. The *National Review* called the commission "a typical venture in ritualistic Liberalism—the thoughtless underwriting of the claim that Sacco and Vanzetti were clearly innocent and clearly railroaded by rampant American hysteria and xenophobia; and the handing of the job over to a noisy, belligerent fellow traveler like Mr. Blitzstein." William F. Buckley, Jr.'s magazine called instead for operas on the martyrs of Communism: "we volunteer to come up with enough names to keep all the musicmakers in the land occupied. . . . Couldn't we make beautiful music writing about them? Or would Mr. Blitzstein's keys stick?" In Washington, J. Edgar Hoover noticed the Washington *Daily News* item about the opera on February 26, and circulated it to his staff. "What do we know about Blitzstein?" he asked.[3]

Nationally syndicated newspaper columnist George Sokolsky was only one writer whose piece "*Sacco and Vanzetti* on the Met Stage?" bore all the earmarks of a timely leak from House Committee on Un-American Activities records—for years Sokolsky had enjoyed privileged access to Hoover's FBI files. Until his article appeared, details of Blitzstein's executive-session testimony on May 8, 1958, had never appeared before the public. Sokolsky fulminated wildly with his theme for the day:

> One would imagine that if the Ford Foundation and the Metropolitan Opera desired an opera on an historic episode in American life, they might have done something on the conspiracy of Aaron Burr or the life of John Brown or the heroism of Robert E. Lee or dozens of subjects that could touch the heartstrings of an American. Instead they seek to have a Rigoletto in a shoe factory worker and a fish peddler who were found guilty in a payroll holdup and executed in 1927 after due process of the law. Why not do an opera on the life of Al Capone or Gyp the Blood or Lefty Louie to say nothing of Jesse James?

Sokolsky proceeded with six paragraphs of background on the "Communist-front" composer, citing the 1958 testimony. How could an opera "about a pair of anarchists" be justified,

> written by one who at a telling period in the history of his country was a Communist which means that he had submitted to the discipline of the Kremlin—a government which since 1917 was an enemy of his country?
>
> I am not, in this article, criticizing Blitzstein. He has done as he chooses; he must assume all the risks which accompany conduct. He was given several opportunities to assist the agencies of his country in safeguarding it from the enemy. He has not done more than he was absolutely required to do by the law. That is his will and his right.
>
> Criticism should indeed be levelled at the Ford Foundation for selecting so poor a theme, so obnoxious and depressing a subject for a subsidized American opera.[4]

Up in Sacco and Vanzetti territory, Edward B. Simmons, local writer for the famously reactionary New Bedford *Standard-Times,* also appeared to have been shown FBI files. In his article "Composer Long Tied to Red Fronts," datelined Washington, Simmons listed various of Blitzstein's old sponsorships and memberships. In the lexicon of antiradicalism, it always seemed more damaging to point to the subject's associations with "front" organizations: At least an honest American Communist would presumably not choose to hide behind them. Simmons particularly delighted in contrasting Blitzstein's claims about injustice in the Sacco and Vanzetti case to the purge trials of the Stalin era, giving the precise date of April 28, 1938, when the *Daily Worker* printed the composer's name in support of the Soviet system.[5]

HUAC, the FBI, and their friends must have expected that a huge public outcry against the commission might result in a formal investigation of the composer on the part of the Met and the Ford Foundation, withdrawal of the money, and a victory for anti-Communism. To be sure, an outpouring of protest letters did arrive in the mailboxes of both institutions, almost every letter a direct result of Sokolsky's column. The Met received batches of letters on the same day, all postmarked from a particular city, followed by another batch a day or two later from somewhere else, a sure sign of the group pressure tactics engaged in by the John Birch Society. Very few letters came from anyone with a connection to the Met or any serious interest in music.

To these letter writers en masse president of the Metropolitan Opera Association Anthony A. Bliss sent a standard response to the effect that the work had not been written yet and the Met remained free to decide about producing the opera. "When submitted, the libretto, as well as the score, will be subject to meticulous scrutiny. In the meantime, since Mr. Blitzstein avows that he no longer maintains his past political affiliations and that the libretto will not be written in an objectionable manner, we do not feel that we should pre-judge the work."

As press director and assistant manager, Francis Robinson also wrote letters on behalf of the Met when a more pointed answer seemed called for. "Neither the Ford Foundation nor the Metropolitan Opera asked Mr. Blitzstein to write an opera on Sacco and Vanzetti. It was he who chose the subject," Robinson replied,

> and I don't think you would want to see our country aligned with Russia and the other dictatorships which tell their artists what and what not to do and suppress works which do not agree with their views. . . . What concerns us most is whether or not the work will be good, and I think you must agree that a subject which still arouses strong feelings more than thirty years after the event must have some dramatic value.

George Sokolsky would not be quieted with Robinson's defense of artistic freedom. He was determined to wrestle the opera to the ground. In a follow-up column, he sneered at Robinson's words and showed his colors as a critic of the arts:

> The Sacco-Vanzetti theme is not good theater. It is not particularly dramatic. . . . The issue has been captured by Communist parties the world over to denounce American justice. Just as the Chessman Case is now being used by the Communists. . . . Will the judge stab himself, as they do in Italian operas, to prove that moral justice lies at the end of a stiletto? . . .
>
> What constructive value can there be in the Sacco-Vanzetti theme, unless it is propaganda against our courts?[6]

The Ford Foundation replied peaceably to the majority of the John Birch-style protests. But to those of obvious position and influence, foundation officers assumed a somewhat less benign attitude. In one letter, president of the foundation and former member of the Loyalty Review Board Henry T. Heald defended artistic integrity free of ideological restraint. But he added, "I don't suppose I have any more enthusiasm for an opera about Sacco and Vanzetti than you have." In another response, John J. McCloy, chairman of the board, reassured his critic, "I doubt that anything will ever come of this particular venture. . . . I agree heartily with you that this is no subject for The Ford Foundation to be dealing with."[7] He may not have known that Henry Ford himself had in 1927 opposed the death penalty for Sacco and Vanzetti.

In an internal foundation memo reporting on the Met's handling of the Blitzstein affair, an officer stated that between Bing and Bliss, "neither of them was acquainted with Mr. Blitzstein's own political past. If they had been aware of all these facts, they would certainly have proceeded more slowly and might not have taken out the option. On the other hand, it is their feeling that Blitzstein has a great sense of theater, perhaps greater than that of many other composers whose music may surpass his." In any case, the memo added, the Met had sought to obtain four or five other commissions in the next half year, "so as to try to have a wide range of new operas among which to choose."[8]

Bing invited Blitzstein to Sherry's for lunch at the end of March to review progress to date on the opera. He advised Blitzstein of the "holocaust" of letters and phone calls, all protesting the opera. One caller from the American Legion threatened to throw up a picket line in front of the Met if they staged any Blitzstein opera about Sacco and Vanzetti. The composer asked the general manager how he felt about such a possibility. Seeming to be reveling in the frisson of scandal almost as much as Blitzstein himself, Bing quipped, "That can only help business!"

Still, having recently seen *Cradle,* Bing asked him to confirm that the libretto would not be inflammatory. "I repeat what I said at our first meeting," Blitzstein told him, sniffing the same case of nerves that infected the Federal Theatre Project. "I guarantee absolutely nothing. As I see it now it will be an overall deep tragedy."

Bing reported that his board also felt "a little jittery" about Blitzstein, though none had actually opposed the project. A few board members, in fact, also happened to be dining at Sherry's that Monday, and Bing made a point of introducing them to the controversial composer. "They all seem very cordial," Blitzstein thought.

When it came time to discuss the actual contract, Bing offered Blitzstein the same figures given to Samuel Barber for *Vanessa:* $750 per performance, and $2,000 for a radio broadcast.

The following day, Bing asked the Metropolitan's lawyer, Lincoln Lauterstein, to prepare the contract. In his instructions, he insisted on keeping the Met's options wide open. "Please make sure that the contract clearly provides—as we had in other cases—'pay or play.' That means to say, *without in any way* 'rubbing it in,' the contract should provide that we are not obliged to perform but only to pay if and when we accept to do the work."[9]

In the weeks following the announcement of the Sacco and Vanzetti opera, hostile reactions—and cautious support—were not all that Blitzstein received. The music critic Paul Henry Lang, who had found Blitzstein's earlier work at the City Opera so amateurish, felt sure that "today, a generation after *The Cradle Will Rock,* he will summon, in his new opera, un-dialectical sentiments and present the tragedy of men rather than that of a milieu."[10] Furthermore, in 1960 many survivors of the case lived on in continuing sympathy with the cause, tirelessly defending the innocence of the two men, searching always for new clues and perspectives.

Gardner Jackson, one of the most persistent members of the Sacco-Vanzetti Defense Committee and an editor of their letters, wrote to Blitzstein at generous length to offer help on the opera. He expressed his "deep rejoicing" that such an opera would be created, and urged Blitzstein to contact Aldino Felicani, a Boston printer and Vanzetti's closest friend, who "knows more about the case than any other living person." At the same time, Jackson wrote separately to Reginald Rose, deep into production of his television dramatization, speculating what Blitzstein as a former Communist might make of the story:

> It's hard for me to suppress anxiety because of my experiences with the CPers during the case. That was my baptism ending with the chairman

> of the Massachusetts CP committee (whom I had helped when he was prosecuted for criminal libel against Governor Fuller) coming to me a few days before our second anniversary memorial meeting (in Old South Church, with Edna St. Vincent Millay, Rabbi Stephen Wise, etc.) and apologetically telling me he would have to call me "one of the murderers of Sacco and Vanzetti" at a rival meeting he had been ordered by the party to stage that night on Boston Common.[11]

Richard Rohman offered to serve as Blitzstein's researcher and co-librettist. One of the first journalists to write about the case and an eyewitness to the events at every stage of the trial and appeals, he was a committed trade unionist and a playwright besides. "I helped bring Miss Vanzetti to this country to plead for her brother's life before Governor Fuller, and I ate my first plate of spaghetti, prepared for me by Rose Sacco herself."[12]

From Washington, D.C., a co-author of *The Legacy of Sacco and Vanzetti,* Louis Joughin, wrote to Rudolf Bing offering to help on the opera. He could provide critical advice not only on the case itself but on the dramaturgy, having spent a quarter of a century teaching drama history and criticism. From Springfield, Massachusetts, Ray M. Wiley, the anarchists' last lawyer, also wrote to offer help.

Blitzstein would listen to little advice on his libretto, however, only seeking out those, such as Aldino Felicani, with an informed point of view on problems he encountered in the writing. He told Bing he had received many letters since the story broke, "some offering real help, others disingenuously wishing to 'get into the act.' I am by this time practically snowed under with research. The work itself begins to move. More than that I dare not say."[13]

Even from Scotland, where news of the commission had made the *Daily Express,* an old friend named Donald McKillop wrote to congratulate Blitzstein: They had met aboard the S.S. *Finland* steaming through the Panama Canal and up the Mexican coast to California many, many years before—the composer was nineteen—passing the time giving impromptu concerts of Scottish ballads.

The Composers' Showcase announced two semistaged concert performances of *No for an Answer* on Monday, April 18 and 25 at the Circle in the Square. Blitzstein and Joseph Liebling, as musical director, assembled a notable cast. Although Michael Kermoyan had been announced for the role of Nick Kyriakos, in the end the original Nick, Martin Wolfson, was available to repeat his performance of nineteen years earlier. Joan Copeland, Arthur Miller's sister, played the role of Clara to Raymond Murcell's Paul. Sophie Ginn, Nancy Dussault, and Philip Bruns had appeared in the City Opera's *Cradle* and came in to *No for an Answer.* Elaine Bonazzi, the Santa Fe Regina, sang the part of Gina. Felice Orlandi, husband of Alice Ghostley, played Joe, and Dino Narizzano, a Method actor and later an Off-Broadway producer, played Max Kraus. Since all the actors had memorized their roles, director Bernard Gersten from the American Shakespeare Festival staged the work almost as a full production.

As in *Cradle,* Blitzstein reassigned the action to the year 1931. He compressed much of the dialogue between the fourteen musical numbers into brief connecting narratives, which he read in the performances. He took the opportunity to restore the "Outside Agitator" number, deleted from the 1941 production but just as timely now, with Southern officials braying about all the Northern civil rights activists working for black voting rights.

Howard Taubman, whose recent review of *Cradle* was lukewarm at best, now claimed that it had had "the vitality of a clean hit. *No for an Answer* is more like a soft pop fly. . . . The serious fault is that the material is essentially heavy-handed and commonplace." It "bogs down in a swamp of proletarian clichés." The *Village Voice* did not consider the work a "credit to Blitzstein's talents." The *Herald Tribune* critic enjoyed the score "exceedingly well. The touching and courageous story . . . contains a lot of sincere fetching music and a book which, to these ears, seemed not to be dated at all." Though selected numbers from the show have been performed numerous times since in a variety of settings, the complete opera has (at this writing) never been heard again.[14]

An editor of *Esquire* who had attended a performance wrote Blitzstein the next day offering to publish the *Sacco and Vanzetti* text. George Braziller of the Book Find Club also said he would be "extremely interested in publishing a reading version of the book."[15]

In the absence of a clear commitment on the stage rights to *Mahagonny,* a concert version of the Blitzstein translation might at least take place. The New York Philharmonic announced it for May 5–8, 1960—under Leonard Bernstein—as part of a three-week Festival of Theatre Music. But Stefan Brecht refused to settle on mutually agreeable terms, and early in March the Philharmonic canceled its plans. Hopes for the Blitzstein *Mother Courage* dimmed perceptibly, but some lingering flickers remained. In early 1960, Lee Paton announced a production of Eric Bentley's translation, but Stefan Brecht challenged her in court, asserting that Bentley did not have the rights. Again he came to the defense of the Blitzstein translation, claiming it was still slated for the Circle in the Square.

To a limited extent, Blitzstein followed through with some of the offers of help on Sacco and Vanzetti, and was himself able to offer his advice to others. On May 15 he traveled out to the NBC studios on Avenue M in Brooklyn to meet with Reginald Rose and Robert Alan Aurthur, producer of the television program. Blitzstein's extensive suggestions on several drafts of Rose's script indicate that his advice had been sought; some of his ideas for cutting, rewording, and on pronunciation apparently found their way into the final script. The day turned into something of a reunion of Sacco and Vanzetti scholars. Gardner Jackson and Aldino Felicani were there. Tom O'Connor, secretary of the Committee for the Vindication of Sacco and Vanzetti, had come down from Massachusetts. Present also was Michael A. Musmanno, a judge on the Pennsylvania State Supreme

Court who wrote extensively on the legal history of the case.* All of these men would continue to encourage the composer.

As summer approached, Blitzstein broke away briefly from his labors on the new opera to write an article for the *Saturday Review.* In "Music's Other Boulanger," he paid tribute to the music of Lili Boulanger, recorded on Everest by the Orchestre Lamoureux and chorus under Igor Markevitch. The young composer had died in 1918 at the age of twenty-four. Her music, Blitzstein wrote, "is more than good. It is extraordinary. Make no mistake: here was an original talent, a talent afire, bold, uncompromising, marvelously in command, impatient with prettiness and triviality . . . masculine in its rugged force, utterly feminine in its purity and lyrical outpouring."[16]

From 36, rue Ballu, her older sister Nadia thanked "Dear Mark" for the appreciation; she was all the more affecting, somehow, for her idiosyncratic use of English:

> You know, I feel, what your article means to me—more than I can ever say. In what has remainded a burning sorrow, it is such an happiness to feel you have been so impressed—and you have said it. To my last day, I shall see my little one saying with a sad smile, soft, accepting her fate: "Is it not strange—every one will have heard this music except myself." And so was it.
>
> Feel how profoundly I am touched—your article is so understanding, so human,—it is for me an unvaluable tribute.
>
> As ever, & with a same, an older affection, I am faithfully your
> Nadia B[17]

For the entire summer, Blitzstein rented a cottage near Lillian Hellman's house at South Beach on Martha's Vineyard. He loved walking up and down the shoreline, bracing himself against the high winds. His arguments with Hellman—both of them were litigious hard drinkers—carried on the entire season. By now happily enjoying the largesse of the Ford Foundation, he alternated his pursuit of Sacco and Vanzetti with work on a three-hundred-dollar commission from Alice Esty for a song cycle. The wife of a prominent New York advertising agency executive who handled the Nescafé and Winston cigarettes accounts, Esty possessed a not bad soprano voice. Though she had no talent for a professional career, she commissioned art songs from leading composers as a hobby. Every year she would offer a program featuring her latest collection.

For his texts, Blitzstein decided to return to E. E. Cummings, titling his set *From Marion's Book,* Marion being the wife of the poet. Work on Cummings recalled the 1920s in several ways. The poetry reflects that same cubistic, nonlinear spirit of the time; its jumbled language could be useful for the composer as

*Though a defender of the two anarchists' rights, Musmanno had a peculiar kind of tunnel vision: As a young law student in Italy, he had publicly praised Mussolini's attacks on the left-wing opposition, and in 1950 he had played a scandalously partisan role in railroading Communist Party members into prison.

training for setting the irregular prose of his immigrant subjects. Musically, too, with the song cycle, he felt liberated from the need to appeal to a popular audience. As were his early treatments of Cummings thirty years before and his opera for the Met, this was musicians' music. One piece included in the set of seven is "when life is quite through with," written in 1929 and altered only very slightly.

In August, the cycle completed, he wrote to Esty and her accompanist David Stimer with his sometimes cryptic breakdown of the songs:

> I. *o by the by:* This is obviously a kite; the image must be kept throughout, of a comical volatility. Poignance at the diving and the climbing, and especially at the "throbbing like . . . singing like. . . ." And then a final frustration (comic again) as the string is let go.
> II. *when life is quite through with:* Elegiac, muted; at the grave of the beloved.
> III. *what if a much of a which of a wind:* A kind of young, roistering paean to the indomitableness of man. It is strophic; the three stanzas are set to exactly the same music, with some tempo variation in the third verse. Watch out for the meaning at the end: "The most who die the more we live" means "the most *of us* who die," so that the sentence is not callous or cutthroat at all; simply stated, there is no nothing, the "single secret will still be man."
> IV. *silent unday by silently not night:* The most ambitious of the lot. Death, purgatory, transfiguration; or, death-not-death, raging breaking-apart, the rising of the phoenix.
> V. *until and i heard:* Possibly the hardest to perform. Light as a feather, yet soaring, with a lyrical rising to the triumphant "grave gay brave bright cry of alive."
> VI. *yes is a pleasant country:* Tiny, slight, but not trivial or facetious. Again affirmation.
> VII. *open your heart:* I like it the best of the lot. We need big climaxes and sudden hushes; and then the last phrases, quieter and quieter, to the endless word "ocean."[18]

The Cummings cycle encompasses worlds in its tight dimensions—seasons of the year, humanity in its interaction with nature, wonder, exuberance, and mortality. Without calling for special vocal devices or any extraordinary feats of contemporary musicianship, the composer asks for concentration on a variety of interpretive moods that together comprise almost a solo scena for the performer. In the keyboard part, he wastes little effort on overburdening the structure with unnecessary pianism. Especially in the spare places, the simple monumentality of Hugo Wolf comes to mind.

Inviting Ned Rorem to come up to the Vineyard for a visit, Blitzstein nevertheless warned, "I'll be lousy company; all work and swimming, that's me this summer. The opera is hard, hard. I do nearly twelve hours a day. I suppose I'll look back on this period of struggle with love and envy." John Gutman of the Metropolitan Opera wrote to Blitzstein in early June with a breakdown of the Met's orchestra, saying, "I hope most of *Sacco and Vanzetti* has been written by now." In reply, Blitzstein confirmed the "considerable struggle, not to say pain" he was experiencing with the composition. He had seen the television show on Sacco and Vanzetti and found it "absorbing, admirable and cold." The Boston station carrying the program had been threatened with pickets and boycotts, and NBC's Robert Aurthur had received a pile of denunciations by mail and by phone. "I have always known that the subject was bound to be a red-hot potato," Blitzstein wrote. "It is also for me the very essence of tragic nobility."[19]

For some time the Committee for the Vindication of Sacco and Vanzetti had fought, with the sympathy of Representative Alexander J. Cella, for a complete reexamination of the case. During this Martha's Vineyard summer, Blitzstein was studying the *Verbatim Record* of the 1959 Massachusetts Judiciary Committee hearing on the case. Tom O'Connor of the Vindication Committee, who had preoccupied himself with the case for nearly forty years, tried to save Blitzstein countless hours by directing him straight to the most critical testimony. But nothing and no one could approach Blitzstein too closely: The libretto would be entirely his own, whatever the cost.

He had become a man obsessed. He accepted no limits on what he demanded of himself to know about the case. How could he be sure that in the next article he read, in the next book he studied, or in conversation with the next expert on the case, he would not discover the key to his opera? Assiduously he underscored significant sentences in his library of source material on the case, pointing out in scrupulous marginalia all of the errors and contradictions, cross-referencing one account to another. He made a reminder to himself written into the book of Sacco and Vanzetti letters: "Take note of *all* underlined passages—not only pages with flap-notes! In fact, take note of *every word* written!!"

At the same time that Blitzstein researched the case, he constructed outlines of acts and scenes, sketched his characters, stated and restated his basic themes, and occasionally jotted a few bars of music.

> I shall start with the two men, burning with idealism; both poor, both "innocents"—but very different, one from the other: Sacco, "physical," the manual laborer, not very articulate, but ebullient, impulsive, gay or moody; married to Rosa, with the child Dante and the infant Ines. Vanzetti is the mental type, intellectual, dreamer, mystic: eloquent yet quiet, a "reasoning man"; not married and lonely; the spokesman for the two.

In his two main characters, not to mention in the cast of their sympathizers, Blitzstein had found another example of the necessary union of the physical with the mental—workers and intellectuals—and he enjoyed thinking of appropriate arias for them to sing. For Sacco, he wrote out the text of an extended solo about piecework on shoes, in which the craftsman laments that unlike in his garden, and unlike making a baby with his wife, his skill is reduced to the low demands of assembly-line, mass-production manufacture:

> *So listen Massachusetts*
> *You taught me what I know*
> *But do not let me use it*
> *Go take my finished edges*
> *And pass them to next man*
> *Is all you let me do*
> *When so much more I can*
> *It gave me such a little satisfaction*
> *Who want to make a whole shoe*
> *Patience, patience.*

He also retrieved the song "With a Woman to Be" from *Reuben Reuben,* rewriting the text as Sacco's disoriented jail house soliloquy of longing for Rosa. For Vanzetti, he imagined an aria about his precious books that were taken away from time to time by the prison authorities.

By now he was convinced of Mina Curtiss's idea: That whatever their personal flaws—and these are required in any definition of tragedy—the two men "grow like thunder in their martyrdom," attaining in their death the nobility life never proposed for them. "By the time we get to the end (the executions), we should have built S and V into the type of 'heroes' . . . whereby the music can take on grandeur *for the first time*—and over and beyond tragedy." Arrested and tried for the wrong reasons, the wrong reasons became the real reasons: They were foreigners, agitators, and radicals. "Who killed them?" Blitzstein asked of himself. "Officialdom? (Gov., D.A., Judge, jury). 'Public' opinion? The sick interaction of both."

As playwright, Blitzstein felt that he needed to balance the principals in the case against images of the man in the street. Here he wanted to show both sides of the public. He portrayed the unconcerned in a speakeasy setting; there, through an alcoholic haze, their consciousness is dominated on the night of the execution by escapist flapper antics. Perhaps, as in the Night Court of *Cradle,* the speakeasy would return at several points in the opera for continued soundings of the public temper. Here the chorus would comment on the action, and there would be room for talk about big money and the Wall Street boom, Prohibition and bootleg whiskey, captured in musical forms such as the Charleston and the shimmy—"the Hello-Suckers, Everybody-Happy? mood and psychology," as he expressed it.

Troubling in their inevitability as the unconcerned bystanders might have been to Blitzstein, the protesters posed a different kind of problem. Worldwide, the main force on the left from the 1920s on had been the Communist parties with their Moscow allegiance. The anarchist and syndicalist movements that survived the First World War could not compete with the allure of the Soviet Union, the world's first socialist state. The Communists in every country had been responsible for organizing a large proportion of the mass demonstrations against the "dollar-justice" being carried out in America. Yet, Blitzstein wondered in Martha's Vineyard, "The making of an international issue—the universal outcry—does it help the defendants, or is it actually (partly) responsible for their inevitable doom?" The authorities could not allow themselves to be seen backing down to such pressure, and they continued unrelentingly on their deadly course. Perhaps no other form of petition could have saved the two men—everything else had been tried. But still, probably for the first time, Blitzstein had to reassess the value of public protest.

Even though he had not seen Gardner Jackson's letter to Reginald Rose about the Massachusetts Communist Party, in numerous other places he read claims that most of the funds collected by the Communists had never reached the Defense Committee. To those not sympathetic with the Communists, the Party seemed more interested in holding up the trial as an object lesson in capitalism, more zealous to promote itself than to save two anarchists from the chair. Indeed, more and more, it appeared, the Party had a greater tactical stake in their deaths than in their lives.

As he read through the various accounts, he found his old loyalties under further attack. Even from their prison cells Sacco and, particularly, the intellectual Vanzetti denounced the authoritarian régime set up by the Bolsheviks in Russia. "This Achilles-heel is part of the nature of many left-wing dissidents in the orthodox left. The real enemy is imperialistic capitalism; but the larger-bulking foe, the immediate antagonist, is the 'Stalinist,' on whom they shower the strongest vituperation." So Blitzstein wrote in a memorandum on the character of Aldino Felicani. But significantly he added: "It works the other way too: cf. CP's vs. Social Democrats; in Germany (pre-Hitler and later), in Spain, etc."

Blitzstein found little to oppose in the anarchist credo Sacco and Vanzetti espoused. Though surely in *Juno* he showed a revulsion against ideological arrogance and an attraction toward a more broadly felt humanism, he had left the Party more than ten years before without adopting any other single point of view. Now he was deep in a confrontation with men on the left committed to a consistent and humane class-conscious position free of the constraints of Marx, Lenin, and Stalin. This may be why he felt the influence of *Mahagonny* so strongly in these years. Engaged, yes. But as he had put it in the *Saturday Review*, "it lends itself to no specific social or political sponsorship."

Lenny and Felicia Bernstein also spent their summers on Martha's Vineyard. Every summer, they took two or three days off from everything they were doing to create a fifteen-minute home movie, usually a parody of some big commercial success. The theme for this year's production was *Exodus*, and its title was "Call Me Moses." Shooting on the beach at Lambert's Cove, they improvised costumes out of bathrobes and sheets, and hats out of lamp shades. Though essentially a Bernstein family affair, visitors and friends played supporting roles. The key roles of Pharaoh and Moses went to Lenny and his brother Burton; their wives played Mrs. Pharaoh and Mrs. Moses. Since Marc was on hand, he played the vicious Egyptian taskmaster who beats the Hebrews into servile submission. At the end, the Hebrews escape across the Red Sea on water skis, while the Egyptians in hot pursuit on their own skis simply fall into the ocean—an effect achieved in the film simply by slowing down the boat until the skiers could no longer stand. It was all great fun, a welcome respite from serious thought, into which Marc threw himself with complete abandon.

When he returned to his opera, Blitzstein found himself in such confusion that he intently considered Hellman's view—that the opera should not even focus on Sacco and Vanzetti themselves. Rather, it should reveal the social dynamic around them that could lead to such a tragedy. Actually, she advised Marc, "Don't think of it as a 'tragedy.' Don't treat it as such. The *satirical* approach, whereby people can be made both funny and touching (which is to say both reprehensible and understandable) could be good." To which Blitzstein thought, "I have *that* talent; and who knows *who* has the rare talent for tragedy?"

From the beginning, self-doubt plagued his every working hour on *Sacco and Vanzetti.* That summer he asked himself, "Do I have 1) the *courage;* 2) the *poetry* to tackle this?"

24

NOSTALGIA DELL'ITALIA

Fall 1960–May 1962

"I break the news, am curiously saddened."

A second wave of protest over the Ford Foundation commission spilled into the press over the summer. Dozens of newspapers across the country picked up a syndicated editorial on the subject; only in a portion of the cases could the foundation know which papers had run it, and of these only some chose to print the foundation's explanatory letter. Many editorials paired Sacco and Vanzetti with the Caryl Chessman case—once again, they snorted, in the name of "due process" or some other legal nicety, the liberals and radicals wanted to make martyrs out of common criminals. The striking similarity of posture indicates the existence of a strong campaign on the part of the John Birch Society, the American Legion, and other ultraconservatives to circulate the George Sokolsky columns to newspaper editors and special-interest groups. William F. Buckley, Jr.'s article in *American Legion Magazine* carried a photograph of Blitzstein, identified as "a composer with a front record," a theme echoed in *U.S. News and World Report*'s coverage of the story. With the National Federation of Music Clubs—private piano teachers, for the most part—they succeeded in having a resolution opposing the commission passed at their national convention that summer, which in turn brought more publicity.

It seemed as though the furor would never quiet down. The more public awareness of the project grew, the more Blitzstein struggled to produce his dangerous work, and the more blocked he became. Musically, his generation had written off the Metropolitan Opera as a den of conservatism, a haven of anti-Semitism, a largely irrelevant repository of standard war-horses. Here was his chance, bigger than anything before, to prove himself as a composer. Politically, the McCarthyites had appeared to be receding, but here they were again, raising their heckling voices against him. This would be his opportunity to "refute" his tendentious past with the Party, reinventing his vision of America in a new affirmation of independent humanism. Now, with the spotlight upon him, where was the opera?

The year before, he had thoroughly relished European living, even if none of his music got performed as a result of his efforts. Partly to flee the public eye in America and escape the usual distractions of New York, partly to absorb the Italian atmosphere he was trying to recreate in *Sacco and Vanzetti,* partly just to enjoy life abroad again, Blitzstein decided on a long residency in Rome. During his absence, he subleased his apartment to Mordy and Irma Bauman. Once again, as he had done before going off to war, he made out a revised will. With thoughts of mortality, he designated the Library of Congress as the site for his collection of papers. He also took the time that fall to visit Alice Esty and coach her on his Cummings song cycle whose premiere in March he would have to miss.

He flew to Paris on November 1, where he purchased a new Peugeot. He was in Florence within the week, staying once again with David Diamond and his Italian companion Ciro.

The night he dined with Francis Thorne and his family, he arrived with at least a couple of drinks already in him and seemed a bit testy. At the dinner table, Ann Thorne asked, "How is *Sacco and Vanzetti* going?"

Without warning, Blitzstein exploded. He raged at her ferociously, "You don't ask a composer a question like that!"

A long pause ensued—embarrassed, terrified silence all around. Then the Thornes' thirteen-year-old daughter Candy innocently offered her opinion, "I think that's a very obvious question to ask a composer." At that, Blitzstein broke into a wild, almost uncontrollable laughter. He could hardly fail to appreciate his own absurd hypersensitivity.

On November 9, Marc, David, and Ciro drove down to Rome, and Blitzstein began looking for a flat. Hellman was in town; he had dinner with her and William and Tally Wyler. A few days later, he found the top-floor apartment he would call home for the next seven months, via della Colonna Antonina, 52. He rented it from the Baronessa Lazzaroni, who had installed all new furnishings, using beams removed from a castle she owned that dated back to the year 1400. The small mansard featured a terrace as large as the apartment itself from which he could enjoy commanding views of the city in almost every direction. He described it to Claire Reis: "I glance out and see the old-tile roofs, the tawny-tanned building in front that is the Camera dei Deputati (made by Bernini), and even the Cathédrale Engloutie (which is St. Peter's) on my left."[1] His piano was a Czech-made baby grand Petrof. His next-door neighbor turned out to be

Clemente Castelbarco Albani, the son of Wally Toscanini; and directly below lived a chief justice who, whenever he saw the *maestro americano,* would burst out in arias from *Werther.*

Blitzstein's first visitors were Jo and Ed, who stayed in Rome for a week. Together they explored Tivoli, Hadrian's Villa, and the Etruscan Museum. A week later, Kit and his family arrived on their way from Spain to Sicily. "I see now how I can manage my daily routine," Blitzstein wrote to Lina. "See just enough people to keep me amused, and nevertheless get the opera moving."[2]

In theory, he planned to take one day off work each week to see the city. He liked stumbling on surprises, such as the plaque on the house where Verdi had lived in Rome during the winter of 1859. Might he have imagined a plaque for himself on via della Colonna Antonina, 52? Above all other sites, he fell in love with Piazza San Ignazio, which he thought the most theatrical place in the world, its baroque contours made for magisterial entrances and exits. And he returned again and again to the Capitoline Museum, just to stand contemplating the marble *Dying Gaul,* the wounded soldier's strength slowly ebbing from a mesmerizing athletic form he could adore without shame. Rome worked its endless fascinations on him far more often than one day a week.

> Mama dear:
>
> Just beside my house is a tiny trattoria, or restaurant. The proprietor is charming, and sends food up to me as I want it; or I go down for lunch. . . . Yesterday, one of the small rooms of his restaurant had only individual men at each table—deputies from the Chamber (lower House of Italy), right across the street. My tavern-owner had evidently told them I was a composer—because they talked back and forth to each other of Vivaldi and Bach, rivalling for my attention. They are all so theatrical here, making an operatic production of the smallest thing. You cannot imagine the excitement in my flat, when finally the Murphy beds (larger ones, changed by the Baronessa expressly for me) managed to enter their grooves properly. Singing and dancing, no less. The people are also cynical, sad, happy and stubborn. I love them.[3]

As always, he loved the challenge of expressing himself in half-known languages. He welcomed the opportunity with the workmen to discuss and understand the vocabulary of their trade. In his notebooks he also jotted down regional slang:

"gay"
frocio } Romano
finocchio }
cazz'impero—(imperial prick)
orecchione ("Queen")—Naples
buaiolo—Firenze
zia (auntie)—all Italy.

Toward the middle of December, Blitzstein noticed that the Teatro Parioli would shortly put on Mino Roli and Luciano Vincenzoni's play about Sacco and Vanzetti. Interest in the case had reawakened among the Italians, too. He met with the actors and producers, attended rehearsals, and studied the content and structure of the play. He clipped all of the coverage on it in the Italian press, even taking the time to translate word for word a lengthy but deeply flawed background article on the case in *Il Successo.* He read interviews with Vincenzina Vanzetti, Bartolomeo's sister. He never tried to locate her, but she knew of his opera—she had written to Aldino Felicani in Boston inquiring when it might be finished.

His own presence on the set of the play itself brought about a certain amount of press attention. Professor Robert Clements interviewed him for an article mentioning various Sacco and Vanzetti activities that he would publish in the fall of 1961 in the *Columbia University Forum.* The Milan weekly *ABC* carried a full-page portrait of Blitzstein on January 8, 1961. The interviewer quoted Blitzstein's pleasure with the Baronessa's apartment. "The only thing that bothers me is the clock," he said, referring to the clock on the Palazzo di Montecitorio just outside his window. "It reminds me too obsessively of the passage of time."[4]

But time is what seemed boundless in the Eternal City, as Blitzstein settled into the casual discipline of his long, underwritten working vacation. A stroll in an unfamiliar quarter, dinner with friends from America, or an excursion out of town would always rescue him from despair. Sundays he would often spend with Beverly Pepper at her studio at Monte Mario. He had met her in the summer of 1959 when he passed through Rome. She had been a painter primarily, but in 1960 after visiting the ancient Buddhist temples at Angkor Wat in Cambodia, she switched to sculpture. Blitzstein did not much care for her abstract forms, but gradually he came to respect the vigors of her working process. "We artists live to work, not work to live," he would say to her. He dissipated his sense of isolation with a stream of letters back home—to Lina, to Mama, to Jo.

Lina was doing some casting for Tony Richardson, who wanted Marc's advice. Did he know of a black dancer-singer-actor in New York?

> I have more-or-less forgiven him his "naughtiness" regarding *Juno*—my god, if I have forgiven Orson all his misbehaviors, who is Tony to imagine himself in *that* class? Orson is here, at Fregene (pronounced Fray-jenay), a seaside village a half-hour away—and I am to go up to dinner with him and Paola next week. Thank heavens there is now no business to talk about—we can be our utter silly selves, and talk just the time of day or poetry or gossip.
>
> Work is fine—I am at that point where solutions for stuck-spots that have lasted months occur suddenly and exactly; and it all comes out as it should. So that's nice.[5]

Mama dear:

. . . I went out to see Orson and Paola (his wife) at their shore-villa in Fregene last night. It's about forty minutes out of town, and Orson insisted on sending his car and chauffeur for me. It turned out to be a comedy all around; his car (a Mercedes-Benz) broke down within two minutes, we had to leave it in a parking-spot, and went after my own car instead. But I'm glad the chauffeur was along; the fog was so thick all the way you had to know the winding road like a book to get anywhere. Orson is fine, plump as a butter-ball on pasta and wine, and still talking big and still the same charmer. Paola is wasp-thin and very beautiful, and a love. The five-year old progeny, Beatrice, is bi-lingual and curtseys English style at the drop of a hat. I had a fine time, and got back at 3 A.M.! So this morning was sort of work-wasted. Never mind. I can afford it.[6]

With Jo in particular he shared his most revealed self—problems with the opera, the occasional breakthroughs, anecdotes of life in Rome:

(December 7, 1960, working on the second act) . . . but keep going back to the first as new thoughts strike me.

(December 11, 1960) There's going to be a good opera here. . . . The whole trick is, as always, concentration.

(December 15, 1960) The music goes like the wind; but the libretto keeps limping, mostly in terms of tone and style.

(January 8, 1961, describing his work) . . . really good . . . I'm pleased. . . . My upstairs watchtower-hideaway-aerie-attico-what have you continues a dream; and makes me into a dream-boy, its only disadvantage.

(January 11, 1961) I have a real hold on the two main characters. The others still elude me somewhat. . . . I am still as happy as a minx-eyed lynx and vice-versa with Rome.

(January 20, 1961, quoting John F. Kennedy's inaugural address) "If a free society cannot help the many who are poor, it cannot save the few who are rich." So THAT is to be the keystone: save the poor *for* the rich. Well, what else did we expect?

Up and down as far as the work goes. The main trouble is that I keep getting new ideas that throw out the old: a sure sign of amateurism. Forget it; I'll get it right.

(February 1, 1961, about a radio interview with Jean Genet) Asked how he liked Rome, he said shortly, "I detest Rome." Pause. "May I ask why?" "Because here everything is for sale, including men and boys." Consternation, the show clipped off the air like a shot, and tango music substituted. I giggled all through dinner. Why can't someone blow up the works like that in New York?

(February 14, 1961) I'm not writing well these days. . . . [It is] not fatigue . . . [Rome is] a temptress if there ever was one. . . . Lumumba's assassination was a shocker even for Belgium. . . . Front-row seat (from my apartment) of the student-riots in front of the Camera dei Deputati. They were fascist-led (so students can be *lumpen* too). . . . I now know what a mob is. Useful too, for at least one scene in S-V.

(February 18, 1961, sending birthday greetings; now the left is demonstrating about Lumumba) This time there were more *polizia* and more cracked heads, of course. . . . I can't give Krushchev much either for trying to break up the UN, clearly his tactic of the moment.

(February 27, 1961) And now in a minute it'll be my birthday. I don't feel a thing, not 56, not 20, not even old. And of course I am, and my pace shows it. This damned work is taking it out of me, I'm free to admit. Or Rome. Or the *scirocco.* When I concentrate it's fine, and I skim along. But I have more, and greater moments of doubt—doubt, hell, revulsion. It's all in the cards, as one used to say; and I'll be smart as a whip when it's finished, and will have forgotten all the soul-wracking (what a high phrase!) hours and days it cost, and will blithely step into the next trap. Peace! (It's wonderful.)

This is just a mood, and I have no business to let it out on you. It isn't my birthday that has sparked it, I assure you: I had it once when I began here, and about once monthly since:—hey! Maybe I'm having my odious version of the climacteric. If so, that's just a bore, and not worth the noting.

As I write, I am looking over my left shoulder (you remember the layout of my room) at the goddamndest sunset anybody ever saw. And I'm not even letting myself react to it; such is the puritanical guilt-gift of my tribe and my environmental conditioning.

Forgive. And love. M.

What you want to know is: AM I HAPPY? Well, of course.[7]

Sweat poured out of him, yet little of the opera hung together right. With an excitement that could be maddening, new thoughts would lead him into completely different approaches, revised scenes, third and fourth drafts. Beverly Pepper heard him howl with hysterical delight, telling the story of how he smoked his first marijuana cigarette. He had always wondered whether it truly made people as productive as they said it did, so one evening he tried a joint offered by an acquaintance. For hours and hours far into the night, he sat at the keyboard and composed. When he awoke from bed the following morning, he hurried to the piano to see what he had written. Exactly one note.

Between the resident Americans and the visitors to Rome that year, Blitzstein kept his social calendar well occupied. Among the music people, some of them in residencies at the American Academy in Rome, were composers Gail Kubik and Otto Luening, translator and musicologist William Weaver, and duo-pianists Paul Sheftel and Joseph Rollino. Marc took readily to Sheftel's wife Sara who, like Felicia Bernstein, was a petite Chilean with a soothing accent, although less petite that winter with a baby on the way. At one party at the Sheftels' in January, Blitzstein embarrassed himself and his hosts by venting his still-vivid thirties anger against another guest, the anti-Stalinist composer and critic Arthur Berger. Yet on successive days, the two composers kept each other company by attending concerts together. Others he met included Fellini, the comedian Shelley Berman, and Janet McDevitt, a photographer with whom he became good friends. Irene Diamond returned to Rome for a visit with Marc. Kermit Bloomgarden showed up, as did Virgil Thomson, Martha Gellhorn, Cheryl Crawford, and Morris Golde.

In April Blitzstein left Rome for a week to attend the Venice Music Festival. Writing to Jo letting her know of his plan to visit the city, he recalled, "I saw it once with Papa in 1926, and once alone on a chill November day of 1932 . . . both times I felt it was an anachronism, full of rats and motor-oil smell." He planned to drive there with the theatrical producer Ethel Reiner and Sylvia Lyons, wife of the columnist. "I'll get the two dames off by themselves when I want to prowl."[8]

In Venice, Blitzstein attended all of the major performances. He saw Britten's *Noye's Fludde* and visited the Isola di San Giorgio for an electronics concert. On April 12 while there, he recorded in his diary, "Gagarin makes first orbital flight-in-space! (USSR)." The main event of the festival, however, was the premiere on April 13 of Luigi Nono's anti-imperialist protest opera *Intolleranza,* set to texts by Brecht, Sartre, Eluard, and Mayakovsky. Neofascists in the audience demonstrated their objections to his "contamination" of Italian music with leaflets, police whistles, and stink bombs, but conductor Bruno Maderna kept it going without interruption. Blitzstein sat in the Teatro Fenice with Ethel Reiner and Ann and Francis Thorne. Exhilarated to be a witness to these extraordinary goings-on, Blitzstein realized he had finally been outclassed. He remarked to his companions, "None of my own scandals can touch this one!"

To comply with the regulations of his tourist visa, Blitzstein had to leave and reenter the country, and he took the opportunity one day to drive his Peugeot over into Yugoslavia via Trieste. He exchanged a bit of money, had lunch with the Yugoslavian customs officer, then returned to Venice. "I really have gone for the city at last," he told Jo. "It's messed-up beauty, but real beauty."[9]

On his return from Venice, he had disturbing news from Jo: Ed was seriously ill. Knowing Jo's stoicism, and perhaps wanting to feel needed, Marc offered to go home if he could be of any help. "Call on me; for once, don't spare me, spare yourself. If you don't want me, I shall also understand."[10] But Kit had returned home to be nearby, and within two weeks Ed had improved.

There was other news from home to deal with. Dashiell Hammett had died in January, and Blitzstein cabled his condolences to Hellman. Not long after, a good friend of Lina's passed away, and Marc wrote to Lina, "Dear, I am so sorry for you. I know very well what a wrench it must be. We know how much death is a part of life, don't we?"[11]

Blitzstein and Morris Golde had been friendly with a talented young radio writer named Bobby Cone. Occasionally they had visited his house on Water Island, off Long Island. The tiny boat Cone used to get back and forth was notorious for its leaks. One time, Blitzstein got angry with Cone when they suddenly had to bail out. How could he dare subject his guests to this kind of danger? One day in April 1960 in the middle of a storm, Cone tried to cross to the mainland. The boat capsized and Cone drowned. When the estate was settled in the spring of 1961, it turned out that Cone had left Blitzstein ten thousand dollars. Feeling guilty with the taint of inherited money, he divided it between Lina and his mother as a contribution toward their support.

The American Shakespeare Festival production of *A Midsummer Night's Dream* had been on tour that fall and winter, opening in Boston in September and closing in Washington, D.C., in February. In light of the company's precarious financial condition, Blitzstein gave up his royalties from the score. In February he celebrated the new status achieved by *The Threepenny Opera*—longest-running musical in American history. He also signed a license for Bobby Darin and Jackie Cooper to perform "Mack the Knife" on television. Advised of the forthcoming thirtieth wedding anniversary party for Louis Schweitzer and Lucille Lortel, one of *Threepenny*'s producers, Blitzstein wrote an eight-stanza parody of "Mack the Knife" for Gerald Price to sing as a surprise:

> *At the opening/ of the new play*
> *Gorgeous glamor/ weaves a spell.*
> *See that couple/ down in Row A?*
> *Mister Schweizer [*sic*],/ Miss Lortel.*
>
> *Now she rarely/ shops for diamonds.*
> *No, the Lady/ known as Lou*
> *Tells the salesgirl:/ "I want something*
> *In a playwright;/ maybe two.*
>
> *"How's your Beckett?/ How's Ionesco?*
> *Is your Genet/ in its prime?*
> *How's your Blitzstein/ out of Brecht-Weill?—*
> *That should last me/ quite a time."*

Alice Esty premiered the Cummings songs at Carnegie Recital Hall on March 13, along with other new commissions from Paul Bowles and Germaine Tailleferre. Martin Bernheimer of the *Herald Tribune* praised Esty's lofty goals in commissioning so much new music, "although her vocal resources are rather limited." One can wonder if with such relatively inauspicious launchings, the music she commissioned truly received the musical and critical attention it deserved. "Mr. Blitzstein's angular *From Marion's Book,* based on lines by E. E. Cummings," Bernheimer reported, "provided the most humor of the evening." In the *Times,* Eric Salzman wrote, "The Blitzstein songs . . . had a kind of bit-of-everything bounce and bite that was sometimes effective."[12] In 1962 Chappell published them, twenty-three pages priced at $2.50, though managing to misprint the dedication "To Alice Estey."

"Work is once again ok," Blitzstein wrote to Mama, trying without much sense of conviction to reassure her of his happiness:

> What a deal, to be at the mercy of oneself! I ought to sit back and enjoy it; instead I lacerate myself, saying (as though I were an accusing someone else): "And where were you these last days?" I now know what a collaborator would be for: a battering-ram, pure and simple, someone to yell at, accuse of incompetence, give the gate to, remain intact. But me, I have to go back on myself. Since I arranged it this way, I have no redress at all. Enough.[13]

There had been something of a sex life for Blitzstein in Rome, brief attachments for the most part, whose continuance he did not encourage. "I'm getting used to 'wounded feelings,' Italian-style," he wrote to Leonard Bernstein.[14] And to David Diamond, then a visiting professor in Buffalo, he wrote:

> No love yet, not that it hasn't been offered. I am too crotchety and old, I guess. I love the genuine affection strewn about by all and sundry; even the most casual encounters produce feelings of hurt and forgiveness which startle and attract me.[15]

For several weeks in the spring of 1961, Blitzstein regularly saw Adolfo Velletri, a man in his late forties, judging from photographs. Overly romantic, histrionic with his emotions but wholly in love with Marc, Adolfo showed up at the apartment at 9 P.M., after the productive hours of the day had ended. It was a relationship Marc's friends encouraged, pleased to see him relaxing with a partner and afraid that otherwise he might fall in with the wrong crowd.

Adolfo knew little English. At first, Blitzstein must have relished the idea of conducting an affair in Italian. But fatigue soon sets in with such adventures. This one with the cloying Adolfo lasted three or four tiresome months. As he described the relationship to David Diamond:

> I have a quiet love-life: not exciting, not right, but full of that uniquely Italian mothering-by-lover that is so touching. Do I want mothering, six slightly wilted carnations on my birthday, almost daily post-cards, the darning of a cigarette-hole in my *impermeabile?* Do I? Clearly I do, in some part of me; or I'd give it up; and I don't. I used to hear that Italy was the place where a woman was made to feel a woman. Apparently they work it on both sides of the fence, and over it and beneath it too. God love them.[16]

"9 P.M. A. Velletri here," Blitzstein wrote in his appointment book for May 19. "I break the news, am curiously saddened."

He ended it. For Blitzstein, love came hard. He found it easier to spread out his emotions and passions diffusely—for his family and friends, for the men at the baths, for his crazy country, for the people, for humanity—than to concentrate all his affections on one other human being.

May 21: "10:30 P.M. Giuseppe here." Marc had met someone else.

May 25: "The letter from Velletri—'help!' " Adolfo had written, "I can't bear it any longer—call me! Don't kill me, I beg you! Forgive me."[17] He came the next day at 9 P.M. Marc wanted to say it again: It was over. Nevertheless, they continued to see one another.

The Italian time was drawing to a close. It might have continued into the fall if Blitzstein had felt able to accept the offer from the American Academy in Rome to remain. Its director, Richard A. Kimball, had become genuinely fond of Blitzstein's visits there. "We should have enjoyed having you around," he wrote, acknowledging Blitzstein's need to return home. "I hope we shall see more of you before the end of your Roman sojourn." Blitzstein planned to spend most of the summer in Brigantine. "A whole part of me is anxious to get there and 'begin' work," he told Mama, "since a great geographical change almost always does that for me." In his last week, Morris Golde and his painter-dancer friend Gene Meyer joined him for a spin down to Positano, near Naples. Filled with thoughts of Eva, he wrote to Jo, "I arranged *not* to go to Capri, wishing my thirty-year-old memory to be kept intact." But he did find things had changed: "I found a new race of young sophisticated natives," he wrote to the Baumans,

> all luscious to the eye, conscious of their sexiness, and ready to receive money for favors from apparently any sex and apparently at any end. I forbore, was the contented observer, which is a bit different from a peeping Tom.[18]

Just before Marc left, Adolfo composed a little musical tribute for his American lover, *Il valzer delle candele,* transforming the tune of "Auld Lang Syne" into a waltz:

Domani tu mi lascerai e più non tornerai,
domani tutti i sogni miei ti porterai con te.
La fiamma del mio amore che sol per te sognavo invan(o),
è lume di candela che, gia si spegne piano pian.

Tomorrow you will leave me, and never come back again,
Tomorrow you will take away every dream I have.
The flame of my love I kept for you alone in vain,
Is candlelight now flickering slowly till it's spent.

Flying homeward on July 10, Blitzstein wrote to Adolfo the following day from New York. He had arrived safely and was sad that his travels had come to an end.

It was a theme Adolfo quickly exploited. *"A che cosa devo alludere la tua tristezza?"* he wrote back to Marc, in care of the William Morris Agency, the only address Blitzstein had given. "What is the reason for your sadness? *Nostalgia dell'Italia?*"[19] There followed almost daily an effusion of picture postcards, and a couple of letters, each in care of the agency, filled with the tugs and taunts and pained pleasures of unanswered love. After two months *devotissimo* Adolfo complained of Marc's silence, and Blitzstein decided finally to respond. He drafted his letter in English, then translated it into his librettoese Italian:

> Dear Adolfo:
> It is useless to write me. I have received all your *cartoline* and your two letters. It is not laziness which has conditioned my silence. It is so much better for both of us, believe me, that this communication be ended, once and for all.
> I wish you well with all my heart.
> Marc
> I shall answer no more letters. One day you will forgive me, even understand. Is it any comfort to you now to know that during the entire writing of this difficult letter, I thought of nothing but you?[20]

No more *cartoline* came from Adolfo after that.

Less than a month into his stay in Brigantine, the Peugeot arrived in Newark. The rest of the summer he spent on the Jersey shore with Mama, Jo, and Ed, continuing research on *Sacco and Vanzetti.* Jo gave him a copy of *The Untried Case,* a study by Sacco and Vanzetti's lawyer Herbert B. Ehrmann in the late stages of the trial. She inscribed the book to "Bartolomeo, Nicola and Marc."

In the fall, he returned to New York: nights at the theatre, at the Philharmonic, at the City Opera, meals with Hellman, Morris Golde, Edward Albee, Irene Diamond, Joe Stein, Claire Reis, Jennie Tourel, and of course, Lina. It didn't help that he lost his wallet one night in September. Where? he wondered in his appointment book. "Luchow's? Bar at Irving Place & 14th St.? Union Square?" Between his social engagements, work for the National Institute grants committee, and the usual distractions, work on the opera bogged down.

A further blow to Blitzstein's chances of ever seeing a production of his *Mother Courage* came with the show *Brecht on Brecht,* a series of brief excerpts assembled by George Tabori into a moving portrait of the poet and playwright and his world. Presented by Lucille Lortel in November 1961 on a program for the New York chapter of the American National Theatre and Academy, it reached the stage of the Theater de Lys just after the turn of the year, lasting 424 performances and later enjoying a wide exposure on a national tour. Produced by Cheryl Crawford, it featured designs by Wolfgang Roth. Lotte Lenya appeared in the cast, with Viveca Lindfors, Michael Wager, Anne Jackson, Dane Clark, and

George Voskovec. Two Blitzstein translations from *Threepenny*, the "Solomon Song" and "Pirate Jenny," were included. In Tabori's translation, Lenya sang the "Song of Mother Courage." Here were Lenya and Crawford and Lortel bypassing Blitzstein's patient efforts.

To add further injury, Crawford announced in mid-January that she intended to present the Bentley translation of *Mother Courage* during the next season, with Anne Bancroft. This time the unpredictable Stefan Brecht insisted on the Bentley, and Crawford could not perceive enough difference between the two scripts to fight for Marc's. This production came about in March 1963, co-produced with Jerome Robbins under Samuel Matlovsky's musical direction. It closed after fifty-two performances.

In the end, no *Mother Courage* or *Mahagonny* as adapted by Marc Blitzstein ever reached performance. But *The Threepenny Opera* continued. In 1960 Carmen Capalbo and Stanley Chase gathered several members of the original cast under Samuel Matlovsky's baton to launch a West Coast production in San Francisco. Anna Sten played the part of Jenny. After four weeks, it traveled to the New Music Box Theatre in Hollywood, with Lenya replacing Sten, and Estelle Parsons as Mrs. Peachum. But it was not a success. Los Angeles was not a theatre town, and the buoyant West Coast sensibility did not respond to the play's mordancy.

As the Weill-Brecht opera began its seventh incredible year in New York, Capalbo and Chase decided to produce a national touring *Threepenny* starring Gypsy Rose Lee. Beginning in September 1961 with a three-week run in Toronto, it would continue on for thirty-five weeks in cities around the country. But after a poor reception in Toronto, the producers cut their losses and closed. It seemed out of place somehow, uprooted from where it belonged—in New York at the Theater de Lys.

While in Rome, Blitzstein had been invited by Robert H. Hethmon, director of the Center for Theater Research at the State Historical Society of Wisconsin, to consider the center the ultimate repository of his papers. Hethmon had already gathered the archives of numerous important figures in the theatre, including the papers of the Playwrights Company. In time, the Wisconsin holdings would expand to include radio and television personalities and production companies. "It is my feeling that a Marc Blitzstein Collection would serve as a permanent and fitting memorial to your work in the American theatre," Hethmon told him. Flattered to be asked for his work, Blitzstein responded with thanks for the suggestion, "and for the fact that you feel me qualified to be a part of your project."[21]

Back in the city, he was able to talk it over with his lawyer Abe Friedman, and to meet with Hethmon. According to the appraiser, the Marc Blitzstein Collection was worth in the neighborhood of eighty-three thousand dollars. Thus, yearly donations to the center could make an appreciable dent in Blitzstein's taxes. He decided to go ahead with the plan, settling on a guarantee that unpublished and uncopyrighted material would be protected and that his approval would have to be granted to anyone conducting research with his papers there. Toward the end of the year, he put in some long sessions of probing through papers and compositions from his earliest years, both in his New York studio and in his third-floor room at Jo's house in Philadelphia. The first shipment of materials going to Wisconsin before the end of the year included scores and working drafts of *Cain* and *The Guests.* He also changed his will, stipulating the Wisconsin site as the final repository of his collection.

The inevitable moment had arrived for a meeting with Rudolf Bing and John Gutman at the Metropolitan Opera. On October 9, he told them he had written enough of both score and text to meet the Met's requirement of three-quarters of the libretto and 40 percent of the music. It was not sufficiently organized, however, and still required extensive revision before he was willing to show it to anyone. He asked them to wait another six months. By now the two years of the commission had come to an end. Would the Ford Foundation possibly extend the commission?

At this juncture, Leonard Bernstein and Rudolf Bing had some dealings about conducting at the Met, and Bing visited Bernstein at home. The subject of Blitzstein's Ford Foundation extension came up. Bing must have been thinking of his board's displeasure with the project when he said to Bernstein, "Oh, let him starve to death! We'll all be better off." Bernstein had never heard such a cruel statement about any composer, much less about his friend. Unable to bear Bing's presence in his home any further, he promptly showed him the door.

An internal Ford Foundation memorandum by Edward F. D'Arms, associate director of the Program in Humanities and the Arts, reported his talk with Blitzstein about a seventy-five-hundred-dollar extension. D'Arms stated that Blitzstein's grant had been "well above the average provided for in the commissioning fund, and is the largest single commission to date." In his November answer to Blitzstein, he did not mention these factors. Rather, he said that the funds set aside for the operatic project were dwindling and that further expenses had yet to come out of them. Therefore, the request was, "with best wishes," denied. In his acknowledgment, ostensibly courteous but with a patent undercurrent of bitterness directed both outward and inward, Blitzstein thanked the foundation for its past support:

> I seem to have miscalculated both the difficulty of the task and the amount of time required to do the libretto, composition and orchestration of the opera. It is hard to feel that I am in a sense being penalized for my miscalculation. I believe that my name and my reputation for conscientious acquittal of assumed obligations speak for themselves.
>
> I have worked, I am working, with all possible speed and energy, solely on the opera. I now see that I shall need certainly another year. And so I shall have to seek financial help elsewhere during the final period of work. Never fear; the opera will get finished.[22]

Help did come in the form of a positive answer to Blitzstein's request to stay at Yaddo for a long working session of several months. Unlike New York or Rome, the distractions in Saratoga would be few. He would live hermitlike there and acquit his conscience. Just after Thanksgiving, he settled into the Pink Room in the West House. From time to time, he might play the piano at a little homestyle musicale, or he might make good conversation with the novelist John Cheever or the black writer Charles Mitchell. Painters there at the time included Elizabeth Sparhawk-Jones and Peter Takal. He had no use for Quaintance Eaton, whom he uncharitably described as "a bitch who writes opera-anecdotes."[23] Interrupted by only a very occasional foray, Blitzstein remained at Yaddo until the end of April.

One of his first ventures out came after only two weeks there. At long last, on December 17, *The Threepenny Opera* closed at the Theater de Lys—making it available for *Brecht on Brecht*—and Blitzstein attended the final performance, number 2,611. That same day he noticed irregular heartbeats. Was it panic at the loss of his steady income from the show; the absence of his name from the New York stage after so many years? He returned to Yaddo the following day, intending to cut back on coffee and cigarettes, but still, he felt pains in his heart.

Tams-Witmark, licensing agency for *The Threepenny Opera,* immediately announced the work's availability to theatre producers all around the country. Within a few months, it was playing everywhere. For promotional purposes, Blitzstein wrote a short article for Tams-Witmark to distribute. "I wish I had written *The Threepenny Opera,*" he opened it, describing some of the work's incredible history. "It is fine to know that what began as a labor of love has blossomed into a nation-wide accolade; and that the *Threepenny Opera* will no longer be just a name on everybody's tongue, but a part of everybody's theatre experience."[24]

Not everybody, of course, appreciated the work. During the summer of 1962, in an incident all too familiar to Blitzstein's career, Philadelphia Mayor James H. J. Tate forced the municipally owned John B. Kelly Playhouse in the Park to cancel its production because he objected to "dirty" shows. As a protest, the Lambertville Music Circus put it on across the Delaware in New Jersey, with Elly Stone in the cast. Ads in the Philadelphia *Inquirer* read "Banned in Philadelphia! Welcomed in Lambertville."

Bernstein had written to Marc at Yaddo telling him how one night at the Met watching *La Forza del Destino,* he imagined seeing *Sacco and Vanzetti* on its stage. "For a 'holiday' evening," Marc answered,

> we sat around Elizabeth Ames' TV and watched your Christmas show, with great compliments all around for you. I liked it too, but worried about how gray and wan you looked. Jamaica helped, I hope.
>
> "Those *Forza* boards" are going to have to wait a bit for my opera. This one will kill me, I think. If only there weren't so much material! The ups and downs of my moods won't bear investigation, much less description. But at last the whole thing is approaching some kind of order.[25]

Mordy and Irma Bauman asked whether they could come for a visit, and Marc said no:

> I have not permitted Lina or my mother or Jo to come, all of whom have asked. I am simply not in condition to receive or talk with anyone. They have all understood; I know you will.
>
> I have reached a turning-point in the opera. It goes both very high and correspondingly low. I don't know what I feel, and I don't want to have to put on a face, even for intimates.[26]

As librettist, Blitzstein approached his task from two directions at once. He broke the scenario into an overall division of three acts, each containing four to seven scenes. In each scene, he determined which characters would advance the story. At the same time, he worked from the inside out, writing dialogue for scenes and arias that might fit in somewhere, discarding them later if they no longer suited the revised outline.

In the first act, a prologue, perhaps the speakeasy scene, would introduce the main conflict of guilt or innocence. In the next scene, set in Sacco's house, Nicola Sacco and his wife Rosa are rehearsing a short scene from Ibsen's *A Doll's House* in Italian, to be presented that evening at an anarchist fundraising event. Vanzetti comes to tell Sacco to get rid of all his left-wing literature; they leave, with guns. Next, they are arrested in a garage, but they do not know for what. Amidst the repressive climate of the Palmer Raids and deportations, they assume they have been picked up for their radicalism. In the Brockton police office, they are interrogated. They lie about several questions concerning their political beliefs and associations, trying to protect themselves and their friends. In the last scene, supporters come to tell the pair that the district attorney is charging them with robbery and murder.

Act Two is the trial. Courtroom scenes alternate with the cells of Dedham Prison. As the trial unfolds, characters continue to develop. Those representing the state are seen to be prejudiced, mean of spirit, concerned with proprieties, symbols, and authority. The two anarchists, seen at first as simple victims, begin to emerge into historic proportions as they challenge injustice. Still, they retain their humanity: Sacco has a mad scene.

Act Three conflates more than three years' time into its several scenes. Motions for appeal are filed and denied. The confession of Celestino Madeiros, indicating the responsibility of the Morelli Gang from Providence in the crimes, is heard and rejected. Sentence is passed; Sacco and Vanzetti each make statements to the court. In the prison yard, Sacco wishes it all to end—he has lost hope. Vanzetti still trusts that the final appeals will bring their release; he makes his remark "If it had not been for these thing" to a visiting reporter. The pace accelerates as worldwide demonstrations call for a halt to the executions. Leading up to the final scene in the death chamber, Blitzstein intended to adapt the process Brecht used in *Galileo,* where the Pope in conversation with the Inquisitor is helped into his robes of office, becoming a public persona along with his attire. In his opera, Blitzstein would have Sacco and Vanzetti shaved, their hair cut, and their pants slit in preparation for the electric chair.

In some such order, subject to constant revision, Blitzstein wanted to tell the story. Yet he was cautious not to be too much the historian. Both *Danton's Death* and *Wozzeck* treated actual history, the former written thirty-five years after the respective events, the latter only eleven. Yet in both cases, the stage work moved "utterly into the poetic-drama world." "Don't be afraid of discontinuity!" he reminded himself. "As a matter of fact, beware of continuity, structural logic (except *basic*)—my ever-loving pitfall." Wanting to move the opera along swiftly, at the same time he did not wish each scene to conclude with a dramatic tag, for example, at the end of Act One when Sacco and Vanzetti realize that they are being held on a murder charge: "extend it into a *static* number! during which the men and the moment are explored!"

Particularly significant for Blitzstein are Sacco and Vanzetti's friends, such as Mrs. Elizabeth Glendower Evans, member of a leading Boston family. In his prison cell, she tells Sacco:

Now why do I wish to help?
I am not a charitable woman.
The heart that bleeds like a leaking faucet,
The waves of pity washed in tears
Tears that spring easily
And turn into money
Dumped from the guilty purse—
These I find ugly
Because they are so pretty.
The world is not soft
And was not meant to be
No. I wish to help
Because I am in peril
And must save myself.
If you are hounded and hindered
If you are punished
For coming to my country, for believing
What you choose while you are here,
Then I am in great danger.
I am then poorer than you
And in greater trouble.
They will free you.
They must. . . .
I dare not think any other thing.

Though he could not have afforded the time to develop a character such as Mrs. Evans from an amorphous sympathizer to a solid fighter for justice, she represents the same type as Clara in *No for an Answer.* In such characters, Blitzstein wanted to show how the cause of the oppressed is at heart inseparable from the interest of all humanity. Not his role to show the working class the way, he directed his appeal toward his own element, the middle class, professionals and intellectuals. He would ask them to examine the banality of lives spent in allegiance to repression.

Musically, Blitzstein was developing some fascinating ideas. In one scene showing Vanzetti's love for classic literature, the prisoner sings the verses he has been writing in terza rima, an austere, elevated poetic form with an aba, bcb, cdc, ded, efe rhyme scheme. Dante used it in *The Divine Comedy,* but it has rarely appeared in English. Aside from the political, historical attractions of his chosen subject, Blitzstein also could use the Italian characters to let himself go with expansive, arioso music that he rarely gave himself the occasion or the permission to write.

Sprinkled among Blitzstein's sketches for the opera are sample tone rows he might have used. He also wanted to extend his technique of American recitative, as developed in the character Mike in *No for an Answer* and in the film *Valley Town.* "Use this as prototype!" he told himself. At the same time, he warned himself, "Watch out for local references (American)! This is a work, remember, to be translated, done elsewhere, in many other languages." "As to words: *multum in parvo*—get rid of that habit of mine of piling on words: concentrate them!"

Blitzstein also thought of using the chorus as a symbolic representation of the Commonwealth of Massachusetts, much like his use of massed voices for individuals in *The Condemned.* He conceived primitive, savage music for a magisterial text:

Now: here: I,
The people,
The Commonwealth:
Nameless servant and lord.
This the sword, the scepter;
These my scales and chart.
Behold me in the chair.

The chorus would take offense at the presumption of two immigrant laborers in a number called "Death to Thought," whose principal idea Blitzstein described in his notes: "There is something so awful, so outside-the-pale, unforgivable, outrageous in a shoe-cobbler, a fish-monger *thinking*—exercising his *brain,* in 'abstract' 'philosophy,' worlds of thought."

In one memorandum, Blitzstein thought of using a taped chorus, played back at a higher speed than recorded, "so that the sound, especially of the soprani, will be higher than voices have ever been heard." The tape might be used a cappella, or with live chorus and orchestra. Curiously, he invented the device before knowing what use he would make of it: "Now what, or whom, does this taped chorus represent, in terms of characters in the opera?"

Other devices he considered included choruses of simultaneous singing and speaking, which he remembered from Schoenberg's *Moses and Aaron.* And he recalled the multiplication of characters in his own *Triple-Sec.* In the verdict scene, "JUDGE THAYER enters in gown. All rise; he sits; all sit. Seven JUDGE THAYERS take seats beside him, dressed and made up exactly like him." Rosa Sacco cries out when the verdict is pronounced, and "8 JUDGE THAYERS rap their gavels in unison." Blitzstein imagined the two protagonists themselves at one point in this kind of multiplicity: At the end, they develop into groups of two or three, then four or five, then eight and twelve, becoming "a small roar."

By now, certain scholars of the case had researched questions relating to the innocence of the two anarchists, beyond what might have been possible in the tense atmosphere of the 1920s. Articles and books were appearing that pointed to the actual guilt of one or the other or both, or if not to their guilt, at least to their propensity toward violence and "propaganda of the deed" as sympathizers of the Galleani branch of the anarchist movement.

In other words, maybe the traditional characterization that liberals and the left had made of them as simple, idealistic dreamers was incorrect. If so, it would throw the opera into an entirely different perspective. What use could be made, for instance, of the note Vanzetti passed to his comrade Felicani shortly before the execution? "*Vendicate la mia morte,*" it read, or in the pluralized form into which it has been translated, "Avenge our death." Could Vanzetti possibly have meant with bombs or assassinations? Blitzstein surely thought about these emerging developments. "Should there be something more clearly anarchistic, *wild,* in S and V's character?" he asked at Yaddo. "For Christ's sake give either S or V (or both) some kind of 'un-saintly' something!"

That spring in Saratoga, three invitations came to Blitzstein that he accepted. In the first, Clarence Q. Berger, dean of University Planning and Development at Brandeis, asked whether he would consent to give the Adolph Ullman Memorial Lecture on music on April 2. Part of the five-hundred-dollar agreement included a videotaping of his lecture the following day at the studios of WGBH, the educational television station in Boston. Although he had vowed to himself not to interrupt his work on *Sacco and Vanzetti,* he wrote to Berger, "I find the chance to come again to Brandeis University well-nigh irresistible."[27] He also felt that if Brandeis was fishing to interest him in a permanent position there, he might as well go and explore the possibilities. He accepted Berger's suggested title, "Mark the Music"—taken from Act V, scene one of *The Merchant of Venice*—incorporating the quotation into his speech:

The man that hath no music in himself,
Nor is not moved with concord of sweet sounds,
Is fit for treasons, stratagems, and spoils;
The motions of his spirit are dull as night,
And his affections dark as Erebus.
Let no such man be trusted.

"And the passage finished," Blitzstein interrupted his recitation at this point, "with grandeur and appropriate scansion,"

Mark the music.

Referring to the Brandeis premiere, Blitzstein emphasized that the work that had given him his greatest success had been "a serviceable translation" of *The Threepenny Opera* and its "Mack the Knife." But now, he said, it was his turn to talk about "Mark the Music"—"myself, a subject dear to my heart. Also one which troubles me much." In the course of the talk, the composer reviewed the major formative works of his theatrical career in a manner similar to his approach on the 1956 Spoken Arts recording. By now, of course, the nature of his former political affiliations had become a subject for national press coverage. At Brandeis and on WGBH television, he chose to redefine the nature of his commitment as "an engaged writer":

> In the days of the thirties it was strict, even sectarian. It is now rather looser, more flexible and broader. But many things remain. I believed then, as I do now, in the right of all men to have no need to ask favors in order to exist with dignity. I felt then, and I do now, that the questions, who we are, how are we to live and by what, and by what values, are the most serious and basic questions there are. And that these questions cannot even be met unless such horrors as the making use of one man by another, one race by another, one class by another, one nation by another, are disposed of. And I do mean by that, gotten rid of.

Blitzstein talked to some extent about his desiderata in music as such:

> About my music technically: I am not an inventor or an experimenter. I say this flatly. I don't seem to insist on finding new ways to say things. I suppose I want to find an exact way to say the thing I wish to communicate, and I am still benighted to think of music as communication.

Having early on rejected serialism as a method for himself, Blitzstein laid out the musical polarities between Schoenberg's system and the music of chance, or aleatory music, the "do it yourself" trend, as he called it.

> I imagine I do lean toward the serialists if anything, although my music doesn't sound at all like it. But I do long for an exactitude, and a control, insofar as my conscious mind will let me. I know very well that try as I may, something which André Gide once called *"la part de Dieu"* will enter in. You can call it what you like—the subconscious, the ineluctable, the accidental, the uncontrolled. I conceive it to be my duty to have it all *the thing known,* and I know that in any case, the unknown will be part of the finished product.

In his conclusion, he returned to the commanding spirit behind his art, leaving a testament of his passion in the minds of his young listeners:

> This is a time when being a philosopher is incumbent upon us all, upon the man on the street, upon the student, even upon the youngster. We have no choice. If there's a single good thing that has happened because of The Bomb, and I include in that word all the perils whereby mankind has arrived at the verge of self-destruction, it is that no one—repeat, no one—can evade the crucial questions, who am I, how am I to live, by what, and with what values?
>
> I have no easy answers for myself, and so I can have no easy answers for you. The one thing we can ask is that our lives have some meaning. I have tried to give you a small look-see into the meaning I have sought in my own life. A much better way for you is to find out what I am like by listening to some of my music sometime. For yourselves, you will have found those questions which stand for meaning in your life. Because meaning has become a necessity.
>
> How does it feel, I ask each one of you, to be a philosopher? Well, I think I know. It isn't happy. It's full of anxiety, or worse, fear. But the basic questions turn out now to be the imperative ones, and asking those questions is what gives meaning to our lives, and makes men of us.[28]

The taping finished, Blitzstein conducted a bit of research in Boston: lunch with Herbert B. Ehrmann, the Sacco and Vanzetti lawyer. He wanted to know more about the kind of anarchism Sacco and Vanzetti truly espoused. Were they disposed toward violence, after all? Ehrmann tried to be helpful, but the meeting produced no sure answers for the composer.

The second invitation Blitzstein received that spring came from Bennington College in Vermont. Wallace Fowlie had broached the idea to President William C. Fels that Blitzstein might accept the John Golden Foundation fellowship to teach playwriting at Bennington for the 1962–1963 academic year. The college would pay for room and board, and the fellowship would be worth five thousand dollars, more appropriate for a younger playwright, Fels admitted, "but Wallace tells me you might not find it impossibly small."[29]

Blitzstein had never written a play, properly speaking, only librettos that he set to music. Indeed, one might say that the primary weakness of his entire career was his failure to seek out the playwriting expertise he obviously needed. The Bennington invitation, therefore, must have struck Blitzstein with some sense of irony. Nevertheless, Blitzstein talked with Fels at the college on March 16 and quickly warmed to the idea of coaching a small number of serious students in an academic setting. The arrangement seemed to be set, but by the beginning of May still no confirmation of the appointment had come. Fels told him then of the college's indecision and, somewhat pointedly at this late date, said that Blitzstein should not turn down other offers waiting for Bennington to come through. In that case, Blitzstein answered, "I think we had better forget the plan for me to come to Bennington next year."[30] By return mail, however, the offer did come, with apologies for the delay, and Blitzstein accepted. His duties at Bennington would start in September.

The third invitation came from the father of Mendy Wager, Meyer W. Weisgal, chairman of the executive council of the Weizmann Institute of Science in Israel. Weisgal was a leading Zionist and an almost ubiquitous link between Israel and American Jewry. Tireless in his approaches to American Jewish intellectuals in an attempt to win their sympathies for the young state, he invited a number of composers to come and get to know the country. He asked whether Blitzstein would be interested in participating in an open American-Israeli dialogue on the creative arts, to be held in Jerusalem in mid-June. After that, he would be free to settle in to Israeli life however he chose for the rest of the summer. With alacrity, Blitzstein agreed to go. "Now I am off to Israel," he wrote to Claire Reis, "first to work on my opera; also to discuss publicly my being a composer, a man, a jew [*sic*], an American."[31]

25

THE THIRTEENTH SCENE

June 1962–January 1964

"*. . . sitting here waiting for any explosion . . .*"

The American Jewish Congress conference took place in Jerusalem, June 12–14, 1962. The American-Israeli dialogue was alliteratively called "New Responses, Responsibilities and Our Reciprocal Relationship." Blitzstein planned to arrive only a day or two before it opened. He packed his *Sacco and Vanzetti* work, a few of his songs—in case he was asked to perform any of them in Israel—and several of his recordings for possible airplay. He left his Peugeot at an apartment building in New Rochelle owned by Aaron Diamond. On the El Al flight from New York, he sat with the satirical painter Jack Levine, who had illustrated Blitzstein's 1946 homecoming articles in *New Masses* and who, also on his first trip to Israel, planned to participate in the conference. "Look, we're here," Levine remarked as the plane landed, "where everybody lives in Jewish."[1]

Once in Israel, Blitzstein's sponsor Meyer Weisgal housed him at the King David Hotel, supplying fresh flowers in the room and placing a limousine at his disposal. The first day of the conference featured a welcoming reception by Ish Shalom, mayor of Jerusalem, greetings from Itzhak Ben Zvi, president of Israel, and a dialogue between Dr. Joachim Prinz, president of the congress, and Abba Eban, ambassador to the United Nations, on the ways Israeli and American Jews see each other. Among the themes to emerge from the discussion was the idea that unlike other societies in the rest of the world, in Israel problems of discrimination, anti-Semitism, and thorny church-state relations did not exist.

On the second day of the conference, an exchange entitled "The Jewish Commitment in the Creative Arts" included, aside from Blitzstein and Jack Levine: Mordechai Ardon, painter; Itzhak Danziger, sculptor; Frank Pelleg, composer; Moshe Shamir, a writer and director of Haifa's municipal theatre; Peter Frye, member of the Theatre of Action and the Group Theatre in New York in the 1930s and now an Israeli theatre director; Meyer Levin, the American novelist and now a resident of Israel; Anna Sokolow, choreographer of the original *Regina,* on a six-month residency in Israel devoted to training a company of dance actors; and Harold Prince, Broadway producer and director.

The panelists reviewed their relationships to their Jewishness. Meyer Levin urged the translation of American Jewish writers into Hebrew. Hearing him whine over the unenthusiastic reception given to his work, Blitzstein considered Levin an "absurd and unattractive ego-maniac sounding off his own horn." Sokolow confessed to a kind of fascination with Israel, this being her ninth trip to the country in as many years. Pelleg affirmed that music is more importantly judged as good or bad, not on its Jewish quotient. Both Jack Levine and Harold Prince stressed the liberal, progressive content to their art, whose antecedents could be found in Jewish tradition. Prince reminded his listeners, or informed them if they did not know it, that the original Jerome Robbins conception of *West Side Story* was the love affair between a Jewish boy and a Gentile girl.

"I consider myself addicted to humanism," Blitzstein remarked, a man who personally identifies as much with the Sacco and Vanzetti plight as with Dreyfus. "I know I am a Jew," he declared, particularly when he encountered anti-Semitism, though he projected a hypothesis that when all anti-Semitism disappeared, he might cease to feel like a Jew. Never having studied Hebrew nor having participated in any facet of organized Jewish life, he now found himself for the first time in a country where he felt at a loss with the language. But in his first days in the country, he already perceived that Hebrew was a new language even for the Israelis, so there might be hope for him, too.

When people found Jewish-sounding music in his work, he continued, he often agreed. Perhaps it was that element of "self-pity," perhaps even—and he admitted it with chagrin—something "mystical." Finally, he claimed to feel the continuity of Jewish life and Jewish survival in the making of a Jewish nation. "I have come here because I want to find out about Israel."[2]

Privately, he viewed his Jewishness more suspectly, for in his notepad he jotted down this thought while listening to the other speakers: "I am a jew (who would know it? Not even I.)" And he continued—surely not out of ignorance but with a perverse sense of deprecation—to use the lowercase *j.*

Blitzstein found himself questioning the assertion that church-state problems had automatically disappeared in Israel. What prompted him was the sculptor Danziger's story of the public destruction of one of his works on the Orthodox religious grounds that by depicting a human figure the sculpture violated the

Second Commandment against graven images. Is this not censorship of art by the church? Blitzstein asked.

Prime Minister David Ben-Gurion gave the evening address on June 13, stressing that while American Jews represented only a group, in Israel the Jews are the whole nation, with no concern for "what the goyim say." Immediately resisting the way the prime minister ignored the non-Jewish populations in Israel, Blitzstein publicly objected: "I found Ben-Gurion's easy disdain of 'goyim' startling." Thinking further about his own place in American culture, he scratched a memo to himself: "What with the jewish-bit and the homosexual-bit on Broadway, I might even think myself belonging to a *majority,* God forbid."

It appears doubtful that he returned to the final sessions the next day—which, apart from a speech by Martin Buber, rehashed the minority vs. majority question and summed up inconclusively with "The Significance of Our Dialogue." For Blitzstein's notebook indicates a full day of visits to the Hadassah Hospital to see the Marc Chagall windows, the National Art Museum, to a falafel stand for lunch, to the Mea Shearim to hear all the Yiddish spoken there, the Mandelbaum Gate, and the university.

From the air-conditioned hostel at the Weizmann Institute of Science, where Weisgal had installed him following the conference, Blitzstein set out in a rented Morris-Oxford sedan to look for a suitable house with an uninterrupted view of the sea for the rest of the summer. Jack Levine went along as a good way to see the country. The stream of letters began to flow, to Mama and most of all to Jo:

> I'm loving it here; but that's in terms of long-term staying; and I'm also being given the VIP treatment. I wonder if you'd like the noise or could stand the food. It is all such a hurled-at-you combination of Miami (Tel-Aviv, noisy, piss-elegant, no swimming-pools and a polluted sea), Cape Canaveral (this Institute, really *run* by Mendy Wager's father Meyer Weisgal, who turns out to be a staggering power in the nation . . .)—and the ancient-ancient Jerusalem (beyond words wonderful and awesome, beautiful, horrifying as to beggars and Chassidim, poignant, and grand in the grand style, but also noisy and obstreperous as everywhere.) We jews!! Conventions all over; the tourists are of course the worst; the natives are marvelous, and spoken Hebrew has a wonderful softness. And the whole is a stupendous effort, and I still don't know on what it basically rests: a United Nations partition decision, which kicked millions of Arabs out to their not-unnatural resentment. But such scholarship, and such building, and such making green what was sandy rock, miles and miles of it. And culture is next to cleanliness (the place *is* clean), which for the young Israeli comes way before godliness, since most of them are free-thinkers, a surprise. They keep ShabBATT (H. pron.) as we do Sunday, not much more. . . .
>
> The "Conference" was depressing and a bust, except for some startling "talking-back" to Ben-Gurion who thinks all American jews ought to be bi-lingual, and then just Hebrew-speaking as they make an "aliya" (mass-migration) here. No wonder he does. Now he has to do with illiterate

> Moroccan and Abyssinian refugees, who keep pulling the standard down like our own Puerto-Ricans. There is also a growing race-problem ("dark jews"). My part of the "dialogue" came off well, and I'm too much of a hit.[3]

The "To Whom It May Concern" letter of introduction Weisgal wrote on Blitzstein's behalf described him as "a very good friend of mine" and "one of the greatest opera composers of our time." Pointing more to his own wish than to Blitzstein's, he said that the composer was presently in Israel with "hopes to get inspiration to write an opera here." "I stand behind any commitments he may make to you in any form whatsoever, and will be very happy to guarantee any financial obligations he may incur."[4]

The opportunity soon arose for the relationship to be tested. Weisgal informed him that three cables Blitzstein had sent from the Weizmann Institute came to fifteen Israeli pounds and eighteen *agurot* [cents], "in case you are interested and wish to pay for" them. The composer promptly sent reimbursement for the fifteen pounds. "I was overwhelmed," Weisgal replied. "As far as concerns the Ag. 18, you can donate it to the Jewish National Fund or to the most convenient *pushke,* whichever you prefer and whichever is easiest."[5]

The search for a place by the sea ended happily on June 21 at Beit Yannai. Named for an Old Testament king and patriarch, the village lay midway between Tel Aviv and Haifa, three miles from the resort town of Natanya. Chief among the virtues of his rented house was its location on a cliff two hundred feet above the Mediterranean: A short scramble down a ravine cut through the slaty stone, and he could be swimming in the tepid aquamarine. The comfortable four-room house featured a huge air-conditioned kitchen, a private garden with trees, and a terrace looking out on flawless sunsets. Stunning drapes, blankets, and rugs created by the owner, a prize-winning weaver, provided the decor. Within the first days, he had a piano installed.

At his back, poor chicken farms housed a mixed population: "the noise from 3 A.M. of crowing cocks, and awakened dogs and donkeys is something," he wrote to Jo. "Kids abound, roaring with energy; neighbors, kids, dogs, roosters, donkeys are all jewish (a couple of Arabs), which means that even in their sleep they moan and sing out."[6]

"Being Jewish among the Jews is still an experience," he wrote again to his sister after two weeks in Israel, now beginning, though still intermittently, to use capital letters.

> I've made no attempt to get at Hebrew; even the alphabet still eludes me. I talk French to my neighbor (Luxembourgeois), who translates into Hebrew what I need from my Arab maid; Italian to the postman (from Tripoli) and the Italian restaurant at Natanya, four minutes away; German to most others; some English, to Americans or Canadians or South Africans, of which there is quite a colony. It is amusing to see the last, having come "home," turning on their darker brethren (the Yemenite or

Tunisian or Moroccan Jew is really dark), just as though they were back in Jo'burg, with the blacks.[7]

Soon he developed a routine of steady work on the opera combined with physical exercise in the water. In his "first Beit Yannai note"—as if a historic value attached to the new place—he wondered whether Sacco and Vanzetti should each have his own musical theme. He described his life to Mama:

> Tel Aviv is some thirty–forty minutes away down the coast, by car; so I go in about once a week, to refresh myself with people, some shopping, a concert or a party. Otherwise I stay put in my "hideaway" cliff-house all day, going into Natanya (only five minutes away) for most of the big meals. My maid (she turns out to be Yemenite-strict-jewish, not Arab, although she is quite dark) does some light cooking for me, preparing stuff like chicken and putting it in the Frigidaire for later. I still do three swims a day, plus about a mile's walking on this heavenly beach. . . . I love it. . . .
>
> They don't drink; really, almost no alcohol seems to be consumed here except by tourists. I have yet to hear a drunken voice; loud they are, but that's just being jewish and in good spirits.[8]

Until nearly the end of July, he encouraged Jo and Ed to come and visit him in Israel. He gave advice on clothes to pack, where to stay, the side trips they might take, the weather. Perhaps they could coordinate their visit with a proposed trip to Israel by Morris Golde, then in Positano. He wanted to show off his "*ambiente,*" and to show them how, amidst all the fascinating distractions, he could continue working. If Jo and Ed came toward the end of the summer, he might return with them via Athens, though, he admitted, "I have a hankering to see Rome once again." But Morris's brother died that summer, and he returned to America. Jo, concerned over an abscess in Mama's eye and herself just back from a trip to San Francisco, never managed to make the trip.[9]

In unexpected places, Blitzstein found interest in himself and his work. An American family comprised of artists and doctors living nearby all knew his music. To his surprise, Mrs. Fink recited the line "Hurry up, hurry up, hurry up, and wait" from the *Airborne* Symphony. Then, after an article on him appeared in the newspaper *Ma'ariv,* he received a letter from a Shoshana Ron in Haifa. She was reminded "that my Grandfather (in Russia) Z[elig] Galanter mentioned often the name of his Sister in Philadelphia Hanna Blitzstein." He visited her, this granddaughter of Babushka's brother—his second cousin—and got on famously with her and her family. He seemed fascinated to learn the names of all his distant relations and something of the family history: Shoshana, just a year younger than he, had left Russia and landed in Palestine as a young Zionist in 1925, leaving two sisters behind; they later settled in Novosibirsk. Their mother, Bontche Rosenblit, died in the Holocaust. Shoshana's son Moshe—Marc's name in Hebrew—was a music-school graduate and piano teacher. "It's a microscopic world," Marc reported to Jo.[10]

In the expected places, there was interest in him as well. He conducted a radio interview that included selections from his recordings. He managed to stir some interest in a Hebrew-language staging of *Regina* by the Israel National Opera; the production never materialized. Additional interviews appeared in *Ha Aretz* and *Davar Hashavuah.* A group of the leading Israeli composers sponsored a gathering in Blitzstein's honor at the Milo Writers and Artists Club in Tel Aviv, one of the few concentrated social-cum-business gatherings in which he took part that summer.

Otherwise, he enjoyed Anna Sokolow's dance performances, a production of Brecht's *Galileo* in Tel Aviv, *Turandot* at the opera, and a party given by the French-Israeli groups on Bastille Day. He saw Jennie Tourel in Israel that summer, and one day was surprised by his old friends Ella Winter and Donald Ogden Stewart, there to visit her son Peter Steffens who had married an Israeli.

He spent one afternoon with Mendy Wager's sister Helen (Chaya), a Communist at that time, to whom Mendy sent all his left-wing, Israel-bound friends. Their conversation helped to fortify the reservations Marc had already expressed about Ben-Gurion's and the religious orthodoxy's type of exclusionary state.

Yet the meaning of a "promised land" did not escape him. Unexpectedly, he found himself regarding Israel with the affectionate, tolerant respect due any society struggling to create a bold new system of human relations, and with an admiration and awe he might have felt for socialism. His old ironic tweak of Leonard Bernstein's sensibilities on the day the State of Israel was founded back in 1948—"And remember, the Jews have a homeland!"—now, if he ever recalled it, must have rung hollow.

Northward excursions to Caesaria, Acre, Tiberias, Nazareth, and Safad completed his tour. He summed it all up for Mama:

> I adore this land, and am moved beyond words. It is a harsh and always-struggling life for everybody; not pretty. "Intellectuals," white-collar people from other lands have plowed in and used their hands and bodies and brains to make an oasis out of a desert. The best fruit I have ever tasted . . . has come out of rock and sand. And the faces of the people all show it: beautiful, with a kind of fierceness. I think I arrived at a moment which will never happen again here, so that the influx from all countries provides a hybrid, multi-lingual, multi-custom population. Later, the other languages and habits will fuse into the Hebrew-speaking and Israel-acting unity which is inevitable. I'm lucky to have hit it right now.[11]

His lifelong sense of the world failed him. Sentiments hardly encountered before touched him in unfamiliar parts of his being. That animal-health quality he loved in people, that resilient ability to cast off fear and neurosis and engage life totally, struck him as the essence of Israel. The crazy-quilt vitality of the new nation, sprung from ancient traditions and from a collective history of such unimaginable pain, produced an unaccustomed effect that he tried to describe to Jo:

I went to a rehearsal of the Yemenite INBAL ballet company, and practically cried at the beauty of the girls and men, the swift simplicity of their story-telling-in-dance, and the severe linear heartbreaking music. I tried to tell Sara [Levi-Tanai], their leader, what I felt. She just patted my hand, and said: write for us. Who knows? maybe. I feel capable of anything now. I am having sex and fun as well as the closest thing I'll ever have to serenity and joy. . . .

Love. You do understand me, don't you?[12]

Whatever his problems trying to create a modern opera, they evaporated in the expansive, sunny ether linking all nature, life, history, and hope in a mystical connectedness that included him. "I'm known as the Monk of Beit Yannai," he wrote in another letter to Jo that fixes the whole Israeli episode as a uniquely satisfying time in his life. "People wonder how I rattle around alone in this house. In fact, it's the most satisfying house I've ever had, better than Rome or Edgartown or Capri; I have to go back to Mallorca for comparisons."[13]

At the end of his stay, Helga Dudman, reporter for the Jerusalem *Post,* asked about his *Sacco and Vanzetti* work and explored his reactions to Israel. "I'm not trying to prove innocence," he responded. "It's not legalistic or journalistic. It's the growth of two men during seven years in jail, and during that time, the decline of the Commonwealth. Did you know that another book appeared on the case just last week?"

To the question of writing consciously Jewish music, Blitzstein answered that the deliberate search for roots often ends up as bad art. "I don't see why I shouldn't write about two Italians. And in the case of Gershwin, though Yiddish themes are to be found, what would have happened to *Porgy and Bess* if Gershwin had been intent on expressing his Jewishness? Even though it was a toss of a coin that decided Gershwin to do *Porgy* rather than *The Dybbuk.*" Finishing with mostly favorable comments on the theatre and music he had experienced in Israel, he admitted to having been "bitten by the well-known bug. I certainly didn't come looking for a home, but in a way I've found one." Dudman's interview, appearing a few days after Blitzstein left Israel, predicted his enthusiastic return.[14]

He could not convert his El Al ticket home (prepaid by the American Jewish Congress) to another airline, and El Al had no available seats on flights from Rome to New York. Thus, he flew home directly with no stopovers. He divided the two weeks before Labor Day between New York and Brigantine, sorting and packing for his fall in Bennington, reuniting with the family, and answering accumulated correspondence. Among the letters he sent was one to Judge Musmanno, reassuring him that Francis Russell's new book on Sacco and Vanzetti had not influenced him to believe them guilty. Musmanno replied with relief.

He paid a brief visit to Boston, where the Charles Playhouse was offering *Threepenny,* and where Ben Bagley had a revue in progress. "I hope you don't become successful," he told Bagley—one problem Blitzstein never had to face. "It'll destroy you." They sat together through a perfectly wretched performance of the Weill work; but afterward, Blitzstein greeted the company backstage and told them all how marvelous they had been.

Once it was announced who had received the John Golden Fellowship at Bennington, students at various levels of accomplishment in the playwriting field asked to be in Blitzstein's course during the 1962–1963 academic year. The "golden fellow," as he enjoyed calling himself, selected five students, meeting with each for a weekly tutorial and together once a week for a "jam session" in which they could all criticize each other's work. During some sessions, he had the students "jam" on *Regina* and his *Mother Courage* translation. Three students chose straight dramatic projects, one a musical theatre piece, and another something in between. Aside from his teaching responsibilities, he also made time for ongoing work on *Sacco and Vanzetti.* He even announced to *The Bennington Banner* that he was still working "fitfully" on *Mahagonny.*[15]

An apartment complete with grand piano, in Swan House, one of the women's dormitories, was his for the year, and the girls regarded him as their housefather. Though he never locked his door, no one ever abused his trust. Indeed, the students used his open door on a weekly basis when the head housekeeper made her inspection rounds: Hearing she was on the way, they scurried to place their illegal pets in his apartment. At one point, his pet population grew to substantial proportions—three dogs, three cats, and a canary. On interrogation, he calmly claimed ownership of them all.

Unlike so many of his composer colleagues, Blitzstein had never spent much time on a college campus. Since he would be at Bennington for only one academic year, he adopted a highly personal approach toward teaching: hard work, high expectations, and generosity with his time and advice combined with brashly direct criticism, intellectual exhibitionism, and impatience with laziness. He would bombard the students with "all the attack, the presumption and the passion [he] could muster." They would simply have to respond, going along or protesting and disagreeing, but in any case with vigor.[16] He consciously underplayed the tactical give-and-take required in an institutional setting, and he rarely made any special efforts to connect with colleagues in the music or other departments. His old friend and orchestrator Henry Brant, a member of the Bennington faculty, saw Blitzstein once at a concert of Brant's music and at the reception afterward, but for the most part Blitzstein kept his distance from the community life of the college.

In the main, his students worked well and he felt proud of them. Of the five, he recommended that one, because he lacked the technical training in music required for his project, not continue the course the second semester. With the administration at Bennington, he labored at cross-purposes for much of the year: Perhaps he never curbed his petulant quarrelsomeness. At one point, explaining that his room and board had to be reported to the IRS as income, the president's assistant apologetically added, "I feel that in some way there has been a lack of real communication between you and the College about your fellowship, for it seems we have never understood what it is that you want from us."[17]

Not long after arriving at the college, the composer and playwright-in-residence met Bernard Malamud, the novelist and storywriter on the Bennington faculty. They soon became friendly, and within weeks Blitzstein had become smitten with the idea of composing one-act operas based on Malamud's short stories. He read and considered ten or more stories. By the middle of October, he had chosen "Idiots First" and "The Magic Barrel"—both with strong Jewish characters and settings—as the two halves of an evening entitled *Tales of Malamud.* Thus did Meyer Weisgal's hope come true—that in Israel Blitzstein would find inspiration for a new opera.

He assured Malamud that the librettos would stay close to the original texts but that he should not expect very "Jewish" music. Nevertheless, he began researching Jewish music sources in a way he had never done before, and he read up on the Jewish minstrels of the Middle Ages. He appreciated the satiric protest, as well as the masochism, of their tradition. He wrote to Bernstein, telling of his need for wedding music and a prayer for the dead in *The Magic Barrel,* and started taking notes on the ancient Kaddish prayer, which he did not know.

Now he directed most of his creative urges into the Malamud operas, taking a "breather" from *Sacco and Vanzetti,* shuffling those papers only when a fresh idea came to mind. The Israel trip clearly had brought Blitzstein nearer to his Jewish identity. A music-theatre work seemed modest enough a contribution for him to make compared to the collective trials of the Jewish people. It is also true, however, that stage works on Jewish themes, particularly themes with a Yiddish inflection, now appeared more frequently in New York. The long period of recoil from the pain of the Holocaust was ending and progressive-minded Jews now felt more secure in reclaiming such authors as Sholom Aleichem and I. L. Peretz. Their intense humanity and their almost timeless understanding of the ambiguous place of the Jew in the world lent a kind of permission to writers, musicians, and actors to express their Jewishness in radical, secular forms. Perhaps on the strength of the Malamud stories, Blitzstein could write a successful work that would temper the climate for his next and greater opera, *Sacco and Vanzetti.* The contract Malamud and Blitzstein signed, giving Malamud one-third of all advances, royalties, and proceeds, went into effect January 1, 1963.

The story "Idiots First" is written in Malamud's typically terse, epigrammatic style. Yet in the course of his eleven pages, the author shifts the scene several times, managing to enfold a striking number of sharply drawn characters set in a New York Jewish milieu. Mendel awakens to the frightening fact that his ticking clock has stopped: It is a clear signal that he is shortly to die. As his last act of mercy on earth, he resolves to place his idiot son Isaac on a train to California, where aged Uncle Leo will meet him and look after him. But before the train departs at midnight, Mendel must raise another thirty-five dollars to purchase the ticket.

To gather the money, Mendel visits a pawnbroker who gives him eight dollars for his gold watch; rich Mr. Fishbein who contributes "only to institutions"; and a rabbi who over his wife's protests gives Mendel a new fur-lined caftan to pawn. In between these stops, Mendel and Isaac ride the subway, sit on a bench in the park, eat in a cafeteria. All the while pursuing Mendel is the specter Ginzburg, an angel of death hurrying the old man on his course. In the end, with Death taking the guise of the recalcitrant ticket collector, Mendel struggles with his last breath to force his way past the gate and send Isaac on his way. This mighty and noble deed accomplished, Mendel emerges from the platform to meet Ginzburg, but Ginzburg is not to be found.

Embedded in the tale lies acute commentary on selfishness and on the chaotic distribution of human resources in our atomized society. The purported communitarian self-help system of the Jews has broken down in this instance. Only the rabbi instinctively understands Mendel's situation and acts like the good angel of the Genesis story who saves Isaac from sacrifice by his intervention.

It is significant that Blitzstein chose to cast the opera in thirteen scenes. Recalling the clock scene in Mussorgsky's *Boris Godunov,* or the clock in Strauss's *Der Rosenkavalier* that beats out a thirteenth chime to reinforce the Marschallin's fear of aging, the final scene in *Idiots First* captures Mendel at the moment of his impending death. But death eludes both the Marschallin and Mendel (not Boris, of course). Blitzstein must have been aware, too, of Schoenberg's almost pathological horror of the number thirteen, and it may be that in this way he wanted to exorcise the demon of twelve-tone music.

Blitzstein added to the opera an incident not found in the Malamud story. In Scene 4, set in a park, Mendel tells an uncomprehending Isaac the story of "How I Met My New Grandfather," a charming tale about meeting his grandmother's new husband for the first time. A touch of humor placed amidst otherwise grim, mystical material, this set piece represents Blitzstein as the familiar creator of character numbers; and it contains a certain amount of autobiographical reference, as his father's marriage to Maddie Leof had indeed given Marc a "new grandfather," as well as a "new grandmother."

As a musical piece, *Idiots First* falls within a continuum of operatic tradition. The rabbi's generous gesture calls to mind the famous coat Colline offers up to the pawnbroker to keep Mimi alive at the end of *La Bohème.* The idiot, or fool, is an important old fixture especially in Russian opera. He makes an appearance in Berg's *Wozzeck* as well. (As librettist, Blitzstein changed Isaac's name to the diminutive form Itzak). Blitzstein found opportunities here to write more "machine music," with the sounds of clocks and watches, doorbell buzzers, offstage radio music, and the subway. Once again, the composer commits his art to protecting and uplifting the awkward, migrant Everyman, out of place in mass society. Programmatically, the Malamud tales show Blitzstein's political consciousness at its least specific, at least among the operas written since the 1930s.

For his musical idiom, Blitzstein used modes strongly suggesting Eastern European Jewish music. Strains of Bartók and Mussorgsky and jazz-derived rhythms enter the score. Minor thirds melt into his experiment with two twelve-tone row themes for the first time in his composing career; they are used to represent Ginzburg (whom he spells as "Ginzberg," following an early published version of the story). Could he have wanted to suggest by this unexpected intrusion into his vocabulary that Schoenberg and the tone-row system meant a kind of death in twentieth-century music; or that his specter somehow haunted musical creativity, requiring constant, conscious struggle to battle back its neurasthenic influence?

In one instance, for Itzak's theme of innocence, Blitzstein reached back into the score of *Cain,* revising Abel's number "The Young Son." In another more telling passage, Mendel's plea with Mr. Fishbein, Blitzstein remembered his 1945 song "Displaced," with its refugee wandering among the smoke and rubble of burned-out doorways. Now the aching tune served to draw the class distinction between supplicant and lord. Closely paraphrasing Malamud's original text, Mendel fights for his son's life:

> *Who will close the door on a neighbor's misfortune?*
> *Where is open the door, there we go in the house.*
> *Mr. Fishbein:*
> *If you will give me*
> *Thirty-five dollars,*
> *God will bless you.*
> *What is thirty-five dollars to Mr. Fishbein?*
> *Nothing. To me, for my boy,*
> *Is everything.*
> *Enjoy yourself, enjoy yourself*
> *To give me everything.*

In these lines, Blitzstein could sum up the catastrophe of life under capitalism, whereby the private patronage system, and more recently the corporate foundations, could dole out charity on an arbitrary basis that only haphazardly coincided with real need.

"The Magic Barrel" is equally mystical in that the external dimensions of the story lend only a sparse form to the protagonist's spiritual quests. Leo Finkle, a studious rabbinical candidate, decides to consult Pinye Salzman, a marriage broker. In succession, each proposed bride is rejected: One is a widow, another too old, a third has a limp. In the course of his search for an appropriate partner, Leo becomes aware of how loveless his life has been, even how empty of love for God. Pinye is a persistent salesman but to no effect. Eventually, among the photographs of prospects he has left behind for Leo to examine, the student finds a drugstore snapshot of a hauntingly moving face. Though mistakenly enclosed in the envelope, this is the one Leo is resolved to meet. She will be his redemption. It turns out to be Pinye's own daughter Stella, a whore for whom Pinye has long ago said prayers for the dead. They meet, Leo filled with the sense that she is the answer to all his searching, but also not without the suspicion that the marriage broker had somehow planned to marry off his own wayward child in this way.

In Malamud's story, "[v]iolins and lit candles revolved in the sky" for Leo when he met Stella, a rich Chagall-like image but surely not much of a musical impetus for operatic treatment.[18] So recently exposed in Israel to the possibilities of using traditional Jewish ceremonial music for contemporary purposes, Blitzstein felt attracted to the wedding theme. He could fill the stage with dances and songs. At the same time, Pinye's mourning for Stella's lost soul would provide opportunities to exploit the somber side of Jewish liturgy. Thoughts of his own marriage to Eva must have returned: marriage not as sexual love or even as a concession to family, but as answer to some unspecified yearnings for union, and brushed by the shroud of death.

Blitzstein thought at first more about the staging of *The Magic Barrel* than about its music. He wanted to revive some of the nonlinear aspects of theatre that he had used in such early works as *Triple-Sec, Parabola and Circula,* and *The Condemned.* Thus he proposed that part of the action onstage take place as if in Leo's mind. As each prospect is mentioned, all of them played by the same singer who portrays Stella, she is lit up in her wedding attire. When Leo learns that she is a widow, or is too old, he dismisses her, and the lights black out. When he learns that another limps, the entire wedding set collapses. Blitzstein thought of using the chorus surrealistically, appearing for as short a time as one note or a bar at these frustrated moments, brought on as a full ensemble only at the end, building to a grand finish. He considered asking the same tenor who sang Itzak in *Idiots First* to sing Leo; and the baritone singing Mendel to portray Pinye.

The first semester at Bennington ended on December 15. Before it closed, Blitzstein had been convicted in Bennington Municipal Court for speeding: Typically, and to the distress of everyone who rode with him, he took out his personal frustrations on the road. The court did not suspend his driver's license but warned him against future violations. He did not reform his habits, however: He tempted the fates every time he sat behind the wheel.

Blitzstein did not have to return until the spring session began in the second week of March. He went back to New York for several weeks of dentist appointments, concertgoing, National Institute meetings, and an almost compulsive daily round of lunches and dinners with friends. Minna Lederman was the victim of one of his outbursts when she innocently asked him during the intermission of a concert of twelve-tone music whether he had finished *Sacco and Vanzetti.* He exploded into a delirious barrage of unintelligible raving; several days later, he inscribed a copy of his newly published Cummings song cycle, *From Marion's Book,* and sent it to her by way of apology.

By New Year's Day, Lina Abarbanell had taken ill for virtually the first time in her life. Two months before, she had visited friends on the West Coast; and only the day before entering Montefiore Hospital in the Bronx, she had taken the subway with Leonora Hays to visit a Harlem dance studio, where she picked out a little girl for some theatre show. On the way to the hospital, she said to a friend, "It's ridiculous, I feel wonderful. I don't know why I'm going in. We're going to Loehmann's as soon as I get better." Dr. Samuel Standard, Blitzstein's own physician and a personal friend, performed a seemingly successful abdominal operation on Lina. On the telephone to Leonora Hays's daughter Julie, the last thing she said was, "I'm going to bring you some candies." Then on January 6, 1963, her heart gave out, three days after her eighty-fourth birthday.

From the hospital, Marc called Lina and Anna Wiman's office assistant, Adrienne Durand Gaiton. "I don't think I could ever live without Lina," Marc said to her.

"But Lina would want you to," she answered. In her mind she concluded that Lina had more or less willed herself to die so as not to become a burden on Marc.

"She understood me," Marc said, "and in no way did she ever show any reproach."

Two days later, friends gathered for a service at the Riverside Chapel. Anna Wiman could not bear to return from Landmark for the funeral nor to enter the office at the Alvin Theatre with Lina gone. Lina's florist sent a bouquet of her favorite violets. The owner of the health-food shop where she bought on an everlasting credit line forgave her debt. Leonora Hays asked the mortician, a former actor whom Lina had given his first job in the theatre, whether Lina should be presented in the open casket with her hat on.

"Yes, of course," he replied, "Lina always wore a hat."

It fell to Marc to clear Lina's room at the Barbizon Plaza and to pay her last bills. When the hotel staff opened her safety-deposit box for Blitzstein, he was horrified to find the container holding her husband Edward's ashes. Since 1934 she had kept them. Employees recalled how often she would open the box and stand simply gazing at them. Now timeless, ageless Lina was gone. Blindly going through the motions, her faithful son-in-law and friend took her body in for cremation—just as he had done nearly thirty years before for Eva—and disposed of her last effects. He was shocked to find a batch of pawn tickets among her things—had she really been that desperate for money? He donated her boxes of papers, including press clippings, rare photographs of her as a performer, and Eva's long letters from Mallorca and elsewhere in Europe, to the New York Public Library. He also sent pictures of Lina to a number of her longtime friends.

Only a few weeks later, he wrote to Jo: "Anna Wiman has died; another fall (in Bermuda), cerebral hemmorhage, out. Poor poor wretch. (She had muttered to me over the phone about Lina: 'She was my mother!')"[19] A combination of alcohol and mourning for Lina had sent her reeling down a flight of stairs at Landmark. She had never returned to New York after Lina died.

During his weeks in New York between semesters, Blitzstein saw the Tony Richardson film *The Loneliness of the Long Distance Runner,* which stimulated fresh thoughts about ordering the action of *Sacco and Vanzetti* in a "dis-chronology." In a memorandum dated March 11, 1963, "The re-assortment of scenes," he projected that the opera might begin with the verdict, then flashback to Sacco and Vanzetti in their cells, then further flashback to the night of the arrest. At the end of Act Three we catch up to the action when the clerk of the court asks, "Gentlemen of the jury, have you agreed upon your verdict?"

A day or two after attending a performance of Hellman's short-lived new play, *My Father, My Mother and Me,* Blitzstein joined the Bernsteins in Miami, along with Jack Gottlieb, composer and scholarly specialist on Bernstein's works, and

Verna Fine, recently widowed after the death of her composer husband Irving. While Lenny rehearsed with the New York Philharmonic, on tour in Florida that February, Marc, Felicia and her daughter Jamie, and Verna and her Joanna sunned and swam all day long at the beach. As he whiled away the hours, Blitzstein penned a parody of a song from *Wonderful Town,* "A Quiet Girl" (whose title Bernstein had borrowed from one of Blitzstein's wartime songs). His facetious new text implies a sense of apartness from Lenny and Felicia's, or anyone else's, happiness:

I love a QUIET GIRL.
She loves a NOISY BOY.
He loves ME, dear:
Whom else but me?
So soft my QUIET GIRL.
So loud her NOISY BOY.
I croon: I'm just in-between:
MEZZO- FOR-TEE.
Love should be answered,
Without asking why.
Breath calls to breath,
And THIGH to THIGH.
So give me my QUIET GIRL.
Give her her NOISY BOY.
Then if NOISY BOY
Doesn't mind three,
Whilst he bangs
[or] beds her,
I can have me.
(Ossia: Give me—to me.)

During the second semester at Bennington, Blitzstein felt less attached to the campus. The spring weather drew him out more and attracted friends to visit him at his rustic post. In early April, close to her birthday, he spent a weekend in Ventnor with Mama. Later that month, he hosted a party for his sister Jo and Irene Diamond. In May he traveled to Washington, D.C., where a Bennington College benefit performance of his *Threepenny* translation at the Arena Stage, directed by Alan Schneider, brought him extensive television and press coverage. He related to Meryle Secrest of the Washington *Post* how the banging he produced on his Chickering piano outdid the noise from the wild Bennington girls. "I'm not a teacher and never expected to be," he told her, "because I am both too vain and too impatient. But curiously enough the girls supply the patience and put up with my vanity . . . and I have discovered that in the act of revealing something to them, I am also revealing it to myself." Speaking of the production at the Arena Stage and of the irony of being best known for another composer's work, he confessed his big secret: "All translations are failures. The best you can do is to find the translation that fails least."[20]

The semester did not end well. At one point, Blitzstein considered giving up his fellowship. Gaunt and irritable, he approached President Fels with his decision. "So I leave. I feel that the girls here are getting a raw deal," he told Fels.

"Do you always turn on your benefactors that way?" the president answered.

Blitzstein deflected the charge: "The only word I find permissible in that sentence is 'you.' " He reconsidered and stayed on.

The college newspaper *The Galley* had published a proposal that the student body give up three meals to benefit the civil rights struggle. A few students protested that such participation be limited to a personal decision and not be obligatory for the entire school. Blitzstein thundered his rejoinder:

> May I, as incumbent fellow (which is to say guest) faculty-member, express my astonishment. It had never occurred to me that civil rights in this country were up for grabs. . . . It is a little like saying "Please decide privately and secretly whether the Bill of Rights Amendments to the Constitution should not be scrapped."
>
> If a simply-arranged collective effort to contribute to the Bennington Civil Rights Committee is to be sniped at, perhaps sabotaged, then I really don't know why I'm here.
>
> You will all be free of my convictions and partisanship shortly. At the moment I am still here; the Galley was placed in my box, it is presumably there for me to read and respond to. You now have my response: Forfeit them 3 Friday dinners like crazy, say I.[21]

The letter shows well his state of mind: Anxious to be free of his teaching obligations and no longer caring how he exposed his sensitivities, he invented a special language of persecution. He interpreted the students' "sabotage" as though they were fifth-column pro-Nazis.

The old ideals returned in another way, too, for one of his playwriting students chose to dramatize an incident from the French Resistance he had related about his trip to the Continent during the closing months of the war. She had invested the play with the Abraham and Isaac theme, a story Blitzstein had always found chilling.

Several of his students failed to submit their finished plays by the end of the semester in June. Well into the fall of 1963, he sent curt, indignant letters to two of them demanding that they complete their last semester's work with him. It hurt him that they apparently felt their year spent with him was so lacking in value.

Another student, Reed Wolcott, had also left her work unfinished. She wrote letters of gushing praise mixed with abject apology:

> Your very presence here last year meant more to me than anything ever has. . . . I've never loved or admired anyone as I do you . . . because you are the finest teacher who has ever taught me and the greatest man I've ever known. . . . Somehow because I knew you, I had something to live for. Because your courage and integrity which was in everything you did

> and said taught me that there are good people left and things to live and fight for.[22]

In June President Fels wrote to Blitzstein, politely claiming, "It was a special pleasure to have you with us this year. I hope you will come to see us often."[23]

All summer and fall, Blitzstein shuttled back and forth to various familiar homes: Mina Curtiss, now living in Bethel, and Brenda Lewis in Weston, both in Connecticut, hosted him for days at a time. Frequently, after a day's work, he would visit Bernstein, also living in Fairfield County. He caught performances of *Brecht on Brecht* at the White Barn in Westport, Connecticut, and *The World of Kurt Weill in Song,* with Martha Schlamme and Will Holt in New York, both of which included some of his translations. "He had his own little apartment over our barn," Brenda Lewis wrote, where he worked on *Sacco and Vanzetti* and the Malamud operas:

> We moved in a piano, filled his refrigerator and gave him keys, and a little car. One of the most amazing things about Marc, given the usual canards about the artistic soul who needs inspiration and is so undisciplined—was his invariable and regimented daily schedule. The six A.M. splash in the pool was on the dot each day—he set off the clucking of the bantam hens and other birds we kept near the barn. He found his daily fresh egg, made his breakfast, and the fresh-perked coffee stirred our household 100 feet away. He would work at his table until lunch—join us for an hour—take another swim, then back to the work table or piano until dinner. Really, until cocktails before dinner. He supervised the making of the drinks, and all had to be chilled and set out for his delicate maneuvers. . . .
>
> He would proudly play and sing for us in his mordant, husky tenor the latest parts that he had written. I remember vividly an excruciatingly moving scene he had written for Sacco, reading letters in his death-cell. It seemed clear that this work would forever put Marc beyond the Broadway Show-Biz frame that he had always been thrust into and judged by.[24]

Later in the summer he spent time in Ventnor and Brigantine. At that time he grew his first beard to go along with his customary mustache. All hoary around the chin, it gave him a dashing, self-assured air. He corresponded with John Orr Hunter, assistant professor of social science at the Niagara County subdivision of the State University of New York, who was beginning research on *The Cradle Will Rock* as a document of the New Deal period. He questioned Hunter's sources of information, such as the work of music historian John Tasker Howard, "who knows next to nothing of what modern composition is about," and the criticism of Virgil Thomson, "whose motives are always suspect whether he is lauding or damning." And he started exchanging letters with Robert J. Dietz, preparing to write his doctoral dissertation on Blitzstein's agitprop period for the University of Iowa. "I am anxious to help," he wrote Dietz, authorizing access to the papers in Wisconsin. "Don't be afraid to ask questions. Your thesis ought to be as complete and accurate as possible."[25]

In October, he met with Mira Gilbert and Lou Norman, who wanted to produce a Blitzstein evening similar in format to the Kurt Weill revue. Encouraging them, he agreed to meet again in a few months once they had devised a program.

But underneath all the frantic coming and going lay a malaise brought on in part by health problems and in part by an inability to settle into work. In July he broke a bone in his right foot, which still needed attention three months later. An elbow bothered him, too, and he saw a physician about his unexplainable loss of weight. His nephew Stephen had moved to a new office with an attractive view of the city from high up in the Pan Am building; he had moved with his family to a new home in New Jersey, but Marc repeatedly made unconvincing excuses and never visited either.

He also made excuses to Rudolf Bing and John Gutman of the Metropolitan Opera as to why, still, he could not show them any *Sacco and Vanzetti* material. To Judge Michael Musmanno he expressed his crushing anxiety: The opera was "a long hard task. . . . Maybe soon there will come a night when the opera is produced, and we can look at each other, and you can tell me if you feel I have let this incredibly grand subject down."[26]

For the month of September, he worked in Brigantine. "The first Malamud opera is done," he wrote to Lenny, exaggerating somewhat, "the second well on its way. *S and VZ* lie in wait."[27]

With the approach of cold weather, Blitzstein began looking southward again. This time, for his swimming, working vacation in the sun, he chose the island of Martinique in the French West Indies. Through her Chapelbrook Foundation, Mina Curtiss provided a substantial grant, large enough to support Marc through the spring. Ella Winter, in New York from her base in London, asked him to reconsider the trip, mostly because she had looked forward to spending time with him during her stay in New York. To other friends he seemed depressed and did not look well. Sam Standard, the physician who had already performed a series of hernia operations on Blitzstein, anticipated that still another might be required and advised him not to go.

Lenny's brother Burton, who had served in the Caribbean as a public information officer in the army a few years before, had nothing good to say about the island. All over the Caribbean, people spoke ill of the place—in part because they disliked its arch petty aristocracy, but mostly because during World War II its Vichy government had allowed German U-boats to use Martinique as a refueling station, thus permitting them to blockade the other islands. And the French possession still seemed as though it were full of unreconstructed Vichy sympathizers.

Through the French Government Tourist Office, Blitzstein secured a letter of introduction from the public relations man to the director of the tourism office in Fort-de-France; it overexcitedly described Blitzstein as "one of the most eminent personalities in the world of music in the United States . . . who, among other works, composed the music for *Three Penny Opera.*" The letter announced that Blitzstein would arrive at the beginning of November and would need to rent a villa or small house for five months. In a postscript, the writer added, "Although

Mr. Blitzstein's present opera has nothing to do with Martinique, one can always hope that the excellent scenery of your beautiful island might perhaps inspire him for a future work."[28]

A week before he left the city, Blitzstein packed into the trunk of his gray Peugeot all his drafts of libretto and music for *Sacco and Vanzetti.* He may have felt they would be safer there than in his vacant apartment. He drove the car to New Rochelle where, as he had done before, he left it at the apartment building owned by Aaron Diamond. He had decided to give the opera a rest during his stay in Martinique, and he took with him only his two Malamud one-acts. Morris Golde hosted a farewell party for Marc on October 28, and Irene Diamond gave another the following night. The day before he left, at Claire Reis's urging, he addressed a new class of artists and performers at the City Center about contemporary music and theatre. He also played through *Idiots First* for David Diamond, telling him that he planned to score the opera while he was away.

Blitzstein's reservation at the Auberge de l'Anse Mitan in Fort-de-France began on November 1. From there, with the help of the tourist bureau, he began his search for a suitable house for the winter. In a letter to Mama, he described the food and the service: "they try to make up by good-will and exertion what they lack in civilized appurtenances. So far it's fun and a little suspenseful."[29]

After several days and no luck in locating a house, he considered giving up on the island. Only weeks before, a cyclone had ripped through Martinique leaving considerable devastation in its wake. Hot water and electricity were undependable, and in any case, the island was not accustomed to tourists and their needs. Still, the place held his interest, "a down-at-heel feudal insouciant island full of charming polite class-ridden lords-and-esnes," he wrote Jo.[30]

After two weeks, he found his spot, a house with three bedrooms and two baths near the town of Frégate-François. His villa, owned by Marcel Hervé and situated directly across the island from Fort-de-France, looked out over the Atlantic Ocean on a point whose vista included a garden with dozens of flowering pear trees and several hilly islets offshore. The water was shallow off his private dock, but the swimming and sunning were more than acceptable. Jacqueline, an eighteen-year-old girl living in a small building on the property, cooked splendidly, cleaned, and laundered for fourteen dollars a month, while Georges, a fourteen-year-old, came on the weekends to garden and clean up outside. "No cushy splendors like Israel or Rome; I've been spoiled," he wrote home. He bought a black 403 Peugeot, arranging to resell it to the dealer at the end of his stay in April less $25 a week; he also bought a grand piano. Now he began asking Jo when she would like to come for a visit with Ed and Irene and Aaron Diamond. "You won't believe it, but it's a beautiful island indeed; when I get to work really, I'll love it, never fear."[31]

Morris Golde visited him during the last week of November just as Blitzstein settled into the house. It was fortunate timing, for only a few days before he arrived, the shocking events in Dallas had aroused in Blitzstein a profound longing to be home with his people. It was the second time the sudden death of a president had caught Blitzstein abroad.

An inquiry for up-to-date news at the American Consulate led him across the street to the Cultural Center run by the United States Information Service, where a wire service ticked off the latest developments. There, he introduced himself to the director, James DeCou, an urbane young man in his thirties who displayed some familiarity with Blitzstein's work. Immediately he let Blitzstein know how much he adored the *Threepenny Opera* adaptation, and quickly they became friends. Later on, DeCou and his wife invited the composer to their home several times.

Blitzstein found solace in the high mass conducted in Fort-de-France for President Kennedy, not failing to note the "14th century choruses by black male-sopranos," and he gravely accepted the natives' expressions of personal condolences with a stoic "*merci*"—the response he had learned under similar circumstances in London back in 1945. With an eerie foreboding, as though he himself were wrapped up in the death trend, he wrote to Irene Diamond that day: "In the middle of all the cataclysmic assassinations that have been happening at home, I am small potatoes indeed." And to Mama he wrote:

> The news from home is so horrible, and we get so maddeningly little of it, garbled by the French or toned down by our own consulate, that I am dazed. It seems somehow a double disgrace, aside from the suspension of all continuities in civil rights, etc. As to what kind of president Johnson will make, and whether he will be re-elected, I don't dare think. Whatever happened to the scandals he was involved in, by the way? And the slimy stalwartstripteaseowner [*sic*] who avenged the murder! It all stinks.[32]

Morris Golde found Marc despondent. As a host, he seemed mannered, shuttling his guest around the island to meet his new friends, particularly George and Lollie Peckham, Americans resident in his little town of François. He argued vehemently about the way the French treated the colonials and about the U.S. investors and tourists who fleeced the natives. At the end of Morris's stay, Blitzstein looked at him with a long, sad expression that Morris had never seen before, and begged him to stay on. Not long after Morris left, Marc wrote him with details of the latest household problems—the plumbing this time. "If I last, I'll love it all. Pray for me," he asked.[33]

To Mama and Jo, as usual, he presented a brighter image, outlining the comfortable daily schedule he had evolved. He rose at six for a swim from the quay, ate breakfast, worked until 11:30, broke for another swim. The local fisherman brought lobsters and mackerel for lunch. Then more work until dinner. "I have French friends, negro friends, some Americans even," he wrote to Mama. "And it's an even keel, and regular routine, and I am at last loving it." He developed a warm friendship with Père Mayer, a Swiss priest and baritone who had sung at Kennedy's high mass. He "smokes, drinks, wears shorts on leave, and curses superbly; he is also a music-fanatic and can talk Schönberg and Boulez with me. We go swimming together at Morris' favorite beach, Les Salines at Ste. Anne (southern tip of the island), which must be one of the glorious untouched beaches of the world."[34]

During these months in Martinique, Blitzstein worked primarily on *The Magic Barrel.* For thematic material, he cast a wide net, remembering old Russian peasant songs, some snatches of Yiddish tunes, and a Haydn round. He also noted down the calls of a tree frog and a bird at his villa, and was prepared to incorporate the defective two notes on his piano into an ostinato yearning motif for the rabbinical student Leo. Following his usual custom, he jumped from scene to scene, gradually shaping the literal translation of Malamud's dialogue into lyrics, and deciding how much he wanted to make it a "number" opera, with spoken dialogue.

Before the year ended, he wrote to Rudolf Bing and John Gutman of the Metropolitan Opera:

> Now that I am happily installed in a seashore house on this beautiful and primitive island, and working well, guilt assails me that I went off without giving you even a taste of what my opera on Sacco and Vanzetti might be like, after all this time. And so, I have copied out an aria (for Sacco, tenor), which I think can safely see the light of day without my personal shepherding.[35]

The aria, called "With a Woman to Be," occurs just before the end of the second act when Sacco is experiencing hallucinations after an extended hunger strike. He imagines himself courting his wife Rosa. Blitzstein derived most of the music and some of the lyrics from *Reuben Reuben.* Clearly, he wanted to give the impression that he was "working well" on the opera for the Metropolitan. Of course, this was not the case: His *Sacco and Vanzetti* materials lay safely packed in the trunk of his gray Peugeot in New Rochelle.

Gutman answered after the first of the new year. He had placed the aria in the hands of a young tenor new to the company, Nicholas di Virgilio, and an audition of the piece would take place shortly. "I envy you for being in such a pleasant neighborhood," Gutman wrote, "and I hope for your sake you will be able to stay there for a long time."[36]

Just before the end of the year, he had a brief stopover visit from Jo and Ed to look forward to: Their cruise ship, the *Olympia,* would allow them a day in Martinique on December 30, and he was anxious to show off his villa.

On the day they arrived, Marc met them at the boat when they disembarked at eight in the morning. He had planned a full day and sped them along the island's jarring roads at seventy miles an hour. They saw his house and private garden, traveled down to the beach at Les Salines, lunched at a tiny inn, and shopped in Fort-de-France in the afternoon. He also introduced them to the Peckhams. Jo had brought Kit's newest book, *Belmarch,* lovingly inscribed to his uncle. The visit came and went "so quickly that four minutes seemed to pass," he reported to Mama the following day. He had not wished to encumber Jo and Ed with any reminders of his melancholy. "I tried to pack as much as I could into the 8-to-5 schedule, and I seem to have succeeded. They have now, I think, a kind of idealistic picture of the island, having just skimmed the cream. . . . It was all too short; but it was good too."[37]

New Year's Eve was a quiet one: He enjoyed cold cuts and champagne with the Peckhams. When he awoke, he skipped his swim and drove into the little town of François. Mama always appreciated Marc's anecdotes about his travels:

> But festivity! (or so I thought)—every bitty bistrot [*sic*] jammed to the door, waiters and waitresses commandeered on the spot, all the gentry (not a woman, all males) in *black velvet hats,* black ties (some butterfly-bows), suits, my God (I mean jackets too)—and a raillery and exuding happiness rarely seen by me here. Of course: a burial. Not only New Year's Day, but someone had the grace to die too.

Unabashed at the eroticism of his imagery, he took additional pains to describe for his mother how François continued to function through a power shortage:

> Quite a discovery: the town bakery; also with its own motor, lights and all, revealing twelve nudes (all male, not really nude, shorts), including two twelve-year-old boys. Now there's a sight, if you remember the figures on these men—all kneading the dough, slapping it from round mounds to long flat-type phalluses, and sending them javelin-like onto the long floury tables.[38]

In other letters, Blitzstein wrote about the local political climate, citing the strength of the Communist Party; about sexual and marital mores in Martinique; often something about the natural life of the island, the insects, frogs, water, or light; and about the daily incidents in the life of a composer abroad. Always in letters to Mama, he inquired after her health. In one letter to his sister, he enclosed a photograph of himself stretched out on the limb of a dead tree at Les Salines: "I seem to be camouflaged by the background, but healthy-looking enough, if skinny. (I'll try to put on some weight in the next few weeks.)"[39] He urged Jo to plan another visit to the island in March, along with Irene Diamond, then in Acapulco.

Jo had been in touch with Marc's surgeon about the need for another hernia operation. "Standard did say it was O.K. for you to wait," she wrote to her brother, "but that's all. Don't get any notion that you can continue too long without the operation. He says, 'This time they'll make it last.' He doesn't seem worried in the least. Of course, it's not his gut."[40]

In his conception of *The Magic Barrel,* "the entire opera should be musically hot and sexy," Blitzstein advised himself, "until the advent of Stella." In late December, he worked on various drafts of "Then," a final-scene aria for Stella, the matchmaker's decadent daughter, whom he compared to *Cradle*'s Moll: "the music can be hard-boiled, the delivery 'pure.' " In the vocal line, the music is a throwback to his style of the 1930s, particularly his blues and torch songs, but the harmony is more advanced. The lyrics, nowhere suggested in Malamud's prose, are entirely Blitzstein's; as in some of his earlier songs, they expose the quiet panic of his longing for love. In mid-January, he copied out this song in a clear hand:

Then
Mountains will tumble;
Big stars will go crazy
And fall in the sea.
They promised me.
Then
Is when it all happens,
With gorgeous explosions
To play around me.
They promised me.
I'm sitting here waiting
For any explosion
And I don't care when.
I'll bet they're wrong.
It's not meant for me.
How long, how old
Must I get to be
Till for me
It's then?

On the night of January 21, 1964, a Tuesday, Blitzstein had dinner in François with George and Lollie Peckham. When he left their house, they expected he would be returning home to nearby Villa Hervé. He decided instead to drive into Fort-de-France to check out the scene down at the waterfront bars where the sailors and merchant seamen liked to drink. Shortly before midnight, he fell in with three such types, two Portuguese and a native Martiniquan, and together they toured several of the low-class dives around the Place de Stalingrad.

As they drank, Blitzstein fished for bills from his wallet, revealing the tidy sum he was carrying. After two or three hours, en route to the next bar, Blitzstein and one of his three companions slipped into a nearby alleyway, the lure of sex in the air. The other two followed. Then suddenly, all three set upon him. They beat him severely, robbed him of his valuables, and left him there in the alley stripped of every piece of clothing but his shirt and socks. Hearing his cries and moans, policemen found him between three and four in the morning and took him to Clarac Hospital.

Blitzstein told the hospital authorities that he had been injured in an auto accident, and this is what they reported to the American consulate in the morning. When consular official William B. Milam appeared at the hospital to see Blitzstein, the victim had already been x-rayed and was sitting up, his mind lucid and his speech clear, waiting for a thorough examination. He told Milam of being robbed and beaten by three Venezuelans, which is what he believed his companions were. He admitted to some sexual advances with the men but requested that this not be publicized. In accordance with his wishes, Milam telegraphed Jo: MARC BLITSTEIN [*sic*] HOSPITALIZED AUTO ACCIDENT YOUR PRESENCE NEEDED IF POSSIBLE TELEPHONE AMERICAN CONSULATE.[41] Marc must have felt his injuries were severe enough to ask for Jo to come and take care of him. Considering the reckless way Marc had spun Jo and Ed around the island that day just three weeks before—and given his penchant for drinking as well—a car crash seemed utterly believable.

An English-speaking doctor examined Blitzstein and found his injuries to be external only, of no serious consequence. By late afternoon when Milam stopped in again to visit, followed shortly by James DeCou and his wife, Blitzstein appeared much worse, however, his face swollen and his color an alarming yellowish green. He still spoke well, referring to "those bastards" who beat him up, but his distress and embarrassment over the manner of his injury were painful, especially with Mrs. DeCou present. Again he asked that the facts of the story not be given to the press. Milam and DeCou both requested the hospital staff's greatest possible attention to his care.

To no avail, however. At about eight that evening, January 22, he died of multiple contusions.

Marc Blitzstein, who had fought all his life for the workers, the underclass, the foreigner, and for meaning in the struggle for decency, now lay dead at fifty-eight, brought down by the very type of men he had held so high. What to three sailors seemed like a merry, drunken episode of beating up a queer and humiliating him by leaving him naked and stealing his money turned fatal under less than ideal hospital conditions to a man with a weak liver and in need of a hernia operation.

In her Philadelphia apartment, Jo had already begun packing her suitcase for a flight out to Martinique the next day when a second telegram from William Milam arrived: REGRET NOTIFY DEATH YOUR BROTHER MARC BLITZTEIN [*sic*] JANUARY 22 IN MARTINIQUE YOUR IMMEDIATE INSTRUCTIONS AND FUNDS REQUIRED FOR DISPOSITION REMAINS ESTIMATED COST LOCAL BURIAL DOLLARS 163 AIR SHIPMENT DOLLARS 420.[42] The following morning when Ed called the American consulate in Fort-de-France, he heard from Milam the true story of Marc's death.

26

THEN

January 1964–March 1965

On Thursday, January 23, 1964, the day following Blitzstein's death, police arrested the three seamen on charges of involuntary homicide and theft. The two Portuguese, both natives of Madeira but now legal residents of Venezuela while working in the Martinique fishing industry, were Armando Fernandes, twenty-six, and Alfredo Mendez Rodriguez, thirty-four. Some four hundred dollars of Blitzstein's money was found in a cabin aboard their vessel. The Martinique boy, only seventeen years old, was Daniel Yves Charles Nicolas.

When Police Chief Georges Fluchaire came around to speak with the American officials, he spoke in confidential tones of his knowledge of Blitzstein as *"un homme de moeurs bizarres,"*—a man of strange morals. James DeCou's look indicated that he was unfamiliar with Fluchaire's euphemism. The policeman translated for him: "Queer." DeCou launched into an extended lecture about the case involving a very distinguished American composer, and about how loose talk and innuendo would be most unfortunate in such a sensitive situation.

Perhaps based on this cautionary advice, the local authorities released few details of the crime for fear that it would reflect poorly on the image both of the island and of the composer. Their public position, according to a U.S. consular report, was that "the victim was visiting those dives to find color for the opera he was writing here."[1]

American newspapers at first picked up the story—fed early on to the local stringers—that death had come in the auto accident. The front page of *The New York Times* carried this version on January 24, correcting the story the next day, but several published obituaries later repeated the initial version.

On the night of the twenty-third, conducting the New York Philharmonic in a program of Vivaldi, Varèse, and Beethoven, Leonard Bernstein announced the grievous news to his audience; he had heard it from Kit's wife, Sonia Davis, earlier in the day. Waiting for their gasps of shock to subside, he then dedicated the *Eroica* to Blitzstein's memory. "The work was performed as if the conductor were re-writing Beethoven as he went along in order to express his personal grief," wrote Eric Salzman in the *Herald Tribune.* "It was an incredible, agonized, unbearable reading which, with its bursts of nervous energy, and wild relentless drive, left detail, clarity, accuracy and indeed everything but anguished, frenetic intensity far, far behind."[2]

Lollie Peckham wrote to Jo—whom she had met briefly only three weeks before—the evening of the twenty-third, reporting that she had been present when the consul opened Blitzstein's house and packed up the manuscripts and clothes for later shipment to the family.

> I would like to tell you how much we loved Marc—and how he has enriched our lives. Oh, we argued and debated and discussed our diverse political and philosophical and yes, religious views—but we learned, and pondered and had respect for his. He was at once an intellect and a humanist.
>
> He loved people—no matter what race, color, creed, nationality, or kind of clothes they wore. Perhaps this inquisitiveness into what makes people tick might have been the cause of his demise. He was wanting to know where and how carnival was *really* celebrated—not by the tourists, but by the *real* Martiniquoise [*sic*].[3]

The American consulate arranged to fly the body to Philadelphia on Sunday the twenty-sixth for cremation. The family held no funeral service. Burial of the remains took place in the suburb of Germantown.

Telegrams and condolence letters poured in to Jo and to Anna Blitzstein, now eighty-one years old. They came from composers and friends, professional organizations, his representatives at the William Morris Agency, his students at Bennington, members of the family, his housekeeper of eleven years, and from old schoolmates, neighbors in Brigantine, and peace activists Jo knew. Numerous donations went in Blitzstein's memory to music schools, hospitals, libraries, and to the organization to which Jo devoted herself, the Women's International League for Peace and Freedom. Someone planted a tree in Israel in Blitzstein's name.

From the little town of François in Martinique, the postmistress expressed her profound regrets. From the secretary at the Fort-de-France branch of the Martinique Tourist Office came a lengthy tribute and a loving recollection of Blitzstein's life on the island: "He often came into the office to see us in the morning, whistling, his beret tipped over his forehead."[4]

The traditional memorial took place on January 31 at the Helen Hayes Theatre on Broadway, just adjacent to the Forty-sixth Street Theatre where *Regina* had opened. One hundred and twenty of Blitzstein's friends and associates attended to hear the remarks of Dr. Sam Standard, José Ferrer, Douglas Moore, Lillian Hellman, and others. Neither Jo nor Anna could bear to be there, but Kit and

Stephen attended. Hellman cited her long, sometimes stormy relationship with Blitzstein. Even in the hour of his death, she referred unrelentingly to the "failure" of *Regina.* Leonard Bernstein could not be present: He was in Boston preparing to conduct the U.S. premiere of—fittingly enough—his *Kaddish* Symphony, following its first performance in Israel the month before.

In the weeks after Marc's death, Jo concerned herself, as executor with Ed of her brother's estate, with settling his affairs. Appreciative of William Milam's efforts in Martinique, she asked him through the State Department to assist in disposing of the black Peugeot Blitzstein had purchased in Martinique and that he was to have resold to the dealer for six hundred dollars. She drafted a letter to Washington in special hopes of recovering a canvas bag she felt might contain *Sacco and Vanzetti* materials and that so far had failed to materialize:

> The trunk of the car & the glove compartment should be checked for personal property. The above mentioned canvas bag may be in the trunk of the car.
>
> We tried to explain to you the importance of the music ms. which was commissioned by the NY Metropolitan Opera Co. on a grant from the Ford Foundation. This represents 4 years work & was nearing completion.[5]

But no material from *Sacco and Vanzetti* could be found, either at Villa Hervé or in the trunk of the Peugeot in Martinique. No one knew that Blitzstein had not even taken the work with him and that it all lay in cartons in the trunk of his own gray Peugeot stored in New Rochelle at Aaron Diamond's apartment-house garage.

As those around Blitzstein resumed their lives, Hellman and Bernstein in particular wished to sponsor a public event honoring the dead composer. They organized a memorial concert at the new Philharmonic Hall at Lincoln Center on Sunday, April 19, 1964, with the additional initial sponsorship of Aaron Copland, Edward Albee, Mrs. Serge Koussevitsky, Gian Carlo Menotti, Dorothy Parker, and Virgil Thomson, and an appended list of over a hundred friends and patrons. Contributions of fourteen thousand dollars raised on the occasion would fund a Marc Blitzstein musical theatre award to be given periodically to a composer, lyricist, or librettist, encouraging the creation of works of merit. The award was to be administered by the National Institute of Arts and Letters. In conjunction with the advance publicity for the evening, Bernstein announced to the press that he would complete and orchestrate *Idiots First,*

The program for the evening was comprised of major scenes from *Regina,* with connective narration by Hellman and with the orchestra conducted by Julius Rudel. Phyllis Curtin, who had never done the role on stage, sang Regina, with Elisabeth Carron, Lee Venora, Carol Brice, Joshua Hecht, George Irving, Emile Renan, and Andrew Frierson also performing. Following *Regina,* Bernstein announced in a speech from the podium that the manuscript materials for *Sacco and Vanzetti* had apparently disappeared. The audience reacted in audible shock.

He repeated his promise to complete and orchestrate *Idiots First,* which the audience applauded. As the centerpiece of the evening, he then conducted Hershy Kay's orchestrations of three Blitzstein songs never heard before, all from the last, unfinished works in progress. Summoning up, in Harold Schonberg's phrase, "a Yiddish accent that would make the blintzes stand up and salute," José Ferrer sang "How I Met My New Grandfather" from *Idiots First;* Anita Ellis sang "Then" from *The Magic Barrel;* and Luigi Alva sang "With a Woman to Be" from *Sacco and Vanzetti,* the only piece of music Blitzstein ever submitted to the Metropolitan Opera.[6]

After the intermission, the audience heard Blitzstein's voice from the Spoken Arts recording telling the story of the opening night of *The Cradle Will Rock,* and then the work itself (minus the Faculty Room scene), with Bernstein directing from the piano. Howard da Silva, Will Geer, and Hiram Sherman repeated their roles from the 1937 production, joined by Betty Comden, Charles Nelson Reilly, Phyllis Newman, Michael Wager, Adolph Green, Heywood Hale Broun, Micki Grant, Jack Harrold, and William Redfield.

The Philharmonic Hall program book contained a collection of remembrances by Aaron Copland, Mina Curtiss, Minna Lederman, Lillian Hellman, Leonard Bernstein, and Claire Reis. As the man who intended to complete *Idiots First,* Bernstein presumed to inherit the dead composer's mantle. He recalled Blitzstein's visit to see *Cradle* at Harvard in 1939: "then we walked, all afternoon, by the Charles River. Now that image leaps up in my mind: Marc lying on the banks of the Charles, talking, talking, bequeathing to me his knowledge, insight, warmth, endlessly. . . ."

Jo did not attend the concert. Ever since Soviet and American women had gathered in Bryn Mawr, Pennsylvania, in 1961 to discuss problems of war and peace, Jo had hoped, as National Literature Chairman of the Women's International League for Peace and Freedom, to attend a reciprocal conference in the Soviet Union. This second conference took place in Moscow during the third week of April 1964, and Jo felt it more productive to go there than to stay at home. Ed went to the concert, however, along with Mama and the rest of the family.

"Close friends, famous colleagues, and anonymous admirers of the late Marc Blitzstein filled Philharmonic Hall right up to its acoustical 'clouds,' " wrote Leighton Kerner in his *Village Voice* review. Gerald Weales, writing for *The Reporter,* contributed a thoughtful essay on Blitzstein's career, analyzing why *Cradle* succeeds as art while so much else of the propaganda art of the 1930s is beyond redemption—the secret lay in the oblique, wry presentation of the good guy, Larry Foreman. Jay S. Harrison in *Musical America* wrote of the aria "With a Woman to Be": "*Sacco and Vanzetti* could easily have become Mr. Blitzstein's major work. It has dignity, it has drama and pulse and it rings like struck steel. That we will know no more of the opera is one of the authentic tragedies of our time."[7]

It was lucky that Bernstein had announced the loss of *Sacco and Vanzetti.* After Blitzstein's death, Aaron Diamond, never thinking to open the trunk, had moved the Peugeot from its New Rochelle storage to a used-car lot in Long Island City, where it was put up for sale. The manager of the lot stumbled on Bernstein's statement in a newspaper account of the concert. On the off chance that he might find something of Blitzstein's there, he looked in the trunk and discovered the cartons. He turned them over to Bernstein, who claimed in a Metropolitan Opera press release that Acts One and Two looked substantially completed, and Act Three sketched.

By the end of the year, however, with the three uncompleted operas in his possession and with people asking him repeatedly about his plans for finishing them, the man to whom Blitzstein had "bequeathed" his knowledge and insight admitted he could not proceed with his appointed project. In an apostrophe written as a commemorative tribute to the missing composer for the National Institute of Arts and Letters, he said that *Idiots First* was

> almost finished. A short scene to be written here and there, ten bars of accompaniment missing here, twelve bars there. It could be done, they tell me. Done? With what notes? Only yours, your own private and mysterious notes. Neither I, nor anyone I know, has access to your luminous caves where those word-notes are forged.

A part of Bernstein reveled in the sagging arc of Blitzstein's career. To a degree, as did Hellman, he relished his mentor's disappointments. He conspicuously skewed Blitzstein's record:

> I have always thought of you as the chief survivor, of the welts of passion, the agony of commitment, of a long chain of beautiful work-failures. Never have I seen such glowing failures, all in a row, like falling (but not fallen) angels. You have rushed, singing but orderly, from one to another: another, another, always singing. . . .
>
> Come back from Martinique, come soon, and make more falling angels. They will look lovely in descending flight, like the sea gulls we used to watch those summers on the Vineyard.[8]

"Make more falling angels"! Bernstein did not even want Marc to enjoy a posthumous success. Though unquestionably Blitzstein's "almost finished" last work as completed by Leonard Bernstein at the height of his renown would have received a very attentive production by the Metropolitan Opera, the New York City Opera, or another first-rate company, Bernstein refused to do it.

Other tributes to Blitzstein included a Bennington College evening in June of songs and excerpts from the stage works, organized by Reed Wolcott, his admiring student. That same month, Minna Lederman's "Memories of Marc Blitzstein, Music's Angry Man" appeared in *Show* magazine, a wise and funny reminiscence that strikes many a true note despite its errors. In November, a Theater Four production of *The Cradle Will Rock* brought Howard da Silva back as director of a young and enthusiastic cast, garnering warm respect for the work. Gershon Kingsley served as musical director, with Bernstein listed as musical consultant. The cast recording of that production appeared on two MGM disks released in the spring of 1965, the only recording commercially available until well into the 1980s.*

Blitzstein's family had little interest in the trial of his assailants. Whatever justice was done or failed to be done, nothing would bring Marc back. Any attendant publicity relating to his death would only bring further sorrow, especially to his mother Anna. Jo and the rest of her family preferred to spare her. But Lillian Hellman bragged widely that the whole story stank and that she was going to Martinique to conduct her own investigation. Many who loved Marc wished her well in her selfless efforts. What actually happened is that she was invited to spend several weeks in the Caribbean on board Sam Spiegel's 250-foot yacht, enjoying his liquor and gourmet meals and the use of his private helicopter, while writing the screenplay of *The Chase* for his studio. Various other guests, such as Oliver Smith and William Holden and his companion, the French actress Capucine, joined Spiegel and Hellman for portions of the trip. When the ship reached Martinique, Hellman took Spiegel ashore to meet the American consul. She let him know how Lenny, she, and Marc were practically the Three Musketeers, and that she was deeply disturbed by Marc's death. She told him how sure she felt that Marc had not been properly cared for. William Milam and James DeCou understood her grief but patiently laid out the facts of the case. It was a confirmation of her worst fears. She invited the consul to lunch on the yacht, and that was the investigation.†

That first summer at Brigantine after Marc's death, Jo could not bring herself to enter Marc's studio. Her sons and grandchildren used the room, but she would not. Having set the tradition, she kept it for all her later years: Until she and Ed sold the property twenty years later, she never again set foot in that holy space where Marc had spent his monkish summers with her. Though she knew life without Marc somehow had to go on, she often felt guilty if she caught herself having too good a time. Once, a few years later, someone asked Mama how she was in Jo's presence. Without a thought, Mama answered, "Oh, it's been the best year of my life!" Jo rebuked her for such a response. How could it have been, with Marc gone?

Meanwhile, the trial of the three sailors proceeded apace in Fort-de-France. On March 31, 1965, all were found guilty of assault and theft. Armando Fernandes received a sentence of three years in prison. Alfredo Rodriguez was sentenced to fourteen months. The trial of the Martiniquan youth, Daniel Yves Charles Nicolas, was held in secret because of his age. He received a fourteen-month suspended sentence and a three-year probation.

*American Legacy Records released a limited edition of one thousand copies of a long-play transcription of the original 1938 *Cradle* cast recording. In addition, JJA Presents (a Box Office Production) issued a long-play disk containing the original *No for an Answer* cast recording on one face, and on the other, Blitzstein's demo of the songs from *Juno*.

†Intrigued by the island, Hellman returned in 1973 to finish writing *Pentimento. Travel and Leisure* published her article "Martinique" in January 1974, pp. 27ff.

Epilogue

"I have no wish to hide the kind of person I was, for I am that person—plus years."

The year after his death, the first $2,500 Marc Blitzstein Award for the Musical Theatre went to composer William Bolcom. Funds raised at the memorial concert were intended to create enough interest for a yearly award, but with only fourteen thousand dollars contributed, this plan had to be abandoned. Opera composer Jack Beeson won the next award three years later. When the Arrow Music Press formally dissolved in 1972 and its publications transferred to Boosey & Hawkes, Aaron Copland, Virgil Thomson and Lehman Engel agreed to add the remaining sum of money in its treasury—$1,353.86—to the capital of the Blitzstein fund. The third award was delayed eight years: The librettist John Olon-Scrymgeour received it in 1976. The award will not be given out again until the capital builds up sufficient interest.

In other ways, Marc's name survives: Mordecai and Irma Bauman had named a son for him, and Blitzstein was his godfather. The tenor Charles Holland, whom Blitzstein had encouraged in his career, named his son Marc, for the composer and for Marc Pincherle, the French music historian. And Blitzstein had practically dissolved when in September 1954 Carmen Capalbo and his wife gave their son the name Marc. Throughout the seven-year run of *The Threepenny Opera,* Blitzstein never failed to ask after the boy. Following the guiding spirit of his namesake, Marc Capalbo grew up and became a composer. The actor Michael Wager named his son, born in 1964, for Marc as well. Also born in 1964 was the third of Kit and Sonia Davis's four daughters—Sonia was pregnant at the time Marc was killed. They named her Emily, the *Airborne* bombardier's girl.

In 1966, twenty years after its premiere and with the Vietnam War raging under Lyndon Johnson, Bernstein programed the *Airborne* Symphony with the New York Philharmonic and recorded it with Orson Welles as the Monitor. Late that year, the two-performer evening of Blitzstein songs that Mira Gilbert had discussed with the composer a week before he left for Martinique opened with Norman Friesen at the Provincetown Playhouse. Lukewarm reviews for both of these productions ushered in a rapid, sure decline in Blitzstein's reputation.

Affixing the gravestone ever more firmly, Joan Peyser wrote what amounts to a musical obituary, "The Troubled Time of Marc Blitzstein," in the *Columbia University Forum* for the winter of 1966, concluding that the composer's style and set of values had long since come and gone. John Gruen's interview with him, conducted shortly before Blitzstein left for Martinique, appeared in Gruen's collection *Close-Up.* "I would be very unhappy," the composer told Gruen after reaffirming his role as protester and rebel, "to think that it was true that my message is more important than my music." But somehow, what comes across in this interview is just that impression. Perhaps beginning to mellow into a more self-forgiving mood, Blitzstein threw the door open to his early works, giving a kind of posthumous permission to exhume them: "I would let anything of mine be produced—even something I didn't like. I have no wish to hide the kind of person I was, for I am that person—plus years."[1]

Among the fresh, creative New Left activists on the cultural front during the 1960s, Blitzstein's name was unknown, unless by some red-diaper babies who had grown up on old recordings from *The Cradle Will Rock* or *No for an Answer.* The new protest music was of another stripe entirely—folk and folk-inspired music, such as the songs of Joan Baez and Phil Ochs, or rock in all its varieties, such as the Beatles, Country Joe and the Fish, and the Mothers of Invention. Blitzstein's sophistication, urbanity, culture, and the times that gave him a singing voice were things of a generation past.

Robert Dietz, who had corresponded with Blitzstein from the University of Iowa about the doctoral dissertation he planned on the composer's work, finished "The Operatic Style of Marc Blitzstein in the American 'Agit-Prop' Era" in 1970. Earlier, in 1965, Paul Myers Talley had earned his doctorate from the University of Wisconsin with a dissertation called "Social Criticism in the Original Theatre Librettos of Marc Blitzstein."

One rare performance of *The Cradle Will Rock* during those years was a 1969 production at Harvard, led by young pianist and composer Leonard Lehrman. A former student of Elie Siegmeister, who called his attention to Blitzstein's work, Lehrman spared no pains to draw the connections between Blitzstein's themes and the university's complicity in the Vietnam War. Still at Harvard, he followed a year later with a triple bill of Bernstein's *Trouble in Tahiti* and Blitzstein's *I've Got the Tune* and *The Harpies.*

In attendance at this performance, Bernstein suggested that Lehrman might be the one to complete *Idiots First.* Lehrman completed this task in 1973 with the approval of both Bernard Malamud and the Blitzstein Estate, and it formed the basis of his master's thesis essay at Cornell University. The finished opera, handled for rental by Theodore Presser, has been produced with a two-piano accompaniment in Ithaca, Bloomington (Indiana), and by the Bel Canto Opera in New York. Some critics hailed *Idiots First* as the composer's finest creation, and it won the 1978 Off-Broadway Opera Award. Reviewing the 1977–1978 musical year in New York, critic Leighton Kerner called the staging of Blitzstein's last opera the "most important event of the season."[2] However, the opera still awaits a full production with orchestra.

The decade after Blitzstein's death was the driest period of interest in his work. In 1975, Kit—Christopher Davis—published his tenth book, a lengthy novel called *The Sun in Mid-Career,* based extensively on his uncle's life. An earlier novel, *A Kind of Darkness,* published while Marc was still alive, also had drawn on Blitzstein's life, particularly on the summer of 1945 at Chadds Ford. In that novel, Kit cast Blitzstein in the role of a fondly remembered dead war hero and he introduced a character modeled on Bill Hewitt. When he read the book, Marc's comment to his nephew had been, "So this is the stuff legends are made of!" For the later novel about Marc, Kit had kept in Philadelphia many of Marc and Eva's letters from the 1930s, and all of Eva's diaries and other writings, incorporating many of their themes into his fictionalized account. Harper & Row, his publisher, hoped to increase sales of the novel by advertising it as Blitzstein's life. The book received a few favorable reviews but in the end failed to gain a readership. Marc's friends were understanding, but mostly disappointed that Kit had fallen short of capturing the man. Eventually, Kit sent all the papers out to Wisconsin for inclusion in the Blitzstein Collection.

By the mid-1970s, Blitzstein's star began to rise again. Richard Maltby, Jr., and Geraldine Fitzgerald revived *Juno* for a Massachusetts production at the Williamstown Theatre Festival in 1974, in which Fitzgerald starred as Juno and Milo O'Shea appeared as Boyle. Significant adaptations, additional lyrics, and the rescoring of the music for a small Irish village band brought the show down to more modest proportions. Director Arvin Brown restaged it as *Daarlin' Juno* at the Long Wharf Theatre in New Haven two years later with the same two leads, but still the show failed to convince the critics. CBS had kept the *Airborne* Symphony recorded in 1966 under Bernstein in its vaults for ten years, until at the conductor's insistence they finally released it in 1976. It did not do well commercially, but it soon became a treasured item in the record libraries of collectors of musical Americana. On CBS television, the independent show "Camera Three" devoted two episodes to Blitzstein's career. Produced by Muriel Balash, these aired in the fall of 1976.

A short story by Truman Capote, "Music for Chameleons," which made reference to Blitzstein's death, appeared in *The New Yorker,* and lent its title to a 1980 collection of stories. "Strange where our passions carry us, flaggingly pursue us," Capote wrote of Blitzstein, "forcing upon us unwanted dreams, unwelcome destinies."[3]

Leonard Lehrman continued to promote *Idiots First.* In addition, as a pianist and concert organizer, he frequently included Blitzstein material in his programs of Jewish songs and American musical theatre. On more than one occasion he has performed the Piano Sonata as well. Beveridge Webster also played the Sonata on a League of Composers-International Society for Contemporary Music concert at Carnegie Recital Hall in 1980.

Regina has come to be seen as an eminently revivable opera. Detroit saw a production in 1977, with George Gaynes in the role of Horace. The Houston Grand Opera mounted a lavish *Regina* in 1980, with Maralin Niska in the title role, the still powerful Elisabeth Carron as Birdie, and Giorgio Tozzi as Ben. The production almost came to the New York City Opera, but in her new position at the helm of the company, Beverly Sills nixed it, reportedly for being "too old-fashioned." The opera has been seen in Boston, Colorado Springs, Kansas City, Chautauqua, Wolf Trap, Augusta, Baton Rouge, New Haven, and in New York City stagings by the Bel Canto Opera, Encompass Theatre, and the Opera Ensemble. The "Rain Quartet" has also been arranged for male voices and performed by the San Francisco Gay Men's Chorus.

At one point in the late 1970s, Leonard Bernstein assigned some researchers to examine all the materials from the opera—from the Broadway version through the two City Opera versions—with the intention of coming up with a new and perhaps definitive score. But the project never got off the ground. If what Blitzstein had in mind is ever to be heard again, an authentic, responsible reconstruction of *Regina* should include all of his original Angel Band music and the Chinkypin material (together with the party guests' dialogue, without which the Chinkypin song makes little sense), restore the onstage ballroom trio, and incorporate the sung recitatives Blitzstein composed for the City Opera. Though audiences have found the bandless version effective musical drama, to perpetuate it as the final form of the opera continues to misrepresent Blitzstein's work, depriving the public of a much more ambitious musical conception.

The Cradle Will Rock has proved the most durable of Blitzstein's works. If there are critics and audiences who find the piece hopelessly out of touch with present reality, they are usually the types of people who actually do not care for social protest on the stage at all. Many others see in it both a vibrant sample of American theatre in one of its most communicative phases and a sharp metaphor for venality in all times, historic and actual. College drama departments tend to be fond of the work for the learning potential it holds, and because youth is traditionally idealistic; and the left-wing theatre companies that come and go will often include it in their repertory. Before he died in 1985, Orson Welles had been trying to raise backing for a film about *Cradle*'s historic debut. Both he and Ring Lardner, Jr., wrote filmscripts, but neither script found a producer. At this writing, Frank Beacham, an assistant to Welles in his last years, has begun producing such a film with Michael Hodges as scriptwriter and director.

Martha Schlamme and Alvin Epstein—the Fool in Orson Welles's *King Lear*—put together a Bernstein-Blitzstein revue directed by Michael Feingold that happily joined a dozen or so songs from each composer. They presented it privately in New York and publicly in Aspen, Colorado, hoping that the show might be taken up on the college circuit. However, Schlamme's voice was already showing a good deal of wear by 1981, and the project did not succeed.

In 1983 John Houseman directed a splendid production of *Cradle* in New York, using a group of handpicked graduates of The Acting Company, starring Patti LuPone as the Moll, with Michael Barrett, pianist and conducting protégé of Bernstein, as musical director. The company included *Cradle* on its subsequent national tour, offering performances in dozens of cities across the country. WGBH filmed the production for television broadcast, releasing it in January 1986. In addition, the company took the show to London for a run at the Old Vic in the summer of 1985. This version was recorded commercially on disk and cassette, the second complete *Cradle* available, a sign of remarkable vitality for such a supposedly "dated" work. The premiere of *Cradle* on the Continent took place in 1984 in Recklinghausen, West Germany, in a translated version presided over by Gershon Kingsley, who rescored it for chamber ensemble, including synthesizer.

As for the Blitzstein adaptation of *The Threepenny Opera,* it continues at this writing as the only authorized version in the United States and Canada for stock and amateur productions. Royalties from it—from the stage, from sheet-music sales, from recordings and other sources—still provide far more income to his heirs than anything else in Blitzstein's catalogue, despite the fact that his English text has never been published for a general readership (naturally, a printed script exists from which the artists learn their lines). Only in the case of producers wishing to mount a first-class staging can other translations be used. In some ways, this is unfortunate: Blitzstein did, after all, make certain changes, such as tightening up the dialogue and transposing certain songs to a lower key, that do alter Weill and Brecht's intentions. And it can defensibly be argued that however effective his adaptation was, and remains, his words do reflect the period of the early fifties in style and wordage. Few translations can stand for all time—as do all works of literature, they, too, show their age.

Still, when other versions crop up, they tend to fare no better. On May 1, 1976, Joseph Papp's New York Shakespeare Festival produced and recorded a translation by Ralph Manheim and John Willett in a musical recasting by Stanley Silverman. In their attempt to drum up enthusiasm for their "real" *Threepenny Opera,* presented "in its original and uncensored form," the promoters attacked Blitzstein savagely for his supposed crime of sweetening Brecht. They ignored any notion of what Blitzstein was able to put on the stage in the 1950s, not to mention what he was able to put on the cast recording; and they failed to consider how outrageous some broadcasters at the time considered the tunes and lyrics from the show. For a number of years following the Manheim-Willett production, many critics wanting to appear au courant with developments in the theatre joined the anti-Blitzstein bandwagon. Only a few protesting voices pointed out at the time that the new "real" version was almost unsingable, clumsy, vulgar far beyond Brecht's intentions, and musically a disaster. After the storm had passed, the pendulum began swinging back to Blitzstein's as the more sensitively conceived version despite its problems. Often times, producers at colleges or in other places not closely monitored by the licensers of the property will on their own make unauthorized changes that have little to do with Brecht, Weill, or Blitzstein—inserting local or timely topical references, for example. For the most part, these intrusions are harmless; in any case, they are impossible to prevent completely. In 1988, Cannon Films began making a new version of *Threepenny*

Opera, directed by Menahem Golan, with a cast featuring Raul Julia, Julia Migenes, Richard Harris, and Roger Daltrey. About a third of the lyrics were Blitzstein's.

On the occasion of Blitzstein's eightieth birthday in 1985, a large assemblage of well-known performers brought together by director Paul Lazarus and Michael Barrett presented, under the banner of Charles Schwartz's Composers' Showcase, a full evening's tribute at Lincoln Center's Alice Tully Hall. The evening went further in some respects than the 1964 memorial concert, in that some of the rarer items in Blitzstein's catalogue came to the surface. Aside from a selection of scenes from *The Cradle Will Rock,* "Then" from *The Magic Barrel,* and "With a Woman to Be" from *Sacco and Vanzetti,* the audience heard songs from *No for an Answer* and *Juno,* excerpts from the *Airborne* Symphony, solo voice settings of E. E. Cummings, "Monday Morning Blues" from *Reuben Reuben,* and "Displaced." The program also included the "Rain Quartet," the "Army Song" from *Threepenny,* and Bernstein's delicious rendition of "The New Suit," his favorite song of Marc's. With the range of styles of composition offered, it was an evening that put Blitzstein back on the map of the New York music scene, exposing almost everyone to at least some unfamiliar material. When Barrett conducted the full orchestra in the final scene of *Cradle,* with Houseman playing Mr. Mister, it marked twenty-five years since the New York City Opera production had allowed the original orchestration to be heard. In Berlin, Albrecht Dümling provided commentary for a long eightieth birthday tribute on SFB Radio, featuring recorded excerpts from Blitzstein's catalogue.

As a champion of Blitzstein, Barrett played the solo part in the composer's 1931 Piano Concerto. Lukas Foss conducted the Brooklyn Philharmonic in January 1986 at the first performances of the work with orchestra. Curiously, the Edwin A. Fleisher Music Collection in Philadelphia, which held a copy of the work, also contained a full set of parts for the concerto, which had been copied out by employees of the Federal Music Project in the 1930s. Fifty years later, Foss's players benefited from this early example of government subsidy. Peter G. Davis of *New York* magazine wrote of the occasion that the composer's "early works should be reassessed and performed, if the Piano Concerto is typical of them. Terse, biting, witty, melodically fresh, and with a disturbing undercurrent of melancholy, it is not that different, in spirit at least, from the familiar Blitzstein of *Regina.*" He pronounced it "a valuable score."[4] Composers Recordings, Inc., taped the concerto for release in 1988. Barrett also conducted *Freedom Morning* in Vienna.

Two recordings released in 1986 revived Blitzstein works. *Where, Oh Where: Rare Songs of the American Theater,* sung by Judy Kaye, anthologized "I Wish It So" from *Juno.* In addition, the pianist Bennett Lerner rediscovered three dance episodes from *The Guests,* which he included on his second album of American piano music on the Etcetera label. The versions of these pieces differ substantially from the recordings Blitzstein made in the late 1940s, however, as Lerner followed alternate and more pianistically interesting manuscripts found in the Blitzstein archive. Lerner also served as editor of one of these pieces,

"Variation II," published in the magazine *Keyboard Classics* (July–August 1986), the first time a solo piano piece by Blitzstein had ever been published.

The pianist Steven Blier has also made a specialty of introducing Blitzstein songs to a number of singers he coaches and accompanies. One of his singers, the baritone William Sharp, won the 1987 Carnegie Hall International American Music Competition for Vocalists. Among the five Blitzstein songs he included in his recital repertoire, unquestionably his rendition of "Zipperfly" ("The New Suit") created a sensation among both his audience and his judges. The applause that greeted this song hailed not only the exquisitely affecting performance but the discovery of a thrilling addition to the American song canon. On the strength of his winning the competition, Sharp is scheduled to commit an entire Blitzstein song recital to disk in 1989.

In the spring of 1986, London celebrated the career of Leonard Bernstein with a series of performances in major theatres and concert halls. Bernstein requested that the repertoire for these concerts include, alongside his own works, the compositions of other men whose music had strongly influenced him: Stravinsky, Shostakovich, Copland, Mahler, Gershwin, Ives, and Britten. He also asked for the *Airborne* Symphony, which received its first European performance on May 4 at the Barbican Centre in the city where Blitzstein had composed it forty years before. John Mauceri conducted, with Terence Stamp as the Monitor.

Revival of interest in Blitzstein's work is part of a more general phenomenon, the rediscovery of worth in all the past epochs of American music. The struggle of twentieth-century composers to be played and heard was a noble and necessary cause. However, once the upstarts, such as Copland, had become more or less established—most would consider themselves less established, of course—the older generation of more conservative musicians tended to get pushed aside. Howard Hanson, Quincy Porter, John Knowles Paine, Edward MacDowell, Charles Tomlinson Griffes, John Alden Carpenter, Henry Hadley, Daniel Gregory Mason, Charles Martin Loeffler—these are but a few of the names once revered in America, then all but forgotten.

Similarly, since he wrote for the better part of his career in a musically conservative, diatonic mode, Blitzstein was consigned to virtual oblivion by the twelve-tone seigneurs of American music in the post-World War II period. In the 1970s and 1980s with the advent of minimalism, the "new romanticism," and other trends breaking down academia's stranglehold, critics and audiences have been able to examine with greater freedom the inherent musical value in creations of the past.[5]

The Cradle Will Rock and *Regina* are destined to retain their attractiveness for future audiences because they are so solid and consistent in conception. The *Airborne* Symphony will probably always have its champions and an occasional performance. The cantata is limited by its period: There is no escaping its always being considered dated, yet it remains the most significant statement in American music to emerge from the Second World War. A society that did not willfully forget its own history would recognize it as *the* musical monument to the fighting men who conquered the skies for democracy.

The rise of a host of gay men's choruses in the 1980s should provide a natural sponsorship for performances of the *Airborne* Symphony, and an established audience for it as well, though as of this writing none of them has yet taken up the call. Though performances should not be limited to gay choruses, they can present it unapologetically as proof of gay commitment to the defense of freedom.

After thirty years without a second hearing, the cantata *This Is the Garden* received a pair of performances in June 1987 by New York's Stonewall Chorale, a mixed chorus of gay and lesbian singers. In his own day, Blitzstein could certainly never have imagined performers openly presenting themselves as homosexuals as a matter of gay pride; but here was an ensemble of more than thirty singers who had discovered his wistful and surely intentional neglect to specify the genders of the unlucky lovers of "In Twos." His message to the future had been detected; interestingly, one member of the Stonewall Chorale, a woman in her fifties, had participated in the premiere back in 1957.

No for an Answer, too, may never entirely rise above its period; but presented honestly and with a bit of judicious cutting, its power could be made to ring again, giving a modern public the opportunity to appreciate the stirring and often sensitive music it contains. At this writing, Maggie da Silva, daughter of Howard da Silva, has plans to revive *No for an Answer* in 1989.

In the long run, the chances for *Juno*'s eventual success are very strong because O'Casey wrote an absorbing play with memorable characters, and the musical captures their spirit with heightened expression. Jaded critics in 1959 killed a powerful work that was truly ahead of its time. With a few changes in some silly lyrics and with a good director's common sense about balancing the intimacy of the Boyles' living room against the larger requirements of a musical, a theatre work that sings out boldly for humanity and against all senseless violence has every reason to live again and enter the accepted canon. Certain critics—and O'Casey himself—wondered whether *Juno* would have made a better opera than a musical. Now that the New York City Opera and many regional opera companies are presenting Broadway musicals as the most evolved forms of musical theatre in America, the time may be right to look at the sophisticated score to *Juno* with an eye toward opera-house production.*

Reuben Reuben has its defenders still among those who saw it in Boston, though as time passes, these become fewer and fewer. Somehow, its gorgeous music ought to be preserved, even if the book would require serious revision before becoming stageworthy. Cheryl Crawford, a producer whose instincts often proved sharper than her audiences' and critics', wrote about *Reuben Reuben* in her memoirs: "So much blood and talent had gone into the show. Today, with the new sounds of music and new styles of writing, I doubt if it would seem at

*In 1988, almost thirty years after *Juno* closed, Agnes de Mille revived large portions of her choreography in her half-hour work for the American Ballet Theatre, *The Informer,* likewise set in the same period of Irish struggle against British rule. Critics viewed it without enthusiasm.

all obscure."[6] If her comment is worth any attention, perhaps the score could be presented in concert version for a public reassessment.

The early operas *Triple-Sec* and *The Harpies* will continue to have a life, mostly in college and opera-workshop productions, because they are tangy, short, and not linked to any particular time period. *I've Got the Tune* has its appeal to those interested in classic agitprop theatre: The Soho Rep offered it in New York in September 1988 with *The Harpies* on an evening called *The Blitzstein Project.* Much of the critical reception agreed with the *Post*'s assessment: Blitzstein's

> didactic, acidic songs of the Depression era, full of oppressed, heroic working men and women and their rapacious oppressors, are generally about as subtle as a *Daily Worker* editorial cartoon. . . .
>
> And yet, and yet . . .
>
> In this fat-cat era of the '80's, in particular when you look around at the gray-on-gray election-year political landscape that's somehow been imposed upon us, the spirit cries out for a salutary taste of the angry '30s. Which is precisely what's being delivered—with great zest and no little joy. . . .[7]

As for the never-performed *Parabola and Circula* and *The Condemned,* the challenge awaits. The former piece is vocally well written in an accessible, undemanding style, making it a suitable vehicle for college productions despite its remote libretto and the fact that Blitzstein cannibalized parts of it for at least five later works. *The Condemned* is a superbly crafted piece of choral writing marred by an unfortunate, unpoetic text. Obviously, it will never become a repertory item, but the composer's idea was original and his music rich in its combinations. The rewards might be substantial enough for at least a hearing, if not a full staging.

Idiots First will be given a fully orchestrated production some day. The measure of Blitzstein as a composer in his most mature phase can then be properly taken. It is indeed shameful that no company with the adequate resources to do so has offered this work in the twenty-five years since Blitzstein's death. "It's discouraging to realize that Marc's best work was his last, *Idiots First,* which he played me just weeks ago," Ned Rorem wrote in his diary on January 27, 1964, a few days after his friend's death. "Malamud would have continued to be his ideal collaborator."[8]

The ballets *Cain* and *The Guests* both contain brilliant music and absorbing scenarios. The latter, at twenty minutes' duration, can easily stand alone as a concert piece. In the smaller forms, the Whitman, Cummings, and Elizabethan songs all have merit, but their present unavailability in print puts them beyond most singers' reach. There is no reason why the little Whitman cantata for women's voices, *A Word Out of the Sea,* should not be given a hearing. The same can be said for Blitzstein's instrumental music—the solo piano works and the string quartets. The film scores, especially for *Valley Town* and *Native Land,* live on in their original form as sound tracks: Each film is a documentary classic that will continue to be shown and appreciated. Unfortunately, it is only their style that appears antiquated: The prolabor, propeople substance remains intact to this day. The *Native Land* Suite might successfully be revived as a concert piece.

The 1986 premiere of the Piano Concerto in its orchestral version, and the welcome reception it won, led the music publishing firm of Boosey & Hawkes to take it on as a rental item. They also took on the other two Blitzstein items in the Edwin A. Fleisher Collection, the never-performed *Orchestra Variations* and the score for the film *Surf and Seaweed,* played only once in 1931. *Variations* was finally given its world premiere on October 9, 1988, on an American Composers Orchestra program at Carnegie Hall, conducted by Dennis Russell Davies. The critics diverged widely about the piece. Peter G. Davis called it an "arid neoclassical exercise," and Will Crutchfield thought that it "does all the right things to its opening theme, but never takes off." Bill Zakariasen, however, regretted that Blitzstein never heard the *Variations,* "since it's one of his strongest works—tough yet expressive, brilliantly orchestrated and amazingly concise."[9]

It is too early to predict what future all this nontheatrical music will have, but it is possible that given a good launching or relaunching, these song cycles, ballet and film scores, and orchestra pieces, including *Lear: A Study,* may come to be performed as frequently as any of Blitzstein's stage works. Because they are more manageable in proportion, not requiring the added complications of a stage production, and because they do not call upon the political or social sympathies of the listener, these compositions may eventually match or even supplant Blitzstein's preeminence as a composer for the theatre. Though the composer could hardly have imagined such a development, he would have been content to note the irony.

In virtually all his work from *Regina* on, and obviously with *Sacco and Vanzetti* and the two Malamud one-acts, Blitzstein had left behind the agitational motive, the need to comment so directly on his own times that his works would soon become mysterious. In many ways, for this composer forever engaged in the pursuit of the right form for his expression, it always looked as though his best work still lay ahead. His tragedy is that as he aged into one of the grand old men of American music, there would indeed have been a newly politicized generation in the 1960s and 1970s and beyond that could appreciate his art; but his singing voice had been stilled, all too soon.

Blitzstein's influence is evident, certainly in Bernstein's music and, either independently or through the Bernstein route, in the music of other composers who seek to marry popular idioms to the formal tradition. Blitzstein was not the only American composer to attempt this union, though he must still be considered among the most successful. Where he particularly excelled was in the purity of his setting of the American language, almost always faithful to its rhythms and cadences and attentive to the speech patterns of all our social classes. His gift takes on added dimension when we remember that in large part he set his own lyrics: His ear for words was as sharp as his ear for melody. His satirical aim was sure, even if some of his targets—musical as well as political—are less recognizable today than when he fired at them.

The British critic Wilfrid Mellers, perhaps the shrewdest of any critic to comment on Blitzstein's work, once remarked after studying the music to *Reuben Reuben:*

> He makes us feel—without minimizing the odds against us—that it is good to be alive. For that reason I feel pretty sure not merely that his historical significance is greater than we can appreciate at the moment: but also that his works will survive the apparent topicality of his approach.[10]

In the realm of social thought expressed in music, the American theatre has yet to produce Blitzstein's equal. To be sure, he did not limit himself to a political agenda, as numerous works attest. Still, no one has produced such a consistent body of works that so effectively challenges other artists and the public alike to examine the role of music and culture in general in this society.

If war and exploitation continue to be a part of the human condition, as it appears they will for a long time to come, Blitzstein's legacy stands as the voice of one who answered No. To honest work and to the chances for youth and peace and love in this world of throbbing possibility, Blitzstein sang:

yes is a pleasant country.

Notes

Preface

1. Marc Blitzstein, "Talk—Music—Dance; New York 1933," *Modern Music* (November–December 1933): 34–40.

Chapter 1: THE BRAT

1. Benzion C. Kaganoff, "A Gem of a Name," *The Jewish Monthly* (June–July 1987): 34. Other Jewish names ending with "stein," such as Rothstein or Bernstein, can also be traced to gemmological origins. I am indebted to Freya Maslow for her assistance on Blitzstein genealogy.
2. Family history is based on interviews with first cousins Josephine Davis, Laura Goldsmith, and Andrew Voynow, all grandchildren of Anna and Marcus L. Blitzstein. Robert Leiter's article, "Opening the Door to the New World," *Jewish Exponent* (Philadelphia), July 13, 1984, presents much useful research concerning the immigrant banks of Philadelphia.
3. Marc Blitzstein, draft of an uncompleted autobiography, 1947.
4. Marc Blitzstein (hereafter MB) to Josephine Davis, July 21, 1929.
5. Madeline Goss, *Modern Music-Makers: Contemporary American Composers* (New York: E. P. Dutton, 1952), pp. 358–369.
6. Elinor Hughes, Boston *Herald,* October 19, 1949.
7. MB to Victor Yellin, April 18, 1949; appended to Yellin, "The Case for American Opera: Virgil Thomson and Marc Blitzstein" (Senior thesis, Department of Music, Harvard College, May 2, 1949).

Chapter 2: STUDIES

1. Journal of Berenice C. Skidelsky, January 20, 1921; courtesy of Joyce K. Davis, Literary Executor of the Estate of Berenice C. Skidelsky.
2. MB to Berenice Skidelsky, November 9, 1921.
3. Particularly in his early years, Blitzstein failed to note exact sources for the clippings he kept. The first citation is from an unsigned review in the Philadelphia *Inquirer,* February 6, 1922; all of the others are unascribed but surely come from Philadelphia and local papers of the following day or days.
4. Journal of Berenice C. Skidelsky, February 19, 1922; courtesy of Joyce K. Davis, Literary Executor of the Estate of Berenice C. Skidelsky.
5. Vera Siloti to MB, September 26, 1923.
6. Anna Blitzstein to MB, April 9, 1924.
7. Donald McKillop to MB, March 13, 1960.

8. MB to William E. Walter, August 18, 1925; Walter to MB, September 10, 1925; courtesy of the Curtis Institute of Music.
9. Marc Blitzstein, "My Lady Jazz," *The Review* (February 5, 1926): 17,29.

Chapter 3: DONNER UND BLITZSTEIN

1. MB to Berenice Skidelsky, October 24, 1926.
2. Ibid.
3. Letter from Nadia Boulanger, January 2, 1928.
4. Roberto Gerhard to MB, February 11, 1963; Marc Blitzstein, "Four American Composers," *This Quarter* (July–September, 1929): 163.
5. MB to William E. Walter, March 19, 1927; courtesy of the Curtis Institute of Music.
6. Undated lecture notes, and notes toward an unpublished article on Schoenberg, from the mid-1930s.
7. Recalled in Blitzstein's notes for Lecture 8, "The Modern Movement in Music," 1928–1929.
8. Marc Blitzstein, Lecture at Brandeis University, April 2, 1962.
9. *The New York Times,* January 8, 1927.
10. MB to Berenice Skidelsky, November 16, 1927.
11. MB to Louis Simon, February 10, 1928; courtesy of Louis Simon.
12. Both reviews are unascribed.
13. MB to Berenice Skidelsky, February 28, 1928.
14. All reviews are unascribed.
15. MB to Berenice Skidelsky, March 3, 1928.
16. Arthur D. Pierce, Camden *Evening Courier,* March 14, 1928.
17. Linton Martin, Philadelphia *Inquirer,* March 14, 1928.
18. Pierce, Camden *Evening Courier,* March 14, 1928.
19. W. R. Murphy, *Musical America,* March 31, 1928.
20. Martin, Philadelphia *Inquirer,* March 14, 1928.
21. MB to Louis Simon, March 20, 1928; courtesy of Louis Simon.
22. Marc Blitzstein, "Hin und Zurück in Philadelphia," *Modern Music* (May–June 1928): 34–36.
23. "Season at MacDowell Colony Best So Far," Peterborough *Transcript,* August 30, 1928.
24. For a more complete treatment of Lina Abarbanell's career, see Eric Gordon, "The Met's First Hansel," *Opera News,* December 24, 1983, pp. 30–31.
25. Journal of Chard Powers Smith, June 14, 1928, Chard Powers Smith Papers, Collection of American Literature, Beinecke Rare Book and Manuscript Library, Yale University, New Haven, Connecticut.
26. Charles Pearce, of Harcourt, Brace and Co., to Eva Goldbeck, May 8, 1935. Reprinted by permission of Harcourt Brace Jovanovich, Inc.
27. Eva Goldbeck to Chard Powers Smith, September 24, 1928, Chard Powers Smith Papers, Collection of American Literature, Beinecke Rare Book and Manuscript Library, Yale University, New Haven, Connecticut.
28. MB to Berenice Skidelsky, September 18, 1928.
29. Marc Blitzstein, Notes for Lecture 1.
30. Marc Blitzstein, Notes for Lecture 3.
31. Marc Blitzstein, Notes for Lecture 4.

32. Marc Blitzstein, Notes for Lecture 5.
33. Marc Blitzstein, Notes for Lecture 7.
34. Journal of Eva Goldbeck, November 13, 1928.
35. Marc Blitzstein, quoted in "Negro Choristers Singing for Copland," *The World,* December 30, 1928.
36. Journal of Eva Goldbeck, December 30, 1928.
37. Arthur Mendel, "First Fruits of the Season," *Modern Music* (January–February 1929): 30–32.
38. Marion Bauer, "A Furious and Outraged Audience, a Debasing Program," *The Musical Leader,* January 3, 1929.
39. Olin Downes, *The New York Times,* December 31, 1928.
40. Samuel Chotzinoff, *The World,* December 31, 1928.
41. Pitts Sanborn, New York *World-Telegram,* December 31, 1928.
42. MB to Louis Simon, January 8, 1929; courtesy of Louis Simon.
43. Marion Bauer, *The Musical Leader,* March 21, 1929; *Musical Courier,* March 21, 1929; MB to Louis Simon, March 30, 1929; courtesy of Louis Simon. In a 1933 lecture-recital on Debussy, Blitzstein played the "Feux d'artifice" ("Fireworks") from the *24 Préludes,* saying it contained "the germ of essence of every subsequent discovery in the matter of piano-technique; the idea of the piano as a percussion instrument, one in which the tones are beaten, struck, like a drum . . . , the first piece to indicate definitely that the piano is to be taken as the symbolic instrument of the new era."
44. MB to Berenice Skidelsky, April 3, 1929.
45. Ibid.
46. H. T. Craven, Philadelphia *Record,* May 7, 1929.
47. Journal of Eva Goldbeck, May 26, 1929.
48. MB to Eva Goldbeck, July 9, 1929; Journal of Eva Goldbeck, August 25, 1929
49. Minna Lederman, "Memories of Marc Blitzstein, Music's Angry Man," *Sho*[illegible] (June 1964): 18ff.
50. MB to Josephine Davis, July 21, 1929.
51. MB to Louis Simon, August 9, 1929; courtesy of Louis Simon.
52. MB to Josephine Davis, August 29, 1929.
53. Journal of Eva Goldbeck, August 26, 1929 (her birthday); September 7, 1929.
54. An often-told anecdote, repeated by Blitzstein himself, has it that as a rash young student he scandalized Schoenberg's class at the Akademie der Künste in Berlin by banging out the hit tunes "Mack the Knife" and the "Jealousy Duet" from *Die Dreigroschenoper,* singing them in his strongly accented German, just as the horrified professor was entering the classroom. Supposedly, as the story goes, the only reason Schoenberg did not throw Blitzstein out of the class at once was that Blitzstein was the only one of his students with enough technique to play Schoenberg's piano pieces. Believably enough, Blitzstein also claims to have seen three or more different productions of the Weill opera in various German cities during his European sojourns. But clearly Blitzstein could not have seen the work before this performance in Wiesbaden, because it had premiered in August 1928 when he was back in America. When he returned to Europe in 1929, he was no longer a student of Schoenberg. Possibly the incident took place on the occasion of a later visit to the Akademie. See Blitzstein's article "On 'Mahagonny,' " *The Score* (July 1958): 11–13.
55. MB to Eva Goldbeck, September 18, 1929.
56. MB to Josephine Davis, October 29, 1929.
57. MB to Josephine Davis, November 25, 1929.

58. Eva Goldbeck to Cecil Goldbeck, November 30, 1930.
59. MB to Berenice Skidelsky, October 31, 1929.
60. Marc Blitzstein, Lecture at Brandeis University, April 2, 1962.
61. MB to Berenice Skidelsky, October 31, 1929; from Blitzstein's notebook on *Parabola and Circula.*
62. MB to Berenice Skidelsky, March 9, 1930.
63. MB to Josephine Davis, November 11 and 21, 1929.
64. MB to Josephine Davis, December 24, 1929.

Chapter 4: EVA

1. MB to Stella Simon, January 28, 1930; courtesy of Louis Simon.
2. Journal of Eva Goldbeck, February 8, 1930.
3. MB to Berenice Skidelsky, March 9, 1930; MB to Louis Simon, April 2, 1930, courtesy of Louis Simon. Numerous details, and a few quotations, concerning the rest of the year 1930 come from a seventeen-page letter from Eva Goldbeck to Cecil Goldbeck, November 30, 1930.
4. Aaron Copland to MB and Eva Goldbeck, February 13, 1930.
5. Only some pencil sketches of this quartet seem to have survived among Blitzstein's papers. A copy Blitzstein later gave to Nadia Boulanger is in her archive at the Houghton Library, Harvard University, Cambridge, Massachusetts.
6. From the scenario to *Cain.*
7. MB to Josephine Davis, June 23, 1930.
8. MB to Stella Simon, April 15, 1930; MB to Louis Simon, April 2, 1930; both courtesy of Louis Simon.
9. Wilella Waldorf, New York *Post,* June 5, 1930.
10. Brooks Atkinson, *The New York Times,* June 5, 1930.
11. MB to Josephine Davis, June 23, 1930.
12. Cecil Goldbeck to Eva Goldbeck, June 19, 1930.
13. MB to Berenice Skidelsky, June 26, 1930.
14. Eva Goldbeck to Cecil Goldbeck, August 26, 1930.
15. MB to Eva Goldbeck, August 11, 1930.
16. Eva Goldbeck to Cecil Goldbeck, November 30, 1930.
17. MB to Eva Goldbeck, November 18, 1930.
18. Eva Goldbeck to Cecil Goldbeck, November 30, 1930.
19. MB to Eva Goldbeck, January 13, 1931.
20. In his *Our New Music: Leading Composers in Europe and America* (New York: Whittlesey House, McGraw-Hill, 1951), Copland called *Cain* "an unusually promising piece," p. 194. Earlier, in a *Modern Music* "Symposium on Neglected Works" (Winter 1946), he had cited *Cain* as an "unproduced dance score from Blitzstein's early period that warrants investigation from a ballet company." No evidence survives that Blitzstein did submit the score of *Cain* to the League of Composers competition; in any event, he did not win it.
21. MB to Eva Goldbeck, January 13, 1931.
22. Marc Blitzstein, Lecture notes, "Modern Music—Latest Developments," February 4, 1931.
23. MB to Eva Goldbeck, March 11, 1931.
24. Aaron Copland to Eva Goldbeck, December 11, 1930, and January 23, 1931.
25. Richard Hammond, "Pioneers of Movie Music," *Modern Music* (March–April 1931): 35–38. As it exists today, the film has no sound track.

26. MB to Eva Goldbeck, March 27, 1931.
27. Ralph Steiner, *A Point of View* (Middletown, Connecticut: Wesleyan University Press, 1978), pp. 12–13.
28. Marc Blitzstein, "New York Chronicle of New Music," *Modern Music* (January–February 1931): 39–42.
29. Marc Blitzstein, "Spring Season in the East," *Modern Music* (May–June 1931): 33–39.
30. Marc Blitzstein, "Dancers of the Season," *Modern Music* (March–April 1931): 38–42.
31. MB to Eva Goldbeck, February 6, 1931.
32. Eva Goldbeck to Cecil Goldbeck, December 31, 1930, January 25, April 20, and May 18, 1931.
33. MB to Eva Goldbeck, April 1, 1931.
34. Claire Reis to MB, March 31, 1931.
35. MB to Eva Goldbeck, March 26, 1931.
36. MB to Eva Goldbeck, June 8, 1931.
37. Cecil Goldbeck to Eva Goldbeck, July 29, 1931.
38. Cecil Goldbeck to Eva Goldbeck, August 7, 1931.
39. MB to Josephine Davis, August 9–12, 1931. In a letter to Stella and Louis Simon, dated August 14, 1931, Blitzstein wrote: "The subject for the choral opera has struck me of a sudden," and he proceeded with a synopsis. His wording suggests that he had been considering, and had already discussed with the Simons, writing a choral opera.
40. Journal of Eva Goldbeck, August 19 to September 25, 1931.
41. Cecil Goldbeck to Eva Goldbeck, August 26, 1931.
42. MB to Eva Goldbeck, September 18, 1931.
43. MB to Eva Goldbeck, September 23, 1931.
44. Josephine Davis to Eva Goldbeck, September 24, 1931; Eva Goldbeck to Josephine Davis, October 4, 1931.
45. MB to Eva Goldbeck, September 28, 1931; MB to Josephine Davis, October 15, 1931.
46. Claire Reis to MB, November 25, 1931.
47. MB to Josephine Davis, December 9, 1931.
48. Leopold Stokowski to MB, March 21, 1932.
49. Eugene Goossens to MB, May 10, 1932.
50. Marc Blitzstein, "Tame Season in New York," *Modern Music* (January–February 1932): 79–85.
51. Marc Blitzstein, "Premieres and Experiments—1932," *Modern Music* (March–April 1932): 121–127.
52. Marc Blitzstein, "Music and Theatre–1932," *Modern Music* (May–June 1932): 164–168.
53. Journal of Eva Goldbeck, March 2 to April 25, 1932.
54. Journal of Eva Goldbeck, March 25 to April 25, 1932.
55. MB, Journal of Eva Goldbeck, May 1, 1932.
56. Alfred H. Meyer, "Yaddo—A May Festival," *Modern Music* (May–June 1932): 172–176.
57. Oscar Levant, *A Smattering of Ignorance,* second edition (New York: Doubleday, 1959), p. 163.
58. Eva Goldbeck, Notes on the Yaddo Composers' Conference, May 2, 1932; Journal of Eva Goldbeck, May 2, 1932.
59. Aaron Copland to MB and Eva Goldbeck, May 18, 1932.

Chapter 5: IN PURSUIT OF FORM

1. Journal of Eva Goldbeck, June 16, 1932.
2. MB to Josephine Davis, October 29, 1932.
3. Journal of Eva Goldbeck, July 24 to September 22, 1932.
4. Vera Siloti to MB, September 1, 1932; MB to Eva Goldbeck, September 29, 1932; MB to Albert Coates, November 27, 1932;
5. MB to Eva Goldbeck, September 29, 1932.
6. Josephine Davis to Eva Goldbeck, undated but late Fall 1932.
7. MB to Josephine Davis, November 14, 1932.
8. Journal of Eva Goldbeck, December 17, 1932; MB to Eva Goldbeck, December 22 and 27, 1932.
9. From Marc Blitzstein's notes on Copland's opinion.
10. Marc Blitzstein, "Popular Music—An Invasion," *Modern Music* (January–February 1933): 96–102.
11. Ibid.
12. Quoted in Virgil Thomson, *Virgil Thomson* (New York: Alfred A. Knopf, 1966), p. 227.
13. Marc Blitzstein, Lecture notes, April 21, 1933.
14. Journal of Eva Goldbeck, February 14, 1933.
15. Journal of Eva Goldbeck, April 21, 1933; MB to Eva Goldbeck, August 26, 1933.
16. Eva Goldbeck, "Marc Blitzstein's Music," p. 3.
17. Ibid., p. 5.
18. Lina Abarbanell to Eva Goldbeck, April 17, 1933.
19. MB to Josephine Davis, June 2, 1933; Eva Goldbeck to Mr. and Mrs. Goldbeck, June 18, 1933; Eva Goldbeck to Josephine Davis, June 24, 1933; Journal of Eva Goldbeck, June 24 to July 5, 1933.
20. Journal of Eva Goldbeck, July 5, 1933.
21. MB to Eva Goldbeck, July 31, 1933.
22. Eva Goldbeck to Mr. and Mrs. Goldbeck, August 27, 1933.
23. David Ewen, "New Blood in American Music," *Musical Courier,* September 16, 1933.
24. MB to Stella and Louis Simon, September 8, 1933; courtesy of Louis Simon.
25. Marc Blitzstein, "Talk—Music—Dance; New York, 1933," *Modern Music* (November–December 1933): 34–40.
26. Marc Blitzstein, "Mid-Season in New York," *Modern Music* (January–February 1934): 99–103.
27. Charles Seeger, "On Proletarian Music," *Modern Music* (March–April 1934): 121–127.
28. Marc Blitzstein, "Towards a New Form," *Musical Quarterly* (April 1934): 213–218.
29. Eva Goldbeck to Lina Abarbanell, March 11 and 14, 1934.
30. Margaret Barr to the Blitzsteins, June 17 and August 4, 1934; Dorothy Elmhirst to MB, July 18, 1934. Though the episode involving Blitzstein is not mentioned, see Michael Young, *The Elmhirsts of Dartington: The Creation of an Utopian Community* (London: Routledge & Kegan Paul, 1982).
31. Marc Blitzstein, "Towards a New Form": 216.
32. MB to Eva Goldbeck, undated but June 1934. The inscription on the manuscript, however, says "for Gene." The piece was originally signed with the name Martin

Eastman, later crossed out and substituted by Blitzstein's own name. Most likely, he had submitted the work to a blind competition at one point. If so, then "Gene" might have been substituted for Eva, as this was the protagonist's name in one of her autobiographical novels.
33. Charles Seeger to MB, July 18, 1934.
34. MB to Josephine Davis, November 29, 1934; Eva Goldbeck to Lina Abarbanell, December 1, 1934.
35. Dorothy Elmhirst to MB, November 26 and December 6, 1934.
36. Marc Blitzstein, "Theatre-Music in Paris," *Modern Music* (March–April 1935): 128–134.
37. Marc Blitzstein, "The Phenomenon of Stravinsky," *Musical Quarterly* (July 1935): 330–347.
38. MB to Kurt Jooss, undated but early December 1934; Jooss to MB, January 3, 1935.

Chapter 6: IN THE VANGUARD

1. Helen Hough to the Blitzstein family, probably April 1945.
2. Eva Goldbeck to Eslanda and Paul Robeson; February 22, 1935. The Blitzsteins' friendship with the Robesons stemmed from Eva's journalism. The Robesons, too, in this period were moving politically leftward.
3. Concert program, May 12, 1935. Originally from Chester, Pennsylvania, Alex North remembered his mother taking money into the M. L. Blitzstein Bank every week to finance her brother's immigration to America.
4. *Daily Worker,* June 11, 1934.
5. Marc Blitzstein, First lecture on "Form in Music," February 1933.
6. Marc Blitzstein, *Daily Worker,* June 12, 1935.
7. Eva Goldbeck, interview in the Brooklyn *Eagle,* April 11, 1935.
8. Eva Goldbeck to Dr. Frankwood E. Williams, undated but early August 1935.
9. Eve Arden, *Three Faces of Eve: An Autobiography* (New York: St. Martin's Press, 1985).
10. Eva Goldbeck to Lina Abarbanell, May 23, 1935.
11. Elliott Carter to Eva Goldbeck, June 3, 1935; Eva Goldbeck to Clifton J. Furness, September 2, 1935; Eva Goldbeck to Lina Abarbanell, August 11, 1935; MB to Wallingford Riegger, August 19, 1935.
12. Eva Goldbeck to Lina Abarbanell, August 26, 1935; Journal of Eva Goldbeck, August 4, 1935.
13. Eva Goldbeck to Lilly Popper, August 19, 1935.
14. Aaron Copland to MB, August 23, 1935.
15. Journal of Eva Goldbeck, August 25 to October 1, 1935; Eva Goldbeck to Clifton Furness, September 2, 1935.
16. MB to Eva Goldbeck, September 13 and 14, 1935.
17. MB to Eva Goldbeck, September 17 and 18, 1935.
18. Eva Goldbeck to MB, September 17, 1935.
19. MB to Eva Goldbeck, September 20, 1935.
20. Bertolt Brecht, "How the Carpet Weavers of Kujan-Bulak Honored Lenin," trans. by Eva Goldbeck, *Daily Worker,* January 21, 1936.
21. Minna Lederman, *The Life and Death of a Small Magazine (Modern Music, 1924–1946)* (Brooklyn: Institute for Studies in American Music, Conservatory

of Music, Brooklyn College of the City University of New York, 1983), pp. 66–75.
22. Eva Goldbeck, "A Thomson Soiree," *Modern Music* (November–December 1935): 50–51.
23. Robert A. Simon, "Musical Events," *The New Yorker,* December 14, 1935, pp. 110–111.
24. Marc Blitzstein, Boston *Evening Transcript* December 9, 1935.
25. Marc Blitzstein, "New York Medley, Winter, 1935," *Modern Music* (January–February 1936): 34–40.
26. Ibid.
27. Ibid.
28. Ibid.
29. Marc Blitzstein, "Music Manifesto," *New Masses,* June 23, 1936, p. 28. See also Marc Blitzstein, "Composers as Lecturers and in Concerts," *Modern Music* (November–December 1935): 47–50.
30. Marc Blitzstein "Les jeunes américains dans la musique," *Revue Musicale* (February 1936): 145–148.
31. Marc Blitzstein, "Chroniques et notes: Etats-Unis," *Revue Musicale* (April 1936): 314–315.
32. MB to Lazare Saminsky, February 10, 1936; Colin McPhee to MB, undated; Virgil Thomson, undated draft but early March 1936; Ashley Pettis to MB, March 17, 1936.
33. Louis Biancolli, *World-Telegram,* April 16, 1936.
34. Colin McPhee, "New York's Spring Season, 1936," *Modern Music* (May–June 1936): 39–42. Earlier, on January 26, 1936, Cazden and Blitzstein had played the concerto on WEVD, with the composer's young new friend David Diamond turning pages for him. Back in November, Marc and Eva had attended the first performance of Diamond's "Formal Dance," with choreography by Martha Graham. The following year, Blitzstein served as the judge for a competition sponsored by *Young Israel* magazine; he recommended that Diamond enter it, and he selected Diamond's "Passover Night" as the prize-winning song. Blitzstein's Piano Concerto shortly found its way into the Edwin A. Fleisher Collection of musical scores at the Free Library of Philadelphia, along with the Suite to *Surf and Seaweed* and the *Orchestra Variations.*
35. Journal of Marc Blitzstein, April 2, 1936.
36. Eva Goldbeck to MB, May 13, 1936.
37. Eva Goldbeck to MB, May 7, 1936. The score exists, but no copy of the film appears to have survived.
38. "The Composer and His Audience," *Unison* (May 1936): 2.
39. Marc Blitzstein, "Coming—the Mass Audience!" *Modern Music* (May–June 1936): 23–29.
40. Dr. Henry A. Murray to Eva Goldbeck, May 25, 1936.
41. Jack London, *Martin Eden* (New York: Bantam, 1986), p. 342.
42. Eva Goldbeck, undated.

Chapter 7: WHEN THE WIND BLOWS

1. Marc Blitzstein, "The Case for Modern Music," *New Masses,* July 14, 21, and 28, 1936.
2. John L. Lewis, "The C.I.O. Crusade" (pamphlet), 1937.
3. Edith Hale, "Author and Composer Blitzstein," *Daily Worker,* December 7, 1938.

This is the only place where Blitzstein ever made the claim that he had met both Eisler and Brecht during his year of study abroad. If so, the meeting was incidental at most.
4. MB to Kurt Weill, November 19, 1936; courtesy of The Kurt Weill Foundation for Music.
5. Marc Blitzstein, "Weill Scores for Johnny Johnson," *Modern Music* (November–December 1936): 44–46. The magazine's contributor notes announced that *Cradle* would be done during the winter season by the Actors' Repertory Theatre.
6. MB to Lina Abarbanell, December 23, 1936.
7. Library of Congress Federal Theatre Project, Oral History interview with Will Geer, June 1, 1976, George Mason University Library, Fairfax, Virginia.
8. MB to Sam and Maddie Blitzstein, March 3, 1937.
9. MB to Josephine Davis, March 27, 1937.
10. Virgil Thomson, "High-Brows Wow Local Public," *Modern Music* (May–June 1937): 233–237.
11. "Blitzstein Opera," *Unison* (Summer 1937): 1–2.
12. MB to Josephine Davis, June 2, 1937, and undated but later June 1937.
13. For certain details, the following account draws from John Houseman, *Run-through* (New York: Simon and Schuster, 1972), pp. 245–279.
14. John Houseman, *Run-through,* pp. 268–69.
15. Charles E. Dexter, *Daily Worker,* June 17, 1937. In subsequent days, however, the *Daily Worker* lent its support to the show.
16. Curiously—this has apparently never been pointed out before—the Federal Theatre Project did not entirely lose interest in *Cradle,* for as many as three different playreaders considered the work favorably for FTP production, perhaps by other units outside New York. Two readings took place in February 1938, and a third as late as December 1938. Library of Congress Federal Theatre Project Collection, George Mason University Library, Fairfax, Virginia. Playreader Report, *The Cradle Will Rock.*
17. Source unknown.

Chapter 8: TUNES FOR THE PEOPLE

1. Howard Barnes, *Herald Tribune,* August 21, 1937; J.T.M., *The New York Times,* August 21, 1937; *Daily Worker,* July 20, 1937; Peter Ellis, "Sights and Sounds," *New Masses,* August 24, 1937.
2. George Antheil, "On the Hollywood Front," *Modern Music* (May–June 1938): 253.
3. Robert Coleman, *Daily Mirror,* October 20, 1937.
4. Richard Gilbert, "Music and Records," *Scribner's* (January 1938): 80–81.
5. *Time,* November 1, 1937; *Radio Daily,* October 26, 1937; Irving Kolodin, New York *Sun,* October 25, 1937; Ben Gross, *Daily News,* October 25, 1937.
6. R. D. Darrell, "Sights and Sounds," *New Masses,* November 9, 1937, p. 28; R. D. Darrell, "Concert Notes," *New Masses,* November 30, 1937, p. 29.
7. Elliott Carter, "In the Theatre," *Modern Music* (November–December 1937): 51–53.
8. Marc Blitzstein, "On Writing Music for the Theatre," *Modern Music* (January–February 1938): 81–85.
9. Heywood Broun, *World-Telegram,* January 6, 1938.
10. Hallie Flanagan to MB, March 5, 1947;
11. Deems Taylor, "The Audience *Is* the Fourth Wall," *Stage* (February 1938):

46–47. Thornton Wilder's Pulitzer Prize-winning play *Our Town,* also staged without scenery, opened in February 1938.
12. Walter Winchell, *Mirror,* December 15, 1937; Brooks Atkinson, *The New York Times,* December 6, 1937.
13. Eric Englander, *Sunday Worker,* December 12, 1937; R. D. Darrell, "Blitzstein Brings New Tunes to Music," *New Masses,* December 28, 1937.
14. MB to Josephine Davis, January 22, 1938.
15. Quoted in Leonard Lyons, New York *Post,* March 27, 1946.
16. Stark Young, "The Mercury and London," *The New Republic,* January 19, 1938, p. 310–311.
17. Alistair Cooke, on the NBC Red Network, January 12, 1938.
18. George Jean Nathan, "Theater," *Scribner's* (March 1938): 70–71.
19. "Mother Bloor Sees 'The Cradle,'" *Daily Worker,* January 12, 1938. Will Geer was married to Mother Bloor's granddaughter.
20. Library of Congress Federal Theatre Project Oral History interview with Howard da Silva, May 24, 1976, George Mason University Library, Fairfax, Virginia.
21. Virgil Thomson, "In the Theatre," *Modern Music* (January–February 1938): 112–114.
22. Quoted in Minna Lederman, "Memories of Marc Blitzstein, Music's Angry Man," *Show* (June 1964): 18ff.

Chapter 9: ODE TO REASON

1. Walter Winchell, *Mirror,* February 19, 1938. Blitzstein wanted Meredith to appear as the lead in *No for an Answer,* which he expected to be ready by summer.
2. "The Moscow Trials: A Statement by American Progressives," *New Masses,* May 3, 1938, p. 19.
3. Tiba Willner to MB, March 15, 1939.
4. Minna Lederman, "Memories of Marc Blitzstein, Music's Angry Man," *Show* (June 1964): 18ff.
5. Henry Cowell to MB, March 6, 1939.
6. Howard Taubman, *The New York Times,* February 7, 1938; Elliott Carter, "Orchestras and Audiences; Winter 1938," *Modern Music* (March–April 1938): 167–171.
7. *Variety,* February 23, 1938.
8. Wilfrid H. Mellers to MB, June 7, 1941.
9. *The New Records* (May 1938); Moses Smith, Boston *Evening Transcript,* May 3, 1938; Musicraft Records to MB, March 3, 1939.
10. MB to Mina Curtiss, July 24, 1938.
11. *The March of the Workers and Other Songs,* (Chicago: Young Workers League of America, n.d. [ca. 1935]).
12. John Gutman, "In the Theatre," *Modern Music* (November–December 1938): 54–58; Ruth McKenney, "Big Themes in the Theater," *New Masses,* November 15, 1938.
13. Quoted in Leonard Lyons, New York *Post,* September 9, 1938.
14. Lyrics to Blitzstein's song "Wish," about sending all the fascists off to some remote island to get them out of humanity's way, appeared in the Theatre Arts Committee magazine in February 1939, along with a photo of Blitzstein at the piano performing a solo rendition of the Purple Shirts' fascist scene from *I've Got the Tune.* In the March

issue, Blitzstein reviewed Aaron Copland's "special and uncommon book," *What to Listen for in Music.*
15. Moses Smith, Boston *Evening Transcript,* May 29, 1939; Elliot Norton, Boston *Post,* May 28, 1939.
16. MB to Leonard Bernstein, June 2, 1939; courtesy of Leonard Bernstein.
17. MB to Mina Curtiss, July 19, 1939.
18. MB to David Diamond, August 15, 1939; courtesy of David Diamond.
19. MB to Herman Shumlin, June 20, 1939, and August 5, 1939, Herman Shumlin Papers, State Historical Society of Wisconsin, Madison.
20. MB to David Diamond, December 1939; courtesy of David Diamond.
21. Constance Askew to Virgil Thomson, ca. February 20, 1940, Virgil Thomson Archives, Music Library at Yale University, New Haven, Connecticut.
22. MB to Henry Moe, March 28, 1940; courtesy of the John Simon Guggenheim Memorial Foundation.
23. Quoted in Leonard Lyons, New York *Post,* March 16, 1946.

Chapter 10: IN THE CLEAR

1. Marc Blitzstein, Notes for a lecture on "Lesser Masterworks," late twenties or early thirties.
2. B. H. Haggin, "Music," *The Nation,* February 15, 1941, p. 194; Paul Bowles, "On the Film Front," *Modern Music* (November–December 1940): 58–61; Henry Cowell, "The League's Evening of Films," *Modern Music* (March–April 1941): 176–178; Elsie Finn, Philadelphia *Inquirer,* February 18, 1941.
3. Marc Blitzstein, "Theatre Music," *Modern Music* (March–April 1940): 181–184.
4. Marc Blitzstein, "Pierrot Lunaire in Lindy's," *Modern Music* (March–April 1940): 196–197.
5. Marc Blitzstein, "On Collaborating With Oneself," *Herald Tribune,* January 12, 1941. In another promotional piece for the *Times,* January 5, 1941, he addressed the question of a co-author again: "I never found one. The nature and problems of collaboration are too complicated to go into here. Let us just say that for the present, and with no prejudice, I remain a lone wolf, having tried various partnerships."
6. Marc Blitzstein, *The New York Times,* January 5, 1941.
7. Josephine Davis to Robert J. Dietz, January 16, 1965, cited in Dietz, "The Operatic Style of Marc Blitzstein in the American 'Agit-Prop' Era" (Ph.D. dissertation, The University of Iowa, 1970), p. 326. In the year *No for an Answer* was produced, Jo and Ed bought a new house in West Philadelphia, which they occupied for about twenty years. Marc had a studio on the third floor. Once their sons Stephen and Christopher had married and established families, Jo and Ed relocated to a downtown apartment, leaving Christopher with the house.
8. Marc Blitzstein, dated March 24, no year.
9. Marc Blitzstein, *The New York Times,* January 5, 1941.
10. Marion Bussang, New York *Post,* January 2, 1941.
11. Muriel Draper to MB, March 21, 1940.
12. Brooks Atkinson, *The New York Times,* January 6, 1941; Virgil Thomson, *Herald Tribune,* January 12, 1941.
13. "Yes for an Answer," *Opera News,* January 13, 1941;
14. Samuel Barlow, "Blitzstein's Answer," *Modern Music* (January–February, 1941):

81–83; Robert Simon, "Musical Events," *The New Yorker,* January 11, 1941, p. 49—no relation to the Robert Simon who played Joe.
15. Ralph Warner, *Daily Worker,* January 7, 1941; "Blitzstein's Music," *New Masses,* January 21, 1941.
16. Aaron Copland, *Our New Music: Leading Composers in Europe and America* (New York: Whittlesey House, McGraw-Hill, 1941), pp. 196–99.
17. Quoted in *PM,* January 10, 1941.
18. Brooks Atkinson, *The New York Times,* January 26, 1941. Atkinson was mistaken about the top ticket price, which was $3.30.
19. Quoted in Leonard Lyons, New York *Evening Post,* April 16, 1941.
20. John Edgar Hoover to Special Agent in Charge, New York, New York, November 8, 1940; FBI document number 100-4753-1, United States Department of Justice, Federal Bureau of Investigation, Washington, D.C. Blitzstein's FBI file, amounting to 168 heavily censored pages, was released to the author on August 22, 1988. Further references to FBI material will list FBI and the document number.
21. Memorandum, April 23, 1941; FBI 100-4753-6. E. E. Kuhnel to Director [J. Edgar Hoover], May 23, 1941; FBI 100-4753-8 (?).

Chapter 11: PHONY WAR, REAL WAR

1. MB to David Diamond, June 21, 1941; courtesy of David Diamond.
2. Charles Glenn, "Hollywood Meets Blitzstein," *Daily Worker,* July 5, 1941.
3. MB to David Diamond, July 11, 1941; courtesy of David Diamond.
4. Marc Blitzstein, *The New York Times,* October 19, 1941.
5. MB to Claire Reis, December 3, 1941; in the Music Division, New York Public Library.
6. MB to David Diamond, February 17, 1942; courtesy of David Diamond.
7. Marc Blitzstein, "Singing Country," *Modern Music* (January–February 1942): 139–140.
8. Virgil Thomson, *Herald Tribune;* Olin Downes, *The New York Times,* both May 11, 1942.
9. John I. McManus, *PM,* May 12, 1942; Bosley Crowther, *The New York Times,* May 13, 1942; *Time,* June 8, 1942.
10. Pete Seeger to MB, May 25, 1942; Stephen Davis, ". . . —and a Dash," *The Overbrook Beacon,* May ?, 1942.
11. Leon Kochnitzky, "On the Film Front," *Modern Music* (May–June 1942): 275–278.
12. Marc Blitzstein, Notes for "Russia Is Singing."
13. MB to David Diamond, August 6, 1942; courtesy of David Diamond.
14. Davidson Taylor to MB, July 6, 1942; Robert W. Horton to MB, July 6, 1942; John Houseman to MB, June 30, 1942; Aaron Copland to Ralph Hawkes and Sir Adrian Boult, August 16, 1942; Brooks Atkinson to MB, July 23, 1942.
15. Nadia Boulanger to MB, undated but summer 1942.
16. Marc Blitzstein, "The Quiet Girl," in Anne Allan, ed., *Sing, America* (New York?: Workers Bookshop): 40–41. This publication was one of the very few times anyone other than Chappell published Blitzstein's music. The song was sung in public, apparently for the first time, in the Lenin memorial stage review "Order of the Day" at Madison Square Garden on January 11, 1943.

17. MB to David Diamond, August 23, 1942; courtesy of David Diamond.
18. Report, October 4, 1943; FBI 100-4753-21.

Chapter 12: EVERY INCH A SOLDIER

1. MB to Leonard Bernstein, August 29, 1942; courtesy of Leonard Bernstein.
2. MB to Josephine Davis, September 13, 1942.
3. MB to Anna Levy, September 13, 1942.
4. Blitzstein told this anecdote in "A Musician's War Diary," *New Masses,* August 13, 20, and 27, 1946. I have drawn on these articles for the war years.
5. MB to Sam and Maddie Blitzstein, October 8, 1942.
6. MB to Josephine Davis (?), October 10, 1942. Like many that followed, this letter did not carry a specific salutation because it was meant as a round robin to the whole family. For consistency, all such letters will be identified as to Josephine Davis (?).
7. MB to David Diamond, December 21, 1942; courtesy of David Diamond.
8. MB to Josephine Davis (?), November 22, 1942.
9. MB to Stephen Davis, November 5, 1942; MB to Josephine Davis (?), November 1, 1942.
10. Alan Bush, in an interview with Leonard Lehrman, October 1971; MB to Josephine Davis (?), November 22, 1942.
11. Alan Bush, *Music in the Soviet Union* (London: Workers' Music Association, 1943).
12. MB to Sam and Maddie Blitzstein, November 18, 1942.
13. MB to David Diamond, n.d., December 1942 and April 28, 1943; both courtesy of David Diamond.
14. Marc Blitzstein, "London: Fourth Winter of the Blackout," *Modern Music* (January–February 1943): 117–120.
15. MB to Josephine Davis (?), November 1, 1942.
16. MB to Claire Reis, December 2, 1942, in the Music Division, New York Public Library. In a *Musical America* article of January 1963, Reis published this letter, with Blitzstein's permission to alter the word *white* to *big.*
17. MB to Josephine Davis (?), December 5–9, 1942.
18. Ibid.
19. MB to Sam and Maddie Blitzstein, December 4, 1942; MB to Josephine Davis, December 13, 1942.
20. MB to Josephine Davis, December 18, 1942. An air enthusiast, Lay had written *I Wanted Wings* in the mid-thirties. After the war, he wrote a memoir of his adventures in *I've Had It: The Survival of a Bomb Group Commander* (New York: Harper and Brothers, 1945), as well as later studies of aeronautical and space-exploration themes.
21. MB to David Diamond, January 13, 1942; courtesy of David Diamond.
22. Anatole Litvak, January 9, 1943.
23. James Dugan to Josephine Davis, July 9, 1965.
24. MB to Sam and Maddie Blitzstein, January 30, 1943.
25. MB to Josephine Davis, February 3, 1943.
26. MB to Josephine Davis (?), February 16, 1943.
27. MB to Sam and Maddie Blitzstein, March 10, 1943.
28. MB to Sam and Maddie Blitzstein, April 2, 1943.
29. MB to Sam Blitzstein, April 1943 (no date).

30. MB to Sam and Maddie Blitzstein, May 14, 1943.
31. MB to Sam Blitzstein, June 18, 1943.
32. MB to Anna Levy, July 27, 1943; MB to Josephine Davis, August 6, 1943. A recorded transcription of two-thirds of the broadcast, including Blitzstein's portion, survives.
33. MB to Josephine Davis, August 6, 1943.
34. MB to Anna Levy, August 12, 1943.
35. MB to Josephine Davis, August 31, 1943. For more on racist attitudes toward blacks, see Graham Smith, *When Jim Crow Met John Bull: Black American Soldiers in World War II Britain* (New York: St. Martin's Press, 1988).
36. Marc Blitzstein, *The New York Times,* October 3, 1943.
37. F. Bonavia, *The New York Times,* October 31, 1943.
38. Gail Kubik, "London Letter," *Modern Music* (May–June 1944): 240–243. Kubik mistakenly referred to the work as *Freedom Song.* Because *Freedom Morning* received its premiere on a largely choral program and because of a certain confusion between it and the *Airborne* Symphony, it has very often wrongly been referred to as a choral work.
39. MB to Josephine Davis, September 30, 1943.
40. MB to David Diamond, May 25, 1943; courtesy of David Diamond.
41. MB to Sam and Maddie Blitzstein, November 1, 1943; MB to Josephine Davis, November 6, 1943.
42. MB to Josephine Davis, November 26, 1943. For a time Blitzstein believed that James Stewart might join Meredith as a co-narrator.
43. MB to Josephine Davis, November 6, 1943. Blitzstein did not explain in his *New Masses* diary why the promotion came through in early November, yet at the November 25 audition he was addressed as "Corporal."

Chapter 13: BILL

1. MB to Anna Levy, February 14, 1944.
2. MB to Josephine Davis, December 6, 1943; MB to Mina Curtiss, June 18, 1943.
3. MB to Sam and Maddie Blitzstein, February 24, 1944.
4. MB to Josephine Davis, March 5, and 9, 1944.
5. MB to Josephine Davis, April 1, 1944.
6. MB to Anna Levy, March 10, 1944.
7. W. H. Haddon Squire, "American Music in London," source unknown.
8. MB to Josephine Davis, April 1, 1944.
9. MB to Josephine Davis, April 6, 1944.
10. MB to Sam and Maddie Blitzstein, April 30, 1944; MB to Josephine Davis, May 5, 1944.
11. Edwin H. Schloss, Philadelphia *Record,* April 15, 1944.
12. Vincent Persichetti, "Some Firsts in Philadelphia," *Modern Music* (May–June 1944): 248–251. Gail Kubik's review of the London premiere, published in the same issue, expressed an opposite opinion.
13. MB to Sam and Maddie Blitzstein, April 30, 1944.
14. MB to Josephine Davis (?), May 21, 1944.
15. Marc Blitzstein, *The New York Times,* April 14, 1946.
16. MB to Josephine Davis, June 6, 1944.
17. MB to Josephine Davis, June 16, 1944.

18. MB to Sam Blitzstein, August 31, 1944.
19. Paul Bowles, *Herald Tribune,* August 5, 1944; MB to Sam Blitzstein, August 18, 1944.
20. MB to Josephine Davis, September 13, 1944.
21. MB to Sam Blitzstein, August 31, 1944; MB to Josephine Davis, October 17, 1944; August 23, 1943; December 27, 1943.
22. MB to Sam and Maddie Blitzstein, October 23, 1944. Interestingly, in 1987 Hewitt denied ever owning records of *The Cradle Will Rock.*
23. MB to Josephine Davis (?), December 4, 1944.
24. Marc Blitzstein, Philadelphia *Record,* December 2, 1945.
25. In his memoirs, *Sun and Shadow* (New York: W. W. Norton, 1977), Aumont mentions this incident. At the end of 1944, Aumont appeared with Claude Dauphin in André Roussin's play *Une grande fille toute simple,* then returned to his military post in January.
26. MB to Josephine Davis (?), December 4, 1944.
27. MB to Josephine Davis, December 14, 1944.
28. MB to Sam and Maddie Blitzstein, December 25, 1944.
29. MB to Josephine Davis, January 7 and February 21, 1945. Hewitt was 24.
30. MB to Josephine Davis, February 21, 1945. Bernstein had made a well-publicized debut conducting the New York Philharmonic in November 1943, and had embarked immediately on a meteoric career guest-conducting dozens of other orchestras. In addition, his first compositions were beginning to be heard.
31. MB to Josephine Davis, undated but beginning of April 1945.
32. MB to William Hewitt, March 27, 1945; courtesy of William Hewitt.
33. MB to Sam and Maddie Blitzstein, April 17, 1945.
34. MB to Anna Levy, April 22, 1945.
35. MB to Josephine Davis and Maddie Blitzstein, May 5, 1945.

Chapter 14: HOME

1. "Army Used 'Reds,' House Group Told," *The New York Times,* July 19, 1945; Howard Rushmore, "Fear Red Spies Beat Army Ban to Atom Facts," New York *Journal American,* March 10, 1946.
2. The full transcript of the panel on music from the day's proceedings is published in *Musicology* (Spring 1946): 167–196.
3. "It Happens in Music," *The New York Times,* March 24, 1946.
4. It is possible that the date of the premiere was selected because it was the last date any new work could be performed to be considered for a Pulitzer Prize in music for 1946. Leonard Bernstein had advised the Pulitzer committee of the premiere of the *Airborne* Symphony back in October.
5. Seymour Peck, *PM,* March 29, 1946.
6. Virgil Thomson, *Herald Tribune;* Olin Downes, *The New York Times,* both April 2, 1946.
7. Grena Bennet, New York *Journal-American,* April 2, 1946.
8. Douglas Watt, New York *News,* April 2, 1946.
9. Louis Harap, *Daily Worker,* April 4, 1946; Sam Morgenstern, *Daily Worker,* April 5, 1946; Wallingford Riegger, "The Airborne," *New Masses,* April 16, 1946.
10. *Musical America,* April 10, 1946. T-B-B=Tenor-Baritone-Bass.
11. Harold Clurman, "Night Life and Day Light," *Tomorrow* (June 1946): 64.

12. Joseph Liss, ed., *Radio's Best Plays* (New York: Greenberg, 1947).
13. From the Archive of the American-Soviet Music Society; courtesy of Betty Bean.
14. Noel Straus, *The New York Times,* May 3, 1946.
15. Charles Mills "Over the Air," *Modern Music* (Summer 1946): 218–220.
16. Olin Downes, "The Force of Art," *The New York Times,* June 16, 1946, reprints most of Ehrenburg's remarks on this occasion about art, music, literature, and peace.
17. Joseph Stein and Norman Barasch, Script for "The Penguin Room," July 3, 1946.
18. Louis Biancolli, New York *World-Telegram,* July 11, 1946.
19. Olin Downes, *The New York Times,* October 20, 1946.
20. Charles Sinnickson, Jr., Philadelphia *Record,* October 23, 1946.
21. Marc Blitzstein, "An Analysis of Prokofiev," *Soviet Russia Today* (November 1946): 23.
22. Director [J. Edgar Hoover] to SAC [Special Agent in Charge], New York, November 22, 1946; FBI 100-4753-23.

Chapter 15. LITTLE FOXES

1. MB to Christopher Davis, October 14, 1946.
2. "Our Music in Other Countries," *Musical Courier,* June 1, 1947. Few copies of the *American-Soviet Music Review* ever found their way into library collections. Vassar College has one.
3. Miles Kastendieck, New York *Journal-American,* May 13, 1947. Robbins revived *Summer Day* for the Ballet Theatre the following December at City Center.
4. Marc Blitzstein, "Notes on the 'Airborne' Symphony," *RCA Victor Record Review* (June 1947).
5. Corbin Patrick, Indianapolis *Star,* June 6, 1947.
6. Willard M. Clark, Springfield (Massachusetts) *Morning Union,* June 5, 1947; Evans Rodgers, New Orleans *Item,* June 6, 1947.
7. Toledo *Times,* June 6, 1947; Houston *Post,* June 15, 1947; S.H., Pittsburgh *Press,* August 17, 1947; *Pic* (September 1947).
8. Martin Roberts, Harrisburg *News,* June 19, 1947; Dyneley Hussey, *The Listener,* June 10, 1948.
9. MB to Serge Koussevitzky, February 8 and April 3, 1947; Koussevitzky to MB, April 1, 1947, Library of Congress, Washington, D.C.
10. MB to Mordecai and Irma Bauman, August 27, 1947; courtesy of Mordecai and Irma Bauman.
11. MB to Mordecai and Irma Bauman, October 4, 1947; courtesy of Mordecai and Irma Bauman.
12. MB, Notes on *Regina,* June 21, 1949.
13. Lillian Hellman to MB, June 27, 1949. Until almost the eve of the production, the "Blues" had been Jabez's, or Jazz's, song. During the rehearsals, Blitzstein gave it to Cal.
14. Leonard Bernstein, "The Negro in Music," *The New York Times,* November 2, 1947.
15. Marc Blitzstein, *Herald Tribune,* November 23, 1947.
16. Olin Downes, *The New York Times,* November 25, 1947.
17. Virgil Thomson, *Herald Tribune,* November 25, 1947.
18. Miles Kastendieck, *Journal-American;* Irving Kolodin, *Sun,* both November 25, 1947.

19. R. S., *Musical America,* December 15, 1947.
20. John Briggs, New York *Post,* November 25, 1947; Cecil Smith, "When the Wind Blows," *New Republic,* December 22, 1947, pp. 35–36.
21. MB to Mordecai and Irma Bauman, early December 1947; courtesy of Mordecai and Irma Bauman.
22. Joan Kahn to MB, December 1, 1947 and January 9, 1948; MB to Joan Kahn, December 3, 1947, and January 6, 1948; The Harry Ransom Humanities Research Center, The University of Texas, Austin, Texas.
23. John Ball, Brooklyn *Eagle,* November 25, 1947.
24. Contracts and financial records from this production are in the Michael Myerberg Collection, Wisconsin Center for Film and Theater Research, State Historical Society of Wisconsin, Madison.
25. Brooks Atkinson, *The New York Times,* December 27, 1947; George Freedley, New York *Telegraph,* December 29, 1947.
26. *Daily Variety; Wall Street Journal,* both December 29, 1947; John Chapman, New York *Daily News,* January 1, 1948; George Jean Nathan, New York *Journal-American,* January 12, 1948.
27. Harold Clurman, "Nightlife and Daylight," *Tomorrow* (March 1948): 51.
28. O. V. Clyde, *Daily Worker,* December 30, 1947.
29. Sidney Finkelstein, "Music," *New Masses,* December 30, 1947, p. 22.
30. Waldemar Hille, ed., *The People's Songbook* (New York: Boni & Gaer, 1948).

Chapter 16: THE PARTY'S OVER

1. "32 'Artists' vs. Uncle Sam," New York *Daily News,* May 4, 1948.
2. MB to Mina Curtiss, May 5, 1948. *The New York Times* published the artists' response on May 24, 1948.
3. Marc Blitzstein, letter to *The New York Times,* October 10, 1948.
4. MB to Mina Curtiss, April 17, 1948.
5. Report, April 22, 1949; FBI 100-3868, p. 6. Report, June 14, 1955; FBI 100-4753-40, p. 4.
6. MB to William Hewitt, October 15, 1948; courtesy of William Hewitt.
7. Walter Terry, *Herald Tribune;* Harriett Johnson, New York *Post;* Robert Sylvester, New York *Daily News,* all January 21, 1949.
8. Henry Cowell, "Current Chronicle: New York," *The Musical Quarterly* (April 1949): 293–296.
9. MB to Mina Curtiss, February 20, 1949.
10. Cheryl Crawford, *One Naked Individual: My Fifty Years in the Theatre* (Indianapolis: Bobbs-Merrill, 1977), p. 173.
11. Lillian Hellman to MB, September 8, 1948.
12. MB to Shirley Bernstein, March 7, 1949; courtesy of Leonard Bernstein.
13. D. Rabinovich, *Dmitry Shostakovich, Composer* (Moscow: Foreign Languages Publishing House, 1959), p. 115.
14. MB to William Hewitt, March 31, 1949; courtesy of William Hewitt.
15. Earl Wilson, Wheeling (West Virginia) *News Register,* November 23, 1949.
16. Papers of Lina Abarbanell, Theatre Division, The New York Public Library.
17. MB to Serge Koussevitzky, June 10 and 23, 1949, Library of Congress, Washington, D.C.

18. Peggy Doyle, *The American;* Elinor Hughes, Boston *Herald,* both October 12, 1949.
19. Elinor Hughes, Sunday *Herald,* October 16, 1949.
20. Lillian Hellman, quoted in "Hellman Week on Broadway," *Cue,* October 1, 1949, pp. 14–15.
21. Leonard Bernstein, *The New York Times,* October 30, 1949.
22. Brooks Atkinson, *The New York Times,* November 1, 1949.
23. George Jean Nathan, New York *Journal-American,* November 14, 1949.
24. Robert Garland, New York *Journal-American;* William Hawkins, *World-Telegram,* both November 1, 1949; *Time,* November 14, 1949; Leonard Lyons, New York *Post,* November 2, 1949.
25. Virgil Thomson, *Herald Tribune,* November 1, 1949.
26. This letter to Houseman probably dates from mid-November 1949. It may indeed never have been sent, as the original was included in a packet of Blitzstein's letters to Curtiss that Curtiss returned to Blitzstein's family years after his death.
27. Cecil Smith, "Regina—Yet Another Opera on Broadway," *Musical America,* December 1, 1949, p. 9.
28. Barnard Rubin, *Daily Worker,* November 8, 1949.
29. Quoted in Leonard Lyons, New York *Post,* December 12, 1949.
30. Walter Terry, *Herald Tribune;* John Martin, *The New York Times,* both November 26, 1949.
31. Quoted in Cheryl Crawford, *One Naked Individual,* p. 174.
32. Arthur Pollock, *The Daily Compass,* January 5, 1950; Oscar Hammerstein and Richard Rodgers, *The New York Times,* January 1, 1950.
33. Paul Moor, "Tradition of Turbulence," *Theatre Arts* (March 1950): 36–38; Crawford, quoted in Lewis Funke, *The New York Times,* December 25, 1949.

Chapter 17: NEW MÉTIERS

1. Marc Blitzstein, *Herald Tribune,* March 7, 1954. In her memoir, *One Naked Individual* (p. 213), Cheryl Crawford wrote that at the time of *Regina,* Blitzstein showed her the work he had completed on *The Threepenny Opera.* "His lyrics were so good that I drove him out to Kurt Weill's home in New City to have Kurt listen to them. He too was impressed and gave Marc the rights to translate the entire work." Crawford further explored with Brecht the idea of producing the opera, but in the end, influenced negatively by its earlier failure in New York, she backed out.
2. Walter Terry, *Herald Tribune,* February 22, 1950.
3. L. J. H. Bradley, " 'The Guests' and 'The Age of Anxiety,' " *Ballet* (September–October 1950): 18–19.
4. MB to Mina Curtiss, May 7, 1953.
5. MB to Leonard Bernstein, January 4, 1950; courtesy of Leonard Bernstein.
6. MB to Mina Curtiss, July 12, 1951.
7. MB to Mordecai Bauman, February 26, 1953; courtesy of Mordecai Bauman. Weill was older than Blitzstein by exactly five years.
8. Marc Blitzstein, record review of Kurt Weill's *Kleine Dreigroschenmusik* and Aaron Copland's *Music for the Theatre, The Musical Quarterly* (July 1954): 454–456.
9. Marc Blitzstein, *Herald Tribune,* March 7, 1954.
10. MB to Leonard Bernstein, April 16, 1950; courtesy of Leonard Bernstein.
11. MB to Leonard Bernstein, May 19, 1950; courtesy of Leonard Bernstein.

12. Letter from *Theatre Arts,* unidentified editor to MB, March 23, 1950.
13. Marc Blitzstein, "Notes on Musical Theatre," *Theatre Arts* (June 1950): 30–31.
14. Arthur Berger, *Herald Tribune,* June 8, 1950.
15. MB to Mina Curtiss, June 16, 1950.
16. Elinor Hughes, Boston *Herald,* November 27, 1950.
17. Elliot Norton, Boston *Post,* November 28, 1950.
18. Brooks Atkinson, *The New York Times;* Howard Barnes *Herald Tribune,* both December 14, 1950; MB to Mina Curtiss, December 15, 1950.
19. Brooks Atkinson, *The New York Times,* December 26, 1950. The clue for LEAR—51 Across in that day's crossword puzzle—read, "Subject of Marc Blitzstein's new music."
20. MB to Alexander H. Cohen and Robert L. Joseph, January 29, 1951; Theatre Division, The New York Public Library.
21. When John Houseman revived *King Lear* for The Acting Company's national tour in 1978, he used Blitzstein's music once again. In *Newsday*'s view, it "suffused the play in a feeling of an age long past"—Leo Seligsohn, April 10, 1978. Clive Barnes, writing in the New York *Post* the same day, said it "admirably combines a sense of the timelessly ancient and modern worlds."
22. Marc Blitzstein, "On Music and Words," *Theatre Arts* (November 1950): 52–53.
23. MB to Mina Curtiss, August 12, 1951.
24. Joan Kahn to John Fischer, November 15, 1950; The Harry Ransom Humanities Resources Center, The University of Texas, Austin, Texas.
25. Marc Blitzstein, notes on *Reuben Reuben,* September 4, 1951.
26. MB to Mina Curtiss, September 18, 1952.
27. MB to Mordecai and Irma Bauman, September 27, 1951; courtesy of Mordecai and Irma Bauman.
28. Eric Bentley to MB, November 9, 1951.
29. MB to Eric Bentley, November 13, 1951; courtesy of Eric Bentley.
30. MB to Mina Curtiss, December 10, 1951.
31. Kurt List, "A Musical Brief for Gangsterism," *The New Leader,* February 4, 1952, and "A Dissent on the 'Dreigroschenoper,' " March 3, 1952.
32. MB to David Diamond, February 14, 1952; courtesy of David Diamond.
33. MB to David Diamond, March 20, 1952; courtesy of David Diamond.
34. Quoted in Lillian Hellman, *Scoundrel Time* (New York: Bantam, 1977), p. 124. Hellman's memory of the events surrounding the *Regina* revival is flawed in some respects. For example, the performance was free, so there was no money to give back.
35. Lillian Hellman, letter to the Hon. John S. Wood, chairman, House Committee on Un-American Activities, May 19, 1952. *Scoundrel Time,* p. 90.
36. Francis D. Perkins, *Herald Tribune;* Douglas Watt, New York *Daily News;* William Hawkins, New York *World-Telegram and Sun,* all June 2, 1952; Arthur Bronson, *Variety,* June 4, 1952.
37. Late in life, and long after Blitzstein's death, Hellman may have mellowed on the subject of the opera's black content. In 1975 Maurice Levine proposed a revival in concert form similar to the 1952 version, but perhaps with Jazz as narrator. Hellman answered him on August 4, 1975, "I particularly like the idea of a black man telling the story." Courtesy of Maurice Levine.
38. Harold Rogers, *Christian Science Monitor;* Howard Taubman, *The New York Times,* both June 16, 1952.
39. Arthur Berger, *Herald Tribune,* June 17, 1952.

40. Elinor Hughes, Boston *Sunday Herald,* June 24, 1952.
41. MB to Mina Curtiss, August 24, 1951.
42. MB to Leonard and Felicia Bernstein, July 19, 1952; courtesy of Leonard Bernstein.
43. MB to Leonard Bernstein, August 15, 1952; courtesy of Leonard Bernstein.
44. Billy Rose to MB, December 3, 1952.
45. MB to Mina Curtiss, February 24, 1953.
46. Carol Brice Carey to the author, June 6, 1981.
47. Howard Taubman, *The New York Times,* April 3, 1953.
48. Richard RePass, "New American Opera," *The Music Review* (August 1953): 224–227; Henry W. Levinger, "Regina in New Version," *Musical Courier,* April 15, 1953, pp. 6–7.
49. Douglass Watt, New York *Daily News,* April 3, 1953; *Variety,* April 8, 1953; *Musical Courier,* April 15, 1953.
50. Ross Parmenter, *The New York Times;* Jay S. Harrison, *Herald Tribune;* Harriett Johnson, New York *Post,* all May 5, 1953. Skitch Henderson conducted the *Airborne* Symphony once again, in the early 1970s in Tulsa, Oklahoma, with Schuyler Chapin as the Monitor and the men's chorus from Oral Roberts University.
51. MB to Mordecai and Irma Bauman, May 17, 1953; courtesy of Mordecai and Irma Bauman.
52. Robert Sabin, "The Harpies," *Musical America* (June 1953): 7.
53. Mina Curtiss to John Houseman, probably mid-November 1949.
54. MB to Leonard Bernstein, November 1, 1953; courtesy of Leonard Bernstein.
55. Marc Blitzstein, quoted in San Antonio *Light,* December 16, 1953.
56. MB to Josephine Davis, December 19, 1953.

Chapter 18: A SMASH, A FLOP

1. Quoted in Emory Lewis, "Musicals Off Beat," *Cue,* April 2, 1954, p. 16; quoted in Kurt Pinthus, "Die Zeit vergeht, *Die Dreigroschenoper* besteht (Time passes, *The Threepenny Opera* remains)," *Aufbau,* February 26, 1954; translation by the author.
2. Robert Coleman, *Daily Mirror;* John Chapman, New York *Daily News,* both March 11, 1954; Olin Downes, *The New York Times,* April 4, 1954.
3. Lewis Funke, *The New York Times,* March 11, 1954; Brooks Atkinson, *The New York Times,* March 21, 1954.
4. Virgil Thomson, *Herald Tribune,* March 21, 1954; Henry Hewes, "Lay on Macheath!" *Saturday Review,* March 27, 1954.
5. Eric Bentley, "Theatre," *The New Republic,* April 5, 1954, p. 21. See also his *The Dramatic Event: An American Chronicle* (Boston: Beacon Press, 1956), pp. 210–211. In later years, Bentley significantly mellowed his view of Blitzstein's translation. In "How Free Is Too Free?," *American Theatre* (November 1985), he still called Blitzstein's the freest of existing translations, but he did not resort to any low swipes. He admitted to a certain "sibling rivalry" with Blitzstein: "Both the brothers wanted to own Dad (BB)," that is, Bertolt Brecht.
6. Bertolt Brecht to MB, June 14, 1955. Brecht's son and heir, Stefan Brecht, refused permission to quote the relevant twelve words from this letter.
7. MB to David Diamond, April 24, 1954; courtesy of David Diamond.
8. MB to Leonard Bernstein, April 21, 1955; courtesy of Leonard Bernstein.
9. Henry W. Levinger, "Jennie Tourel," *Musical Courier* (April 1955): 23; Ubiquitous, "Along 57th Street," same issue, p. 5.

10. Marc Blitzstein, Notes on *Reuben Reuben,* April 15, 1950.
11. Blitzstein, Notes, April 8, 1951.
12. Blitzstein, Notes, April 1951?
13. Blitzstein, Notes, April 15, 1951.
14. Blitzstein, Notes, August 11, 1953.
15. Blitzstein, Notes, February 7, 1952.
16. Blitzstein, Notes, April 1951.
17. Blitzstein, Notes, January 7–11, 1952.
18. Blitzstein, Notes, February 1951?
19. MB to David Diamond, September 29, 1954; courtesy of David Diamond.
20. MB to Leonard Bernstein, July 8, 1954; courtesy of Leonard Bernstein.
21. MB to David Diamond, September 29, 1954; courtesy of David Diamond.
22. MB to David Diamond, February 13, 1955; courtesy of David Diamond.
23. MB to Leonard Bernstein, April 21, 1955; courtesy of Leonard Bernstein.
24. MB to Leonard Bernstein, March 23, 1955; courtesy of Leonard Bernstein.
25. Leonard Bernstein to MB, March 20, 1955.
26. Victor de Sabata to MB, March 27, 1955.
27. MB to Leonard Bernstein, April 5, 1955; courtesy of Leonard Bernstein.
28. Leonard Bernstein to MB, April 17, 1955.
29. MB to David Diamond, February 28, 1956; courtesy of David Diamond. I have not presumed to offer a comprehensive study of the harrowing legal and contractual details concerning the Brecht-Weill works that Blitzstein adapted. Such a complicated project falls well outside the range of a Blitzstein biography. By the same token, I may as well say that neither have I chosen to rekindle the line-by-line debate carried on by zealous partisans on several sides about the merits and demerits of Blitzstein's translations. I happily yield that pedantic endeavor to the Brecht specialists.
30. John Lewis Carver, *Top Secret* (June 1955).
31. MB to Mina Curtiss, September 3, 1955.
32. MB to Mina Curtiss, October 20, 1955.
33. Elinor Hughes, Boston *Herald,* October 12, 1955.
34. Cyrus Durgin, Boston *Globe;* L. G. Gaffney, Boston *Record,* both October 12, 1955.
35. George E. Ryan, Boston *Pilot,* October 15, 1955; Elliot Norton, Boston *Post,* October 11, 1955; Hollywood *Daily Variety,* October 12, 1955; Elinor Hughes, Boston *Herald,* October 12, 1955.
36. Elliot Norton, Boston *Post,* October 16, 1955.
37. George Clarke, Boston *Record,* October 14, 1955.
38. Quoted in Mary X. Sullivan, Boston *Advertiser,* October 16, 1955.
39. Robert Anderson, critical notes on *Reuben Reuben,* October 12, 1955.
40. Quoted in Elinor Hughes, Boston *Herald,* October 18, 1955.
41. Robert Lewis to MB, October 20, 1955.
42. MB to Robert Lewis, October 21, 1955; Robert Lewis to MB, October 22, 1955.
43. Quoted in Cheryl Crawford, *One Naked Individual,* p. 179.

Chapter 19: TIME OF THE FRIGHT

1. Marc Blitzstein's notes on a conversation with Orson Welles, October 30, 1955.
2. Orson Welles to MB, December 4, 1955.
3. Music for the Theatre, 1967 catalogue.
4. Edward Cole to MB, August 18, 1956.

5. Marc Blitzstein, letter to *The New York Times,* November 25, 1956.
6. Marc Blitzstein, "Richard Mohaupt: Double Trouble," *Notes* (March 1955): 319; Marc Blitzstein, "Gian-Carlo Menotti: The Saint of Bleecker Street," *Notes* (June 1956): 521–523. Menotti's opera and *Reuben Reuben,* conceived during the same period, both featured brightly lit night scenes from the San Gennaro Festival in New York's Little Italy, as well as scenes in subway stations. Blitzstein mentions the San Gennaro scene, but without reference to his own work.
7. MB to Carmen Capalbo and Stanley Chase, from Brigantine, N.J., undated.
8. Quoted in Andrew Porter, "Responding," *The New Yorker,* April 14, 1986.
9. MB to David Diamond, September 10, 1956; courtesy of David Diamond.
10. MB to Irma Bauman, January 26, 1957; courtesy of Irma Bauman.
11. John Briggs, *The New York Times,* April 28, 1957.
12. Reported in *The New York Times,* April 10, 1957.
13. Harriett Johnson, New York *Post;* Jay Harrison, *Herald Tribune;* Howard Taubman, *The New York Times,* all May 6, 1957.
14. Robert Sabin, "Marc Blitzstein Writes Cantata," *Musical America* (August 1958): 26.

Chapter 20: BIRD UPON THE TREE

1. Sean O'Casey, quoted from a letter to Joseph Stein in Stein, "A Visit with O'Casey," *The Theatre* (February 1959): 12–13.
2. Joseph Stein to MB, June 22, 1957.
3. Sean O'Casey, quoted in "Personality Cult Scored by O'Casey," *The New York Times,* August 25, 1957.
4. Eileen O'Casey to Joseph Stein, May 18, 1958; Sean O'Casey to Stein, May 21, 1958.
5. MB to David Diamond, October 9, 1957; courtesy of David Diamond.
6. Paul Dessau to MB, January 29, 1958.
7. John Willett to MB, September 9, 1958; MB, "Primer on Brecht," *The Nation,* September 12, 1959, pp. 137–138.
8. MB to David Diamond, January 13, 1958; courtesy of David Diamond.
9. Harold C. Schonberg, *The New York Times;* Jay Harrison, *Herald Tribune,* both February 28, 1958; Harriett Johnson, New York *Post,* March 2, 1958.
10. Anna Blitzstein to MB, February 27, 1958.
11. MB to David Diamond, March 4, 1958; courtesy of David Diamond.
12. Quoted in Vivien Leone Mazzone, *Entertainment Off Broadway,* early Spring 1958.
13. Robert Coleman, *Daily Mirror,* April 18, 1958; *Variety,* April 23, 1958.
14. John M. Conly, "Record Reviews," *Atlantic Monthly* (September 1959); Virgil Thomson, "From 'Regina' to 'Juno,'" *Saturday Review,* May 16, 1959, pp. 82–83.
15. Murray Schumach, *The New York Times,* March 1, 1959.

Chapter 21: WE'RE ALIVE

1. Quoted in *The New York Times,* June 16, 1958.
2. *The New York Times,* June 17, 1958.
3. Harold Clurman, "Theatre," *The Nation,* July 5, 1958, pp. 19–20; John Chapman, *Daily News,* and Herbert Whittaker, *Herald Tribune,* both June 23, 1958; Brooks Atkinson, *The New York Times,* July 21, 1958.

4. Harriett Johnson, New York *Post,* August 13, 1958.
5. Tony Richardson to MB, October 22, 1958.
6. Melvyn Douglas and Tom Arthur, *See You at the Movies: The Autobiography of Melvyn Douglas* (Lanham, Maryland: University Press of America, 1986), p. 104.
7. Melvyn Douglas, quoted in Jesse Zunser, "A Daarlin' Man," *Cue* (February 21, 1959): 10.
8. Papers of Lina Abarbanell, Theatre Division, The New York Public Library.
9. Tom Donnelly, Washington *Daily News,* and Jay Carmody, Washington *Evening Star,* both January 19, 1959; Richard L. Coe, Washington *Post and Times Herald,* January 18, 1959.
10. *Variety,* January 21, 1959; Richard L. Coe, Washington *Post and Times Herald,* January 18, 1959; Tom Donnelly, Washington *Daily News,* January 19, 1959.
11. Richard L. Coe, Washington *Post and Times Herald,* January 18, 1959; Tom Donnelly, Washington *Daily News,* January 19, 1959.
12. Jay Carmody, Washington *Sunday Star,* January 25, 1959.
13. Melvin Maddocks, *Christian Science Monitor;* Peggy Doyle, Boston *Evening American,* both February 5, 1959.
14. Elliot Norton, *Daily Record,* February 5, 1959.
15. Elinor Hughes, Boston *Herald,* February 5 and 15, 1959.
16. Brooks Atkinson, *The New York Times,* March 10, 1959.
17. Kenneth Tynan, *The New Yorker,* March 21, 1959.
18. John McClain, *Journal-American,* March 10, 1959.
19. John Chapman, New York *Daily News,* March 10, 1959.
20. Victor Samrock to Roger L. Stevens and Oliver Rea, March 16, 1959, The Playwrights Company Collection, Wisconsin Center for Film and Theater Research, Madison, Wisconsin.
21. S. G., *Hi Fi Review* (July 1959).
22. Quoted in Joseph Stein to MB, April 20, 1959.
23. Robert Emmett Dolan to MB, March 28, 1959.
24. SAC [Special Agent in Charge], New York to Director, FBI, December 18, 1958; FBI 100-4753–46, p. 2. Director, FBI to SAC, New York, January 6, 1959; no document number.
25. Report, March 27, 1959, p. 3; no document number. Report, March 27, 1959, p. 2; FBI 100-4753–48.

Chapter 22: PART OF THE GANG

1. Stefan Brecht to MB, March 27, 1959. Stefan Brecht refused permission to quote from this letter.
2. Marc Blitzstein, "On 'Mahagonny,' " *Saturday Review,* May 31, 1958, pp. 40ff. An alternate version of the article, focusing more on the opera itself and less on the recording, appeared in the British magazine *The Score,* July 1958, pp. 11–13.
3. MB to Helene Weigel, May 24, 1959.
4. Virgil Thomson to the National Institute of Arts and Letters, September 25, 1958.
5. MB to Glenway Wescott, April 1, 1959.
6. Laurence Pawell, *New Mexican,* July 30, 1959.
7. MB to Josephine Davis, July 17, 1959.
8. MB to Ned Rorem, August 6, 1959; courtesy of Ned Rorem.
9. *Composers of the Americas,* volume 5, 1959, pp. 22–28.

10. MB to the Ford Foundation, February 15, 1960; courtesy of the Ford Foundation.
11. MB to George Freedley, February 19, 1960; Theatre Division, The New York Public Library.
12. Leonard and Felicia Bernstein to MB, February 11, 1960.
13. Paul Henry Lang, *Herald Tribune;* Miles Kastendieck, New York *Journal-American;* Howard Taubman, *The New York Times,* all February 12, 1960.
14. Douglas Watt, New York *Daily News;* Harriett Johnson, New York *Post,* both February 12, 1960; Goth, *Variety,* February 17, 1960.
15. Harold Clurman, "Theatre," *The Nation,* March 12, 1960, p. 236.
16. Tammy Grimes to MB, March 23, 1960; Jack Harrold to MB, March 12, 1960.

Chapter 23: LOYALTY UNDER ATTACK

1. "Music," *Time,* p. 74; "Opera—Strange Venture," *Newsweek,* p. 65, both March 7, 1960; Don Ross, *Herald Tribune,* February 29, 1960.
2. Rudolf Bing to MB, March 7, 1960.
3. *National Review,* March 12, 1960, pp. 157–158. J. Edgar Hoover, memorandum, February 26, 1960; FBI 100-4753-56.
4. George Sokolsky, New York *Journal-American,* March 3, 1960.
5. Edward B. Simmons, New Bedford *Standard-Times,* March 29, 1960.
6. George Sokolsky, *Kennebec Journal,* April 23, 1960. Sokolsky quotes the Francis Robinson letter.
7. Henry T. Heald to John S. Miller, August 17, 1960; Ford Foundation Archives, PA60–118. Heald included this comment in several letters. John J. McCloy to Henry S. Booth, April 27, 1960; Ford Foundation Archives, PA60–118.
8. Edward F. D'Arms, Memorandum to Records Center, May 2, 1960; Ford Foundation Archives, PA60–118.
9. Rudolf Bing to Lincoln Lauterstein, March 29, 1960; Metropolitan Opera Archives.
10. Paul Henry Lang, *Herald Tribune,* April 3, 1960.
11. Gardner Jackson to MB, March 15, 1960; Gardner Jackson to Reginald Rose, March 19, 1960. Reginald Rose Papers, Wisconsin Center for Film and Theater Research, Madison, Wisconsin.
12. Richard Rohman to MB, February 29, 1960.
13. MB to Rudolf Bing, March 12, 1960; Metropolitan Opera Archives.
14. Howard Taubman, *The New York Times,* and Lester Trimble, *Herald Tribune,* both April 19, 1960; Nancy K. Siff, *Village Voice,* April 27, 1960.
15. George Braziller to MB, February 29, 1960.
16. Marc Blitzstein, "Music's Other Boulanger," *Saturday Review,* May 28, 1960, p. 60.
17. Nadia Boulanger to MB, June 9, 1960.
18. MB to Alice Esty and David Stimer, August 19, 1960.
19. MB to Ned Rorem, June 29, 1960; courtesy of Ned Rorem. John Gutman to MB, June 9, 1960. MB to John Gutman, June 12, 1960; Metropolitan Opera Archives.

Chapter 24: NOSTALGIA DELL'ITALIA

1. MB to Claire Reis, December 17, 1960; Music Division, The New York Public Library.

2. MB to Lina Abarbanell, December 14, 1960.
3. MB to Anna Blitzstein, December 6, 1960.
4. MB to Josephine Davis, January 11, 1961. The *ABC* article is unsigned.
5. MB to Lina Abarbanell, January 8, 1961.
6. MB to Anna Blitzstein, February 1, 1961.
7. MB to Josephine Davis, multiple letters, December 1960–February 1961.
8. MB to Josephine Davis, April 4, 1961.
9. MB to Josephine Davis, April 17, 1961.
10. MB to Josephine Davis, April 21, 1961.
11. MB to Lina Abarbanell, March 17, 1961.
12. Martin Bernheimer, *Herald Tribune;* Eric Salzman, *The New York Times,* both March 14, 1961.
13. MB to Anna Blitzstein, March 7, 1961.
14. MB to Leonard Bernstein, March 8, 1961; courtesy of Leonard Bernstein.
15. MB to David Diamond, February 11, 1961; courtesy of David Diamond.
16. MB to David Diamond, March 7, 1961; courtesy of David Diamond.
17. Adolfo Velletri to MB, May 24, 1961.
18. Richard A. Kimball to MB, May 25, 1961; MB to Anna Blitzstein, June 3, 1961; MB to Josephine Davis, May 10, 1961; MB to Mordecai and Irma Bauman, May 12, 1961, courtesy of Mordecai and Irma Bauman.
19. Adolfo Velletri to MB, July 31, 1961.
20. MB to Adolfo Velletri, undated draft, but probably September 1961.
21. Robert H. Hethmon to MB, March 17, 1961; MB to Robert H. Hethmon, March 25, 1961.
22. Edward F. D'Arms, Memorandum to Records Center, October 16, 1961; Edward F. D'Arms to MB, November 7, 1961; MB to Edward F. D'Arms, November 8, 1961; all Ford Foundation Archives, PA60–118.
23. MB to Mina Curtiss, December 9, 1961.
24. Marc Blitzstein, "On the *Threepenny Opera,*" *Musical Show* (October 1962): 2.
25. MB to Leonard Bernstein, December 27, 1961; courtesy of Leonard Bernstein.
26. MB to Mordecai and Irma Bauman, January 5, 1962; courtesy of Mordecai and Irma Bauman.
27. MB to Clarence Q. Berger, late February 1962.
28. The WGBH film of Blitzstein's talk is at the Brandeis University Library, Waltham, Massachusetts.
29. William C. Fels to MB, February 14, 1962.
30. MB to William C. Fels, May 8, 1962.
31. MB to Claire Reis, June 5, 1962; Music Division, The New York Public Library.

Chapter 25: THE THIRTEENTH SCENE

1. MB to Josephine Davis, July 1, 1962.
2. Quoted in (American Jewish) *Congress Bi-Weekly,* September 24, 1962, pp. 37–38.
3. MB to Josephine Davis, June 18, 1962.
4. Meyer Weisgal, "To Whom It May Concern," June 19, 1962.
5. Meyer Weisgal to MB, July 4, 1962.
6. MB to Josephine Davis, June 22, 1962.
7. MB to Josephine Davis, July 1, 1962.

8. MB to Anna Blitzstein, July 11, 1962.
9. MB to Josephine Davis, July (misdated June) 11, 1962.
10. MB to Anna Blitzstein, July 3, 1962; Shoshana Ron to MB, July 30, 1962; MB to Josephine Davis, August 2, 1962; Shoshana Ron to Eric A. Gordon, March 20, 1988.
11. MB to Anna Blitzstein, August 7, 1962.
12. MB to Josephine Davis, July 26, 1962.
13. MB to Josephine Davis, August 7, 1962.
14. Quoted in Helga Dudman, Jerusalem *Post,* August 26, 1962.
15. Quoted in *The Bennington Banner,* October 12, 1962.
16. Marc Blitzstein, Memorandum on his year at Bennington College, October 10, 1963.
17. Edith Stewart to MB, February 20, 1963.
18. Bernard Malamud, *The Magic Barrel* (New York: Vintage, 1960), p. 214.
19. MB to Josephine Davis, March 28, 1963.
20. Quoted in Meryle Secrest, Washington *Post,* May 14, 1963.
21. MB to Jeannie Nicholas, Marianne Stafne and Sally Wolter, May 21, 1963.
22. Reed Wolcott to MB, October 7, 1963.
23. William C. Fels to MB, June 27, 1963.
24. Brenda Lewis, program notes to the Acting Company performance of *The Cradle Will Rock,* West Hartford, Connecticut, January 1984.
25. MB to John Orr Hunter, Fall 1963; MB to Robert J. Dietz, July 23, 1963.
26. MB to Michael Musmanno, July 17, 1963.
27. MB to Leonard Bernstein, September 7, 1963; courtesy of Leonard Bernstein.
28. Myron Clement to Henry Joseph, October 21, 1963; translation by the author.
29. MB to Anna Blitzstein, November (misdated October) 6, 1963.
30. MB to Josephine Davis, November 9, 1963.
31. MB to Josephine Davis, November 22 and 15, 1963.
32. MB to Josephine Davis, December 3, 1963; MB to Irene Diamond, November 25, 1963, courtesy of Irene Diamond; MB to Anna Blitzstein, December 5, 1963.
33. MB to Morris Golde, December 9, 1963.
34. MB to Anna Blitzstein, December 5, 1963; MB to Josephine Davis, December 11, 1963.
35. MB to Rudolf Bing and John Gutman, late December 1963.
36. John Gutman to MB, January 4, 1964.
37. MB to Anna Blitzstein, December 31, 1963.
38. MB to Anna Blitzstein, January 4, 1964.
39. MB to Josephine Davis, January 9, 1964.
40. Josephine Davis to MB, January 21, 1964.
41. William B. Milam to Josephine Davis, January 22, 1964.
42. Ibid.

Chapter 26: THEN

1. Arva C. Floyd, U.S. consular report, February 3, 1964; courtesy of the Department of State.
2. Eric Salzman, *Herald Tribune,* January 25, 1964.
3. Lollie Peckham to Josephine Davis, January 23, 1964. The Martiniquans begin Carnival festivities shortly after New Year.
4. Josephe Pierre-Louis to Myron Clement, January 29, 1964.

5. Josephine Davis, undated draft to the Department of State.
6. Harold C. Schonberg, *The New York Times,* April 20, 1964.
7. Leighton Kerner, *Village Voice* April 30, 1964; Gerald Weales, "The Cradle Still Rocks," *The Reporter* (May 21, 1964): 46ff; Jay S. Harrison, "Jay S. Harrison Covers the New York Music Scene," *Musical America* (May 1964): 33–34.
8. Leonard Bernstein, *Findings* (New York: Simon and Schuster, 1982), pp. 225–26.

Epilogue

1. Quoted in John Gruen, *Close-Up* (New York: Viking Press, 1968), pp. 168–69.
2. Leighton Kerner, *Village Voice,* June 19, 1978.
3. Truman Capote, "Music for Chameleons," *The New Yorker,* September 17, 1979, p. 131.
4. Peter G. Davis, *New York,* February 10, 1986.
5. As of this writing, the musicologist Dee Baily is under contract with Greenwood Press to write *Marc Blitzstein: A Bio-Bibliography,* a book consisting of a short biographical overview, annotated bibliography of writings by and about the composer, discography, work list, and a selection of critical reviews of Blitzstein's works. Date of completion was unknown at the time *Mark the Music* went to press.
6. Cheryl Crawford, *One Naked Individual,* p. 179.
7. Jerry Tallmer, New York *Post,* September 21, 1988.
8. Ned Rorem, *The Final Diary* (New York: Holt, Rinehart and Winston, 1974), p. 88.
9. Peter G. Davis, *New York,* October 24, 1988; Will Crutchfield, *The New York Times,* October 12, 1988; Bill Zakariasen, *Daily News,* October 11, 1988.
10. Wilfrid Mellers, "Music, Theatre and Commerce: A Note on Gershwin, Menotti and Marc Blitzstein," *The Score* (June 1955): 76.

*List of Works by Marc Blitzstein**

FOR THE STAGE, INCLUDING BALLET

King Hunger (Leonid Andreyev), incidental music, 1924.

Svarga, 1925. Ballet.

Jigg-Saw, 1928. Ballet.

Triple-Sec, 1928. Libretto (l.), Ronald Jeans. Piano-vocal score published by Schotts Söhne.

Parabola and Circula, 1929. l., George Whitsett.

Cain, 1930. Ballet.

The Harpies, 1931. l., Marc Blitzstein (MB).

The Condemned, 1932. l., MB.

The Cradle Will Rock, 1936. l., MB. Songs published: "The Cradle Will Rock," "Doctor and Ella," "Gus and Sadie Love Song," "The Freedom of the Press," "Leaflets"/"Art for Art's Sake," "Croon-Spoon," "Drugstore Scene," "Honolulu," "Joe Worker," "The Rich," "Nickel Under the Foot"; "The Cradle Will Rock" and "Nickel Under the Foot" in *The Chappell Collection of Great Theatre Composers,* volume one, n.d. Entire script, including six songs (some in different keys), published by Random House, New York, 1938. Recordings: Musicraft, album 18, 1938 (rereleased on American Legacy Records T1001, n.d.); MGM Records, 1965 (rereleased on Composers Recordings, Inc. CRI SD 266, n.d.); Polydor 0704 and cassette, 1985. Evelyn Lear, "Nickel Under the Foot," and Roddy McDowall, Alvin Epstein, and Jane Connell, the Hotel Lobby Scene, *Marc Blitzstein Discusses His Theater Compositions,* Spoken Arts 717, 1956.

Julius Caesar (William Shakespeare), incidental music, 1937. Text, Shakespeare. Published: "Orpheus." Recording: Muriel Smith, "Orpheus," *Marc Blitzstein—Songs for the Theatre,* Concert Hall Society CHC 24, 1950? The broadcast transcription of Orson Welles's Mercury Theatre radio production, released on Ariel SHO 9 with five references to Blitzstein's music, in fact includes no music.

FTP [Federal Theatre Project] Plowed Under, 1937. l., MB.

Danton's Death (Georg Buechner), incidental music, 1938. Texts, MB. Recording: Muriel Smith, "Ode to Reason," Concert Hall Society CHC 24.

No for an Answer, 1937–1940. l., MB. Published: "The Purest Kind of a Guy," *People's Songs* (August 1947), and *Sing Out!,* volume 27, no. 2 (1978). Recordings: Keynote,

*Juvenilia and individual songs from stage works are omitted, except those published or recorded. All publications are by the Chappell Music Company unless otherwise stated.

album 105 (rereleased on Box Office Production, JJA 19772, n.d., and American Entertainment Industries 1140, 1982); Paul Robeson, "The Purest Kind of a Guy," *Songs of Free Men,* Columbia M534-3, 1943 (and subsequent rereleases); Muriel Smith, "In the Clear," Concert Hall Society CHC 24; Charlotte Rae, "Fraught," *Songs I Taught My Mother,* Vanguard VRS 9004; George Gaynes and Evelyn Lear, "Francie," and Joshua Shelley, "Penny Candy," Spoken Arts 717.

Goloopchik, 1945. l., MB. Incomplete. Recordings: Muriel Smith, "Mamasha Goose" and "Displaced [Song of the D.P.]," Concert Hall Society CHC 24.

Androcles and the Lion (George Bernard Shaw), incidental music, 1946.

Another Part of the Forest (Lillian Hellman), incidental music, 1946.

The Guests [originally *Show*], 1946–1948. Ballet. For publishing and recording information, see For Piano Solo.

Regina, 1946–1949. l., MB, based on *The Little Foxes* by Lillian Hellman. Piano-vocal score published; also six songs: "Blues," "Chinkypin," "Greedy Girl," "Summer Day," "What Will It Be?," "The Best Thing of All"; "The Rain" for mixed chorus. Recordings: 1958 New York City Opera version on Columbia/Odyssey Y3 35236; Brenda Lewis, "Birdie's Aria," Spoken Arts 717.

King Lear (Shakespeare), incidental music, 1950.

Reuben Reuben, 1949–1955. l., MB. Published: "Be with Me," "The Hills of Amalfi," "Monday Morning Blues," "Miracle Song," "Never Get Lost"; "The Hills of Amalfi" also in *The Chappell Collection of Great Theatre Composers.*

King Lear, incidental music, 1956.

Volpone (Ben Jonson), incidental music, 1956.

Juno, 1957–1959. Book, Joseph Stein, based on *Juno and the Paycock* by Sean O'Casey; lyrics, MB. Published: "My True Heart," "The Liffey Waltz," "One Kind Word," "My True Heart"; "My True Heart" and "I Wish It So" in *The Chappell Collection of Great Theatre Composers.* Recordings: Columbia OL 5380; *Original Demo Sung and Played by Marc Blitzstein,* Box Office Production, JJA 19772; Judy Kaye, "I Wish It So," *Where, Oh Where: Rare Songs of the American Theater,* Premier PRLP 001, 1986.

A Midsummer Night's Dream (Shakespeare), incidental music, 1958. Published: See *Six Elizabethan Songs* under Songs and Cantatas.

The Winter's Tale (Shakespeare), incidental music, 1958. Published: See *Six Elizabethan Songs* under Songs and Cantatas.

Sacco and Vanzetti, 1959–1964. l., MB. Incomplete.

Toys in the Attic (Lillian Hellman), incidental music, 1960.

The Magic Barrel, 1962–1964. l., MB, based on "The Magic Barrel" by Bernard Malamud. Incomplete.

Idiots First, 1962–1964. l., MB, based on "Idiots First" by Bernard Malamud. Completed by Leonard J. Lehrman.

FOR RADIO AND FILM

Hände [*Hands*] (Stella Simon), film score, 1927.

Surf and Seaweed (Ralph Steiner), film score, 1931.

Chesapeake Bay Retriever (Mrs. Milton Erlanger and Thomas T. K. Frelinghuysen), film score, 1936. Film lost.

The Spanish Earth (Joris Ivens), sound montage, with Virgil Thomson, 1937.

I've Got the Tune, 1937. Radio song-play. l., MB. Piano-vocal score published. Recording: Musicraft GM 212/218.

Twelfth Night (Shakespeare), incidental music for Mercury Theatre radio production, 1939. Recording: Columbia, 1939.

Valley Town (Willard Van Dyke), film score, 1940.

Native Land (Leo Hurwitz), film score, 1941. Recording: Walter Scheff, "Dusty Sun," with the *Airborne* Symphony, RCA Victor DM 1117.

Night Shift (Garson Kanin), film script and score, 1942. Unproduced. Published: "Turn the Night into Day."

Labor for Victory, 1942 radio programs. Published: "Quiet Girl," in Anne Allen, ed., *Sing, America,* 1943.

The True Glory (Garson Kanin and Carol Reed), film score, 1944–1945. *Movie Music* (suite). Lost?

SONGS AND CANTATAS*

Walt Whitman settings: "As If a Phantom Caress'd Me," "After the Dazzle of Day," "Joy, Shipmate, Joy," "What Weeping Face," all 1925; "Gods," 1926; "O Hymen! O Hymenee!," "As Adam," both 1927; "I Am He," "Ages and Ages," both 1928.

A Word Out of the Sea (text, Whitman), cantata for women's chorus, 1928. Three (of five?) movements complete.

E. E. Cummings settings, *Is 5,* 1929: "When life is quite through with," "After all white horses are in bed," "You are like the snow," "Mister, youse needn't be so spry," "Jimmie's got a goil." Published: "Jimmie's got a goil," Cos Cob Press, 1935 (subsequently, Boosey & Hawkes).

"What's the Matter with Me?," 1929? Text, MB.

"Into the Streets May First," 1934. Text, Alfred Hayes.

Workers' Kids of the World Unite! [*Children's Cantata*], for children's chorus, 1934. Text, MB.

"First of May," 1935. Text, Eva Goldbeck.

"War Department Manual, Volume 7, Part 3," 1935. Text, *War Department Manual,* adapted by MB.

"Send for the Militia," for *Parade,* 1935. Text, MB.

"Stay in My Arms," 1935. Text, MB.

"The Way You Are," 1935. Text, MB.

"Who Knows?," 1938. Text, MB.

"Smoking Glasses," 1938. Text, MB.

"Invitation to Bitterness," male chorus with altos, 1939. Text, MB. Published by Arrow Music Press (subsequently Boosey & Hawkes).

*For solo voice unless otherwise stated.

"Modest Maid," 1943. Text, MB. Recording: Charlotte Rae, Vanguard VRS 9004.

"The New Suit [Zipper Fly]," 1945? Text, MB.

The *Airborne* Symphony, cantata for male chorus, 1943–1946. Text, MB. Published: "Emily"; "Ballad of Hurry Up" (male chorus). Recordings: RCA Victor DM 1117, 1947; Columbia M 34136, 1976.

"Chez Eitingon," 1946. Text, MB.

This Is the Garden, cantata for mixed chorus, 1956–1957. Text, MB. Published.

Six Elizabethan Songs, 1958. "Sweet Is the Rose" (Amoretti), "Shepherd's Song" (Shakespeare), "Song of the Glove" (Ben Jonson), "Court Song" (Anonymous), "Lullaby" (Shakespeare), "Vendor's Song" (Shakespeare). Published.

E. E. Cummings settings, *From Marion's Book,* 1960: "o by the by," "when life is quite through with," "what if a much of a which of a wind," "silent unday by silently not night," "until and i heard," "yes is a pleasant country:," "open your heart:." Published.

FOR PIANO SOLO

Sonata, 1927.

Percussion Music for the Piano, 1929.

1930 Scherzo ["Bourgeois at Play"], 1930.

Piano Solo, 1933.

Le monde libre, 1944. Published by Chappell London.

The Guests [*Show*], suite for piano, 1946–48. Published: "Variation II," *Keyboard Classics* (July–August 1986): 23. Recordings: Marc Blitzstein, "Variation Three" and "Three-Four Dance and Finale," Concert Hall Society B9 (*American Composers at the Piano*), 1947; Bennett Lerner, "Variation II," "Pas de Deux," "Three-Four Dance," *American Piano Music,* volume II, Etcetera Records 1036, 1986.

"Innocent Psalm," 1953.

"For Kit's Wedding—June 6, 1953."

"Wedding Piece for Joyce and Stephen," 1955.

INSTRUMENTAL WORKS

String Quartet ("The Italian"), 1930.

Romantic Piece for Orchestra, 1930.

Piano Concerto, 1931. Recording: Composers Recordings, Inc. CRI CD 554 compact disk and cassette, 1988.

Suite for *Surf and Seaweed,* 1931.

Serenade (string quartet), 1932.

Orchestra Variations, 1934.

Freedom Morning, 1943. Recording: Supraphon H 18130, 1946.

Suite from *Native Land,* 1946; revised 1958.

Lear: A Study, 1958.

TRANSLATIONS AND ADAPTATIONS

Bertolt Brecht, *The Threepenny Opera* (music, Kurt Weill), 1950–1954. Published: *Vocal Selections from The Threepenny Opera,* New York: Warner Bros. Publications, 1984 and several sheet music issues of "Mack the Knife." Recordings: MGM SE-3121 OC (rereleased on subsequent analogs); at least two dozen versions of "Mack the Knife."

Three Offenbach Songs ("Canary Song," "Hermosa's Song," "Duettino"), music by Jacques Offenbach, 1955. Published.

Bertolt Brecht, *Rise and Fall of the City of Mahagonny* (music, Kurt Weill), 1957–1962. Incomplete.

Bertolt Brecht, *Mother Courage* (music, Paul Dessau), 1956–1962.

Index